THE PUBLICATIONS OF
THE CHAMPLAIN
SOCIETY

ONTARIO SERIES
IV

THE
PUBLICATIONS OF THE CHAMPLAIN SOCIETY

THE WINDSOR BORDER REGION

TORONTO
THE CHAMPLAIN SOCIETY

Six Hundred Copies of this Volume have been printed for the Champlain Society. Fifty are reserved for editorial purposes. The Remaining Five Hundred and Fifty are supplied only to Members of the Society and to Subscribing Libraries

This Copy is No. 206

A further Fifteen Hundred Copies have been printed and bound separately for the Ontario Government, which is sponsoring the Ontario Series

THE WINDSOR BORDER REGION

Canada's Southernmost Frontier

A Collection of Documents

Edited with an introduction by

Ernest J. Lajeunesse, C.S.B.

Professor of French
Assumption University of Windsor

TORONTO
THE CHAMPLAIN SOCIETY
1960

All rights reserved
by the Champlain Society

FOREWORD

THERE IS only one locality in the Province of Ontario that can claim a continuous settlement antedating the British conquest. That locality is the Windsor area on the Canadian side of the Detroit River. About the middle of the eighteenth century, when the flag of France was flying over the fort at Detroit, French settlers began to clear the first ribbon-like farms on the east shore of the strait. Within a few decades these farm lots filled nearly all the water frontage along the upper part of the river. After the American Revolutionary War this frontier region became a haven to United Empire Loyalists. These new residents settled near the mouth of the river and on the north shore of Lake Erie in what is now known as South Essex. The descendants of these two pioneer groups—the one of French and the other mostly of British stock—constitute a large proportion of the present population of Essex County. These factors alone give me confidence that wide interest will be aroused by the documentary history of this frontier region as prepared by the Reverend E. J. Lajeunesse, C.S.B., of Assumption University of Windsor.

Father Lajeunesse's volume is the fourth in the "Ontario Series" of documentary historical works prepared under the direction of the Champlain Society and the sponsorship of the Government of Ontario—all aimed at providing a documentary record of the early years of various regions of Ontario supplemented by useful commentaries from the very able historians who have been chosen to edit them. Much valuable research into Ontario's past has been undertaken by the Ontario Archives, interested persons, groups and communities, but I have always felt that the Province itself should be instrumental in ensuring that the fruits of such research be made available to the public in published form. The arrangement behind this series, therefore, has been a happy one. The Champlain Society, which has been publishing Canadian historical documents for over half a century, has the responsibility of choosing and guiding the editors. The Ontario Government meets the editorial expenses and publication costs.

This volume, like its predecessors, is not intended to provide an interpretation of history. Its primary purpose is to bring together for historians and the general reader the rich heritage that is to be found in Ontario's early records and documents. In the introductions and commentaries supplied by the editors of each work, these documents have been given perspective within the area and period to which they relate. Any opinions expressed in these volumes are, of course, those of the editors.

The first volume in the Ontario Series, *The Valley of the Trent*, edited by Edwin C. Guillet, appeared in 1957. The two succeeding volumes, *Royal Fort Frontenac*, by Professors Leopold Lamontagne and Richard Preston, and *Kingston before the War of 1812*, edited by Professor Preston, which documented the first two hundred years of the development of the Kingston area, were published in 1958 and 1959. Under preparation are volumes on the early histories of York, the Muskoka-Haliburton region and the Grand River Valley.

I should like to express my deepest appreciation to the Champlain Society and Father Lajeunesse for making possible the completion of another milestone in this unveiling of our historic past.

May 12, 1960

LESLIE M. FROST
Prime Minister of Ontario

PREFACE

AFTER VISITING the Detroit River region in 1679, Father Hennepin wrote with prophetic appropriateness these memorable lines: "Those who shall be so happy as to inhabit that noble country cannot but remember with gratitude the men who have discovered the way by venturing to sail upon an unknown lake for about one hundred leagues." Would not the hearts of today's inhabitants overflow with gratitude also for the pioneer settlers of the eighteenth century who transformed that noble wilderness into fruitful fields, if only that story were known? The present volume, while not pretending to be complete interpretative history, represents an effort to assemble the ingredients of that story, and to set them in perspective by means of a short introductory narrative.

Even this much would have been a hopeless task for the present writer but for the assistance received from many quarters. To all who have helped he desires to express hearty thanks. First of all it is a pleasant duty to acknowledge gratefully the direction and encouragement received from three men who have devoted a major portion of their long lives to historical pursuits and collection in the Detroit River region: Mr. George F. Macdonald who made available his rare collection, and also gave freely of his accumulated store of information; Rev. George Paré who offered expert counsel on many occasions, and placed at the writer's disposal material that proved to be of great assistance; Dr. Milo M. Quaife whose suggestions have been of immeasurable benefit, and who gave permission to make use of any material found in his numerous writings.

It is impossible within the conventional limits of a preface to give adequate expression of indebtedness to the directors and staffs of several archival depositories visited in Canada and the United States. These faithful servants constitute such a long list that it behooves to name only the institutions: Quebec Chancery Archives; Quebec Seminary; St. Mary's College, Montreal; Montreal Municipal Library; Public Archives of Canada, Ottawa; Ontario Provincial Archives, Toronto; Toronto Public Library, Reference Division; George F. Macdonald Collection, Windsor, Ontario; Archives of Assumption Church, Windsor, Ontario; Burton Historical Collection, Detroit; Wayne County Registry Office, Detroit;

William L. Clements Library, Ann Arbor, Michigan. Without in any way reflecting upon the generosity of others, however, it is fit to single out for special thanks the personnel of the Burton Historical Collection, where a major portion of the present work was compiled. Mrs. Elleine H. Stones and Mr. James M. Babcock, successive directors, and their efficient staff were always eager to devote time and service far beyond the ordinary requirements of courtesy or duty.

It is a pleasure to express a great indebtedness to the officials of the Champlain Society, Dr. W. Kaye Lamb, the President, and Dr. P. C. T. White, the Editor, whose patient guidance and competent supervision have proven invaluable. The figures and maps appearing in this volume were drawn under the direction of Major C. C. J. Bond, Army Headquarters, Ottawa, whose contribution of exquisite craftsmanship is hereby gratefully acknowledged. Lastly an expression of sincere thanks is due to the directors of Assumption University of Windsor for granting the writer leave of absence to make possible the preparation of this work.

A word of explanation about the documentation found in this volume will be helpful to the reader. Corresponding to the eight chapters of the Introduction, the Documents section also contains eight divisions lettered "A" to "H." Generally the documents appear in chronological order, but a logical sequence is observed when distinct topics are developed under the same heading. Throughout this section it has been deemed advisable to refrain from the liberal sprinkling of *"sic"* that would be required to mark the numerous mistakes in grammar, spelling, and punctuation. The original text of the French and Latin documents will be found in Appendix I. Some of the English translations of these documents are taken from cited published sources and are reproduced without alteration. In the translations made by the author the aim has been to convey the precise meaning without any attempt at achieving a literary excellence that is not found in the original texts. It will be noticed that a large proportion of the records comes from ecclesiastical sources. All the material available was examined, and the compiler alone is responsible for the selection.

Manifesting perhaps more local pride than common prudence, quite untrained in historical research, the writer undertook this publication as a labour of love—a task that turned out to be a very rewarding experience. Many times he was led to realize the wisdom contained in the lines inscribed near the entrance of the William L. Clements Library: "In the darkness dwells the people which knows its annals not." In presenting this volume his great hope is that it may serve at least as a small candlelight to dispel some of the darkness that in the past two centuries has gathered over this oldest continuous settlement in the Province of Ontario. It will be more than ample compensation if this "gathering up of the fragments lest they be lost" should help to interest some future writer in the preparation of a work that will do full justice to the greatness of the subject.

E. J. LAJEUNESSE, C.S.B.

CONTENTS

FOREWORD TO THE ONTARIO SERIES BY THE HONOURABLE LESLIE M. FROST, PRIME MINISTER OF ONTARIO vii

PREFACE ix

INTRODUCTION

    A. VISITORS BEFORE 1700 xxix
    B. THE FOUNDING OF DETROIT AND THE HURON MISSION ... xli
    C. SETTLERS COME TO THE SOUTH SHORE lii
    D. THE PIONEER SETTLERS AND THEIR FARMS lxvi
    E. GOVERNMENT AND LAW UNDER BRITISH RULE lxxvi
    F. RELIGION AND EDUCATION AFTER 1760 xc
    G. LOYALISTS AND LAND BOARDS cii
    H. FIRST TOWNS—SANDWICH AND AMHERSTBURG cxvii

DOCUMENTS

    A. VISITORS BEFORE 1700

      A 1 Extracts from the Relation of 1640–1 by Jérôme Lalement at Ste. Marie among the Hurons 3
      A 2 Extracts from the Relation of 1640–1 by Jérôme Lalement at Ste. Marie among the Hurons 3
      A 3 Extracts from Galinée's Narrative (1669–70) 4
      A 4 Act of Taking Possession of the Lands of Lake Erie (October 1669) 8
      A 5 Tonti's Visit to the Strait of Lake Erie 8
      A 6 Hennepin's Description of the Strait by which Lake Orleans Empties into Lake Conty 9
      A 7 Denonville to Monsieur Du Lhut (Duluth) 10
      A 8 Act of Retaking Possession of the Land in the Neighborhood of the Strait between Lakes Erie and Huron 11
      A 9 Frontenac to the Minister 12
      A 10 Cadillac to the Minister 13

CONTENTS

B. THE FOUNDING OF DETROIT AND THE HURON MISSION

B	1	Callières to Pontchartrain	17
B	2	Description of the Detroit River by M. de Lamothe, the Commandant there	18
B	3	Germain to Cadillac	19
B	4	Extracts from Cadillac's Description of Detroit in 1702	20
B	5	Extracts from Cadillac's Report of Detroit in 1703	22
B	6	Memorandum on Indians at Detroit	24
B	7	Extracts from the Answer of Mm. Vaudreuil and Bégon to Cadillac's Petition to Be Put in Possession of Detroit	26
B	8	Charlevoix at Detroit	26
B	9	La Richardie to Retz	27
B	10	Extract from the Journal of the Most Interesting Occurences in Canada 1746–7	29
B	11	Extracts from the Account Book of the Huron Mission	30
B	12	Extracts from the Potier Manuscript	35
B	13	Extracts from the Potier Gazette	37

C. SETTLERS COME TO THE SOUTH SHORE

C	1	The Journey of Joseph Gaspard Chaussegros de Léry to Detroit in 1749	42
C	2	Instructions for the Surveyor of Detroit	45
C	3	Names of Inhabitants to Whom Were Granted Lands of 3 Arpents Frontage by 40 Arpents in Depth in the Year 1749	45
C	4	Léry's Report of his Journey to Detroit	46
C	5	Contract of Jean Baptiste and René LeBeau to Conduct a Canot to Detroit	48
C	6	Extracts from the Cicotte Book	49
C	7	Census of the Inhabitants of Detroit on September 1st, 1750	54
C	8	Extract from Father Bonnecamps' Report	57
C	9	Grant of Land to Chevalier de Longueuil	57
C	10	Grant of Land to Alexis Delisle	58
C	11	Grant of Land to Pierre Réaume	59
C	12	Grant of Land to Widow Vien	59
C	13	The Captivity of Charles Stuart	59

C	14	Gift of Land—Pontiac to Maisonville	62
C	15	Louis Gervais Takes Possession of Land	62
C	16	Extract from the Census of All the Inhabitants of Detroit Made by Philip Dejean in the Year 1768	63
C	17	General Gage to Commander at Detroit	64
C	18	Gift of Land from the Ottawas to Charles Réaume	66
C	19	Lieutenant-Governor Hamilton to General Carleton	67
C	20	Lieutenant-Governor Hamilton to General Haldimand	67
C	21	Notes on a Survey by T. Smith of Lots Opposite Peach Island	68
C	22	Major De Peyster to F. Comparé	68
C	23	A Survey of the Settlement of Detroit Made by Order of Major De Peyster in 1782	69
C	24	General Haldimand to Lieutenant-Governor Jehu Hay	74
C	25	Lieutenant-Governor Hay to General Haldimand	74
C	26	Census of the Families and Farms of Petite Côte	75
C	27	Extracts from the Minutes of the Land Board of the District of Hesse	77

D. THE PIONEER SETTLERS AND THEIR FARMS

D	1	Baptisms of French Children at the Mission of the Hurons	78
D	2	Marriage Contract	79
D	3	List of the Inhabitants Living on the Detroit River, Who Have Engaged to Furnish Provisions for His Majesty's Troops at this Post and Yearly, Specifying the Quantity and at What Rate	80
D	4	Inventory of the Estate of Joseph Pillet	81
D	5	A General Return of All the Inhabitants of Detroit Taken by Phillip Dejean, 1773	82
D	6	Contract of Purchase between Claude Landry and Benjamin Chaput	83
D	7	Lieutenant-Governor Hamilton to the Earl of Dartmouth	84
D	8	Petition for Water-Mill on Turkey Creek	85
D	9	Reverend J. F. Hubert to General Haldimand	86

E. GOVERNMENT AND LAW UNDER BRITISH RULE

- E 1 Marquis de Vaudreuil to Commander Belestre .. 88
- E 2 Extract from the Journal of Robert Rogers 89
- E 3 Extract from George Croghan's Journal 1759–63 93
- E 4 Extracts from the Pontiac Manuscript 94
- E 5 Major Henry Gladwin to Sir Jeffery Amherst 98
- E 6 Commission to Jacques Campeau 100
- E 7 Appointment of Philip Dejean as Justice of the Peace etc. 100
- E 8 Appointment of Philip Dejean as Judge 101
- E 9 Major Henry Bassett to General Haldimand 101
- E 10 Award by Arbitrators 102
- E 11 Lord George Germain to Governor Haldimand .. 102
- E 12 Calculation of Rum Necessary per Day for Detroit, Taken from the Issues between 25th December 1778 and 24th June 1779 103
- E 13 General Haldimand to Lieutenant-Colonel Mason Bolton 103
- E 14 Major De Peyster to General Haldimand 103
- E 15 Extract from the Account of the Expedition of Lieutenant-Governor Hamilton 104
- E 16 Major Mathews to General Haldimand 104
- E 17 Extract from the Proclamation Forming the District of Hesse 105
- E 18 Appointment of Justices and Officers for the District of Hesse 105
- E 19 Judge Powell to Bishop Hubert 106
- E 20 Extract from the Copy of a Journal Dated Detroit June 8, 1791 107
- E 21 Accounts of the Sheriff of the District of Hesse .. 107
- E 22 D. W. Smith to John Askin 108
- E 23 Smith to Askin 110
- E 24 Smith to Askin 111
- E 25 Election Expenses of David W. Smith 112
- E 26 Smith to John Askin 113
- E 27 Copy of an Account of the Sheriff's Expenses for the Election of Members for the Counties of Suffolk & Essex 113
- E 28 Askin to Alexander McKee 114
- E 29 Askin to McKee 115

CONTENTS

E 30 Captain Wm. Mayne to Major General Anthony Wayne 115
E 31 Wayne to Mayne 116

F. RELIGION AND EDUCATION AFTER 1760

F 1 Report of Father de Launay, Procurator of the Canadian Missions, to the Superior-General 117
F 2 Sale of Land—Potier to Marantet 117
F 3 Potier to Briand 118
F 4 Extract from the Account Book of Assumption Parish for 1775–1781 118
F 5 List of the Inhabitants of Petite Côte in 1778 119
F 6 Gift of Land from the Hurons to Father Potier 120
F 7 Death and Burial of Father Potier 120
F 8 Affidavit of Francis Pratt 121
F 9 Inventory of the Effects of the late Father Potier 121
F 10 Major De Peyster to Major Lernoult 123
F 11 Minutes of a Meeting of the Church Wardens 124
F 12 Speeches of the Principal Huron Chiefs in Council with Major De Peyster, Commandant of Detroit &c, July 29, 1781 124
F 13 Extracts from the Account Book of Assumption Parish for 1781 126
F 14 Gift of Land from the Huron Indians to Reverend F. X. Hubert and the Sisters of the Congregation 131
F 15 Re a Foundation of the Congregation of Notre-Dame at Detroit 132
F 16 Hubert to Bishop Briand 134
F 17 Fréchette to Hubert 134
F 18 Dufaux to Hubert 136
F 19 Dufaux to Hubert 139
F 20 Dufaux to Hubert 141
F 21 Dufaux to Hubert 142
F 22 Dufaux to Hubert 145
F 23 Wm. Monforton to Alexander McKee 145
F 24 Dufaux to Hubert 145
F 25 Copy of a Letter from His Excellency John Graves Simcoe to the Reverend Edmund Burke, Vicar-General of Upper Canada 147

F 26 Dufaux to Hubert 148
F 27 The Inhabitants of L'Assomption to Hubert 149
F 28 The Reverend E. Burke to the Parishioners of the Church of the Assumption 150
F 29 Marchand to Hubert 151
F 30 Extract from the Minutes of the Executive Council (Lands) 153

G. LOYALISTS AND LAND BOARDS

G 1 Indian Deed to Jacob Schieffelin 154
G 2 Captain Alexander McKee to Sir John Johnson 155
G 3 Captain Bird to Captain Mathews 156
G 4 General Frederick Haldimand to Sir John Johnson 157
G 5 Haldimand to Lieutenant-Governor Hay 157
G 6 Hay to Haldimand 158
G 7 Haldimand to Hay 159
G 8 Hay to Philip Fry, Deputy Surveyor 160
G 9 Certificate of Philip Fry, Deputy Surveyor 161
G 10 Extract from the Minutes of Council of Upper Canada 161
G 11 Report of Land Committee re the Grant of a Certain Marsh at Detroit 162
G 12 Extracts from the Diary of David Zeisberger 163
G 13 The Chiefs of the Ottawa and Chippewa Nations of Detroit Ceding Land at River Canard and Bois Blanc 165
G 14 Major Robert Mathews to Haldimand 166
G 15 List of Disbanded Troops and Loyalists to Be Settled on the North Side of Lake Erie 167
G 16 List of Disbanded Troops and Loyalists Settled at the Mouth of the River Detroit 170
G 17 Indian Deed of Present Southwestern Ontario to King George III 171
G 18 Indian Speech to Sir John Johnson at Huron Village 173
G 19 Minutes of a Meeting of the Land Board for the District of Hesse 173
G 20 Schedules of Lots in Two Connected Townships 174
G 21 Minutes of a Meeting of the Land Board for the District of Hesse 176

G 22	Minutes of a Meeting of the Land Board of the Counties of Essex and Kent	176
G 23	Minutes of the Land Board Meeting, re the Claims of the Inhabitants of L'Assomption Settlement for a Second Concession	177
G 24	Minutes of a Meeting of the Land Board of Hesse, re the Petition of the Inhabitants of Petite Côte for Their Continuations	178
G 25	D. W. Smith, Secretary of the Land Board, to P. McNiff, Deputy Surveyor	178
G 26	McNiff to D. W. Smith	179
G 27	Minutes of a Meeting of the Land Board for the District of Hesse re the Side Lines at Petite Côte	180
G 28	D. W. Smith to Captain Monforton	180
G 29	E. J. O'Brien, Secretary of the Land Board, to McNiff	181
G 30	Report from McNiff	182
G 31	Order of Survey for Lots on Streams Flowing into Lake St. Clair	183
G 32	Report from the Deputy Surveyor Re Lots on Streams Flowing into Lake St. Clair	184
G 33	R. G. England to D. W. Smith	184
G 34	Agreement of Sale from William Smith to John Askin	185
G 35	Deputy Surveyor Iredell to Surveyor General's Office	185
G 36	Certificates for Lots of Land Bought by Askin	186
G 37	Askin to D. W. Smith at Newark	186
G 38	Askin to the Honorable Richard Cartwright at Yorke	187

H. THE FIRST TOWNS—SANDWICH AND AMHERSTBURG

H 1	Lists of Persons Residing in Detroit in 1796 who Elected to Remain British Subjects	189
H 2	A Memorial from Several Magistrates of Detroit to Colonel Sargent	190
H 3	Peter Russell to Robert Prescott	191
H 4	Prescott to Russell	191
H 5	Russell to Prescott	191
H 6	Prescott to Russell	192

CONTENTS

H	7	Lists of Persons Who Have Drawn Lots in the Town of Sandwich	193
H	8	Minutes of the Executive Council (Lands) re Lots Adjoining the Baby Mill	194
H	9	Directions Respecting Reserves and Surveys in the Town of Sandwich	194
H	10	Certificate of First Houses in the Town of Sandwich and Assignment of Park Lots	195
H	11	Minutes of the Executive Council re Gaol and Court House for the Western District	195
H	12	Prideaux Selby to Russell	196
H	13	Russell to the Duke of Portland	197
H	14	Schedule of Timbers Contracted for by Mr. Augustin Roy for the Purpose of Building a Gaol and Court House at Sandwich	198
H	15	Russell to the Anglican Bishop of Quebec	199
H	16	The Anglican Bishop of Quebec to Russell	199
H	17	Russell to the Duke of Portland	199
H	18	Marriage Register for the Western District	200
H	19	Report of Grand Jury re Town of Sandwich	203
H	20	Alexander McKee to Russell	204
H	21	Sir John Johnson to Russell	204
H	22	Captain Thomas McKee to Captain William Claus	205
H	23	Sale of the Huron Church Reserve	205
H	24	Extract from Gother Mann's Report to Lord Dorchester	209
H	25	Minutes of the Land Board of Hesse re George Town	210
H	26	Memorandum by Gother Mann to Lieutenant-Governor Simcoe	211
H	27	Lieutenant-Colonel R. G. England to Simcoe	212
H	28	Dorchester to Simcoe	212
H	29	England to Green	212
H	30	England to Green	213
H	31	England to James Wilkinson	213
H	32	Captain Wm. Mayne to Green	214
H	33	Captain Hector McLean to Green	215
H	34	McLean to Green	217
H	35	Requisition for Stores Proposed as Presents for Indians Resorting to the Post of Amherstburg for the Year 1797	217

CONTENTS

H 36	Return of Provisions and Rum Issued to Indians at Amherstburg and Chenail Ecarté from 25 June 1797 to 24 June 1798	220
H 37	McLean to Green	221
H 38	McLean to Colonel Alexander McKee	221
H 39	McLean to General Robert Prescott	222
H 40	Prescott to Russell	222
H 41	McLean to Green	223
H 42	McLean to Green	225
H 43	McLean to Green	225
H 44	Names of Lot Holders in the Town of Amherstburg 1799	226

Appendixes

I. Original Texts of French and Latin Documents

A 1	Extraits de la Relation de 1640–1 par Jérôme Lalement à Ste-Marie-aux-Hurons	229
A 2	Extraits de la Relation de 1640–1 par Jérôme Lalement à Ste-Marie-aux-Hurons	229
A 3	Extraits du voyage de MM. Dollier et Galinée 1669–70	230
A 4	Acte de prise de possession des terres du Lac Erié	233
A 5	Visite de M. de Tonti au détroit du Lac Herié	233
A 6	Description par Hennepin du détroit par lequel le Lac Orléans se décharge dans le Lac Conty	234
A 7	Lettre du Marquis de Denonville à Greysolon du Lhut (Duluth)	234
A 8	La Durantaye renouvelle la prise de possession des terres des environs du détroit des Lacs Erié et Huron	235
A 9	Frontenac au ministre	236
A 10	Lamothe Cadillac au ministre	236
B 1	Callières au ministre	239
B 2	Description de la rivière du Détroit par le Sieur de Lamothe Cadillac qui y commande	240
B 3	Lettre du Père Germain à Lamothe Cadillac	241
B 4	Extraits d'une description du Détroit par M. de Lamothe	242

B	5	Extraits d'une lettre de Lamothe Cadillac à Jérôme Pontchartrain	244
B	7	Extraits de la réponse des Sieurs de Vaudreuil et Bégon	245
B	8	Charlevoix au Détroit	245
B	9	La Richardie ad Retz	246
B	11	Extraits du livre de compte de la mission des Hurons du Détroit	247
B	12	Extraits du Manuscrit Potier	251
B	13	Extraits de la Gazette du Père Potier	253
C	1	Extrait du journal de la campagne que le Sr. de Léry a faite au Détroit en l'année 1749	257
C	4	Rapport de Joseph Gaspard Chaussegros de Léry sur son voyage au Détroit en 1749	259
C	5	Contrat de Jean Baptiste et René LeBeau pour conduire un canot au Poste du Détroit	262
C	6	Extraits du Registre Cicot	262
C	8	Extrait du rapport du Père Bonnecamps	266
C	9	Concession au Chevalier de Longueuil	267
C	10	Concession à Alexis Delisle	268
C	11	Concession à Pierre Réaume	268
C	12	Concession à la veuve Vien	269
C	15	Louis Gervais prend possession d'une terre	269
C	18	Donation des Ottawas à Charles Réaume	269
C	22	Le Commandant De Peyster à F. Comparé	270
D	2	Contrat de mariage	270
D	4	Inventaire des biens de feu Joseph Pillet, habitant établi à la côte du sud	271
D	6	Contrat d'acquest entre Claude Landry et Benjamin Chappue	272
D	8	Pétition pour un moulin à eau à la Rivière aux Dindes	273
D	9	Le Révérend J.-F. Hubert au Général Haldimand	274
E	1	Le Marquis de Vaudreuil au Commandant Belestre	274
E	4	Extraits du journal de la conspiration de Pontiac	275
E	19	Powell à Hubert	278

CONTENTS

E	20	Extrait de la copie d'un journal daté Détroit 8 janvier 1791	278
F	1	De Launay, Proc. Miss. Canad. ad Superiorem Generalem	279
F	2	Vente de terre — Potier à Marantet	279
F	3	Potier à Briand	280
F	4	Extrait du livre de compte de l'église de l'Assomption 1775-81	280
F	6	Donation des Hurons au Père Potier	281
F	7	Mort et inhumation du Père Potier	281
F	8	Déclaration de François Pratt	281
F	9	Inventaire des effets du feu Père Potier	282
F	11	Procès-verbal d'une assemblée des marguilliers	284
F	12	Discours des principaux chefs hurons en conseil au Major De Peyster commandant au Détroit &c. 29 juillet 1781	285
F	13	Extraits du Registre des Comptes, Elections &c. de la paroisse de l'Assomption, 1781 —	286
F	15	Etablissement de la Congrégation de Notre-Dame à Détroit	291
F	16	Hubert à Mgr. J.-O. Briand	293
F	17	Fréchette à Hubert	293
F	18	Dufaux à Hubert	294
F	19	Dufaux à Hubert	297
F	20	Dufaux à Hubert	299
F	21	Dufaux à Hubert	300
F	22	Dufaux à Hubert	303
F	24	Dufaux à Hubert	303
F	25	Traduction française de la susdite lettre	304
F	26	Dufaux à Hubert	305
F	27	Les habitants de l'Assomption à Hubert	306
F	28	Le Révérend E. Burke aux paroissiens de l'église de l'Assomption	307
F	29	Marchand à Hubert	308

II. FRENCH COMMANDANTS AT DETROIT 1701-60 ... 310

III. DOUBLE NAMES OR SOBRIQUETS ... 311

IV. ABSTRACTS FROM THE DETROIT NOTARIAL RECORDS .. 312

V. GENEALOGIES ... 335

CONTENTS

VI. SUMMARY OF THE MARRIAGES RECORDED IN THE PARISH OF THE ASSUMPTION 1760–81 343

VII. BRITISH COMMANDING OFFICERS AT DETROIT 1760–1796 356

VIII. MARGUILLIERS OR WARDENS OF THE PARISH OF THE ASSUMPTION 356

IX. HOLDERS OF FARM LOTS IN ESSEX COUNTY ABOUT 1794 357

BIBLIOGRAPHY 361

INDEX 365

ILLUSTRATIONS

Maps

1. SANSON'S MAP OF CANADA OR NEW FRANCE, 1656 .... *facing page* xxxii
2. SECTION OF MAP OF GALINÉE'S VOYAGE, 1670 xxxiv
3. MAP SHOWING THE LOCATION OF INDIAN AND PRE-INDIAN VESTIGES IN ESSEX COUNTY AND VICINITY xxxviii
4. MAP OF DETROIT ERIÉ BY COMMANDANT DE BOIS-HEBERT, *c.* 1730 xliv
5. IMAGINATIVE DRAWING OF FORT PONTCHARTRAIN, *c.* 1740 l
6. MAP OF THE DETROIT RIVER BY CHAUSSEGROS DE LÉRY, *fils,* 1749 liv
7. TOPOGRAPHICAL MAP OF DETROIT BY CHAUSSEGROS DE LÉRY, *fils, c.* 1754 lviii
8. PLAN OF DETROIT WITH ITS ENVIRONS BY JOHN MONTRESOR, 1763 lxii
9. SECTION OF MCNIFF'S SURVEY OF 1791 SHOWING LOCATION OF WINDMILLS ALONG THE DETROIT RIVER lxxiii
10. PLAN OF J. B. FERÉ'S WATER-MILL ON TURKEY CREEK BY T. SMITH, 1798 lxxv
11. THE BOUNDARIES OF THE COUNTIES OF ESSEX, KENT, AND SUFFOLK IN 1792 lxxxvi
12. PLAN OF THE HURON RESERVE AND MALDEN BY P. MCNIFF, 1790 cvi
13. THE CESSION OF THE INDIANS TO KING GEORGE III ON MAY 19, 1790 cx
14. MAP OF ESSEX COUNTY SHOWING THE WATER-FRONTAGE SURVEYS OF THE 1790's .... *facing page* cxvi

ILLUSTRATIONS

15. PLAN OF THE PURCHASE OF THE HURON RESERVE FOR THE TOWN OF SANDWICH BY A. IREDELL, JULY 12, 1797 cxix

16. PLAN OF FORTIFICATIONS OPPOSITE THE ISLAND OF BOIS BLANC IN 1796 cxxv

17. SKETCH OF THE POST AT AMHERSTBURG BY A. COOPER, 1797, AND THE WORKS OF DEFENCE ORDERED TO BE CONSTRUCTED IN 1799 BY GOTHER MANN cxxvii

18. HOLDERS OF LOTS IN THE TOWN OF AMHERSTBURG, 1799 cxxviii

Plates

(Between pp. lxiv and lxv)

I. FATHER PIERRE POTIER, S.J.

II. COLONEL ALEXANDER MCKEE

III. THE RECTORY AND HALL OF ASSUMPTION PARISH BUILT IN 1784

IV. THE MATTHEW ELLIOTT HOMESTEAD BUILT IN 1784

V. THE HURON CHURCH OR CHURCH OF THE ASSUMPTION OPENED IN 1787

(Between pp. xcvi and xcvii)

VI. THE NORTH BLOCKHOUSE OPPOSITE THE UPPER END OF BOIS BLANC ISLAND

VII. THE STOREHOUSE FLANKED BY TWO SMALL BLOCKHOUSES IN FRONT OF THE WHARF OPPOSITE THE ISLAND OF BOIS BLANC

THE WINDSOR BORDER REGION

INTRODUCTION

A. VISITORS BEFORE 1700

THIS historical survey is intended to serve as an introduction to a series of documents relating to the exploration and settlement of Canada's southernmost frontier. A glance at the map of Canada suffices to locate that frontier—the Detroit River region.[1] At 42° latitude the eye quickly focuses on a 20-by-30-mile rectangular peninsula whose south, west, and north shores are washed by the waters of Lake Erie, the Detroit River, and Lake St. Clair respectively. Today this peninsula is Essex County in the Province of Ontario. Local Chambers of Commerce refer to it as the Sun Parlour of Canada. A recent book which records the development of the county and its chief city, Windsor, during the past century is entitled *Garden Gateway to Canada*. These last two appellations indicate its frontier position, its mild climate, and its fertile fields.

The exploration of the Detroit River region was retarded by the warring expeditions of the Father of New France. In 1609 and 1615, when Champlain accompanied Algonquin and Huron Indians on forays against their Iroquois enemies, whose strongholds were located between the Hudson and Genesee rivers in the present State of New York, he sealed the friendship between the French and the Hurons and Algonquins. At the same time, however, he provoked later alignments of the Iroquois with their Dutch and English neighbours of the Atlantic seaboard, because the savages became convinced that the French were the allies of their Indian enemies. Because of this enmity of the Iroquois for the French, for half a century the French explorers and missionaries could not follow the St. Lawrence River and Lake Ontario in their westward journeys. Instead they paddled and portaged up the Ottawa River to Lake Nipissing, then down the French River into Georgian Bay at a point directly east of the Straits of Mackinac, connecting Lakes Huron and Michigan. As a consequence all the upper lakes were explored before Lake Erie.

Despite the Iroquois road-block on the Lake Ontario route to the interior of the continent, the historical beginnings of the strait between Lakes Huron and Erie reach back into the first half of the seventeenth century. By the Ottawa route Father Jean de Brébeuf

[1]The French word *détroit* means a strait. The early explorers considered the whole water connection between Lakes Huron and Erie as *Le Détroit*, Lake St. Clair being only a bulge in the strait.

xxix

and his companions in 1626 reached the country of the Hurons on the southern shore of Georgian Bay. These Indians had been chosen as the object of the first Jesuit missionary effort in the West because they were less migratory than the other tribes. While striving to evangelize this nation, the blackrobes did not close their eyes to other possible fields of apostolic endeavour which lay beyond the boundaries of Huronia. As early as 1640 they had detailed knowledge of the territory to the south, where were located the villages of the Neutral nation,[2] and at least a general notion of the strait between Lakes Huron and Erie (A 1). Where had they obtained this information? Some of it had likely come from Joseph de La Roche d'Aillon, Recollet missionary, who in 1626 had spent some time among the Neutral nation, "of which the interpreter (Bruslé) has told wonders."[3] Information might also have been supplied by Etienne Brûlé himself, who is believed to have been the first European to gaze upon the waters of Lake Erie. Moreover, the Relation of 1640–1[4] tells of many Frenchmen from Huronia who, in the past, had penetrated into the country of the Neutrals for purposes of trade. On their return these traders were no doubt interrogated and any geographical knowledge thus obtained was entered on maps drawn at the mission headquarters of Ste. Marie among the Hurons.[5]

These reports about the extent of this nation to the south kindled the zeal of the Jesuits, and in the fall of 1640 Fathers Brébeuf and Chaumonot left the country of the Hurons to spend the winter preaching the Gospel to the Neutrals. The Relation of 1640–1

[2]Some historians relying mostly on early maps assign to the Neutral nation the whole northern shore of Lake Erie from the Niagara to the Detroit rivers. Others basing their opinion on written documents tend to restrict the villages of the Neutrals to the Niagara district (both sides of the river) and a small area at the western end of Lake Ontario.

[3]For an account of La Roche d'Aillon's excursion into the Neutral country, see Father Christian Leclerq, *First Establishment of the French in New France*, I, 263–70.

[4]The Jesuit missionaries in North America sent every year to their Canadian Superior at Quebec an account of their activities. These letters were combined into a long narrative called a Relation, which was sent to the Provincial in Paris. There they were printed by Sebastien Cramoisy. The Relations proper begin in 1632 and continue to 1673. In 1858 the Dominion government published in French a three-volume edition of these Jesuit Relations. From 1896 to 1901 Reuben Gold Thwaites edited a page-for-page translation of the Relations, to which he added a mass of related documentary material. This imposing publication comprising seventy-three volumes is known as *The Jesuit Relations and Allied Documents*, hereafter referred to as Thwaites, *Jesuit Relations*.

[5]On the right bank of the River Wye, about three miles east of the town of Midland, Ontario.

INTRODUCTION   xxxi

describes this winter tour of the missionaries, and states that they were well received by a certain strange nation at a village called Khioetoa,⁶ which they renamed the Mission of St. Michel (A 2). On his return to Huronia in March 1641, Chaumonot drew a map of this journey, but no copy can be found today.

However, that map very likely served as a basis for two others that were issued within the next two decades. In 1656 Sanson d'Abbeville, geographer to the King, published at Paris a map showing the full extent of Lake Erie and its connection with Lake Huron through what are now known as the Detroit River, Lake St. Clair, and River St. Clair (see Fig. 1). Therefore, as early as 1656, and possibly much earlier, certain persons had explored the strait sufficiently to make a fairly accurate map of the waters and the adjacent land. In 1660 the Jesuit historian Du Creux issued a map which differs only slightly from Sanson's. On both these maps Lake St. Clair is named Lac des Eaux de Mer (Salt Water Lake), which suggests that some of the information had come at least indirectly from the Indians, who were always willing to "oblige" the explorers looking for the South Sea. Information was also derived from the Jesuits, possibly from Chaumonot's map, because on both maps there is marked the location of a number of their missions. The Mission of St. Michel is located on the Canadian side of the Detroit River near the present city of Windsor. Hence we must reckon with the possibility that Fathers Brébeuf and Chaumonot may have reached the Detroit River region in the winter of 1640–1.

The Relation of 1641–2 reveals that the Jesuits were withdrawn from such outlying missions as a consequence of Father Lalemant's policy of concentrating all missionary efforts among the Hurons until the entire tribe should be converted.⁷ The result of this policy was that some 3,000 persons were baptized in the two years prior to the spring of 1649.⁸ This was the year of the martyrdom of the Jesuits and the destruction of the Huron villages by the Dutch-armed Iroquois.

The remnants of the Hurons fled in every direction. Some three hundred of them, after various sojourns, settled at Lorette near Quebec, and their descendants are there to this day. Others made their way to the islands in Georgian Bay and to the northern shores of Lakes Huron and Michigan and even to Wisconsin. After the

⁶It is important to note that the village of Khioetoa was inhabited by a strange nation, not by Neutral Indians. Hence its location near the Detroit River cannot be used to establish the extent of the territory of the Neutral nation.
⁷Thwaites, *Jesuit Relations*, XXIII, 179–81.
⁸*Ibid.*, XXXIII, 69, 257.

dispersal of the Hurons, the Iroquois carried the terrors of their ferocious prowess southwest to the Petuns or Tobacco nation and then southward to the land of the Neutrals. By 1651 the whole of western Ontario including the Essex County peninsula was nothing but the unpopulated hunting grounds of the Iroquois.

In 1666 the Iroquois spirit was temporarily tamed when the Mohawk strongholds were destroyed by the Carignan-Salières Regiment. The St. Lawrence and Lake Ontario route was now open to the French, and the explorers and missionaries lost little time in taking advantage of it. In 1669 Robert Cavelier de La Salle was preparing near Montreal an expedition to the southwest in order to explore the Ohio River, which was believed to empty into the South Sea, and thereby find a way to China. Governor Rémy de Courcelles urged François Dollier de Casson, a Sulpician priest, to join the expedition. René Bréhant de Galinée, a deacon, was sent as Dollier's companion[9] and recorded the events of the journey.

Galinée's Journal unfolds one of the most interesting stories of early American exploration (A 3). On July 5, 1669, twenty-one men in seven canoes left Montreal. After a voyage up the St. Lawrence River, they followed the south shore of Lake Ontario where they obtained a guide at a Seneca village. In September they arrived at an Iroquois hunting camp called Tiwanatawa, formerly the site of a Neutral village, located a dozen miles northwest of the present city of Hamilton, Ontario. There they talked with a man named Jolliet,[10] who was returning to Quebec from Lake Superior where he had been sent by Courcelles to discover the location of copper mines and to find an easy route for bringing the ore to Montreal—a vision of a commercial highway along the chain of lakes and rivers. An Iroquois prisoner whom Jolliet had saved from the Ottawa Indians had offered to show him a new passage to the St. Lawrence. It proved to be the straits connecting Lakes Huron and Erie—a way that Sanson had mapped out in 1656, and which had been described in the Jesuit Relations as early as 1641. Jolliet is, however, the first white man known to have paddled down the Detroit River.

---

[9]Why historians employ the name Dollier instead of Casson, but Galinée rather than Bréhant, is one of those quirks frequently associated with French-Canadian names.

[10]It has been generally assumed that this man was Louis Jolliet, who later explored the Mississippi River with Marquette. However, in the light of recent investigation it is more probable that it was Adrien, brother of Louis, with whom the missionaries conferred. See Jean Delanglez, S.J., "Louis Jolliet—Early Years," in *Mid-America*, XXVII, 3–29.

INTRODUCTION

At Tiwanatawa Jolliet drew for Dollier a rough sketch of the route he had followed. He told the Sulpician that in the north country he had heard of a numerous tribe called the Potawatomi. No missionary had as yet visited them. Here was a definite objective for Dollier's zeal. He would find the Potawatomi and begin his missionary work among them.[11] With seven men in three canoes Dollier and Galinée made their way to Lake Erie *via* the Grand River, and then followed the northern shore of the lake. Towards the end of October they had reached what is now the Port Dover region, where they wintered. On Passion Sunday, March 23, 1670, they took possession of all the surrounding country (southwestern Ontario) in the name of the King of France (A 4). Three days later they resumed their journey westward. They landed at Pointe Pelée[12] (in what is now Essex County) and in a storm during the night lost nearly all their belongings, including their entire altar service. These are the first white men known to have set foot on the soil of that county.

In spite of their misfortune they decided to continue their journey to Sault Ste. Marie in order to return to Montreal by way of the Ottawa River. They entered the Detroit River and after proceeding six leagues they came upon the camp sites of Indians who had come to pay homage to a stone idol located on the shore. The Iroquois had urged the two Sulpicians to honour this great Captain; instead the clerics destroyed it. The record does not state whether or not any pilgrimages of red men were present at that time but it is unlikely, since they would not have tolerated peaceably the destruction of their revered graven image. After four more leagues the Dollier-Galinée party entered a small lake, called by M. Sanson the Salt Water Lake, but they saw no signs of salt in it. This episode marks the first recorded advent of white men to the strait between Lakes Huron and Erie. Galinée's chart of the journey is the earliest map that discernibly delineates the shoreline of the peninsula of the present County of Essex (see Fig. 2).

In 1679 the restless La Salle reappeared on the scene of western exploration in a more pretentious effort. This time the canoes were replaced by a large sailing vessel—the first to come to the upper

---

[11]This objective did not accord with La Salle's plans. The party broke up and some of his men returned to Montreal and were afterwards referred to as "the men from China," and La Salle's domain near Montreal is said to have been called La Chine (Lachine) in derision of its master's dream of discovering a short cut to China.

[12]The French word *pelé(e)* means peeled or bare, and this tongue of land was so named by the French on account of the absence of trees on its east shore.

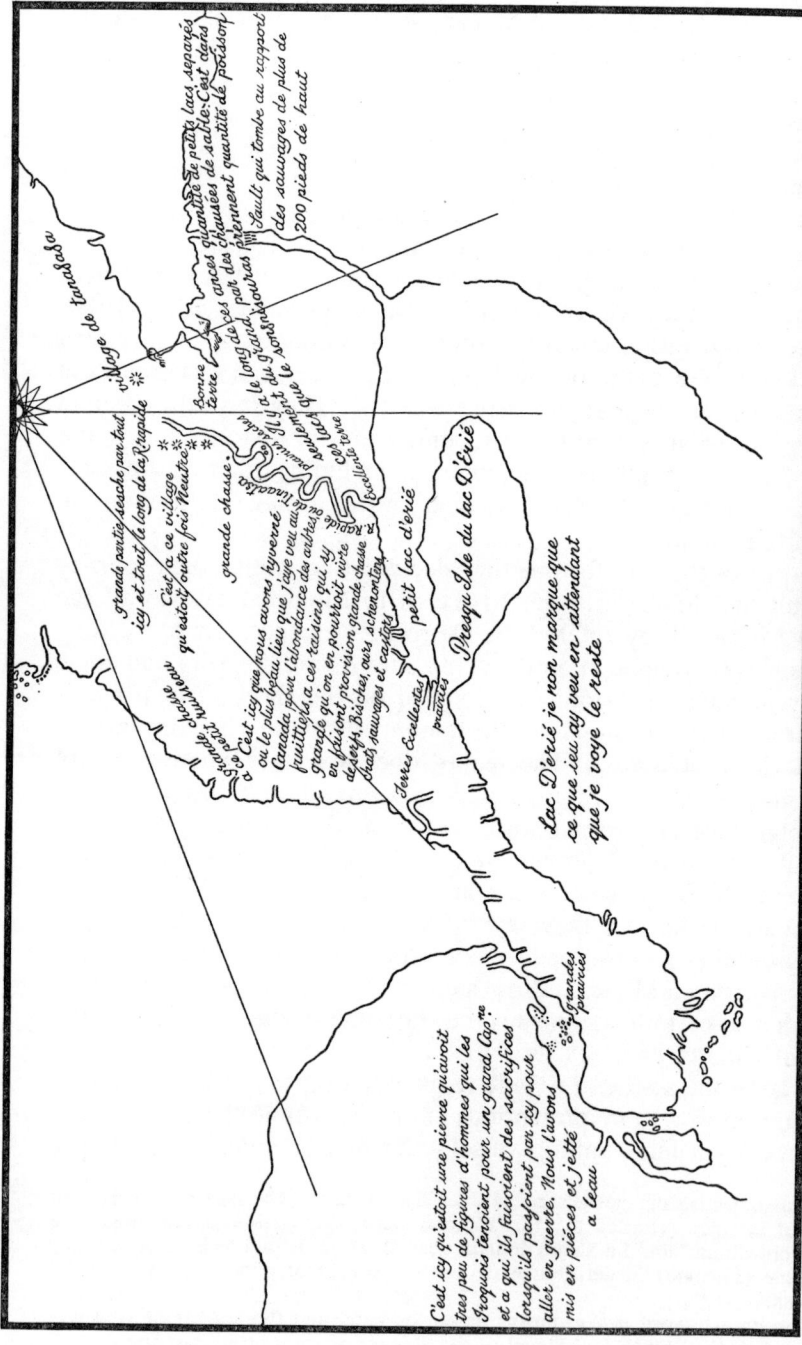

FIG. 2. SECTION OF MAP OF GALINÉE'S VOYAGE, 1670. [Copy in Public Archives of Canada.]

lakes. The falls at Niagara presented a major obstacle. Accordingly, early in 1679, at the mouth of Cayuga Creek (above the falls), La Salle built the *Griffon*, a sailing vessel of about forty-five tons' burden. While it was being constructed two groups from the shipyard visited the Detroit River region. In the winter La Salle sent an advance party of fifteen men to the Illinois tribes to prepare the way for his voyage. Then in early summer he sent his first assistant, Henri de Tonti, with five men to reconnoitre the coasts and lands "six times twenty" leagues ahead. Tonti stopped along the Detroit River and inquired about the earlier scouts from Niagara. He learned that they had gone farther. Unfortunately, he did not reveal whether his informants were Indians or white men. He returned to Niagara just in time to embark on the *Griffon*'s western voyage (A 5).[13]

With a party of thirty-two on board, including Father Louis Hennepin who was the historian of the voyage, the *Griffon* set sail on August 7, 1679. The winds were favourable, and on the feast of St. Lawrence (August 10) the first sailing vessel entered the Detroit River. Hennepin has left a promised-land description of the strait, wherein there is no mention of the presence of any inhabitants, red or white (A 6).

On the feast of St. Clare of Assisi (August 12) the *Griffon* entered the lake that washes the northern shore of the present Essex County. Accordingly its company named this body of water Lake Ste. Claire.[14] Head winds delayed their ship several days at the mouth of the St. Clair River. On August 23 they entered Lake Huron, and five days later (August 27), after weathering a very severe storm, they reached the Straits of Mackinac. After a few days of reconnoitring in the region, where they encountered some members of the advance party, they sailed into Lake Michigan and headed for its western shore to take on a cargo of furs. La Salle and Hennepin, still thirsting for new horizons, continued their explorations southward in canoes. On September 18 the *Griffon* started back for Niagara, but she was never seen again. After this tragedy

[13]In a Relation that is considered more authentic, Tonti and his men are said not to have returned to Niagara, but to have boarded the *Griffon* off a sandy point near the mouth of the strait. See "Relation de Henri de Tonty écrite de Québec le 14 novembre, 1694," in Pierre Margry, *Découvertes et établissements des Français dans l'ouest et dans le sud de l'Amérique septentrionale, 1614–1754*, I, 573–616.

[14]The lake was named after St. Clare of Assisi whose feast is kept on August 12. The French name is Claire, and local historians can give no satisfactory explanation of the actual spelling. In some later records it even appears as Lake Sinclair.

no sailing vessel is known to have passed through the Detroit River until after the British occupation eighty years later.

Although they are unrecorded there can be little doubt that numbers of the famed *coureurs de bois* visited the strait in the last half of the seventeenth century. The King of France wanted the fur trading with the distant tribes to be transacted along the St. Lawrence River and laws were passed with heavy penalties forbidding trading "in the woods." Nevertheless, attracted by the lure of large profits and an independent life, many bush rangers defied all edicts of the King and his representatives. Later, since it was impossible to prevent this surreptitious commerce, an attempt was made to control it. It was decided that each year there would be issued a limited number of *congés* or licences for trade with the distant tribes. It was to superintend this commerce, to form alliances with the Indians, and to keep them in check that a garrison was sent to Michilimackinac in 1683, of which Olivier Morel de La Durantaye was named the Commandant.

Michilimackinac was the chief meeting place of the *coureurs de bois* in the upper lakes. In 1680 when Hennepin was rescued from the Sioux Indians and brought to the Michilimackinac Indian mission, he found about fifty Frenchmen wintering there. Many of these adventurers joined the Indian tribes and settled among them. They consolidated the French influence in the West and helped to retain for France that part of the continent. From their headquarters these carefree and betimes wild men of the woods ranged far and wide, wherever furs could be obtained. Some of them probably visited the Detroit River region, for according to early travellers that area abounded in all game and fur-bearing animals to an extent not surpassed by any other place.

In 1686 Marquis de Denonville, Governor of New France, ordered Greysolon du Lhut (Duluth) to go from Michilimackinac with thirty soldiers to establish a fort at the strait between Lakes Huron and Erie in order to keep the English from trading on the upper lakes (A 7). The fort was named St. Joseph and was located at the northern end of River St. Clair (now the site of Port Huron, Michigan). It is reasonable to suppose that Duluth made a reconnaissance of the full extent of the strait before deciding upon a location for this fort.

The next recorded visitors to the district came in 1687. On June 7 of that year La Durantaye, leading a number of Indians, fur traders, and soldiers from Michilimackinac to Niagara, stopped on the west shore of the Detroit River long enough to take possession of the territory in the name of the King of France (A 8). In that deed there is mentioned the fact that La Salle had done so before "to facilitate his journeys by barge from Niagara to Michilimackinac." La Durantaye envisioned an early settlement in this area. He directed that several dwellings be built for the establishment of the French and the Miamis and Chouannons, "the former owners of the land at the strait, who had withdrawn from this place for some time for their greater convenience."[15]

Three months after La Durantaye's visit, Baron de La Hontan, a French army officer and a prolific writer, passed through the strait on his way to relieve Duluth at Fort St. Joseph. Strangely enough his description of the locality is very scant and contains nothing new.[16] There is no mention of encountering any villages of Indians along the shores of the river. La Hontan abandoned and burned Fort St. Joseph in 1689 when information reached him that the English and the Iroquois were preparing to move against it from their newly acquired position at Niagara.

English traders also visited the strait before the end of the seventeenth century. In 1686 Governor Denonville protested to the English Governor Thomas Dongan at New York the incursions of English traders in the upper lakes. Dongan replied that the King of England had as much right to trade in those parts as the King of France. To substantiate his claims Dongan equipped a considerable expedition composed of two flotillas, the first commanded by one Rooseboom and the second by Colonel McGregory. In spite of the fort at the head of the St. Clair River one party reached Lake Huron. On his way from Michilimackinac to Niagara in June of 1687, La Durantaye met and captured the Rooseboom party on Lake Huron. Among the prisoners taken were thirty Englishmen. Continuing his way, after stopping at Detroit, La Durantaye captured the McGregory group on Lake Erie.[17] This double defeat, however, did not discourage the English. In 1700 Robert Livingstone, Secretary for Indian Affairs at Albany, wrote to the Earl of Bellomont, Governor of New York, as follows:

We shall never be able to rancounter the French except we have a nursery of Bushlopers as well as they. . . . The best way to effect this is to build a

---

[15]The earlier presence of these tribes at the strait does not preclude the possibility of the Neutral Indians also abiding there at the same time. The river could have been the dividing line between the two nations. For locations of vestiges of Indian civilization in the present County of Essex, see Figure 3.

[16]M. le Baron de la Hontan, *Nouveaux Voyages de M. le baron de Lahontan dans l'Amérique septentrionale*, I, 108–9.

[17]E. B. O'Callaghan, ed., *Documents Relating to the Colonial History of the State of New York*, IX, 363. In future references this work will be designated as N.Y.C.D. (New York Colonial Documents).

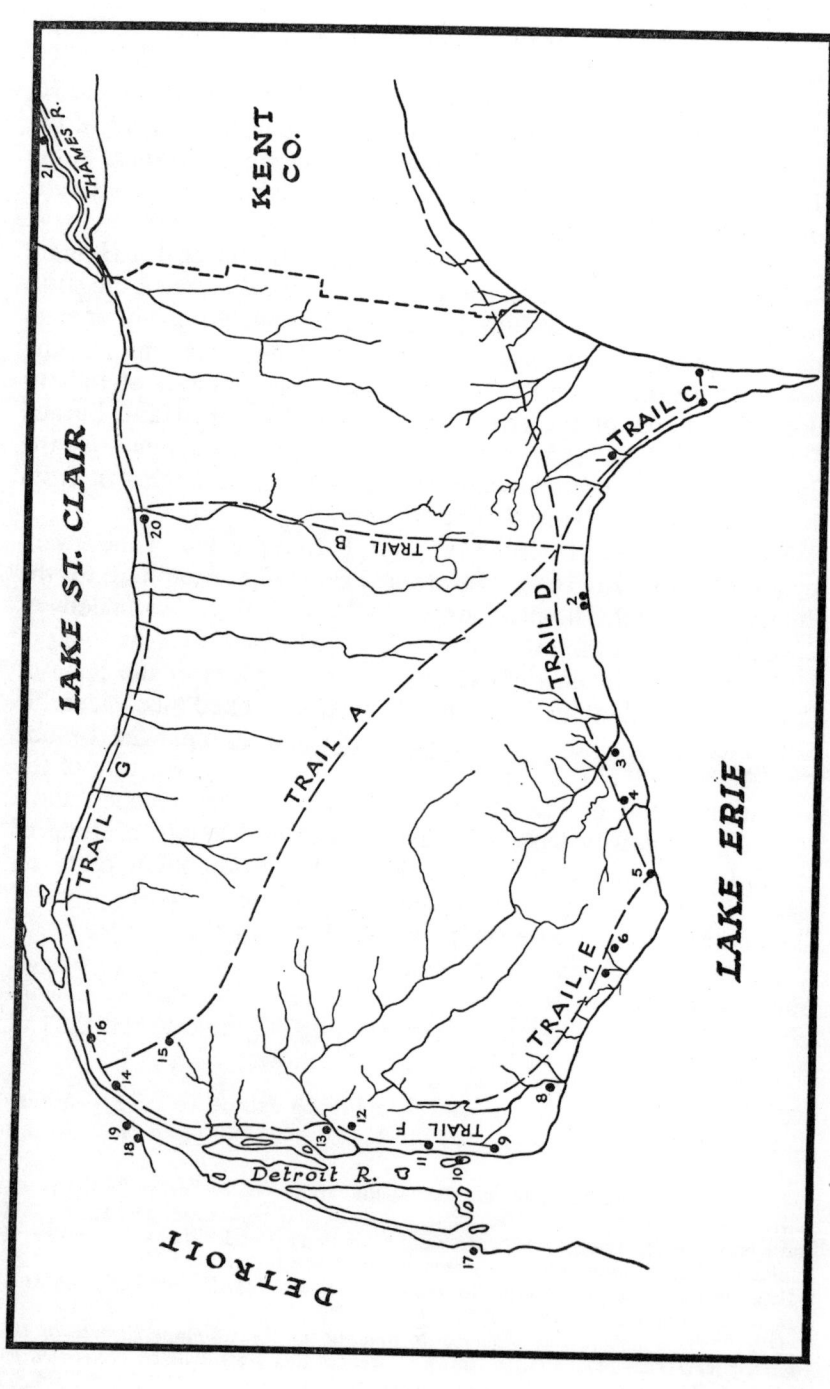

fort at Wawyachtenok called by the French DeTroett the most beautiful and plentiful inland place in America by all relations, where there is arable land for thousands of people, the only place of beaver hunting, for which our Indians have fought so long and at last forced the natives to fly.[18]

More than a year before Livingstone wrote this letter, Antoine Laumet, Sieur de Lamothe Cadillac, a typically grandiloquent Gasconian who had been commandant at Michilimackinac from 1694 to 1697, was in Paris, with a recommendation from Governor Frontenac (A 9),[19] pressing for quick action to ward off the grow-

[18]*Ibid.*, IV, 650.
[19]This recommendation appears in the Cadillac Papers—documents relating to Detroit in the French régime which Mr. Clarence M. Burton had copied and translated from the originals in the archives at Paris and Quebec. These transcriptions are preserved in the Burton Historical Collection of the Detroit Public Library. This enormous collection of material bearing on the history of Detroit will be designated as B.H.C. in all future references.
The English translations of the Cadillac Papers have been published in volumes XXXIII and XXXIV of the *Michigan Historical Collections*. This work, also known as the *Michigan Pioneer Collections*, published between the years 1877 and 1929, comprises forty volumes of materials and writings on the history of Michigan. Hereafter it will be indicated as *M.H.C.*

FIG. 3. MAP SHOWING THE LOCATION OF INDIAN AND PRE-INDIAN VESTIGES FOUND IN ESSEX COUNTY AND VICINITY. [Prepared by George F. Macdonald and John Lee.]

KEY TO INDIAN AND PRE-INDIAN VESTIGES FOUND IN ESSEX COUNTY AND VICINITY: (1) village, cornfields, and portage, Point Pelee (plan by A. Iredell, 1799); (2) two Indian entrenchments, Gosfield Township (plan by McNiff, 1794); (3) village on Cedar Creek, entrenched, Gosfield Township; (4) village, Colchester South Township; (5) Indian encampment, Colchester Township (McNiff, 1794); (6) village and mound, Daniel Wright farm, Colchester Township; (7) several mounds, Colchester Township; (8) village, Big Creek (plan by Iredell, 1796); (9) former village of the Hurons abandoned in 1748 (map by Chaussegros de Léry, *fils*, 1749); (10) camping site used by all tribes, Bois Blanc Island; (11) village above Fort Malden (McNiff's map of 1790); (12) Huron village, Anderdon Township (McNiff, 1790); (13) cornfields, Anderdon Township (McNiff, 1790); (14) Huron village, Huron Church Line; (15) burial mound, Huron Church Line and Third Concession, Sandwich West Township (excavated by W. J. Wintemberg for National Museum of Canada, 1936); (16) Ottawa village and cemetery, Louis Avenue, Windsor (Léry map, 1754); (17) Huron village, Brownstowe, Wayne County, Michigan; (18) the great mound at the mouth of the Rouge River, Wayne County, Michigan; (19) circular mound and several smaller mounds at old Fort Wayne; (20) Indian village, Ruscom River, Rochester Township (plan by Col. Burwell, 1823); (21) Chippewa town reported by Major E. B. Littlehales in 1793.
KEY TO INDIAN TRAILS AND PATHS: (A) Talbot Road, through the county from beyond Wheatley to Sandwich (shown on McNiff's map of 1791); (B) from Lake Erie to Lake St. Clair, following the Ruscom River (Burwell's map, 1823); (C) from Point Pelee to Talbot Road; (D) Lake Erie trail connecting shoreline settlements; (E) from Lake Erie shoreline to Amherstburg area; (F) river shore path, now Highway 18; (G) river and lake shoreline to the Thames River and eastward, followed by Governor Simcoe in 1793.

ing danger of English infiltration in the Great Lakes region. His plan called for shifting the centre of importance from Michilimackinac, where the climate was too severe, to the shores of a deep clear river south of the pearl-like Lake St. Clair where the climate was mild and a crop of corn was assured each year. According to him this veritable paradise, known hitherto only as Le Détroit, was the real hub of the Great Lakes country, the one spot best suited to hold in check both the English and the Iroquois. To accomplish this double purpose it was necessary to establish in this fair locality not only a trading and military post as at Michilimackinac but also an agricultural colony, which would give permanency to the foundation (A 10).

By the close of the seventeenth century, therefore, the Detroit River region, no man's land between the English and Iroquois on one hand and the French, Algonquins, and Hurons on the other, had been sufficiently explored and visited to make both the French and the English burn with desire to occupy that most beautiful and strategic position on the world's finest system of interior waters. Who would win the race for the coveted prize? The answer was not long awaited.

B. THE FOUNDING OF DETROIT AND THE HURON MISSION

CADILLAC'S plan won the general approval of the King of France and it was referred to Quebec for immediate execution. Governor Callières of New France ordered the author of the plan to prepare the expedition for the spring of 1701. Early in June of that year, with Alphonse de Tonti as assistant and accompanied by fifty soldiers and an equal number of civilians, the visionary Cadillac left Montreal headed for Detroit (B 1). In order not to ruffle the Iroquois with whom a definitive peace treaty was being negotiated, the party followed the Ottawa River route with its many portages. Seven weeks later, on July 24, the flotilla of twenty-five canoes had reached its destination, a place described by Cadillac as a fabulous land of plenty (B 2). After exploring the river to its mouth in search of the best location for the fort, the party spent the night on Grosse Isle. The next day they paddled upstream and chose a site on the north shore[1] above the bend where the river is narrow and the banks are high on both sides. This was the most commanding situation on the river—a high place, free of islands, where the cannon of the future fort could most easily defend the stream against all the enemies of France.

At that spot they measured off one square arpent[2] of land on which they soon erected dwellings, a warehouse, and a place for divine worship. The church at the fort later became known as Ste. Anne's of Detroit. This little village was surrounded by a bastioned palisade twelve to fifteen feet high. The enclosure was named Fort Pontchartrain in honour of Louis Phélipeaux Comte de Pontchartrain, who had been Minister of the Marine until 1699, and who was then Chancellor of France.[3]

[1]The expression "north shore" and its opposite require some explanation. The general direction of the Detroit River is north-south, but at a point about two-thirds of the way upstream there is a decided bend to a course that is almost east-west. The present city of Windsor, Ontario, is directly south of the city of Detroit, Michigan. Confusion arises because the term "south side" was employed to designate the Canadian shore even below the bend, where the river runs north-south. East shore would have been a more accurate description of that part of the strait.

[2]The French word *arpent* is a land measure approximating 191.8 English feet in length. The square *arpent*, or French acre, is a square having sides of this length, equivalent to about .85 of the English acre. Ten *perches* (poles) make one linear *arpent*. In Canada a *perche* was eighteen French feet in length. The French foot was the equivalent of about 1.0658 English feet.

[3]For some time the place was called Fort Pontchartrain du Détroit. Gradually

In proof of Cadillac's determination to found a stable settlement at Detroit, in the fall of 1701 Madame Cadillac and Madame de Tonti travelled the 800 miles from Quebec to Detroit (*via* Lake Ontario, peace with the Iroquois having been concluded in August of that year) in order to come and live with their husbands (B 3). The appearance of these two white women to grace the first homes at the strait helped to settle the minds of the Indians concerning the plans for Detroit (B 4). This establishment of a permanent colony in the wilds of America at the beginning of the eighteenth century is one of the most important events in the history of the continental interior.

Even with Cadillac's enthusiasm and utopian dreams, however, the growth of the colony at Detroit was slow. Development was hampered by opposition from the Jesuits and the Montreal merchants (B 5),[4] as well as by constant interference by the home government. Cadillac's royal charter had given him a monopoly of the trade at the new post. During the first year of the establishment this exclusive right was revoked in favour of the Company of the Colony, only to be returned to Cadillac in 1704.[5] Moreover, it was not until 1708 that grants of land were made to the settlers, and then on conditions that tended to discourage any persistent efforts at farming. The result was that by the year 1710, when the disillusioned Cadillac was transferred to the governorship of Louisiana, there were only sixty-three white men, exclusive of soldiers, residing at Detroit.[6] After the founder's departure the office of commandant became a rotating political preferment with which the governors-general could reward their friends and favourites (Appendix II). These men, in charge only temporarily, were for the most part not very ambitious for the development of the colony.

Two events with similar consequences contributed towards turning the next two decades into a period of dwindling importance for Cadillac's village. In 1712, when Charles Regnault, Sieur Dubuisson, was in command, the foundation barely escaped total destruction from a sudden attack by the fierce Outagami or Fox Indians from central Wisconsin. Only the timely arrival of friendly tribes made it possible to administer a crushing defeat upon the savage

the name Pontchartrain was dropped, and the name Détroit remained to designate both the post and the settlement.

[4]For the Memorial of the Montreal merchants, see Margry, *Découvertes*, V, 180–7.

[5]*Ibid.*, V, 195, 341.

[6]See G. Paré, *The Catholic Church in Detroit, 1701–1888*, p. 160n. Also *M.H.C.*, XXXIII, 492–5.

foes.⁷ Fear of new attacks caused some settlers to venture into more promising fields. In 1716 the court party at Paris succeeded in obtaining an order setting aside as void all the deeds that Cadillac had made. The discouraged farmers or householders began to leave the place, and there was even serious thought of abandoning and destroying the fort. For more than another decade Detroit remained little more than an isolated trading post on the fringes of civilization with a small garrison to protect it.

About 1730, however, numbers began to increase as *voyageurs* made their headquarters at Detroit. Encouraged by Governor Beauharnois, immigrants and discharged soldiers took up land in the vicinity of the fort. Concessions of land made to them began to figure in the official dispatches as early as 1734. Cadillac's dream of establishing an agricultural colony at the strait slowly began to be realized.⁸

Fur was the prime article of trade when Detroit was founded, and to assure an ample supply of it Cadillac invited the Indian tribes of the lakes region to come to that hunting ground from which the natives had fled under pressure of the Iroquois. An unknown observer has supplied an interesting description of the life and habits of the four tribes of savages that came and stayed at Detroit (B 6). These were a branch of the Ottawas (8ta8ais)⁹ from the northern part of Lower Michigan, the Potawatomi from Lake Michigan, the Hurons (also called Wyandots) from Michilimackinac, and the Chippewas or Ojibways from Sault Ste. Marie, who were joined by a number of Mississaugas. The villages of the first three of these tribes can be located on a map of the Detroit River area drawn by Commandant Boishebert about 1730, of which a copy is in the Public Archives of Canada. On it the Hurons and the Potawatomi are located below the fort on the north side. Opposite the fort and slightly upstream is the village of the Ottawas about three miles above La Pointe de Montréal at the river's bend (see Fig. 4).¹⁰

---

⁷For a detailed account of the Fox attack on Detroit, see "Report of Sr. Dubuisson to M. de Vaudreuil" in *M.H.C.*, XXXIII, 537–52.

⁸The increase of settlers at this time is reflected in the number of baptisms recorded in Ste. Anne's Church. From 1701 to 1730 there were 143 baptisms; from 1731 to 1740, 156 baptisms; and from 1741 to 1750, 235 baptisms.

⁹The figure 8 designates a sound in the Indian language approximating a guttural "ou."

¹⁰It is suggested that the name was given by the French in the fort at Detroit because the boats coming from Montreal could first be seen at that spot. In this connection it is interesting to note that at Fort Frontenac (now Kingston, Ontario) there was also a Pointe de Montréal a short distance downstream from the fort.

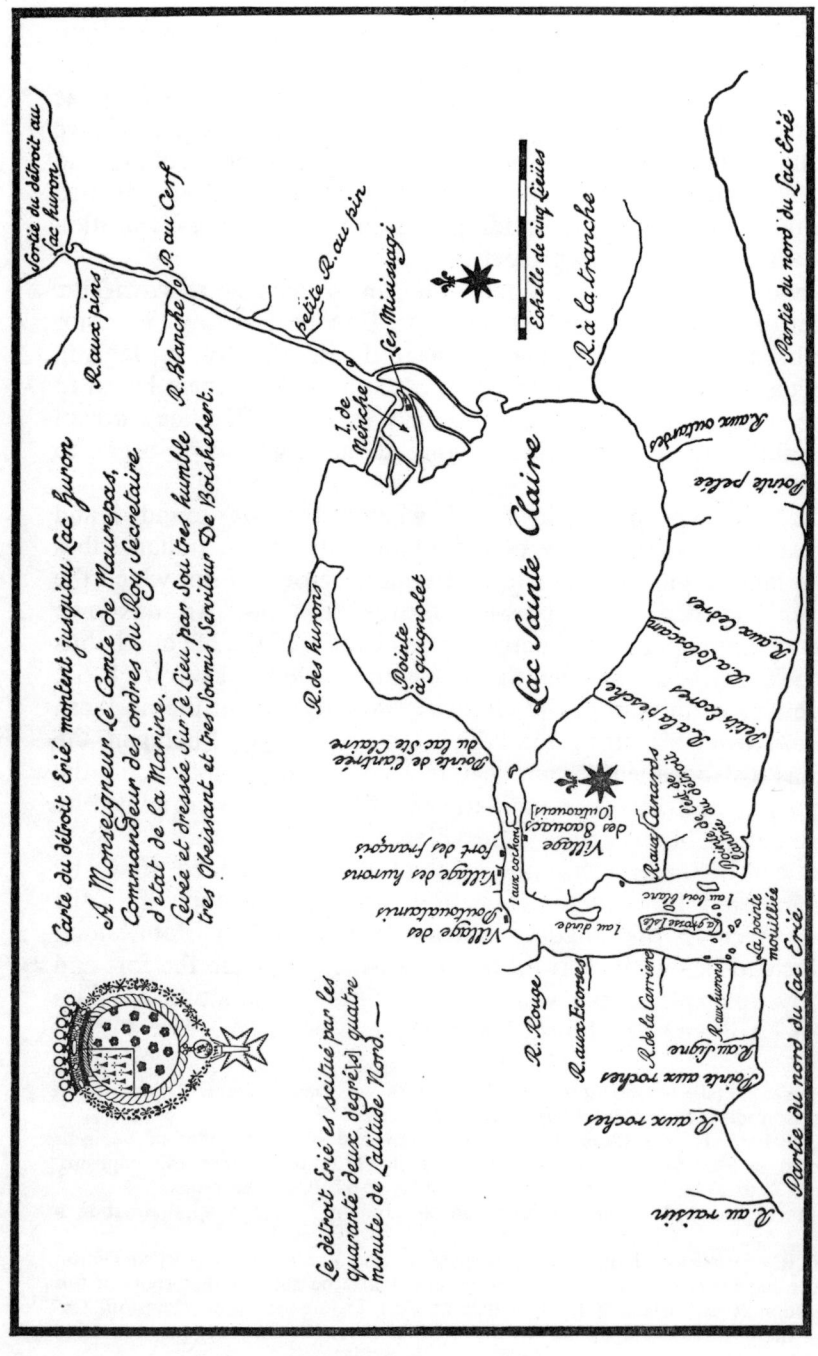

FIG. 4. MAP OF DETROIT ERIÉ BY COMMANDANT DE BOISHEBERT c. 1730. [Copy in Public Archives of Canada.]

The site of the Chippewa-Mississauga band is not indicated on this map. They were constantly on the move, hopping from one place to another. In 1721 their encampment was located on the south side of Lake St. Clair, twelve leagues from the fort (B 7). At the time of this map they were probably sojourning along the Thames River, whence according to tradition they chased the Iroquois from their usurped hunting grounds.[11] There they stayed long enough to acquire a later claim to proprietary rights in the land along that stream. By the middle of the century they had made their abodes on the shores of Lake St. Clair, River St. Clair, and also on the southern part of Lake Huron. Because the Chippewas came from Sault Ste. Marie they were called Saulteurs (Sauteurs), that is, Jumpers. Sauteurs they were in name and in deed.

Cadillac invited the Jesuits to transfer their Indian mission from Michilimackinac to Detroit, but they refused. A bitter controversy had been waged at the upper lakes post between Cadillac and the missionaries. Besides the clash of personalities (Cadillac *versus* Carheil), matters of policy were involved. There was the liquor question. The bartering of brandy to the Indians, who would certainly drink too much, was immoral in the eyes of the Jesuits and rendered useless all their efforts at civilizing them. Cadillac replied that if the French stopped this practice the Indians would trade with the English who were bartering rum for furs. Cadillac also wanted to try to gallicize the savages by intermarriage and by teaching them agriculture and the French language and customs. The Jesuits claimed this plan was not feasible. They believed it necessary to bring the Indians into the pale of the Church before initiating them to the white man's civilization. This controversy accounts for the fact that it was not a Jesuit but a Recollet priest who came to Detroit with Cadillac as chaplain of the expedition.[12]

[11]Major E. B. Littlehales, who accompanied Lieutenant-Governor Simcoe on his overland trip to Detroit in the winter of 1793, wrote in his diary: "From Dolson's we went to the mouth of the Thames in carioles, and, about twelve miles on we saw the remains of a considerable town (Chippewas) where it was reported that a desperate battle was fought between them and the Senecas, and that the latter were totally vanquished and abandoned their dominions to the conquerors. Certain it is, that human bones are scattered in abundance in the vicinity of the Ground, and the Indians have a variety of traditions relative to this transaction." E. A. Cruikshank, *The Correspondence of Lieut. Governor John Graves Simcoe,* I, 292. In future references this work will be cited as *The Simcoe Papers.*

[12]Father François Vaillant de Gueslis, a Jesuit, also accompanied Cadillac to Detroit, but apparently only for the purpose of making an appraisal of the place as a future Indian mission. On his way back to Montreal that same year he stopped at Fort Frontenac, where on September 23 he encountered Madame Cadillac who was making her way to Detroit. See *M.H.C.,* XXXIII, 106.

When Father P. F. X. Charlevoix visited the strait in 1721 as an envoy of the King of France to report on the French colonies in America, the Huron village was located on the north shore of the Detroit River a short distance below the fort, where it appears on the later Boishebert map. His report bemoaned the fact that this nation, although Christian, had no missionary, and he urged that the situation be remedied (B 8). In 1726 and 1727 the Hurons themselves asked Governor Beauharnois for a blackrobe to minister to them. Their petition was granted in 1728.

On October 1 of that year Beauharnois wrote to the Minister of the Marine that the Jesuits had sent a missionary to the Hurons at Detroit who seemed well fitted to carry on this mission and to curb the proud spirit of that tribe.[13] This was Father Armand de La Richardie, S.J., who had spent some time with the Hurons at Lorette near Quebec in order to familiarize himself with the Huron tongue. He found it very slow and discouraging work trying to bring these Indians back to the practice of their religion. However, in 1735 Father Nau at Sault St. Louis (near Montreal) was able to write to his Superior that all the scattered Hurons had been reunited at Detroit and that the whole tribe was now Christian.[14] Very likely he had obtained this information from Father de La Richardie himself while the latter was on his way to spend the winter of 1734-5 at Quebec. In 1741 the missionary at Detroit wrote to the Superior-General of the Jesuits that "the sacred edifice, though seventy cubits long, scarcely contains the multitude of christians." This letter is of special interest because it is headed: "The Mission of the *Assumption* of the Blessed Virgin Mary among the Hurons." This is the oldest known record that gives the title of the mission—a title that later followed it to its permanent location on the south shore of the river (B 9).

In 1738 the Hurons warned the Flathead Indians, who lived far to the southwest, that the other tribes of Detroit were going to raid them. In this way the Hurons earned the enmity of their neighbours and had to withdraw from Detroit. Numbers went to their winter hunting grounds near Sandusky on the south shore of Lake Erie. At the request of Governor Beauharnois an attempt was made to

[13]*Ibid.*, XXXIV, 49.
[14]Thwaites, *Jesuit Relations*, LVIII, 281-3; also Camille de Rochemonteix, S.J., *Les Jésuites et la Nouvelle France au XVIIe siècle*, V, 57-8. This work consists of two series. The first, dealing with the Jesuits of the seventeenth century, comprises three volumes published in 1895-6. The second series, dealing with the Jesuits of the eighteenth century, has two volumes issued in 1906. For the sake of convenience the work is here quoted as a continuous series of five volumes.

persuade them to move to Montreal. When this proved fruitless Father de La Richardie suggested that they be given Grosse Isle, an island near the western shore at the mouth of the Detroit River. The Governor refused. Thereupon the missionary settled most of the tribe on the neighbouring Isle aux Bois Blancs[15] and on the adjacent mainland on the east side of the river. This event took place on October 13, 1742.[16] The mission house located on the island was the first place of Christian worship in the territory that now constitutes the County of Essex.

The troubles of the past few years and the strain of unremitting toil were taking their toll, and the weary Jesuit asked to be relieved of his charge. In the summer of 1743 Father De Gonnor (Degonor) came to replace him, but sickness forced him to return to Quebec the following year. On September 25, 1744, Father Pierre Potier, who had spent eight months at Lorette studying the Huron language, arrived at the Bois Blanc mission. His coming proved to be very timely, for in the spring of 1746 while he and Father de La Richardie were at the Huron wintering place south of Lake Erie, the latter suffered an attack of paralysis and returned to Quebec that summer.

On May 20 of the following year, some rebel Hurons who had remained at Sandusky under Chief Nicolas, who had contacts with the English and Iroquois, plotted with the help of some other disaffected Indians to seize the missionary and the commandant of Detroit, then to massacre all the French in the post (B 10). Before their plot was discovered the mission at Bois Blanc had been destroyed. Those Hurons who were not in sympathy with the plot sent a delegation to Governor de La Galissonière at Quebec requesting that Father de La Richardie, who had great influence over the Indians, be sent back to the mission. The Governor agreed and the expedition left Quebec on August 23, 1747, and reached Detroit on October 20. Order was restored, but the Hurons remained divided between Detroit and Sandusky.

La Galissonière was anxious to have the Detroit Hurons settle closer to the fort, at La Pointe de Montréal on the south shore. At that place a tract of land about seven arpents wide by forty deep was granted without written title by the Indians to the missionaries. The lodges of the Hurons were erected just below this property, near the road now known as Huron Line. In order to help the

[15]In later documents the name often appears with "Blanc" written in the singular, Bois Blanc Island. Today it is popularly known by the unrecognizable phonetic name of Bob-Lo, and it is the scene of an amusement park.
[16]See below, Potier Gazette (B 13).

undertaking, the Governor contributed five thousand livres[17] to build a church and house.[18] These buildings were started in 1748 and the church was opened for divine service on September 8 of the following year.[19] After vain efforts to win back the rebels on the south shore of Lake Erie, Father de La Richardie returned to Quebec in the summer of 1751, again leaving Father Potier in full charge of the mission.

Father Potier was much given to writing, and fortunately for local historians a large number of his manuscripts are extant. Chief among them is the account book of the mission for 1733–51, preserved in the Burton Historical Collection of the Detroit Public Library.[20] Penned in microscopic but very legible handwriting with ink that has stood the test of more than two centuries, it contains many interesting items relating to the operations of the share-crop farm, the forge, and the store connected with the mission at Bois Blanc Island and at La Pointe de Montréal (B 11). Father de La Richardie had appointed Mr. René de Couagne, a wealthy merchant at Montreal, as factor of his establishment. Each year in the protected convoy of bateaux the factor shipped to the mission store stocks of goods—blankets, powder, lead, iron, vermilion, cutlery, arms, cotton, wampum, beads, and trinkets. In return he received packs of furs to be disposed of to the account of the missionary. There is evidence of a brisk trade between the mission and the people living in the fort in lumber, iron, grain, brandy, and hides, and the various transactions in these commodities make up the greater part of the record. One ironic item refers to the difficulty and high cost of bringing salt to that area—the site today of one of the best salt mines in the world.

Numerous items in the account book provide information on the costs of various goods and labour at Detroit around the middle of the eighteenth century. The following is a list of some of the items

[17]The *livre* was the ordinary money of account. This was the *livre parisis* (struck at Paris), worth 1¼ *livre tournois* (struck at Tours) which later became the French franc. The franc is rarely mentioned in the account books of the period. The *livre* was divided into twenty *sols (sous)*. The *sou* was divided into twelve *deniers*. Three *livres* made one *écu*; ten *livres* made one *pistole*; twenty *livres* made one *louis*.

[18]Public Archives of Canada, C 2, 93, p. 31. Hereafter this depository of documents at Ottawa will be designated as *P.A.C.*

[19]See below, Potier Gazette (B 13).

[20]The account book of the Huron Mission was published in Thwaites, *Jesuit Relations*, LXIX, 241 sqq. It also appeared edited by Richard Elliott in Fraser, *Fifteenth Report of the . . . Archives . . . of Ontario*, pp. 691–712. The same *Report* also contains a Huron grammar and vocabulary written by Father Potier, as well as a number of homilies and sermons in the Huron language.

INTRODUCTION

that could be purchased for four livres or one "castor":[21] four chickens; twelve to fifteen pounds of beef; one bushel of peas; one gallon of brandy; two hundred large nails; two cords of wood; six or seven planks; two days of labour. It is quite evident that there was not much currency in circulation; trade was usually carried on by barter, and most of the transactions are recorded on a credit basis. After listing a number of items that he owes and that are owed to him, Father Potier tallies up as follows:

> Adding up all the above items I owe here 335 livres and there is owed to me 120 livres. This includes the 72 livres that le P. Bon owes me.[22] Niagara would not collect this sum from him. I owed the said sum to Niagara and I have been obliged to borrow them from Valet to whom the said Niagara owed them.

Other writings from the pen of Father Potier cast light on the story of the Huron mission. The Gagnon Collection of the Montreal Municipal Library possesses two small books written in the missionary's distinctive penmanship. One is filled with Huron-French vocabularies; the other contains a census of the Indians at Bois Blanc Island in 1747 showing 534 persons plus a number of children living in 33 cabins (B 12). In the Archives of St. Mary's College, Montreal, there is deposited a collection of heterogeneous material under the title of Potier Gazette, which includes a chronology of events at the mission and a number of letters to or from Father Potier (B 13).

Two entries in the Gazette allude to the possibility of other residents on the east shore of the strait:

> [October 28, 1744] Went to La Rivière aux Canards—Navarre had been there for five days; I did not see him.

> [September 22, 1745] . . . I went to the fort with Mr. Navarre; we slept at La Rivière aux Canards.

The question arises: Who were at La Rivière aux Canards? A band of Huron Indians? White settlers? Both theories are possible, but the writer believes that the key to the answer lies in the time of the

---

[21] The economic life of the country was bound up with the fur trade to such an extent that furs were used as a medium of exchange. Beavers were so numerous that the beaver or castor became the unit of measurement. The skin of the buck or male beaver was worth four livres, twice as much as the skin of the doe beaver. It is the buck that came to be recognized as the money unit, and is used to this day as slang for a dollar. It would be interesting to find out if the word "dough" for money comes from the homonym "doe," worth half a buck.

[22] P. Bon. is an abbreviation for Père Bonaventure Liénard, Recollet, pastor of Ste. Anne's Church from 1722 to 1754.

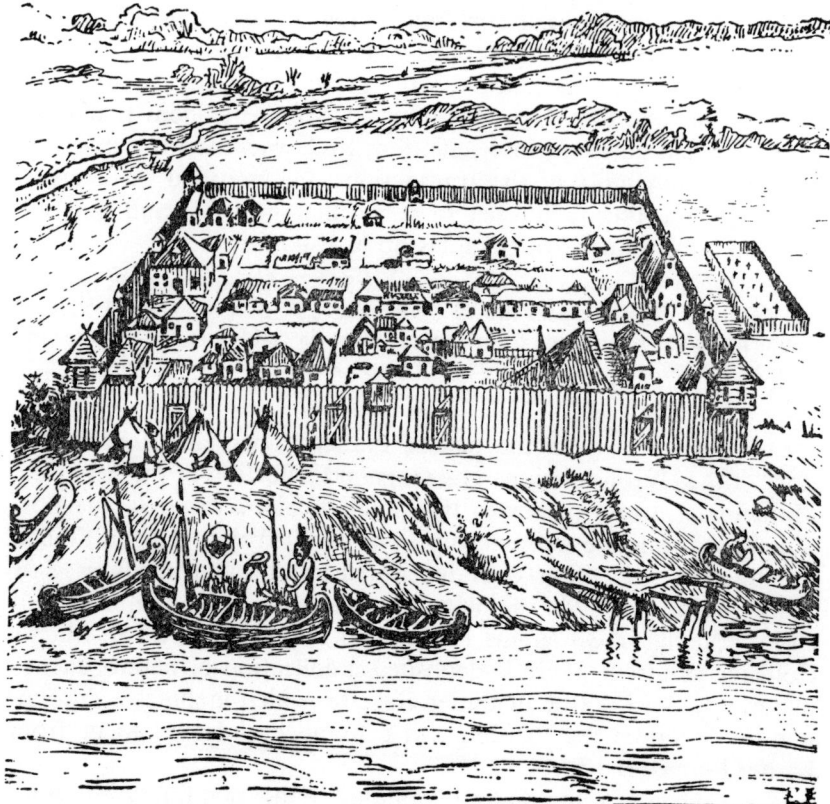

FIG. 5. IMAGINATIVE DRAWING OF FORT PONTCHARTRAIN ABOUT 1740 FROM INFORMATION SUPPLIED BY C. M. BURTON. [By courtesy of the Director of the Burton Historical Collection, Detroit, Michigan.]

year at which these visits occurred. Both were in the fall. And what would be going on in the wide fringes of reedy marsh at the mouth of La Rivière aux Canards in the fall of the 1740's? The very name of the place suggests the answer—duck-shooting, the same thing that has been taking place every year for over two centuries in that habitat of waterfowl. Lacking definite proof of the presence of Hurons or of white settlers at that place, it is easy to believe that on these two occasions Father Potier visited and stayed with hunting parties from the town of Detroit, and that up to 1748 the personnel connected with the Huron mission were the only white residents on what is now the Canadian side of the Detroit River.

The first half of the eighteenth century had witnessed along the Detroit River two events of major importance to this story. On the north side a fort, a trading post, and an agricultural settlement had been firmly established. The south side was still a wilderness inhabited by two tribes of barbarous Indians—the Ottawas and the Hurons. But adjoining the Huron village a Jesuit mission was now safely set up within sight of the fort. These two foundations, one on each side of the river, formed the basis for fast approaching events that would see settlers come to the south shore to establish habitations for themselves by converting patches of wilderness into fields of wheat, oats, and corn.

C. SETTLERS COME TO THE SOUTH SHORE

THE early settlement at Detroit was on the north shore for the protection of the fort, but contemporaneous with the transfer of the Huron village and mission to La Pointe de Montréal settlers came to the south shore. This was occasioned by the decision of the government at Quebec to check the infiltration of British traders and Iroquois Indians along the Ohio River, the lifeline of communications to the Mississippi, and thence to Louisiana and the Gulf of Mexico. In 1748 Governor de La Galissonière wrote to the French government his plan to achieve this purpose:

The establishing of a few posts on the Ohio is one of the most urgent expenditures, but at the same time it is believed that these posts will succeed only in so far as the forces of Niagara and Detroit are increased. This latter place presently demands the greatest attention. If it should come to have a population of one thousand it would feed and defend all the others.[1]

In 1749 the Governor proceeded to implement his twofold plan to build forts in the Ohio country and make Detroit the bulwark and granary of these outposts. To clinch the claims of New France to the Ohio country, he sent Céloron de Bienville (Blainville) with a detachment of 250 men to take formal possession of the territory and to establish military posts along the main streams. At the same time he directed Joseph Gaspard Chaussegros de Léry, *fils*, a military engineer, to accompany the newly appointed Commandant de Sabrevois to Detroit in order to ascertain the actual condition and strength of the post at that place and also to draw up an exact account of the position and quality of the lands and of the things needed to farm them. His diary of the journey has been preserved at Quebec (C 1).

The Governor's determined effort to increase the population of Detroit did not wait for Léry's report. In the spring of that same year (1749) the following proclamation was read in every parish along the St. Lawrence River:

Every man who will go to settle at Detroit will receive gratuitously one spade, one axe, one ploughshare, one large and one small auger. Other tools will be advanced to be paid for in two years only. The settler will also be given a cow, which he shall return at the time of the increase; the same for a sow. Seed will be advanced the first year, to be returned at the third harvest. The women and children will be supported for one year. They will

[1] N.Y.C.D., X, 230.

be deprived of the liberality of the King, who shall give themselves up to trade instead of agriculture.[2]

The first families from Lower Canada that responded to this call came in the convoy that brought Léry and Sabrevois to Detroit in the summer of 1749. These newcomers were joined as settlers by other civilians who had been living in the fortified town of Detroit and also by soldiers discharged from the garrison at that place. Land and provisions were given them as promised. An entry in Léry's Journal, who was at Detroit from July 25 to August 26, 1749, notes that lands of 3 by 40 arpents were granted to 22 settlers along the river from Le Ruisseau de la Vieille Reine[3] to La Rivière aux Dindes. There is evidence that the survey of this area was made somewhat inaccurately (C 2).

A Léry map of the Detroit River area drawn up at Quebec in October of that year shows this survey, which is entitled "New French Settlement of 1749," located in the 2½ mile stretch of Detroit River frontage between the two streams (see Fig. 6). This map has been preserved at the Ministère de la France d'Outre-mer in Paris. Attached to this map is a list of names of the settlers to whom were granted farms of 3 arpents in front by 40 arpents in depth in 1749 (C 3).

Léry's report dated October 22, 1749, has also been preserved in Paris (C 4). It was favourable to the government's plan and stressed the urgency of the matter because the Indians dwelling at the strait could not be trusted. It also recommended that there should be a settlement and a small fort at the mouth of the river opposite Bois Blanc Island where there was a village of the Hurons in 1748.

On January 2, 1750, the proclamation calling for settlers for Detroit was renewed by the newly appointed Governor, La Jonquière. These two proclamations had little immediate effect in the Districts of Quebec and Three Rivers. Later on, settlers did come from those regions, as is known from the later marriage records of Assumption Church, Windsor, and St. Anne's Church of Detroit—records that note the home parish of the parents of the bride and groom. However, a goodly number of people from the District of

[2]Translation from the French quoted in Rameau de Saint-Père, *La France aux Colonies*, p. 301.
[3]La Vieille Reine was the name of the head of cabin 9 in the large Huron village at the Island of Bois Blancs. See Potier Manuscript (B 12). It has been suggested that La Vieille Reine may have been the grandmother of Sastaretsy, hereditary chief of the Hurons. The stream known by the name of La Vieille Reine emptied into the Detroit River near the southern limit of the present city of Windsor.

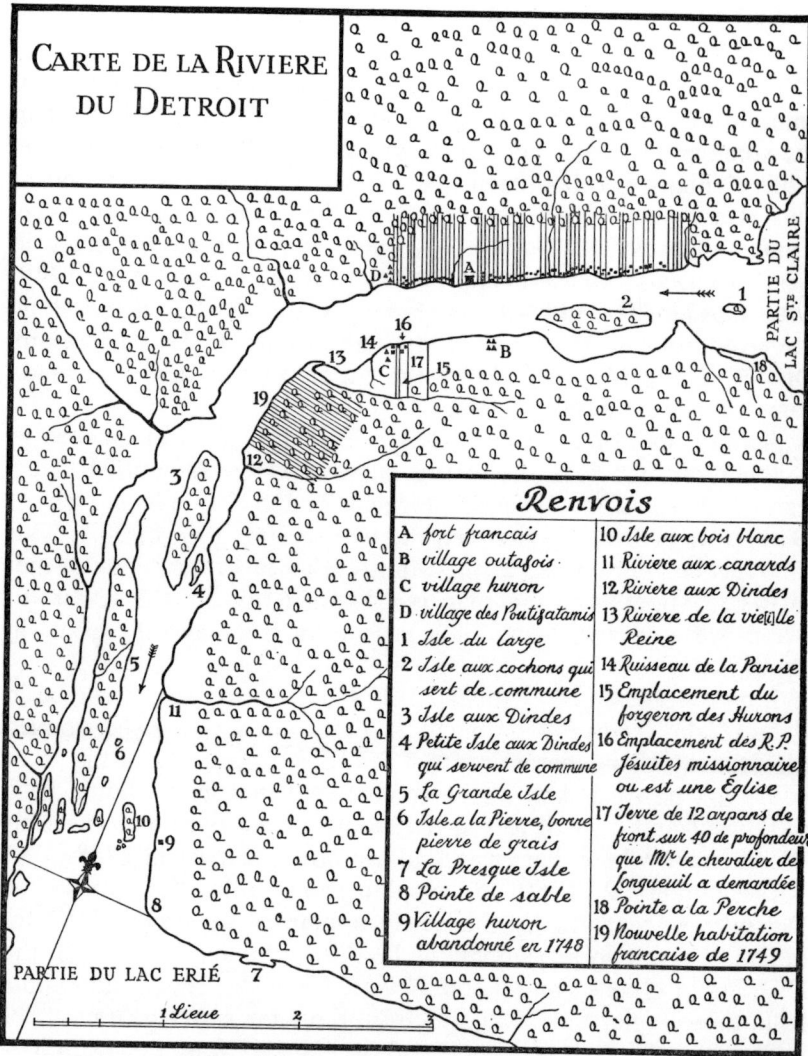

FIG. 6. MAP OF THE DETROIT RIVER BY CHAUSSEGROS DE LÉRY *fils*, 1749. [Archives du Ministère des Colonies, Paris.]

Montreal took up the government's offer and came to Detroit in bateaux.

For some of the men who came at this time and during the next decade, it was not a journey into an unknown country. In previous summers, as canoemen or *voyageurs* they had manned canoes or bateaux laden with provisions for Detroit and had returned to

Montreal with cargoes of furs. From the notarial records for this period in the Palais de Justice at Montreal one can read the contracts they made with the merchants of Montreal or of Detroit for the journey to the west country (C 5).

The names of the settlers who took advantage of the government's offer are entered in a ledger known as the Cicotte Book, now in the Burton Historical Collection of the Detroit Public Library. Grantees on both sides of the strait for the years 1749–51 are entered along with a description of their lands and an account of the supplies, animals, and rations they received (C 6). By the proclamation of 1750 the rations for one year promised to the settlers were extended to cover a period of eighteen months. Those who came in 1749 shared in this extension of bounty. A typical entry is that of Louis Plichon (C 6).

The entry indicates that the farm granted to Louis Plichon was immediately south of the land of Louis Gervais. The latter was a captain of the militia who had taken residence on his lot that same summer (C 15). It is likely that, in preparation for the coming of settlers to the south shore, a captain of the militia had been stationed there. Besides the regular French troops in the garrison every able-bodied Canadian from sixteen to sixty belonged to the militia. Each *habitant* had his gun, powder, and lead, to be used for fighting as well as for hunting purposes. Fifteen minutes after receiving his captain's orders he was expected to be ready to leave. Besides the martial duties of organizing and training his local company, the captain of the militia also had civic responsibilities such as supervising roads and fences and making provision for other public services.

Captain Gervais' residence was at the southwestern limits of the present city of Windsor, just south of McKee Road on land now occupied by the Hydro Generating Station. Gervais owned a sawmill twenty-five leagues upstream (Léry Journal) and was able to build a better-than-average dwelling. Le Ruisseau de La Vieille Reine which emptied into the Detroit River a little above that place was thereafter called La Rivière à Gervais.

In the Cicotte Book the location of some of the grants is not clearly defined, but twenty-five of them for the three years 1749–51 are definitely listed on the south shore, that is, the Canadian side of the river. Some entries give the approximate location of the grant. That of Louis Antoine De Hêtre (Deshêtres) is said to be located "near the village of the Ottawas of whom he is the interpreter." Today Louis Avenue in Windsor runs along this tract of land. The cemetery of the Ottawas was immediately east of the De Hêtre concession, and their village was situated a little farther upstream. A report issued in 1752 indicated that twenty-three grants were made that year at Detroit.[4] No doubt a number of these were on the south side. The same source stated that it would not be possible to send any families to Detroit the following year on account of the shortage of supplies.

A comparison of the lists of proprietors attached to the Léry map of 1749 with the entries in the Cicotte Book for that year reveals great differences and discrepancies. However, it must not be assumed that a different name means a different person. Sobriquets, double names, and variant spellings were very common (see Appendix III). Léry's St. Louis is the Louis Plichon of the Cicotte Book. Likewise St. Etienne denotes Pierre Dinan (*dit* St. Etienne). Dinan is a variant spelling of Bineau. The majority of these people could not write or spell their names, and the notary or priest spelled them according to sound. Hence, Bineau also appears in records of the period as Bino, Binot, Dineau, Guignan, Guignard, Druignan— all at least remotely assonant but very confusing to the unwary reader. Fortunately a "*dit* St. Etienne" was attached to these variants —a peculiarity that frequently assists in tracing the identity of names otherwise obscure.

A major discrepancy appears in the number of proprietors. Léry indicates that in 1749 lands were granted on the south shore to twenty-two settlers. The Cicotte Book lists only ten for that year. This variance can be reconciled. Grants were conditional on establishing a "hearth and home" within one year. The Cicotte Book, which from internal evidence is known to have been compiled two or three years later, likely lists only those who actually took possession of their lands. This hypothesis finds support in the census of Detroit for September 1, 1750 (C 7). Allowance being made for double names, sobriquets, and variants, some of the grantees on the Léry list do not appear at all. The farms of others whose names appear on both the census and the Léry list, judging by the amount of land under cultivation, refer more likely to old farms located on the north side (for instance, LeDuc, Labadie).

From another source it is known that there were a number of defections and abandonment of property during the first year. This information is supplied in a report issued by Father Bonnecamps. This Jesuit mathematician and hydrographer had been on the Céloron de Bienville expedition to the Ohio River. Before returning to Quebec he took a side-trip to Detroit, arriving at the fort on

[4]Rameau, *La France aux Colonies*, p. 301.

October 6, 1749. In his report issued on October 17, 1750, he bemoaned the fact that some of the settlers who had been sent to Detroit the previous year had gone to seek fortune elsewhere (C 8).

One can obtain a picture of the development of the settlement in the first five years by referring to a copy of another Léry map, which is undated but was probably made in 1754 (see Fig. 7). Léry was at Detroit working on the strengthening of the fort from August 5, 1754, to March 11, 1755. During the winter he measured the width of the river on the ice, and indicated corrections to be made on the scale of his map. That map with a partial list of proprietors shows the survey on the south shore extending nearly three miles below La Rivière aux Dindes with nineteen lots in that new area.[5]

A fairly accurate description of the district in 1756 comes from Charles Stuart, an American colonist who had been captured in Pennsylvania by a band of Indians and ransomed by Father Potier. Stuart paid off his ransom by working eight months at the Huron mission. A few years later he made a statement of his observations to the military authorities at New York. It reveals that there were 27 or 28 families in the settlement below Le Ruisseau de la Vieille Reine (La Rivière à Gervais) (C 13).

Two later documents provide additional information about the development in the 1750's. A list of proprietors prepared in 1792 by William Monforton, Notary and Captain of the Militia, gives the years in which the various parcels of land at Petite Côte (below La Rivière à Gervais) were granted or occupied (C 26). According to this document all the farm lots down to La Rivière aux Dindes were granted without title by M. de Sabrevois who was at Detroit 1749–51. Eight new grants with written titles made by M. Céloron in 1755–6 filled up the river frontage for a mile southward to the present Sunnyside area. The date or the name of the grantor is incorrect because Céloron was at Detroit in 1751–4. The same source indicates that the lands lying in a two and one-half mile stretch immediately below Sunnyside were occupied, some before and some after 1760.

In the Minutes of the Land Board of Hesse it is indicated that the twelve farms immediately south of the present Martin Lane were part of French grants (C 27). According to that information, by the year 1760 the settlement on the south side extended for six

---

[5]This map is sometimes called the Collot map. With later information added it was prepared for the intelligence of the French General Victor Collot for his reconnoitring tour of the Mississippi valley in 1796.

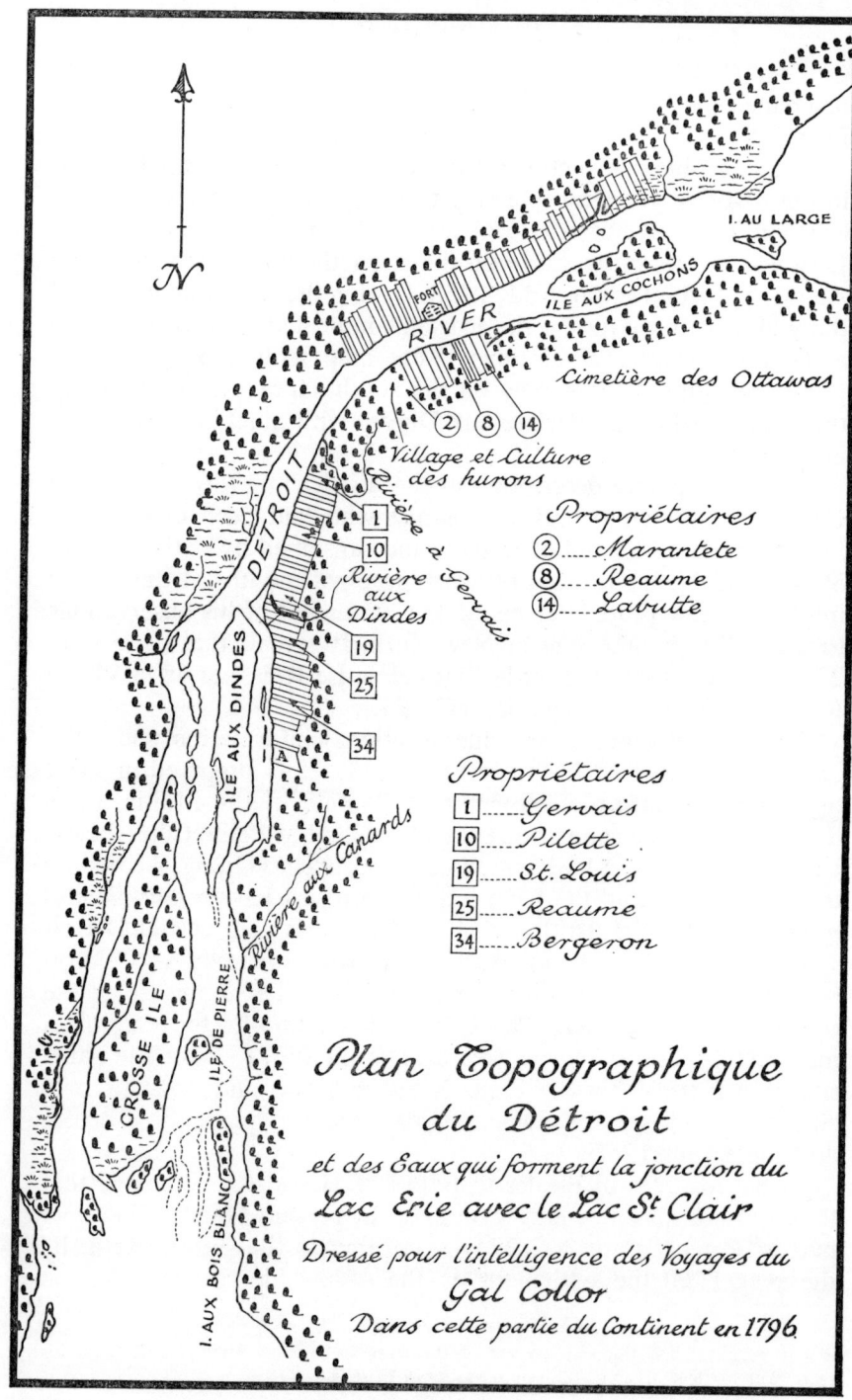

FIG. 7. TOPOGRAPHICAL MAP OF DETROIT BY CHAUSSEGROS DE LÉRY, *fils*, *c.* 1754. [Copy in Burton Historical Collection, Main Library, Detroit.]

miles downstream, from La Rivière à Gervais to a point less than a mile from the present dividing line between North and South Essex. This French colony at Petite Côte which started in 1749 is the oldest continuous white settlement in the Province of Ontario.

So much for the settlement below the bend in the river, that is, below La Pointe de Montréal. Above this place the river frontage between the village of the Hurons and the village of the Ottawas, a three-mile stretch over which Fort Pontchartrain frowned its protection, was granted a little later than the first grants in the Petite Côte area. These lands seem to have been allocated to people on preferred lists, not to newcomers from Lower Canada. On April 1, 1750, a tract twelve arpents wide by 40 arpents deep was granted to Chevalier de Longueuil, former Commandant at Detroit (C 9). This property is described in the deed as bordered on the west-southwest by the lands of the Huron mission and on the east-northeast by lands not yet granted.[6] This grant was made by the Crown *en roture*—the only one so made on the south side of the river. On the Léry map of 1749 it was listed as land "requested" by Chevalier de Longueuil, and it was the only lot marked between the mission lands and the Ottawa village.

There is no list with dates of the grants east of the Longueuil tract. However, a careful examination of the notarial records of later transfers of property reveals copies of some of the original grants annexed to the conveyances. For instance, the record of a transfer of property notarized on July 5, 1771, makes clear that the Bouron farm was granted on November 24, 1751, by Commandant Céloron to Alexis Delisle dit Bienvenu (C 10), and that Charles Bouron purchased it in 1752.[7] The 1751 grant to Delisle is said to be bordered on the west-southwest by the land of Hyacinthe Réaume and on the east-northeast by lands not yet granted. But

---

[6]The streets between Askin and Curry in the city of Windsor are on that tract of land.

[7]Bruce and Janette streets in Windsor run along that property.

NAMES OF THE PROPRIETORS ON THE SOUTH SHORE OF THE RIVER: 1. Marentette; 2. Longueuil; 3. Desnoyers; 4. Mayeux; 5. Janisse; 6. Bouron; 7. Godet; 8. Reaume; 9. Goyau; 10. Goyau; 11. L'Esperance; 12. Parent; 13. Langlois; 14. DeHetre; 15. DeHetre.

NAMES OF THE PROPRIETORS ON THE EAST SHORE OF THE RIVER: 1. Gervais; 2. Lafleur; 3. Lafleur; 4. Joseph Henri Etienne; 5. LeGrand; 6. Baptiste Lebeau; 7. LeBeau fils; 8. Leronde; 9. Robert; 10. Pilette; 11. Meloche; 12. Drouillard; 13. Baby; 14. Grenom; 15. Campeau; 16. Tamisier; 17. L'Esperance; 18. . . .; 19. St. Louis; 20. . . .; 21. Jadot; 22. . . .; 23. . . .; 24. . . .; 25. Reaume; 26. Pare; 27. . . .; 28. . . .; 29. . . .; 30. . . .; 31. Drouillard; 32. Binot; 33. St. Remy; 34. Bergeron.

the 1752 transfer from Delisle to Bouron mentions Jacques Gaudet (Godet) as owner of the lands east-northeast of the property. The grant to Jacques Gaudet must have been made on November 24, 1751, for on the same day Commandant Céloron granted to Pierre Réaume a lot three arpents wide adjoining on the west-southwest the lands of Jacques Gaudet and on the east-northeast lands not yet granted (C 11). This grant was made to Réaume to compensate him for his two-arpent frontage next to the fort that was being expropriated for reasons of security.[8]

From a copy of the original grant attached to a transfer of property dated August 21, 1768, it is clear that on November 24, 1751, a parcel of land was granted by Commandant Céloron to Madame Vien, widow of J. St. Aubin (C 12).[9] This lot is described as bounded on the west-southwest by the land of Chauvin and on the east-northeast by lands not yet granted. Hence Chauvin must have received his lot on the same day between the grants made to Pierre Réaume and Madame Vien.[10]

By the end of November 1751, lands had been granted above the Huron village at least as far as the present Goyeau Street in the city of Windsor. It is quite possible that the next four lots were also added on November 24, 1751, for it is apparent that Commandant Céloron was in granting mood that day. None of these cessions above the Longueuil tract appears in the Cicotte Book because its entries of grants end in September of 1751. It has already been noted that earlier in that year Louis Antoine De Hêtre had been granted a parcel of land near the Ottawa village. The Léry map of 1754 shows farm lots comprising all the frontage from the Huron mission to the Ottawa town, and lists the following proprietors: Marentette, Longueuil, Desnoyers, Mayeux, Janisse, Bouron, Godet, Réaume, Goyau, Goyau, L'Esperance, Parent, Langlois, De Hêtre, De Hêtre. A careful study of the notarial records of the period reveals that some of the landowners listed on the 1754 Léry

---

[8] Later this Réaume grant became the Baby farm in the very heart of the city of Windsor. The wife of Jacques Duperon Baby was the daughter of Pierre Réaume and she lived there after the death of her husband in 1789. When she died it passed over to her son, François Baby, who erected on it a substantial brick house in 1811–12. In 1957 this house was renovated and became the Hiram Walker's Historical Museum housing the George F. Macdonald Collection.

[9] The Vien property was sold to Vital Goyeau. Today Goyeau Street, Windsor, is on part of that land.

[10] Ouellette Avenue, the main street of Windsor, runs along the Chauvin lot. It was sold to Baptiste Goyeau and then came into the possession of Vital Dumouchel who married Goyeau's daughter. Jean Baptiste Ouellette married Vital Dumouchel's daughter who inherited the farm lot, whence the name Ouellette Avenue.

map did not come into possession of those lots until a much later date, for example, Marentette in 1767 (Appendix IV). Hence it may be concluded that the names were added no earlier than that date. All available information, however, indicates that the map with the outlined farm lots is correct for the year 1754.

The earliest evidence names the grantees, but it is more difficult to tell exactly how many of these people actually resided on their land. As noted before, the grants were made on condition that a "hearth and home" be established within a year. The disbanded soldiers and the settlers who came from Lower Canada had no other place to go, and it can be presumed that if they remained at Detroit they occupied their land immediately. People who had been living in the town of Detroit as tradesmen or merchants, on the other hand, may not have taken up residence immediately. Building a house on the property and installing a hired man in it would have satisfied the conditions of the grant. In his description of Detroit in 1756 Charles Stuart indicated that between the two Indian villages there were three plantations belonging to three French merchants who lived in the fort of Detroit. This account was not written on the spot but from memory a few years later. Hence its accuracy may be questioned. Still it cannot be assumed that all the grantees were necessarily residents.

Hardly had the French settlers on the south shore of the Detroit River begun to feel secure in their possessions wrested from the wilderness when the Seven Years' War broke out in America. In the struggle for the possession of the Ohio Valley, with few exceptions the numerous tribes of the lakes and Mississippi regions were on the side of the French. At Braddock's defeat near Fort Duquesne on July 9, 1755, Hurons, Ottawas, and Ojibways took part in the battle. Father Potier was away from his mission during that year. It is not clear whether he accompanied the Indian war parties to Pennsylvania or simply went to Sandusky to minister to the Hurons at that place. This war followed by the British occupation of Detroit put a brake on the extension of the settlement.

For some years after the change of government the Ottawa village remained the eastern limit of the occupied frontage. Captain John Montresor's map of the Detroit River made in 1763 pictures the amount of land under cultivation above the Huron village, and it shows no farms above the Ottawa town (see Fig. 8). However, there is evidence that the Ottawas had entirely moved away by the summer of 1765. In September of that year at a meeting held in Detroit, Pontiac, Chief of the Ottawas, told George Croghan,

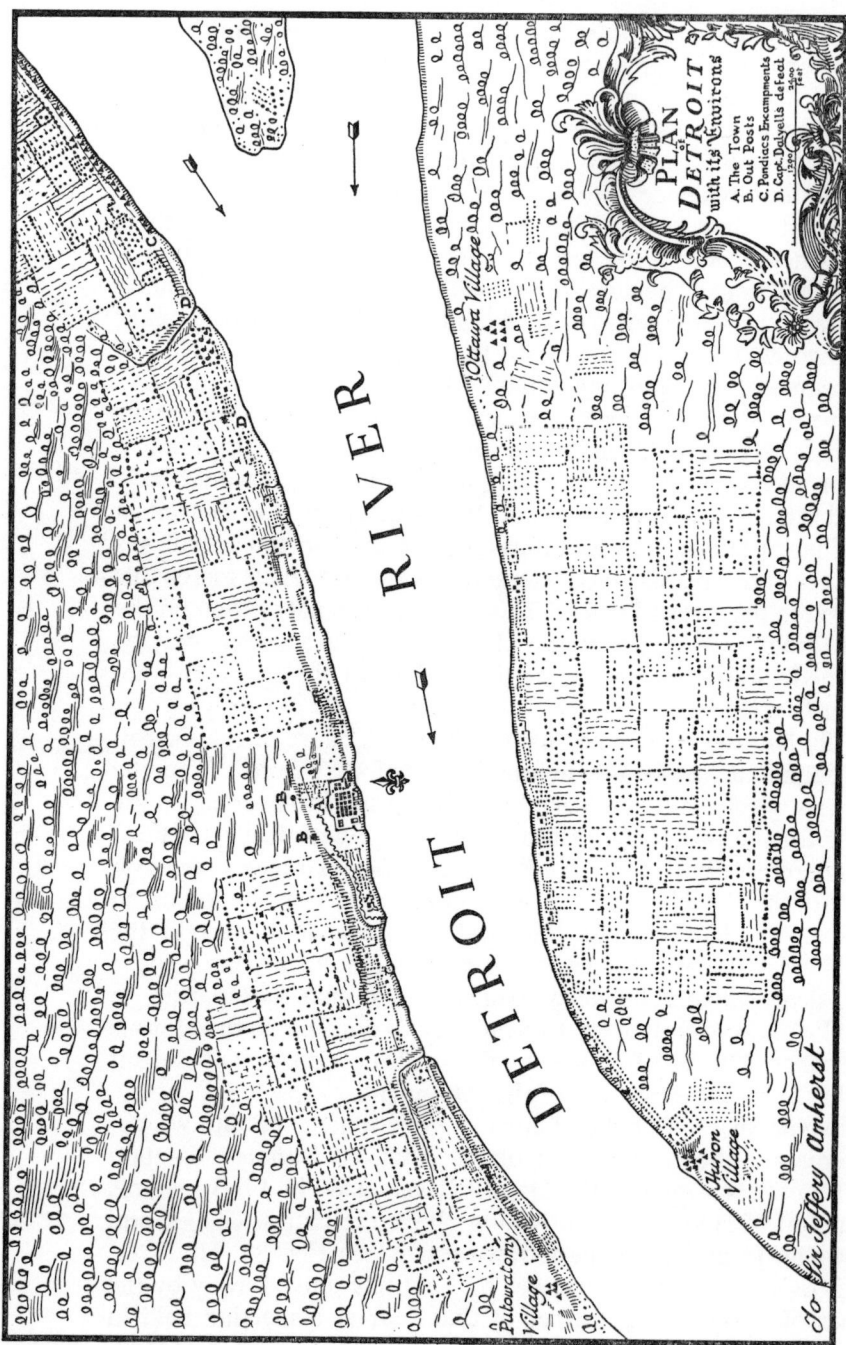

FIG. 8. PLAN OF DETROIT WITH ITS ENVIRONS BY JOHN MONTRESOR, 1763. [By permission William L. Clements Library, Ann Arbor, Michigan.]

Deputy Superintendent for Indian Affairs, that his people were now settled on the Maumee River.[11] That same year he gave deeds of land located at the site of the former Ottawa village to several residents of Detroit (C 14). General Thomas Gage, Commander-in-Chief of the British forces in America, in a letter of April 8, 1771, pointed out that such gifts were to be considered null and void unless made with the King's permission and authority (C 17). From later transfers of these properties, however, it appears that the titles were considered secure, the deeds having been made in the presence of the Deputy Superintendent for Indian Affairs.

The sixty-one names on the south side listed in the Dejean census of Detroit for 1768 also point to the Ottawa town as the limit of the settlement (C 16). It is worthy of note that at this date the Longueuil tract above the Huron mission had not yet been subdivided. The census data tally with the information contained in a letter of Father Potier to the Bishop of Quebec in 1768 stating that his parish comprised some sixty families on the south shore of the river.[12]

The 1770's saw the beginning of development towards Lake St. Clair. Expansion was necessary to provide farms for the natural increase in population, for the second generation was coming of age. Of the forty-five marriages at Assumption Church during this decade twenty-seven of the grooms' names appear as heads of families on the south side in the 1782 census of Detroit (C 23). Immigration from Lower Canada also played a part in the need for extending the boundaries of the settlement. On October 2, 1770, Father Bocquet of Ste. Anne's Church of Detroit wrote to the Bishop of Quebec as follows: "I estimate that soon Detroit will be larger than Montreal. Every day families are arriving from that direction and they say that some are still on the way."[13] It is not unlikely that some of these families located on the south shore.

In spite of the pressing need, the extension of the settlement was slow because of the difficulty in obtaining grants of land. The British government showed great delicacy in respecting the rights of the Indians to the ownership of the land, and restricted the manner of their disposing of it (C 17). Contrary to these restrictions some gifts of land were made by the Indians, but they could not be registered at the notarial office at Detroit (C 18). There is also

[11]The Maumee River empties into the western end of Lake Erie at the present city of Toledo, Ohio.
[12]Quebec Chancery Archives, E.U., V-15. For further reference purposes this source of documents will be designated as Q.C.A.
[13]*Ibid.*, E.U., V-21.

evidence that in 1774 Commandant Bassett gave permission to settlers to occupy land opposite Peach Island[14] at the entrance to Lake St. Clair (C 21). Moreover, in 1778 Lieutenant-Governor Henry Hamilton at Detroit reported that he had given permits to till land to some needy persons, but with the understanding that they must not be considered as grants (C 19, C 20). In the census of Detroit for 1779[15] the Longueuil tract above the Huron mission has been divided into five farm lots, but not more than ten improved farms can be located above the former Ottawa village.

Hamilton's successor, Major Arent De Peyster (1779-84), appears to have been less scrupulous in the matter of grants and to have countenanced the cessions by the Indians to certain individuals (C 21, C 22), even a 5,000-acre tract to himself. In some cases these lands were subsequently divided and farm lots were sold to settlers. Because the holdings originated in irregular Indian gifts the titles were questionable, and sales were made with this condition: "If dispossessed by Indians or others only money paid will be refunded. Improvements made will be lost." (See Appendix IV.) Complaints of De Peyster's improper procedure reached Quebec, and in 1784 General Haldimand ordered the notarial register of Detroit to be taken to Quebec "for an investigation of the grants which individuals have received from Indians and Commanding Officers" (C 24, C 25).[16]

De Peyster's laxity gave impetus to the expansion along the Detroit River. This development was very timely as this decade (1781-90) witnessed ninety-one marriages at Assumption Church. From the census of Detroit for the year 1782 (C 23) it appears that the settlement then extended upstream to land opposite the lower end of Hog Island,[17] with some scattered settlers as far east as the

[14]Peach Island should be called Fishing Island, a translation of Isle à la Pêche. (It was also known as Isle du Large.)
[15]P.A.C., B 122, p. 318 sqq.; *M.H.C.*, X, 312-27.
[16]This register remained at Quebec until 1789. During the interval the records of Detroit were kept by Guillaume Monforton in his capacity of Notary Public. The entries for the first two years are missing, having been stolen from his office. The records for the remaining years are contained in the Monforton Register preserved in the Public Archives of Canada. A copy was made for the Burton Historical Collection and it is incorporated in its Notarial Records of Detroit.
[17]Hog Island (Isle aux Cochons) is now known as Belle Isle, and is an amusement park owned by the city of Detroit. There is a popular legend that the island was infested with rattlesnakes, and that a large herd of swine was placed on it to destroy the reptiles, whence the name Hog Island. Its Indian name was Kouishkouishki. At the beginning of the present century it was not uncommon to hear the French farmers along the Detroit River employing the sounds "kouish, kouish" in calling their hogs. "Kouish" is still heard as baby talk for "pig." Possibly these expressions have come from the Indians.

PLATE I. FATHER PIERRE POTIER, S.J. [Reproduced from the *Detroit News* of April 26, 1891.]

PLATE II. COLONEL ALEXANDER MCKEE. [Reproduced from original oil painting made at Pittsburg in 1757, now in possession of Mr. Raymond W. McKee, Los Angeles, California.]

PLATE III. THE RECTORY AND HALL OF ASSUMPTION PARISH BUILT IN 1784. [From a photo by A. Phil. E. Panet taken in 1892.]

PLATE IV. THE MATTHEW ELLIOTT HOMESTEAD BUILT IN 1784. [From a photo taken in 1912 preserved in the Museum of the Fort Malden National Historic Park, Amherstburg, Ontario.]

PLATE V. THE HURON CHURCH OR CHURCH OF THE ASSUMPTION OPENED IN 1787. [From a water-colour painting by Dr. Edward Walsh in 1804 entitled "A View of Detroit and the Straits Taken from the Huron Church." Original in the William L. Clements Library, Ann Arbor, Michigan. Reproduced by courtesy of the Director of the Library.]

area facing Peach Island at the entrance to Lake St. Clair. Unfortunately the notarial records of 1784–6 are missing. But later surveyors' lists show that in these few years about forty frontage lots were occupied in this area, and before 1790 the settlement had pushed its way solidly to Lake St. Clair. In addition Monforton's 1792 lists of landholders at Petite Côte noted that in 1789 six farm lots at the southern end of that settlement were granted by the Indians (C 26). These grants extended the occupied frontage southward to the present boundary line between North and South Essex.

Excluding the Huron reserve near Assumption Church, a survey of the upper part of the Detroit River in the late 1780's would have shown a hundred and fifty farm lots covering all the frontage from a point four miles below La Rivière aux Dindes to Lake St. Clair. This development had been effected within four decades after the south shore had been opened to settlers in the middle of the century in an effort by the government to make Detroit the granary of the West, thereby laying the foundations of the only white settlement in the present Province of Ontario that reaches back continuously to the last decade of the French régime in Canada.

D. THE PIONEER SETTLERS AND THEIR FARMS

MUCH of the information concerning the pioneers and their families is to be found in the baptismal and marriage records of the parishes of Assumption and Ste. Anne. It must not be forgotten that during the French régime Ste. Anne's on the north side of the river was the parish church for all the French living on both sides of the river, and that until 1761 it was the ordinary place for baptism of their children even though they were born on the south shore. The Huron Mission of the Assumption at La Pointe de Montréal was intended for the Indians only, but the French were allowed to attend divine services and to receive the sacraments in that chapel. Very likely only those children who, for some reason or other, could not be taken across the river were baptized at the mission. Written in Latin and incorporated in the account book of the mission are seventeen entries of baptisms of white children for the years 1751-6 (D 1). Marie Louise Villers, baptized on October 4, 1751, heads the list.[1] From 1756-61 there is a gap in the records. An easy explanation is that the pages for those years have been lost.

Marie Louise Villers is the first white child known to have been baptized at the Huron Mission of the Assumption at La Pointe de Montréal, but she is not the first white child born in the settlement on the south shore of the Detroit River. An entry in the Cicotte Book states that in July 1749 Louis Plichon arrived at Detroit with his wife and two children to take up the land assigned to him on the south shore. In the census of Detroit for September 1, 1750, Louis Plichon is listed with three children under the age of fifteen. An examination of the records of Ste. Anne's Church, Detroit, shows that a Plichon, son of Louis Plichon and Marie Louise Pimparé, was baptized there on November 26, 1749, and given the name of François. In the light of present evidence, François Plichon must be considered the first white child born in what is now Essex County.

[1]Because the last digit of 1751 is somewhat blurred at the base, this entry was published in Thwaites, *Jesuit Relations*, LXX, 75, as 175 (4?—illegible), and transposed among the entries of that year. Under a magnifying glass the year can be identified as 1751. The 1754 date is certainly erroneous because, according to the records of Ste. Anne's Church, the Villers have another daughter (Jeanne) born and baptized on November 24, 1754. If the record is consecutive, as it appears to be, the date of 1751 fits its position at the head of the list of entries and also accords with the date of Marie Louise's death and her age then. According to the Assumption Church register, Marie Louise Villers, wife of Jean Thomas Pajot, died on January 9, 1814, at the age of sixty-two years.

From 1761 there are continuous records in the archives of the Church of the Assumption. For twenty years (1761–81) in his characteristic copperplate handwriting Father Potier kept a faithful record of the baptisms, marriages, and burials of his spiritual children. The names of the sponsors for baptisms and witnesses for marriages are also entered. It is worthy of note that in matters of record a wife did not take her husband's name. Even in the record of her burial she retained her maiden name.

It is interesting to study in the baptismal registers of the parish the names of the pioneer families. Their descendants constitute a large percentage of the French-Canadian population of Essex County today. Frequently enough, in the non-urbanized areas along the Detroit River, they retain parcels of the land cleared by their eighteenth-century forefathers. Heading the list of surnames were Drouillard, Langlois, Réaume, Meloche and Godet (Marantet). The tally of French names in a recent issue of the telephone directory for Essex County shows these five families still amongst the first ten, having been surpassed by Renaud, Bondy, and Ouellette and joined in the honour roll by Parent and Dupuis—all family names that appeared in the first generation of settlers on the south shore (see Appendix V). The records of baptisms also supply information regarding the increase of the population in the locality. From them have been compiled the following quinquennial statistics: 1761–5 inclusive, 83 baptisms; 1766–70, 103 baptisms; 1771–5, 164 baptisms; 1776–80, 193 baptisms.

The rate of infant mortality was high. In the ten-year span of 1771–80 inclusive, there were 357 infant baptisms. Over the same period of time there were 72 burials of children under one year of age. But in spite of these losses the average family was reckoned as six.

There is evidence that slavery was quite common along the Detroit River in the eighteenth century. This practice was founded on the assumed right of selling captives taken in war. Many families held Indians and Negroes as slaves and employed them as house servants or as drudges in the fur trade. So many of the Indian slaves were Pawnees, an Indian tribe that lived on the Missouri River, that the name "pawnee" or "panis" (fem. panise) became synonymous with Indian slave. In the parish records there are several entries of "le panis, or la panise de N." There are also a few records of "le nègre or la négresse de N." Most of the Negro slaves had been captured by the Indians in their war depredations on the southern plantations. In the census of Detroit for 1750 there are 33 slaves;

for 1773 there are 83 slaves, nine of which are on the south side; for 1779 the total jumps to 138 with 24 on the south side; for 1782 are listed 179 slaves, 35 of whom are held by families residing on the south shore of the river.[2] In 1793 the importation of slaves into the Province of Upper Canada was prohibited by law. The actual slaves, however, remained as such, but their children were to be freed when they reached the age of twenty-five.

The marriage records contain much historical data (see Appendix VI). Each entry gives the date, the publication of banns, the ecclesiastical dispensation if any, the names of the bride and groom as well as the names and place of residence of their parents, usually a parish along the St. Lawrence River. Except in the case of the discharged soldiers the pioneer settlers did not come to the Detroit River region directly from France. There was a stopover of one or more generations in the lower part of Canada. By collating the dates of the marriages with the baptismal records of the bride and groom, one finds that the popular age for marriage for girls was sixteen or seventeen. Some were only fourteen or fifteen, so great was the demand for eligible maidens on this frontier of civilization. The men, however, usually waited until their twenties before contracting matrimony. The names of the official witnesses to the marriages are also given. Very few of them were able to write. They made their mark (X) alongside their names inscribed by the priest. The witnesses were always men. There is no trace of bridesmaids in the Assumption Church records of the eighteenth century.

Notwithstanding the brotherly spirit between the French and the Hurons who worshipped together in the parish of the Assumption, intermarriage was not frequent. Such alliances did not form part of the Jesuit plan for Christianizing the Indians, hence they would find no encouragement from Father Potier. In his parish records for 1761–81, out of 82 marriages of the French two are with halfbreeds and one is with a panise to legitimize the children, and none with a Huron.

When the marriage was between persons belonging to prosperous families, it was preceded by a long formal contract drawn up by a notary and agreed to before many witnesses. These contracts do

[2]The following original bill of sale of an Indian slave woman is preserved in the George F. Macdonald Collection, Windsor, Ontario (translation from the French): "I certify that I have sold and delivered to Mr. Badichon Labadie a panis slave woman named Mannon, for and in consideration of eighty bushels of wheat which he shall pay me whenever he has a supply between now and next spring. Given under my hand this 10th day of October, 1775.
    Witness   John Porteous   James Sterling"

not appear in the church records, but can be found in the notarial registers of the period (D 2).

In the early years of the settlement the people were very poor. On December 2, 1760, Captain Donald Campbell, first British Commandant of Detroit, wrote to Colonel Henry Bouquet at Fort Pitt that "the *habitants* seemed pleased with the change of regime but that they were in great destitution of all things."[3] Very likely the last part of the sentence explains the first. Reduced almost to famine by their contributions for the support of the armies during the last few years of French rule, the inhabitants were happy to have a moment of truce, but their hearts, for the most part, remained loyal to France. In a letter to General Thomas Gage dated May 31, 1766, Captain John Campbell wrote from Detroit that the people were so wretchedly poor that they had not been able to pay half of their taxes.[4]

A part of this destitution could be attributed to the settlers' own improvidence. On April 8, 1768, writing to the Bishop of Quebec about Father Potier's parishioners on the south shore, the pastor of Ste. Anne's Church, Detroit, says: "More than half of them have already wasted all their wheat in drink, and I believe that the priest and people will not have sufficient to last them till the harvest."[5] The immoderate use of drink was typical of frontier society in America at that time.

These pioneers, whose descendants have become renowned as farmers and market gardeners,[6] have sometimes been criticized for having been unprogressive, not improving their methods of cultivating the soil, being satisfied to fish, hunt, and trade for their livelihood. A partial explanation for this apparent lack of enterprise can be found in a study of the settlers' background. Some of these men had been *voyageurs* and consequently were always eager for adventure. A trip to the wilderness in quest of furs, a military foray, or some other activity of a similar nature was enough to draw them away from farming. Besides, quite a number of the others had been soldiers in the garrison at the fort or tradesmen living in the village of Detroit. *Voyageurs*, soldiers, and artisans are not easily transformed into sedentary farmers.

Another contributing factor for some of the colonists on the south shore was the location of the first settlement, between Le Ruisseau

[3]P.A.C., A 15, p. 278; *M.H.C.*, XIX, 45.
[4]William L. Clements Library, Gage Papers, American Series, vol. 52. Hereafter this depository will be referred to as Clements Library.
[5]Q.C.A., E.U., V-12.
[6]The famous Petite Côte radishes provide one of their most lucrative crops.

de la Vieille Reine and La Rivière aux Dindes. This site must have been selected for its sandy beach, which afforded an easy approach to the farm lots, rather than for the fertility of the land. In most of that area the soil is yellow sand with a very thin cover of loam. It was not long before the locality came to be known as La Côte de Misère (Misery Settlement). Those who wanted to cultivate land seriously moved farther south or above the former Ottawa village towards Lake St. Clair.

The main reason, however, for this agricultural indolence lies in the light demand and consequent low price for products of the farm. Shipping was very expensive and the only market within hundreds of miles was the provision stores of His Majesty's troops at the Post of Detroit. Its lists of 1766 indicate that the farmers on the south shore had contracted for only 27,900 pounds of flour, 81 bushels of peas, and 1,340 pounds of pork (D 3). One or two good farms could have supplied all these products. Consequently a large number of the inhabitants did not produce beyond their own needs (D 4), and found it easier and more pleasant to gain the rest of their livelihood with gun and line rather than with the hoe and the plough (D 9). In 1773 there were only 1,424 acres of land under cultivation on the south shore, indicating that after more than two decades the narrow farms, on an average, were not being tilled for more than six or seven arpents in depth (D 5).

Few of the French farm grants at Detroit actually received confirmation of the King, although this was required by the *Coutume de Paris*, which was then the law of the country. Permits to occupy, or grants, were given by the Commandant at the fort. There was a yearly rental, *cens et rentes*—one *sol* of *cens* plus a quarter bushel of wheat per arpent frontage, and *one* sol of *rente* per square arpent. This was usually paid on St. Martin's Day (November 11). When the property was transferred by sale, exchange, or inheritance there was a fine of alienation, *lots et ventes*. According to article 76 of the *Coutume de Paris* this fine amounted to one-twelfth of the estimated value of the land.

After the British occupation in 1760, the landowners were taxed two cords of wood for every arpent of frontage. In 1765 this tax was changed to ten shillings, New York currency. However, the tax could be paid in firewood at the rate of eight shillings per cord. The census of 1768 (C 16) indicates that the taxes were reduced to the following scale: one arpent frontage—three-quarters cord; three arpents—two cords.

In matters of taxes and in other official transactions at the fort, pounds, shillings, and pence replaced the French livre. This was in keeping with General Thomas Gage's order to Major Henry Gladwin on January 9, 1764: "The French *livre* must no more be heard of."[7] However, this order was not observed in general practice. Even in legal transactions such as transfers of property the amount of money involved was usually expressed in both units, being translated from one to the other at the rate of fifteen livres for one pound New York currency. In the account books of Assumption Church the term pounds (paonds) occurs very rarely, and the French livre was regularly used as the money of account throughout the eighteenth century.

Because the river was necessary to each settler as a means of communication and as a source of food, the grants were laid out into farms of narrow fronts of three arpents along the river and running back forty arpents or more. At the beginning of the settlement the depth did not matter. Except for a small area of so-called meadows near the shore, the tract was inaccessible and covered with woods and swamps. Later on when the first forty arpents were cleared of firewood, the settlers were given continuations or extensions of their farms for another forty or eighty arpents. In time these ribbons of land became narrower as the farm lots were divided among the children, and the river front resembled a single village street.

Orchards of apples, pears, and cherries were to be found on nearly every farm. Situated in the southernmost part of Canada, and being almost surrounded by water, the frontier peninsula possessed exceptional advantages in this branch of horticulture. From these orchards came many noted kinds of apples, especially spies, russets, and snows. As cider fruit these apples maintained a high reputation. The Detroit census for July 1782 reported prospects of a thousand barrels of cyder (*sic*) being made that year. The crowning glory of these orchards was the pear tree. Nearly every farm had one or more of these giant trees that each year produced at least twenty-five to thirty bushels of fruit that was used for stewing and preserving. Although they have been called Jesuit pear trees, their origin is unknown, and like the orchards they have all but disappeared from the scene.

The houses of the early settlers were very small. In 1774 St. André sold to Ben Chappus a log house sixteen feet by seventeen feet located on the south shore (D 6). The largest houses described in other transfers of property are twenty feet square. Some of these

[7]Clements Library, Gage Papers, American Series, vol. 12.

were of logs; others were of lighter construction. The walls were only seven or eight feet high. A bark roof was proof against the weather. Glass panes for windows were available at the mission store as early as 1750. From the 1768 inventory of the estate of an apparently prosperous *habitant*, it is possible to catch a glimpse of the scanty furnishings of these pioneer homes (D 4). Cook stoves were not invented early enough to be used by the first settlers. The family baking was done outside in public ovens made of clay. In 1751 there was an oven at the mission capable of handling twenty-four pounds of bread per batch. In 1781 a new bakery, sixteen feet square, had been constructed in the yard of the Church of the Assumption. The yards around the houses were enclosed by high picket fences to protect from wild animals not only the children but also the cattle, hogs, and chickens.

Strung bead-like along the river and linked together by a narrow road running along the edge of the water, these farmhouses formed what was called in Canadian language a *Côte*. *Petite Côte* was the name applied to the earliest settlement below Le Ruisseau de la Vieille Reine—a settlement which later extended southward along the Detroit River to the present base-line between North and South Essex. The stretch of frontage above the Huron Church was known as *La Côte des Hurons*. To the settlement from the village of the Ottawas to Lake St. Clair was applied the name of *La Côte des Outaouais*. The isolated position of these *Côtes* and the proximity of the houses fostered mutual dependence and sociability among the inhabitants. The *coup-de-main* or bee was a popular way of doing big jobs such as hauling logs, threshing grain, or raising a building. Frequently these were occasions for copious libations of wine and brandy followed by much joviality.

A familiar sight along these *Côtes* in the eighteenth century was the windmills with their sweeping arms and flapping sails, where the farmers brought their grain to have it ground. These were tower-shaped buildings about thirty feet in height and about twenty feet in diameter. The roof was conical and to it were attached long arms or wings fixed to an axle fitted with small sails. A map dated 1791 indicates six windmills along the river between Turkey Creek and the lower end of Hog Island (see Fig. 9). Maisonville's Mill was a well-known landmark at Windmill Point at the foot of the present Lincoln Road in the city of Windsor.

Although the topography in the peninsula of Essex County is remarkably flat, an attempt was made to harness springtime water-power in one of the streams that flow into the Detroit River. Since

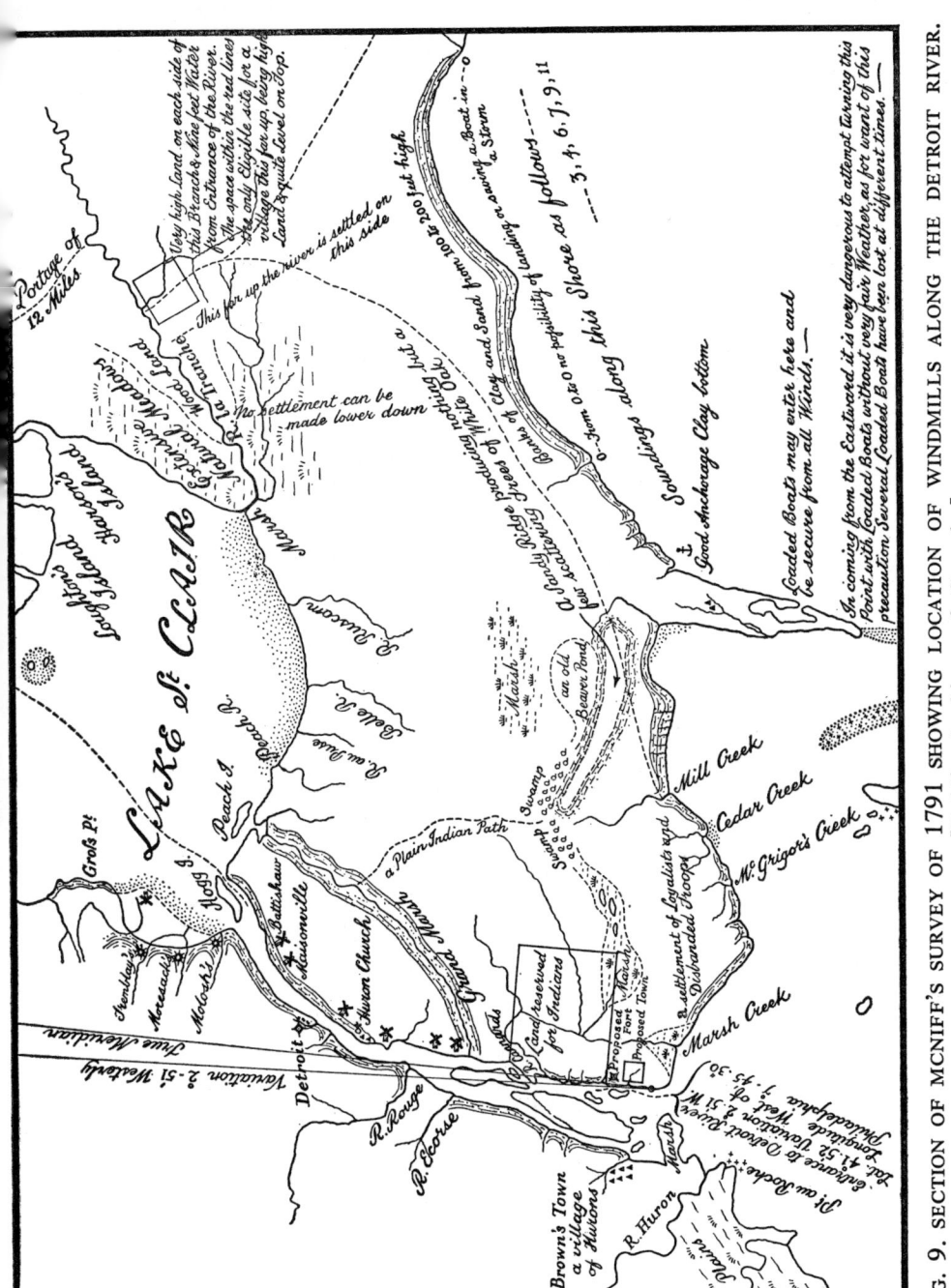

FIG. 9. SECTION OF MCNIFF'S SURVEY OF 1791 SHOWING LOCATION OF WINDMILLS ALONG THE DETROIT RIVER. [Public Archives of Canada.]

mill sites were reserved to the government, it was necessary to obtain permission from the Commandant for their development. Upon petition of a group of settlers at Petite Côte, dated July 1, 1780, Commandant De Peyster authorized the construction of a water-mill on La Rivière aux Dindes in favour of Simon Drouillard (D 8). This mill was located just below the present Malden Road. Later it came into possession of J. B. Feré and was known for a long time as the Feré Mill (see Fig. 10).

A surveyor's map of 1790 marks two other mill sites. One is located on La Rivière à Gervais about a mile from its mouth. The other is indicated as being about four miles up La Rivière aux Canards "to which loaded bateaux can go." Even though a 1797 map shows a mill on La Rivière à Gervais, there is no evidence that either of these two mill sites was ever developed.

A letter written in 1776 by Lieutenant-Governor Hamilton at Detroit to the Colonial Secretary gives a good description of the south side of the river. He mentions that the French farmers were settled for eight miles along the shore, that the houses were of log or of frame construction, and most of them had orchards adjoining. Very informingly he writes in part as follows: "The Inhabitants may thank the bounty full hand of providence for Melons, Plums, Pears, Apples, Mulberries and Grapes, besides several sorts of smaller fruits. . . . Almost every farmer has a calash for the summer and a carriole for the winter. They use Oxen and Horses indifferently for the Plough. . . . The farmer, in a few hours, with gun and line will furnish food for several families." (D 7.)

It appears that in 1776 the name of the locality known, up to that time, as La Pointe de Montréal was changed to L'Assomption. Until August of that year Father Potier signed himself as "pastor of tho Church of the Assumption at La Pointe de Montréal du Détroit." After that date La Pointe de Montréal was omitted in his official title. Civil records as well as letters of the period indicate that in the last quarter of the eighteenth century the whole territory from the Huron Church to Lake St. Clair was generally known by the name of the Settlement of L'Assomption or simply L'Assomption—the title of the old Mission of the Hurons founded at Detroit by Father de La Richardie in 1728.

To the slaves and prisoners brought to Detroit during the American Revolutionary War the east bank of the river offered the prospect of two settlements of narrow farms—one at Petite Côte and the other at L'Assomption. On these partly cultivated farms, the

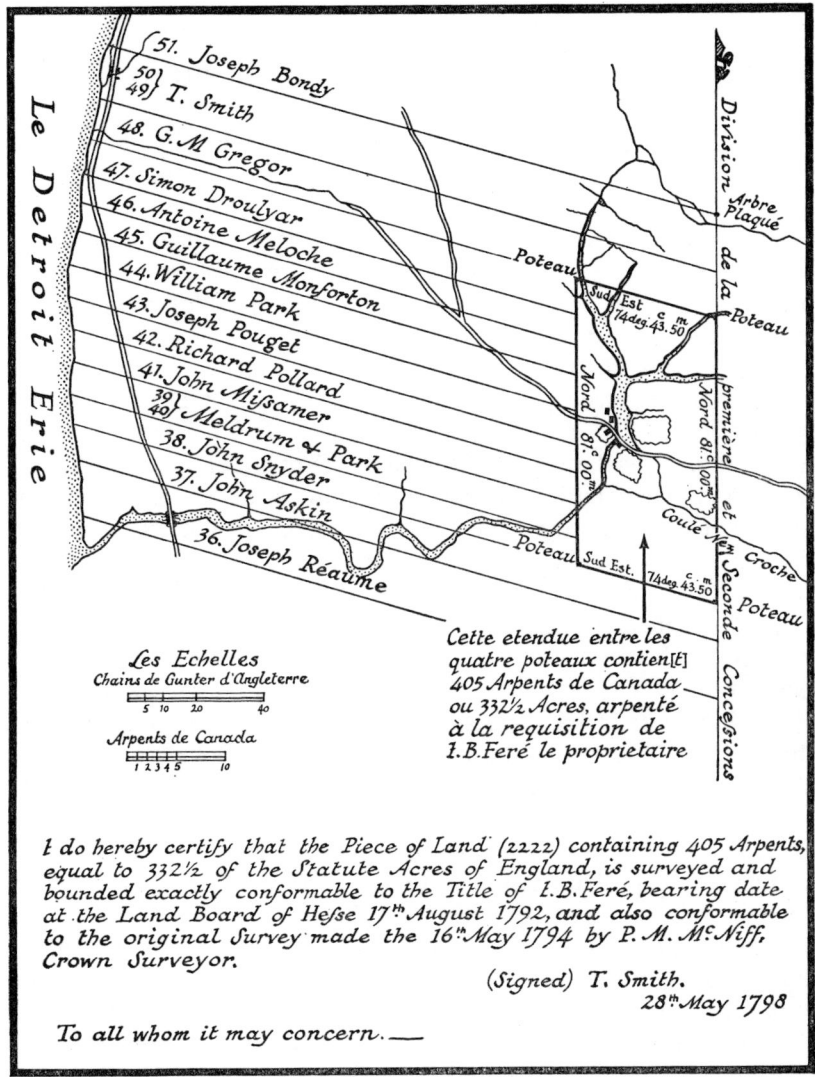

FIG. 10. PLAN OF J. B. FERÉ'S WATER-MILL ON TURKEY CREEK BY T. SMITH, 1798. [Public Archives of Canada.]

small houses surrounded by orchards were occupied by almost a hundred pioneer French families totalling some six hundred souls —the first generation of white settlers along the so-called south shore of the Detroit River.

E. GOVERNMENT AND LAW UNDER BRITISH RULE

BEFORE 1760 the Detroit River region was ruled by the French Commandant at the fort. Matters of controversy were settled by him. The inhabitants had been accustomed to submit to his decisions which were based on the *Coutume de Paris*. This Code contained the legal forms for conveying real estate or personal property by deed or will, for marriage or other contracts, and for many other instruments. In each settlement of New France there was an appointed royal notary who drew up all these legal papers. During the last twenty-five years of French rule at Detroit, Robert Navarre filled this position.

By the capitulation of Montreal (September 8, 1760), the western posts including Detroit came into British possession. The interchange of garrison and flags was accomplished without fighting, and almost without warning, on November 29, 1760 (E 2). A British occupation force of more than 200 soldiers arrived at Detroit in nineteen bateaux and whale-boats, led by Major Robert Rogers who bore a letter of capitulation from Marquis de Vaudreuil, the last French Governor of Canada, to the French Commandant F. M. Picoté de Bel(l)estre at Detroit (E 1). Waiting on the south shore a half-mile below the town, Rogers gave Bellestre until four o'clock in the afternoon to surrender. There was nothing to do but submit, and the British colours were hoisted atop the fort. Thus came to an abrupt end three-score years of French rule at the place founded by Cadillac's vision at the beginning of the century in an effort to hold back the English from the upper lakes.

After taking possession of the fort, Rogers ordered the thirty-five French soldiers to be sent to Philadelphia *via* Fort Pitt for embarkation for France. Then he summoned the Canadian (that is, French-Canadian) militia, disarmed it, and administered the oath of allegiance (E 3). The militia included every able-bodied man between the ages of sixteen and sixty. The loss of guns was a great hardship because many of the habitants depended on hunting for food. Later these regulations were eased, guns were returned, and French captains of militia were recommissioned (E 6).

The coming of the British opened an era of marked progress in lake navigation. There had been no sailing vessels on Lake Erie since the ill-fated maiden voyage of La Salle's *Griffon* in 1679. The very first year after the conquest the schooner *Huron* was built on an island (later called Navy Island) in the Niagara River above the falls. The next year this shipyard launched a sloop named *Michigan*.[1] When not occupied for military purposes these two ships were employed in the carrying trade. It was not long, however, before this embryonic British fleet of the upper lakes was tested in actual warfare.

The British occupation of Detroit, so calmly accepted by its French settlers, soon met resistance from the Indians. The influx of British traders and soldiers into Indian territory was resented by the red men. Missing the old *camaraderie* and the presents they had known in their dealings with the French officers and traders, the Indians began to realize the disdain in which they were held by their new masters. The French element still in the West on the Mississippi, promising them that help was coming from their father Onontio,[2] played upon the Indians' discontent. The spring of 1763 saw the breaking point.

At Detroit the gathering resentment of the Indians against the English was epitomized in the person of Pontiac. On April 27, 1763, this great Ottawa Chief assembled the tribes of the region for a council at an Indian burial ground on the west shore of the river. There, upon the graves of their dead, by his eloquence and personality he aroused in the hearts of the living the will to resist their oppressors.

Pontiac, who was then staying on Peach Island at the entrance to Lake St. Clair, reserved for himself the capture of Fort Detroit. With 800 warriors he encamped on the north side, east of Parent Creek about a mile and a half above the fort. The house of his old friend, the late Pierre Meloche, served as his headquarters. From there he besieged the British garrison of 120 soldiers mustered in the stockade. The story of the siege which lasted from May to October, and the stubborn resistance by forewarned Major Gladwin is well known. Therefore, relation will be confined to a few highlights, especially those that affected the south shore, which are

[1] In 1765 four vessels were built at Navy Island. All were owned and operated by the government. In 1771 a shipyard was established at Detroit which became the chief naval station on the upper lakes. For a detailed treatment of this subject, see "The Royal Navy of the Upper Lakes" by M. M. Quaife, *B.H.C. Leaflet*, II, no. 5.

[2] The term "Onontio" meaning "Big Mountain" was first applied by the Indians to the second French Governor of New France, Charles Hualt de Montmagny. Later it became the usual name for the Governor, and was extended to apply to the chief sovereign, the King.

described in the Pontiac Manuscript[3] (E 4) and in other contemporary documents.[4]

No fighting took place on the south side, but there was plenty of activity all along the shore. At that time the Hurons were living under two separate chiefs. One received the war-belts[5] from Pontiac with shouts of joy, while the other refused. On May 11, the eve of the Feast of the Ascension, Pontiac crossed the river with four chiefs and held a council at the Huron village, at which he threatened to massacre all those who would not throw in their lot with him. Having only sixty warriors the recalcitrant band promised to join the fray after Mass the next day. During the siege the landing of plunder and prisoners captured by the Indians on Lake Erie and at the mouth of the river were also moments of great stir and movement in the village.[6] Along the *Côtes* roving parties of savages went about the French farms stealing or killing horses, cows, and pigs. When grain was needed the Indians either stole or requisitioned it. The settlers living outside the protection of the fort had no choice. They surrendered their provisions in order to save their lives, but with few exceptions they maintained that they could not enter the war on account of the oath they had taken.

[3]The Pontiac Manuscript is a contemporary account of the siege written in French, probably by Robert Navarre, who had been Royal Notary under the French régime, and was continued in office by the British. The original manuscript is in the B.H.C. Translated by R. Clyde Ford, it was published by Clarence M. Burton under the title of *Journal of Pontiac's Conspiracy, 1763*.

[4]Franklin B. Hough, ed., *Diary of the Siege of Detroit*. This day-by-day account of the war was written by Lieutenant Jehu Hay. The original manuscript is in the William L. Clements Library, Ann Arbor, Michigan.

In the same volume there is also published "Journal of the Siege of Detroit," a collection of notes taken by Major Robert Rogers from the officers who were in the fort. The report, which ends on July 4, 1763, was sent to Sir William Johnson and was found among his papers.

The Journal of John Montresor, preserved among Amherst papers in England, was published in the *Transactions of the Royal Society of Canada*, Series III, vol. XXII (1928).

For a full treatment of the war, see Howard H. Peckham, *Pontiac and the Indian Uprising*.

[5]Since the Indians did not have a written language they were compelled to rely upon symbols. At their councils the speaker would raise in his hands a calumet, a belt, a skin, or some wampum, and he would tell his hearers what the article was intended to represent. The acceptance of the emblem constituted a contract to remain in force until the symbol was returned.

[6]The largest capture made by the Indians took place on May 28 at Point Pelee on Lake Erie. In an ambush some Hurons and Potawatamis intercepted Lieutenant Abraham Cuyler's detachment bound for Detroit from Niagara. The Indians succeeded in capturing twenty to thirty British soldiers and eight barges carrying munitions and provisions. Two days later to the accompaniment of death cries they reached the Huron village with their prizes of war. Burton, *Journal of Pontiac's Conspiracy*, pp. 136–44.

An important phase of the war revolved around the efforts to maintain water transportation. Fortunately for the besieged, at the outbreak of hostilities the schooner *Huron* and the sloop *Michigan* were anchored in front of the fort whose approaches they protected on the river side. Even though some English boats were captured on Lake Erie and on the river, the two armed sailing vessels kept open the lines of communication with Niagara. At the end of May the schooner left Detroit, and returned a month later loaded with men and provisions. On its way up the river it was attacked by the Indians off Isle aux Dindes (hence named Fighting Island), but it succeeded in reaching the fort. A month later when Captain Dalyell was sighted below the Rouge River with 280 men in 22 barges, it was this same vessel that escorted them to their destination. Two days after his arrival, on July 31 Dalyell rashly attempted to inflict a crushing defeat on Pontiac. He was defeated and killed in the historic battle on the banks of Parent Creek (afterwards called Bloody Run). Throughout August and September there were intermittent skirmishes by the Ottawas and Ojibways, which failed to dislodge the British garrison. On October 3 Captain John Montresor reached the fort with supplies in the schooner *Huron*. This was the turning point of the war. The assistance received from the recently constructed armed vessels had enabled the beleaguered garrison to withstand the attacks of the red men until they became exhausted. The Indians had failed to strike a decisive blow quickly, which they needed in order to succeed. To provide supplies for a long campaign was not part of their way to life. On October 12, the hunting season being at hand and ammunition running low, some of the Indians sued for peace with a view to renewing the war in the following spring.

On October 30 French messengers came to Detroit with a letter from M. Neyon, Commandant of Fort Chartres on the Mississippi, advising Pontiac to expect no assistance from the French as they and the British were now at peace. The very next day Pontiac sent a note to Gladwin saying that the Indians had buried their hatchets. Thereupon Pontiac withdrew to the Maumee River and peace was restored along the shore of the Detroit River.

On November 1 Gladwin wrote to General Amherst advising against pursuing the Indians (E 5). In that letter he suggested that an easy and inexpensive way of punishing them for their mischief would be to permit a free sale of rum, which would destroy them more effectively than fire or sword. However, instead of retaliating by rum or gun, it was decided to try to cultivate their friendship by the lavish distribution of presents, provisions (including rum), and ammunition for hunting. Because the purchased friendship of the savages lasted only as long as they could see the purchase price, this business of presents was an ever recurring one, and was accompanied by many abuses (E 12, E 13). The Indians sold their presents for more rum. They were indolent as long as they could obtain provisions. Nevertheless the distribution was maintained because it was the only language undertsood by the red men. Under the able direction of Sir William Johnson, diplomat of the forest, this policy kept the savages loyal to the British in the American Revolution.

In accord with the Proclamation of 1763 the western boundary of the new Government of Quebec was fixed the following year on a line drawn from the southern end of Lake Nipissing to the point where the 45th parallel crosses the St. Lawrence River. The territory lying west of this boundary was to be kept as Indian Country. Therefore, the vast expanse west of Quebec Province remained outside the pale of civil government (E 9). Detroit, that is, both sides of the river, which was the most important place in that whole district continued to be an isolated settlement, the capital of a wilderness, where the transient commanding officers or commandants exercised the functions of both a civil and military ruler (see Appendix VII).

In the administration of justice and in the settling of matters of controversy among the inhabitants of this area, the Commandant was aided by a justice of the peace. The first one under the British régime was probably St. Cosme. The Pontiac Manuscript of 1763 mentions that Mr. LeGrand, Justice of the Peace, succeeded Mr. St. Cosme.[7] This Gabriel LeGrand had come to Detroit in 1752 as surgeon of the French garrison. After 1760, besides continuing to practise medicine, he served as notary and justice of the peace.[8]

Philip Dejean, appointed in 1767 justice of the peace and second judge (the Commandant presumably being the first judge), is one about whom more information has come down to us, information that sheds some light on the administration of justice (E 7, E 8). Although Dejean's authority as justice was never clearly defined, he was determined that the dignity of his office be recognized. On

[7]*Ibid.*, p. 113.
[8]At least four of LeGrand's children were baptized at the Church of the Assumption between 1761 and 1772—strong evidence that he resided for some years on the south shore, where he had obtained land in 1760 (Appendix IV). To him, therefore, may be due the honour of having been the first resident surgeon or notary in the present County of Essex.

June 22, 1770, he wrote to Bishop Briand of Quebec complaining that the privileges of a judge were not accorded to him by the wardens of the church.[9] Not satisfied with the answer, he visited the Bishop in Quebec. The prelate demanded a certificate of good standing from the pastor of Ste. Anne's Church. It was granted but with the notation that court fees in Detroit were so exorbitant that few inhabitants could afford to have their wrongs redressed.[10]

In 1774 the Quebec Act extended the boundaries of the Province of Quebec to the Ohio and Mississippi rivers, and such courts as were created by the Act were to be provided at Detroit. The ordinance establishing the new courts of justice was sent from Lord Dartmouth, Secretary of State, to Sir Guy Carleton, Governor of Canada, in December 1774, and was to have been acted upon before May 1, 1775. To implement these governmental and judicial changes Henry Hamilton was appointed Lieutenant-Governor of Detroit in charge of civil affairs. The American Revolutionary War, however, interfered with the establishing of the new judicial arrangements, and the Court of Common Pleas at Montreal, with its long delays and heavy expenses occasioned by the great distance, continued to be the only judicial resort for or against the western merchants.

This prolonged unsatisfactory state of affairs had brought an uncommon form of procedure for settling differences in matters relating to property. When controversies arose, the parties called upon the Justice of the Peace or the Commandant to take charge of the matter, and three or five arbitrators were chosen by agreement or indiscriminately from a select panel (E 10). Although the refractory parties could not be compelled to abide by the decision of the arbitrators, the dread of the consequences of refusing to do so gave force to the award. Those who would not obey could maintain no suit to recover debts and the Commanding Officer refused to grant them permits to engage in trade, and on occasion even threatened to send them down the country, that is, to Montreal.[11] Losers in awards who lived in Detroit submitted or lived there as outlaws.

In the unfavourable conjunction of the time criminal cases continued to be heard by Dejean who without any legal authority meted out justice, sometimes high-handed. In 1778 he and Lieu-

---

[9]Q.C.A., E.U., V-19. This letter is printed in full in G. Paré, *The Catholic Church in Detroit*, pp. 220–1.
[10]Q.C.A., E.U., V-26.
[11]B.H.C., Detroit Notarial Records, liber C, p. 281.

tenant-Governor Hamilton were indicted by a Montreal grand jury. The charge against Dejean was for "having acted and transacted divers unjust and illegal, tyrannical and felonious acts contrary to good government and the safety of His Majesty's liege subjects."[12] The charge against the Lieutenant-Governor was that "the said Hamilton both not only remained at Detroit aforesaid and been witness to the several illegal acts and doings of him, the said Philip Dejean, but has tolerated, suffered and permitted the same under his government, guidance and direction." Among the many charges in the presentment was one dealing with the illegal execution of one Jean Contencineau (Coutinenceau). This Frenchman and a Negro woman, Ann Wiley, were found guilty of robbery and were sentenced to death. Dejean and Hamilton offered the woman her freedom on condition that she would hang her accomplice. This she agreed to do readily enough.[13] Dejean and Hamilton were found guilty of using illegal authority but were not sentenced, because it was believed they were acting in the interests of security under the circumstances, that is, the unsettled state of affairs during the American Revolutionary War and the fact that no courts had been set up at Detroit (E 11).

In the war, no actual fighting took place along the Detroit River. However, a new fort was built, called Fort Lernoult after the officer commanding at the time. War parties, red and white, went out to do battle from this place—the chief seat of British power in the West. In August 1776, Lieutenant-Governor Hamilton at Detroit wrote to the Earl of Dartmouth that some Ottawas, Chippewas, Hurons, and Potawatamis were joining the Six Nations at Niagara under orders of Lieutenant-Colonel Caldwell.[14] In 1778 Hamilton, although by appointment only a civil ruler, personally headed an expedition to recapture Fort Vincennes (in the present State of Indiana) with the aid of the French militia—an expedition from which he never returned to Detroit. At the request of the mistrustful Lieutenant-Governor, Father Potier went to the fort to remind the men of the sacredness of their oath and to renew it before starting from Detroit. On the campaign they showed themselves more faithful to their oath of allegiance than had been expected by Hamilton (E 15). It appears that the French residents were largely indifferent to the issues of the war between the colonies and the mother country. Out of 140 militiamen who were in Captain Bird's army

[12]P.A.C., B 42, p. 36; *M.H.C.*, X, 293–4.
[13]C. M. Burton, *The City of Detroit*, I, 193–4.
[14]P.A.C., Q 12, p. 212; *M.H.C.*, X, 269.

of invasion of Kentucky in 1780, only 30 are listed as volunteers. The remainder had to be "ordered to go" on the expedition.[15] These people were not anti-British or pro-American, just neutral (E 20). This view is corroborated by the fact that not one of the French residents of the south shore moved across the river when American rule was established at Detroit in 1796.[16]

The independence of the United States was recognized by the Treaty of Paris on September 3, 1783. Under its terms all the territory lying south of a line drawn through the Great Lakes and connecting rivers was awarded to the United States. The British agreed to evacuate this territory "with all convenient speed." However, for commercial and diplomatic reasons relating to the interests of the Indians as well as of the British, the border posts of Detroit, Niagara, Mackinac, Oswegachi, and Oswego were not immediately abandoned. Indeed, the British occupation of these posts, continued for another thirteen years.

After the treaty, still hopeful that something might happen, British agents went among the Indians and encouraged them to hold the land north of the Ohio against the American invasion. This opposition of the Indians to American expansion into their land continued for more than ten years after the treaty that had ended the war. In their struggle the Indians, led by Colonels McKee and Elliott, were backed by the British at Fort Miamis, which at one time was partly garrisoned by some militia from Essex County. The rest of the militiamen in the county were put in a state of readiness to march (E 28, E 29). The maintaining of this fort in the Indian country was a veritable powder-keg and only the timely signing of the Jay Treaty in 1794 prevented a serious rupture in Anglo-American relations. Indian resistance was ended by the battle of Fallen Timbers, August 20, 1794, where they were decisively defeated by the forces of General Wayne, who two years later ordered his army to occupy the town of Detroit.

Although another lieutenant-governor, Jehu Hay, was appointed for Detroit in 1782 and assumed office two years later, for five years after the Treaty of Paris the Detroit area still remained without the advantage of duly established local courts (E 14, E 16). Finally, by a proclamation of July 24, 1788, Lord Dorchester created four Judicial Districts in the present Province of Ontario—Luneburg,

[15]See Macomb, Edgar and Macomb ledger for 1779–80 in B.H.C. It contains the names and rates of pay of all the men in Bird's army. Privates received four shillings a day.

[16]Q.C.A., E.U., V-113, Parishioners of Assumption Church to Bishop Hubert, dated February 1, 1797.

Mecklenburgh, Nassau, and Hesse (E 17). At the same time he appointed justices and officers in each District. The Detroit area was in the District of Hesse, which later became known as the Western District. It consisted of all the territory from Long Point on Lake Erie westward to Detroit and northward to the limits of the province. The following were appointed judges of the Court of Common Pleas to sit at Detroit: Jacques Duperon Baby, Alexander McKee, and William Robertson (E 18).

The people of Detroit did not want merchants as judges. A petition signed by nearly all the important citizens was taken to the Governor at Quebec by Baby and Robertson, who at the same time presented their own resignations. After much consideration it was decided to appoint one lawyer as judge with the title of First Justice and to give him the same jurisdiction as the three judges in the courts of the other districts, and to pay him a salary of 500 pounds sterling. The man appointed to this unique office was William Dummer Powell. His arrival at Detroit in 1789 marked the complete transfer of judicial authority from military to civil control.

In acknowledgement of the terms of the treaty of 1783, sittings of the court were held on the Canadian side of the river even though a large majority of the cases tried concerned citizens dwelling on the American side. The first sessions were held in the *salle des habitants* or hall attached to the rectory of Assumption parish and in the old church. In a letter dated December 26, 1789, Judge Powell wrote to Bishop Hubert of Quebec expressing his great indebtedness to Father Dufaux who had offered him the hall of his presbytery for a courtroom while the old church was being readied for sittings (E 19).[17] At the end of the following year, however, court sessions were being held in a room of a neighbouring house (E 21). The record book of these assizes has been preserved and is now in the Archives of the Province of Ontario.[18] The initial session is dated L'Assomption, July 16, 1789. The record shows that Powell's judicial authority extended to the Court of Oyer and Terminer and General Gaol Delivery. He continued to preside over all these tribunals at L'Assomption until the Court of Common Pleas was abolished by the King's Bench Act of 1794. This legislation effected a centralization of the law in the capital of the province, and Powell's jurisdiction in the Western District automatically came to an end. He was immediately appointed the first Puisne Justice of the newly created Court of the King's Bench.

[17]See also Powell to Dorchester, July 29, 1789, Powell MSS, B 81, p. 1, in the Reference Division of the Toronto Public Library.
[18]Published in Fraser, *Fourteenth Report of Archives of Ontario*, pp. 23–190.

In 1794 the Court of the Western District was directed to hold its sittings on the other side of the river at Detroit, the district town of the County of Kent. But this arrangement lasted only two years. On June 3, 1796, the so-called Exodus Act was passed providing for the departure of British authority from Detroit. This Act called for the holding of Courts of Quarter Sessions and County Courts in the parish of the Assumption until "such time as it may seem expedient to the justices to hold the same nearer to the Isle of Bois Blanc." This last provision was never carried out. The courts remained in the parish of the Assumption (later Sandwich).

In the meantime the Constitutional Act of 1791 had divided the Province of Quebec into the Provinces of Upper and Lower Canada with a lieutenant-governor, an appointed executive council, an appointed legislative council and an elected legislative assembly for each province. John Graves Simcoe was the first Lieutenant-Governor of Upper Canada. Alexander Grant, James Baby, and William Robertson were members of the Executive Council. It is indicative of the relative importance of the Detroit area in the province that no less than three out of five members of the Executive Council came from the banks of the Detroit River. The home government was anxious that there should be on the first Executive Council of Upper Canada at least one representative of His Majesty's new subjects, as the French Canadians were called at that time. That is the reason James Baby was chosen.

British-minded Simcoe patterned the government of the new province after the governmental system of England. Even the names he gave to the counties evidence his desire to transplant a bit of England to Upper Canada. By proclamation of July 16, 1792, the four districts were divided into nineteen counties for representation in the House of Assembly. The Western District (formerly District of Hesse) was divided into the Counties of Kent, Essex, and Suffolk. The town of Detroit, as well as a strip in the present County of Essex four miles deep along the upper part of the Detroit River and along Lake St. Clair, belonged to the County of Kent.

The County of Essex was bounded on the south by Lake Erie from Pointe aux Pins to the Detroit River, on the west by the Detroit River to Maisonville's Mill, thence by a line running parallel to the Detroit River and Lake St. Clair, at the distance of four miles until it meets the River Thames, thence up the said river to the carrying place to Pointe aux Pins. These boundaries of Essex lasted until the end of the century. A proclamation was issued January 1, 1800, bringing into operation an Act for the better division of the Province of Upper Canada, being chapter v of the Second Parliament of the

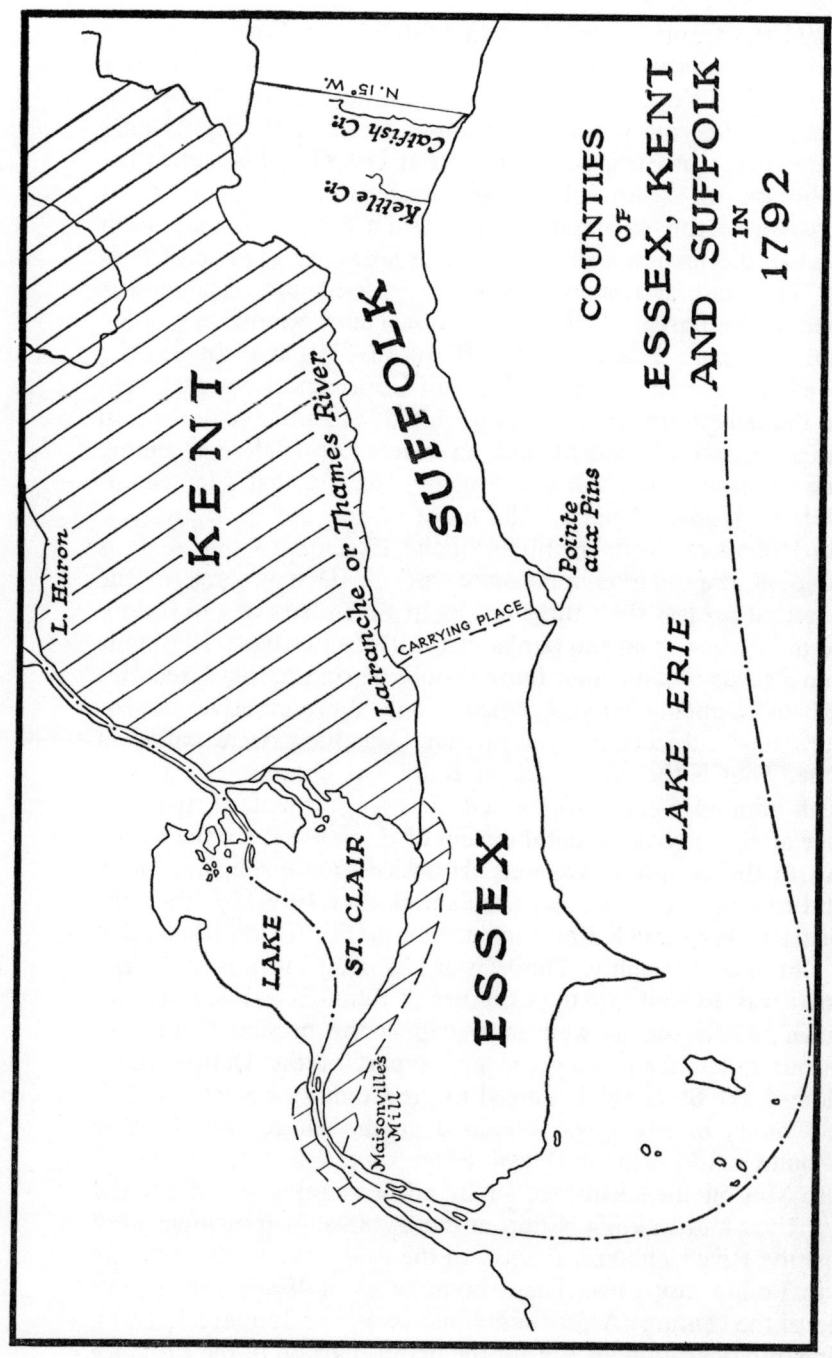

FIG. 11. THE BOUNDARIES OF THE COUNTIES OF ESSEX, KENT, AND SUFFOLK IN 1792. [Maps and Surveys Division of the Lands and Forests, Toronto.]

thirty-eighth year of George III. Section 39 of this Act reads as follows: "And be it further enacted by the authority of the aforesaid that the townships of Rochester, Mersea, Gosfield, Maidstone, Sandwich, Colchester, Malden and Tracts of land occupied by the Huron and other Indians, upon the strait, together with such of the Islands as are in Lakes Erie and Sinclair [sic] or the straits, do constitute and form the County of Essex." (See Fig. 11.)

The proclamation that divided the province into counties stipulated that for the purposes of representation in the sixteen-member House of Assembly, the County of Kent which included a four-mile strip along the Detroit River and Lake St. Clair, now in the present County of Essex, would send two representatives, and the Counties of Essex and Suffolk together (there were no inhabitants in Suffolk at the time) would be represented by one member (E 22). The first representatives of these counties were elected in August 1792. They were Wm. Macomb, Detroit merchant, and Francis Baby, brother of James, for Kent and David W. Smith, lieutenant of the Fifth Regiment of Foot, for Essex and Suffolk. These gentlemen took their seats in the first parliament of Upper Canada held at the town of Newark (Niagara) on September 17, 1792.

There has been some confusion with regard to the first representative from the County of Essex. Some writers have assigned Baby to Essex and Smith to Kent. The confusion seems to have arisen from the fact that it had been anticipated that Smith and Baby would oppose each other in Essex. When it became apparent that there was only one candidate in Kent, a deal was arranged whereby Smith was "set up" in Essex and Baby in Kent (E 23). The hustings for Kent were held at Detroit during the week ending August 21, 1792. Since the town at Detroit controlled the Kent vote we have the strange situation of an American territory sending representatives to a Canadian parliament.

Much of the material available on this first election in Essex County is to be found in the John Askin Papers. John Askin, Detroit merchant, was the manager of Smith's campaign. Smith, who had lived in this area while his regiment was stationed in Detroit, qualified to run for election by being a freeholder on the south bank of the Thames. At the time of the campaign he was with his regiment at Niagara, and sickness prevented him from visiting his constituency. From Niagara he wrote several letters to Askin wherein it was evident that he was prepared to go to great lengths in order to attain his objective. He counted heavily on the voters from River Thames and Lake Erie settlements, but did not expect much help from the French if Francis Baby opposed him. The week before the voting his illness had changed to a severe case of election fever. He requested Askin to supply conveyance, boats if necessary, to the hustings for the English gentry—"the French people can easily walk." In the same letter he also wrote: "Have proper booths erected for my friends at the Hustings . . . be sure [to] let the Wine be good & plenty." In the event of success he wanted Askin to arrange for a big bonfire on the Commons where an ox could be roasted and plenty of rum supplied to the crowd—"The more broken heads and bloody noses there is the more election like" (E 24).

The hustings were erected somewhere near the mouth of the Detroit River by Henry Botsford and the voting was held during the week ending August 28 (E 27). Only freeholders, or leaseholders to a minimum of forty-five shillings, and possessors of French grants *en roture* had the right to vote. There were no ballots. Voters exercised their franchise orally by calling out the name of their candidate. The voter's name was taken down, and his qualifications for suffrage were indicated. Richard Pollard was the returning officer.

Smith was elected to the Assembly and Askin shortly submitted an itemized bill of expenses incurred on his behalf. It amounted to 233 pounds, 4 shillings, 5 pence, New York currency—or about 600 dollars (E 25). In scrutinizing Askin's bill it is necessary to know that in plain English the major item listed as sundries meant liquor and entertainment.

From letters written after the election we learn that Askin's efforts were repaid by the influence Smith was able to exert in the first parliament "to get his (Askin's) wishes gratified." In one very important matter, however, Smith's efforts were of no avail. "In order to promote an aristocracy so necessary in this country,"[19] Simcoe appointed lieutenants and deputy lieutenants of counties that were sufficiently populous. Their duties consisted in recommending persons, tavern keepers excepted, to act as magistrates and officers of the militia, and to supervise their activities. Alexander McKee was named for the County of Essex and James Baby for the County of Kent. Askin had coveted the position awarded to Baby. In explanation Smith confessed that his efforts to help Askin had failed because of influence at Quebec (E 26).

[19]Cruikshank, *The Simcoe Papers*, I, 249–51, J. G. Simcoe to Henry Dundas, November 4, 1792.

The appointment of Baby became the source of much trouble. Jealousies were aroused by the nomination of the "young Frenchman." The Commandant of the fort at Detroit found himself under the command of one who knew nothing about military matters and he was provoked. His supporters tried to make the *habitants* believe that Baby had no authority and that they should not obey him. The quarrel even reached the precincts of the Church of Ste. Anne. To convince the parishioners that he was the highest ranking official, Baby usurped the pew of honour that was occupied by Mrs. Hay, widow of the former Lieutenant-Governor at Detroit. The quarrel was referred to Father Edmund Burke who was in the area with the title of Vicar-General for the Province of Upper Canada. His sympathies were on the side of Baby. However, before he made a ruling in the case, the death of Mrs. Hay put an end to the controversy.

For some thirty years after the British ensign had supplanted the French flag above the fort at Detroit, the quasi-military rule of the Commandants and Lieutenant-Governors continued to prevail in the area. Even the end of the American War of Independence with the Treaty of 1783 specifying the middle of the Detroit River as the international boundary brought no appreciable change in the administration of law and order on either side of the strait. In 1789, however, civil judicial authority was introduced with the arrival of the first judge of Detroit to preside over the newly established court. Then in 1792, the inauguration of the Province of Upper Canada saw the establishment of constitutional representative government. For four years the town of Detroit, although in American territory, functioned as part of the County of Kent and sent representatives to the Assembly of Upper Canada. Finally in July 1796, without fighting, even with a friendly loan of pork (E 30, E 31), the flag above the fort was changed again, this time to the American Stars and Stripes, and the Detroit River became in fact the political boundary between Canada and the United States.

F. RELIGION AND EDUCATION AFTER 1760

Religion

WHEN it is realized that for two centuries the religious element had been present in all the wars between France and England, it is easy to understand why the French Catholic inhabitants in the Detroit area were apprehensive of threats to their freedom of worship at the time of the conquest. The letter from Vaudreuil assuring them of the free exercise of their religion was welcome news indeed. During the period of British occupation the settlers were permitted to live their religious lives pretty much as before, on condition of swearing the oath of allegiance to the British Crown.

Generally speaking the people took the oath readily enough. One notable exception was Jacques Duperon Baby. He left Detroit, and went to Fort Pitt and then to Montreal with the intention of going to France. Later he changed his mind and decided to throw himself on the mercy of the conquerors and swore allegiance to the British Crown. From that moment His Britannic Majesty never had a more loyal subject. He soon became a most useful servant of the government, particularly in dealing with the Indian tribes whose language he spoke and over whom he had acquired a marked ascendancy.

Father Potier had special reasons for apprehension. There was the fear that the rigours of English law against Roman Catholic priests might be introduced into the conquered province. In January 1761, a month after the occupation of Detroit by the British, he left his mission and went to the Illinois country. Unless the journey had been planned and arranged before the arrival of the British forces, it is difficult to account for this move at such a critical moment except that he feared for his person or that his priestly ministrations would have to come to an end at Detroit.

A report on the Canadian missions sent from Paris on February 16, 1762, to the Superior-General of the Jesuits, and now in the Jesuit Archives in Rome, links his name with two other missionaries who went to the Illinois country in fear of the enemy which was occupying by force of arms the entire region of Canada (F 1). According to the church records Father Potier was back at the Mission of the Hurons in July 1761, where he remained until his death in July 1781.

Later in the summer of 1761, when Sir William Johnson, the Indian Commissioner, visited Detroit, he assured the inhabitants of His Majesty's protection as long as they continued to behave as good subjects. During his stay both Father Bocquet, pastor of Ste. Anne's Church, and Father Potier were invited to dine with him—"an invitation that was accepted cordially and as cordially enjoyed."[1] Whatever may have been Father Potier's feeling at the time of the British occupation, it is clear that ten months later he had accepted the new order.

It was not long before the allegiance of the *habitants* and their priest was put to the test. In the Pontiac revolt of 1763 the support of the French settlers would have been sufficient to turn the tide in favour of the Indians. The sympathies of the French must have been with the Indians, for their habits of thought and loyalty to the *fleur-de-lis* could not have changed overnight. Since the terms of the treaty of peace between France and England were not yet known at Detroit,[2] it was only natural that some would still be cherishing vague hopes of being restored to the old allegiance. On the advice of Fathers Bocquet and Potier, the French with a few exceptions did not enter the fray. There is evidence that some of them, led by Baby, took some badly needed provisions to the short-rationed garrison in the fort. Major Gladwin, while acknowledging aid from a few Frenchmen, was under the impression that the great majority of them were not neutral, and that "one half of the settlement deserves a gibbet, and the other half ought to be decimated."[3] James Sterling, Detroit merchant in the fort, was more conservative in his estimate of gallows-birds among the French: "We have made sufficient discovery already to hang at least a dozen of them."[4] On the other hand Pontiac also reproved the French for having "given comfort to the English by reporting to them all that the Indians do and say."[5] Gladwin's condemnation notwithstanding, the French of the Detroit area as a group, even if not indifferent in their hopes, had refrained from active intervention in the Indian uprising.

Although the conquest made little change in the religious life of the French Catholic inhabitants of the south shore, a definite change

---

[1] W. L. Stone, *Life and Times of Sir William Johnson*, II, 463.

[2] News of the treaty reached Detroit June 2, 1763. See Burton, *Journal of Pontiac's Conspiracy*, p. 155; *M.H.C.*, VIII, 310.

[3] Clements Library, Amherst Papers, II, Gladwin to Amherst, July 8, 1763; P.A.C., A & W 981, p. 305.

[4] Clements Library, James Sterling Letter Book, pp. 110–11, Sterling to John Duncan Esq. & Co., Detroit, August 7, 1763.

[5] Burton, *Journal of Pontiac's Conspiracy*, p. 195; *M.H.C.*, VIII, 324.

in the care of souls took place after Father Potier's return from the Illinois in the summer of 1761. Beginning in July of that year he kept in Latin a register of the French children baptized at the Mission of the Hurons.[6] During the next six years there were 111 entries. For the same period the marriage vows of fifteen French couples were witnessed by him. From the number of baptisms and marriages it is safe to conclude that at that time the French settlers on the south shore had been placed in charge of the missionary of the Hurons. This was a special arrangement between Fathers Potier and Bocquet. The latter's letters to the Bishop of Quebec make it clear that his infirmities and dread of water prevented him from attending properly to the needs of the people on the south shore. Consequently he had given the Jesuit missionary permission to act in his place, and had surrendered to him nearly all the tithes in that locality because "he [Potier] had nothing on which to live."[7]

In 1765 some sixty families living on the south shore petitioned for a church of their own. Most of them could not give much money, but they could and did give the work of their hands. They built a new chapel sixty by thirty feet to replace the mission church of 1749 which was now falling into ruin. In the same year Father Potier obtained permission from his Jesuit Superior at Quebec to sell the mission lands in order to satisfy the debts of the church and to provide for his own living. In granting the permission the Superior mentioned the fact that "the land has become useless to you."[8] Apparently the farming experiment started in 1748 at La Pointe de Montréal had been abandoned. So had the mission store, which might have provided a livelihood. The Seven Years' War for the possession of the Ohio Valley had set a temporary check upon all trading activities and the store had petered out. After the conquest, trade at Detroit was handled exclusively by British merchants with the one exception of Jacques Duperon Baby.

In a letter of August 7, 1767, the Bishop of Quebec wrote to the pastor of Ste. Anne's: "I consent to give to Father Potier charge of all the south shore, and assign it to his care, to perform all functions and to receive all emoluments."[9] On October 21, 1767, Father Bocquet wrote to the Bishop: "I have placed Father Potier in charge of his new parish and I thank you with all my heart for the very great relief you have procured for me."[10] Up to

[6]Original in Assumption Church Archives, Windsor, Ontario; published in Ontario Historical Society, *Papers and Records*, VII (Toronto, 1906), 32 sqq.
[7]Q.C.A., E.U., V-5.
[8]See extract of letter attached to document F 2 below.
[9]Q.C.A., E. de Q., I, 117.
[10]*Ibid.*, E.U., V-10.

October 1767, Father Potier had signed the registers as "missionary of the Hurons at La Pointe de Montréal du Détroit." Beginning October 3, 1767, he signs himself as "Jesuit missionary performing the pastoral duties in the Church of the Assumption at La Pointe de Montréal du Détroit." Thus came into being the parish of the Assumption—the first parish in what is now the Province of Ontario.[11]

Immediately the pastor strove to set his financial house in order. On October 15, 1767, the sale of four arpents of church land to François Marentet was notarized for the price of 1,600 livres, money to be paid later (F 2). To this parcel of land one perche (one-tenth arpent) was added on July 2, 1768, and one arpent and one perche the following summer without mention of any increase in the price. Thus by 1769 a total of five arpents and two perches of the original grant to the missionaries had been disposed of to support the newly constituted parish.[12]

In a letter to the Bishop of Quebec acknowledging his appointment as pastor of the parish of the Assumption, Father Potier promised that as soon as the debt on the church was paid he would establish a *fabrique* to administer the temporalities of the parish (F 3). This corporation was composed of the pastor and a number of laymen called *marguilliers* or wardens. There were usually three *marguilliers* in active service. A new one was chosen each year at a parish election, and the oldest in point of service retired into the honourable body of past *marguilliers*. These men retained a vote for the election of the future wardens, and when the parish was faced with some serious problem they were invited to the meetings as advisers (Appendix VIII).

The parish revenue administered by the *fabrique* came from various sources. There were stipends for various services in the church such as high masses, weddings, and funerals. Collections were taken up on Sundays and holy days but these did not amount to very much. Listed among the receipts in the church collections are pieces of porcelain, spangles, and pieces of silver-plated metal— the offerings of the Indians. These trinkets were allowed to accumulate in the *coffre*, the strong box of the church, to be sold when the quantity was sufficiently large. A substantial income was derived from the rental and sale of the pews (F 4, F 5). When a pew became vacant, the fact was announced for two or three Sun-

[11]For fuller treatment of this subject, see E. C. Lebel, "History of Assumption, the First Parish in Upper Canada," *Report of the Canadian Catholic Historical Association* (Ottawa, 1954).

[12]Sunset, California, and Askin streets in the city of Windsor now occupy this tract of land.

days, and then it was auctioned off at the door of the church to the highest bidder.

Another important source of income was *la quête de l'Enfant-Jésus*—the Child Jesus collection. During the days between Christmas and Epiphany (January 6), the pastor made the rounds of his parish, driven by the first *marguillier*. On the occasion of this visit the priest was offered a present according to the giver's means. It might be in the form of money, but generally it was in goods—food or grain. In the Province of Quebec this collection was intended for the support of the pastor. At Assumption it was entered in the account book as a parish revenue.

In addition to his share of the casuals derived from the offerings for the various services, the pastor was supported by *dîmes* or tithes that the parishioners were bound to render. Although the word properly means a tenth, the obligation was reduced to one twenty-sixth part of the grain harvest. This grain was stored in the priest's granary, and from its contents he supplied his needs and those of the church by sale, or, as was usually the case, by barter.

In many ways the church did the work of the modern newspaper. People gathered early before the service in front of the church or in *la salle des habitants,* and exchanged information and views on matters of the day. Even though only a few of the people could read, notices of importance were posted on the church door. After the service the *crieur* would stand on the steps of the church to give out the news and read aloud public announcements or ordinances from the Commandant (F 23).

On July 16, 1781, Father Potier, S. J., died from a fall on an andiron, after having spent thirty-seven years at the mission and parish of the Assumption (F 7). He was the last Jesuit missionary to the Indians, and the first pastor of the newly constituted parish. His death ended the story of the Jesuit mission on the shores of the Detroit River—a story possibly begun by Fathers Brébeuf and Chaumonot in the winter of 1640–1.

It is of interest to note that Father Potier, a Jesuit, was at Assumption Church at the time of the Brief suppressing the Society issued by Pope Clement XIV in 1773. And of greater interest is the fact that he remained there as a Jesuit until his death eight years later. The explanation lies in the fact that the Brief of Suppression went into effect whenever the Bishop of the diocese promulgated it. Bishop Briand of Quebec did not promulgate it because Governor Carleton wanted the Jesuits to remain. Towards the end of 1774 the Bishop assembled the four Jesuits who were at Quebec and told them he had the Brief and the order to make it known. On November 8, 1774, Bishop Briand wrote to Cardinal Castelli (Pope Clement XIV having died on September 22) that the Governor did not want any exterior change. For that reason he had named the same superior and procurator to continue administering the Jesuit property under his orders. This was not in accord with the detailed prescriptions of the Brief. There is no evidence that the Brief was even made known officially to Jesuits such as Father Potier living outside of Quebec.

None the less, the Jesuits in Canada were doomed to extinction. Under the terms of the Capitulation of Montreal, they had not been permitted to receive new members. The result was that, at the time of the suppression, their members were only thirteen in number. These were allowed to remain at their posts until their death. A careful watch was kept on them and their property was seized for the Crown as soon as they died. In 1778 Lieutenant-Governor Hamilton at Detroit wrote to Governor Carleton at Quebec: "That as the Jesuit missionary at this place is advanced in years and very infirm, I have directed that in case of his death all his papers to be secured and sealed up till I have Your Excellency's orders to their possession."[13]

At the time of Hamilton's letter Father Potier had only debts. However, he was enabled to settle most of his accounts two years later by the sale of church lands. In 1780 the Huron Indians gave him a written title to the remaining two arpents' frontage of the original grant made in 1747 (F 6). Shortly afterwards, while retaining only two small lots between the river and the *coulée*, on which were located the church buildings and cemetery, he sold the rest of this parcel to Francis Pratt in order to pay his debts.[14] By an oversight the reservation was not mentioned in the deed, but it was subsequently acknowledged by the purchaser (F 8). Nevertheless, later on these two lots became the object of much litigation.

On Father Potier's death the parish house was sealed and after the funeral a detailed inventory was made of everything in the house, church and yard. This list has been preserved in the Quebec Chancery Archives along with the account of the disposal of the moneys found (F 9, F 10). Three days after his death, the wardens of the church deputed one of their number and a companion to wait on the Bishop of Quebec and ask that he leave them not too long without a pastor (F 11). The Huron Indians also sent a plea

[13]P.A.C., B 122, 123; *M.H.C.*, IX, 432.
[14]Patricia Street in Windsor runs along this property.

for a missionary (F 12). The Bishop sent his Vicar-General, Reverend Jean François Hubert, who arrived at Assumption on November 8, 1781.

Immediately the new pastor devoted himself to the task of building a new church and presbytery. His active zeal is reflected in the parish account book which began to be kept in due form with balances struck each year (F 13). Because nearly all the church property had been sold, it was necessary to acquire land. Again the Hurons came to the assistance of their missionary. On March 4, 1782, they made a donation of a tract of land six arpents wide by forty arpents deep adjoining the Pratt farm on the east and the Indian lands on the west (F 14). This was a joint donation to Father Hubert and to the Sisters of the Congregation of Notre Dame of Montreal who, it was hoped, would come to establish a school. Today the eastern half of this tract of land forms the site of Assumption Church and a part of the campus of Assumption University of Windsor.

In 1785 Father Hubert was chosen Coadjutor to the Bishop of Quebec and left Assumption parish in October of that year. Before his departure he had the satisfaction of seeing the presbytery completed (F 16). To it was attached a hall, known as *la salle des habitants*, wherein the parishioners gathered before and after the church services (see Plate III). The energetic pastor did not stay long enough, however, to see the erection of the church towards which he had contributed the princely sum of 12,642 livres. Its construction started during the short incumbency of his successor, Father Pierre Fréchette (F 17), who apparently was not happy at Assumption. When Father François-Xavier Dufaux, a Sulpician, arrived in Detroit in October 1786 to take charge of Ste. Anne's, Father Fréchette prevailed on him to exchange parishes. At that time the church was well on its way to completion. So energetically did the new pastor push the work that, in spite of the scarcity of money, he was able to dedicate it in the summer of 1787 (F 18, F 19) (see Plate V). The church was built of timbers and lasted until the present edifice, which was opened in 1846, was built. The pulpit, which was the work of a man named Frerot, has been preserved and now graces the present church of the Assumption. The bell was a gift of the government to the Hurons.[15]

The parishioners helped to defray the expenses from their meagre means, but again it became necessary to sell some of the church lands. The western half of the lands granted by the Hurons in 1782

[15]P.A.C., B 123, p. 422, Haldimand to Hay.

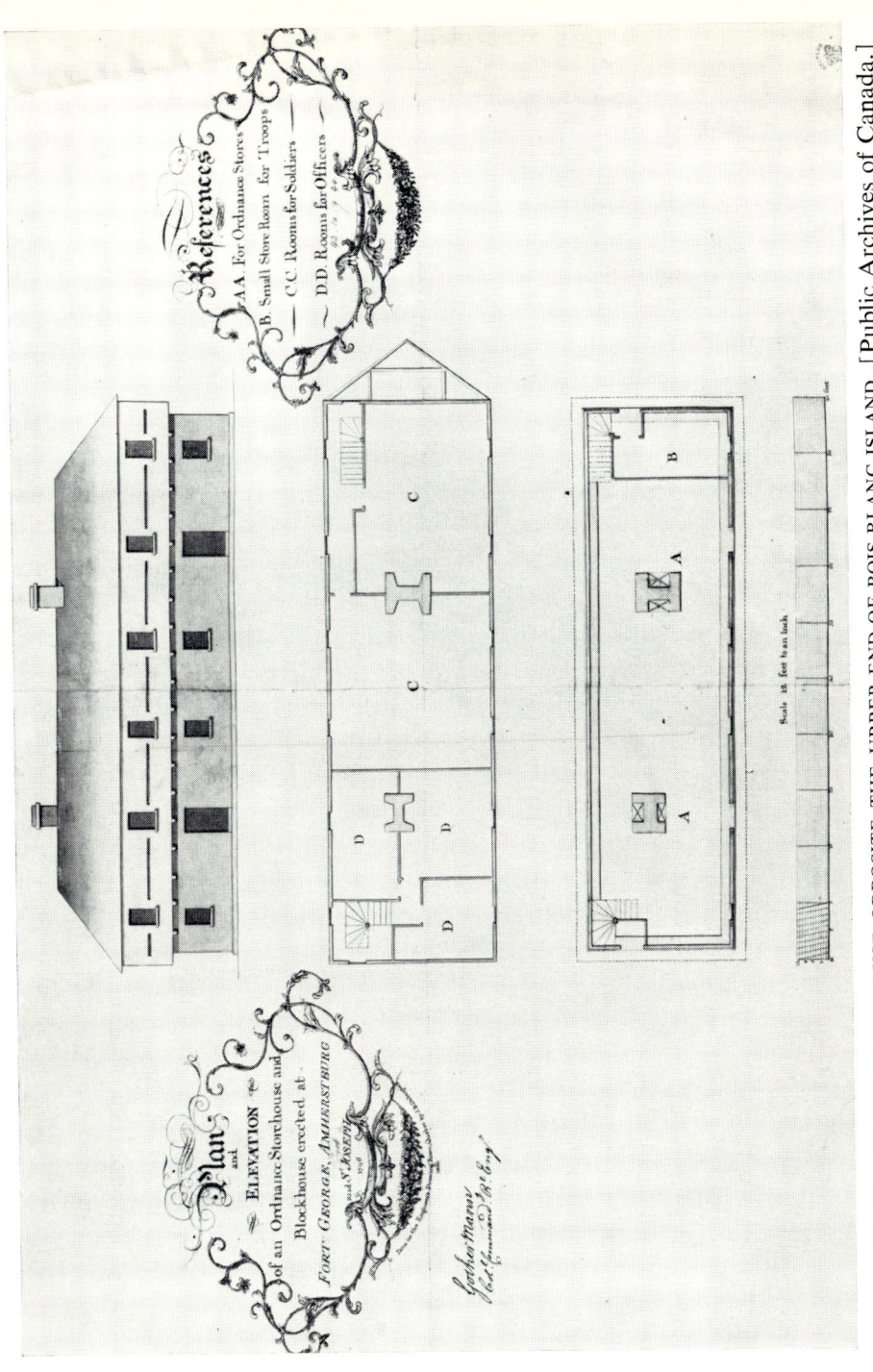

PLATE VI. THE NORTH BLOCKHOUSE OPPOSITE THE UPPER END OF BOIS BLANC ISLAND. [Public Archives of Canada.]

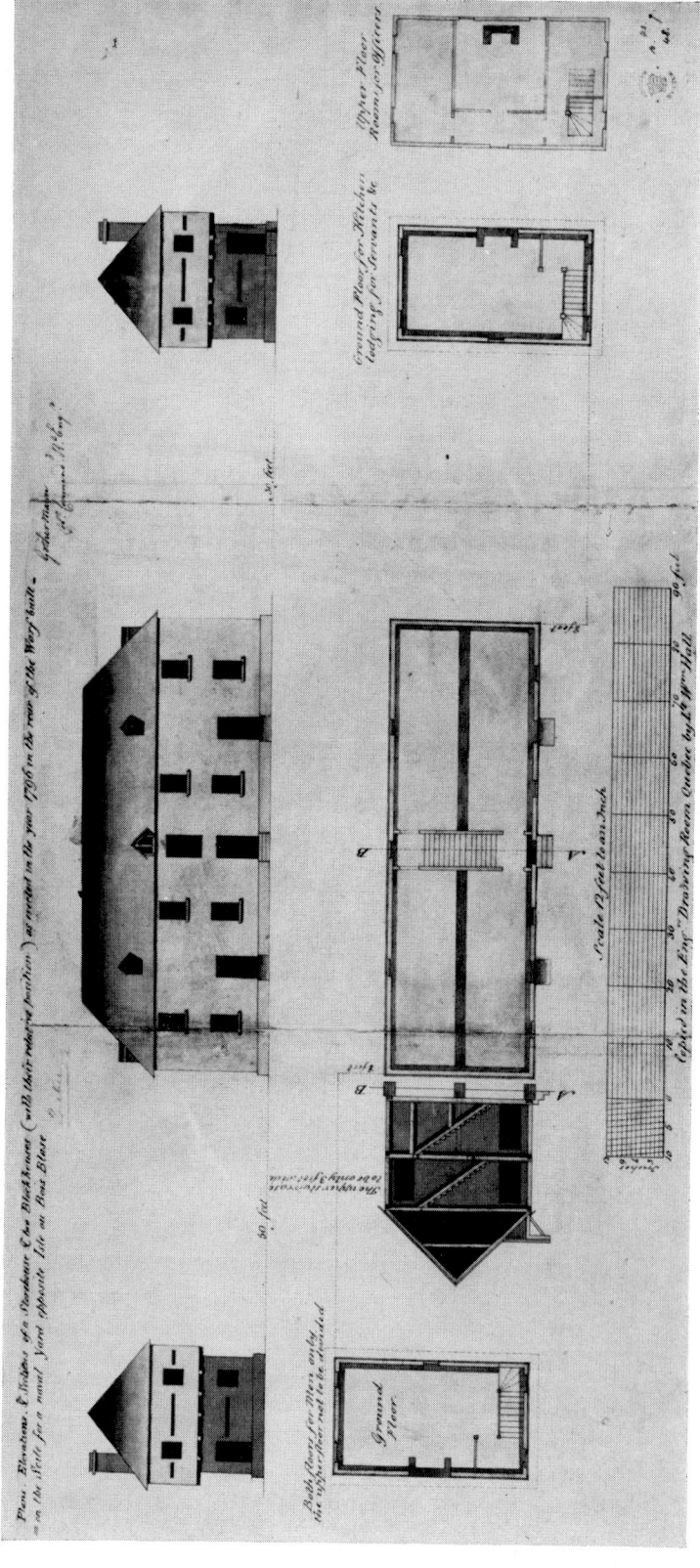

PLATE VII. THE STOREHOUSE FLANKED BY TWO SMALL BLOCKHOUSES IN FRONT OF THE WHARF OPPOSITE THE ISLAND OF BOIS BLANC. [Public Archives of Canada.]

was sold to Thomas Pajot to pay the debt on the buildings (F 30). The mighty pillars of the Ambassador Bridge now rest on the eastern edge of that property. Another grant of four by forty arpents at Petite Côte made by the Hurons on May 1, 1787, was sold within a fortnight for 7,600 pounds of flour (Appendix IV). The formula for financing church projects was a simple one—obtain grants of land from the Indians and sell them to the settlers. Within two decades the formula had been applied four times.

In return for their contribution of land the Hurons continued to share in the new church. At a meeting of *la fabrique* on September 9, 1787, it was decided that a section of the church would be reserved for the pews and seats of the Indians "in gratitude for their zeal and their contributions as far as was in their power" (F 13). The decision to set aside for them only about a quarter of the church was dictated by the large increase of the French and the dwindling number of the Indians in the parish. For the years 1787–91 while there were 232 baptisms of French children, only sixteen are recorded of the children of the Hurons. So few Hurons remained near the church that they did not even bother erecting pews in their reserved section, and it was not long before the whole church was occupied by the settlers.

What had become of the Hurons? Gradually they had withdrawn from their reserve near the Church of the Assumption and the majority were scattered along the western shore of Lake Erie, while some had pushed on westward as far as the present State of Kansas. Only a few still had their lodges at La Rivière aux Canards—the meagre remnant in the peninsula of the savages who had come to the strait at the beginning of the century. Economics, the factor that had brought them to the area, had also pushed them out as the Detroit River region was transformed from a fur-trading to a predominantly agricultural economy. In this instance the advancing tide of white settlement had not stopped at the usual encroachments on the red men's hunting grounds, but by sheer force of numbers it had taken practically full possession of the Indian mission church which had played such an important part in the early years of the settlement.

Although the church congregation was now almost entirely composed of white settlers, a division of a different nature raised its ugly head among the parishioners. In 1795 a quarrel over a pew broke out that threatened to cause a minor schism. Francis Baby, brother of James, was Deputy-Lieutenant of Essex County, acting in the place of Colonel Alexander McKee. With the support of

Father Burke, Vicar-General of Upper Canada, who was on a special mission to the Detroit area, he requested a pew of honour in Assumption Church and had one erected in the fall of 1795 (F 24). Encouraged by mutinous leaders from across the river, a clique of jealous troublemakers was formed to oppose it. Baby claimed that their opposition stemmed from his family's too great attachment to the King. Be that as it may, the rebellious group threw the pew out of the church. Father Dufaux did not oppose them, probably because Father Burke was in favour of Baby. In letters to the Bishop of Quebec there is ample evidence of friction existing between the two priests.

The matter was referred to the Bishop who left it to Lieutenant-Governor Simcoe to name the highest ranking representative of the government. He named Francis Baby, Deputy-Lieutenant of Essex (F 25). The letters of the Bishop and of the Lieutenant-Governor were read in church (F 28). Baby then erected the pew once more. The following Sunday the mutinous group threw it out again. Baby wrote to the Bishop that he had more supporters than the opposition led by Maisonville, Pratt, and Parent, and could force the issue, but he did not want to be the cause of any scandal in the church.[16] This ended the threat of a serious split in the parish of the Assumption.

While this quarrel was raging, important ecclesiastical changes took place along the Detroit River. When the fort at Detroit was occupied by the Americans in July 1796, Ste. Anne's parish automatically ceased to belong to the diocese of Quebec and became part of the diocese of Baltimore (F 26). The river served not only as a political but also as an ecclesiastical boundary line. Ahead of the advancing American troops, Father Burke scurried across the border and made his way to Niagara. Father Dufaux, however, crossed the line in the opposite direction in order to pay a friendly visit to the newly arrived officers. Later, when General Wayne made his appearance at Detroit, the pastor of Assumption was invited to wine and dine with him.[17] Unfortunately, Father Dufaux was not destined to enjoy for long the neighbourly relations so happily begun. On September 11 he died in the arms of his confrère, Father Levadoux, pastor of Ste. Anne's, leaving behind a reputation for kindliness and holiness of life. The tearful parishioners sent a delegation to implore the Bishop of Quebec not to let them languish without a spiritual guide (F 27). At Niagara the

[16]Q.C.A., E.U., V-135.
[17]*Ibid.*, E.U., V-134.

messengers encountered Father Burke who was still Vicar-General of Upper Canada. Immediately he hurried to Assumption to take charge of the parish temporarily. Once more the Bishop turned to the Sulpicians for assistance, and their choice fell upon Jean Baptiste Marchand, Superior of the College of Montreal. On Christmas Day, 1796, in the evening, the inhabitants joyfully welcomed to Assumption the priest who was to rule over the destinies of the parish for the next thirty years (F 29).

EDUCATION

In the eighteenth century, education was not considered a function of the community. Rather it was a matter attended to, if at all, by private individuals or by the Church. It is difficult to believe that a scholar like Father Potier, a member of a society renowned for its learning, did not make some effort for the elementary education of the children in his parish. In this connection it is necessary to take into consideration the fact that when he became pastor of the French in 1767 he was already in his sixtieth year, and his dominant interest was still in the Indians. Although there had been schools on the other side of the river since 1760 and possibly before, there is no evidence of any attempt to start a school in the parish of the Assumption until 1782.

When Father Hubert, a former Superior of the Quebec Seminary, arrived at Assumption as pastor in the fall of 1781, he wasted no time before trying to remedy the educational situation. In March 1782 he offered the Sisters of the Congregation of Notre Dame of Montreal a house and a tract of land three by forty arpents to support a school for girls. In May of the same year he sent 2,400 livres to defray the expenses of the journey of the Sisters to Detroit. After much deliberation the Congregation declined the offer and the land was returned to the parish (F 15). This is the tract of land that was later sold to Thomas Pajot to pay the debt incurred by the building of the church and rectory. The 2,400 livres were probably returned to the pastor personally although this money transaction does not appear in the account book. During the same year (1782), through the intermediary of Governor Haldimand, Father Hubert was promised the services of a lay teacher for the boys and of "Sisters of the Church" for the girls.[18]

From these two efforts nothing resulted during Father Hubert's tenure of four years. But what he had been unable to accomplish

[18]P.A.C., B 67, p. 86; *M.H.C.*, XX, 48.

as pastor of Assumption he helped to realize later when he was the Coadjutor to the Bishop of Quebec. In October 1786, on his advice, two teachers from Quebec (the Misses Ademard and Papineau) came to Detroit to open a school for girls in Assumption Parish (F 18). To lodge them and their boarding students it was decided to transport near the presbytery a small house that had been inhabited by the family of the pastor's servant. Spurred on by Father Dufaux's treats of brandy, within three weeks seven or eight men had moved, repaired, and fitted the building to serve as a dormitory for the two teachers and their eight boarders. The hall attached to the presbytery served as a classroom. Thus the first school known to have been conducted in the parish of the Assumption opened its doors to a group of young girls in the fall of 1786.

Father Dufaux paid all the current expenses of the house and schoolroom. For their salary the teachers kept all the revenue which for the first year was as follows: three boarders who paid two pounds a month; three others who were to pay what they could; two other boarders "who promised that God would keep their account" (F 18). Besides the eight boarders there were five day students. The teachers were devoted and the parents recognized the benefit of an education for their children. But they were so poor that they could scarcely supply them with clothing, let alone send them away to school. Father Dufaux's letters inform us that the years 1786-91 were very bad for the inhabitants of the area. There was no sale for their products and many farms had to be sold or mortgaged with interest at 7 per cent to satisfy the creditors. From the notarial records of the time it is clear that, for the most part, these creditors were the merchants at Detroit. Nevertheless the school was continued at the pastor's expense. In the summer of 1788 he reported to the Bishop that the prospect for the next year indicated there would be only eight or ten students. He decided the time had not yet come to undertake the erection of a school building (F 20). In 1789-90, when the classroom also served on Thursdays as the courthouse for the first judge of Detroit, there were still only seven or eight pupils (F 21). But in 1792 the numbers had risen to twelve boarders and five or six day students, and Father Dufaux was making plans for improving the educational facilities (F 22). Humble indeed were the beginnings of the first school on the Canadian side of the Detroit River.

Besides the extreme poverty of the settlers there were two other factors that militated against the development of this first school—

its location and the fact that it was not the practice in the diocese of Quebec to have coeducational institutions. Apparently the school had been located near the church with a view to getting the Sisters to come from Montreal. A large portion of the parish was located south of La Rivière aux Dindes, five miles away. It was impossible for these children to come daily to their classes and their parents could not afford to board them at or near the school. Another major portion of the parish extended along the river from the church to Lake St. Clair. Again it was impossible for those children who lived more than two or three miles away to attend as day students. The problem of education might have been solved better by the establishment of two coeducational schools—one at Petite Côte and another two or three miles east of the church. It sounds paradoxical to say that two schools might have succeeded when it was so difficult to keep one operating, but it is reasonable to suppose that a different arrangement would have produced very different results by providing educational opportunities within reach of nearly all the children of the settlement.

The promise of freedom of worship made to the French Catholics in the Articles of Capitulation of 1760 was honoured by the various British rulers at Detroit. As a result the religious life of the French settlers went on undisturbed. On arriving at Assumption Church to assume charge of the parish in 1796 the new pastor was able to report to his Bishop that a total of 150 families of whites and a few lodges of Huron Indians constituted the flock of that far-away fold—the oldest parish in the Province of Ontario.

G. LOYALISTS AND LAND BOARDS

For more than twenty years after the conquest nothing was done to bring British colonists to the Detroit area. Only merchants, traders, and sutlers followed in the wake of the occupation troops. A few of them later became gentlemen farmers. Substantially Detroit remained a French settlement but it was overlaid with a thin veneer of British officials, military and mercantile. However, the close of the Revolutionary War in 1783 brought to Canada an influx of United Empire Loyalists who came seeking new homes under the old flag. As a reward for their patriotism and as a recompense for the losses they had sustained in the war, the King's Instructions of 1783 provided for them generous allotments of the waste lands of the Crown, free from any expense, with aid in the form of provisions and tools. All land grants were made for the purpose of settlement and improvement within a year and not for speculation.

For the Detroit River region this Loyalist immigration meant a second birth. The first to take advantage of the King's bounty in the present County of Essex were Captains Matthew Elliott and William Caldwell. In 1783 they took up tracts of land on the east side of the Detroit River. Elliott's location was opposite the lower end of Bois Blanc Island, on the old Huron village site that had been abandoned in 1748. Caldwell located opposite the middle of the island in the southern section of the present town of Amherstburg. In 1784 other lots between the upper end of Bois Blanc Island and the mouth of the river were occupied by Indian officers and interpreters. This was the beginning of the present Township of Malden at the southwestern corner of the County of Essex.

A questionable transaction almost prevented this early Loyalist settlement. On October 13, 1783, the Ottawa Indians ceded all this land (approximately seven miles square) by secret treaty to Jacob Schieffelin, Secretary of the Indian Department at Detroit (G 1). This grant is probably the first conveyance of land in South Essex. However, Alexander McKee, Deputy Superintendent of Indian Affairs, received information about it even before the deed had been drawn up, and in a letter to Sir John Johnson he objected to its confirmation (G 2). At the same time Captain Bird of Detroit wrote a letter of protest to Robert Mathews, secretary to Lieutenant-Governor Hamilton at Quebec (G 3). The cession was not recognized by the Crown (G 4). In order to protect the

Indians from being iniquitously deprived of their lands and also in order to obtain clear titles, the King's Instructions stipulated that any sale or transfer of land held by the Indians would not be legal until the land had first been ceded to the King. Schieffelin had not conformed to the Instructions. Moreover, there is evidence that he had used foul means to achieve his purpose. Biter bitten, he did not relinquish his claim without a long and determined effort.

McKee and Bird had good reasons for objecting to the grant of this land to Schieffelin. Along with other officers, interpreters, and Loyalists they were making overtures for the same territory in order to begin a settlement (G 5, G 6). In this they were successful. In June 1784 the Huron Indians and "other neighbouring Chiefs" deeded the same tract to certain officers and others of the Indian Department who had served with them in the recent war. The next step was to get this new cession confirmed by the Crown. In the same summer Captain Caldwell went to Quebec to press the point. In August 1784 Governor Haldimand directed Lieutenant-Governor Hay of Detroit to give every encouragement to those officers and men to make immediate settlement on the tract, at the same time promising that their portions of the gift from the Indians would be confirmed to them in due time by proper deeds according to the King's Instructions (G 7).

A memorandum of 1785 from Lieutenant-Governor Hay to Ensign Fry, a surveyor, supplies the names of some of the original proprietors, and also the information that the lots of Captains Bird, McKee, Caldwell, and Elliott were to be six acres wide and the rest only four acres (G 8, G 9). Later it was found that these four captains actually occupied a frontage of ten acres each, that is, the whole length of the island of Bois Blanc "by special promise from the Indians." They were confirmed in these possessions in 1788 by Major Robert Mathews, Commanding Officer at Detroit, acting under written instructions from Lord Dorchester. Major Mathews accompanied by Captain McKee and a Mr. Hughes as surveyor extended the lines to ten acres. The actual lines of the lots were not disturbed because those men had made their improvements under reiterated approbation of persons having authority.

On January 8, 1793, Lieutenant-Governor Simcoe requested that a township be surveyed at the mouth of the Detroit River to be called the Township of Malden (G 10). He advised that because Malden consisted of land deeded by the Indians to their officers in 1784, Colonel McKee and Captains Elliott and Caldwell were to be the patentees of the township. For a limited time they had the privilege of recommending petitions for land in that area. The Indian officers also had it at their option to complete their quota of land in the said township. Iredell's survey dated April 17, 1796, containing nineteen riverside lots occupied all the water frontage from the Huron Reserve at La Rivière aux Canards to the Big Marsh. This latter was a tract of marsh lands containing 3,050 acres at the entrance of Lake Erie that had been granted by Order-in-Council of December 29, 1788, to Captain Caldwell's sons, William and James (G 11). To the rear of these nineteen river lots and the marsh the survey shows an additional 84 parcels of land, making a total of 103 lots in the Township of Malden.

An Order-in-Council of December 24, 1793, increased Captain Elliott's holdings to 3,000 acres in the Township of Malden.[1] This tract was developed with the aid of slaves that he had imported from his former Virginia plantation. Travellers and visitors were unanimous in relating the hospitality accorded them by Mr. Elliott. His log house was the best in the township and possessed two large fireplaces and chimneys, the remnants of which are still standing (1958). (See Plate IV.)

Among the visitors at this place, special mention must be made of a group of pacifist Moravian missionaries and some 150 of their Delaware Indian converts. Fleeing from the American-Indian war zone in the Ohio Country, they spent almost a year on the McKee and Elliott plantations. From the diary of their leader, David Zeisberger, we learn that their first services were held in the open air at which were present "whites and blacks from the neighbourhood" (G 12). Shortly after their arrival they built a meeting-house, complete with benches and bell, in which they were able to hold their first service on Trinity Sunday, June 19, 1791. This is the first record of a Protestant place of worship in the present County of Essex.[2] There is evidence that the missionaries also conducted a school during their sojourn at the mouth of the river. Two Dolson children from Detroit attended this school from September 1791 to April 1792.

Unfortunately, this religious and educational influence was of short duration on the Canadian shore of the Detroit River. The missionaries did not like the environment. On April 12, 1792, the Moravians and Delawares left the district to go and found a settle-

[1] Fraser, *Third Report of the Archives of Ontario*, p. 248.
[2] At this time John Messemer, an itinerant Baptist preacher, was holding meetings in various homes along the north shore of Lake Erie, but he had no fixed meeting-place. See below, *Diary of David Zeisberger* (G 12) for May 29, 1791.

ment at Fairfield far up the River Thames in an effort to get away from Indian war parties and white rum-pedlars who had begun to lead astray their Christian converts.

Immediately north of Malden lies another tract about seven miles square that constitutes the present Township of Anderdon. For a long time it was known as the Huron Reserve at La Rivière aux Canards. On May 15, 1786, the Indians ceded this tract of land to Colonel McKee in trust for the Crown in order to prevent encroachments by the white settlers in the neighbourhood (G 13). However, in 1789 McKee sought to have the grant to himself ratified by Lord Dorchester so that he might have it in his power "to place such loyal subjects upon it as he may conceive worthy of such an indulgence."[3] Then on May 14, 1790, McKee withdrew his request, just one week before he purchased, from the Indians on behalf of the Crown, all the territory from Long Point on Lake Erie to Chenal Ecarté,[4] at the mouth of the St. Clair River. In this purchase the tract at La Rivière aux Canards was retained as a Huron Reserve. Throughout the eighteenth century this whole frontage saw no settlement, and the small Huron corn fields near the mouth of La Rivière aux Canards were the only part of this large area under cultivation (see Fig. 12).

This Indian reservation between settlements, however, did not altogether interrupt land communications along the strait. For a long time there had been a road as close to the Detroit River as practicable, and in 1793 a contract for a bridge over La Rivière aux Canards was completed at a cost of 240 pounds.[5] Seven years later a right of way for a road through the reserve was deeded to the government, but this was merely to permit the improving or rerouting of the existing roadway in the most convenient place without any danger of interference from the Indians.

In 1784 Captain Caldwell's Company of Colonel Butler's Rangers, which had seen service at Detroit during the war, was disbanded at Niagara. These former Loyalist soldiers had little hope of being able to return to their homes in the thirteen colonies. Caldwell invited them to come and settle near him at the mouth of the Detroit River. At the same time a general invitation with an offer

[3]*Third Report of the Archives of Ontario*, p. 40.
[4]This channel is now known as Snye Carty—a splendid example of name corruption by phonetic transcription. Chenal Ecarté means an out-of-the-way channel, but what signification can be attached to the words Snye Carty?
[5]Cruikshank, *The Simcoe Papers*, V, 40, P. Selby to Alex. McKee, May 9, 1793. This bridge was destroyed in 1812 to halt the American General William Hull on his march towards Fort Malden.

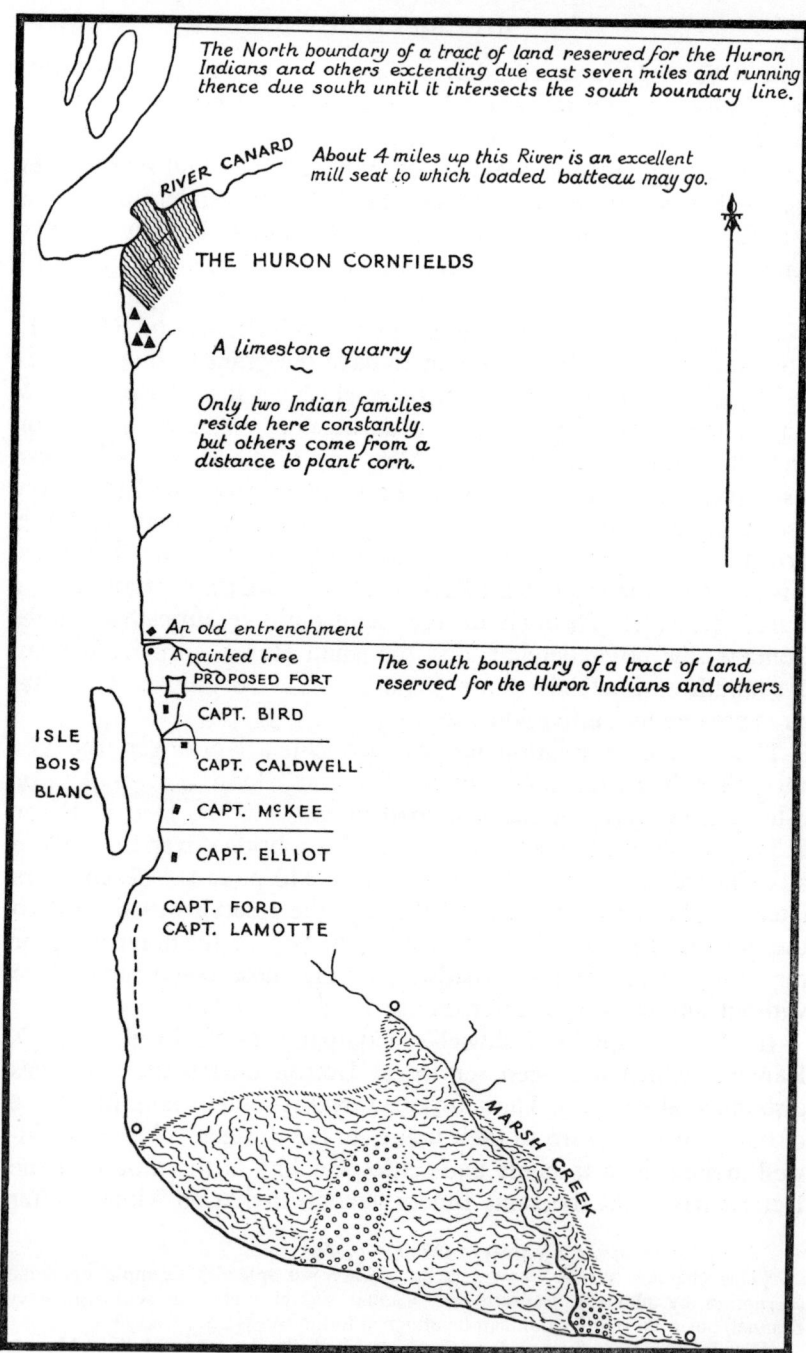

FIG. 12. PLAN OF THE HURON RESERVE AND MALDEN BY P. MCNIFF, 1790. [Original in Ontario Bureau of Archives, Toronto.]

of tools and provisions was extended by the government to other Loyalists and sympathizers in the United States. When the prospective settlers arrived, a great disappointment awaited them. All the lands along the river near its mouth were occupied by Indian officers and interpreters.

To remedy the situation Caldwell obtained from the Indians a parcel of land on the north shore of Lake Erie. It was called the New Settlement to distinguish it from the old settlement at Petite Côte and L'Assomption. In 1787 this tract of land was given to Major Mathews on behalf of the government (G 14). As surveyed that summer by T. Smith working under direction of Major Mathews, this settlement consisted of ninety-seven lots on the north shore of Lake Erie, between a creek four miles from the mouth of the Detroit River to a small creek (Mill Creek)[6] about a mile and a half east of Cedar Creek. In this survey lots 68, 69, and 70 were reserved by the Crown for a town plot.[7] This was the first town plot to be laid out in the present County of Essex. Later the town of Colchester was founded on that land.

This frontage was occupied under licence of the Commandant at Detroit under authority from the Governor-in-Chief. A letter from the Deputy-Surveyor of the District of Hesse (Mr. Patrick McNiff) dated September 21, 1790, addressed to the Deputy Surveyor-General at Quebec (Mr. John Collins) described the settlement as follows: "The people forming the New Settlement in question were composed of disbanded soldiers and loyalists and were settled by authority from the Government in 1787, when ninety-seven lots were laid out in the best manner that could then be done by the best surveyor they then could find (not so professionally)."[8] The names and occupations as well as the locations of these newcomers have been preserved in lists approved by Major Mathews of the fort at Detroit (G 15).

When this stretch of water frontage was exhausted, additional lots were made available by running a second concession to the rear. Under date of December 15, 1788, Major Close, Commanding Officer at Detroit, signed a list of 45 settlers attached to a survey containing 52 lots in the back concessions (G 16). There is no evidence that any of these lots were occupied by the end of 1794. In 1789 Major Murray gave permission to certain individuals to take up unoccupied lots in the first concession.

[6]Where the town of Kingsville is now situated. Nearby is the internationally famous Jack Miner Bird Sanctuary, the stopping place for thousands of migrating Canada geese each spring and fall.
[7]*Third Report of the Archives of Ontario*, pp. 74–5.
[8]*Seventeenth Report of the Archives of Ontario*, p. 186.

In 1790 the name of the settlement was changed to the Two Connected Townships in the New Settlement, Lake Erie. That year twelve lots were added east of Mill Creek on Lake Erie. The settling of this 18-mile stretch of lake frontage constituted the nucleus of the Townships of Colchester and Gosfield. The establishment of townships was to aid in clarifying land titles and not for the purpose of local self-government.

Among these new settlers on the north shore of Lake Erie we find a number of names of German origin. Some of them were members of the Hessian regiments who had seen service during the American Revolution. Others came from the old German settlement of Pennsylvania, men who had actually sided with the British or at least whose political sympathies had been with them during the war.

In order to make sure that the King's Instructions would be followed and to settle all matters of dispute relating to lands, land boards were appointed for each District. The personnel of the Land Board for the District of Hesse, appointed by Lord Dorchester, April 2, 1789, was as follows:

> Farnham Close, Esq., or Officer Commanding at Detroit
> William Dummer Powell, Esq.
> Duperon Baby, Esq.
> Alexander McKee, Esq.
> William Robertson, Esq.
> Alexander Grant, Esq.
> Adhemar de St. Martin.

On May 1, 1791, the names of John Askin, George Leith, and Montigny de Louvigny, and the officer of the Royal Corps of Engineers at Detroit were added to the Board. Five members were to make a quorum. By July 22, 1791, the Board was reduced to the actual residence and attendance of only five members. A request was sent to Quebec that three members might be sufficient to form a quorum. During his visit of the four Western Districts of the Province of Quebec in the summer of 1790, Sir John Johnson, Superintendent of Indian Affairs, sat as president of the different land boards, wherever he might be present. He presided over the meeting of the local Board on July 16 and on August 11 and 12. The Board usually met on Fridays at eleven o'clock before noon at the Commandant's quarters at Detroit, three members forming a quorum. Thomas Smith was the first secretary.

The Land Board of Hesse ran into difficulties that obstructed the progress of the settlement on the important southernmost frontier of Canada. The main obstruction was that the Board had no land at its disposal free from the claims of Indians and others. In the proclamation of 1764, which followed the Treaty of Paris, the British Government recognized the title of the Indian tribes of Canada to the land they occupied. Before the creation of land boards, Indian officers and Loyalists and emigrants from the United States had been authorized by the lieutenant-governors and commanding officers at Detroit to take up lots on the land ceded by the Indians at Malden and at the New Settlement. This practice was now discontinued. No location certificates could be granted by the Board before the right of soil had been purchased from the Indians for the use of the Crown.

Alexander McKee, Deputy Agent for the Indian Affairs, was instructed to purchase for the Crown all the land from Long Point on Lake Erie to Chenal Ecarté at the mouth of River St. Clair. On May 21, 1790, he reported to the Board that the "Cession from ye Indians to the Crown" had been completed at the bargain price of trade goods to the value of 1,200 pounds Quebec currency, excepting the reserve near the Huron Church and the reserve at La Rivière aux Canards (G 17). (See Fig. 13.)

At the Land Board meeting the following day, McKee explained why these two areas had not been included in the purchase. He thought it impracticable to press for their inclusion at this time because it might have jeopardized the greater deal. Moreover, he was complying with the express wish of the Governor "that all possible regard be had to the ease and comfort of the Indians." The Board was not satisfied. Besides the need of land for settlers on lakes or rivers, the Board insisted that the reserve at La Rivière aux Canards would retard the settlement on the Detroit frontier, interfere with the future town and fort, interrupt communications, and seal up the only source of limestone on the east side of the strait. In return the Board offered to grant to the Huron Indians a tract of land of equal extent at Chenal Ecarté at the mouth of the St. Clair River, and also to make such compensation as might appear necessary to accomplish this object.[9] McKee remained adamant. His position was reiterated by the Indian Chiefs to Sir John Johnson when he visited the area a few months later (G 18).

Even after the large cession of May 1790, the Board could not issue certificates before it received a survey of the present purchase.

[9]*Ibid.*, p. 176.

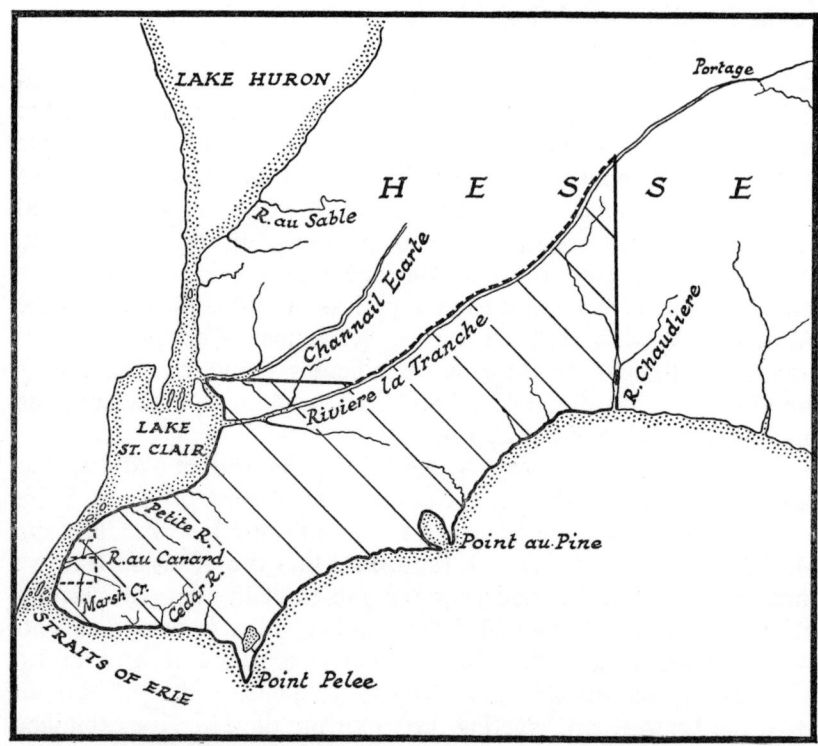

FIG. 13. THE CESSION OF THE INDIANS TO KING GEORGE III ON MAY 19, 1790. [Department of Indian Affairs, Ottawa.]

Patrick McNiff was the only surveyor, and a vacillating one in the face of the difficulties he encountered. Delays were also occasioned by the friction between the Board and the inefficient surveyor. The correspondence of the surveyor mentions difficulties he had in obtaining from the Board precise orders of survey and requisitions such as boats, men, paper, and even lead pencils.[10]

On May 22, 1790, McNiff was directed by the Board to expedite a survey of the recent purchase. After having waited fourteen days after the return of McNiff from his voyage of survey, the Board commanded his attendance at a meeting. At that time he informed the Board that having proceeded to the survey under a written order of the Commandant at the post, he could not communicate to the Board his progress, which by general instructions must come to them through the office at Quebec. Thereupon the Board gave him

[10]*Ibid.*, p. 215.

definite instructions to report a survey of the frontage of the tract lately ceded to the Crown, starting from Long Point on Lake Erie and continuing to the beginning of the old French settlement on the Detroit River. McNiff raised difficulties about proceeding with this survey. There was no point fixed for the beginning and end. Moreover, he did not know the extent of the grants made to the Indian officers (Malden). If they extended seven miles they would encroach upon the farms of other settlers of the New Settlement. The Board issued an order to begin to run his lines north from the lake at the western boundary of lot 97 occupied by John Cornwall.

This survey was not laid before the Board until July 30. Even then the Board had no land ready for disposal in the present County of Essex along the water frontage of Lake Erie or the Detroit River. The New Settlement covered all the suitable shore frontage of Lake Erie and the present Malden Township was taken up by the Indian officers. Continuing up the river front was the Huron reserve at La Rivière aux Canards. This extended to the old settlement at Petite Côte, which was completely inhabited. North of that was the other Huron reserve that comprised the tract of land up to the Huron Church. From the church to Lake St. Clair all the river frontage was occupied.

In the meantime the Board invited all persons having claims to any part of lands in the District to communicate their titles and pretensions. These claims might be in the nature of grants from the French King, or permission to occupy from the commandants or private purchase or gifts from the Indians, countenanced by the commanding officers and lieutenant-governors at Detroit, who had received the rents and fines on these holdings and speculations.

The Board also continued to receive and file petitions for new land. A large number of these requests were for lots at Rivière La Tranche (Thames River). Impatient with the delays encountered, some of the emigrants, unable to obtain land, were obliged to return to the United States after having expended the little property they had brought with them.

On September 10, 1790, the Board finally got down to the business of issuing certificates for lots of 200 acres, more or less (G 19). The first was issued to Alexander Clarke to secure him in his improvement of lot 2 in the New Settlement after having confirmed his claim and after having "administered the oath of fidelity and allegiance as by law directed." Twelve certificates in the New Settlement were completed that day. In order to accommodate the people who were so far from their homes, a meeting of the Board was held on the following day at which seventeen certificates in the same locality were delivered (G 20). On October 22 ten certificates were issued for lots east of Mill Creek (G 21).

This disposed of the immediate land office rush because a large number of those who had received location tickets in 1787 were not settled on their lots. In January 1789 Major John Smith reported that in the New Settlement only 29 lots were settled, 22 were occupied by sham settlers, and on the remaining lots no improvement had been made.[11] McNiff's survey, made in the summer of 1790, tells of numerous transfers and abandonment of property.[12] In some cases the non-improvement and abandonment of property were attributable to the withholding of provisions and implements which the settlers had expected from the government.[13] It is also known that crop failures were general in the area during the first three years of the settlement (F 30). These factors account in part for the fact that only a little more than a third of the original ticket holders appeared before the Board in the fall of 1790 to claim lots awarded to them in 1787.

The Board was confronted with many problems in considering petitions for the unoccupied lots. It took two years to clear up the confusion, during which time some of the original ticket holders, or their transferees, presented themselves. Usually the 1787 tickets were honoured unless transfers of property were shown to be in order, and as having taken place before the appointment of the Land Board. In the Heads of Enquiry previous to granting lots in the Two Connected Townships, several names were frequently given as petitioners for the same parcel of land. Lot 1 at Mill Creek is an example in case, where the names of Thomas Curtis, William Cook and Peter Williams appear in succession.[14] Why Curtis did not obtain a certificate is not indicated. Cook made no improvement and the lot was promised to Williams who, it was thought, had returned to the United States. Finally on December 30, 1793, upon the petition of several settlers, the land was granted to Andrew Alcock, a miller, so that he might develop a mill-seat on the stream to grind their grain (G 22).

There was much instability in the infant settlement on the north shore of Lake Erie. Even after the Board had disposed of all the available lots in the New Settlement, cases of lack of improvement

---

[11]*Third Report of the Archives of Ontario*, pp. 271–90.
[12]*Ibid.*, passim.
[13]*Seventeenth Report of the Archives of Ontario*, p. 143.
[14]*Third Report of the Archives of Ontario*, p. 271.

were common enough. On January 18, 1793, the Board notified those who had not cultivated their lots in the Two Connected Townships, Lake Erie, to produce proof of their compliance with the regulations within four weeks, otherwise the Board would grant the said lots to such claimants as would reside on them and conform to the rules and regulations.[15] Requests for approval of transfers or exchange of property were also numerous. The McNiff survey of 1794 gives an accurate picture of the proprietors as of that date—only a little more than half of the names corresponding to the original ticket holders of 1787, and not more than three-quarters tallying with the original receivers of certificates from the Land Board (Appendix IX).

Some of the petitioners for lots along Lake Erie who were disappointed, or who resigned their lots, petitioned for land at Rivière La Tranche (Thames River). Unable to secure certificates many of them settled at that place without obtaining the consent of the Board. Owing to frustrating delays in the preparation of proper surveys, they had to wait until late in the summer of 1792 before the Board could confirm them in their holdings.

The Board also examined the claims of the landholders in the old settlements of Petite Côte and L'Assomption and issued certificates to the actual bona fide occupants of such improved farms. From these settlers the Board also entertained requests for continuations, that is, land in the second and third concessions at the rear of their farms (G 23, G 24). The reason given in the petitions was the need of wood for fuel and fences. These requests were usually granted for the second concession only, provided that it did not interfere with any improvement already made.

Surveys of the front as well as of the rear concessions were ordered. At the same time the direction of side lines was defined and set, and space was marked for side roads to be opened between concessions (G 25, G 26, G 27, G 28). This heralded the end of the era when rivers and lakes were the only highways and streams the only roadways to the hinterland. Because of its swampy nature very little of this hinterland was fit for agricultural purposes, and its general development had to wait until proper drainage was provided.

When Canada was divided into two provinces by the Constitutional Act of 1791, the authority to grant the waste lands of the Crown passed over to the provinces. By a proclamation of Lieutenant-Governor Simcoe, dated February 7, 1792, land boards

[15]*Ibid.*, p. 217.

received instructions to continue functioning as before.[16] In these instructions it was stipulated that "no farm lot be granted to any one person which shall contain more than 200 acres." Petitions for larger grants had to be addressed to the Lieutenant-Governor. On July 16, 1792, the jurisdiction of the Land Board at Detroit was limited to the newly constituted counties of Essex and Kent.

Because the available water frontage along Lake Erie and the Detroit River was practically all occupied, the surveyor was requested to explore the possibilities of locating settlers in the back concessions (G 29). On March 8, 1793, the Board received a report from Surveyor McNiff regarding the difficulties he encountered while attempting to survey the fourth and fifth concessions south of the Huron Church (G 30). The swampy condition of the soil forced him to abandon the work. Therefore he proceeded to explore the possibilities of establishing settlements along the rivers emptying into Lake St. Clair—Rivière aux Pêches (Pike Creek), Rivière aux Puces, Belle Rivière, and Rivière Ruscom. He reported that the conditions in that area were favourable. On March 29, 1793, he was directed by the Board to survey these streams (G 31). On April 11, 1793, he reported the results of his inspection (G 32). Although the President of the Land Board was not satisfied with the small number of lots made available by the sketchy survey (G 33), the Board gave public notice that on May 16 it would proceed to grant lots of land along these streams to those "whose services, loyalty and conduct entitled them to the bounty of the Government."

There was a delay in the granting of the lots—perhaps the Board was awaiting an answer from the Lieutenant-Governor to its query about the "Usual Reserves." The Canada Act of 1791 as interpreted and the proclamation of February 7, 1792, directed that two-sevenths of the land granted be reserved for the Protestant clergy and the Crown. This had not been done in the Lake Erie or Detroit River settlements because those areas had been occupied before the Act of 1791. The answer in this case must have been to make the Reserves. Before the Board began to issue certificates for these lots it held back two lots on each side of each stream for "the use of the Crown and Clergy Reserves agreeable to the Instruction of His Excellency the Lieutenant-Governor and Council."[17] McNiff's survey had one thing in its favour, having seven lots on each side of the stream facilitated setting aside two-sevenths of the land for the

[16] *Ibid.*, pp. civ-cviii.
[17] *Ibid.*, pp. 231–2.

Reserves. Lots 3 and 6 on Rivière aux Puces and lots 1 and 7 on the other streams were earmarked for this purpose.

The President of the Land Board, Colonel England, had reason to believe that more lots were available in that region. In the same year Wm. Harffy was granted lots 8 and 9 (unsurveyed) on the west side of Rivière aux Pêches. Other lots were soon made available for on January 17, 1797, Wm. Smith sold to John Askin lots 8, 9, and 10 of 200 acres each on the west side of Belle Rivière, for sixty pounds New York currency (G 34). Moreover, in the rear of the farms fronting on these rivers a number of lots with lake frontage were later surveyed—four lots between Rivière aux Pêches and Rivière aux Puces, three lots between the latter and Belle Rivière, and eight lots between Belle Rivière and Rivière Ruscom. The lots fronting on Rivière aux Pêches and Rivière aux Puces and those on the west side of Belle Rivière, along with the lots with lake frontage between these rivers, form the basis of Maidstone Township. The lots fronting on the east shore of Belle Rivière and on both sides of Rivière Ruscom compose the origins of Rochester Township. To the rear of the lots fronting on the east side of Rivière Ruscom lies Tilbury West Township. In the first survey made of this territory the lots all fronted on Lake St. Clair (G 35). In the summer of 1798 nine lots had already been located. When the plotting of this frontage was completed it comprised twenty-two lots. Thus McNiff's sketchy survey of these streams initiated the development of the three townships situated on the southern shore of Lake St. Clair.

That extension of the settlement completed the allocation of all the water frontage in the present County of Essex with the exception of Point Pelee and Pelee Island. In May 1788 these two large tracts of land were leased by the Chippewa and Ottawa Indians for 999 years renewable at the rate of three bushels of corn annually or value thereof. The lessees were James Allan and William and J. Caldwell for the Point, and Thomas McKee for the Island (Appendix IV). From contemporary schedules and surveys, and from the minutes of the Land Board it has been possible to chart and list as of 1792–4 the owners of the lots along Lake Erie, the Detroit River, Lake St. Clair, and the streams emptying into that lake (see Fig. 14 and Appendix IX). In quest of additional land for settlers, eyes were again turned to the interior of the county. In a letter to the Land Board dated February 4, 1794, D. W. Smith, Acting Surveyor-General, wrote: "I am informed of an eligible ridge for settlement which runs somewhere in the rear of the Huron Church towards Point Pelee. Should this be the case the opening of a road or concession line there would have double advantage, because it would afford more convenience to the settlers on Lake Erie."[18] But it was not until the second decade of the next century that this ridge was opened up as a continuation of the Talbot Road through the present centres of Leamington, Ruthven, Cottam, Essex, and Maidstone.

After the dissolution of the Land Board on November 6, 1794,[19] recommendatory power for locations of 200 acres or less was in the hands of the magistrates of the District, settlement duties were not strictly enforced, and the system laid itself open to the evils of speculative development. Adventurers simply complied with the regulations up to the point where possession was possible, and then sold out to the first bidder, often a speculator. In the next few years the titles to nearly all the surveyed lots fronting Lake St. Clair as well as a considerable number of the lots along the streams emptying into it were acquired by John Askin, Detroit merchant (G 36, G 37, G 38). With much justice he could have been dubbed the Count of Kent, since a four-mile strip along Lake St. Clair was then part of the County of Kent.

On August 21, 1795, a proclamation of Lieutenant-Governor Simcoe directed all holders of certificates or tickets of occupation to deposit same with the Clerk of the Peace of the District within six months in order that grants might be issued under the Seal of the Province to the rightful claimants. Either the applications were slow in coming in or the processing was delayed, for by December 31, 1798, only eighty-four title deeds for land in Essex County had passed the Seals of the Province.[20] Even so, security of tenure was now possible for both the old and the new holders of the farm lots that now rimmed the three exposed sides of the Sun Parlour of Canada. Before the end of the eighteenth century the evolutionary force of human progress had practically completed the work of changing the wilderness of the Indians on the periphery of Canada's southernmost frontier into the secured fertile fields of its Garden Gateway.

[18]*Ibid.*, p. 249.
[19]*Ibid.*, pp. cviii–cix.
[20]Cruikshank and Hunter, *The Russell Papers*, III, 159.

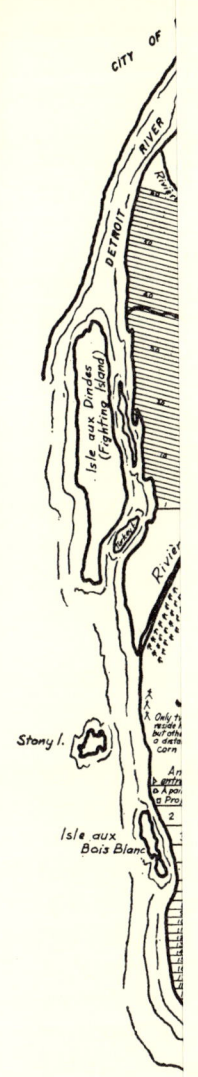

H. FIRST TOWNS—SANDWICH AND AMHERSTBURG

THE end of the American Revolution with the Treaty of 1783, which made the middle of the Detroit River part of the international boundary, also led to the founding of the first two towns along the Canadian side of the Detroit River—Sandwich and Amherstburg. In preparation for the handing over of Detroit to the Americans, the Settlement of L'Assomption (later Sandwich) was chosen as the seat of government for the Western District, and land opposite the Island of Bois Blanc (later Amherstburg), because of its strategic position commanding the entrance to the river, was selected as the place where the military post and naval station would be established.

In the interval between the Treaty of Paris (1783) and the evacuation of Detroit (1796) a number of British adherents living in the town of Detroit crossed the boundary and settled on what is now the Canadian side of the river, mostly in the Township of Malden and in the section of Petite Côte north of La Rivière aux Dindes where the original French settlement had started in the middle of the century. Residents who stayed in Detroit in 1796 were given a year to make a declaration of their intention to remain British subjects living in American territory. Otherwise, they would be considered American citizens. A good number made the declaration, enough to alarm the American officials at Detroit (H 1, H 2). Many others, however, moved across the river, preferring to live under the British flag. These included merchants and government officials who contributed much to the development of the business, social and cultural life of the area.

SANDWICH

For the convenience of these citizens, in the summer of 1797 the Honourable Peter Russell, President of the Executive Council, bought on the Canadian side of the Detroit River the Reserve at the Huron Church containing 1,078 acres (H 3, H 4, H 5, H 6). This land had been characterized by Surveyor McNiff in 1791 as "of no consequence being only a barren sandy plain."[1] It consisted of a triangular tract of land whose base extended along the river nearly two miles from La Rivière à Gervais to the Huron Church. One side of this triangle ran along the church lands for about two miles. The

[1]Fraser, *Seventeenth Report of the Archives of Ontario*, p. 193.

other side was formed by a straight line from this apex to the point of beginning. An area of sixty-one acres along the river near the church was reserved for the use of the Huron Indians. Also excluded from the purchase were the improved lands of Wm. Hands and Thomas Pajot at the easterly limits of the triangle.

A part of the purchased tract lying near the river was divided into one-acre lots for settlement. It is worthy of note that two of the three streets paralleling the river were named after the buyer—Peter Street and Russell Street. The other was called Bedford, probably in memory of the fact that Russell's ancestors were from Bedford County in England, or that the Duke of Bedford was an illustrious relative. This town plot extended from Detroit Street to South Street. The other cross-streets were Mill (so called because it led to the Baby Mill opposite lot 3 of Russell Street), Huron (now Brock), and Chippewa. The four corner lots at the junction of Bedford and Huron streets (now Sandwich and Brock) were reserved for the public. Drawn by A. Iredell, dated July 12, 1797, the first plan of Sandwich shows the town nestling snugly along the river in its protective triangle (see Fig. 15).

The negotiations with the Indians for the transfer of the property could not be completed immediately. This fact, however, was not permitted to interfere with the development of the new town. A draw for the lots in the town of Sandwich was held on July 7, 1797, and approved by the Council at Newark on August 14 of the same year (H 7).

Of great interest to local historians is the fact that lot 5 on Russell Street, where the present James Baby House stands, was drawn by Colonel McKee. James Baby did not come into possession of this lot until 1807. On the house at the corner of Mill and Russell streets there is a plaque that reads: "This dwelling was erected about 1790 by Hon. James Baby, Legislative Councillor." This is clearly an error. By coincidence or by arrangement, James Baby's lot was number 3 on the east side of Russell Street, facing the Baby Mill on the shore of the Detroit River (H 8).

To encourage building in the town of Sandwich, Russell, under date of August 19, 1797, directed that those settlers who built the first houses should be given park lots of twenty-four acres to the rear of the townsite (H 9). The first four to receive this bounty were John McGregor, Richard Pattinson, Robert Innis, and William Park, all on March 5, 1798 (H 10). On December 9, 1797, Russell wrote, somewhat optimistically, to Simcoe: "The British merchants at Detroit having solicited me to give them a town on the river,

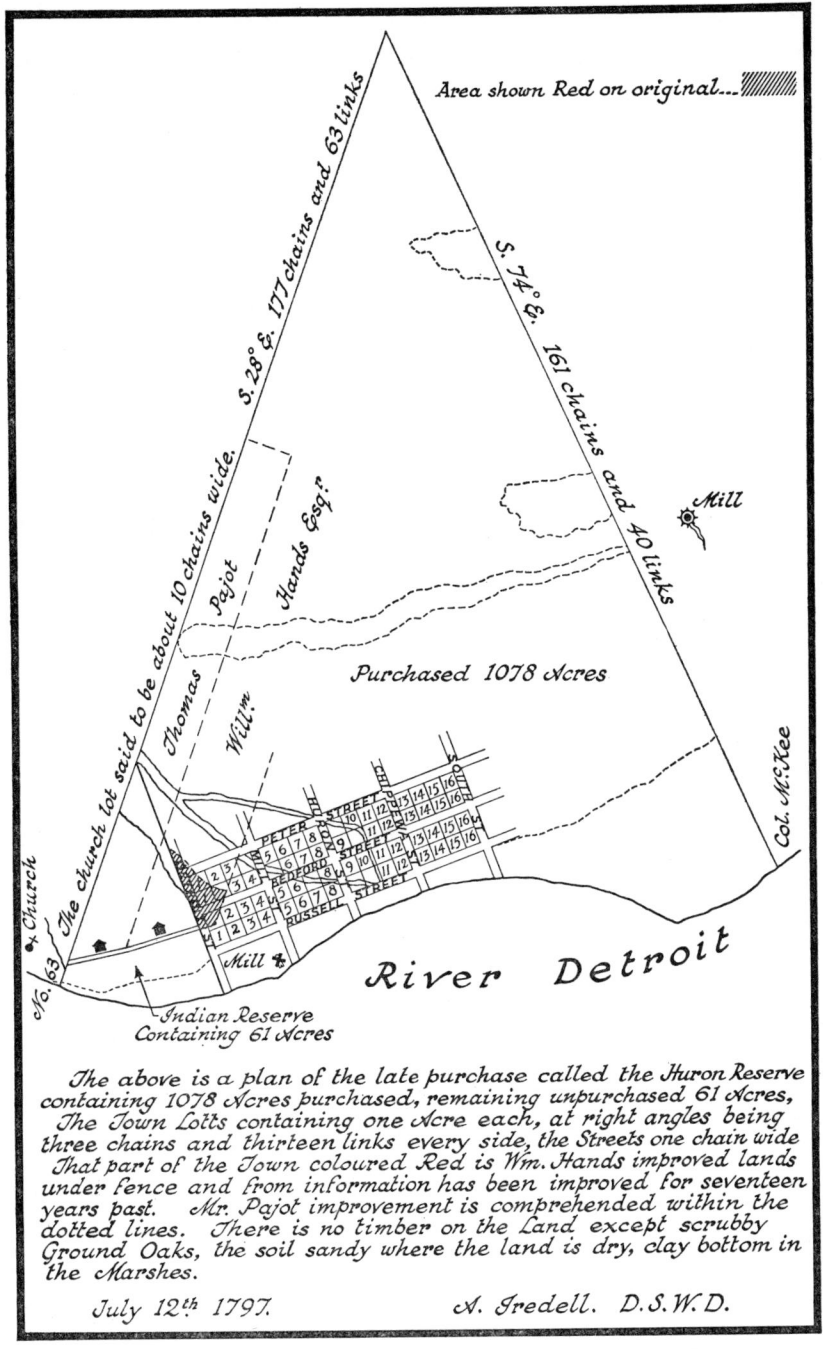

FIG. 15. PLAN OF THE PURCHASE OF THE HURON RESERVE FOR THE TOWN OF SANDWICH BY A. IREDELL, JULY 12, 1797. [Public Archives of Canada.]

where they may reside and carry on their trade with equal convenience, I purchased from the Indians the Gore near the Huron Church for their accommodation and named it Sandwich,[2] and I am informed that several houses have already been built there and that it promises fair to become soon the most beautiful town in the Province."[3]

When the courts were transferred from Detroit to the Settlement of L'Assomption there was immediate need of a building to serve as a gaol and court house. The magistrates in General Quarter Sessions petitioned the government for a loan of £750 as part payment for the erection of this building (H 11). On December 12, 1796, the Council at Newark resolved to offer the magistrates of the Western District a storehouse built by the government at Chatham to be used as a prison "either at the place where it now stands or to be removed to any more proper situation." This building was erected in Sandwich in 1797. In December of that year when nearing completion it was burned (H 12). Until it was replaced, the vessel *Dunmore* was brought up from the naval station at the mouth of the river to house the prisoners who in great part were deserters from the American army (H 13, H 14).

A church was needed for the non-Catholic residents of the area. Except for the temple that the Moravian missionaries erected during their short sojourn at the mouth of the Detroit River, there had been no Protestant place of worship on either side of the strait. The American occupation of Detroit with the river serving as an actual political boundary brought attention to the urgency of placing "a discreet Clergyman at Sandwich and giving him a Church there." In an exchange of letters between Peter Russell and the Right Reverend Jacob Mountain, Episcopal Bishop of Quebec, it was emphasized that the religious and moral instruction of the inhabitants was urgently needed as an antidote to that "most dangerous contagion" of American soldiers deserting to the Canadian side (H 15, H 16). In 1798 Russell sent £200 to the wardens of Sandwich to enable them to build an Episcopal Church in that town (H 17). There is no evidence that the building was erected immediately. At first Richard Pollard, as a layman, conducted religious services in the court house or in private homes. In conformance with an act of 1793, there being no person or minister of the

---

[2] Very likely named after the town of Sandwich in the county of Kent, England, thus following the pattern set by Simcoe of naming counties, townships, etc., after their counterparts in England.

[3] Cruikshank and Hunter, *The Russell Papers*, II, 38.

Church of England living within eighteen miles, marriages were validated or solemnized before justices of the peace (H 18). It was not until May 1802 that, as a deacon, the Reverend Mr. Pollard began to keep the register of marriages, christenings, and burials by the Church of England at Sandwich. This was the beginning of the parish of St. John, the mother parish of the Protestant Episcopal Church of the Western District and also of the State of Michigan.

With the erection of public buildings and government inducements for private housing, one might have expected with Russell that the town would experience an immediate building boom. But such was not the case. In 1800 a report was received by the Council at York from the Grand Jury of the Western District, asserting that a great number of town lots in Sandwich granted in 1797 still remained unimproved although the time stipulated for such improvements had passed (H 19). As a result, it was stated, the settlement of the town had been greatly impeded, streets had not yet been opened, and only seven or eight houses had been built. Slow indeed was the initial development of the capital town of the Western District.

Slow also was the finalizing of the purchase of the townsite. Negotiations with the Huron Indians dragged on for three years (H 20, H 21, H 22). Colonel Alex McKee having died in January 1799, the deed was finally executed by his son, Captain Thomas McKee, in September 1800, for the bargain price of goods to the value of £300 Quebec currency—today's price of a small building lot in the same locality (H 23).

Amherstburg

As early as 1784 the land opposite Bois Blanc Island was being considered as a site for a town and a fort. In July of that year Lieutenant-Governor Hay of Detroit wrote to Governor Haldimand at Quebec: "I am informed several of the reduced Provincial Officers and many of the Soldiers wish to settle on the South Side of Detroit rather than anywhere else. Several have built upon and improved lands who have no other pretensions than the Indians' consent to possession. Captains Bird and Caldwell are of the number at a place they have called Fredericksburg." (G 6.) Very likely the name was chosen in honour of Governor Frederick Haldimand. On August 14 of the same year, after having been briefed in Quebec by Caldwell, Haldimand wrote to Hay that because the intended settlement at the mouth of the river was at a place where it might thereafter be necessary to establish a post, two thousand yards from the centre should be reserved on all sides for that purpose (G 7). These are the earliest suggestions of a future town and fort opposite the Island of Bois Blanc.

Four years elapsed before the next trace of activity in this matter. On May 29, 1788, Lord Dorchester ordered Gother Mann, Captain Commanding the Royal Engineers, to proceed without loss of time to survey all the fortifications on the Great Lakes. At Detroit besides the inspection of Fort Lernoult, he was directed to "examine the Post on this side at the entrance of the River, where there is a new Settlement and the Island of Bois Blanc opposite to it."[4] Mann made a careful study of the water communication, and in his report dated December 6, 1788, he advised that the best situation for a post would be on the main shore opposite the north end of the Island of Bois Blanc (H 24).

On August 28 of the same year Dorchester also asked Major Mathews, former Commanding Officer at Detroit, to state his ideas fully about what might be done to establish a military post at the strait. The reply, which did not come until 1790, was in general agreement with the views of Gother Mann: "Should this Post [Detroit] be given up and another taken, the most convenient place will be at the entrance of the river upon a point at present occupied by some officers and men who served in the war as Rangers with the Indians. The channel for ships runs between this point and the Isle of Bois Blanc, which should be fortified, the distance from each to mid-channel about 200 yards."[5]

In the meantime on May 15, 1789, Henry Motz, secretary to Dorchester, wrote a letter to Major Close, member of the Land Board of Hesse, respecting the laying out of a township opposite the Island of Bois Blanc, to be called George Town according to the plan sent, wherein certificates would be granted for town and farm lots according to the general instructions. This was a general town and township plan prepared at Quebec.[6] The site indicated was Caldwell's lot, number 3. Upon inquiry the Board found that the land at that place had been deeded by the Indians to officers and others in 1784. Therefore they resolved to forbear any order to the Deputy-Surveyor on the subject of the proposed town opposite the Island of Bois Blanc until further instructed (H 25). A letter from

[4]P.A.C., C 381, p. 16; *M.H.C.*, XXIII, 371–2.
[5]P.A.C., Q 49, p. 317; *M.H.C.*, XXIV, 94.
[6]For a specimen of plan see *Third Report of the Archives of Ontario*, p. lxxxiii.

Dorchester received October 16, 1789, without any mention of George Town, instructed the Board to give certificates to the actual bona fide occupants of such improved farms.

On January 8, 1793, when the Executive Council at Newark ordered the laying out of a township to be called Malden, it also resolved that the land lying between Captain Bird's lot and the Indian land (Huron Reserve at La Rivière aux Canards) be reserved for the government (G 10). Thus within a decade after the Treaty of Paris (1783) three names had been mentioned successively in connection with a town or fort opposite the Isle of Bois Blanc—Fredericksburg, George Town, and Malden.

It is worthy of note that Lieutenant-Governor Simcoe was not in favour of erecting any new fortifications along the strait. He believed that such action would be politically unwise, because it could cast suspicion upon the British iterations of a desire for a cordial alliance; moreover, such a move could very easily be rendered militarily useless if the United States moved their fort downstream to the mouth of the River Rouge. In the event of ceding the Post of Detroit, he simply proposed that the garrison be transferred into barracks directly across the river.[7] His views, however, did not prevail in the councils at Quebec or London.

The Jay Treaty, concluded in London on November 19, 1794, and ratified by the United States the following summer, stipulated that the fort at Detroit be evacuated June 1, 1796. Upon notification preparations were begun in earnest for moving the British military post and naval station to the ground opposite the Island of Bois Blanc. Late in 1795 orders were received at Detroit to proceed with the erection of two blockhouses, two storehouses, a magazine, and a wharf at the new location near the mouth of the river (H 26, H 27, H 28). Assembling of material was begun immediately. In the following spring the frame of a shed for the temporary deposit of the stores, timbers from the naval yard, pickets from the fort, and other materials were floated eighteen miles downstream to the new site (H 29, H 30). In June 1796 the buildings were reported "in great forwardness" and ready for the transfer (H 31).

The "great forwardness" of the buildings proved to be true in a very restricted sense only. From a letter written on September 8, 1796, by the newly arrived Commanding Officer William Mayne, we learn that the gunpowder had to be kept in the hull of a sailing vessel until the completion of the temporary magazine (H 32). The

[7]See letter of J. G. Simcoe to Henry Dundas, dated Quebec, April 28, 1792, Cruikshank, *The Simcoe Papers*, I, 138–9.

following summer the same officer wrote that on his arrival at the post (July 1796) he and his officers had to put up board sheds in which they lived for three months, because the only building on the ground at that time was the south blockhouse.[8] Before the winter set in, however, the north blockhouse opposite the northern end of the Island of Bois Blanc was occupied with troops above, and ordnance stores and fixed ammunition below (see Plate VI).

Towards the end of July 1797, Hector McLean became Commanding Officer at the post. On August 3 he wrote: "Neither the Officers' nor the men's Quarters are as yet finished. The magazines but begun a few days previous to my arrival. The Frame of the Store House not yet up and the wharf only begun." (H 33.) His appearance on the scene must have accelerated construction, because two weeks later he reported that for security reasons he was considering the transfer of the troops and gunpowder to the two small blockhouses and stores half a mile downstream from the north blockhouse (H 34). (See Plate VII.)

Such were the scant and unsatisfactory facilities that were provided for the troops and stores when the British evacuated Detroit on July 10, 1796. They were located on the Military Reserve which occupied lot 1 of Malden Township and Captain Bird's lot (number 2 of Malden Township) which was repossessed for the Crown with much consequent litigation (see Fig. 16). In the year 1800 "because the ground about His Majesty's Garrison at Amherstburg was too small and confined," the Indians ceded a strip five hundred yards wide extending the full depth of the Huron Reserve (H 23).

The Indian stores were also transferred from the town of Detroit to the mouth of the river. Malden became the centre of British influence among the Indians of the lakes region as large assemblies of red men came thither to hold council meetings and to receive great quantities of provisions and presents from their English father, the King (H 35, H 36).[9] In the beginning no accommodation for the stores was available at the garrison. A room was rented from Colonel Elliott at sixty pounds per year. Presents to the Indians were distributed from that place—about a mile and a half below the fort. The location made supervision difficult and abuses crept in (H 37, H 38, H 39). To remedy the situation McLean obtained the summary dismissal of Elliott as Deputy Agent for Indian Affairs,

[8]P.A.C., C 250, p. 550; *M.H.C.*, XX, 515–16, Mayne to Green, Amherstburg, June 28, 1797.

[9]For an eye-witness description of one of these assemblies, see Isaac Weld, *Travels through the States of North America and the Provinces of Upper and Lower Canada in the years 1795, 1796, 1797*, pp. 356–9.

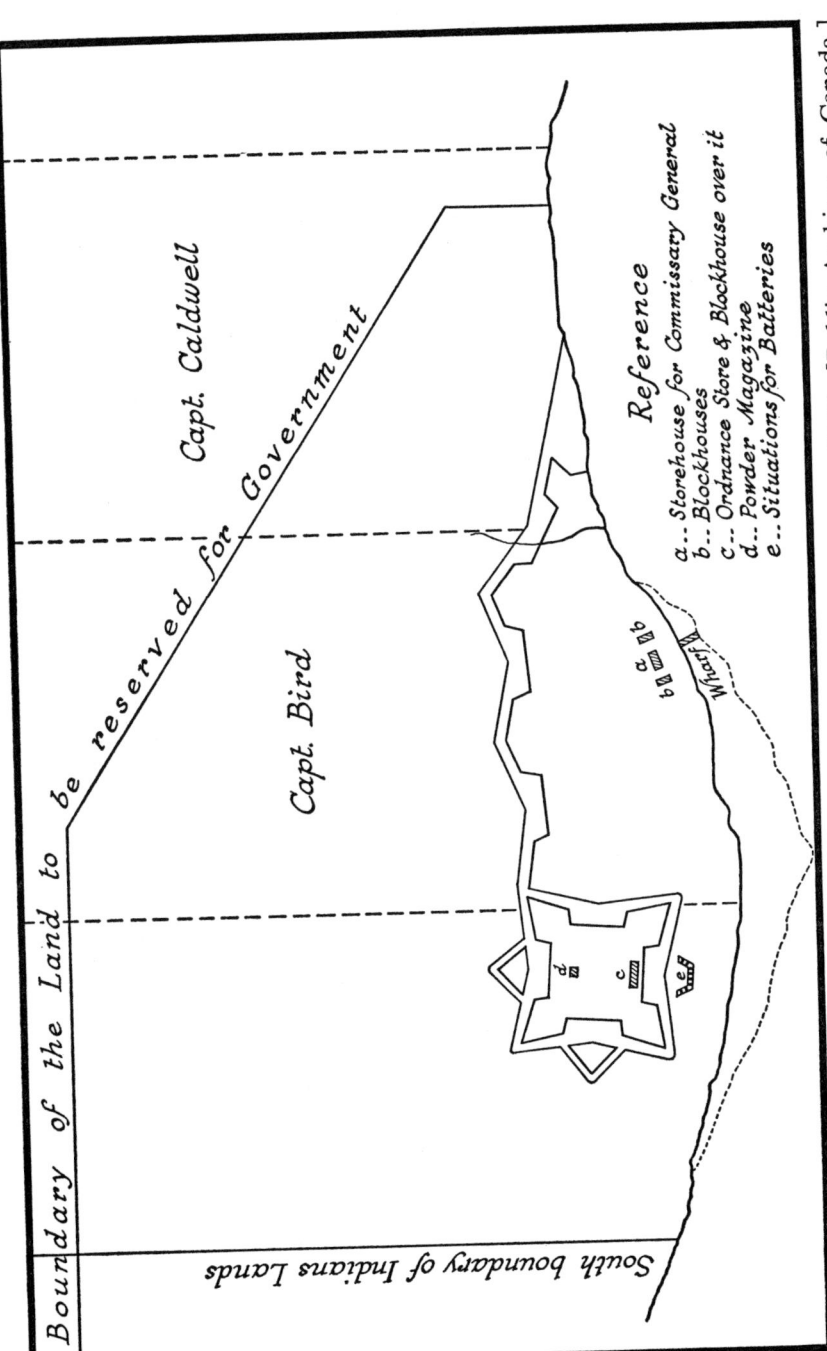

FIG. 16. PLAN OF FORTIFICATIONS OPPOSITE THE ISLAND OF BOIS BLANC IN 1796. [Public Archives of Canada.]

and transferred the stores to a room in the garrison (H 40, H 41). McLean's voluminous correspondence to Quebec supplies us with a running description of the feud between himself and Elliott, and at the same time furnishes interesting details about the infant town of Amherstburg.

If insufficient preparations at the mouth of the river had been taken for transfer of the army and navy services and Indian stores before the summer of 1796, still less were made for the accommodation of the civilians. On May 7, 1796, Detroit merchants petitioned for a town opposite the Island of Bois Blanc. On September 8, 1796, Captain Mayne wrote to the military secretary at Quebec: "I do not know of any vacant land in the vicinity of this Garrison. . . . I . . . enclose for the Commander in Chief's inspection, a plan of a Town laid out by Colonel Caldwell on his own land, who could sell his lots to much advantage to British Subjects wishing to leave the territory of the United States . . ." (H 32.) This projected town containing 363 lots would have been located in what is now the southern part of Amherstburg. From a later plan it is clear that lot 3 (Caldwell's) was not developed.

The first town plan of Amherstburg dated 1797 contains only about fifty building lots. It occupies the southern half of the original Bird lot, and is actually within the proposed boundary of the Military Reserve (see Fig. 17). On February 2, 1798, Captain McLean wrote that "he already had more applications than there were lots from merchants and others chiefly mechanics" (H 41). Additional lots were provided (H 42, H 43). In the 1799 plan the "new town" is extended eastward to a total of about eighty lots. Fortunately a map of that year furnishes the names of the holders of nearly all these lots (H 44). Amherstburg quickly mushroomed into the leading town on the eastern side of the strait, a position it held for more than half a century.

A fourth name, Amherstburg, has just been mentioned in connection with the downriver town. Where did it come from? When was it first used? Doubtless it was given in honour of General Amherst, leader of the British forces at the time of the conquest and first British Governor of Canada. On February 9, 1797, there appears a requisition for stores proposed as presents for Indians resorting to the post of Amherstburg (H 35). This is the first time the name Amherstburg appears in an official document, and it likely came from the Military Department at Quebec. In corroboration of this statement there is a letter written by Mr. Peter Russell to Robert Prescott at Quebec dated West Niagara, February 28, 1797. In part

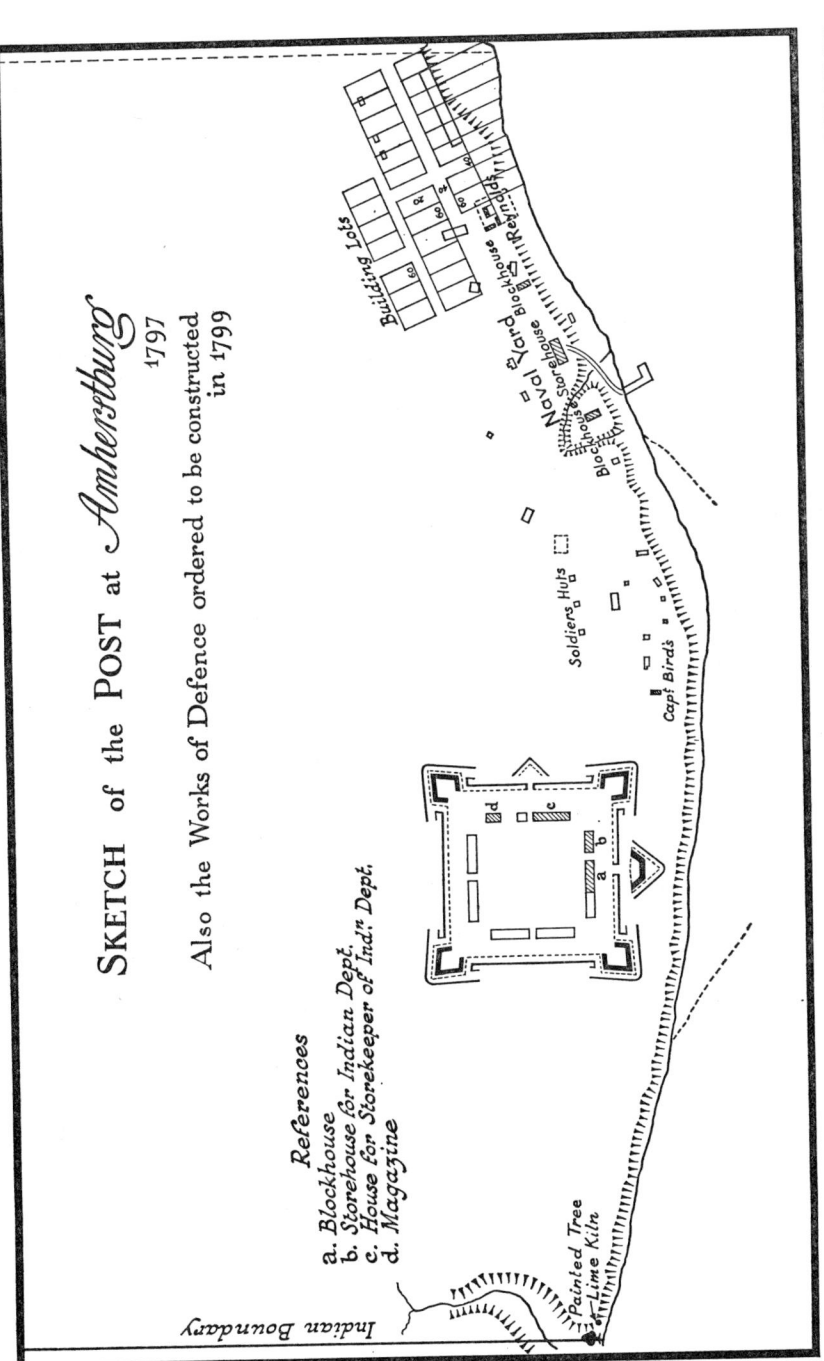

FIG. 17. SKETCH OF THE POST AT AMHERSTBURG BY A. COOPER, 1797, AND THE WORKS OF DEFENCE ORDERED TO BE CONSTRUCTED IN 1799 BY GOTHER MANN. [Public Archives of Canada.]

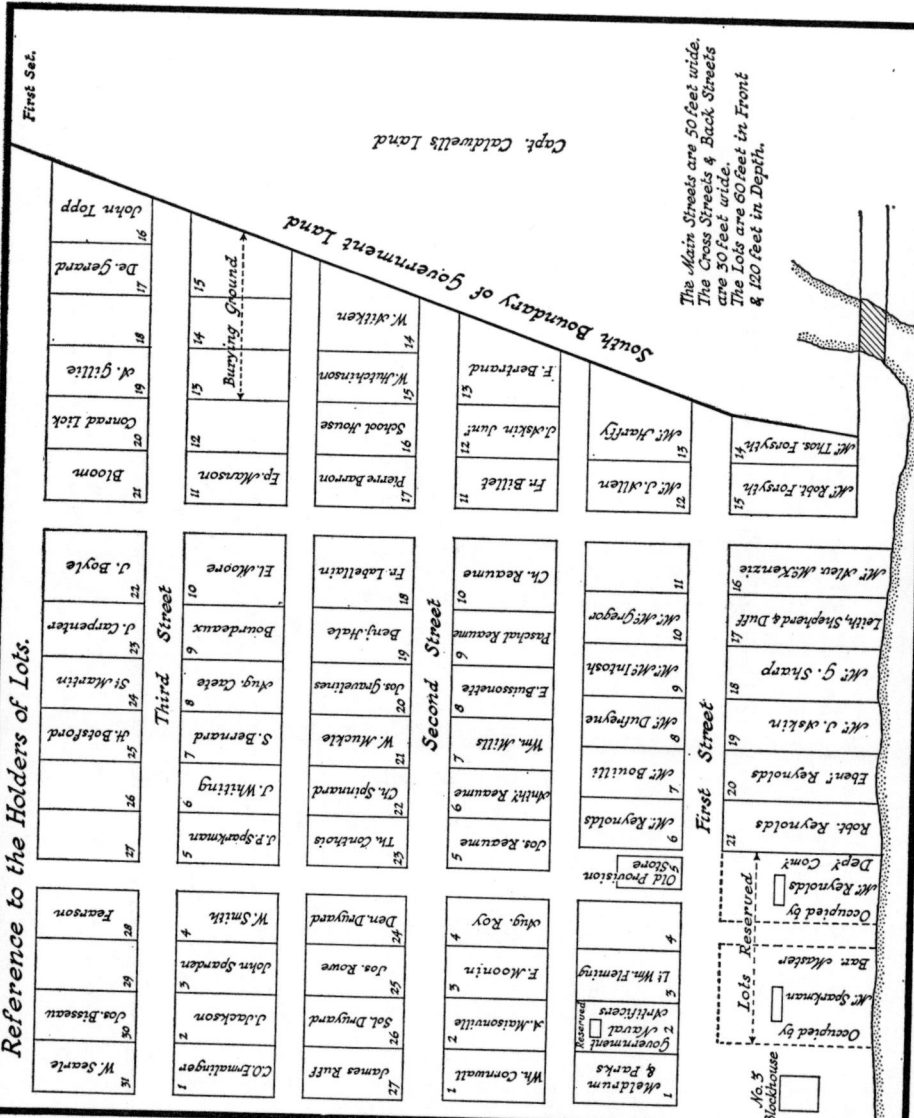

FIG. 18. HOLDERS OF LOTS IN THE TOWN OF AMHERSTBURG, 1799. [Public Archives of Canada.]

it reads as follows: "I have communicated to the Civil officers of the government the names which your Excellency has been pleased to give to the Military Posts opposite to Fort Niagara and the Island of Bois Blanc."[10] Since February 1797 Amherstburg has been the name of the town that lies opposite the Island of Bois Blanc, a town that has retained in many ways the military and marine spirit that prevailed at its inception.

The founding of the two towns of Sandwich and Amherstburg towards the end of the eighteenth century as centres of civil and military authority ended what might be called the pioneer settlement period on Canada's southernmost frontier. The transformation from an Indian wilderness to a fruitful county divided into townships and towns had been effected mainly in two waves of immigration—one of French stock which in the middle of the century laid the foundation of the oldest continuous white settlement in the present Province of Ontario, the other mostly of British and German ancestry which after the American Revolutionary War brought to the area a population of unquestioned attachment to the British Crown. The change was completed within fifty years after the first white men had come to settle on the south shore of the strait, and within a century after Cadillac's vision had established a fort, a trading post, and a colony at the strategic hub of the Great Lakes—the Detroit River region.

[10]*The Russell Papers*, I, 149.

THE WINDSOR BORDER REGION

DOCUMENTS

A. VISITORS BEFORE 1700

A 1 EXTRACTS FROM THE RELATION OF 1640-1 BY JÉRÔME LALEMENT AT STE. MARIE AMONG THE HURONS[1]

[*Thwaites*, Jesuit Relations, *XXI, 189*]

. . .

From the first village of the Neutral Nations[2] which one finds on arriving there from this place, and continuing to travel south or southeast it is about four days' journey to the entrance of the so celebrated River of that Nation, into the Ontario or lake of St. Louys. On this side of that River, and not beyond it, as a certain map indicates, are the greater part of the villages of the Neutral Nation. . . .

This stream or River is that through which our great lake of the Hurons, or fresh-water Sea, empties; it flows first into the lake of Erie, or of the Nation of the Cat, and at the end of that lake [jusques là], it enters into the territory of the Neutral Nation, and takes the name Onguiaahra, until it empties into the Ontario or lake of St. Louis, whence finally emerges the river that passes before Quebec, called the St. Lawrence. So that, if once we were masters of the coasts of the sea nearest to the dwelling of the Iroquois,[3] we could ascend by the river Saint Lawrence without danger, as far as the Neutral Nation, and far beyond, with considerable saving of time and trouble. . . .

A 2 EXTRACTS FROM THE RELATION OF 1640-1 BY JÉRÔME LALEMENT AT STE. MARIE AMONG THE HURONS
[*Thwaites*, Jesuit Relations, *XXI, 223, 231*]

. . .

The Fathers [Brébeuf[4] and Chaumonot[5]] in their journey passed through

---

[1]Hurons or Wyandots. Indian tribe racially and linguistically related to the Iroquois, but for some unknown reason their bitter enemies. In the first half of the seventeenth century they were located at the southern end of Georgian Bay.

[2]Neutrals or Attawandarons. Indian tribe that served as a buffer nation between the Hurons and the Iroquois. Most of their villages were near the Niagara River and at the western end of Lake Ontario.

[3]Iroquois. An Indian confederacy comprising the following tribes: Mohawk, Oneida, Onondaga, Seneca, Cayuga, and later Tuscorara. Their villages were in the territory of the present State of New York.

[4]Jean de Brébeuf (1593-1649), a Jesuit who came to Canada in 1625, and the following year was sent to the Huron country. After the capture of Quebec by the British in 1629 he returned to France. In 1633 he came back to Canada with Champlain and resumed his work among the Hurons. There he laboured until his death (excepting 1641-4, when at Quebec). He was captured by the Iroquois and cruelly put to death on March 16, 1649.

[5]Pierre Joseph Chaumonot (1611-93), Jesuit, was assigned to the Canadian missions in 1639 and immediately went to the Huron country, where he laboured

eighteen hamlets or villages, to all of which they gave a Christian name, which we shall use hereafter when occasion arises. They made a special stay at ten, where they gave instruction as often as they could find a hearing. They estimated about five hundred fires, and three thousand persons, that might be contained in these ten villages in which they set forth and published the Gospel. . . .

During all these gusts and tempests, the Fathers had not failed to provide for the salvation of the little children, the old men, and the sick, whom they could approach and whom they found fitted therefor. In all the eighteen villages which they visited, there was found only one, to wit, that of Khioetoa, surnamed St. Michel, which had given them the hearing that their Embassy merited. Some years ago, through fear of their enemies, there took refuge in this village a certain strange Nation, who had dwelt beyond the Erie or Cat Nation, called Awenrehronon; and they seemed to have come in these quarters only to enjoy the good fortune of this visit, and to have been led by the providence of the good Shepherd, that they might hear his voice therein. They were sufficiently instructed; but the Fathers did not think it expedient to go still further, and baptize them. The Holy Ghost will cause this seed that has been dropped into their hearts to ripen, and, in his own time, the harvest that has already been watered by so many tears will be gathered.

It is in this Nation that the Fathers administered the first Adult Baptism, in the case of a good old woman, who had already nearly lost her hearing. A remarkable thing at her Baptism was the devotion of a good woman of the same cabin, who served the Fathers as interpreter, making known to her the mysteries of our Faith, more clearly and effectually than the Fathers had to herself in the first place, so they said. The poor woman had nothing to reply, except that, as she was now old, she would have too much trouble to reach heaven; besides, she had nothing of which she could make the Fathers a present, and she must await her children who were hunting, so as to have the necessary garments to adorn herself. It was easy to satisfy her regarding these things, and she was, at last, happily baptized. Two or three other adults participated in the happiness of this visit, and a small number of children, who have gone early to heaven.

A 3 Extracts from Galinée's[6] Narrative (1669–70)
[*Bibliothèque Nationale, Paris; Margry, Découvertes, I, 112–66;*

until the dispersal of the Hurons by the Iroquois in 1649. The following year he accompanied a number of refugee Hurons to Quebec. He spent most of the next forty-three years with the Huron colony at Quebec. He is best known for his works on the Huron language, especially his *Huron Grammar*.

[6]René François Bréhant de Galinée (–1678), a Sulpician, arrived in Canada in 1668. The following year he explored the Great Lakes with Dollier de Casson. He is renowned as the author of the narrative of that journey. He returned to France in 1671.

translated and edited by James H. Coyne in Ontario Historical Society,
Papers and Records, IV (Toronto, 1903)]

...

At last we arrived at Tiwanatawa on the 24th of September, and found that the Frenchman who had arrived the day before was a man named Jolliet, who had left Montreal before us with a fleet of four canoes loaded with goods for the Ottawas,[7] and had orders from the Governor[8] to go up as far as Lake Superior to discover the situation of a copper mine, specimens from which are seen here that scarcely need refining, so good and pure is the copper. After finding this mine he was to find out an easier route than the ordinary one to transport it to Montreal. M. Jolliet had not been able to see this mine, because time pressed him for his return; but having discovered amongst the Ottawas some Iroquois prisoners that these tribes had taken, he told them that Onontio's intention was that they should live at peace with the Iroquois, and persuded them to send one of their prisoners to the Iroquois as a token of the peace they wished to have with them.

It was this Iroquois who showed M. Jolliet a new route, heretofore unknown to the French, for returning from the Ottawas to the country of the Iroquois. However the fear this Indian had of falling again into the hands of the Antastoes led him to tell M. Jolliet he must leave his canoe and walk overland sooner than would have been necessary. . . .

Meanwhile M. de la Salle's[9] illness was beginning to take away from him the inclination to push further on, and the desire to see Montreal was beginning to press him. . . . Moreover the route M. Jolliet had taken, with the news he brought us—that he had sent some of his party in search of a very numerous nation of Ottawas called the Pottawattamies,[10] amongst whom there never had been any missionaries, and that this tribe bordered on the Iskoutegas—and the great river that led to the Shawanons, induced M. Dollier[11] and me to wish to go and search for the river into which we wished to enter by way of the Ottawas

[7]The Ottawas included many tribes of the Algonquin family. They lived in the region of the upper lakes. The Ottawa River led to their country.

[8]Daniel Rémy de Courcelles (1626-98) was Governor of New France from 1665 to 1672. He took part in expeditions against the Iroquois.

[9]Robert Cavelier, Sieur de La Salle (1643-87) arrived at Quebec in 1667. He was granted the Seigneury of Lachine by the Sulpicians. In 1673 he was appointed commandant at Cataraqui. In 1679 he sailed up to the western shore of Lake Michigan, then paddled to the Illinois River where he built Fort Crèvecœur. In 1681-2 he explored the Mississippi River to the Gulf of Mexico. In July 1784 he left France with a flotilla to reconnoitre the mouth of the Mississippi. The expedition was a failure that ended in mutiny and La Salle was killed somewhere along the shore of Texas or Louisiana.

[10]Pottawattamies (Potawatomi). Indian tribe that had been driven out of the land between Lakes Huron and Michigan by the Iroquois. They had settled first on some islands at the entrance of Green Bay, and later on the Wisconsin mainland. When the Iroquois menace abated they moved southward around the end of Lake Michigan and into the valley of the St. Joseph River.

[11]François Dollier de Casson (1636-1701), a Sulpician who came to Canada in 1666. After a voyage of exploration on the Great Lakes 1669-70, he became

rather than by that of the Iroquois, because the route seemed to us much easier and we both knew the Ottawa language.

... M. Jolliet offered us a description he had made of his route from the Ottawas, which I accepted, and I reduced it at the time to a marine chart, which gave us a good deal of information as to our way. ...

...

We set out then from Tinawatawa on the 1st of October, 1669, accompanied by a good number of Indians, who helped us to carry our canoes and baggage, and after making about 9 or 10 leagues in three days we arrived at the bank of the river which I call the Rapid, because of the violence of its current. ...

...

At last we arrived on the 13th or 14th, at the shore of Lake Erie, which appeared to us at first like a great sea, because there was a great south wind blowing at the time. ... We proceeded three days along this lake. ... At the end of three days during which we made only 21 or 22 leagues, we found a spot which appeared to us so beautiful, with such an abundance of game, that we thought we could not find a better in which to pass our winter. ... We looked for some favorable spot to make a winter camp, and discovered a very pretty river at the mouth of which we camped. ...

We could not pass the winter on the lake shore because of the high winds by which we should have been buffeted. For this reason we chose a beautiful spot on the bank of a rivulet, about a quarter of a league in the woods, where we encamped. ...

...

We could not help longing for the season of navigation, so as to get to the Pottawattamies at an early date, and that I might be able to return this year to Montreal, in order to send back to M. Dollier the things that he would require in his mission.

On the 23rd of March, Passion Sunday we all went to the lake shore to make and plant a cross in memory of so long a sojourn of Frenchmen as ours had been. We offered our prayers there, and seeing that where we were was almost clear of ice, we resolved to set out on the 26th of March, the day after Annunciation.

But as the river by which we had gone to the place of our wintering was still entirely frozen, it was necessary to portage all our baggage and our canoes as far as the lake, where we embarked after living in that place 5 months and 11 days. ...

...

We loaded ourselves in this place [Pointe Aux Pins] with fresh and smoked meat and proceeded as far as a long point, which you will find marked on the map of Lake Erie. We landed there on a beautiful sand beach on the east side of the point. We had made that day nearly twenty

---

Superior of the Seminary of St. Sulpice at Montreal. He is the author of *Histoire de Montréal*.

leagues, so we were all very tired. That was the reason why we did not carry all our packs up on the high ground, but left them on the sand and carried our canoes up on high ground.

Night came on and we slept so soundly that a great north-east wind rising had time to agitate the lake with so much violence that the water rose six feet where we were, and carried away the packs of Mr. Dollier's canoe that were nearest the water, and would have carried away all the rest if one of us had not awoke. Astonished to hear the lake roaring so furiously, he went to the beach to see if the baggage was safe, and seeing that the water already came as far as the packs that were placed the highest, cried out that all was lost. At this cry we rose and rescued the baggage of my canoe and of one of M. Dollier's. Pieces of bark were lighted to search along the water, but all that could be saved was a keg of powder that floated; the rest was carried away. Even the lead was carried away, or buried so deep in the sand that it could never be found. But the worst of all was that the entire altar service was lost. We waited for the wind to go down and the waters to retire, in order to go and search along the water, whether some debris of the wreck could not be found. But all that was found was a musketoon and a small bag of clothes belonging to one of our men; the rest was lost beyond recall. Even our provisions were all lost except what was in my canoe.

This accident put it out of our power to have the aid of the sacraments or to administer them to the rest. So we took counsel together to know whether we ought to stop with some tribe to carry on our mission there, or should return to Montreal for another altar service, and other goods necessary to obtain provisions, with a view to returning afterwards and establishing ourselves in some spot, and this suggestion seemed to us best. As the route to the Ottawas seemed to us almost as short from the place where we were as the way we had come, and as we purposed to reach Sainte-Marie of the Sault, where the Ottawas assemble in order to descend in company, before they should leave, we thought we should descend with them more easily. Add to this, moreover, that we were better pleased to see a new country than to turn back.

We pursued our journey accordingly toward the west, and after making about 100 leagues on Lake Erie arrived at the place where the Lake of the Hurons, otherwise called the Fresh Water Sea of the Hurons, or Michigan, discharges into this Lake. This outlet is perhaps half a league in width and turns sharp to the north-east, so that we were almost retracing our path. At the end of six leagues we discovered a place that is very remarkable, and held in great veneration by all the Indians of these countries, because of a stone idol that nature has formed there. To it they say they owe their good luck in sailing on Lake Erie, when they cross it without accident, and they propitiate it by sacrifices, presents of skins, provisions, etc., when they wish to embark on it. The place was full of camps of those who had come to pay their homage to this stone, which had no other resemblance to the figure of a man than what the imagination was pleased to give it. However it was all painted, and a sort of face had been formed for it with vermillion. I leave you to imagine whether we avenged upon this idol, which the Iroquois had strongly recommended us to honor, the loss of our chapel. We attributed to it even the dearth of provisions from which we had hitherto suffered. In short, there was nobody whose hatred it had not incurred. I consecrated one of my axes to break this god of stone, and then having yoked our canoes together we carried the largest piece to the middle of the river, and threw all the rest also into the water, in order that it might never be heard of again. God rewarded us immediately for this good action, for we killed a roe-buck and a bear that very day.

At the end of four leagues we entered a small lake, about ten leagues in length and almost as many in width, called by M. Sanson The Salt Water Lake, but we saw no sign of salt in it. . . .

A 4   ACT OF TAKING POSSESSION OF THE LANDS OF LAKE ERIE
(OCTOBER 1669)
[*M.H.C., XXXIII, 36*]

We, the undersigned, certify that we have seen, on the lands of the lake named Erie, the arms of the King of France attached to the foot of a cross, with this inscription: "The year of salvation 1669, Clement IX being seated in the chair of St. Peter, Louis XIV reigning in France, Monsieur de Courcelles being Governor of New France, and Monsieur Talon[12] being Intendant therein for the King, two missionaries of the Seminary of Montreal arrived at this place accompanied by seven other Frenchmen, who [are] the first of all European people [to] have wintered on this lake, of which they have taken possession in the name of their King, as of unoccupied territory, by affixing his arms which they have attached here at the foot of this cross". In witness whereof we have signed the present certificate.

(Signed)   François Dollier, priest of the Diocese of Nantes,
in Brittany.
De Galinée, Deacon of the Diocese of Rennes,
in Brittany.

A 5   TONTI'S[13] VISIT TO THE STRAIT OF LAKE ERIE (1679)
[*Tonti*, Dernières Découvertes, *pp. 35–9*]

. . . While waiting for spring, he (M. de La Salle) wanted to spend the rest of the winter gathering peltries, and all sorts of munitions to defray the expenses of his trip. These reasons obliged him to return to

[12]Jean Talon (1625–94) was appointed Intendant of Canada in March 1665. He came to Canada that summer with Governor Courcelles. Under his administration the country prospered. He returned to France in 1672.

[13]Henri de Tonti (Tonty) (1650–1704) came to Canada in 1678. He accompanied La Salle on his first explorations. He built Fort St. Louis on the Illinois River, where he remained until 1700. He died at Mobile, Alabama, of yellow fever.

Frontenac on the ice; beforehand he ordered fifteen men to go ahead of him in search of the Illinois, and to prepare the way for him, and he left me as commandant at Niagara with thirty men and a Recollet Priest. . . .

. . . He ordered me to go six times twenty leagues from there [Niagara] in order to reconnoitre the coasts and the lands that lie beyond the Lakes towards the north-east. I embarked in a canoe with five men; after two days of navigation, I arrived at the strait of Lake Erie. It is a channel about thirty leagues long, by which this Lake is joined to that of the Hurons. I landed on the north shore. While there I inquired immediately about our people. I learned that they had gone on further; the desire to meet them made me make a careful examination of the country; it was a sort of a heart-shaped peninsula enclosed between these three Lakes. After having scoured these lands I returned in my canoe in order to go and render an account of my commission to M. de La Salle, who during the space of my little trip, had returned to Frontenac, where he brought some new merchandise, and from where shortly afterwards he brought back new provisions and new people to Niagara. He arrived on the 7th of August in the year 1679 accompanied by three Recollet Priests. . . .

Having returned to Niagara, M. de La Salle prepared everything for the continuation of his work. About forty persons boarded his new bark about the middle of August, and having happily crossed Lake Erie, we entered the Lake of the Hurons, which is much larger than the first two. On account of the bad weather it took us the rest of the month to go over it, and after having weathered the worst storm that can be experienced on the most stormy seas, we finally came to a harbour in the country called Missilimackinac.[14]

A 6 HENNEPIN'S[15] DESCRIPTION OF THE STRAIT BY WHICH LAKE ORLEANS (HURON) EMPTIES INTO LAKE CONTY (ERIE) (1679)
[*Hennepin*, Description de la Louisiane, *pp. 91–2*]

. . . Our voyage was so fortunate that on the tenth day [of August], the feast of St. Lawrence, we reached the entrance of the strait by which Lake Orleans empties into Lake Conty, and which is one hundred leagues distant from the Niagara River. This strait is thirty leagues long and almost everywhere a league wide, except in the middle where it expands and forms a lake of circular form, and ten leagues in diameter,

[14]Missilimackinac. Variant for Michilimackinac. Today it is known as the Straits of Mackinaw, connecting Lakes Huron and Michigan.

[15]Jean Louis Hennepin (1640–1705), a Recollet friar, arrived in Canada with La Salle in June 1675. He was the first European to describe the Falls of Niagara from actual view and to publish a picture of them, whence Hennepin Point on the American side of the falls. He went back to France in 1682 where he published his *Description de la Lousiane nouvellement découverte* (Paris, 1683), and *Nouvelle Découverte d'un très grand pays situé dans l'Amérique* (Utrecht, 1697). Many historians question the veracity of some of his writings.

which we called Lake St. Claire, on account of our passing through it on that Saint's day.

The country on both sides of this beautiful strait is adorned with fine open plains, and you can see numbers of stags, does, deer, bears, by no means fierce and good to eat, turkey hens and all kinds of game, swans in abundance. Our guys were loaded and decked with several wild animals cut up, which our Indian and our Frenchmen killed. The rest of the strait is covered with forests, fruit trees like walnuts, plum and apple trees, wild vines loaded with grapes, of which we made some little wine. There is timber fit for building. It is the place in which deer most delight. . . .

A 7   DENONVILLE TO MONSIEUR DU LHUT (DULUTH)[16]
[*Margry,* Découvertes, *V, 23–5;* M.H.C., *XXXIII, 40–1*]

At Ville Marie the 6th of June 1686.

Although I wrote you word this autumn to come to me for the purpose of conferring with us on many matters which cannot be written, as the Revd. Father Anjalran[17] has come here and will have to return to Michilimaquina as soon as the restoration of the prisoners has been made, your presence with the Outaouax is much more necessary. Thereby I hereby send you word not to come down, but to join M. de la Durantaye[18] who is to be at Michilimaquina to carry out the orders I am sending him for the safety of our allies and friends.

You will see from the letters which I am writing to M. de la Durantaye that my intention is that you should occupy a post at the strait of Lake Erie with fifty men, that you should choose a post in an advantageous spot so as to secure this passage to us, to protect our savages who go hunting there, and to serve them as a refuge against the designs of their enemies and ours; you will do nothing and say nothing to the Iroquois, unless they venture on any attempt against you and against our allies.

You will also see from the letter I am writing to M. de la Durantaye that my intention is that you should go to this post, as soon as ever you can, with about twenty men only, whom you will station (there) under

---

[16]Daniel Greysolon Duluth (Du Lhut) (1636–1710) was a military officer, *coureur de bois*, and explorer who came to Canada in 1676. In 1678 he explored the Sioux country and returned to Quebec in 1681. In 1686 he established Fort St. Joseph at the northern end of River St. Clair. In 1696 he was appointed commandant at Fort Frontenac. The city of Duluth, Minnesota, is named in honor of this great explorer.

[17]Jean Anjalran (Enjalran, Angeliran), (1639–1718), a Jesuit who came to Canada in 1676. The next year he was sent to the Ottawa mission at Michilimackinac, of which he was superior from 1681 to 1688. In 1687 he accompanied Commandant La Durantaye to Niagara. He returned to France in 1688, but was back in Canada before 1701.

[18]Olivier Morel, Sieur de La Durantaye (1640–1716) arrived in Canada in 1665 with the Carignan-Salières Regiment. He seized Fort Frontenac in 1683. That same year he was appointed Commandant at Michilimackinac.

the command of whichever of your lieutenants you may choose as being the fittest for the command, and the one which suits you best.

After you have given all the orders you think necessary for the safety of this post, and have strictly commanded your lieutenant to be on his guard, and enjoined obedience on the others, you will repair to Michilimaquina to wait for the Revd. Father Anjalran there, and receive from him the information and instructions as to all I have communicated to him concerning what I wish from you. After (that) you will return to the said post with thirty more men, whom you will receive from M. de la Durantaye to take the said post. You will be careful to see that everyone provides himself with the provisions necessary for subsistence at the said post, where I have no doubt some trade in furs might be done; hence your men will not do badly to take some few goods there.

I cannot recommend you too strongly to keep up a good understanding with M. de la Durantaye, without which all our plans will come to nothing, and yet the service of the King and the public will suffer greatly from it.

The post to which I am sending you is of all the more importance as I expect it will put us in connection with the Illinois, to whom you will make known the matters of which the Revd. Father will inform you. Depend upon it, nothing could be so important as to apply yourself to carrying out well all that I send you word of, and that I will inform you of through the Revd. Father on his return from Michilimaquina.

I send you the necessary commissions for the command of this post, and for your lieutenant.

I say nothing to you about your own interests, but you may count on my doing, with pleasure, all that may be necessary for your benefit after this; but I will repeat once more that you cannot be too diligent to succeed in all that I wish from you for the interests of the King's service.

I should be very glad if your affairs would permit of your brother being with you next spring, for as he is an intelligent fellow and would be of great assistance to you, he might also be of great use to us.

I beg you to say nothing about our plans, which you may catch a glimpse of, but to evade all that.

A 8   ACT OF RETAKING POSSESSION OF THE LAND IN THE NEIGHBOURHOOD OF THE STRAIT BETWEEN LAKES ERIE AND HURON
[*P.A.C., C2 A, 10;* M.H.C., *XXXIII, 41*]

7th of June, 1787

Ollivier Morel Esquire, Sieur de la Durantaye, Commandant for the King in the lands of the Outaouax, Miamis, Poutouamis, Sioux and other tribes, under orders of the Marquis de Dennonville,[19] Governor-General of New France.

[19]Jacques René de Brisay, Marquis de Denonville (1643–1710) was Governor of Canada from 1685 to 1689. He organized a campaign against the Iroquois in

This seventh day of June, one thousand six hundred and eighty-seven, in the presence of Rev. Father Angeliran, Superior of the missions to the Outaouax at Missilimackinac de Ste. Marie du Sault, to the Miamis, to the Illinois, to the Puans of the Baye,[20] and to the Sioux; (in the presence) of M. de la Forest, formerly commandant at the fort of St. Louis with the Illinois; of M. de Lisle our Lieutenant; and of M. de Beauvais, Lieutenant of the fort of St. Joseph, at the strait between Lakes Huron and Erie, we declare to all whom it may concern that we came to the margin of the St. Denys River situated three leagues from Lake Erie on the strait between the said Lakes Erie and Huron to the south of the said strait and lower down towards the entrance to Lake Erie on the north, on behalf of the King and in his name to repeat the taking possession of the said posts, which was done by M. de la Salle to facilitate the journeys he made, and had made by barge from Niagara to Missilimackinac in the years . . . . at which said stations we should have had a post set up again with the arms of the King, in order to mark the said re-taking possession, and directed several dwellings to be built for the establishment of the French and savages, Chaouannous and Miamis,[21] for a long time owners of the said lands of the strait and of Lake Erie, and from which they withdrew for some time for their greater convenience.

The present deed executed in our presence signed by our hand and by the Rev. Father Angeliran of the Company of Jesus, by M. M. de la Forest, De Lisle and de Beauvais.

Angeliran, Jesuit   Le Gardeur   de Beauvais
De la Durantaye   F. de la Forest

A 9   FRONTENAC[22] TO THE MINISTER
        [M.H.C., *XXXIII, 96*]

Quebec, this 10th October, 1698

The Sr. de la Mothe Cadillac,[23] captain of the Marines, will give you my letters, and will tell you more particularly all that relates to the

---

1687. Two years later he ordered the destruction of Forts Frontenac and Niagara, and was recalled to France.

[20]Puans of the Baye. Tribe of Indians living near Green Bay on the western shore of Lake Michigan. Green Bay was then known as La Baye des Puans, or simply La Baye.

[21]Miamis and Chouanons (Chouannous). Elements of the Illinois tribe which settled at the southern end of Lake Michigan.

[22]Louis Buade, Comte de Frontenac (1622–98) was appointed Governor of New France in 1672. In 1673 he built Fort Cataraqui, later called Fort Frontenac. He was in France 1682–8. He returned as Governor of New France 1689–98 and restored Fort Frontenac 1695. He was antagonistic towards the Jesuits. He died at Quebec.

[23]Antoine Laumet, Sieur de Lamothe Cadillac (1658–1730) arrived in Canada in 1683. He was Commandant at Michilimackinac 1694–7 and the founder of

condition of this country, of which he is fully informed. I am convinced you will be pleased with the account he will give you of it if you will graciously permit him to speak with you about it. He has already done his duty thoroughly well in all matters of the King's service, as I have already informed you in several of my letters, and particularly in the command of the Outaouais, where he was for three years. He is a man who certainly deserves the honor of your patronage.

A 10 CADILLAC TO THE MINISTER
[M.H.C., XXXIII, 96–100]

Quebec, October 18, 1700

It is my duty to give you an exact account of all that I have done regarding the establishment of Detroit since it was referred to you at the time when I was in France, and concerning which you were good enough to converse with me.

M. de Pontchartrain[24] having referred it this year to MM de Calliere[25] and de Champigny[26] to press it on at once, provided there were no important objections, they both approved of it and retained me to carry out the establishment of this Strait which separates Lake Huron from Lake Erie.

It is greatly to be feared that the execution of this scheme has been delayed too long, from the news we have that the English have fortified themselves on a river which discharges itself into Lake Ontario, and that they will extend their posts towards Lake Erie.

If our Colony were not full of envy, disunion, cabal and intrigue, no opposition would have been offered to taking possession of a post (which is) so advantageous that, if it were separated from all those we (now) have, we should be compelled in a short time to abandon all; for it is that alone which will make the Colony and its commerce entirely safe, and cause the certain ruin of the English colonies. For that reason it is very important that it should not pass into other hands, which would be inevitable if we deferred taking it any longer.

The objections which have been raised also at the wrong time, in the belief that this post might cause us to be forever at war with the Iroquois, are now removed by the peace which has been concluded with them.

Detroit 1701. After leaving Detroit in 1711 he became Governor of Louisiana. In 1717 he went back to France where he died.

[24]Louis Phélypeaux, Comte de Pontchartrain (1643–1727). French statesman who became Intendant of Finances in 1687. He was Minister of the Marine and Secretary of State 1689–99, and Chancellor of France 1699–1714.

[25]Louis Hector, Chevalier de Callières (1646–1703) came to Canada in 1684 as Governor of Montreal. In 1689 he was appointed acting Governor of New France in the absence of Count Frontenac. In 1698 he succeeded Frontenac, and signed the peace agreement with the Iroquois in August of 1701.

[26]Jean Brochart de Champigny (c. 1659–1720) was Intendant in New France from 1686 to 1702. He was a close friend of Count Frontenac.

That tribe was not in a position to keep up the war any longer, and will not be able to begin it again very soon; therefore there could not be a more suitable time for establishing Detroit, which will be fortified more quickly than the Iroquois can make up the loss of their numbers.

It is an incontestable fact, that the strength of the savage lies in the remoteness of the French, and that ours increases against them with our proximity. For it is certain that, with a little Indian corn, these people have no difficulty in traversing two hundred leagues to come and take some one's life by stealth; and when we want to get to their lands, we are obliged to provide ourselves with stores of all kinds and to make great preparations, which involves the King in extraordinary expenses, and always with very little effect since it is like beating drums to catch hares.

But, on the contrary, when we are the neighbors of that tribe and are within easy reach of them, they will be kept in awe and will find themselves forced to maintain peace since they will be unable to do otherwise unless they wish to ruin themselves irretrievably.

It would be in vain to establish this post if they would not comply with my memorandum, for if only a garrison pure and simple were kept up there, it would be liable to the revolutions which usually take place in the frontier posts, and it would make no impression on the minds of the Iroquois and of our allies, and much less still on those of the English. In order to succeed thoroughly, it would be well (in my opinion) to adopt the following measures.

1.

To go and station ourselves there with a hundred men, one half of whom should be soldiers and the other Canadians. In order to carry out this expedition with all necessary despatch, and to undeceive the Englishmen at once as to (their) having any claim there and to take from them all hope of establishing any relations with our allies, this strength is sufficient for the first year. For this number is absolutely necessary to me for fortifying (the place) and for taking the proper steps for the subsistence of those who wish to settle there subsequently.

2.

The year after, the fort being secure from insult, it is well to allow twenty or thirty families to settle there, and to bring their cattle and other necessary things which they will willingly do at their own cost and expense; and this may be continued as it is permitted in all the other settlements of the Colony.

3.

It is no less necessary that the King should send two hundred picked men who should, as far as may be, be of different trades and also rather young.

4.

It is not advisable that I, any more than the other officers, soldiers and inhabitants, should do any trade with the savages, in order to take away from the people of the other established posts their cause for complaint, as to which they are very active. But (it is advisable) to unite this business to that of the general company which is formed; in which (case) it will keep up a warehouse to supply all the goods needed by the savages, our allies, and the Iroquois, while letting them have them at a better price than in the past, which can easily be done by conveying them by boats. But as it would be impossible for me to live without doing any trading and with only the 1000 livres pay which I have, which will barely suffice for making the head men of the savages eat and drink at my table so as to attach them to our interests by this good treatment, I hope you will be so good to me as to inform M. de Pontchartrain of this indispensable necessity for increasing it (i.e. the pay), lest I should become absolutely unable to continue my services in the style due to His Majesty.

5.

We must establish at this post missionaries of different communities such as Jesuits and other Fathers, and ecclesiastics of the foreign missions; they are laborers in the vineyard, and should be received without distinction to labor at the vine of the Lord, with orders in particular to teach the young savages the French language (that) being the only means to civilize and humanize them, and to instil into their hearts and their minds the law of religion and of the monarch. We take wild beasts at their birth, birds in their nests, to tame them and set them free. But in order to succeed better in that, it would be necessary for the King to favor these same missionaries with his bounty and his alms, in proportion as they instruct the children of the Savages at their houses, on the evidence which the Commandant and other officers give of it.

6.

The third or fourth year we shall be able to set Ursulines there, or other nuns, to whom His Majesty could grant the same favors.

7.

It would be important that there should be a hospital for sick or infirm Savages, for there is nothing more urgent for gaining their friendship than the care taken of them in their illnesses. The hospitallers of Montreal seem to me well fitted for that, because they know beforehand the temper and the preferences of the Savages (from) often having them with them.

8.

It would be absolutely necessary also to allow the soldiers and Canadians to marry the savage maidens when they have been instructed in religion and know the French language which they will learn all the more eagerly (provided we labor carefully to that end) because they always prefer a Frenchman for a husband to any savage whatever, though I know no other reason for it than the most ordinary one, namely that strangers are preferred, or, it were better to say, it is a secret of the Almighty Power.

9.

Marriages of this kind will strengthen the friendship of these tribes, as the alliances of the Romans perpetuated peace with the Sabines through the intervention of the women whom the former had taken from the others.

We shall find, in the execution of this scheme, not only the glory of His Majesty but also that of God magnificently extended; for by this means his worship and his religion will be established in the midst of the tribes, and the deplorable sacrifices which they offer to Baal entirely abolished.

I am unable to tell you fully enough how my enemies have bestirred themselves to take away from me the honor of carrying out my scheme; and this appears not to have ceased. But MM. de Caliere and de Champigny have not opposed it; on the contrary they have retained me for that so as to begin it next spring. When it was seen that they had resolved on this, everything possible was done to persuade them that my memorandum is impracticable, and I have seen twenty parties formed to upset it. I venture to assure you there is nothing to fear and that everything will be favorable to this undertaking; I (will) answer for it with my life. Monsieur de Pontchartrain will no sooner have given his decision than the whole country will applaud it, according to the policy of all men, who are very glad to find difficulties in all that does not originate with them.

As I am taking my son with me to Detroit, I beg the Minister to be so good as to grant him an ensigncy or an order for the first vacancy; that of my company has been given to the son of M. de Ramezay, with which I am satisfied. I hope you will have the kindness to say a word in my favor to M. de Pontchartrain regarding it. . . .

B. THE FOUNDING OF DETROIT AND THE HURON MISSION

B 1 Callières to Pontchartrain
[M.H.C., *XXXIII, 107*]

Quebec, October 4, 1701

I have already had the honor of notifying to you, My Lord, in my first letter of the 6th of August, that I had sent the Srs. de la Motte, de Tonty,[1] Duqué and Charcornacle[2] on the 7th of June with more than a hundred men, soldiers or Canadians, to establish the post of Detroit, with a recollet as almoner to the soldiers, and a Jesuit as missionary to the savages. You will see from the speeches of Teganisorens and of the other men of importance who accompanied him, which I have inclosed with this letter, under the index letter D, that he opposed it to me, telling me to wait until the chiefs who were to come to Montreal for the peace had arrived. But, as it appeared to me that he had not been commissioned to speak to me on this point, I still proceeded with that enterprise; for I feared lest, if those chiefs had requested me not to establish that post, and I had refused them, that might have given rise to some opposition to the peace, whereas, if they found the matter settled by the departure of the Sr. de la Motte, they would not speak of it; and that is what happened, I having made them approve of the reasons for (forming) that post, in spite of the distrust which the English inspired them with, although they had the intention of going there themselves, as I learnt in the winter, which was yet another reason for hastening the departure of the Sr. de la Motte and for making his detachment as strong as it is, for fear lest the English might anticipate me. I also made the Sonnontouans promise, when they returned to their villages, to take Indian corn there, on the news I had received that the Sr. de la Motte would not find any at Missilimakinac.

The Sr. de Chacornacle has just arrived now from the fort of Detroit, and has brought me letters from the Sr. de la Motte; but, as we are giving you an account, in our joint letter, of what we have learnt from them I will not repeat it for you here.

You will see, My Lord, from what we have the honor to inform you of in the said joint letter, that when we handed over the trade of this fort to the Company, it pledged itself to pay the 6000# [that is, livres]

---

[1] Alphonse de Tonti (Tonty) (1659-1727) was a brother of Henri de Tonti who accompanied La Salle to Lake Michigan on the *Griffon* in 1679. He came to Canada in 1685. He commanded at Detroit 1704-6, at Fort Crèvecœur 1706-8, and again at Detroit 1717-27. He died at Detroit November 10, 1727.

[2] Duqué (Dugué) and Chacornacle were officers in *les troupes de la marine*.

which you were good enough to have decided upon for the relief of the poor families of this country. You have thereby done a very charitable thing, because of the need they have of it; and they are greatly indebted to you for it.

B 2 DESCRIPTION OF THE DETROIT RIVER BY M. DE LAMOTHE, THE COMMANDANT THERE
[M.H.C., *XXXIII, 111–12*]

October 8, 1701

Since the trade of war is not that of a writer, I cannot without rashness draw the portrait of a country so worthy of a better pen than mine; but since you have ordered me to give you an account of it I will do so, telling you that Detroit is, probably, only a canal or a river of moderate breadth, and twenty-five leagues in length according to my reckoning lying north-north-east, and south-south-west about the 41st degree (of latitude), through which the sparkling and pellucid waters of Lakes Superior, Michigan and Huron (which are so many seas of sweet water) flow and glide away gently and with a moderate current into Lake Erie, into the Ontario or Frontenac, and go at last to mingle in the river St. Lawrence with those of the ocean. The banks are so many vast meadows where the freshness of these beautiful streams keep the grass always green. These same meadows are fringed with long and broad avenues of fruit trees which have never felt the careful hand of the watchful gardener; and fruit trees, young and old, droop under the weight and multitude of their fruit, and bend their branches towards the fertile soil which has produced them. In this soil so fertile, the ambitious vine which has not yet wept under the knife of the industrious vine-dresser, forms a thick roof with its broad leaves and its heavy clusters over the head of whatever it twines round, which it often stifles by embracing it too closely. Under these vast avenues you may see assembling in hundreds the shy stag and the timid hind with the bounding roebuck, to pick up eagerly the apples and plums with which the ground is paved. It is there that the careful turkey hen calls back her numerous brood, and leads them to gather the grapes; it is there that their big cocks come to fill their broad and gluttonous crops. The golden pheasant, the quail, the partridge, the woodcock, the teeming turtle-dove, swarm in the woods and cover the open country intersected and broken by groves of full-grown forest trees which form a charming prospect which of itself might sweeten the melancholy tedium of solitude. There the hand of the pitiless mower has never shorn the juicy grass on which bisons of enormous height and size fatten.

The woods are of six kinds,—walnut trees, white oaks, red, bastard ash, ivy, white wood trees and cottonwood trees. But these same trees are as straight as arrows, without knots, and almost without branches except near the top, and of enormous size and height. It is from thence that the fearless eagle looks steadily at the sun, seeing beneath him enough to glut his formidable claws.

The fish there are fed and laved in sparkling and pellucid waters, and are none the less delicious for the bountiful supply (of them). There are such large numbers of swans that the rushes among which they are massed might be taken for lilies. The gabbling goose, the duck, the teal and the bustard are so common there that, in order to satisfy you of it, I will only make use of the expression of one of the savages, of whom I asked before I got there whether there was much game there; "there is so much" he told me, "that it only moves aside (long enough) to allow the boat to pass."

Can it be thought that a land in which nature has distributed everything in so complete a manner could refuse to the hand of a careful husbandman who breaks into its fertile depths, the return which is expected of it?

In a word, the climate is temperate, the air very pure; during the day there is a gentle wind, and at night the sky, which is always placid, diffuses sweet and cool influences which cause us to enjoy the benignity of tranquil sleep.

If its position is pleasing, it is no less important, for it opens or closes the approach to the most distant tribes which surround these vast sweet water seas.

It is only the opponents of the truth who are the enemies of this settlement, so essential to the increase of the glory of the King, to the spread of religion, and to the destruction of the throne of Baal.

B 3 Germain[3] to Cadillac
[M.H.C., *XXXIII, 104*]

At Quebec, this 25th Augt. 1701

Although we have not yet had positive and certain news of your arrival at Detroit, we have nevertheless conjunctures strong enough for (us) to judge that you must have arrived there safely in the month of July. As you know, Sir, that I take great interest in whatever concerns you, allow me to congratulate you and to pray our Lord, as I do with all my heart, graciously to bless all your plans for the good of the missions and of the Colony. So long as you have these two things in view, you cannot fail to have good success in your undertakings not only as regards public matters but also in your private concerns. Everyone here admires the magnanimity of these two ladies who certainly have courage to undertake so laborious a journey to go and join their husbands, without fearing the great difficulties or the fatigue or other

---

[3] Joseph Germain (1633–1722), a Jesuit, arrived in Canada in 1687. For the next twenty years he taught theology at the College of Quebec. He was acting Superior of the Canadian missions in 1699, and was appointed Superior in 1710, a post he filled for five years.

inconveniences which must be endured by roads so long and so rough for persons of their sex. Well! Sir, is it possible to show more sincere conjugal affection or a firmer attachment?

Some one said pleasantly to them the other day that they would pass for heroines. But on some other ladies, more fastidious, saying to Madame de la Mothe, in order to dissuade her from this journey, that that would be well if they were going to a pleasant and fertile country, where they could always get good company as in France, but they could not understand how people could make up their minds to go to an uncultivated and uninhabited place where they could not but have a very dull time of it in such great solitude, she very discreetly replied that a woman who loves her husband as she ought to do has no attraction more powerful than his society, in whatever place it may be; all the rest should be indifferent to her; those are her opinions. I do not send you other news, she herself will tell you by word of mouth better than I could in writing everything new we have learnt since your departure. Be assured, Sir, that I often recommend your two dear daughters to the Ursulines, and that I will try to contribute to their education as far as it may lie in my power. Young Cadillac promised me to embrace his brother once for me when he arrives at Detroit; if he forgets to do me this little service, reprimand him lightly. I am not writing to any of our Fathers, because I have no doubt that Father Vaillant will have set out to return here before Madame de la Mothe arrives at Detroit, and I do not know whether any other will be allowed (to go there) in his place. Do me the favor to grant me some share in your good-will and the justice to believe that I shall ever be with all possible respect, Sir, your very humble and very obedient servant.

B 4 EXTRACTS FROM CADILLAC'S DESCRIPTION OF DETROIT IN 1702
[M.H.C., *XXXIII, 133–51*]

Quebec, Sept. 25, 1702

... This country, so temperate, so fertile, and so beautiful that it may justly be called the earthly paradise of North America, deserves all the care of the King to keep it up and to attract inhabitants to it, so that a solid settlement may be formed there which shall not be liable to the usual vicissitudes of the other posts in which only a mere garrison is placed. ...

... You will see annexed the plan of Fort Pontchartrain which I have had built at Detroit—I have thus named it by the order of the Chev. de Calliere—and the map of Detroit. The houses there are of good timber, of white oak, which is even and hard and as heavy as iron. This fort is in no danger provided there are enough people there to defend it.

Its position is delightful and very advantageous; it is (at) the narrowest part of the river, where no one can pass by day without being seen.

You know that I set out from Montreal on the 2nd of June, 1701, with 100 men and three month's provisions; that I arrived at Detroit on the 24th of July, having gone by the ordinary route of the Utauais, by which I made only 30 portages, in order to try it.

After the fort was built, and the dwellings, I had the land cleared there and some French wheat sown on the 7th of October, not having had time to prepare it well. This wheat, although sown hastily, came up very fine and was cut on the 21st of July.

I also had some sown this spring, as is done in Canada; it came up well enough, but not like that of the autumn. The land having thus shown its quality, and taught me that the French tillage must be followed, I left orders with M. de Tonty to take care to begin the sowing about the 20th of Sept., and I left him 20 arpents of land prepared. I have no doubt he has increased it somewhat since my departure.

I also had twelve arpents or more sown this spring, in the month of May, with Indian corn which came up eight feet high; it will have been harvested about the 20th of the month of August, and I hope there will be a good deal of it. All the soldiers have their own gardens.

I believe we shall have 60 arpents of land sown this next spring, hence I count on having a large quantity of corn; and I will have a mill built on the spot, so as to be absolutely independent of Canada for provisions. I have also a fine garden in which I have put some vines, and some ungrafted fruit trees. It is one arpent square, and we shall enlarge it if necessary. In all this I have only complied with the orders of the Governor-General.

All that is no easy task, especially as everything has to be carried on the shoulders, for we have no oxen or horses yet to draw (loads) nor to plough; and to accomplish it, it is necessary to be very active.

I have also had a boat of ten tons burden built which will be useful for many purposes in the river.

On the right of the fort, at a good distance, there is a village of the Hurons to which I have granted lands in the name of His Majesty, according to my order. The chief of this tribe, with four of the most important men, in accepting them shouted "Long Live the King" three times with me; and I have myself set up the landmarks, and marked out the place where I wished them to build their fort and their village. By this means I have set all the tribes on the track of asking me for lands, and for permission to settle there. Having shown the others the way, this tribe has cleared up to the present about 200 arpents of land, and will make a great harvest.

There is also, on the left of the fort, a village of Oppenago, that is, of Wolves, to whom I have likewise granted lands, on condition, however, of giving them up to me if I want them afterwards, on granting them others further off; the spot where they are might be useful for a common land hereafter. These are the most tractable and most peaceable of the savages. I am convinced that, if only a little care is taken of them, they will very soon become Christians. They dress like the French, as far as they can; they are very caressing; they even make rough attempts at our language as far as they can. They have also made fine fields of wheat.

Above this village, half a league higher up, there is a village made up of four tribes of the Outavois, to whom I have likewise granted lands; they have made some very fine fields of Indian corn there. Thus, within the space of one league, there are four forts and four hundred men bearing arms with their families, besides the garrison.

Before I set out from the fort, eighteen Miamis came, on behalf of their tribe, to ask me for lands and to beg the savages who are there to approve of their coming to settle there and joining them. Thus the settlements could not promise better; these having prepared the way, the others will not be long before they come there, especially as, before I left, we learnt that the corn at Missilimakinak had been killed this year by the frost as it was the preceding (year), a thing which very often happens at that place.

Last year, my wife and Mme. Tonty set out on the 10th of Sept. with our families to come and join us there. Their resolution in undertaking so long and laborious a journey seemed very extraordinary. It is certain that nothing (ever) astonished the Iroquois so greatly as when they saw them. You could not believe how many caresses they offered them, and particularly the Iroquois who kissed their hands and wept for joy, saying that French women had never been seen coming willingly to their country. It was that which made the Iroquois also say that they well knew that the general peace which the Chev. de Calliere had just made was indeed sincere, and that they could no longer doubt it since women of this rank came amongst them with so much confidence. If these ladies gave favorable impressions regarding us to the Iroquois, those our allies received from them were no less so. They received them at Detroit under arms with many discharges of musketry. They looked upon this move as the most important that could be made to prove to them that we wished to settle there in earnest, and that we wished to make it a post to dwell in, and a flourishing settlement. . . .

B 5 EXTRACTS FROM CADILLAC'S REPORT OF DETROIT IN 1703
[M.H.C., *XXXIII, 161–81*]

Fort Pontchartrain, Aug. 31, 1703

. . . It is for you, My Lord, to consider whether you wish me to continue to get the savages to settle here, and for this post to be preserved and maintained in a flourishing state. If those are your opinions as I believe, I am perhaps fitted to have them carried out; but I venture to tell you that the intentions of the Jesuits of this country are entirely opposed to yours, at least on that point.

All that has not prevented the Sauteurs and Mississaguez from coming this year and forming another village on this river. These two tribes have united and incorporated (themselves) with one another, having followed my advice in that, and done my will. I thought this advisable, considering that their union will be an advantage to them, and to us if any rupture occurred with the enemies of the State and of the Colony.

Thirty Hurons from Missilimakinak arrived here on the 28th of June to incorporate themselves with those who have settled here. Thus only about twenty-five of them remain at that place, where Father de Carheil,[4] their missionary, remains ever resolute. This autumn I hope finally to tear this last feather from his wing; and I am convinced that this obstinate vicar will die in his parish without having a parishoner to bury him.

Several households and families of the Miamis have also settled here, as well as some Nepissiriniens; the first have incorporated themselves with the Hurons and the others with the Outavois, and the Oppenago or Wolves.

The rest of the Sinago Outavois, who are still at Missilimakinak, have secretly sent me a belt to tell me they will come and join their brothers of Detroit after they have gathered their harvest. Six large households of the Kiskakouns have sent to me to say the same thing. I replied to them by a belt that I was going to mark out the lands where they may make their fields.

... It is right that you should be informed that, more than fifty years ago, the Iroquois drove most of the tribes by force of arms to the end of Lake Superior, that is, five hundred leagues to the north of this post, which is a barren and fearful country; and that about thirty-two years ago we brought them together again in the district of Missilimakinak which is also unfruitful, where they have been reduced to the necessity of living on fish only as I explained to you in a short description when I was in France, with which you were good enough to tell me you were well pleased. It appears, therefore, that God has raised me up like another Moses, to go and deliver this people from its captivity, or like another Caleb to bring it back to the land of its fathers and its former dwelling place, of which only feeble recollections still remained to it.

But Montreal plays the part of Pharaoh here; it cannot witness this migration without a shudder, and arms itself to confound it. ...

... What does Montreal complain of concerning the post of Detroit since it was an abandoned country, the possession of which had remained with the neighboring district, and brought its hides, beaverskins, and small furs to the English. This is an unanswerable fact, and anyone must be filled with obstinacy and injustice to deny it. Then I have chosen my

---

[4]Etienne de Carheil (1633–1726), a Jesuit who came to Canada in 1666 and laboured among the Iroquois. In 1686 he was assigned to the mission among the Hurons and Ottawas at Mackinac. He returned to Quebec in 1703. He left two MS volumes on the Huron languages entitled "Racines Huronnes."

time well for beginning this settlement; the Iroquois have entirely withdrawn or, if any remain, they are incorporated with our allies. All the hunting is done by our savages, and all the trade falls to us. It is therefore an advantage to our kingdom, and a possession which we have withdrawn and snatched from England. Private individuals complain that the Company of the Colony profits by it; I do not deny it, I leave them free to complain. Only I wish they had eyes, to be able to see that this is not the fault of the post nor of him who originated the plan for it. . . .

B 6 MEMORANDUM ON INDIANS AT DETROIT[5]
[N.Y.C.D., *IX, 887–8*]

The village of the Poutouatamies adjoins the fort; they lodge partly under Apaquois, which are made of mat grass. The women do all this work. The men belonging to that nation are well clothed, like our domiciled Indians at Montreal; their entire occupation is hunting and dress; they make use of a great deal of vermillion, and in the winter wear buffalo robes richly painted, and in summer, either red or blue cloth. They play a good deal at La Crosse in summer, twenty or more on each side. Their bat is a sort of little racquet, and the ball with which they play is made of very heavy wood, somewhat larger than the balls used at tennis. When playing, they are entirely naked, except a breech cloth, and moccasins on their feet; their body is completely painted with all sorts of colors, Some, with white clay, trace white lace on their bodies, as if on all the seams of a coat, and at a distance it would be taken for silver lace. They play very steep (for heavy stakes) and often. The bets sometimes amount to more than eight hundred livres. They set up two poles and commence the game from the center; one party propels the ball from one side and the others from the opposite, and whichever reaches the goal wins. This is fine recreation and well worth seeing. They often play village against village; the Poux against the Outaouacs or the Hurons, and lay heavy stakes. Sometimes Frenchmen join in the game with them.

The women cultivate Indian corn, beans, pease, squashes and melons, which come up very fine. The women and girls dance at night; adorn themselves considerably, grease their hair, put on a white shift, paint their cheeks with vermillion, and wear whatever wampum they possess, and are very tidy in their way. They dance to the sound of the drum and Sisiquoi, which is a sort of gourd containing some grains of shot. Four or five young men sing and beat time with the drum and Sisiquoi, and the women keep time and do not lose a step; it is very entertaining and lasts almost the entire night. The old men often dance the medelline; they resemble a set of demons and all this takes place during the night.

[5]This is an extract from a longer article entitled "Memoir on the Indians between Lake Erie and the Mississippi." The memoir is dated 1718, and is anonymous.

The young men often dance in a circle and strike posts; it is then they recount their achievements, and dance, at the same time, the war dance, and whenever they act thus they are highly ornamented. It is altogether very curious. They often perform these things for tobacco. When they go hunting which is every fall they carry their Apaquois with them to hut under at night. Everybody follows, men, women and children, and winter in the forest and return in the spring.

The Hurons are also very near; perhaps the eighth of a league from the French fort. This is the most industrious nation that can be seen. They scarcely ever dance, and are always at work. They raise a very large amount of Indian corn, peas, beans; some grow wheat. They construct their huts entirely of bark, very strong and solid; very lofty and very long, and arched like arbors. Their fort is strongly encircled with pickets and bastions, well redoubled, and has strong gates. They are the most faithful nation to the French, and the most expert hunters that we have. Their cabins are divided into sleeping compartments, which contain their Misirague, and are very clean. They are the bravest of all the nations, and possess considerable talent. They are well clad; some of them wear close-fitting coats. The men are always hunting, summer and winter, and the women work. When they go hunting in the fall, a goodly number of them remain to guard the fort. The old women, and throughout the winter those women who remain, collect wood in very large quantities. The soil is fertile; Indian corn grows there to the height of ten to twelve feet; the fields are very clean, and very extensive; not the smallest weed is to be seen in them.

The Outaoues are on the opposite side of the river, over against the French fort. Their cabins resemble somewhat those of the Hurons. They do not make use of the Apaquois except when out hunting; their cabins in this fort are all bark, but not so clean nor so well made as those of the Hurons. They, likewise, have a picket fort. They are well dressed, and very laborious, both in their agriculture and hunting. . . . Their dances, juggleries and games of ball and of the Bowl are the same as those of the Poux. Their game of Bowl consists of eight small pebbles, which are red or black on one side, and yellow or white on the other; these are tossed up in a bowl, and when he who holds the vessel tosses them and finds seven or the whole eight of the same color he gains . . . and continues playing as long as he achieves the same thing. When the result is different, the adverse party takes the bowl and plays next, and they risk heavy stakes on all these games. They have likewise the game of the Straws, and all the nations gamble in like manner.

The Hurons number one hundred men; the Poux, 180; the Outaouaes about one hundred men and a number of women. . . . Twelve leagues from Fort Detroit, always going up the river, you will find the Misisague Indians, who occupy a beautiful Island where they raise their crops. They are about 60 or 80 men. Their language resembles that of the Outaouae; there is very little difference between them, Their customs are the same, and they are very industrious. All these nations construct a great many bark canoes, which is a great assistance to them; they occupy themselves in this sort of work; the women sew the canoes with roots; the men finish them and make the ribs, smoothen and floor them, and the women gum them. It costs some labor to build a canoe; it requires considerable pains and preparations, which are curious to behold.

B 7 EXTRACTS FROM THE ANSWER OF MM. VAUDREUIL AND BÉGON[6] TO CADILLAC'S PETITION TO BE PUT IN POSSESSION OF DETROIT
[M.H.C., *XXXIII,679-80*]

Quebec, Nov. 4, 1721

To the south-west of the fort, inclining towards Lake Erie, are the Hurons and the Poutouatamis who occupy a league of the above stretch (of frontage). To the south on the other side of the river, are the Outaouais who, together with the Hurons and Poutouatamis have made wastes containing about two leagues frontage by eight arpents deep. Above the Lake St. Clair, twelve leagues from the fort on the south side is a village of Mississagues and Sauteurs whose waste lands contain about three quarters of a league frontage by fifteen arpents deep. . . .

The tribe of the Outaouais consists of 130 men; that of the Poutoutamis, of 150 men; that of the Hurons of 120; and that of the Mississagues and Sauteurs of 100.

B 8 CHARLEVOIX[7] AT DETROIT
[*Charlevoix, Journal d'un voyage, V, 376-83*]

Fort Pontchartrain, June 8, 1721

On the fourth [of June] we spent a good part of the day on a point which runs north and south three leagues, and which is called Pointe Pelée. It is however well enough wooded on the west side, but the east side is a sandy tract of land with nothing but red cedars that are quite small and not in an abundant quantity. . . . There are a great number of bears in this part of the country, and last winter more than four hundred were killed on Pointe Pelée alone.

On the fifth . . . we entered the Straits an hour before sunset, and spent the night above a beautiful island called the Island of Bois Blanc. . . .

Before you arrive at the fort, which stands on the left, a league below the island of St. Claire [now Belle Isle], you find on the same side two

---

[6]Vaudreuil and Bégon. Governor (1703-25) and Intendant (1712-26) of New France respectively.

[7]Pierre François Xavier Charlevoix (1682-1761), a Jesuit, arrived in Canada in 1705. In 1721 he visited the French colonies in America. He returned to France the following year. In 1744 he published a history of New France.

pretty populous villages very near each other; the first is inhabited by the Tionnontatez, a tribe of the Hurons, and the same who after having wandered to and fro for a long time, first settled at the falls of St. Mary and at Michillimackinac; the second is inhabited by the Potawatomi Indians. On the right, somewhat higher is a third village of the Ottawas, inseparable companions of the Hurons from the time that both of them were driven from their country by the Iroquois. There are no Christians at all amongst these last, and few, if any, among the Potawatomis; the Hurons are all Christians, but have no missionaries. It is said they will admit of none, but is only true of a few of their principal men who have not much religion, and who do not suffer the others to be heard, who have been a long time desirous of having missionaries sent them.

For a long time the strategic position, even more than the beauty of the land about the Straits, has made people desire that a large settlement be established at that place. A fairly good start was made on it fifteen years ago, but for some unmentioned reasons it has been reduced to practically nothing. . . .

The following day I visited the two Indian villages near the fort. I began with that of the Hurons where I found all the matrons, amongst them the grandmother of Sasteratsi, in much affliction for being so long deprived of every spiritual succour. Many circumstances which I learned at the same time confirmed me in the opinion that certain private interests were the sole obstacles to the desires of these good Christians. It is to be hoped that the last orders of the council of the Marine will remove all those obstacles; Monsieur de Tonti assured me he was going to set about it in an effectual manner.

B 9   LA RICHARDIE[8] TO RETZ[9]
[*General Jesuit Archives, Rome, Gal. 110, vol. II, folios 348-9;*
Thwaites, Jesuit Relations, LXIV, 50-4]

21st June, 1741, Mission of the Assumption of the
Blessed Virgin Mary among the Hurons

Since Father Girandeau has frequently informed me that it would please your Paternity, were I to compose a brief account of the beginnings and progress of the Huron Mission, I gladly fulfil the duty of a most obedient son, considering that that alone above all is most pleasing to your Paternity which contributes to the glory of God. Let your paternity know that the first charge given me was the instruction of children among the Iroquois. After two years among them, Reverend

[8] Armand de La Richardie (1686-1758), Jesuit, came to Canada in 1727. The following year he was sent to Detroit as missionary to the Hurons. There he laboured until 1751 when he returned to Quebec. He died at Quebec on March 17, 1758.

[9] Franciscus Retz (1673-1750) became Superior-General of the Jesuits on November 30, 1730—a post he filled for nearly twenty years.

Father Du Parc,[10] at that time superior of the mission, under divine inspiration as the outcome showed, desired to discover whether the Huron people were far from the kingdom of God and commissioned this district to me, though most unworthy. How many years did I labour without winning any souls!—though in my opinion my work was not good. Finally a ray of divine grace shone through and the fire of the Holy Spirit softened their adamantine hearts.

When I came, I did not find even one barbarian who professed the Christian faith, although some of the older people, having been once upon a time the victims of disease, had been baptized by the first missionaries. Almost forty years ago, shaking the dust from their feet, these missionaries had abandoned this people, uncircumcised at heart. One, Hoosiens by name, having embraced the christian faith after much delay, was such an example to all his kinsmen, that of his whole family not even one resisted the Holy Spirit. But after a short time, he was taken from among the living and scarcely the slightest hope remained of bringing this barbarous throng to the sweet service of Christ. Indeed I myself, forgetful of the depth of divine knowledge, was almost ready to leave, thinking that with the death of this leading man, who was the indefatigable protector of the christian cause, the hope of promoting the glory of God was also dead. While my discouraged spirit hovered amid such uncertainty, the kindness of our Saviour appeard, for barbarians of both sexes and of every age, contrary to all my hopes and after many futile attempts, hastened to attend the exposition of christian doctrine and the public conferences held at the cross-roads. Under the impulse of divine grace, the work of God so flourished that scarcely three years after the death of that illustrious leader, not even one pagan remained among the whole people.

As for the present, Very Reverend Father, I believe that all things are safely under control. A barbarous people seem to profess the faith with unfeigned heart. The sacred edifice, though seventy cubits long, scarcely contains the multitude of christians. Three times a day we gather to pray and to listen to an instruction; four times on feast days, when especially there scarcely remains time to eat, a witness to their fervour in approaching the sacred tribunal. Our daily labour consists in visiting the sick, settling controversies, correcting the delinquent, holding conferences, instructing the children and administering the sacraments. Having pity on me, now nearly sixty years old, Reverend Father St. Pé,[11] superior of the mission, has provided me with an associate who gives himself entirely in the care of this vineyard of the Lord. Now an old man, with almost no health left, I deeply regret, Very Reverend Father, that I find myself incapable of learning the languages

---

[10]Jean Baptiste Du Parc (1676–1742), Jesuit, came to Canada in 1707. He was Superior of the Canadian missions 1726–32.

[11]Jean Baptiste St. Pé (1686–1763), Jesuit, was at Mackinac 1735–6, and Superior of the Canadian missions 1739–48.

of the barbarians who dwell around about and who have not yet been washed in the sacred font. Now that there is someone left to care for God's work in this mission, I would gladly go to other peoples lest I experience a complete loss of that memory which I formerly enjoyed. However, I have every hope for their conversion in view of the fact that Reverend Father St. Pé is afire with zeal for God's glory; while I regretted that his zeal was almost extinct before he was placed in charge, I now rejoice that it is reviving.

May the merciful God grant that your Paternity give him as superior to this most beloved mission as long as he shall live, so that thus religious discipline may flourish in the houses of the Society. I observe zeal in the missions. But if it should please your Paternity that I pursue the care of the Huron mission for a longer time, I shall obey your instructions.

Secretary's summary:
1741 Canadian Missions
From the Mission of the Assumption of the Blessed Virgin among the Hurons, June 21.
Father Armand de la Richardie writes that already in his mission not even one pagan remains etc. . . .
A letter full of edification and consolation; it has been made known to the Holy Father
Answered Jan. 18, 1742.

B 10   Extract from the Journal of the Most Interesting Occurences in Canada 1746–7
[N.Y.C.D., *X, 114–15*]

We are in receipt of letters both from Montreal and Detroit; those from Detroit are very interesting. Chevalier de Longueuil,[12] commanding the post, writes us on the 23rd June, that some Hurons of Detroit, belonging to the tribe of the war chief Nicolas, who, some years since, had settled at Sandoske, have killed five Frenchmen who were on their return from the post at the White River, and stolen their furs; that all the Indians of the neighborhood, except the Illinois, had formed the design to destroy all the French of Detroit on one of the holidays of Pentecost, and afterwards to go to the fort and subject all to fire and sword; that some Hurons having struck too soon, the plot had been discovered by a Huron squaw who came to give Chevalier de Longueuil notice of it; that this conspiracy is the fruit of belts the English have had distributed among all the tribes by the Iroquois of the 5 Nations; that on this notification he caused all the settlers to retire within the fort in order to

[12]Paul Joseph Le Moyne, Chevalier de Longueuil (1701–78) was Commandant at Detroit 1743–8. Subsequently he was named Governor of Three Rivers and then Commandant at the Citadel of Quebec.

be prepared for any new treachery. The Outaouas have spoken at Detroit, and have given assurances that they had no participation in this bad business. Other Hurons of Sastaredsy and Taychatin's Tribe came also to speak to Mr. de Longueuil, and have, in like manner, assured him that they had no share in the misconduct of Nicolas' people, meanwhile asking pardon they endeavour to exculpate themselves, and propose settling near Detroit. Mr. de Longueuil has given them no positive answer, and has referred them to the General. Nicolas' tribe continues nevertheless to reside at Sandoske, where, says Mr. de Longueuil, they doubtless expect not only to maintain themselves but even to harass Detroit by small war parties. They have attached to them several families of vagabond Iroquois, Loups &c. 'Tis even asserted that there are some Saut Indians among them. Father Potier,[13] the Jesuit Missionary, has abandoned the village on Bois Blanc Island, and retired to Detroit where he is to remain.

B 11 Extracts from the account Book of the Huron Mission [B.H.C.]

[1743]

I owe Meloche[14] for all the buildings that he has erected and that he is to erect for me 3100 livres.

I owe Janis[15] for the masonry of the said buildings 600 livres............ also to the same 10 livres for the farmer's house and stable............also to the same 100 livres for minor repairs and for what he did for the blacksmith. This last item is to be paid only in 1744. Also 30 livres for the partitions. On which I have paid him 48 livres in wheat. Also paid to the same 160 livres. Also 100 livres that he accepts on what Cecile owes me. Also 227 livres. The 635 livres are paid. Hence I do not owe Janis anything for the church and the house. I still owe him for the farmer's house and other work the sum of 200 livres less 21 livres and 15 sous. The said sum is paid.

I gave Lesperance on his wages 100 livres. I still owe him 34 livres and 10 sous. I owe Prisq. 56 livres. I have finished paying Lesperance.

I have paid Meloche for my buildings 985 livres that he got from Cuillerier who owed them to me; 4 livres from Valet who owed them to me; 101 livres in racoon skins that I gave him. Total amount given to

[13]Pierre Potier (1708–81), Jesuit, arrived at Quebec in 1743. The following year he was sent to the Huron mission at Detroit, where he laboured for 37 years. He died at l'Assomption du Détroit, July 16, 1781.

[14]Pierre Meloche was the contractor for the timber and framework of the buildings. His sawmill was on the south side above the village of the Ottawas, while his residence was on the north side above the fort, near Parent's Creek.

[15]Nicolas François Janis who did the stone and mason work was married to Meloche's sister, and at this time he also resided on the north side.

the said (Meloche) 1090 livres. The same has received from the Carons to my credit the sum of 300 livres. Total 1390 livres. From Binau for my farm 1900 livres. The said Meloche is paid for all that I owed him except 90 livres that Mini or Binau will pay him next year 1744, as the said Meloche has agreed. Also to the same 10 masses which he asked me to say for Saguin.

This mission owes nothing except for the shipment of goods that Sir de Couagne sent me this year 1743.

I loaned St. Martin the 161 livres coming to me from his work in the forge for Le Roy. This is to be paid at Montreal.

On this day, July 2, 1743, Sir Jean Bapt. Goyau, resident of the post of Detroit, has agreed to move here with all his family during the month of September to take charge of the farm of the Jesuit mission on the following terms:

1. The said Fathers lease the said farm to the said Goyau for a term of six years; should he not be satisfied with the Reverend Fathers or vice-versa, either party shall be free to terminate the agreement by giving notice to the other one year in advance.

2. The said Reverend Fathers shall supply the said Goyau with the seed for all the grain that he will sow on the farm, and they will share with him in equal portions the produce of the said seed, and the said Goyau shall not be at liberty to sow on the said farm anything at all for himself or his family without sharing the said produce, except some corn that he may want to plant for his own use. And in order that the Reverend Fathers may not lack any (corn), he will plough for them each year two arpents of land in which they may be able to plant some for their own use.

3. An inventory shall be taken of all the implements and the cart and plough harnesses that the said Reverend Fathers will hand over to the said Goyau in order that he may return them all in the same state and condition as that in which he received them.

4. As regards the animals, he shall be obliged to return at the end of the lease the same number in the same condition as he received them, or may hereafter receive, together with one half of the increase of these animals.

5. He shall make a suitable enclosure for the keeping and pasturing of the said animals, and shall keep in order the fences on the farm that will be handed over to him, which he shall leave in good condition at the end of his lease.

6. The said Reverend Fathers agree that the said Goyau may use their animals for carting and ploughing both for the French and the Indians.

The whole is on condition that he shall haul every winter forty cords of wood for their fuel and for their share of the blacksmith's forge. Moreover the said Goyau shall be obliged to lend the said animals to the said Reverend Fathers for hauling and carting whenever they shall need the same.

I gave to Goyau when he started working this farm of the Island of Bois Blancs: 6½ bushels of peas for seed, 5 bushels of oats for the same purpose, and 14½ bushels of wheat for seed, which seed he shall return when he leaves the farm. Besides I have given to the same a brand new plough complete with wheels, a cart with almost new wheels, a new sled, 3 Illinois oxen with a cow of the same breed, 2 mares each worth 80 livres. The whole cost 400 livres. Besides I gave him two cows bred in this part of the country and a yearling heifer.

To replace the 3 cows that died or were killed while in Goyau's keeping, I have given him 2 Illinois heifers, one of which cost 40 livres and the other 75 livres. I also gave him an Illinois heifer which I exchanged for a cow that had not calfed that year.

Madame Goyau began to do the laundry-work and the baking for this mission on the feast of St. Michael 1743 for the sum of 100 livres per year.

Madame Goyau has received a shirt worth 3 livres 10 sous; a quart of brandy—3 livres; a quart of brandy—3 livres; 3 livres; a pair of molleton leggings; a pair of molleton leggings; a quart of brandy; 2 bushels of peas—18 livres; 6 blankets—54 livres; a pair of leggings—3 livres. Madame is paid in full for the first year.

I lent Mallet 3 quarts of brandy............3 pounds of powder............5 pounds of shot............one blue blanket............3 large shirts............3 small shirts (P. Degonor[16]).

Received from Mallet 6 roebucks............16 turkeys............6 bustards ....1 swan............8 ducks............1 hind quarter of a bear............5 or 6 partridges............2 small beavers &c. (P. Degonor).

. . .

[1748]

I have contracted with Meloche for the framework of my church, house, roof, &c. for the sum of 1000 livres............also for boards and planks at 60 livres a hundred, and for what he will saw for me at 30 livres a hundred.

---

[16]Nicolas De Gonnor (1691–1759), Jesuit, came to Canada in 1725. Two years later he went to the Sioux mission. Besides the one year spent at Detroit (1743–4) he laboured at the Lorette mission near Quebec and at the Iroquois mission at Sault St. Louis near Montreal.

Item with Janis for two stone chimneys and hearths; for lathing, roughcasting, plastering and white-washing the whole of the above that Meloche is to build for me; for the sum of 850 livres and three bushels of corn. If he plasters the outside, I shall have to pay him 1300 livres extra.

Item with Parent for all the carpentry of the said buildings for the sum of 1000 livres and 2 bushels of corn. Of the 1000 livres, 400 are payable here, and the other 600 are payable at Montreal.

I owe Regis 5½ bushels of corn that I took from his share. I owe him also 6 pounds of deerskin.

I shall owe Morand for 100 pieces of sawed pine 250 livres. To Mini for the frame of the church, and for roof and frame of the house 400 livres in notes. To Claude and Niagara for carting boards and planks 40 livres. Also to the same for the carting of Mini's raft 100 livres less 10 sous.

The Commandant has paid Mini 500 livres.

Niagara took over the farm of this mission September 1, 1748, on condition of sharing all the produce thereof with the Fathers of the said mission. I have supplied him 30 bushels of wheat seed, 4 bushels of peas, a new plough equipped with new wheels and plough share. I gave him 4 Illinois oxen, 4 cows of the same breed, a young horse and an old mare. I also advanced to him 150 livres to build himself a house and a stable. The whole on condition that he shall haul every winter 40 cords of firewood, and that he shall plough each year 3 arpents of land for planting corn for the benefit of the mission. Besides I have advanced to the said Niagara the sum of 200 livres for doing our laundry and baking for two years. On the expiration of these two years he will be obliged to do our laundry and baking throughout the duration of his lease in consideration of 100 livres per year which the mission will pay him at the end of his lease. He shall give back the implements in the same condition as he received them. The same for the animals, and he will share the increase thereof. The original stock (of animals) shall also be returned.

[1749]

On April 10, 1749, Mr. Chauvin took over the forge of this mission on the following conditions:

1. That all the implements of the forge be handed over to him.
2. That he receive the steel and files that will come from Montreal each year.
3. That he will build himself a forge at the said mission and a house whenever he can.

4. That on being supplied with iron he will be obliged to make or repair anything necessary for the buildings and use of the mission, and even weapons—the whole free of charge. In consideration of the above the mission gives him all the profit of the said forge, provided he pay to the missionaries a yearly sum of 300 livres.

Boards—Robert has sawed 126 boards for me; also 57 boards; 7 livres, 10 sous for carting, 47 livres, 10 sous for sawing. Niagara brought here from Meloche's mill 253 boards; also 90 planks; also 293 boards—total 560. Carting 39 livres. Regis carted for me from Meloche's 192 planks of white pine; also 40 planks 15 feet long.

Parent took at our house in the fort: 21 planks or boards; 15 here; 7 more here; 4 at Meloche's; 14 at Robert's, and 12 that Regis gave him.

I paid Moran 250 livres for the sawed lumber that I received from him.

I paid Claude Campeau 82 livres for what I owe him for carting and a boat-load of stone.

Barthe and Dumouchel have paid me in full for the steel that I sold them.

I received from widow Caron 33 livres through Paget, and 140 pounds of shot.

Meloche—I have paid him in small furs 100 livres less 10 sous on account of his work. Also 30 livres paid to my credit by Madame Caron. Also 100 pistoles paid to him on my account by Sir Carignan, trader at Detroit. Also 300 livres paid to the aforesaid by Mr. Navarre. He is paid in full.

Janis—I have paid him in small furs 39 livres, 10 sous on account of his work. Also 160 livres that Pierrot Labute and Carignan paid him. Also 60 livres that Madam Caron paid him for me. Also 10 livres that I paid him. Also 268 livres paid him to my credit by Sir Gouin, trader at Detroit. Also 259 livres to the aforesaid by Mr. Navarre. He is paid in full.

Parent—112 livres paid to him on my account by Mr. Godefroi. Also 63 livres paid to him by Father Bon. Also 232 livres paid to him on my account by Sir Gouin, trader at Detroit. Also 5 livres for some masses. Also 600 livres by Mr. Navarre. He is paid in full. He received 12 livres more than what was coming to him.

I paid Lesperance, the younger, the sum of 59 livres to be deducted from the 50 écus that I owed him for the year that he worked for me. I have finished paying the aforesaid the 50 écus that I owed him.

. . .

I have paid Nicholas Catin the sum of 150 livres which he will receive at Montreal by means of 412 livres in notes at the rate of 30%, on which transaction I owe him 43 livres payable here in the month of May 1750. The said sum pays Niagara in full.

...

[1750]

I have remitted to Chauvin, the blacksmith of this mission, the sum of 100 livres out of the 300 livres that he is to pay to the said mission each year, as compensation for the steel and iron that I was unable to give him this year, 1750.

I have given to Mr. Roy, a voyageur, 3 packs to be delivered to Mr. René de Couagne at Montreal. The freight on these three packs amounts to 36 livres, including the portage. One pack is made up of beaver skins weighing 92 pounds; the other contains 150 racoon skins covered over with two beaver skins; in the third pack there are 48 lynx, 75 otter, 28 racoon and 43 pounds of beaver skins. The freight for two of the three packs was paid here by means of a covered kettle. August 20, 1750.

...

Seed sown in 1750—37 bushels of (———— wheat?); 6 bushels of oats; 3 pecks of peas.

Nota: The crop amounted to 1050 sheaves. It takes 7 sheaves for a bushel. Consequently there must be 150 bushels. Deduct 40 for seed, and there remain 110, of which 55 belong to us as our share.

The crop of wheat was 150 bushels. The crop of corn was 40 bushels, of which 7½ bushels were side-ears. Regis took a third of it. The crop of oats amounted to 16 bushels. There were two bushels of peas.

Onions—800 in hanks; 553 not in hanks; 347 chives. Total 1600. 240 garlic plants of which 180 are in hanks.

B 12   Extracts from the Potier Manuscript
[*Montreal Municipal Library, Gagnon Collection*]

[p. 195]

Huron village of the Island of Bois Blancs in 1747—33 cabins or lodges

The Small Village (19 cabins)

On the right on entering the village   [persons][17]
1. The La Forêt woman—tall male............Temiskan   [44]
2. Skutache............Nicolas............one-armed man............
     Angelique   [34]
3. The Iroquois cabin   [7]

On the left on entering............Nota: 1 indicates the cabin in the street............2 the one behind it............3 and so on.

---

[17] The numbers of persons were obtained from another part of the manuscript.

1. Taęchiaten............(French house) [9]
1. The old Coin woman (not here, stays at Etionnont8t)
1. Mathias (new house) [11 and some children]
2. The old S8ndak8a woman [9]
3. Kinench8e [7]
1. The man Bijou............The Busquette woman [5]
1. The 8aron woman............8asanion............8kaes............
   Babi, the Caliere woman............beadle [44 and some children]
2. Aa8as............Tiok8oink [51]
1. The old Flathead woman [7]
2. Sastaretsi............old Catherine............The mitasse
   woman............Anien8indes............Misting8in's wife [40]
1. Bricon............Sondekon............The Christofle woman [11]
2. L'Onnonsio (or) the old dark woman (or) the
   woman with the sore lips............8a8ananta [9]
1. The man Glorieux............Ozane [13]
1. Ang8irot (janus quirinus) drunkard............not here
1. Enien8indes............blood-shot eye............Enons
   Skanaret............Sachendoa (good drunkard) [27 and many children]
2. Nicholas............one-armed man (new house) [not yet inhabited]

The Large Village (15 cabins) [persons]

1. Anne's daughters [4]
2. The Delongchamps woman [7]
1. The doctor............his nephew............the woman who
   is blind in one eye [5]
1. The old Piponnette woman............3 nephews of Bapt.
   Piponnette [21 and many childen]
2. Widow Ang8irot [6]
1. The chattering woman............Sent8anne [28]
1. The three daughters of Toussaint (a Huron from
   Lorette) [6]
1. The tall Aoes............Tonti [7]
1. The old queen............Ondechonti, his son [6]
2. N'Ondaentons (no one at home, at Etionnont8t)
1. The old Sadendora woman............tall male [10 and some children]
1. The old Andatorenha woman............old Marie............ [32 several young and
   the wolves   old not baptized]
1. The old Quarante Sous woman............The man blind
   in one eye............The flea woman............Lawrence
   &c [72 and some children]
2. Aronissa (French house, burned)
1. The man called Brutal (at Etionnont8t) [12]

Etionnont8t (or) The Little village

1. Nicholas   5. Ta8ita
2. Brutal   6. Sandotes
3. Naendaentons   7. The Caliere woman
4. The old Coin woman 8. The Lorretain man

Aaae or White River or Belle Riviere; 8 cabins

1. Makons
2. Sadendora
3. 2 sisters of the chattering woman
4. The Canerin woman

[p. 200]

The Three Huron Bands Divided into Ten
1. Oskennonto—the deer band divided into three
   1) es8ntennonk—Sastaretsi ⎫
   2) eangontr8non—Mathias ⎬ hontaxen
   3) hatinnionen—aa8as ⎭
2. Andia8ich—the turtle band divided into four
   1) ennchensiaronnon (aron-issa) (Saens8at)
   2) eronhisseronnon (orontondi—the one-armed man)
   3) atierronnon—babi
   4) entihoronnon—ang8irot—S8nnonkanien
3. Hannaarisk8a—the wolf band divided into three
   1) hatinaarisk8a—Taechiaten—hondatorinke
   2) hatindesonk (the hawks)
   3) (hotiraon (the sturgeons) Brutal
      (Hataensik (make only one band)

The Three Big Chiefs of the Huron Nation

    1. Sastaretsi   2. Saents8at   3. Taechiaten

B 13   Extracts from the Potier Gazette
[*Archives of Le Collège Ste-Marie, Montreal*]

p. 84   Chron: &

(1743)
July 18   Left La Rochelle
August 5   Attacked on sea by three English vessels
Oct 1   Arrived at Quebec where I spent two weeks
16   At Lorette for 8 months and 8 days

(1744)
June 26   Left Quebec for Detroit
Sept 25   Arrived at the Island of Bois Blanc
28   Held my first divine services (the offering was 40 sous)
Oct 11   Went to the fort for the first time (saw Mr. Navarre on the 12th)
*   The Huron Mission was transfered to the Island of Bois Blancs on October 13, 1742
28   Went to La Rivière aux Canards—Navarre had been there for five days; I did not see him
Nov. 3   Went to the fort with Mr. de Longueuil in weather that was windy &&—Navarre called at the Island of Bois Blancs on his way hunting; he lunched, stopped in again the next day with 12 turkeys

(1745)
Feb. 2   I began to make some casseaux[?] &
March 23   Lightning struck the chapel of Lorette, wounded one soldier
July 29   Lightning struck near our house
Aug. 20   Arrival of Mr. de Muys with the news of the capture of L'ile-Royalle &. He left the fort on the 27th, and left here on the 29th
28   Cuillerier called here leading 20 Frenchmen to defend Niagara
Sept 22   About this time I went to the fort with Mr. Navarre; we slept at La Rivière aux Canards

Oct. 19	I left for the wintering place, where I stayed 6 months and 18 days. This same day Brother Latour was wounded from a gun-shot by Regis
Dec. 2	I baptized a woman of the wolf tribe at Etionnont8t who died on the 11th

(1746)

Jan. 31	Departure of Hondatorenha for war
March 1	Enons' cabin burned
15	Crossed a river on the ice
20	A dog drowned among the ice floes at River Ostand8ski
25	During the night of the 24–25th Father de la Richardie suffered an attack of paralysis
April 4	I had a colic. I read a letter in Huron addressed to the Ancients. General Council
16	Left Ontietsi &. Went by the portage at Etionnont8t where I stayed until the 30th, and on May 5 I arrived at the Island of Bois Blancs
28	Navarre left Cedar Point after having waited for me six days
May 21	The fever struck me this morning, and it lasted 14 months
27	I buried the Ladouceur woman (first funeral)
June 6	The corn froze
14	Departure of the Ottawas, Potawatomis & Chipewas for Montreal in Préjan's canoe
Aug. 20	Father Du Jauny[18] made a retreat at the Island of Bois Blancs
Nov. 6	Navarre and Pierrot Chêne passed by on their way to hunt
14	Went hunting at Presqu'ile.
22	Arrival of some Hurons from Montreal with 4 chev. [roebucks?]
Dec. 20	Navarre and Pierrot Chêne spent 7 or 8 days at the Island of Bois Blancs

(1747)

Jan. 2	Arrival of Mr. Sac-epée, Jr. with the Cross of St. Louis for Mr. de Longueuil
18	Aron-issa's house burned
23	Mr. de Longueuil and Cuillerier came on the ice to the Island of Bois Blancs in a bitter cold
Feb. 15	Departure of 22 Frenchmen for the Chouannons
March 19	Arrival of an Onondaga Indian at the Island of Bois Blancs with the news of the defeat at the Cedars; he left on the 16th for the fort, and on the 17th Mr. de Longueuil hastened after the 22 Frenchmen to make them abandon the expedition
	Went to the fort; found the river full of ice at La Pointe de Montréal
31	Arrival of 32 persons from Montreal to stir up the nation
April 16	Left for Etionnont8t, arrived there on the 20th. started back on the 24th, and arrived at the Island of Bois Blancs on the 29th
May 20	Arrival of Nicolas at the Island of Bois Blancs with his warriors. I reached the fort a half hour after midnight
31	About this time Antoine Chapoton, Tousignan and LaBorde were killed by some Ottawas near Saguinaw

---

[18]Pierre Luc Du Jaunay, Jesuit, arrived in Canada in 1737. The following year he was missionary at St. Joseph River on the southeastern shore of Lake Michigan. He laboured at Michilimackinac from 1747 to 1765, when he returned to Montreal. He died in 1781.

[p. 90]
Father Marcol[19] to me—letter of June 19, 1749—received on October 23 by the chiefs of the Ouiatanons

Reverend Father, may the peace of Christ be with you—

Nothing could have given me greater pleasure than your expressed determination to make a last effort to improve yourself in the Huron tongue. Please do so, Reverend Father; spend a lot of time with the Indians, go into their cabins and let them always find easy access to you. That is the way to win them over. It is difficult, I admit; but the good of souls and the glory of God demand of us that sacrifice. Let us often recall those sentiments of zeal and fervor with which, on leaving Europe and our families, we came to this country seeking a life of suffering or an early death. Hear confessions, preach, instruct and teach catechism. Since Father de la Richardie is no longer able to endure the fatigues of the mission, and since I expect him to return here at the first opportunity, I pray the Lord to fill you with his spirit, and to grant you all that is needed to conduct, govern and develop a large mission. I am in union of prayers respectfully yours,

Marcol Jes.

At Montreal June 19, 1749

To Father Marcol   Sept. 29, 1749, by Mr. Dubuisson

Reverend Father, may the peace of Christ be with you—

I have received your letters of May 13 and June 19. I appreciate deeply the offers of help contained in the first, and I shall try to profit by the advice that you give me in the second. Although the progress that I have made in the Huron tongue, since the last letter that I had the honor to write to you, has not been great, nevertheless I expect to be able to manage next spring should Fr. de La Richardie return (to Quebec). That Reverend Father continues to enjoy fairly good health. He has retained Brother Gournay because old crotchety St-Come did not keep his word. Nicolas and his partisans (except for a few families who have returned to the mission) still persevere in their schism, and I hope that they will continue in it, because, even by the admission of the Hurons who are here, they are such difficult and ill-intentioned people that, if they returned to this village, they could not help but cause misunderstandings. Hence, on account of their obstinacy Father de La Richardie has decided to abandon them to their reprobate sense. Generally speaking the Hurons of the upper country are impudent rascals—knaves, drunkards, a superstitious and devilishly proud lot. Nevertheless it must be admitted that there are some good ones among them, but they are—rari montes in gurgite vasto—and for the love of this small number I consent to live and die with them. We are now completely re-established except for a section of the chapel floor and ceiling. That did not prevent us from saying Mass in it for the first time on the Nativity of the Blessed Virgin. We expect Mr. de Céloron from day to day, but we have not heard from him for two weeks, when an Ottawa brought letters from him dated August 24. He was then on the point of leaving the Chaouannons of Sonnioto to go to La Rivière à la Roche in order to visit the rebel Miamis. The

[19]Gabriel Marcol (1692-1755), Jesuit, came to Canada in 1723. He was Superior of the Canadian missions 1748-54.

season is far advanced, and I fear that the army will have to winter at Detroit. Should this be the case, I pity Father Bonnecamps and your reverence who no doubt need him. I remain in union of prayers obediently yours &c.

[pp. 90-1]
Potier to de Longueuil, Sept. 29, [1749], by Mr. Dubuisson

Sir,

It was with great regret that I saw you leave this place. The regret was followed by grief when I learned of the unfortunate incidents on your trip from Detroit to Montreal. I was especially indignant at Point Pelee for the bad trick that it played on you. But my grief was dispelled by the news of your promotion. Already on two occasions I have had the honor of congratulating you upon your elevation; permit me to do so for the third time, and doubly so on your account and that of your brother. Heaven grant that you may rise still higher.

Nicolas is still the same and at the same place. It is rumoured that he is planning to return to Sandusky, but I hope that our authorities will oppose it. Sir Tahatie arrived recently from Orange with a large collar addressed to Nicolas from the governor of Boston, to thank him for having used Onontio's hatchet against Onontio himself, and to invite him to go to Boston or Chouagen, with the promise that all the stores will be open to him so that he may take freely anything he pleases. Mr. de Sabrevois has worked . . . (the rest of the letter is missing).

[p. 91]
Mr. de Céloron[20] to me, Sept. 9, 1750, brought by Jean Marie and Cahousa at 8:30 P.M. I had been in bed for an hour.

I learn some new facts that make me fear for Fr. de La Richardie. Baby has just admitted to Chauvin the fugitive Hurons are not well intentioned, and that your Father Superior is exposing himself to danger. Briefly this is what Baby says: he repeats what the Miami woman has already declared; he does not say that they are going to kill, but he admits that it is too bad [c'est de valeur]. Interpret if you can that Indian expression. Why would Baby start such a story? Is he afraid that Nicolas' Hurons will degrade him and dethrone Sastaredzy if they return to the mission? It is not necessary to consider the matter too deeply. I do not believe that this line of action will take place. We must rather believe that the Hurons of Yahague are still rascals and that impunity for their crime renders them more insolent than ever. I did not want to use my authority to prevent the Superior's trip. I simply gave him advice and I believe that it should have sufficed in the present circumstances, after warnings so often repeated by the Hurons themselves.

[20]Pierre Joseph Céloron, Sieur de Bienville (Blainville) (1693-1759), was twice Commandant at Detroit in 1743-4 and 1751-4. In 1749 he led an expedition down the Ohio River for the purpose of taking formal possession of that country for France. Céloron Island, at the mouth of the Detroit River, is named in his honour.

I am entreating Fr. de La Richardie once more. Join me in trying to persuade him not to do anything that might give the rebels an occasion of rendering themselves more guilty.

Father must hold a council with the Hurons that are accompanying him. It is in their interest to act prudently, all the more so because they share in the threats that have been made and will likely share in the blows that may be struck. I am addressing to you a letter for Father and I ask you to send it to him by Le Roy's son who is to leave tomorrow. I would regret very much seeing his zeal and boldness bring harm upon himself.

Respectfully yours
Céloron

Sept. 9, 1750, at Detroit

[p. 94]

Potier to Marcol, Oct. 13, 1750, by Mr de Raymond

Reverend Father—

Father de La Richardie left here on September 7 to go the country of fugitive Hurons, accompanied by three Frenchmen who are his canoemen. The two principal chiefs of this nation, along with two other esteemed persons and a few young men left the next day to join the Father. Hardly had they left when the rumour spread that the whole group of ambassadors were going to be scalped. Alarmed at this rumour Mr. de Céloron immediately dispatched some messengers with a letter for the priest. They found the chiefs at three leagues from Detroit, gave them the letter and returned the same evening. Since the bad rumour was increasing hourly, Mr. de Céloron wrote another letter to the Father. I also wrote to him to give him the news of this place.

He left 35 days ago and we have not heard from him. Did he go to the village of the rebels, or did he not? That's what we do not know. I think that he probably stopped at the Vermillion River, a three-day march from the place of the fugitives, and from there he may have sent runners to the rebel chiefs inviting them to come to a parley. In any case I cannot believe that the Nicolas partisans will dare attempt to take the Father's life.

Father Bon has had trembling fever for two weeks. The quinine that I gave him took it away. I hope that it will not return. I recall having spoken disparagingly about this Reverend Father in my last letter. I now retract. Mr. de Céloron is trying to assemble the Miamis, but I doubt that he will succeed.

I would have many things to tell you about the mission, but that will be for another occasion. In union of prayers I am

Obediently yours

p.s. I have just received a letter from Fr. de La Richardie. He informs me that he stopped at the Vermillion River, where he is daily awaiting the rebel chiefs.

C. SETTLERS COME TO THE SOUTH SHORE

C 1 THE JOURNEY OF JOSEPH GASPARD CHAUSSEGROS DE LÉRY[1] TO DETROIT IN 1749

[*Archives du Séminaire de Québec; published in Roy,* Rapport de l'Archiviste de la Province de Québec pour *1926-7, pp. 334-48*]

[On May 26, 1749, Léry received his instructions from Governor de La Galissonière[2] to go to Detroit. He went in a convoy composed of families of settlers and merchants conducted by Mr. de Sabrevois,[3] who was going to be Commandant at Detroit. At Montreal, Léry prepared slips of vines, fruit stones, pips, and seeds of all kinds to take to Detroit. The convoy left La Chine on June 6, 1749. It followed the north shore of Lake Ontario. In his Journal Léry noted that a French settlement and a trading post should be established at the mouth of the Credit River (Port Credit) in order to keep the Indians from Lake Huron from going to trade with the English at Chouanguen (Oswego, N. Y.). At the end of Lake Ontario he noted a bay (Burlington Bay) whence there is a portage to the Grand River which empties into Lake Erie and another portage to the River Duluth (Thames?) which empties into Lake St. Clair. On July 2, he reached Fort Niagara where he inspected the fortifications and ordered repairs to be made. On Lake Erie he also followed the north shore and on July 23 arrived at Pointe aux Pins.]

July 24, we left before daybreak; at 10 o'clock in the morning I portaged over la Pointe Pelée; one league from the end of the said Pointe this portage is ¾ of a league long. It is necessary to carry the canoe for six arpents in order to enter into a marsh where there is enough water, and on getting out of it you have to make another portage of 14 arpents. Then you are on the other side, a league and a half from the tip of la Pointe Pelée. Thus you have saved 1¾ leagues of travel and you have by-passed the most dangerous point of the lake. This portage could easily be arranged so that the ¾ league crossed by water in the marsh would be easy by cutting the trees that have fallen down in it. Some canoes that tried to round la Pointe Pelée were wrecked. Even though

---

[1]Joseph-Gaspard Chaussegros de Léry (1721–97) was a military engineer. Not to be confused with his father of the same name, who was also an engineer at Quebec, and who was responsible for the plans of many fortifications and public buildings. After the British conquest our subject remained at Quebec, where he became an executive and legislative councillor.

[2]Roland Michel, Marquis de La Galissonière (1693–1756) was Governor of New France 1747–9. He reinforced the western posts including Detroit, where he also increased the settlement. He returned to France in September 1749.

[3]Jacques Charles de Sabrevois was Commandant at Detroit 1749–51.

the wind was not very strong, the waves break with great force. It is necessary to go a half a league out because the tip of the point is rocky. Some of the rocks are submerged. Sometimes sand banks form at that place. From the place where we slept [at la Pointe aux Pins] to the portage of la Pointe Pelée the distance is 14 leagues; from la Pointe Pelée to la Rivière Perthuis—4 leagues; from la Rivière Perthuis to a place called Gros Cap (where there is no cape)—two leagues, and from the said Gros Cap to la Rivière aux Cèdres (Cedar Creek) where we encamped—2 leagues. This day we covered 22 leagues. The shores of the lake are as on preceding days [i.e., sandy banks] and the trees are also the same [i.e., firs and hard woods].

. . .

July 25, in the morning, we left la Rivière aux Cèdres. After having travelled 1½ leagues we came to la Rivière Amaconce. 1½ leagues beyond the said river is the Presqu'isle. One league beyond the Presqu'isle is the entrance to the Detroit River. The distance from la Rivière aux Cèdres to the entrance to the Detroit River is 4 leagues. ¾ of a league from the entrance of the Detroit River we came to the lower end of l'Isle au Bois Blanc where was located the former village of the Hurons. L'Isle aux Bois Blanc is ½ of a league long and shaped like a rectangle with rounded corners. At a league from the lower end of l'Isle au Bois Blanc we found the mouth of la Rivière aux Canards. One league upstream is the middle of la Petite Isle aux Dindes where we encamped. It is about one fifth of a league long.

. . .

July 26, ¾ of a league from l'Isle aux Dindes, i.e., the little one, for there is a large one in the middle of the river opposite the little one, which is a league long and which serves along with the little one as a commons for the animals of the inhabitants, we came upon la Rivière aux Dindes [Turkey Creek]. One league upstream is le Ruisseau de la Vieille Reine, and half a league from the said stream is the Village of the Hurons with the Church and the house of the missionaries.[4] We continued for another half league and we were opposite the fort, where we crossed the river bearing north by northwest. . . .

. . .

July 27, I began surveying and obtaining the necessary information for rendering an exact account of the position, the quality of the lands and the things to be done in order to farm them.

. . .

There are places at Detroit where the clay is good for making brick. In 1749 it was worth 50 l. a thousand. It is very good along the shore opposite the fort. The brick is of excellent quality. There are no fir trees or cedars at the fort of Detroit. It is necessary to bring some 25 leagues from along the above mentioned Rivière Duluth where the great pinery

---

[4]The missionaries are Fathers La Richardie and Potier, who had transferred the Huron mission to La Pointe de Montréal in 1748.

is located. On the said river there is a saw-mill belonging to Mr. Gervais, a resident of Detroit, who brings planks and joists to the post in timber rafts. The current is favorable for this method of transportation in which the lumber runs no risk.

There is no stone at the fort of Detroit. It is necessary to go and get it four leagues downstream at la Rivière à la Carrière. In order to obtain beautiful stone it is necessary to go into the woods a quarter of a league on the south shore of the said river. It resembles the stone at L'Ange Guardien of Quebec. 4¾ leagues below the fort there is an island that is about ¼ of a league in circumference where the stone is as beautiful as that of la Rivière à la Carrière, and it is of the same quality as the stone found at La Pointe aux Trembles in Quebec. Hence the island is called l'Isle à la Pierre [Stoney Island]. They transport the stone from the above-mentioned places in large boats made for that purpose. These boats are propelled by oars and sails. The boats can anchor opposite the fort at a distance of 54 fathoms.

From a spot 60 rods [perches] below Campeau's mill to a small creek above the Huron Village . . . the width of the river at high water is 115 rods of 18 feet in length which make altogether a distance of 11½ arpents. The channel of the Detroit River is closer to the western shore. . . . Lands of 3 arpents in front by 40 arpents in depth were granted to 22 inhabitants along the river starting at le Ruisseau de la Vieille Reine to la Rivière aux Dindes which you will find marked on map 40 between rivers marked 33 and 32.

LOCATION OF THE INDIAN VILLAGES

The village of the Hurons is on the south shore of the Detroit River a half a league below the fort and it is marked E.

The village of the Ottawas is on the same side ½ of a quarter of a league above the fort and marked on the map D.

The village of the Potawatamis is ½ a league below the fort on the north shore, marked B.

. . .

August 26, I left the fort of Detroit with two boats, each one manned by five men. I had taken the precaution to place in each boat a copy of the papers containing the observations of my voyage in case that some accident might befall one of the said boats. I spent the night at the mouth of the Detroit River at six leagues from the fort.

August 27, I spent the night at la Pointe Pelée, at 15 leagues from the mouth of the Detroit River.

[From La Pointe Pelée Léry followed the north shore of Lake Erie to Niagara. Then he proceeded along the south shore of Lake Ontario in order to visit the English fort at Chouaguen (Oswego, N.Y.). This he did on September 15 and 16. On September 21, he reached Montreal.

On the twenty-fifth he arrived at Quebec where he learned that La Galissonière had been replaced as Governor by La Jonquière.[5] One month later he had completed his report and maps. They were dated October 22, 1749, at Quebec. One copy was sent to the Minister of the Marine at Paris.]

C 2 INSTRUCTIONS FOR THE SURVEYOR OF DETROIT
[M.H.C., VIII, 460]
[undated]

...Second Observation.
The lands which Mr. de Sabrevois has ceded in 1749, on the territory south of this river below the Huron Mission, opposite the mouth of the River Rouge, going down the narrows, have been laid out and squared by a line north-northeast and south-southwest in the front, and by a line which runs east-southeast and west-northwest, the winding of the narrows being the cause of the difference of these to those that are in the surroundings of the French fort. These lands have been laid out by Messrs. de Sabrevois and de Lery, in no great regularity. I believe they will be found fully three arpents too large.

In case an examination of these limits shall be made in the future, the defects of this survey can only be attributed to the negligence, ignorance or bad faith of the peasants who carried the poles which have been used for measuring these cessions.

C 3 NAMES OF THE INHABITANTS TO WHOM WERE GRANTED LANDS OF 3 ARPENTS FRONTAGE BY 40 ARPENTS IN DEPTH IN THE YEAR 1749 (NOMS DES HABITANS A QUI L'ON A CONCEDÉS DES TERRES DE 3 ARPANS DE FRONT SUR 40 DE PROFONDEUR EN L'ANNÉ 1749)
[Archives du Ministère des Colonies, Paris]

SCAVOIR (NAMELY)
Louis Gervais
St. Louis
St. Etienne
Drouillard
Lafeuillade
Baptiste LeBeau
Bequette
Rene LeBeaux
Contois dt. Coussin
Francois LeBeaux

Pillet
Des Lignes
St. Jacques
Jean Leduc
Pierre Descompes dt. Labadie
Charles Campeault
Pataine
Lareine
St. Louis
Lafleur

[5]Pierre Jacques, Marquis de La Jonquière (1685–1752) was Governor of New France 1749–51. He continued the work undertaken by La Galissonière of reinforcing the upper posts.

C 4 Léry's Report of His Journey to Detroit
[Archives de la Marine, Paris]

[Quebec, Oct. 22, 1749]

The lands along the Detroit River are for the most part very good, and there is nothing more advantageous for us than their settlement, especially in the case of a future war. The last war[6] proved to us that the Hurons, Ottawas and the Potawatamis who are the three nations of Indians dwelling there along with a village of Chippewas [Sauteurs] located at the entrance to the strait along the shore of Lake Huron, are more inclined to give its [the Strait] possession to the English than to conserve it for us. There are no means that they have not used not only to drive us out, but even to massacre all the French at the post.

The three villages are about ½ a league from the French fort. Some of them could be located along the Ecorce River and at the Grande Presqu'isle [above Grosse Pointe on shore of Lake St. Clair]. But the number of French who dwell along this river is not yet sufficiently large to remove those Indians out of sight from the fort. They could again perpetrate some treacheries.

In their present location within view from the fort, their least movements can be observed and remedies taken. Moreover the Hurons and the Ottawas, who are the worst nations, live on the opposite shore to our fort and to cross the river requires preparations that can be observed.

The Potawatomis on the same shore as the fort leave us nothing to fear. Of all the Indians they are the most faithful to the French even though they do not receive any more presents from them—of which fact they seemed to complain greatly.

It would be necessary to begin by settling the Bay of the Detroit River, that is the bay opposite Bois Blanc Island, where in 1748 was located the village of the Hurons.

For that purpose it would be well to chose in the Government [District] of Quebec where the farmers are the best landowners in Canada, families whose heads have the reputation of being good workmen, and give them the following benefits, without which, it seems to me, it would be difficult for them to be in a position to form a new colony at Detroit.

In the first place it would be necessary for the King to transport at his expense the settlers and their goods to Detroit. Then it would be necessary that he feed them for two years from the provisions at Detroit. Finally, it would be necessary that he give them singly or severally the following articles:

> One plough equipped for two inhabitants
> One ox for each inhabitant
> One cow for two inhabitants

[6]The attempt of Chief Nicolas to destroy Detroit in 1747.

SETTLERS COME TO THE SOUTH SHORE

One horse for two inhabitants
One pig for two inhabitants
One pit-saw, one cross-cut saw and one stone-cutter's saw for every six inhabitants.

To each inhabitant:

One axe [une vache—apparently an error for une hache].
One hoe
One Plane
One iron tool (ferrée)
One adze
One 1-inch auger
One kettle

Two pairs of shoes
One gun
8 lbs of powder and 24 lbs of lead
One tomahwak
One pair of leggings
One 4-point blanket
Seed for one year for the land they will have improved during their first year.

All the Canadian inhabitants know how to use the above-mentioned tools and possessing them they will be in a position to build their houses, barns and stables and even wooden forts if needed.

As for the cattle needed, it is possible to get some from the Illinois Country at a small expense.

The distance from the mouth of the Detroit River to the fort is six leagues. We could build a little fort with battery at the entrance of the said river. Another fort on Lake Erie would watch the passage. Considering the present condition of affairs, it would not be difficult for the enemy to prevent the convoys and the runners from reaching the French fort. That would place the old and the new establishments along the river in a way of being totally ruined.

The lands on the east side of the river are bordered by prairies in such a way that the inhabitants have no wood to cut in order to clear their fields and sow their grain. It is only necessary to plough the land and to cut down some shrubs [fredoches]. The lands are good and grow wheat, barley, oats, peas and in general all sorts of grains. Fall wheat is grown at that place.

On August 1st, I planted some French grape vines that I had brought from Montreal. They had a good start and were growing well when I left. There were three plants of white and four of purple grapes.

In this garden there are peaches, pears and apples that are very good. The inhabitants also have some on their lands, as well as vegetables and other garden produce that abound there.

The inhabitants of the place say that it is not possible to settle the newcomers in a village on account of the large number of starlings that eat the grain. It is true that there are many of them and that people are needed to watch them. It is also true that the inhabitants of Detroit at present do not like work. This year, however, they have a fine crop.

Both for the safety of the French fort and in order to awe and frighten the Indian nations it would be necessary to have at Detroit the following artillery:

8 pieces of cannon of 4-lb. calibre } with cannon balls and gun
2 pieces of cannon of 3-lb. calibre } carriages.
18 swivel guns

    The transportation of this artillery is not as difficult as one might think. From Fort Niagara it is possible to have boats [bateaux] transported into Lake Erie and have the artillery placed on them.

    The steep incline of the portage at Niagara is not an obstacle. Part of it can be avoided by detouring the road into the woods. As far as I'm concerned I believe the matter feasible and that transportation necessary for the safety of Detroit.

    The English who have now entered upon the route of the Grande Rivière can continue their way to Detroit and attack it without Fort Niagara knowing anything about it. That would place us in a position of not being able to bring any help.

    It is necessary then to garrison Detroit and make it proof against unpleasant events. There is no doubt that if this post falls into the hands of the English, the Upper Country will be lost to us.

    But, if troops, settlers and artillery are placed there, we can be assured that no matter what attempts our enemies might make, they will not be able to succeed, even if the Indians should happen to give them a hand. But they will not do this when they see troops, artillery and settlers.

    If this post is well garrisoned we shall be in a position to hold the Upper Country, and from the produce of the lands that will be farmed to nourish the garrison of Detroit and even that of Fort Niagara, by means of a barge on Lake Erie. It could be constructed on the Detroit River or on Lake Erie. There is enough timber-wood to build a large number of vessels of all sizes.

    Once Detroit is set up it will be able to provide at any moment detachments to remedy situations that might arise at Niagara, at Ouatanon, at the Miamis, at Michilimackinac, at St. Joseph by water and by land, at the Baye and generally in all the posts, even at Louisiana.

    The present enclosure of the fort at Detroit is of upright stakes. In time it could be made of stone. It is very good here and so is the lime and the sand.

C 5   Contract of Jean Baptiste and René Lebeau to Conduct a Canot to Detroit
[*B.H.C., Montreal Papers, vol. XII, p. 4088*]

[Montreal, July 2, 1747]

In the presence of the undersigned Royal Notaries of the city and Royal jurisdiction of Montreal, residing at that place, were present Jean

Baptiste and René LeBeau, father and son, (voyageurs) living in this city. They recognized and confessed having contracted and by these presents do contract with Sir Jean Baptiste Godefroy, Esquire, living in this city in his house situated on St. Jean Baptiste Street, here present. The above named agree that at his first request they will leave this city in a canot laden with merchandise, will help to conduct it to the post of Detroit on Lake Erie, and be free on arrival at the said place. They agree that during the whole journey they will take care of the canots, merchandise, peltries, provisions, utensils, and they will work for the profit of the said Sir, and avoid any loss or damage to him, and to notify him if any should come to their knowledge, and to obey in everything licit and honest that will be commanded, and finally to do everything that can and should be done by good and faithful voyageurs, without being permitted to quit the service under the penalties of the service and also of losing their wages. This agreement is made for and in consideration of the sum of one hundred and fifty livres,[7] i.e., one hundred livres to the said LeBeau, senior, and fifty livres to the said LeBeau the son, all in money current in this country—which the said Sir Godefroy promises and agrees to give and pay to the said engagés for their wages and salaries as soon as the said engagés arrive in that place. (Word illegible) of all expenses, damages and interest. All agreed to this contract made at Montreal in the office of the said undersigned notaries in the year seventeen hundred and forty-seven, the second day of July in the afternoon, and all have signed with the exception of the above-mentioned voyageurs, who have declared they could not write or sign their names. The contract was read to them according to the ordinance.

          Signed: Godefroy
                  A. Dehemar
                  Fr. Simonnet, notaire royal

C 6   Extracts from the Cicotte Book
[B.H.C.]

LOUIS PLICHON—was sent from Montreal and arrived at Detroit on July 26, 1749, with his wife and two children to take up the land that had been granted to him. It is 3 arpents wide by 40 arpents deep, and it is situated on the south shore abutting on the north-east the land of Louis Gervais, and on the south-west the lands not yet granted. The fifth ration which is mentioned on the opposite page was granted to one of his wife's brothers who came to stay with him in 1750.

[7]This contract was for the one-way journey from Montreal to Detroit. The pay for the round trip was usually between 200 and 300 livres for steersmen and about 125 livres for middlemen. As the return trip to Montreal was downstream and less laborious, it was the practice among traders and merchants to drop one or two of the men at Detroit in order to save wages and food. In this case, however, it is known from the Cicotte Book that Jean Baptiste LeBeau had been a resident of Detroit, but not his son René.

He received as a donation: 4 rations from July 26, 1749, to July 26, 1750, and five rations from July 26, 1750, to January 26, 1751. He also received:

2 roebucks for meat	2 augers
2 lbs. of flour	1 sow
1 hoe	7 chickens
1 axe	80 roofing nails
1 plough complete	4 pounds of powder
1 scythe	6 pounds of lead

He received to be returned or paid for:

    20 bushels of wheat (R)   1 cow (R)
    1 bushel of corn (R)   1 ox (R)

June 5, 1755. he received the loan of one of the King's cows. It was killed by the Hurons.

Received from the said Plichon:

    2 bushels of wheat which he delivered to Pierre Mongardon dit Brindamour on . . . 1754 according to the note that he is to bring in.
    18 bushels of wheat on the 10th of March.

PIERRE DINAN—was sent from Montreal and arrived at Detroit on July 26, 1749, with his wife and three boys and three girls to take up land that has been granted to him. It is 3 arpents wide by 40 arpents deep and it is situated on the south side, abutting on the north-east [the land of] Louis Plichon and on the south-west the lands not yet granted. He received as a donation: 8 rations for 8 persons from July 26, 1749 to January 26, 1751. [Then are listed the usual tools, provisions, animals, etc.]

JEAN BAPTISTE DROUILLARD—was sent from Montreal and arrived at Detroit on July 26, 1749, with his wife, five boys and three girls to take up the land that has been granted to him. It is 3 arpents wide by 40 arpents deep, and it is situated on the south side, abutting on the north-east (the land of) Pierre Dinan, and on the south-east the lands not yet granted. He received as a donation: 10 rations for 10 persons from July 26, 1749, to January 26, 1751. [Then are listed the usual tools, etc.]

JEAN BAPTISTE LEBEAU—had been living at Detroit for several years when they sent up his family which he had left in Canada. Since he was considered an inhabitant of the place, Mr. de Sabrevois decided not to give him the ration. There has been granted to him a land of three arpents abutting on the north-east (the land of) the neighbor of Drouillard and on the south-west the lands not yet granted. [On list attached to the Léry map of 1749 Lafeuillade is neighbour of

SETTLERS COME TO THE SOUTH SHORE

Drouillard.] He received as a donation: 3 rations for his wife, one boy and one girl from July 26, 1749 to January 26, 1751. [Tools etc.]

PIERRE BECQUET—His wife with two boys and one girl arrived at Detroit on July 24, 1749. Pierre was at the Ouabache country. She was granted a piece of land, but because she was unable to clear it herself, Mr. de Sabrevois gave her permission to go and get her husband. The husband died and the grant of land did not take place. She received 4 rations for 4 persons from July 24, 1749 to October 24 next. [Tools etc.]

JACQUES PILET—had been in Detroit for a number of years when his family, that he had left at Boucherville, came to settle with him. Since he was considered to be a resident at Detroit, Mr. de Sabrevois did not want to give him a ration. Rations were granted to his wife, his son Joseph and his three daughters whom she had brought with her. To the said Joseph was granted a land of 3 arpents situated on the south side and also some agricultural implements. The father was satisfied to cultivate a small piece of land which he does not own on Hog Island. The family received 5 rations for 5 people from July 26, 1749 to January 26, 1751. [Tools etc.]

LOUIS EDELINE—arrived at Detroit with his son to settle on a land granted to him. It is 3 arpents wide by 40 arpents deep and it is situated on the south side. He received 2 rations for 2 persons from July 26, 1749 to January 26, 1751. [Tools etc.]

FRANÇOIS LEDUC dit PERSIL—arrived in the convoy on July 26, 1749. He was granted a land of 3 arpents on the south side. He received a ration of 18 months and provisions according to the regulations. He received one ration from July 26, 1749, to January 26, 1751. [Tools etc.]

LOUIS VILLERS—soldier, married at Detroit, obtained land in 1749 on which he settled the same year on the south side. Louis Morain, his brother-in-law, obtained a grant of 3 arpents abutting [Louis Villers' land]. Villers annexed this property to his grant according to the pleasure of Mr. Céloron. That is why 2 hoes and 2 axes are mentioned on the opposite page. Louis Morain was to use them as well as Villers to clear the land. He received 2½ rations from November 1, 1749 to May 1, 1751 for himself, his wife and a child. [Tools etc.]

RENÉ LEBEAU—bachelor who came to Detroit on July 26, 1749, to settle on land granted to him on the south side. He went back to Montreal in 1751, married and brought back his wife who has been granted a ration. He received a ration from July 26, 1749 to January 26, 1751. His wife received a ration from August 10, 1752, to February 10, 1754. [Tools etc.]

BAPTISTE MALLET—was a shoemaker at Detroit. In 1749 he went to Montreal with his wife and one son. The following year be obtained permission to return with his family in the King's convoy on the promise of settling on a farm of three arpents granted to him on the south side. He received 3 rations from August 3, 1750, to February 3, 1752. [Tools etc.]

FRANÇOIS MALLET—a widower who came to Detroit in 1750 with one daughter and one son to settle on three arpents of land granted to him on the south side. The son disappeared in 1752. He received three rations from August 3, 1750 to February 3, 1752. [Tools etc.]

LOUIS BINEAU—came to Detroit in 1750 with his wife and seven children to settle on a farm of three arpents granted to him on the south side. He received 5½ rations from August 3, 1750, to February 3, 1752. [Tools etc.]

JACQUES BIGRAS—arrived on August 19, 1750, with a numerous progeny. At first he was given land on the north side. His remonstrances won for him a transfer to land on the south side where his widow is living at present. Three big boys who should have been the support of their mother abandoned her. This induced her to marry Antoine Brizard who has entered into all the rights of the deceased on assuming all his debts. The family received 8 rations from August 19, 1750, to September 1, 1751. After this date they received 4½ rations. [Tools etc.]

NICOLAS TAVERNIER dit ST. MARTIN—soldier who was sent to Detroit for garrison duty. He obtained permission to marry the daughter of Bigras and to settle on a farm of 3 arpents on the south side. He died within 8 months of his marriage leaving a widow without children. He received one ration from January 9, 1751, to the time of his death in August 1751. [Tools etc.] [The entry also indicates the receipt of one coffin. His wife later married François LeBeau.]

JOSEPH METEIER—came to Detroit on August 19, 1750, with his wife and small daughter. He was granted a land of 3 arpents on the south side. He received 2½ rations from August 19, 1750, to February 19, 1752. [Tools etc.]

PIERRE DUFOUR—living at Detroit with his wife, five boys and two girls. Upon his request he was granted land on the south side opposite Turkey Island. He received 5½ rations from September 1, 1750, to March 1, 1752. [Tools etc.]

LOUIS ANTOINE DESHÊTRES, JR.—came from St. Joseph with his father [i.e. Antoine DesHêtres who settled on the north side along the shore of Lake St. Clair]. Louis was granted land on the south side near the village of the Ottawas of whom he is the interpreter. He received one ration included in the eight mentioned elsewhere.

SETTLERS COME TO THE SOUTH SHORE

LOUIS REVEAU—from the town of Vif in the parish of St. Jean at two leagues from Grenoble. He had been in the Detroit garrison for several years when he obtained permission to marry the eldest daughter of Pierre Dinan. He received a grant of land 3 arpents wide on the south side on which he has settled. His wife received her ration through her father in 1749 and 1750. To him is granted one ration from January 1, 1751, to July 1, 1752. [Tools etc.]

PIERRE DURAND dit MONTMIREL—soldier who came to Detroit in 1750 for garrison duty. He obtained permission to marry the daughter of Pierre Dinan in order to settle on a farm which has been granted to him on the south side where he has made a small clearing. He received two rations starting in January 1751. [Tools etc.]

JEAN VALE dit VERSAILLES—same as Montmirel. He received two rations from January 9, 1751, to July 9, 1752. [Tools etc.] He also received 5 bushels of wheat to pay Drouillard for cutting the lumber and raising his house.

JEAN FRANÇOIS LEBEAU—same as Baptiste LeBeau, a Canadian who came to Detroit in 1749 as a passenger in the Merchants' Canoes. He obtained a grant of land but was not to be given a ration until he got married. Nicolas Tavernier above-mentioned having died, he married the widow and then received a ration from September 20, 1752, to March 20, 1754. [Tools etc.]

FRANÇOIS PRUDHOMME—came from the District of Montreal to Detroit in 1751 with a rather large family to settle on a farm granted to him opposite Turkey Island. He received 5 rations for 7 persons from September 1, 1751 to March 1, 1753. [Tools etc.]

JOSEPH ST. AUBIN—same as Prudhomme. He received 5½ rations from September 1, 1751, to March 1, 1753. [Tools etc.] He also obtained 10 lbs. of tobacco and 5 lbs. of powder to pay for the hauling of his house.

CHARLES CAMPAU—can be called a child of Detroit. In consideration of work that he has done on a farm and of his marriage to Prudhomme's daughter, he was given a ration from September 14, 1752, to March 14, 1754. [Tools etc.]

CHARLES BUTEAU—came from Montreal in 1751, examined the country and received land on the south side. In 1752 he went back to Montreal and returned with his family. He received 5 rations from August 23, 1752, to February 24, 1754. [Tools etc.] He also received 3 lbs. of powder and 9 lbs. of lead to have his house hauled by Deline.

SIMON BERGERON—In consideration of the fact that he married the daughter of J. B. LeBeau, he received one ration. His wife received her ration on her arrival from Montreal.

C 7 CENSUS OF THE INHABITANTS OF DETROIT ON SEPTEMBER 1ST, 1750

[P.A.C., Series G 1, vol. 461, p 28]

	Women	Boys 15 years and over	Girls 15 years and over	Boys under 15 years	Girls under 15 years	Slaves	Arpents of land under cultivation	Sheaves of wheat	Sheaves of oats	Arpents of land in corn	Horses	Oxen	Cows	Hogs	Poultry
Yacinthe Réome	1	1	1	3	2	.	.	500	.	.	2	.	3	1	30
Forville	1	.	.	1	.	.	.	450	.	.	2	.	2	.	.
Demouchelle	.	.	.	.	.	.	.	.	.	.	.	.	.	.	.
Cecire	1	.	3	1	1	.	20	.	100	.	3	2	14	6	40
Gaudet	1	.	.	1	1	1	25	510	130	1	2	2	5	.	.
Meloche	1	2	.	1	2	.	15	450	150	.	4	2	12	16	70
Gamelin	1	1	3	2	3	1	50	1500	300	3	5	6	8	3	32
Jean Pilet	1	.	.	2	2	2	54	1160	430	4	3	4	3	.	.
LaSelle	1	.	.	.	.	.	12	800	200	.	.	4	.	.	.
L. Parent	1	1	.	3	4	.	.	.	.	.	2	4	2	5	22
Le Duc	1	1	.	1	2	2	40	1800	300	.	3	16	3	4	40
Chauvin	1	1	.	4	2	1	60	2050	430	3	5	2	20	8	50
Chêne père	1	.	.	2	2	1	100	4000	550	2	3	4	25	4	.
Beaubien	1	.	.	.	2	2	46	.	.	.	2	.	14	6	.
Deruissaux	1	1	.	1	1	.	45	1200	190	.	3	4	3	2	80
Cicot	1	.	.	1	1	.	80	2500	700	6	4	.	6	3	24
Gilles Parent	1	2	.	2	1	.	50	2000	430	2	4	4	3	1	12
Seguin	1	3	1	.	.	.	30	1100	200	1	4	2	8	3	.
Cardinal	1	.	.	2	3	.	.	.	.	.	2	2	3	5	24
I. Chêne	1	.	.	2	1	.	42	1400	180	2	4	2	2	1	40
Peltier	1	.	.	1	5	.	32	1500	200	.	5	2	1	3	.
Jac. St. Aubin	1	.	.	2	3	.	25	1800	370	.	2	4	3	5	60
Nicol Campau	1	.	.	.	.	1	.	.	.	.	.	.	4	1	30
Pierre Réome	1	2	1	.	.	.	40	1360	270	.	5	2	5	6	48
Barthe	1	.	.	.	1	1	.	.	.	.	1	.	3	4	60
Claude Campau	1	.	.	1	.	.	.	.	.	.	1	.	2	13	30
Belperche	1	.	.	.	.	.	.	.	.	.	.	.	2	.	50
Janisse	1	.	1	.	1	1	.	.	.	.	.	2	5	4	24
Franc. Roy	1	.	.	.	.	.	.	.	.	.	.	.	7	2	.
LaButte	1	.	.	.	.	.	.	.	.	.	.	2	3	4	.

[54]

C 7 (cont'd.)

	Women	Boys 15 years and over	Girls 15 years and over	Boys under 15 years	Girls under 15 years	Slaves	Arpents of land under cultivation	Sheaves of wheat	Sheaves of oats	Arpents of land in corn	Horses	Oxen	Cows	Hogs	Poultry
Bte. Mallet	1	1	1								1	4	10	1	
Bte. Campau	1	1	1	4	1	3	150	3000	500	4	5		6	2	150
L. Campau	1			2	2	1	120	4500	380	7	3	10	30	15	80
Marsac		2	2									8	22	6	
Poupard	1			3									1		12
Godefroy	1	1	1			1	20	400	150		2	1	4	2	20
Delisle	1			2								2	1	1	24
De lemothe	1		1	2	1	2	30	700	200	4	2	4	6	3	
De Quindre	1			1	1	1	50	1200	303		3	4	13	2	30
Gouin	1		1		2						1		2	2	
Chapoton	1	3									3	4	10	4	50
Gervais	1			1	2		45	1800	300	7				1	
Navarre	1												6	2	
Despeltaux	1		1			1	50	1300	190	3	3	4	16	5	190
Claude Audry	1	1				1	50	1030	460	4	4	8	18	3	30
Cuillerrier	1		1				100	4000	290	2	4	6	18	2	15
Champagne	1	1		1		2	27	730	138	1	3	4	6	1	80
La Bady	1		1		2		42	1500	230		4	4	10	7	16
Barrois	1	1		2		1	50	200	350		2	4	18	2	30
St. Cosme	1				2		28	550	100		1		3	2	35
Ante. Robert	1	1			1		5	300		2	1	2	2	5	18
Jacq. Pilet	1			1	2		10	450	200		3	2	3	4	
Paul Campau				2	2		8	230	190		2	5	1		
Charl Campau	1						28	800	300			4	20	3	48
Jean Chauvin						1	40	930	430	3	3	2	6	2	30
Miny	1				2		50	1630	260	4	2	2	1	6	60
La ve. Esteve	2	2		2			50	1200	200	3	4	2	4	1	30
Clau. Bino				1	2		60	1350	280	3	4	2	3	7	60
Charl. Casse	1	1			3		48	1500	230		3	2	6	3	40
Pierre Boyer	1		1	1			30	750	180	1	2	2	2	6	30
Gabriel C asse	1	1			1		46	1200	340		2	4	2	4	
Noel Casse	1			2	1		18	400	160		2	2	3	2	36
Loson	1	1		1	1										
Duchesne				2	1										

C 7 (cont'd.)

	Women	Boys 15 years and over	Girls 15 years and over	Boys under 15 years	Girls under 15 years	Slaves	Arpents of land under cultivation	Sheaves of wheat	Sheaves of oats	Arpents of land in corn	Horses	Oxen	Cows	Hogs	Poultry
Joseph Seguin	1						20	600	200		1	2	1		
Crêtel	1						16	360			2	2	2	3	40
Comtois							4	180		3			2	1	6
Jean Cardinal	1	1		2	1						1	2	2	1	6
F. Denoyer	1				1								2	1	6
Patel	1				1								2	1	
St. George	1				1									1	6
Bigras	1			2	2						1		1	1	6
Jenette		3													
St. Germain	1												2	1	
Courville	1		1										1		
Pier. Tremblay	1										1	2	1	1	6
Ambroise	1	1		3	1		10	200	140			1	1	1	6
Augustin	1			3	2			230	230		2	1	2	1	6
Laforest	1	3	1	2	1		12	280		3		2	2	3	6
Lafeuillade	1	2		1	3		30	800	130	3		1	4	1	6
Plichon	1						6	200					3	1	6
Dinan	1		1	1	1						1	2	2	8	40
Drouillard	1			2	2						3	1	3	2	12
Michel Campo	1	2		1	2		10		150	2		2	2	1	6
Le Bau	1				1			300					1		
Louis Bino	1	1		4	3							2	1	1	6
F. Mallet	1											1	1	4	35
Revau	1			1	2							4	4	1	6
Monmirelle	1			4	1							2	2	1	5
Villers	1	1		1	3			300				1	2	3	30
Meteyer	1												2		
Dufourd	1				1								1		
Jean Goyau	1	1	4	4			30	1180	300		4	4	10	3	30
Bte. Goyau	1			1	1								1		
Ant. Campau	1													6	
Ignace Boyer	1														
96	80	49	33	97	95	33	1020	55200	2581	94	150	211	471	251	2187

[56]

C 8 EXTRACT FROM FATHER BONNECAMPS'[8] REPORT
[*Thwaites*, Jesuit Relations, *LXIX, 150–99*]

... I remained at Detroit too short a time to be able to give you an exact description of it. ... It is the Touraine and Beauce of Canada. ...

Moreover, Detroit must be considered as one of the most important posts of the colony. It is in a position to give help to Michilimackinac, to River St. Joseph, to the Baye, to the Miamis, to the Ouitanons,[9] and to Belle Rivière (Ohio River) provided that people settle there. Hence you can send any number of people to that place. But where shall we find these people? It is not in Canada (Lower Canada). The settlers that you sent there last year contented themselves with eating the rations that the King gave them. Some amongst them, carried away by their natural fickleness, left the area and went to seek fortune elsewhere. How many poor peasants in France would be delighted to find a land that would reward them abundantly for their sweat and toil!

C 9 GRANT OF LAND TO CHEVALIER DE LONGUEUIL
[*Detroit Notarial Records, Liber A, pp. 44–5*]

[Quebec, April 1, 1750]

Marquis de Lajonquière, Knight of the Royal and Military Order of St. Louis, Captain of his Majesty's ships, Governor and Lieutenant General for the King in New France and Louisiana—

Francois Bigot, Counselor of the King in his Council, Intendant of Justice, Police, Finance and Marine in said countries—

Upon the request made to us by Chevalier de Longueuil of the Royal and Military Order of St. Louis, Lieutenant of the King in the city and castle of Quebec, to grant and concede to him a tract of land twelve arpents wide by forty arpents deep, situated on the Detroit River of Lake Erie, adjoining on the W.S.W. the lands of the Mission of the Hurons and on the E.N.E. the lands not yet granted, bounded on each side by a line running N.N.W. and S.S.E., in front by the Detroit River and in the rear by a line running E.N.E. and W.S.W. separating it from the lands not yet granted.

In virtue of the power jointly granted to us by his Majesty, we have given, granted and conceded, do give, grant and concede, subject to quit rent [cens et rentes] from this time forward and forever, to the said Sieur de Longueuil, for himself, his heirs and assigns, a grant of land situated on the strait of Lake Erie, containing twelve arpents in front by forty arpents in depth, bounded by the lines hereabove de-

[8]Joseph Pierre Bonnecamps, S.J., came to Canada in 1741, and taught hydrography at the College of Quebec from 1749 to 1759.
[9]The village of the Ouitanons was on the site of the present city of Lafayette, Indiana.

signated; for the said Sieur de Longueuil, his heirs and assigns to have, hold and dispose such lands, subject to charges, clauses and conditions hereinafter mentioned, that is to say that the said Sieur de Longueuil, his heirs and assigns shall be bound to take their grain to be ground at the common mill when any such shall be established, under the penalty of the confiscation of such grain, and also of an arbitrary fine; to establish or cause to be established on this land an actual residence within one year from this day at the latest; to protect the clearings of his neighbors whenever it shall be needed; to cultivate the said land; to allow to pass through such roads as may be deemed necessary for the public utility; to make the division fences according to the regulations; to pay each year to the receiver of his Majesty's domain in this country or to the clerk of said receiver residing at Detroit, one sol of "cens" for each arpent in front and twenty sols of "rente" for every square arpent, making for the said twelve arpents in front by forty in depth twelve sols of "cens" and twenty-four livres of "rente", and in addition three bushels of wheat for the said twelve arpents in front, the whole payable each year on the day and feast of St. Martin, the first year's rent falling due on the eleventh of November, one thousand seven hundred and fifty-one, the said "cens" being subject to taxes on sales, defaults and fines with all other Royal and Seignorial rights whenever the case may happen, agreeable to the custom of the provostship and viscountship of Paris. It will, however, be lawful for the said Sieur de Longueuil to pay the said twenty-four livres of "rente" and twelve sols of "cens" in furs at the Detroit market price until a money currency shall have been established; reserving in the name of the King on the said land all the timber that his Majesty shall need for the construction and erection of any buildings or forts that he may hereafter establish, as well as the ownership of mines, ores and minerals if any should be found in the extent of the said concession; and the said Sieur de Longueuil, his heirs and assigns are bound to have the said concession surveyed, measured and bounded in its whole width and depth at his own expense, and to execute the clauses and conditions mentioned in the present title, and to take a patent of confirmation from his Majesty within two years, the whole under the penalty that otherwise these presents shall be null and void.

C 10   GRANT OF LAND TO ALEXIS DELISLE
[*Detroit Notarial Records, liber A, p. 346*]

[Detroit, Nov. 24, 1751]

CÉLORON, MAJOR COMMANDANT AT DETROIT ERIE AND SOUTHERN POSTS In virtue and in accordance with the orders of Messrs. General & Intendant we have granted to Alexis Delisle a parcel of land two arpents wide by forty deep, on the south side of this river, situated on the shore of the Detroit River, abutting on the west-southwest [the land of] Hyacinthe Réaume, and on the other side i.e., east-northeast the lands not yet granted, limited by a line running south-southeast, and north-northwest, to possess it in the same way as in the contracts formerly granted at this place, and especially on condition that he will clear and cultivate the said land, and will establish thereon a hearth and home within a year from this day under penalty of nullity of this title.

C 11 GRANT OF LAND TO PIERRE RÉAUME
[*P.A.C., G 1, New France & Detroit, p. 10*]

[Detroit, Nov. 24, 1751]

CÉLORON, MAJOR COMMANDANT AT DETROIT & SOUTHERN POSTS

In accordance with the orders of Messrs. General and Intendant we have given to Pierre Réaume, in the place of a former grant of two arpents that was made to him near this fort and whose too great proximity is contrary to the reiterated orders of the General by which he enjoins us to keep a clear space of five arpents around this fort, another grant on the south shore of this river, three arpents wide along the river and forty arpents deep, abutting on the west-southwest [the land of] Jacques Gaudet and on the east-northeast the lands not yet granted, limited by a line running south-southeast north-northeast [*sic*], to possess it in the same way as in the contracts formerly granted to the inhabitants of this place, and especially on condition that he will clear and cultivate the said land and establish thereon a hearth and home within a year from this day under penalty of being deprived of it, and by these presents [be it known] that no property remains to him of the two arpents that had been granted to him near this fort.

C 12 GRANT OF LAND TO WIDOW VIEN
[*Detroit Notarial Records, liber A, p. 313*]

[Detroit, Nov. 24, 1751]

In accordance with the orders of the General & Intendant we have granted to Widow Vien a tract of land two arpents in width along the south shore of the Detroit River, by forty arpents in depth, abutting on the west-southwest the land of Mr. Chauvin, and on the east-northeast the lands not yet granted, limited by a line running south-southwest and north-northwest, to possess it in the same way as in the contracts formerly given at this place, and especially on condition that she will clear and establish the said land within a year from this day under penalty of nullity of this title.

(signed) Céloron

C 13 THE CAPTIVITY OF CHARLES STUART
[*Library of Congress, Washington, D.C., The Force Papers; Mississippi Valley Historical Review XIII, 1 (June 1926)*]

[In 1755 a company of Delaware, Mingo and Shawnee Indians raided a settlement near the present city of McConnellsburg, Pennsylvania.

Among their captives was Charles Stuart with his wife and two children. The prisoners were hurried westward to Kittaning, where Stuart and his wife were presented to the Wyandot Nation of Indians. These new masters took them to the Wyandot town at Sandusky. In the following spring the prisoners were transported to Detroit and were compelled to pay for their ransom by working for Fathers Potier and Bocquet. In 1757 they were sent as prisoners to Quebec, whence they were transported to England, and finally they landed back in New York. On his return Stuart evidently dictated a statement of his observations to the military authorities, from which the following passages have been extracted:]

... Sandusky, call^d by the Indians Canuta is a Small Indian Town Containing 11 Cabbins in it, only 3 of wch are constantly Inhabited, the whole were formerly Inhabited by Wondots who Built a Stochad Fort in it to defend them against the Cherokees & Catawbas, but the Fort is now entirely decay^d and Broke down,—Said Sandusky is now used as the Head Quarters of the Wondot Hunters dureing the Winter Season, who Hunt on the Borders of the Head Branches of Sioto. The Hunters leave the Cheif Wondot Town (wch is ab 2 miles distant from Fort Detroit on the East Side of the river or Strait that comes down From Lake Huron) ab^t the Latter End of October and Proceed with their Familys in Canoes round the West End of Lake Erie keeping close to the Shore Till they go Round to Stony Creek wch is ab^t 18 miles, or one Days Paddle of Canoes to the Eastward of the River that comes From the Small Lake near wch Sandusky or Canuta Stands. ...

In time of Hunting the Wondot Town (Sandusky) is Entirely Deserted Except a Few Poor Women who have no relations or Freinds to take care of them and they are left to take care of the Town and Provis^s are left with them to Support on till the Hunters return—The Wondots Hunting Ground Begins at the West End of Lake Erie where the River that Comes from Fort St. Joseph Emptys into the Lake, ab^t 40 miles from the mouth of the Strait that comes from Detroit to Lake Erie—this River from St. Joseph divides the Hunting Ground of the Wondots from the Hunting Ground of Outotowas. The Wondots Hunts and Traps for Beaver &c Dureing the Whole Winter Season From the Latter End of October Till the middle of April and By ab^t the 1st of May They are generally all returned to their Towns—

From Lake Erie up to the Strait that Emptys Lake Huron there are no French or Indians Settled on Either Side Till you get ab^t 11 miles up where is one Family Settled on the East side; then 2 miles Higher up Begins the French Settlements wch extend ab^t 4 miles in Length along the Strait or river, their Plantations are Laid out on the River 3 Acres in Breadth and 100 Acres in Depth from the River, Each Plantation Containing 300 French Acres wch Seemed rather Larger than the English Acres—a Square Cont^g 10 Perches on Every Side is a French Acre—a French Perch is 7 Ells Long. Each Ell is a yard & Quarter

English measure—The French that are settled in said 4 miles amount to ab^t 27 or 28 Familys—the Wondot Corn Fields are Higher up the river and Join on the Side next the French to Capt Jarvis's [Gervais] Plantation (S^d Jarvis is a French Capt of Militia). ab^t 2½ miles Higher up than Capt Jarvis's is the Wondot Town Containing ab^t 60 or 70 Houses and at the Upper End of the Town Towards Lake Huron Stands their church, and Joining to it is the Priests House Garden and Plantation. . . . The Wondot Town contains ab^t 230 Warriors, ab^t 70 of wch are Boys from Ten to Seventeen Years of Age, for Such they carry out to War with them—When they go to War They have a Camp at some remote Corner from where they do the mischief ab^t 15 miles distant and there they Leave so many Boys with some older People and Two Women to Take Care of their Camp and To it They Bring their Plunder.

About 2 miles above the Wondot Town Stands the Tawaw Town. between these Two Towns Lives Three French Familys—there are also Three Plantations in this distance Belonging to three French Merch^{ts} who live in Fort de Troit—The Tawaw Town contains ab^t 90 Houses or Indian Cabbins But No Church for the Tawaws are a Heathen Nation & not Proselyted to the Roman Catholick Religion—. . . . They are a Barbarous Savage Nation and very wicked. . . . The Tawaw Warriors are not numerous haveing Lost many in the Wars they haveing been very much Concern^d in the Incursions and Attacks made on the English of Pennsylv^a, Virginia &c—I saw 2 Companys of them going to War ag^t the English, one of ab^t 25 Warriors and Another of ab^t 35 Warriors, One Company went ab^t 5 days after the other, these 2 Companys I suppose Contain^d most their Warriors. . . .

Mr. Stuart got to Sandusky Decr 21st 1755 and Continued there Till Christmas and then he was carried to the Popish Preists House on the Little Lake where the Indians had a great Council at wch the Preist and the Head Indian Traders Assisted and it was determin^d that Mr. Stuart and his wife was to be carr^d by the Indian Traders to the Place where they Lived wch he supposed was at Fort St. Joseph, But by the next morning the Indians alter^d their determinations & Concluded to Keep him among themselves wch they did Till Ap^r 27, 175(6) and then they Carr^d him & his wife wth them to the Wondot Town at Detroit where They Lived and the 25th of June 1756 They were Sold to Two Popish Preists One of wch was a Jesuit who lived at the Wondot Town, and with these Preists they remain^d Till they had workt out their Ransom money wch am^{td} to about 24 Pennsylv^a Moneys worth of European Goods as they sell it retail Price in the Country Stores, The Ransom Money was work'd Out By the 1st of March 1757 After wch they workt one month for 30 French Livres and on the 13th of Ap^r they wth Capt Smith. Richd Joyce, Thom^s Millaken, Wm. Brattin and John Gill were Sent off By the Govr of De Troit to Montreal where They continued 4 Days Prisoners and were then Put on Board a Schooner for Quebeck at wch They were imprison'd (all of them but Capt. Smith) for 2 m^o

and then on July 23, 1757 Were Put on Board a French Cartel and arriv^d Augst 21: 1757 in 28 days Passage at Plymouth old England From whence they were sent to New York. . . .

C 14   GIFT OF LAND—PONTIAC TO MAISONVILLE
[*Original Deed in George F. Macdonald Collection, Windsor, Ont.*]

[Detroit, Sept. 18, 1765]

Know all men by these Presents that I Pontiack, Chief of the Ottawa Nation of Indians, do for myself & by the consent of the whole of the said Nation in the Presence of George Croghan Esqe. Superintendant for Indian affairs, for the good will I bear, and is borne by the whole of the said Nation, unto Alexis Masonville, Inhabitant of Detroit, Grant Give and Release & by these Presents doth Grant Give and Release unto the said Alexis Masonvile his Heirs Exrs. Admrs. & Assigns for Ever, a Certain Tract or Parcell of Land Situate lying and being on the South side of Detroit River begining at the East side or point of land now Granted to Lieut. Edward Abbott of the Royal Artillery, from thence runing up the River the Length of four Acres, from then runing back from the River towards or into the Woods, Eighty Acres keeping in Every part the Breath of four Acres all French Measure, to Have & to Hold his Heirs and assigns for Ever, & I do hereby acquit for myself and the said Nation of Indians, & our Heirs all Claim to the aforesaid Tract or Parcell of Land, but gives it to the aforesd. Alexis Masonvile, as a free gift without any Lett, Hindrance or Molestation from us or our Heirs.

Sealed & Delivered in the presence of
J. B. Chapoton
Barthe

Given under our Hand and Seal at Detroit this 18th day of Septr. Anno Domini one thousand and seven hundred & Sixty Five
Pontiac his Mark
Ocquichion his Mark

C 15   LOUIS GERVAIS TAKES POSSESSION OF LAND
[*George F. Macdonald Collection, Windsor, Ont.*]

I certify that in the year one thousand seven hundred and forty-nine there was granted to Louis Gervais by Mr. Sabrevois, Commandant at Detroit, a farm lot of three arpents in front, adjoining the Huron lands, of which he took possession in the same year, and did pay rent to the King, according to the receipts which I gave, in virtue of my commission as rent-collector, the truth of which I attest. I also certify that I measured the said land myself by order.
Done at Detroit, the 24th of May, 1766

(Signed) Navarre

C 16 Extract from the Census of All the Inhabitants of Detroit Made by Philip Dejean[10] in the Year 1768 on January 23rd [South Shore Only]

[Enclosed in Turnbull to Gage, Detroit, February 23, 1768, William L. Clements Library, Gage Papers, American Series, vol. 74]

Name	Acres of land	Boys	Girls	Oxen	Cows	Hogs	Wheat	Wood
Cloutier	3	...	...	...	...	...	....	2
Grenon	4	3	2	...	...	...	....	2½
St. Andre	3	...	1	2	...	4	60	2
Pajeau	3	...	...	2	1	2	50	2
Tamizir	3	...	...	...	...	...	....	2
Prudhome	3	4	5	...	1	5	200	2
Touranjeau	3	2	2	4	6	2	150	2
Bergeron	3	2	2	2	2	6	50	2
St. Remy	3	1	3	2	4	1	70	2
Binau	3	2	2	...	2	4	100	2
Bte Drouillard	3	5	1	2	4	19	50	2
Vaudry	3	...	...	4	4	5	150	2
Lesperance	3	4	1	2	3	4	140	2
Fr. Lebeau	3	2	2	2	1	7	40	2
Tamizir	3	...	...	...	...	...	....	2
Estne. Jacob	3	...	...	2	35	3	80	2
Suzor	3	...	...	2	2	4	40	2
Ladéroute	3	1	2	2	...	3	30	2
Réaume	3	...	...	...	...	...	....	2
Moran	3	...	...	...	...	...	....	2
Lisle Ronde	3	2	1	2	2	3	50	2
Laffontaine	2½	2	...	2	3	6	40	1¾
Baby	3	...	...	...	...	...	....	2
Peter Pond	2	...	...	...	...	...	....	2
St. Louis	3	4	4	2	2	5	56	2
Lajeunesse	3	4	3	2	2	14	60	2
Patoca Lesperance	3	3	1	2	2	5	50	2
Tamisir	3	...	...	...	...	...	....	2
Papiche Meloche	3	...	...	2	1	2	40	2
Manchet	3	...	...	...	...	...	....	2
Simon Drouliard	6	2	3	4	12	5	150	4
Pre Meloche	6	5	3	2	2	6	200	4
Charron	3	2	2	6	2	6	200	2
Bondy	3	...	...	...	...	...	....	2
Decoigne	3	...	...	2	2	2	....	2
Jn Bte Rau	3	1	...	2	1	1	30	2
Jn Bte Lebeau	3	...	...	4	3	3	10	2
Gravel	3	...	...	...	...	...	....	2
Jn Bte Estienne	3	...	...	2	3	2	100	2
Jn Bte Pare	3	...	...	4	2	3	55	2
Laboise	3	2	...	4	6	...	50	2
Rivard	3	...	1	2	2	3	40	2
Fr. Drouliard	3	...	1	...	4	2	....	2
Gme Goyau	3	4	3	...	3	5	60	2
Marantet	1	2	...	...	2	4	....	¾

[10]Philip Dejean (1734–   ) came to Canada in 1761. He moved from Montreal to Detroit in 1768, and began a career as notary and local judge. In February 1779 he joined Lieutenant-Governor Hamilton of Detroit on the Vincennes campaign, and was taken prisoner along with his leader. He returned to France about 1782.

C 16 (cont'd.)

Name	Acres of land	Boys	Girls	Oxen	Cows	Hogs	Wheat	Wood
Longueuil	12	...	...	...	...	...	...	8
Dénoyer	3	1	2	2	3	...	150	2
Mailloux	3	1	1	2	...	3	300	2
Janis	3	3	2	4	3	2	50	2
Oualet	2	1	...	1	...	2	10	1½
Bouron	4	1	...	2	3	4	60	2½
Dussault	3	1	1	2	2	2	50	2
Réaume	3	...	1	4	4	16	150	2
Gme Grau [Goyau]	3	...	...	2	1	1	30	2
Vital Goyau	2	...	...	2	1	1	50	1½
Lesperance	2	...	2	2	2	7	100	1½
Parent	2	3	5	2	3	5	100	1½
Langlois	2	4	...	2	3	6	150	1½
Labutte	4	4	5	2	5	12	150	2½
Dehêtre	2	1	1	2	3	5	120	1½
Bonvouloir	2	2	3	2	2	5	...	1½
TOTALS—Both Sides of River	514¼	211	147	264	336	567	9789	344½

C 17   General Gage[11] to Commander at Detroit
[*P.A.C.*, *B 27*, *pp. 184–8;* M.H.C., X, 245–6]

New York April 8th 1771.

Your letters of the 14th and 18th December are very full on the subject of Grants, & Lands at the Detroit. I am to explain to you that the King has not invested any Person whatever with the power of granting Lands in America, except to his Governors, within the limits of their respective Provinces, & under certain forms and restrictions, and where any Purchase is made of the Indians tho' within the limits of the Provinces they are not valid, unless permission is given so to do, & the purchase made in presence of the Governor & His Majesty's Superintendent of Indian Affairs. From hence you will know the power of granting Lands at Detroit remains solely in the King, & that no Purchase can be made of the Indians but with the King's permission & authority.

It may be needless after the above explanation to inform you that all grants made by Lieut: Colonel Gladwin, Major Bruce or any other British Commander are null & void & of no value.

[11] Thomas Gage (1721–87) came to Canada as a lieutenant-colonel in General Braddock's force and was wounded in Braddock's defeat near present Pittsburg on July 8, 1755. On the capture of Montreal by the British in 1760 he was appointed Governor of that place. From 1763 to 1772 he was Commander-in-Chief of the British forces in America, with headquarters at New York. In 1774 he was named Governor of Massachusetts, where he failed to stay the course of the American Revolution, and returned to England in October 1776.

As for the French grants in general unless approved of by the Governor General of Canada & registered accordingly they were not valid but as for Monsieur Belestre's grants in the year 1760, they cannot be deemed any other than fraudulent, and are by no means to be looked upon as valid.

And as for the Indian purchases they were not allowed by the French, nor are they allowed by the English Government but under the Restrictions I have already mentioned.

Monsr Navarre's Declaration or Certificate may be in part true, but it is not the whole truth. The first settlers with Mr. Sabrevois, were not perhaps enjoined to the conditions imposed afterwards, respecting their titles—The Govt was glad to get any people to begin the settlement. But Monsr Navarre's conclusion is vague & ill founded. I am well informed in those matters, was Three years in possession of the Books wherein the Titles were registered & received information upon them—The very time in which Mr. Belestre's Grants were made sufficiently points out their being invalid & that they would not be registered when the whole Govt of Canada was on the point of surrendering to the King & the Capital possessed by his troops so early as September 1759. Monsr Belestre was not ignorant of those circumstances and his grants are fraudulent.

I am now to require of you, as soon as this is received annul & make void by Public Act every concession made by Monsr Belestre in the year 1760, every grant made by every British Commander, without exception, and all Indian Purchases whatever or Indian Deeds not obtained by the King's permission and authority—And that you do not suffer any settlements to be made with the above Titles or any new settlements to be begun on any pretense whatever, and that you pull down as fast as any Person shall presume to build up—And that you do seize and send down the Country all Persons who shall be endeavouring to settle among the Savages.

I imagine the Indians will be set upon to talk to you upon these subjects, you will answer them that the King is tender of their property & has made regulations to prevent their being cheated and defrauded. That His Majesty has been induced to make these Rules upon the frequent complaints of the Indians against the white People who have defrauded them of their lands by making a few of them drunk, & getting them in that condition to give away their country to the great disgust of the rest of the Nation, and that by such means the Indians have represented that the White People have taken a great part of their hunting grounds.

This has happened to many Indian Nations & unless you stop it in the beginning at the Detroit, the same thing will happen there.

Mr. Grant has engaged to build two vessels for the King, in which business you will please assist him, and give him such help as your Garrison affords whenever he shall demand it. As for the Merchants they may build what vessels they please, but you will not suffer Mr. Grant's Artificers or Sailors to be taken from him. You have acted very properly in that respect already. I understand there is very good Cedar to be had which Mr. Grant will make use of for the King's vessels, and if you find it necessary you will reserve the Cedar and suffer no person to cut it, but when it is to be used in the King's service.

I hope that you have received the orders about fitting out the old vessels for this years service.

You must continue to take every precaution against accidents from Fire, if Mr. Baibe's Stables are so near the Magazine as you represent it must be deemed a nuisance & removed accordingly,

p.s.—The Merchants alledge that there is Cedar to be had in the greatest plenty. If that is the real case I can have no objection to their cutting as much as they want of it, and you will not obstruct them, on that or any other business not detrimental to the service.

C 18 Gift of Land from the Ottawas to Charles Réaume
[Original in possession of Mrs. Frank Fortin, 2317 Riverside Drive, Windsor, Ont.]

We, the principal chiefs of the different bands of the village of the Ottawas of Detroit, undersigned with our mark, in our name as well as in the name of the whole nation, DECLARE in the presence of William Tucker, one of our interpreters, that in consideration of the sincere friendship and affection that we have for Charles Réaume we have freely given, granted and surrendered, do give, grant and surrender to the said Charles Réaume, to him, his heirs and assigns, a land of three arpents in frontage along the south shore of the Detroit River, and of eighty arpents in depth; [this land] is bounded in the front by the said Detroit River and in the rear by lands not yet granted, and adjoins on one side the land that we have given to Pierre Réaume Sr. and on the other side the land given to Jean Baptiste Meloche. Which land he shall have and hold, use and dispose as being in the full ownership of him, his heirs and assigns. We promise in our name and in the name of the whole nation never to disturb or trouble him in the peaceful possession of the said land now given.
Done at Detroit on June 10, 1776.

    Isidore Chene   Egouchi8ay   his mark [animal]
        witness   Michimandac   his mark [animal]
                               Chamyanda8a his mark [fish]
                                                           [fish]
                                                           [bird]

C 19 LIEUTENANT-GOVERNOR HAMILTON[12] TO GENERAL CARLETON[13]
[*P.A.C., B 122, p. 31;* M.H.C., *IX, 433*]

Detroit, January 15, 1778

... As there has been a restraint laid upon the granting of land to settlers at this place whose farms are small and families numerous, the consequence has been, young men growing to age engage as Canoe men, go off to distant settlements and in general become vagabonds, so that the settlement does not increase in numbers as may be seen by comparing the recensement of 1776 with that of 1766. ...

C 20 LIEUTENANT-GOVERNOR HAMILTON TO GENERAL HALDIMAND[14]
[*P.A.C., B 122, p. 153;* M.H.C., *IX, 474*]

Detroit, September 9, 1778

... I am to observe to your Excellency, I have never taken upon me to grant lands at this place, on the contrary I convened the principal inhabitants and the chiefs of the neighboring nations, read to them the Proclamation relative to purchases from the Indians and told them that no deeds should be considered as valid till passed by the authority of the Chief Governor, registered at Quebec and entered at the office in this place, further that they should be drawn out fair on parchment and publicly witnessed by the Chiefs of the respective nations. 'Tis true I have allowed necessitous persons with large families to till land for present subsistence, but with this caution that they must not look on that temporary indulgence as a grant, and that any buildings or fences they should raise would be destroyed or removed whenever it was thought necessary.

[12]Henry Hamilton (–1796) came to America as a soldier in the Seven Years' War. He served under Amherst at Louisburg and under Wolfe at Quebec. Soon after the start of the American Revolution he was appointed Lieutenant-Governor of Detroit, arriving there November 9, 1775. In the autumn of 1778 he led an expedition that recaptured Fort Vincennes from the Americans. Two months later he was taken prisoner and sent to Virginia. He was kept in prison until 1781, when he was exchanged and returned to England. The following year he was back in Canada as Lieutenant-Governor at Quebec, where he remained until 1785. In 1790 he became Governor of Bermuda, and gave his name to its capital city. He died in 1796 while serving as Governor of Dominica, and was buried on the island.

[13]Guy Carleton, Lord Dorchester (1724–1808) served under Wolfe at Quebec. In 1766 he was appointed Lieutenant-Governor and the following year Governor-General of Quebec. In 1778 he was succeeded in the governorship by General Haldimand. In 1786 he was again appointed Governor of Canada, an office he held until 1796.

[14]Sir Frederick Haldimand (1718–91) was born in Switzerland. He entered the British Army in 1754. In 1756 he was appointed Lieutenant-Colonel of the Royal American Regiment. From 1778 to 1784 he was Governor and Commander-in-Chief in Canada.

C 21　Notes on a Survey by T. Smith of Lots Opposite Peach Island
[Original in George F. Macdonald Collection, Windsor, Ont.]

The settlement opposite to Peach Island began about the year 1774 by permission of Major Basset of the 10th Regiment of Foot, then Commandant at Detroit, and in the year 1780, F. Porlier Benac acting Surveyor under authority of Major De Peyster[15] of the 8th Regiment of Foot also Commandant run the lines South $+ 14°$ East and gave certificate of survey to each proprietor—the following is a copy: viz.

Trois arpents de front sur quatre vingt de profondeur. Je soussigné duement authorisé certifie avoir mesuré le front de la terre que les Ottawas ont donné au Sieur Louis Peltier (No. 134) de trois arpents de front, laquelle terre tient au ouest à Jacques Peltier (No. 133) et à l'Est à J. B. Paré (No. 135) y avoir planté des piquets sur le bord du chemin dessigné pour le chemin du Roy. Pour la ditte ligne de profondeur cour au Sud $+ 10°$ Est. En foy de quoi j'ai donner le present pour servir ce que de raison. Detroit le 20 juin 1780.

Signe　J. Porlier Benac

[Translation: Three arpents in front by eighty arpents in depth. I, the undersigned, being duly authorized, certify that I measured the front of the land that the Ottawas gave to Mr. Louis Peltier (No. 134) of three arpents' frontage, which land adjoins on the west the land of Jacques Peltier (No. 133) and on the east the land of J. B. Paré (No. 135). I also planted some pickets on the side of the road designated as the King's Road. The side line of the said land runs south 10° east. In witness whereof I have given the present to serve as needed. Detroit June 20, 1780.

[Signed　J. Porlier Benac]

C 22　Major De Peyster to F. Comparé
[Detroit Notarial Records, liber C, p. 352]

[Detroit, Oct. 24, 1781]

François Comparé Sr.

In accordance with a certificate from Mr. Bénac, surveyor, and other proofs with regard to the lands granted at Little River by the Ottawas, you are hereby ordered to move back your house, barn, fences, and other buildings so as to leave for Pierre Meny a farm three arpents wide between your land and that of Antoine Robert Sr., according to the intentions of the said Indians.

[15]Arent Schuyler De Peyster (1736–1832) was born in New York City. At the age of nineteen he joined the Eighth Regiment. He rendered notable service in the Northwest during the Revolution. He was Commandant of Mackinac from 1774 to 1779, when he was promoted to the command at Detroit. He continued in that position until 1784. The following year he accompanied his regiment to England.

C 23 A Survey of the Settlement of Detroit Made by Order of Major De Peyster the 16 Day of July 1782 [South Shore Only]

[*P.A.C., B 123, pp. 260–273; M.H.C., X, 601–13*]

Heads of Families	Married Women	Widows & Hired Women	Young & Hired Men	Boys	Girls	Male Slaves	Female Slaves	Horses	Oxen	Cows	Steers & heifers	Sheep	Hogs	Flour, lbs.	Wheat, bushels	Indian Corn, bushels	Wheat sown, bushels	Indian corn sown, arpents	Oats sown, bushels	Arpents, clear land
Francois Prudhomme	.	.	.	.	.	.	.	.	.	.	.	.	.	.	.	.	5	.	.	40
Charles Fontaine	1	.	.	.	2	.	.	2	2	1	2	.	3	.	.	.	.	.	.	40
Jacques Bésere	1	.	.	4	1	.	.	1	2	4	2	.	4	.	.	.	18	6	.	160
Antoine Soumande	1	.	.	2	1	.	.	3	.	1	1	.	2	.	.	.	57	2	14	120
Pierre Meloche Junr	1	.	.	.	.	.	.	1	.	1	.	.	.	.	.	.	20	.	.	40
Pierre Fouquerau	1	.	1	3	2	.	.	1	2	3	1	.	4	.	.	.	20	5	8	60
Ettienne Lavoilette	1	.	.	5	2	.	.	3	.	1	4	.	2	.	18	.	23	6	5	48
Joseph Cotté	1	.	.	4	1	.	.	2	2	1	.	.	3	.	.	.	10	4	4	16
Louis Montmeney	1	.	.	3	3	.	.	5	3	2	.	.	10	250	.	.	18	6	4	32
Antoine Meloche	1	.	.	.	3	.	.	3	2	2	.	.	4	.	12	.	22	6	4	64
Jean Baptiste Gigniac	1	.	.	1	.	.	.	4	2	4	2	.	10	.	30	.	11	.	6	32
Jean Baptiste Antilliya	1	.	1	2	2	.	.	8	4	4	2	.	10	.	20	.	17	6	11	48
Thomas Pagotte	1	.	1	3	5	.	.	2	2	2	.	.	2	.	.	.	16	4	.	50
Charles Renaud	1	.	.	4	1	.	.	2	.	1	.	.	.	.	.	.	18	.	.	50
Jean Beaushomme	.	.	1	1	2	.	.	3	2	.	.	.	.	.	.	.	17	.	.	50
Pierre Prudhomme	1	.	.	.	3	.	.	3	.	1	2	.	2	.	.	.	10	.	.	55
Amable Gerard	1	.	1	2	.	.	.	3	2	.	1	.	4	.	.	.	20	4	7	60
Jean Louis Reveau	1	.	2	.	.	.	.	3	.	2	.	.	.	.	.	.	17	2	.	60
François Lesperance	.	.	.	.	.	.	.	3	2	.	.	.	.	300	20	.	18	5	8	60

[69]

C 23 (cont'd.)

Heads of Families	Married Women	Widows & Hired Women	Young & Hired Men	Boys	Girls	Male Slaves	Female Slaves	Horses	Oxen	Cows	Steers & heifers	Sheep	Hogs	Flour, lbs.	Wheat, bushels	Indian Corn, bushels	Wheat sown, bushels	Indian corn sown, arpents	Oats sown, bushels	Arpents, clear land
Pierre Proux	1	.	1	1	3	.	.	2	.	2	.	.	4	300	.	.	18	5	16	55
Antoine Rousseau	1	.	.	.	1	.	.	2	2	3	2	.	12	.	.	.	18	5	8	55
Charles Bernier	1	.	1	2	1	.	.	3	.	3	1	.	3	.	.	.	9	.	.	.
Antoine Boufard	2	.	.	5	1	.	.	3	2	4	2	.	6	.	.	.	30	6	6	100
René Cloutier	1	.	.	1	2	.	.	4	.	1	.	.	7	.	5	.	8	2½	4	50
Zachary Cloutier	1	.	1	4	4	.	.	2	2	2	.	.	12	.	.	.	16	4	5	100
Michael Roy	1	.	.	2	1	.	.	2	.	1	1	.	5	.	.	.	18	3	.	.
François Mouton	1	.	1	1	4	.	.	.	.	1	.	11	5	.	.	.	.	.	.	.
Ettienne Jacob	1	.	1	5	4	.	.	4	2	5	.	.	5	.	.	.	22	8	.	75
Louis Sousore	1	.	.	2	3	.	.	3	4	4	1	15	5	.	25	.	20	4	.	75
Mrs. Bissonnette	.	1	2	3	5	.	.	10	.	2	.	.	12	.	6	.	.	.	.	.
Jean Baptiste Begras	1	.	.	.	3	.	.	.	.	.	.	.	6	.	.	.	10	3	5	40
François Belaire	1	.	2	2	4	.	.	2	2	5	5	.	1	.	.	.	20	6	26	60
Paul Campau	1	.	1	2	2	.	.	6	4	6	2	.	7	.	.	.	13	.	10	75
Louis Lajeunesse	1	.	2	1	5	.	.	6	2	4	5	.	9	.	.	.	25	6	4	240
Joseph Pouget	1	.	3	2	4	.	.	5	2	6	.	.	10	.	.	.	47	6	.	180
Jean Bte. Taurenjau	1	2	4	2	1	.	.	4	.	4	.	.	8	.	.	.	5	3	3	120
Jean Saliotte	1	.	1	1	1	.	.	12	6	2	.	.	4	.	.	.	4	6	10	.
Guillaume Monforton	1	.	1	1	2	1	1	2	.	.	1	.	2	.	80	12	16	5	.	120
Joseph Drouillard	1	.	1	1	2	.	.	3	2	5	.	.	4	1000	.	.	8	8	.	120
Jean Bte Lebeau	1	.	1	.	3	.	.	7	2	2	.	.	10	.	.	.	12	5	15	75
Pierre Campeau	1	.	1	1	2	.	1	3	4	2	.	.	2	300	.	.	5	8	.	.
Joseph Nattade	1	.	.	.	2	.	.	3	.	.	.	.	2	.	.	.	2½	6	.	.
Simon Drouillard	1	.	2	3	4	.	.	2	4	5	.	.	12	.	.	.	8	.	.	120
Pierre Meloche	1	.	1	6	2	.	.	6	4	4	2	.	8	300	.	20	10	2	7	160

C 23 (cont'd.)

Heads of Families	Married Women	Widows & Hired Women	Young & Hired men	Boys	Girls	Male Slaves	Female Slaves	Horses	Oxen	Cows	Steers & Heifers	Sheep	Hogs	Flour, lbs.	Wheat, bushels	Indian Corn, bushels	Wheat sown, bushels	Indian corn sown, arpents	Oats sown, bushels	Arpents, clear land
Jacques Belleperche	1	1	.	1	.	.	.	5	2	2	.	.	5	.	.	.	.	.	4	120
Antoine Robert Junr	1	.	.	1	2	.	.	3	2	.	.	.	4	.	.	.	.	.	.	120
Louis Robidoux	1	.	.	3	3	.	.	10	.	9	.	30	.	.	.	.	.	.	.	120
Joseph Bondy	2	.	3	2	5	.	.	5	6	.	1	.	7	.	.	.	25½	.	.	120
Jean Bte Drouillard	1	.	.	1	.	.	.	2	.	.	5	.	2	.	.	.	3	3	.	.
Jean Bte Drouillard Senr	1	.	.	.	.	.	.	5	.	3	.	.	.	100	20	40	22	3	.	120
Pierre Cocquillard	1	.	3	.	3	.	1	2	.	.	2	.	3	.	.	.	11	3	6	120
Jean Bte Parrey	1	.	2	2	.	.	.	2	.	1	.	.	3	.	.	.	8	5	.	120
Augustine Toranjeau	1	.	3	1	4	1	.	2	.	3	5	.	5	.	.	.	10	2	.	120
Theophil Lemay	1	.	.	.	1	.	1	4	4	4	2	.	4	.	.	.	26	4	12	120
Charles Reaume	1	.	1	3	2	.	.	5	4	4	.	.	4	.	.	15	23	4	.	120
Louis Lajoye	1	.	.	5	2	.	.	4	2	9	.	.	.	.	.	.	18	6	.	120
George Knaggs	1	.	.	3	3	.	1	7	3	7	4	.	.	.	.	.	7	5	6	120
James Rankin	1	.	.	1	1	.	1	5	.	2	1	.	3	.	.	.	5	2	.	160
François Pratt	.	1	.	.	.	.	.	4	2	2	.	.	.	.	.	.	.	.	.	.
François Marentete Gaudet	1	.	1	5	2	1	2	10	8	5	.	25	12	300	.	.	50	.	15	200
Charles Robidoux	1	.	1	.	.	.	.	1	.	.	.	.	.	.	.	.	.	.	.	.
Jacques Parent	1	.	1	4	.	.	1	10	4	4	4	.	6	600	.	.	18	8	12	120
Laurent Parent	1	.	1	3	2	.	.	6	2	2	2	.	10	400	.	.	20	4	10	120
Claude Reaume	1	.	1	5	2	2	2	5	2	3	4	.	10	600	.	.	26	5	9	80
Joseph Mathieu	.	.	3	2	.	.	.	2	.	.	.	.	4	.	.	.	15	.	.	.
Philip Leduc	1	.	1	4	2	2	2	9	2	3	1	10	12	200	15	.	30	4	10	120
Ettienne Rodidoux	1	.	.	3	1	.	.	3	.	2	.	.	.	.	.	.	.	.	.	.
Jean Bte. Leduc	1	.	1	3	1	.	.	2	4	2	1	.	6	400	10	.	26	3	8	120

[71]

C 23 (cont'd.)

Heads of Families	Married Women	Widows & Hired Women	Young & Hired men	Boys	Girls	Male Slaves	Female Slaves	Horses	Oxen	Cows	Steers & heifers	Sheep	Hogs	Flour, lbs.	Wheat	Indian corn, bushels	Wheat sown, bushels	Indian corn do arpents	Oats do bushels	Arpents of clear land
Joseph Duschene	1			4	1			2	2				4				8	2	4	
Joseph Maillou	1	1		2	1			4	4	4	1	3	6				30	3	6	120
François Janesse		1		2	1			5	4	3	3		10				25	3	15	120
Jean Ouillette	1	2	2	3	2			10	2	3	3		9	500	8	5	15	4	12	80
André Bennetau	1			3	1			1		1			2	200			12	1	8	
François Bennetau	1	1		1	3			1	2	1			6	150	25	5	10	1		80
Charles Bourond	1							6	2	3	3		3	300			40	1	20	80
Joseph Larente			1					1		1				100						
Jean Bte. Tourneux	1				1		1	7	2	5	2		5	200			40	2½	15	120
Pierre Reaume	1	2		1				7	3	3			20	400	80		50		20	120
Ignace Duvalle	1		2	3	2		1	2	2		5		8				30	2½	12	120
Vittal Demouchelle	1		1	3	4			6		3	3		13	300	20		26	2	14	40
Louis Gouyou			2	1	1			3		1	1		8	400	35		32	6	10	80
Jacques Charon	1		1	1	1		1	10	2	2	1		3				33	4½	14	80
Joseph Lesperance	1	1	2	1	2			3	4		2		7	800			27		12	80
Julien Parent	1		2	3	2		1	5	4	3			15				40	4	20	80
Nicolas Langlois	1			1	2			6	2	1	3		10		100		70	4	30	80
Pierre Labute	1		1			2	1	6	4	3			1	400			65	4	33	160
François Gaudette	1			1	1			2		2	1		2	800			25		8	120
Hyacinth Dehêtre	1		2	1			1	2		1	1	1	6				18		8	60
Charles Delisle	1							3	2	1	3		5	400	50		20	5		80
Antoine Langlois	1	1		1	2		1	4	1	3	2		6				30	1½	12	120
Jean Bte. Beaubien	1	1	1	5	2			3	2	2	1		3				22	3	10	105
Joseph Beaubien	1	1		2	2			3	2	3					10		20			90
Joseph Cecire	1	1		4									2					4		
Fontenay Dequindre	1		1		1			4		1							7		3	

[72]

C 23 (cont'd.)

Heads of Families	Married Women	Widows & Hired Women	Young & Hired Men	Boys	Girls	male slaves	Female Slaves	Horses	Oxen	Cows	Steers & Heifers	Sheep	Hogs	Flour, lbs.	Wheat, bushels	Indian corn, bushels	Wheat sown, bushels	Indian corn sown, arpents	Oats sown, bushels	Arpents, clear land
Alexis Maisonville	1	.	.	4	.	2	2	11	7	7	8	44	15	.	300	.	104	5	37	280
Antoine L. Labady	.	.	.	3	3	1	1	17	4	3	13	.	12	2000	200	.	40	10	24	240
Bonaventure Reaume	1	1	2	4	3	.	.	5	2	3	1	.	7	.	50	.	36	3	10	80
Joseph Gaudet	1	.	2	1	2	.	1	3	2	1	4	.	4	.	20	.	18	.	11	80
Joseph Bertiaume	1	.	.	1	.	.	.	1	1	1	1	3	6	.	16	.	35	3	6	80
Pierre Reaume Jr	1	.	2	.	2	1	1	4	.	1	.	.	2	500	5	.	23	.	10	40
Jean Bte. Sancrainte	1	2	2	2	.	.	.	4	3	5	.	.	4	.	.	.	25	5	20	150
Francois Meloche	1	.	4	3	4	.	5	4	2	1	3	.	11	400	14	.	20	3	12	150
Mrs. Levril	.	.	1	2	5	.	.	4	.	.	.	.	.	200	.	.	.	8	.	15
Pierre Geirou	.	.	1	.	3	.	.	2	.	1	.	.	4	.	8	.	4	1½	.	18
Guillhaume Gouyou	1	.	.	.	1	.	1	9	3	4	.	.	5	.	.	.	.	1½	.	.
Nicholas Petit	1	.	.	3	2	.	.	1	2	1	2	.	3	400	10	.	23	4½	11	24
André Pettier	1	.	1	3	4	.	.	4	.	1	1	.	10	.	.	.	13	2	7	20
Jean Bte. Lapointe	.	2	2	2	5	.	1	3	2	6	.	.	3	.	.	.	12	5	.	48
Pierre Letrouneau	1	.	.	3	3	.	.	4	2	3	2	.	3	.	.	.	18	5	10	33
François Drouillard	1	.	1	2	1	.	.	2	2	3	.	.	10	100	30	.	18	.	.	33
Louis St. Louis	1	.	.	4	3	.	.	6	2	2	3	.	6	.	.	.	18	.	.	36
Pierre Leverseur	1	.	1	2	.	.	.	2	2	5	.	.	6	.	.	.	22	3	8	36
Francois Sourdellet	1	.	.	1	1	.	.	6	2	3	3	.	6	.	.	.	14	2	4	42
Joseph Valcour	1	.	2	3	3	.	.	3	4	5	3	.	3	500	.	.	20	.	6	66
Jean Bte. Parrey	1	.	1	2	2	.	.	3	4	2	4	.	6	.	.	.	13	.	5	66
Joseph Beauchamp	.	.	3	4	3	.	.	2	.	3	1	.	2	.	.	.	16	4	6	66
Antoine Robert	1	.	.	.	.	.	.	4	.	.	.	.	5	.	.	.	.	.	.	.
Totals	98	19	95	218	196	10	25	462	193	263	143	141	610	13600	1217	82	1654	324	761	8723

[The rest of the survey pertains to the north shore]

CENSUS
STATE OF THE SETTLEMENT OF DETROIT TAKEN THE 20TH OF JULY 1782

321	Heads of families	⎫ Exclusive of them	447	Sheep
254	Married Women	⎪ employed in the	1370	Hogs
72	Widows & married [hired?] women	⎪ King's service and are in the	29250	wt Flour
336	Young & Hired Men	⎬ Indian Country	1804	Wheat—bushels
526	Boys	⎪ —say—100—	355	Indian corn do
503	Girls	⎭	4075	bushels wheat sown last fall
78	Male Slaves		521	Acres under Indian Corn
101	Female slaves		1849	ditto [bushels?] under Oats
1112	Horses		13770	ditto under Cultivation
413	Oxen		3000	Bushels Potatoes supposed to be in the ground
807	Cows			
452	Heffirs & Steers		1000	Barrel Cyder ditto will be made

C 24   GENERAL HALDIMAND TO LIEUTENANT-GOVERNOR JEHU HAY[16]
[*P.A.C., B 64, pp. 199–200;* M.H.C., *XX, 249–50*]

Quebec 31st August 1784

I have received your Letters of the 16. & 22. of July in answer to the former Mr. Williams has my Permission to resign his Employments, and inclosed you have a Warrant of Appointment from Henry Caldwell Esq. the acting receiver Genl. authorizing the person whose name you shall insert, to demand of and oblige all Persons to pay to him their arrears of Lots and Ventes & all other dues. As Lt. Govr. of Detroit, you will give him due Assistance in the Execution of his office.

Lieut. Smith of the 31st Regiment has my orders to repair to Detroit for the purpose of receiving the records of that Place, of which you will cause an Inventory to be made, for which Lieut Smith will give you a receipt. These Records are to be lodged in the office of the Clerk of the Council at Quebec, to be forthcoming whenever a committee shall be appointed to Examine & report upon the Grants which Individuals have received from either Indians or Commanding Officers. . . .

C 25   LIEUTENANT-GOVERNOR HAY TO GENERAL HALDIMAND
[*P.A.C., B 75–2, p. 202;* M.H.C., *XX, 265*]

Detroit October 9th 1784

The 4th Instant in the Evening I had the Honor of receiving your Excellency's Letters of the 31st of August and 3d of September by

---

[16]Jehu Hay (–1785), was the second and last Lieutenant-Governor of Detroit. A native of Chester, Pennsylvania, who in 1758 enlisted in the Royal American Regiment, he served at Detroit as a lieutenant in 1762–3, and later was appointed commissary in the Indian Department. In 1776 he became Deputy Indian Agent and Major of Detroit militia. He was on Hamilton's fateful expedition to Vincennes in 1778. He accompanied his chief to Virginia as a prisoner of war, and was exchanged in 1781. The following year he was appointed Lieutenant-Governor of Detroit, but did not assume office until the summer of 1784. He died at Detroit on August 2, 1785.

SETTLERS COME TO THE SOUTH SHORE

Lieut. Smyth of the 31st Regiment, In consequence of which I informed Mr. Williams of your Excellency's permission to resign his Employments, and directed an Inventory to be made of the Records, which were delivered to Lieut Smyth and his receipt taken for the same.

The people express some concern at their being sent from the place, and say many must suffer in their private affairs for want of reference to them for so long a time as must necessarily pass before they can be returned.—I am informed there are many old settled Farms in this Settlement and some Grants from Indians, which will not be found in the Register not having being recorded.

C 26 CENSUS OF THE FAMILIES AND FARMS OF PETITE CÔTE ON APRIL 22, 1792, BY GUILLAUME MONFORTON,[17] CAPTAIN OF THE MILITIA

[*Ontario Historical Society*, Papers and Records, *1927, XXIV, 95–7*]

Name of inhabitant	Boys 15 and over	Boys under 15	Girls	Arpents in front	Arpents in depth	Remarks
Colonel McKey [McKee]	..	..	..	3	40	All the farms from
Jean Bt Pare	..	..	..	3	40	River Gervais to
Frederick Arnold	3	1	5	3	40	Turkey Creek opposite
Isaac Dolson	..	..	..	3	40	the end of Turkey
Mathew Dolson	..	..	..	3	40	Island were granted
Juge Powell	..	..	..	3	40	by Mr. de Sabrevois
Philipp Fox	3	4	2	3	40	
Thomas Smith	..	1	2	3	40	Mr. de Lajonquiere
Joseph Bondy, Senior	1	2	2	3	40	Commander-in-chief
Thomas Smith	..	..	..	2	40	in 1751 granted
Major McGregor	..	..	..	4	40	provisions for three
Simon Drouillar	2	1	..	3	40	years to the first
Antoine Girardin	..	..	1	3	40	settlers in 1752 and
Guillaume Monforton	2	1	3	3	40	1753, without any
Meldrum & Park	..	..	..	3	40	title.
Joseph Pouget	2	..	3	3	40	
Richard Pollar	..	..	..	3	40	
John Messomer	..	2	4	3	40	
Meldrum & Park	..	..	..	3	40	
John Snider	..	..	..	3	40	
John Askin	..	..	..	3	40	
Joseph Reaume	3	..	4	5	40	

[17]Guillaume Monforton (1735–1814) was a notary and Captain of the militia at Petite Côte. He spent some time at Kaskaskia, Illinois, and at Mackinac before coming to Detroit in 1778. From 1784 to 1792 the notarial records of Detroit were kept by him in his capacity of Notary Public. These records are contained in the so-called Monforton Register now resting in the Public Archives of Canada at Ottawa. About the years 1805–7 he was in prison for debt. John Askin befriended him in his misfortune, and some piteous letters on the subject are reproduced in the John Askin Papers.

C 26 (cont'd.)

Name of inhabitant	Boys 15 and over	Boys under 15	Girls	Arpents in front	Arpents in depth	Remarks
RIVIERE AUX DINDES [TURKEY CREEK]						
Pierre Ladebauche	1	..	4	4	40	All these farms were
Jn B. Bigras	..	..	..	..	..	granted in 1755–56
Zacharie Cloutier	1	3	3	2	40	by Mr. de Celoron
Antoine Bouffar	2	3	3	6	40	who gave tickets of
Martin Durocher	1	1	1	6	40	grant to the first
Antoine Bouffar	..	..	..	3	40	settlers on them.
Veuve Rousseau	..	..	..	3	40	[Date incorrect;
Veuve Grould	1	1	3	3	40	Céloron was at
Joseph Rochelo	2	..	..	3	40	Detroit 1751–4.]
Benjamin Chaput	1	2	2	3	40	These farms were
Pierre Meloche	7	..	..	3	40	occupied by several
Joseph Pouget	..	..	..	3	40	individuals, partly
Jn Louis Revau	..	2	2	3	40	before and partly
Pierre Girard	1	3	5	3	40	after the Conquest of
Bte. Gignac	..	3	3	3	40	Canada; the persons
Pierre Prudhomme	..	1	1	3	40	herein mentioned possess
Charles Renau	3	5	2	3	40	them at present by purchase or exchange and
Thomas Pageau	1	2	4	3	40	the majority of them
Jn Bte Antaillau	3	2	5	5	40	have no titles to
Joseph Bondy	..	..	..	2	40	produce....
Antoine Meloche	1	1	2	4	40	
Joseph Mainville	2	3	1	2	40	
Gerv. Hodienne	..	1	..	4	40	
Francois Beneteau	..	1	4	3	40	
Louis Bourassa	..	..	5	2	40	
Guillaume Monforton	..	..	..	1	40	
Jacques Beser	1	1	1	2	40	
Simon Bergeron	..	..	..	2	40	
Charles Renau	..	..	..	4	40	These farms were
Joseph Rocheleau	..	..	..	2	40	granted by the
Joseph Bondy, fils	..	2	2	3	40	Indians about three
Gabriel Bondy	..	1	2	4	40	years ago. The last
Antoine Meloche	..	..	..	4	40	one was listed by Mr.
Louis Bourassa	..	..	..	2	40	McNiff for Laurent Bondy, Louis Bourassa being absent.

C 27 Extracts from the Minutes of the Land Board of the District of Hesse

[*Fraser,* Third Report of Archives of Ontario *(1905), pp. 193–5*]

Friday, the 27th day of July, 1792

Petite Cote . . .

The Board examined Simon Bargeron, the present possessor of Lot No. 7, part of a French Grant, previous to the Conquest, confirm his Grant and having administered the Oath, direct a Certificate to be given him for a continuation in the second Concession. . . .

The Board examined Jacob Bazor, the present possessor of Lot No. 8, part of a French Grant previous to the Conquest, confirm his Grant. . . .

The Board examined Mr. Monforton, (Captain of Militia) the present Possessor of Lot No. 9, part of a French Grant and confirm his Grant. . . .

The Board examined Jarvais Houdienne, the present Possessor of Lot No. 10, part of a French Grant and confirm his Grant. . . .

The Board examined Louis Bourisseau, the present Possessor of Lot No. 11, part of a French grant. . . .

Friday, 3rd August, 1792

The Board proceeded to examine Francis Bennetto, the present Possessor of Lot. 12, part of French Grant and confirm his Grant. . . .

The Board having on the 27th of the last month examined Jervais Houdienne, the present Possessor of Lot No. 13, part of a French Grant confirm it. . . .

The Board proceeded to examine Joseph Menville, the present Possessor of Lot, No. 14, part of a French Grant, and confirm it. . . .

The Board examined Anthony Molosh, the present Possessor of Lot No. 15, part of a French Grant previous to the Conquest, and confirm it. . . .

Joseph Bondy Senior, the present Possessor of Lot No. 16, part of a French Grant, being sick and incapable of attending, the Board deferred. . . .

The Board proceeded to examine Jean Baptiste Antolia, the present Possessor of Lot No. 17, part of a French Grant, confirm it. . . .

The Board proceeded to examine Augustin Lhuissier who purchased Lot No. 18[18] from Thomas Pajot, part of a French grant, confirm him in it. . . .

[18]Lot 18 is immediately north of the side road now known as Martin Lane. The other lots mentioned lie in the mile stretch southward.

D. THE PIONEER SETTLERS AND THEIR FARMS

D 1 BAPTISMS OF FRENCH CHILDREN AT THE MISSION OF THE HURONS

[*B.H.C., Account Book of the Mission of the Hurons 1733–51*]

SAMPLE ENTRY IN EXTENSO:

Ego hodie baptizavi Mariam Ludovicam recens natam ex conjugibus Ludovico Viller et Maria Joseph. Morin; nomen dederunt Petrus Morin et Maria Ludovica Becquemont. . . .

4 Oct. 1751   Pet: Potier M.J.

TRANSLATION:

This day I baptized Marie Louise recently born of the marriage of Louis Viller and Marie Joseph. Morin; Pierre Morin and Marie Louise Becquemont gave the name. . . .

Oct. 4, 1751   Pierre Potier M.J.

Date	Name	Parents	Godparents
1751			
Oct. 4	Marie Louise	Louis Viller Marie Joseph. Morin	Pierre Morin Marie Louise Becquemont
Oct. 12	Jean François	Louis Reveau Jos. St. Estienne	Jean Claude LaSalle Susanne Bienvenue
1752			
Aug. 31	Jean Baptiste	——— Dufour Charlotte Roque	Poligny Langlois
1753			
Jan. 1	François	Louis Viller Marie Jos. Morin	François Janis Marguerite La Durantaye
March 3	Marie Joseph	François LeBeau Marie Jos. Bigras	Amable Bigras Catherine LeBeau
April 2	Michel	Paul Campeau Charlotte DuMoulin	Michael Campeau Marie Jos. Morin
July 13	Michel	Charles Buteau Marie Marguerite Gautier	Michel Campeau Elizabeth Rapin
Dec. 4	Jean	Jean Brisar Marie Angelique	François LeBeau Thérèse Meloche
1754			
Jan. 2	Marie Amable	Joseph Levron Marie Jos. Custeau	Charles Campeau Charlotte Montreil
Feb. 5	Joseph Marie	Jean Valade Marie Eliz. De Rouillard	Joseph Guignan dit St. Etienne Marie Charlotte Dufour
July 31	Thérèse	Michel Campeau Joseph. Buteau	Louis Delisle Marguerite Gautier
Sept. 20	Jean René	François LeBeau Marie Jos. Bigras	Jean René LeBeau Judith Cuillerier

Date	Name	Parents	Godparents
1756			
Jan. 28	Marie Charlotte	Joseph Levron dit Metayer	Joseph LeBeau Marie Charlotte Montret
May 31	Louis	Joseph Custeau Louis Campo Charlotte Des Moulins	Louis Viller Charlotte Campo
July 29	Marie Elizabeth	Michel Campeau Joseph. Buteau	Louis Gervais Elizabeth Rapin
Dec. 5	Jean Louis	not certain Marie Rose Bigras	Jean Brisart Jeanne Belleperche
Dec. 10	Bonaventure	Louis Clermont Louise Bouron	Valère Clermont Thérèse Bequette

NOTE: These entries are all undersigned P. Potier, M.J., with the exception of the entry for May 31, 1756, which is signed by Jean B. Salleneuve, S.J.

D 2 MARRIAGE CONTRACT
[Detroit Notarial Records, liber B, p. 96]

Before Philippe Dejean, notary public residing at Detroit, were present Jean Bte. Gignac also residing at the said place of Detroit, a native of the parish of Cap Santé in the diocese of Quebec, son of age of Joseph Gignac and of Magdeleine Galernau, his parents, stipulating for him and in his name, of the first part; and Sir Jean Bte. Le Beau, widower of the late Catherine Dudevoir stipulating for Lady Catherine LeBeau, their daughter, widow of Simon Bergeron deceased at this post, here present and accepting for her and in her name, of the second part; who in the presence and with the advice and counsel of their relatives and friends here assembled, i.e., on the part of Jean Bte. Gignac—René Cloutier, François Drouillard and François Langlois; and on the part of the above named Catherine LeBeau—the above named Jean Baptiste Le Beau, her father, Thomas Pageau, Antoine Rouchau dit Lafond, Jean Bte. Antaya and Victor Morisseau, son-in-law of the said Catherine Le Beau, have agreed and contracted for marriage as follows: The above mentioned Jean Baptiste Le Beau has promised and promises to give the said Catherine Le Beau, his daughter, to the said Jean Baptiste Gignac, who promises to take her for his future and lawful wife by the laws of marriage, and to have the same celebrated and solemnized before Our Mother, the Holy, Catholic, Apostolic and Roman Church, as soon as convenient or whenever either party asks it of the other.

The future husband and wife shall hold all property in common, both movable and immovable as acquired, according to the usage and custom of the viscounty of Paris, expressly relinquishing all contrary laws and customs. The said future husband and wife will take each other with the goods and rights belonging to them, whatever they may be, without any need of mentioning them here.

The said future husband has endowed and does endow the said future wife with the sum of three hundred livres to have and to take as soon as in every respect reasonable, and this to be secured by any and all property of the said future husband now in his possession. The said future wife shall own and possess the said jointure without being bound to request it by law, and the said jointure shall belong to the children who shall be born of the said future marriage, and if there are no children it shall belong to the said future wife.

In the case of the dissolution of the future marriage by the death of the said future husband, the said future wife shall have and possess as her preferred claim the sum of one hundred and fifty livres Tournois and it will be permissable for her and for her children if there are any, and in case there are none, for her closest heirs, to accept the said common ownership or renounce it, in which case she will take with her all that she brought to the said marriage along with her clothes, jewelry and her room furnished, as well as the goods that may have come to her through inheritance.

And to have the present contract registered with the clerk's office of the above mentioned Detroit and any other place where necessary, the said parties have chosen the bearer of these presents their general and special procurator and to whom they give power to obtain a certificate of same.

For thus it has been agreed between the parties, promising, obliging, renouncing etc. Executed at Detroit in the office of the said notary, in the year one thousand seven hundred and seventy-seven, on the twenty-first day of September in the forenoon. The said future husband and wife have declared they could not sign their names, and after having heard the reading thereof have made their mark in the presence of their relatives and friends.

Catherine + Le Beau	Jean Baptiste + Gignac	René + Cloutier
J. Bte + Antaya	François + Langlois	Antoine + Rouchau
Victorin + Morisseau	Largeau	Thomas + Pageau
	P. Dejean, Notary	

D 3   LIST OF THE INHABITANTS LIVING ON THE DETROIT RIVER, WHO HAVE ENGAGED TO FURNISH PROVISIONS FOR HIS MAJESTY'S TROOPS AT THIS POST AND YEARLY, SPECIFYING THE QUANTITY AND AT WHAT RATE

[Enclosed in Campbell to Gage, Detroit, May 31, 1766, William L. Clements Library, Gage Papers, American Series, vol. 62]

Inhabitants' Names [south side of river]	Flour at £1.13.4d NYCY p cwt Cwts	Pease at 10/p Bush. Bushels	Pork at 1/p lb. Lbs
Tourrenjeau	500	..	100
Charles Lamar	1000	4	....
St. Etiene	300	..	....
J. Baptiste La beaux	200	4	....
Widow Pilete	1000	..	....
Pierre Moloche	1000	..	140
Lesperance	1000	..	100

PIONEER SETTLERS AND THEIR FARMS 81

Inhabitants' Names	Flour	Pease	Pork
Lewis Vilers	300	10	....
Lewis Jadot	3000	14	200
Lelorond	5000	..	100
Lewis Susor	3000	..	....
Etiene Jadquo [Jacob]	300	..	....
Francis Lebeaux	500	..	100
Francis Rochelo	600	..	....
Michael Vodris [Vaudry]	600	..	....
Baptiste Drouillard	1000	..	....
Lewis Binot	400	..	....
Nichs Langlois	500	6	100
G. Gauyeau	1000	5	....
Joseph Dusaux	500	5	100
Charles Bouron	500	10	100
Pierre D'Noie [Desnoyers]	1000	5	100
Joseph Maillous	500	3	....
Vital Gauyeau	400	..	....
J. Baptiste Goualaite [Ouellette]	200	3	....
Pierre Javire	600	..	....
Pierre La Bute	3000	12	200
	27900	81	1340

Detroit May 24th 1766

(Signed)
John Campbell Lt Col. 17th Regt

The above list of people are of opinion that they may dare venture to promise they will be able in a year or two to furnish a due proportion of Fresh Pork and pease (Baring unforeseen accidents) tho' at present they cannot engage for any quantity worth taking notice of.

D 4 INVENTORY OF THE ESTATE OF JOSEPH PILLET
[Detroit Notarial Records, liber A, p. 317]

June 10, 1767

A farm 6 by 40 arpents, with a house, a new barn, an old barn, a shed and other small buildings valued at	4,000 livres
4 draw oxen and 2 bulls	700
3 cows and 2 heifers	400
3 calves	100
1 old horse	50
2 mares, a filly and a colt	250
8 hogs	160
6 little pigs	10
30 chickens	30
1 pot	30
3 tubs	20
1 iron stove	230
1200 lath mails	12
1 pie dish with cover	40
1 spade, 3 axes, 1 crock, 1 saw, etc.	80
5 old kettles	15
1 old pie dish	6
1 pot	20
3 kettles	15
2 frying pans	6
2 irons, 1 toaster, 2 tripods, 1 large spoon, 1 meat fork, and 1 lantern	12

		livres
23 pounds of pewter	23	
50 pounds of iron	37	10
2 andirons, 1 shovel, 1 pot-hanger	20	
1 old caleche	40	
1 carriolle	25	
1 cart, another without wheels	40	
1 plough	35	
1 feather tick, 1 pallett, 1 blanket	40	
1 feather tick, 1 pallett, 1 blanket, and 1 quilt	80	
Harness, straps, chains, etc.	50	
1 chain for hauling logs	15	
2 tables, 1 kneading-trough, 1 old chest, 6 chairs, 1 cupboard	40	
1 mirror	6	
Cash	6637	10
Bills Receivable	162	
Bills payable 1160	876	10
	6516	

J. B. Faignan
Pierre Meloche
Nicolas Langlois
Charles Morand
Joseph Pouget

D 5 A General Return of All the Inhabitants of Detroit Taken by Philip Dejean, Justice of the Peace for the Said Place on the 22nd Day of September 1773
[*P.A.C., B 122, p. 2; M.H.C., IX, 649*]

	Men	Women	Young Men Ten to 20	Boys from 1 to 10	Young Women Ten to Twenty	Girls from 1 to 10	Servants	Men Slaves	Women Slaves
South Side	107	81	33	112	30	76	27	6	3
North Side	124	107	45	137	24	134	36	26	22
The Fort	66	36	6	35	4	30	27	14	4
On Hog Island	1	1	..	...	..	...	3	..	..

	Oxen	Cows	Heifers	Sheep	Hogs	Acres of land in front	Acres of land cultivated	Houses	Barns
South Side	222	203	117	21	390	228	1424	93	63
North Side	211	306	241	424	602	284	1175½	117	93
The Fort	20	83	22	62	45	...	....	68	..
On Hog Island	20	17	32	121	30	...	....	2	1

N.B.—The troops and Naval Dept., with their cattle, etc., are not included in the above. The men servants are generally more numerous, several being now hunting and at the Indian Villages.

D 6 CONTRACT OF PURCHASE BETWEEN CLAUDE LANDRY AND BENJAMIN CHAPUT
[*Quaife,* The John Askin Papers, *I, 61–4*]

BEFORE US, Gabriel Legrand, notary residing at Detroit and there resident, was present the undersigned, Claude Landry dit St. André, living on his land southwest of the said Detroit, whither we went for the purpose following, viz: That the said Claude Landry declares that of his own free will and without constraint of any kind, also with the consent of his wife, Angelique LeDuc, who gives him authority to act for her in this respect, he has sold, released, ceded and given over, henceforth and forever, with right of disposal and guaranty from all troubles and hindrances whatsoever that may arise from any action of his own, a tract of land of three arpents in front by forty in depth located and situated on the south bank of the river of the said Detroit, adjoining land of Gignac on the northeast and of LeVeillié on the southwest, and unceded lands in the rear, with all its dependencies, also a log house on the above land, sixteen by seventeen feet, the whole without reserve such as it is and as it extends on every side, to Benjamin Chaput, farmer, by these presents accepting the same for himself, his heirs and assigns, who also says that he knows the said land, having seen and examined it, and that he is content and satisfied therewith, the said land being the property of the said vendors, who took it back from Charles Bergante to whom Pierre Coquillard had sold it, and by default of payment the said St. André has re-entered into possession of his land and he hereby binds himself to place all documents concerning the said land into the hands of the said purchasers, their heirs and assigns, that they may, by the sale thus made, have full use of the said land forever, with power for its disposal, subject to the charges of cens et rentes, seigniorial rights and customary service, the said land being holden from the domain of the King, and a further charge of one hundred minots of wheat and sixty minots of corn which have been paid in full, and from which the said St. André and his wife give the said purchasers unconditional release, wherefore the said St. André has assigned to the said Benjamin Chaput, his heirs and assigns, all his rights of ownership, real or pretended, upon the said land, that the said purchasers may enter into good and peaceable possession and seizin hereby, and that it may belong to them by virtue of these presents, irrevocably substituting for that purpose the bearer hereof in his place, in giving to them his power hereby, &c., promising &c., obliging, &c., renouncing &c. Duly executed at Detroit, in the house of the said St. André, by us, the notary undersigned, on the afternoon of July the ninth, one thousand seven hundred and seventy-four, in the presence of Jacques Godfroy, resident of Detroit, and of Jean LaRue, living on the south side [of the river] both witnesses who have signed, and the said Claude Landry and Angelique LeDuc, his wife, who have testified that they cannot sign, have made their customary mark after hearing these presents read, and in the original is written, Jacques Godfroy, Jean LaRue, by mark, St. André and Angelique LeDuc, also by their marks, and Notary Legrand, who has delivered the present copy, which is a true copy and conformable to the original, this twenty-second day of April, one thousand seven hundred and seventy-six.

D 7 LIEUTENANT-GOVERNOR HAMILTON TO THE EARL OF DARTMOUTH[1]
[*P.A.C., Q 12, pp. 212–22;* M.H.C., *X, 264–7*]

Detroit, August 29, 1776

Tho sensible that a multiplicity of affairs must engage your Lordship's attention at present, and that the importance of them ought perhaps to deter me from trespassing on your time, yet my Duty informs me, that I should not lose an opportunity of laying before your Lordship the state of this Post and Settlement....

As I have been closely attached to the Fort since my arrival, and my time been much employed in attention to the Savages, it would be improper for me to attempt giving your Lordship any but a general idea of the state of this settlement. I hope to be able when the present troubles subside, to make such enquiries, and gain such Information as not to be entirely at a loss, should your Lordship honor me with your commands—I shall yet be apprehensive of failing in my desire to convey information to your Lordship, and tho' on the spot, shall be happy to have objects of enquiry pointed out to me.

The Industry and enterprising Spirit of the traders of this Post, so far outgo the Canadians, that I am persuaded the latter will in a very few years be dependants on or bought out of their possessions by the former—The Navigating the Lakes in large Vessels, is entirely in the hands of the new Settlers, the new Settlers manage their farms to the best advantage—The Canadians are mostly so illiterate that few can read, and very few can sign their own names. 'till the surrender of the country to the English the breeding of sheep was not known here and horned cattle were very rare, at present I am told there are about 2000 sheep and 3000 head of black cattle in the Settlement.

This backwardness in the improvement of farming has probably been owing to the easy and lazy method of procuring bare necessaries in this Settlement—Wood was at hand, the Inhabitants therefore neglected to raise stone and burn lime which is to be had at their doors—The straight (which at the Town of Detroit is 1000 yards over) is so plentifully stocked with variety of fine fish that a few hours amusement may furnish several families, yet not one French family has got a seine—Hunting

---

[1]William Legge, Second Earl of Dartmouth, was Secretary of State for the Colonies 1772–75; then he became Lord Privy Seal.

and fowling afford food to numbers who are nearly as lazy as the Savages, who are rarely prompted to the chase till hunger pinches them. The soil is so good that great crops are raised by careless & very ignorant farmers, Wheat, Indian Corn, Barley, Oats, Pease, Buck Wheat yield a great increase—Yet there is no such thing as yet, as a piece of land laid down for Meadow, and the last Winter, indeed a remarkable severe one from this country to the Illinois several of the Cattle perished for want of Fodder—There are very extensive Prairies in the Settlement, but so many natural advantages have hitherto appeared rather to encourage sloth than excite Industry—The great advantage to be drawn from the management of bees, has never induced any to try them here, tho there are wild bees in great numbers, and the woods are full of blossoming shrubs, wild flowers and aromatic herbs—As to the Climate, tis by far the most agreable I have ever known. The heat of Summer tho great, does not overpower, and is not attended with either the ruinous gusts of wind experienced to the Southward, or the unwholesome vapours complained of usually by those who live near the Great Waters. The Lakes are as free from stagnation as the sea, and this vast straight, has a swift current yet knows scarce any difference as to the fullness of its Bed in Summer and Winter—The Inhabitants may thank the bounty full hand of providence, for Melons, Peaches, Plumbs, Pears, Apples, Mulberries and Grapes, besides several sorts of smaller fruits— several of these grow wild in the woods, those which have got a place in gardens are after being stuck in the ground committed to the care of the climate and soil, so are perpetually degenerating—Hemp & Hops seem natives of almost all America, they might be greatly improved here— There are Salt Springs at a little distance from this place, but I have not yet had time to visit them—

The number of Settlers whites, is about 1500. They build on the borders of the Straight, and occupy about 13 miles in length on the North, and 8 on the South side—the houses are all of Log or frame Work, shingled, the most have their orchard adjoining, the appearance of the Settlement is very smiling. On Holydays one would be tempted to think the Inhabitants were fond of cleanlyness, for they in general dress beyond their means, almost every one has a calash for summer and a carriole for winter. They use Oxen and Horses indifferently for the Plough. . . .

D 8   PETITION FOR WATER-MILL ON TURKEY CREEK
[*Detroit Notarial Records, liber C, p. 8*]

We, the undersigned, all inhabitants of Petite Côte in the Parish of L'Assomption of Detroit, consider that for the public weal it would be necessary to have at the said place a water-mill that might grind the grain in the seasons most advantageous to the said inhabitants, and that there is a place suitable for this purpose only on Turkey Creek in the King's Domain, and knowing the capability of Simon Drouillard to build and operate the said mill, we beseech you, Sir Commandant, to grant him permission to build the said mill and to possess it for himself and his heirs. In witness whereof we have signed these presents at Detroit the first day of July [in the year] One thousand seven hundred and eighty.

Signed:

J. Bondy	+ Antoine Cloutier	+ Charles Renot
Charles Pouget	+ J. Baptist Lebeau	Pierre Belaire
Charles Reaume	Pierre Meloche	+ Charles Fontane
+ Rene Cloutier	+ Pierre Parrez	J. B. Baushomme
+ Teofil Lemay	+ Touranjeau	+ J. B. Faignant
+ Jacques Belleperche	+ J. B. Drouillard	+ Augus Pinparre
+ ——— Tuotte	+ J. B. Pitre	+ Francois Lesperance
+ Antoine Lafont	+ ——— Charron	+ Francois Dufour
Baptist Dufour	Geo. Knaggs	+ Pierre Proux
		+ Louis Reveau

In accordance with a petition signed by several inhabitants of Petite Côte, I grant permission to Simon Drouillard to have a water-mill erected on Turkey Creek.

Given at Detroit this 11th day of July 1780
(signed) At. S. DePeyster

D 9   Reverend J. F. Hubert[2] to General Haldimand
[*P.A.C., B 74, pp. 225–6*]

La Pointe de Montréal, December 21, 1781

Your Excellency having honored me with the permission to write to him, it is for me a duty to do so. I inform him of my arrival at Detroit on the 8th of November last. I stayed 22 days at Carleton Island occupied in giving to the Canadian sailors the spiritual help which they had long requested. The journey, although long, has been very pleasant; it seemed to me that your Excellency's letters to the commandants of the different posts transmitted to them the kind sentiments with which your Excellency has honored me.

In his History of Canada Father Charlevoix did not exaggerate in saying that everything in this part of the country is beautiful—beautiful climate, beautiful rivers, prairies & forests, but above all beautiful and fertile land. Your Excellency then has reason to be surprised that it does not support its inhabitants. I believe that I have found the cause in the price of wheat being too low. Eight years ago it was worth only

---

[2]Jean François Hubert (1739–97), a native of Quebec, was ordained July 20, 1766. For many years he was secretary to the Bishop of Quebec, and for five years Superior of the Seminary at that place. Pastor of Assumption Church 1781–5; Coadjutor-Bishop of Quebec 1786–8; Bishop of Quebec 1788–97.

five livres. An inhabitant found it quicker and more to his taste to make the five livres with his gun or line than with his bushel of wheat. Hence the farms were neglected. But now that wheat sells for a louis, he willingly leaves the gun and the line to take up the plough. I believe it is an evil for a good that wheat is dear; it makes everybody want to grow some. Gradually men will turn to the cultivation of the land, will train their servants and children in it, and in this way the latter will lose their taste for travelling and hunting, and will be forced to become useful farmers instead of lazy hunters.

Time not having permitted me to make any other observations on this part of the country, I close this letter by wishing a long and happy life to Your Excellency, and assuring him of the profound respect with which I am, dear general,

E. GOVERNMENT AND LAW UNDER BRITISH RULE

E 1 Marquis de Vaudreuil[1] to Commandant Belestre[2]
[Archives du Séminaire de Québec, Viger, "Ma Saberdache," M, tome I, pp. 158–60]

Montreal, September 9, 1760

I notify you, Sir, that I was forced to capitulate yesterday with General Amherst's army. This town is, as you know, without dedence, our troops were considerably diminished, our means and our resources totally exhausted. We were surrounded by three armies which together numbered not less than thirty thousand men. On the 6th of this month General Amherst was in view of the walls of this town; General Murray was within range of one of our suburbs, and the army from Lake Champlain was at La Prairie and Longueuil.

Under these circumstances we had no hope of success from the efforts and even from the sacrifice of the troops. I wisely decided to capitulate with General Amherst on very advantageous terms to the colonists and particularly for the inhabitants of Detroit. They retain the liberty to practice their religion, keep possession of their household goods and real estate, and also their furs &c. Moreover they have the same trading privileges as the subjects of the King of Great Britain. The same conditions are accorded to the soldiers and they can appoint attorneys to act in their interests during their absence. They and the citizens in general can either dispose of their goods to the English or the French, and have the revenue sent to France or take it with them if they think proper to return there at the peace. They keep their Negro or Panis slaves but are obliged to give back those taken from the English.

The English General has declared that the Canadians become subjects of His Britannic Majesty, and for this reason the people have not been kept in the "Coutume de Paris". With regard to the troops he has imposed on them the condition of not serving during the present war and of laying down their arms. They shall be sent back to France.

You will therefore, Sir, assemble the officers and men who are at your Post, make them lay down their arms, and go with them to whatever seaport is designated for embarkation to France. The citizens and inhabitants of Detroit will be consequently under the command of the

---

[1] Pierre François Rigault, Marquis de Vaudreuil (1698–1793) was born in Canada, the son of a former Governor of Canada of the same name. In 1733 he was Governor of Three Rivers, and from 1743 to 1753 of Louisiana. In 1755 he became Governor of Canada, and continued in office until the British conquest.

[2] François Marie Picoté, Sieur de Belestre (1719–1793) was the last French Commandant at Detroit, 1758–60. After the treaty of 1763 he became member of the Legislative Council of Lower Canada. In 1775 he opposed the American invasion at St. Jean.

officer whom General Amherst shall have destined for that Post. You will send copies of my letter to the Miamis and to the 8cactanons if some soldiers remain there in order that they and the inhabitants may conform to it.

I count on having the pleasure of seeing you in France with all your men. Madame de Belestre is enjoying perfect health.

E 2 EXTRACT FROM THE JOURNAL OF ROBERT ROGERS[3]
[*Published in* Bulletin of New York Public Library, *XXXVII, no. 4 (April 1933), 267-72*]

November 19, 1760: From this place [near Sandusky, Ohio] I detached Mr. Brehme with a Letter to Monsr Belestre the french Commandant in theese Words.

Sir:

That you may not be Alarm'd at the Approach of the English Troops under my Command, when they Come to Detroit; I send forward this by Liut^t Brehme to Acquaint you that I have General Amherst's[4] Orders to take possession of Detroite; and such other parts as are in this District, which by Capitulation Agreed to and Signed by the Marquis de Vaudreuil and his Excellency Major General Amherst, the Eighth of September last now belong to the King of Great Britain.

I have with me the Marquis de Vaudreuil's Letters to you directed for your Guiddance, on this occasion, which Letters I shall deliver you at my Arrival; at or near your Post, and shall Incamp the Troops I have with me at some distance from the Fort, untill you have reasonable time to be made Acquainted with the Marquis de Vaudreuill's Instructions & the Capitulation which Captain Campbell[5] who Commands at Detroite this Winter has with him.

To
  Captn Belestre or the
  Officer Commanding at Detroit

I am
Sir
  Your humble Servt
  Robert Rogers

November 24, 1760: This Night Sixty of the Indian Party Came to our Camp [west end of Lake Erie], Congratulated our Arrival in their

[3]Major Robert Rogers (1724-84?) was the leader of Rangers during the Seven Years' War. Upon the surrender of Canada in 1760 he was commissioned to take possession of Detroit and the other western posts from the French. He was back at Detroit during the Pontiac siege in 1763. In 1766-7 he served as Governor of Mackinac and dependencies. In the Revolutionary War he organized and commanded the Queen's Rangers (1775-6) and the King's Rangers (1779).

[4]General Jeffery Amherst (1717-97) became Commander-in-Chief in North America in 1758. He marched to Montreal 1760 and received its capitulation. He became Governor-General of British North America until 1763, when he returned to England.

[5]Major Donald Campbell of the Royal American Regiment came to Detroit with Rogers in 1760 and served as Commandant of the post until the arrival of Major Gladwin in 1762. He was cruelly murdered during the Pontiac conspiracy of 1763.

Country, & Offered themselves as an Escort to Detroite; from whence they came the day before.

They added that Mr Brehme and his Party were Confined, & that Mr Besleter had Set up a high flagg Staff with a Wooden Effigy of a Man's Head on the Top, & upon that a Crow, that the Crow was to Represent himself, the Man's Head mine, and the Meaning of the Whole that he would scratch out my Brains. This Artifice had no Effect for the Indians told them as they said, that the Reverse would be the true Explanation of the Sign.

After we had proceeded Six Miles North East, On the 25th we Halted at the Request of the Indians who desired me to Call in the Chief Captains of the Party at the Streights Mouth. I did so and Spent the 26th at the same place in Conciliating their friendship.

The Morning on the 27th Mr. Belester sent me the following Letter by Mr Babbee[6] [translation p. 92].

Monsieur.   Detroit ce 24e Novembre 1760

J'ai receue la Lettre que vous m'avés ecrit par un de vos Officiers, Comme je n'ai point d'Interprete Je ne puis faire la Reponse Amplement.

L'Officer qu'il ma remis la Votre me fit sçavoir qu'il etoit detaché afin de m'annoncer de votre Arrivé pour prendre possession de Cette Garnison, selon la Capitulation fait en Canada, que vous avés Conjointement avec une Lettre de Monsr de Vaudreuill à mon Adresse.

Je vous prie Monsr d'areter vos Troupes a l'entrance de la Riviere, jusques à ce que vous m'envoyés la Capitulation & la Lettre de Monsr le Marquis de Vaudreuill afin de pouvoir y Conformer

Je suis bien Surpris qu'on ne m'a pas envoyé un Officier françois avec vous selon la Coutume.

A Monsr Monsr
Rogers Major et
Commandant le
Detachment Anglois

J'ai l'honneur d'estre &^cc
De Besleter

Shortly after a French Party under Captn Barringer beat a Parley on the West Shore, I sent M^r McCormick to know his Business who Returned with the Officer and this Letter [translation p. 93].

Detroit ce 25 Novembre 1760

Monsieur

Je vous ai deja marqué par Monsr Berranger les raisons pourquoy, je n'ai pu répondre en Detail a la Lettre qui ma Etés remis le 22eme du Courant par l'Officier que vous m'avés Detaché J'ignore les raisons pourquoy cet Officier n'a pas voulu retournier aupres de vous.

J'envoye mon Interprete Huron ches cette Nation que l'on me dit Etre Attroupé sur le chemin afin de les Contenir ne Scachant positivement s'il, cest a vous ou a nous a qu'ils en veuillent, et pour leurs dire de ma part,

[6]Probably Jacques Duperon Baby.

Q'uils [sic] ayent a Se tenir Tranquils, que je Scavois que je devois a mon General, et que des lors que l'Acte de la Capitulation seroit en Regle, j'etois Obligé d'Obeir; ce dit Interprette a ordre de vous Attendre, et de vous Remettre la presente.

Ne Soyés point Surpris Monsieur Sy le long de la Coste vous trouverés nos Habitans sur leur Garde, on leur a Annoncé qu'il y avoit beaucoup de Nations à votre Suitte, a qui on avois promis le pillage, et que les dittes Nations estoient mesme determiner a vous le demander; Je leur ai promis de se garder, c'est pour votre Conservation et Seurté [sic] ainsy que pour la nôtre en cas que les dittes Nations vinssent a faire les Insolents, Seul vous ne Seriés peut être pas dans les Circonstances presentes en Etat de les Reduire.

Je me flatte Monsieur qu'avant que darriver vous voudriés bien m'envoyer par quelqu'un de vos Messieurs et la Capitulation, Et La Lettre de Monsieur de Vaudreuill.

A Monsieur: Monsr Rogers Major et Commandant le Detachement Anglois au bas de la Riviere	J'ai l'honneur D'estre Monsieur, Vostre très humble et Obeissant Serviteur Piquotu de Beslestre

We Encamped next day Six Miles up the River having rowed against the Wind, and on the 29th I dispatched Captn Campbell, with Messrs Barringer, & Babée, & their Parties, and this Letter.

Camp at the Island 28: Novr 1760

Sir:

I Acknowledge the Receipt of your two Letters, both of which were delivered to me Yesterday; Mr Brehme has not yet Returned; the Inclosed letter from the Marquis de Vaudreuill will Inform you of the Surrender of all Canada to the King of Great Britain and of the great Indulgence granted to the Inhabitants, as also of the terms granted to the Troops of his Most Christian Majesty, Capt Campbell whom I have sent forward with this Letter will Shew you the Capitulation; I desire you'll not detain him, as I am determined Agreable to my Instructions from General Amherst— Speedilly to releive your post. I shall Stop the Troops I have with me at the hither end of the Town, till four o Clock, by which time I expect your Answer, Your Inhabitants under Arms will not Surprize me as yet I have Seen no other in that Position but Savages Waiting for my Orders; but this I tell you that the Inhabitants of Detroite shall not be Mollested, they and you Complying with the Capitulation but be protected in the peacable and Quiet possession of their Estates, neither Shall they be pillaged by my Indians nor by yours that have Joined me

I am & ca &ca
Robert Rogers

To
    Captn Besletre

Captain Campbell returned with Mr Besleters Compliments, Signifying that he was under my Command.

We rowed Eight Miles, and at half a Mile short of the Fort and fronting it I drew up my Detachment on a Field of Grass; from hence I sent Liut^t Lesley's & McCormick with Thirty Six Royal Americans to take possession of the Fort.

The French Garrison laid down their Arms; English Colours were hoisted and the Enemys taken down, At which 700 Indians gave a Shout, Merrily exalting in their Prediction that the Crow represented the English.

They seemed Amazed at the Submissive Salutations of the Inhabitants expressed their Satisfaction at our Generosity in not putting them to Death, and Said they would allways fight for a Nation thus favoured by him that Made the World.

I went Into the Fort Received a Plan of it with a list of the Stores from the Commanding Officer, and by Noon of the 1st December we had Collected the Militia Disarmed them & Administred the Oaths.

The Interval from this time to the 9th was Spent in preparing Several Measures that Appeared to be Necessary.

I put Mr Besletre & the other Prisoners under the Care of Liut^t Holmes and thirty Rangers to be Carried to Philadelphia, Captn Campbell and his Company took possession of the Fort & It's Magazines. Liut^t Butler, and Ensign Wait were sent with a Detached Party of Twenty Men to bring the French Troops from the Forts Miami, and Yatanois.

I Ordered that if possible a party should Subsist at the former this Winter, and give the Earliest Notice at Detroite, of the Enemy's Motions in the Country of the Illinois. I sent M^r McGee [Alexander McKee] with a french Officer for the french Troops at the lower Schwanese Town on the Ohio and as Provisions were scarce directed Captn Brewer to Repair with the greatest part of the Rangers to Niagara detaining Liut^t McCormick and Thirty Seven More to go with me to Missilimakinac.

[BELESTRE TO ROGERS (translation)]

Detroit, Nov. 24, 1760

I received the letter that you sent to me by one of your officers. Since I have no interpreter I cannot give a full answer.

The officer who brought me your letter informed me that he was sent ahead to announce to me your arrival for the purpose of taking possession of this garrison according to the Act of Capitulation made in Canada which you have in your possession along with a letter from Mr. Vaudreuil addressed to me.

I pray you, Sir, to halt your troops at the entrance of the river until you have sent me the Act of Capitulation and Mr. Vaudreuil's letter so that I may be able to conform to it.

I am much surprised that a French officer was not sent with you according to custom.

Detroit, November 25, 1760

I have already pointed out by Mr. Berranger the reasons for not being able to reply in detail to the letter that was delivered to me on the 22nd inst. by the officer that you sent to me. I do not know why that officer has chosen not to return to you.

I am sending my Huron interpreter to that Nation which is said to be gathered along the way in order to restrain them, not knowing for certain whether they are lying in wait for you or for us; I also want to tell them to maintain peace, that I know my duty to my general and that if the Act of Capitulation is in order I am obliged to obey. The said interpreter has orders to wait for you and to deliver to you this letter.

Do not be surprised, Sir, if along the shore you find our inhabitants on their guard. It has been reported to them that accompanying you were many nations to whom pillage had been promised, and that the said nations were determined to demand it. I promised [permitted?] them to arm themselves. It is for your protection and safety as well as for ours in case the said nations should act insolently. Alone you might not be able to restrain them in the present circumstances.

I trust, Sir, that before your arrival you will be good enough to send me by one of your men both the Act of Capitulation and Mr. Vaudreuil's letter.]

E 3   EXTRACT FROM GEORGE CROGHAN'S[7] JOURNAL 1759–63
[*Published in the* Pennsylvania Magazine of History and Biography, *LXXI, no. 4 (October 1947), 393–4*]

26th [*November 1760*] The Wind blew so hard as to prevent our going out of the Cove [west end of Lake Erie] the Messengers sent off Yesterday Return'd and informed us—that the French were much displeas'd with the Indian Nations for meeting us, and threatened to burn their Towns, that they wou'd not suffer the English to come to D'Troit untill they had Orders from the Governour of Canada and hear'd the Terms of the Capitulation.

We then assured them that any damage they shou'd sustain from the French on that account shou'd be repaired by us.

The 27th [*November 1760*] in the morning a Cannoe with two Interpreters and 4 French came to our Camp with Letters from Mr. Belleater. some short time after we Decamped and made the mouth of the D'Troit River, where we met the Chiefs of the Wyandotts, Ottaways and Putawautamies who bid us wellcome to their Country and Joyn'd us, and we proceeded up the River about 6 Miles and were met by a French Officer who hois'd a flagg of Truce and Beat a Parley, here we encamped

---

[7]George Croghan migrated in 1741 from Ireland to the Pennsylvania frontier, where as a trader he soon acquired a knowledge of Indian habits and languages. His influnece among the western tribes led to his appointment in 1756 as Deputy Superintendent of Indian Affairs under Sir William Johnson—a position he ably filled until his resignation in 1772. He died near Philadelphia on August 30, 1792.

on an Island and sent for the Officer who acquainted us with his business.

The 28th [November 1760] Captain Campbell set off with a Flag of Truce to give Mr. Belleater his Orders to Surrender the place, soon after his departure we sailed further up the River and encamped at an Indian Village, at night Captain Campble Return'd and Reported that Mr. Belleater behaved very Polite on seeing Mr. Vodrels Orders, and desired we wou'd March in tomorrow and take Possession of the Fort and Country.

The 29th [November 1760] We Set out and at 12 o'Clock arrived at the Place where we Landed and Relieved the Garrison.

The 30th [November 1760] Part of the Militia laid down their Arms and took the Oath of Fidelity.

December 1st [1760] the remainder of the Militia laid down their Arms and took the aforesaid Oath.

The 2nd [December, 1760] Lieut. Holmes set out with Mr. Belleater and the rest of the Garrison for Fort Pitt with whom I sent English Prisoners that I had got from the Indians.

E 4 EXTRACTS FROM THE PONTIAC MANUSCRIPT[8]
[B.H.C.]

... The two nations [Ottawa and Potawatomi] together comprised about four hundred men. This number not yet seeming large enough, it was a question of drawing into their project the Hurons who were divided into two bands under two different chiefs of different character. However, the same Jesuit father, their missionary, controlled them both.

The two chiefs of this latter nation were called the one Takay, who was like Pontiac in character, the other Teata, who was a very cautious and prudent man. The last named, not of a disposition to do wrong, was not easily won over. Not caring to listen to Pontiac's messengers he sent them back as they had come. They then went to the other band of the Hurons who listened to them and received from them war-belts to Join Pontiac and Ninivois. ...

May 12. Thursday: Feast of the Ascension of our Lord.

... Pontiac who knew neither feast nor Sunday and regarded all days as alike, not making profession of any religion, early in the morning ordered all his men to hold themselves ready so that as soon as the Hurons came they could attack all together. For fear that the Hurons would not keep their word he sent one of his chiefs with several young

[8]Extracts from translation by R. Clyde Ford in C. M. Burton, *Journal of Pontiac's Conspiracy, 1763.*

GOVERNMENT AND LAW UNDER BRITISH RULE

men to their camp to tell them not to fail, and as soon as their missionaries had finished service to come and join the Pottawattamies, as he only awaited their arrival to attack. The Hurons promised and kept their word.

Although Pontiac was waiting for the Hurons in order to begin the attack upon the Fort, still he had some of his men advance in order to take possession of the barns and stables around the Fort from the rear, so as to be ready to make an onslaught at the first signal and hinder anybody's leaving.

Teata and Baby, both chiefs of the good Hurons, who had preserved neutrality up to the present time and would have liked to do so longer, seeing themselves coerced by threats, ordered their band about sixty men in number to assemble, and they thus addressed them:

"My brothers, you see as well as we do the risks that we are running, and that in the present state of affairs we have nothing else to do but to side either with our brothers, the Ottawas and the Pottawattamies, or else abandon our lands and flee with our wives and children—a rash thing to do. We would hardly get started to leave before the Ottawas and the Pottawattamies, and even those of our own nation, would fall upon us and kill our wives and children and then compel us to assist them. Instead of that, by co-operating now, we make sure that our families will be left in peace in our village. We do not know what the designs of the Master of Life towards us may be. Is it He who inspires our brothers, the Ottawas, to war? If it is not He who commands it He will well be able to make his desires known, and we shall yet be able to withdraw without being stained by the blood of the English. Let us do what our brothers demand of us, and spare not".

Immediately after that harangue each chief took a tomahawk and chanted the war-song, and asked his men to do likewise while waiting for the hour of mass; after which their wives sang the mass and they listened with great devotion. When mass was over each went to his cabin and armed himself with the necessary weapons for the attack, and then they crossed the river in twelve canoes straight to the Pottawattamies who uttered yells of joy at seeing them arrive. These cries were a signal to Pontiac of the arrival of the Hurons whose fire was more effective than that of all the other Indians put together. . . .

(May 14) Father Potier, Jesuit missionary to the Hurons, by virtue of his calling and the power that he had over them had kept a part of them, especially the good band, within the bounds of neutrality by refusing them the sacrament. In order to succeed in restraining them all, he needed help, and asked Mr. Laboise, a resident of the Fort but who for some time had been living at his house, to be kind enough to cross the river and invite for him the oldest and most sensible of the settlers whom he knew the Indians loved and esteemed to come and join him in trying to arrest the course of that storm, which in threatening the

English, seemed also to threaten the French. This was done. These settlers who knew and respected the Jesuit father for a worthy priest and regarded him as a saint upon earth, hastened at this call to assemble at his place and deliberate over what should be done to mollify Pontiac, and what representation should be made to get him to end this internal war....

May 17, Tuesday

Pontiac who had not taken care in the beginning of the war to lay in any provisions for the sustenance of his warriors, was obliged to resort to fraud in order to live,—he and all his followers. To this end he and four chiefs of his nation visited all the settlers of the shores to levy contributions of food, saying they could give voluntarily or under compulsion,—if not they would have their live stock killed, a thing which was already begun. In spite of the fact that there were settlers who were already feeding as many as twenty Indians, this did not keep them from committing depredations.

The settlers who feared that the Indians would combine against them agreed to the demand of the chiefs, and each one supported the savages who lived in his vicinity: Pontiac and his people derived their supplies from the north shore, Ninivois and the Pottawattamies from the southwest, and the Hurons from the east and south....

June 16. Thursday.

About three o'clock P.M. the chiefs of the good Huron band, who had not taken any part in hostilities since Father Poitier in order to restrain them had refused them the sacrament, came for a parley. They entered the Fort by a false gate and discussed terms of peace with the Commandant, making many excuses for what they had done. The Commandant listened to them and gave them a flag which they accepted in sign of union, and they departed without any other conclusion than the flag....

June 18. Saturday.

At noon of the same day Father Dujonois,[9] the Jesuit missionary of the Ottawas from Michillimackinac, arrived with seven Indians of this nation, and eight Chippewas of the same place in command of one Kinonchamek, son of the great chief of the nation. People learned through these of the defeat of the English at this post on the second of the month by the Chippewas. The Jesuit father was lodged with his confrere, the missionary to the Hurons....

June 23. Thursday.

The Indians did not come to fire on the Fort during the day, as they were occupied with a project for the capture of the sloop which they

[9] Father Pierre Du Jaunay, S.J., was missionary at L'Arbre Croche (near Harbor Springs, Michigan) and Michilimackinac from 1747 to 1765.

GOVERNMENT AND LAW UNDER BRITISH RULE 97

knew to be at the entrance to the lake. Early in the morning they passed in large numbers in the rear of the Fort to go to join those who had left two days before; they all collected on Turkey Island which is a sort of narrow strait because at this point the river is very narrow. The Indians had constructed on the island an intrenchment with tree trunks which they had felled and piled upon the shore of the river on the side where the sloop had to pass. They also heaped up earth and strengthened it with branches in such a way that if they were seen in their fortifications they had nothing to fear from balls. In this retreat they waited the coming of the sloop. . . .

July 7. Thursday.

During the time that a part of the English were visiting Pontiac's camp with terror, the Pottawattamies came with Mr. Gammelin for the purpose of making peace with the Commandant; their request was granted on condition that they would remain neutral and surrender their prisoners,—a promise they made but did not keep.

The same day both the Huron bands held a council between themselves with the object of coming to the Fort to make peace with the Commandant. . . .

July 8. Friday.

Toward two o'clock in the afternoon the Hurons came to treat with the Commandant in accordance with the council they had held in their village the night before. At the Commandant's order the gate was opened for them and they were admitted into the Fort; they held a council on the drill-ground and asked for an opportunity to make peace with the English. They were told that if they would return all the prisoners and merchandise in their lodges, all their errors would be pardoned and the past forgotten. They said they wished to return to their village and make the same announcement to their brothers and get them to consent; they then withdrew willing to do all that was required. . . .

July 9. Saturday.

The Hurons as they had promised the day before, came about four o'clock bringing with them seven prisoners,—five men, one of whom was the commandant of Presqu'Isle, a woman, and a child; they handed these over to the Commandant and asked to make peace. They were told in reply that they must return all the merchandise which they had taken from the traders, even to a needle, and then terms of peace would be granted them. They withdrew promising to restore all the merchandise they had in their village. . . .

July 11. Monday.

Toward ten o'clock in the morning the Hurons came to fulfill their promise and brought all the merchandise which had been plundered from the traders upon the lake and on the river, and peace was concluded between them and the English. . . .

E 5   MAJOR HENRY GLADWIN[10] TO SIR JEFFERY AMHERST
[*British Museum, ADD. 21, 649 folio 430 ff; M.H.C. XXVII, 675–7*]

Detroit Nov. 1st. 1763

On the 12th. October, The enemy sued for Peace in a very submissive manner: at that time I was so circumstanced for want of flour, that I must either abandon my Post, or hear them: Of the two I chose the latter, thinking it of the utmost consequence to keep possession of the Country: Nevertheless I made them no promises, I told them the affairs of Peace lay wholly in your breast, But I did not doubt, when you was thoroughly convinced of their sincerity Every thing would be well again, upon which hostilities ceased, and they dispersed to their hunting grounds, this gave us an opportunity to get flour from the country, to Serve us from hand to mouth.

Yesterday Mr. Dequinde a Volunteer arrived with Dispatches from the Commandant of the Illinois, Copie of which I inclose you. The tenor of that to Pontiac is somewhat Extraordinary. The Indians are pressing for peace. I inclose you my answer to their demands. I believe as things are circumstanced it would be for the good of His Majesty's Service to accomodate Matters in the Spring; by that time the Savages will be Sufficiently reduced for want of Powder, and I don't imagine there will be any danger of their breaking out again, provided some Examples are made of our good Subjects the French who set them on. No advantages can be gained by prosecuting the War owing to the difficulty of catching them, add to this the Experience of Such a War, which if continued, the entire ruin of our Peltry Trade must follow, and the loss of a prodigious Consumption of our Merchandises. It will be the means of their retiring, which will reinforce other Nations on the Mississipi, whom they will prejudice against us, and make them our Enemy for ever; Consequently they will ["make" crossed in text] render it extremely difficult (if not impossible) for us to possess that Country, as the French have promised to supply them with every thing they want.

They have lost between 80, and 90, of their best Warriors; But if your Excellency still intends to punish them further for their Barbarity, it may be easily done without any Expence to the Crown by permitting a free sale of Rum, which will destroy them more effectually than Fire & Sword. But on the contrary if you intend to accomodate matters in the Spring, which I hope you will for the above Reasons, it may be necessary to send up Sir William Johnson.

[10] Henry Gladwin (1730–91) came to America in 1755, and was wounded at Braddock's defeat that year. In 1761 he accompanied Sir William Johnson to Detroit. He returned to Detroit the following summer. After his stubborn defence of Detroit against the attack by Pontiac, he returned to England in 1764.

I shall write your Excellency fully concerning every thing in this Department by Lieut. Montresor. This comes by Aron a Mohawk whom I shall direct to wait at Fort Pitt for your answer. This moment I received a message from Pontiac telling me that he should send to all the Nations concerned in the War to bury the Hatchet, and he hopes your Excellency will forget what has passed if not, I believe he will retire to the Mississipi.

In a few days I shall send a Duplicate of this by Andrew a faithful Huron; He has a great deal to say with the Delawares; He will try to make matters easy that way. I shall direct him to assure them of a Peace provided they remain quiet during the winter, which may perhaps ease our frontiers of those Villains, and in the Spring your Excellency can do as you please with them.

No news of the Troops, nor of the Vessels which sailed from hence the 7th., of last month, if the Troops don't come very soon, they will scarcely have time to return to Niagara. But I hope they will come time enough to destroy that nest of Thieves at Sandusky.

When things are accomodated, if your Excellency allows an exclusive trade for a Year or Two, to those merchants who have suffered so much by this unhappy affair, they will be amply paid for their loss.

Endorsed: Copy of a letter from Major Gladwin to His Excell: Sir Jeffery Amherst dated Detroit 1st. Nov. 1763 letter open for my perusal.

[The copy of Gladwin's letter continues with the following:]
Copie de la Lettre adressé à Mr le Commandant du Detroit par Pontiac le 30e Octobre 1763.

Mon Frere
La Parole que mon Pere m'a envoyée pour faire la Paix, je l'ai aceptée tous mes jeunes gens ont enterré leur Cassetetes: Je pense que tu oublieras les mouvaises choses que sont passées il y a quelque tems: de meme j'oublierai ce que tu veux m'avoir fait, pour ne penser que de bonnes. Moi, les saulteurs, les Hurons, nous devons t'aller parler, quand tu nous demanderas. Fais nous la reponse. Je t'envoye ce Conseil a fin que la voyes. Si tu es bien comme moi tu me feras response. Je te souhaitte le bon Jour
Signé Pondiac

Reponse
J'ay recu le Lettre de cette date. Si j'avais commencé la guerre j'aurais pu faire la paix, maus comme vous l'avais commencée il faut que vous attend la volante du General là desus: Je ne suis pas maitre mais je marquerai au General vos dispositions pacifiques à present et que vs souhaittez de vivre en paix. ainsi si vous comporté bien à l'avenir ausitot que le General en sera convaincu, je ne doute pas que tout ne soit bien. quand je recevrai la Reponse, Je vous en ferai part. Je te souhaite le bon soir
Signé Gladwin

[PONTIAC TO GLADWIN (translation)]
I have accepted the advice that my Father has sent me to make peace. All my young men have buried their hatchets. I believe that you will forget the mischief that has taken place lately. In the same way I shall forget what you tried to do to me, in order to think only of pleasant matters. I, the Sauteurs, and the Hurons will have a parley with you whenever you send for us. Give us an answer. I am sending you this message for your consideration. If you are as well disposed as I am you will send me an answer. I bid you good day.

GLADWIN TO PONTIAC (translation)
I received your letter of this date. If I had started the war, I could have concluded the peace. But since you started it you must wait for the General's wishes in the matter. I am not the ruler but I shall inform the general of your present peaceful dispositions and that you wish to live in peace. So if you behave well in the future, I have no doubt that everything will be settled as soon as the General is convinced of your conduct. When I receive the answer I shall let you know. I bid you good night.]

E 6 COMMISSION TO JACQUES CAMPEAU
[*Detroit Notarial Records, liber A, p. 187*]

[Detroit, Aug. 27, 1764]

By John Bradstreet Esqr.[11] Colonel and Commander in Chief of all His Majesty's forces on the Western District etc. ....

To James Campeau Esq.

Having special confidence in your attachment to his Majesty George the third and the interest of the English, I do hereby constitute and appoint you Capt. of Militia to be raised in the District of Detroit. You are therefore carefully and diligently to discharge the Duty of Capt. by exercising and well Disciplining both the inferior officers and soldiers of that company, and I hereby command them to obey you as their Capt. and you are to obey and follow such orders and directions from time to time as you may receive from his Majesty the Commander in Chief of all the King's forces in America, myself or any other superior officer according to the rules and discipline of war.

E 7 APPOINTMENT OF PHILIP DEJEAN AS JUSTICE OF THE PEACE ETC.
[*Detroit Notarial Records, liber A, p. 36*]

[Detroit, April 24, 1767]

By George Turnbull Esqr, Captn. in the 2nd Battn. of his Majesty's 60th or Royal American Regiment, Commandant of Detroit and Dependencies.

To Philip Dejean Merchant in Detroit.

I do hereby nominate and appoint you Justice of the Peace to Inquire

[11]John Bradstreet (1711–72) attacked Fort Frontenac in 1758. He visited Detroit in 1764 while conducting a mission of pacification to Pontiac and other rebel Indians.

unto all complaints that shall come before you, for which purpose you are hereby authorized to examine by oath such evidences as shall be necessary that the Truth of the matter may be better known, Provided always that you give no judgment or final award, but at their own request, and which by bond they bind themselves to abide by, but settle the matter by arbitration, which they are likewise to give their bond to abide by, one or two persons to be chosen by each and if they cannot agree and have named only two you name a third, and if four a fifth, and their determination or award to be approved by me before put into execution. I further authorize and empower you to act as chief and sole Notary and Tabellion by Drawing all wills, Deeds, etc. proper for that Department the same to be done in English only, and I also appoint you sole Vendue Master for such sales as may happen here in the usual and accustomed manner. . . .

E 8 APPOINTMENT OF PHILIP DEJEAN AS JUDGE
[*Detroit Notarial Records, liber A, p. 36*]

[Detroit, July 28, 1767]

Whereas it has been represented to me by the Trading People and others Residing at Detroit that some Tempery form of Justice for the Recovery of debts etc. was become absolutely necessary, and having taken the matter into consideration and finding the utility of such an Establishment, I have accordingly granted them a tempery Court of Justice to be held Twice in every month at Detroit to decide all actions of debts, Bonds, Bills, Contracts and Trespasses above the sum of Five Pounds New York Currency. And confiding in Philip Dejean, for his uprightness and Integrity, I do hereby nominate and appoint him the second judge of the said Court of Justice at Detroit. . . .

Signed Rob. Bayard
Major Commg. at Detroit.

E 9 MAJOR HENRY BASSETT[12] TO GENERAL HALDIMAND
[*P.A.C., B 70, pp. 214–16; M.H.C., XIX, 310–11*]

Detroit, 29th of August, 1773

. . . For want of a Civil Government being established here the Commanding Officer is very much employed, with the disputes and difficulties which must naturally happen between the Inhabitants. I'm so uncomfortable as not to speak French, or understand it sufficiently without an Interpreter. Hitherto I have been under an obligation to Mr. Stirling Mercht, who has been ready on all occasions to attend, has wrote & answered all my French letters without any gratuity, a French interpreter when the Inhabitants amount to near 1300 Souls, I should conceive, with submission to Your Excellency, Government would not

[12]Major Henry Bassett of the Tenth Regiment commanded the post of Detroit 1772–4.

object to, more particularly as I am informed one is paid at the Illinois; should your Excellency allow me one here I beg to recommend Mr. James Stirling, who is the first Mercht. at this place, & a gentleman of good character, during the late war, through a Lady that he then courted, from whom he had the best information, was in part a means to save this garrison, this gentleman is now married to that Lady & is connected with the best part of this Settlement, has more to say with them than any one here; the Indians can't well begin without his having information of their designs; if your Excellency disapproves of adding a third Interpreter, mine for the Hurons is a drunken idle fellow, scarcely worth keeping except out of Charity, if your Excellency will appoint Mr. Stirling, French & Huron Interpreter, he'll oblige himself to find a proper person for that Nation. Mr. Stirling tells me he has the honor to be known to your Excellency, having served under you as commissary of provisions, in the year 1759 at Oswago, & at Fort Augustus in 1760. ...

E 10 Award by Arbitrators
[Detroit Notarial Records, liber A, p. 300]

Whereas Messrs Sterling, Baby, Porteous & Chapoton were nominated and appointed arbitrators to determine between John Peck and François Millehomme, for the said Millehomme having stabbed the said Peck, with a knife in the stomach and said arbitrators not agreeing in their award Wm. Edgar being chosen umpire is of the following opinion to which the aforesaid Sterling, Baby, Porteous & Chapoton having agreed, that said Francois Millehomme do pay unto the said John Peck sixty pounds N.Y. currency and give such security for his future behaviour as the Commandant may think proper.

Detroit March 21, 1775
P. Dejean J.P.
Note: Placed under bond of 300 pounds for one year.

Wm. Edgar
James Sterling
D. Baby
John Porteous
B. Chapoton

E 11 Lord George Germain[13] to Governor Haldimand
[P.A.C., B 50, p. 27; M.H.C., X, 336]

Whitehall, 16th April 1779

... The presentments of the Grand Jury at Montreal against Lieut. Govr. Hamilton and Mr. DeJean are expressive of a greater degree of jealousy than the transaction complained of in the then circumstances of the Province appeared to Warrant.

Such stretches of authority are however only to be excused by unavoidable necessity and the Justness and fitness of the occasion & you

[13] George Germain was Secretary of State for the Colonies 1775–8.

will therefore direct the Chief Justice to examine the proofs produced of the Criminal Guilt, and if he shall be of the opinion that he merited the Punishment he met with, tho' irregularly inflicted, it is the King's Pleasure that you do order the Attorney General to grant a nole prosequi, & stop all further proceedings in the matter.

E 12   Calculation of Rum Necessary per Day for Detroit, Taken from the Issues between 25th December 1778 and 24th June 1779
[*P.A.C., B 192, p. 41;* M.H.C., *XIX, 440–1*]

	Gallons	Pints
Issued to Seamen & Carpenters from 25th Dec. to 24th March	500	5
Issued to Indians, Labourers at the works and other extras	2995	1½
Loss by Leakage	279	5
Issues to Seamen & Carpenters from 25th March to 24th June	534	7
Issues to Indians & Extras............do	4071	5
Loss by Leakage............do	368	4
182 days	8750	3½

48 gallons and near 1 pt per day

Saml. Fleming, Dy. Commissary

E 13   General Haldimand to Lieutenant-Colonel Mason Bolton[14]
[*P.A.C., B 104, p. 38;* M.H.C., *XIX, 451–2*]

Quebec 23 July, 1779

... The Expence and the Expenditure of Rum at Detroit is beyond comprehension. I wish some means could be fallen upon to prevent the merchants from carrying up such quantities, for while the Indians or even the soldiers know it is there, they will continually importune those who have the power of supplying them, and such a quantity of Rum must be hurtful to men's health independent of the loss to the Government. The Rum I have sent up will for the future ease this Expence. I hope you have issued orders to the different posts that no rum is to be bought from Traders while any remains in the King's stores from whence Rum for the Indians and all extraordinaries is to be supplied. ...

E 14   Major De Peyster to General Haldimand
[*P.A.C., B 123, p. 17;* M.H.C., *X, 462*]

Detroit 3rd April 1781

Sir, I take the liberty to trouble your Excellency with the enclosed petition from the Merchants of Detroit, I sincerely wish that some method could be fallen upon to oblige the inhabitants to pay their just debts without the parties being obliged to go down the country for the recovery of every trifling sum. Formerly summons's were issued by the

---

[14]Mason Bolton was Acting Commandant at Detroit.

Justice and decisions given, but since we have learned that they have no such power, that mode has ceased—I am confident that many wish for a Revolution in order to wipe off their scores, who otherwise would be very easy under the present Government. This is greatly the case at Detroit & will I hope apologize for my troubling you.

E 15   EXTRACT FROM THE ACCOUNT OF THE EXPEDITION OF LIEUTENANT-GOVERNOR HAMILTON
[P.A.C., B 123, pp. 56-7; M.H.C., IX, 491]

July 6, 1781

Pere Potier the Jesuit Missionary a man of respectable character and venerable figure, came to the head of our little encampment on the common of Detroit, and having attended to the reading of the Articles of War, and the renewal of the Oath of Allegiance to His Britannick Majesty, he gave the blessing to the Catholics present, conditionally upon their strictly adhering to their oath, being the more engaged thereto as the indulgence and favor of their prince merited their best Services and had exceeded their most sanguine expectations. The subsequent behavior of these people has occasioned my recalling this circumstance.

E 16   MAJOR MATHEWS[15] TO GENERAL HALDIMAND
[P.A.C., B 76, pp. 288-9; M.H.C., XX, 288]

Detroit, 3rd of August, 1787

. . . In Trade the lowest of the profession resort to these obsure places, they are without education or sentiment & many of them without Common honesty—these are perpetually over-reaching one another, knowing that they are too distant for the immediate effects of the Law to overtake them. The only resource in all matters in dispute, is the commanding officer, for our Justices of the Peace, it seems, are not authorized to take cognizance of matters relating to property, on which, almost every difference arises, so that if the Commanding officer is indolent or indifferent, he will not hear them at all—or if he does hear & decide, his Judgment tho perhaps equitable may be very contrary to law and hereafter involve him in very unpleasant consequences—besides that, acting in the capacity of a Judge, his whole time is so employed, that he cannot pay the necessary attention to his professional duties. It is much to be wished that some mode for the prompt & effectual administration of Justice were established, for the want of it is a temptation to many to take advantages & commit little chicaneries disgraceful to society & distressing to trade & Individuals—In all matters where I cannot clearly decide I make the parties refer to arbitration, binding themselves to submit to the decision. . . .

[15]Major Robert Mathews was Commandant at Detroit for one year, 1787–8. For several years he served as military secretary to General Haldimand.

E 17 EXTRACT FROM THE PROCLAMATION FORMING THE DISTRICT OF HESSE
[*P.A.C., Q 39, p. 122–4;* M.H.C., *XI, 620–1*]

George the Third, by the Grace of God, of Great Britain, France and Ireland, King, Defender of the Faith, &c. To all our Loving Subjects, Greeting: Whereas our Province of Quebec stands at present divided only into two Districts, and by virtue of two certain Acts or Ordinances, the one passed by our Governor and the Legislative Council, in the twenty-seventh year of Our Reign, and the other in the present year, provision is made for forming and organizing one or more new Districts. Now therefore know ye that our Governor of our said Province, by the advice and consent of our Council of our said Province, and in pursuance of the Acts and Ordinances aforesaid, hath formed and doth hereby form the several new Districts hereinafter described and named, to wit, the District of Luneburg . . . ; and also one other District to be called the District of Mecklenburg . . . ; and also another District to be called the District of Nassau, extending . . . as far Westerly as to a North and South Line, intersecting the extreme projection of Long Point into Lake Erie, on the Northerly side of the said Lake Erie; and also one other District to be called the District of Hesse, which is to comprehend all the residue of Our said Province, in the Western or inland part thereof, of the entire breadth thereof, from the Southerly to the Northerly boundaries of the same. . . .

In testimony whereof We have caused these our Letters to be made Patent, and the Great Seal of Our Province to be hereunto affixed.

Witness Our Trusty and Well-beloved Guy Lord Dorchester, Captain-general and Governor in Chief of Our said Province, at Our Castle of Saint Lewis, in Our City of Quebec, the twenty-fourth day of July in the Year of Our Lord, One thousand seven hundred and eighty-eight, and of Our Reign the Twenty-eight.

                (Signed)   D
                (Signed)   Geo. Pownall Secy.

E 18 APPOINTMENT OF JUSTICES AND OFFICERS FOR THE DISTRICT OF HESSE
[*P.A.C., Q 39, p. 134;* M.H.C., *XI, 621–2*]

Quebec, 24th July 1788

His Excellency the Governor has been pleased to make the following appointments: . . .

District of Hesse

Justices of the Court of Common Pleas —Duperon Baby[16]
    Alexander McKee
    William Robertson
} Esquires

[16]Jacques Duperon Baby (1731–89) was a descendant of Jacques Baby who

Justices of the Peace	—Alexander Grant[17] Guillaume La Motte St. Martin Adhemar William Macomb Joncaire de Chabert } Esquires Alexandre Maisonville William Caldwell Matthew Elliot

Sheriff —Gregor McGregor Esqr
Clerk —Thomas Smith Esqr
Coroner—George Meldrum

E 19   JUDGE POWELL[18] TO BISHOP HUBERT
[Q.C.A., E.U., V–65]

Detroit, December 26, 1789

Out of consideration for Justice and Equity, I cannot permit Mr. Dufaux to reply to the letter he has just received from his bishop without adding, for what it may be worth, my testimonial of this man ever since I have had the honor of knowing him.

Nothing can be further removed from an attack on this man's loyalty than his conduct on all occasions when it is permitted a good subject to show his attachment. He does not limit himself to precepts, he adds example. In the scarcity that threatened the garrison of this post, he sacrificed his own interest by surrendering at the assessed price all his wheat, even to the point of being in want himself.

Upon my arrival seeing the difficulty I had in finding a court-room, he offered me the old church, and until it could be readied he let me use the large room of his rectory. This was a mark of respect for the King's commission and for the public weal, which almost resulted in a lawsuit with his parishioners that was avoided by his prudence and firmness.

---

came to Canada with the Carignan Regiment in 1665. In the Seven Years' War our subject led the Indians in forays along the Ohio frontier. At the close of the war he settled at Detroit, where he married Suzanne Réaume on November 23, 1760. Two of their many children, Jacques (James) and François, played important roles in the early government of the Province of Upper Canada. Jacques Duperon Baby made his home in the town of Detroit.

[17]Alexander Grant (1734–1813) was a native of Scotland who came to America in 1757 with Montgomery's Highlanders. From 1763 to 1778 he directed the naval establishments on all the Great Lakes. In 1778 his naval command was confined to the upper lakes, where he was popularly known as the "Commodore." He built a fine country home known as Grant Castle in modern Grosse Pointe Farms, Michigan, where he continued to reside until his death. His body was interred in St. John's churchyard, Sandwich (now part of Windsor), Ontario.

[18]William Dummer Powell, a native of Boston, Mass., came to Detroit in 1789 as the first Judge of the Court of Common Pleas. He resided for some time at Petite Côte. In 1794 he was transferred to the capital of the province where he became first Puisne Judge of the Court of the King's Bench and Acting Chief Justice of Upper Canada. He died in Toronto on September 6, 1834.

There is proof that he was moved thereto only by an eagerness to do his duty. At the time I did not have the honor of being known to him. I do not doubt that the return mail has cleared him in the mind of Lord Dorchester, and has chased from the mind of your Lordship the shameful suspicion that has been aroused, but I would feel guilty if I did not make known my conviction that this man will do honor to his order.

E 20   EXTRACT FROM THE COPY OF A JOURNAL DATED DETROIT 8TH JUNE 1791
[*P.A.C., Q 51–2, pp. 790–1; M.H.C., XXIV, 252–3*]

... The inhabitants of the fort of Detroit as well as those on this side of the fort answered that they would always be ready, as they had always been to defend the Government & their property & would obey the first order of my Lord or of his representatives. That if this meeting had perchance been called by merchants who desired in the interest of their commerce to engage them in a war in which the Indians alone shared, and which had not perhaps the sanction of my Lord, they would not go. The company of Maisonville and that on the other shore, had made about the same answer, had objected that they had no horses, the illness among the animals having been considerable, they complained much that the Indians had destroyed their animals, & robbed many houses of flour & other things, that they said was in the power of no one to indemnify them for, which had always been done before, and that they would not willingly after that assist them, but that when real service required it, they would not do less than they had already done, fifty-two having been at the Post with Hamilton.

E 21   ACCOUNTS OF THE SHERIFF OF THE DISTRICT OF HESSE
[*P.A.C., Q 58–2, pp. 282–3; M.H.C., XXIV, 343–4*]

Council Chamber Monday 13th June 1791.

At a meeting of a Committee of Council for examining the Public Accounts for the half year ending the 10th April last upon a further Reference from His Excellency, Lord Dorchester dated the 8th Instant.

Present—Messrs. Dunn
                   Harrison
                   Grant

The Committee took into consideration the accounts referred to them of Gregor McGregor Esqr Sheriff of the District of Hesse amounting to £28 12s 6d currency articles as follows vizt.

Government in the Province of Quebec
   To the Sheriff in the District of Hesse Dr.

	£	s	d
To amot of Witnesses charges as per accot herewith	13	10	0
To paid Madam Pratt for hire of a Court Room as per Receipt 15 Yk. Curry	9	7	6

To paid John Smith Bailiff for summoning Jurors &c as per accot & Receipt		4— 5—0
To paid Henry Botsford for Repairs done to the Court room as per Receipt & accot 2—8—0		1—10—0
Halifax Curry		28—12—6

Detroit 3rd May 1791   (signed)   Gregor McGregor
                                                                                      Sheriff

E 22   D. W. SMITH[19] TO JOHN ASKIN[20]
[*Quaife*, The John Askin Papers, *I, 416–19*]

Niagara. 26. July. 92

My dear Sir! The Governors proclamations are arrived dividing the upper Country. The 18 County is called Essex, & is bounded on the East by the Carrying place from point au pins, to the River la tranche— bounded on the South by Lake Erie, & on the west by the River Detroit to Maisonvilles Mill; from thence by a line running parralel to the River Detroit & Lake St. Clair, at the distance of 4 miles, until it meets the River la tranche—thence up the said River to where the Carrying place from point au pins strikes that River. This said County of Essex, with the adjoining County of Suffolk (in which there are no Inhabitants) sends one Member. those who have certificates, only, I understand can vote. this tract comprehends the new settlers on Lake Erie who have generally certificates. Monfortons Company, who have none except they have recd them since my departure—& Maisonvilles Company to the Mill; in this last Space there are Inhabitants on 12 acres front just above the Church, who can vote by reason of their having French deeds, "En Roture" & those settled on the South side of R. la tranche, a few of whom have certificates, & where I myself am a freeholder! This damned Election business seems to bind me to the County, for You know I am not fond of deserting any Cause I undertake, & that of the public is most dear to me.

Should I be returned without an undue Election, or the appearance of party or bribery, I shall be most happy, & in that Case I beg an Ox

---

[19]David William Smith (1764–1837) was an officer in the Fifth Regiment of Foot of which his father was Major. While still holding his commission he was appointed Surveyor-General of the Province of Upper Canada. In 1792 he was elected to the Assembly as representative for Essex County, and later became Speaker. A collection of his personal manuscripts is preserved in the Reference Division of the Toronto Public Library.

[20]John Askin (1739–1815) was born at Strabane in the County of Tyrone, North Ireland, of Scottish descent. He came to America during the Seven Years' War. After the conquest he was one of the first British traders to venture into the Northwest, moving from Albany to Mackinac in 1766. Fourteen years later he transferred his activities to Detroit, where he remained until his death. From 1802 to 1815 he resided on the Canadian side near the foot of the present Strabane Street in Windsor, Ontario. The John Askin Papers have been edited by Milo M. Quaife, and published by the Detroit Library Commission (Detroit, 1928).

may be roasted whole on the common & a barrel of Rum, be given to the Mob, to wash down the Beef. You will draw on me for the Amount. I should have great pleasure in helping to frame Laws, for Lands which I have had so much pleasure in laying out. Mr. Pollard who is appointed Sheriff, is returning officer. The writs are issued this day & returnable the 12 Sepr.

I depend a good deal on your goodness, favor & affection in this business, & hope I need not make many apologys on that Score. as I have begun the canvas, I am determined to go through with it, & should I succeed, I hope to support my Character afterwards; we shall not certainly leave the province these 4 Years, so that wherever the seat of Government may be, or whatever may be the destination of the Regt I make no doubt but I shall be able to attend the Council & assembly Yearly. My having done the settlers business without emoluments from any Quarter should be some inducement to them, on the score of Gratitude to return me!

I rather think it is intended that the people who have french Grants on the Garrison Side should vote; as the Description of the County of Kent comprehends a great deal & sends 2 Members. it is said to contain all the Country (not being territories of the Indians) & not already included in Essex & the several other Counties described, Extending norward to the boundary line of Hudsons Bay, including all the territory to the Westward & southward of the said line to the utmost Extent of the Country commonly called or known by the name of Canada.

Should Candidates to represent this County go a begging & you find I have no chance for Essex, I shall be proud to be returned for this County, but as the french people know little of me, I have not any hopes on that score. I am very ill at present myself, or I would certainly go up to Detroit, but if the people are sincere, that is unnecessary; & this will give it a fair tryal. You will do me a Service by delivering to Mr. Pollard, the Names of those capable to vote, which you can get from a small Register in the Land Office marked or rather endorsed "Certificates Granted," and another endorsed, "French Grants "en Roture".

If any of Monfortons or Maisonvilles Companys have received Certificates since my departure, I will be thankful to you to use yr influence with them. Col. McKee has promised me his Interest, so has the Commodore, & I think I may depend on Cap Elliot, George Leith, & a few others.

When I wrote you last it was Expected that Grossile, Rivers Raisin & Rouge would have voted with the New Settlers, but that is not the Case.

Jacque Parent, Laurent Parent, Claude Rheaum, Bapte le Duc, & John Bap Hoilette, just above Huron Church, may probably ask for an Explanation to my Letters to them, they hold Lands "en roture" formerly granted to Monr Longueil & they of course have indisputably votes; I have therefore addressed them separately. these are the only french deeds acknowledged by the "Tableau des terres "En Roture". on that Side of the water.

I am sure you will forgive me for Encl(os)ing so large a pacquet to you, The most of them are for the freeholders on Lake Erie, all whose Names, I could recollect, the others, You will have great goodness by putting in train for their destinations. . . .

E 23 SMITH TO ASKIN
[*Quaife,* The John Askin Papers, *I, 420–1*]

Niagara, 6 August 1792

My dear Sir: Your Letter, which you honored me with gave me great satisfaction. I hope I may not be too much buoyed up with the hopes you give me of succeeding to the election. Your doubts about the right of voting on your side of the water will be removed before this. If therefore there is any difficulty in bringing me in for Essex, & one of the Kent seats goes abegging I should be flattered to be returned for that County. Mr. Baby tells me, he wrote to his Brother François to set up for Essex, this may perhaps Cause some Confusion, as the French people no doubt will vote for him; & Capt Caldwells Interest may perhaps gain him the Settlers on Lake Erie. Their Sentiments will I hope be sufficiently know[n] before hand, that I may not be set up without chance. Mr. Baby told me however that he rather thought François would decline setting up; in which Case I should have his Interest; & at all Events, if François had made a party previous to his Arrival in Essex, & was likely to succeed; he would then give me his Interest in Kent.

I leave the weight of the transaction on your shoulders, & whatever you do for me therein, I shall be perfectly satisfied & I believe I know You well Enough to think you do not require many apologys from me, for so much trouble. I will endeavour to repay You in the house of Assembly; if I succeed!

I wrote you in my last, in Case of Success to have an ox Roasted on the Common & to give the Mob a barrel of Rum. Mr. Pollard tells me the hustings will probably be held for Essex somewhere about the Rivers Mouth. this therefore may perhaps be a better scite for the Beef & Rum. I am excessively unwell for a long time. I hope however to weather through the winter, & should I be elected, I shall pay You a visit in the Spring, to be chained! The Judge I think while here did not wish to give me any hopes of the french people, for very plain & substantial Reasons, & for this Candid behaviour I am obliged to him; as it has prepared me for the worst. I forgot to tell you that before the Governor arrived he wrote to my father, that he adopted all that he had recommended on the score of the Land business, which was nearly a Counterpart of the Boards Report, so that I hope Everything will go as smoothly with you there.

We are all excessively happy at the idea of Seeing You here. if you make any house at Niagara your hotel, other than the Majors, You are not the same John Askin you used to be.

Leith will give me credit for any little Sums you may find it necessary to require, such as putting up the Hustings, Boards &c, Cake & wine, Returning Officer's fee &c &c &c

Love to the Good family. . . .

E 24 SMITH TO ASKIN
[*Quaife*, The John Askin Papers, *I, 427–8*]

Niagara, 14 August 1792

My Dear Sir: All the Letters I get from Detroit give me favourable hope, except those I receive from McNiff. they assure me of the Interest and Influence of Messrs McKee, Macomb, Park, Leith, Sharp, McIntosh, Elliot, Lamothe, McDonnell & several others for Essex. There is I understand however powerful Influences against me; however if I have fair play I dont fear, as I am assured that the Settlers, on Lake Erie and River la tranche will vote for me "nemine contradicente," at least those are the words in which their assurances are represented to me. Perhaps I should have done better to have set up for one of the Seats in Detroit, as I hear only of Mr. McComb who is to be proposed; but I did not then know they would be entitled to vote; besides were I thrown out on the 20th I might have had a chance on the 28th. The french people can easily walk to the Hustings, but my gentry will require some conveyance; if boats are necessary you can hire them & they must not want beef or Rum, let them have plenty, and in case of success I leave it to you, which you think will be best to give my friends a public dinner, & the ladies a dance, either now, or when I go up. if you think the moment the best time You will throw open Forsyths Tavern, & call for the best he can supply. I trust you will feel very young on the occasion, in the dance, & I wish that Leith and you should push about the bottle, to the promotion of the Settlements on the Detroit. The more broken heads and bloody noses there is the more election like, and in case of Success (damn that if!) let the White Ribbon favors be plentifully distributed, to the old, the Young, the Gay, the lame, the cripple and the blind—half a score cord of wood piled hollow, with a tar barrel in the middle, on the Common, some powder, pour tirer, & plenty of Rum. I am sure that you will preside over & do ev[er]ything that is needful, as far as my circumstances will admit. there must be no want & I am sure you will have ev[er]ything handsome & plentiful.

Elliot I am sure will give you a large red flag to be hoisted on a pole near the Bon fire, and some blue colored tape may be sewn on in large letters

ESSEX. . .

Leith tells me you have written to me but the opposite party have got hold of the Letter because they guessed its Contents. Have proper booths erected for my friends at the Hustings, employ Forsyth to make large plumb Cake, with plenty of fruit &ca & be sure let the Wine be good & plenty. Let the peasants have a fiddle, some beverage & Beef.

If my absence merely should be mentioned as a Bar to my election, You may assure the World that if there is time between the Returns bei[n]g made & the meeting of the assembly, I will come up to take the Sentiments of the County, & I will annually pay Detroit a visit, before I go [to] the Metropolis to meet the Assembly.

forgive me, I worry you out. I have quite an election fever; however it will soon be coold, & let the determination be as it will I shall be perfectly satisfied, & equally obliged to all my good friends.

God bless you & yours, & believe me unfeignedly faithfully & Affectionately Yours whilst. . . .

E 25 ELECTION EXPENSES OF DAVID W. SMITH
[*Toronto Public Library, Reference Division, D. W. Smith Collection, B 4, pp. 111–13*]

Date		Item	£ s d	Total
August 11	To	½ piece green ribbon	16 0	
" 11	"	½ " pink "	18 0	
" 11	"	1 cag Spirits, 8 gals	6 8 0	£ 8 2 0
" 18	"	1 piece green ribbon	1 12 0	
" 18	"	2 pieces pink "	3 12 0	5 4 0
" 24	"	2 gallons spirits	1 12 0	
" 24	"	1 Cag for ditto	3 0	
" 24	"	6 loaves bread	6	2 1 0
"		To cash paid Ellem the constable for 4 days' service, and the Ferry's taking letters to inhabitants of new settlements, the 13th inst.		2 0 0
" 27		To 1 bottle rum and 1 loaf to Roch for taking a letter to Mr. Selby	7 0	
" 27		To ditto and 2 loaves to men going over the river	6 0	0 13 0
" 31		To Wm. and David Robertson for amount of their account for sundry articles furnished by them and paid Mr. Dolson		103 3 11
Sept. 8		To amount of Thomas Smith's account, Tavern keeper, paid him		5 10 6
10		To amount of Wm. Surrell's account for sundries furnished by him		58 7 6
		To James May for sundries per acct pd		12 15 6
11		To paid Wm. and David Robertson for hogshead porter	18 0 0	
		Paid ditto account Wm. Scott	17 7 0	35 7 0
				£233 4 5
1792 21		By your draft on Messrs. Auldjo & Co., at 31 days sight for		200 0 0
Sept. 24		By Messrs. George Leith & Co. for balance		33 4 5
		N. Y. Currency		£233 4 5

E 26 Smith to Askin
[*Quaife,* The John Askin Papers, *I, 446–7*]

Niagara, Novr. 13, 1792

My very good friend. I have received your letter of 2d November, which gave me its usual satisfaction. I do assure you upon my honor, I have done everything in my feeble power to get your wishes gratified; I am bound to it for I consider my self much in your debt, but I am sorry to say my interest seems very feeble to the accomplishment of your desires. I am afraid you have conceived I am a favorite with the Governor; so far as a discharge of the trusts committed to my care, entitles me to it; I believe I am, but beyond that, I know nothing of the Cabinet. however I have not failed to oppose the measures which seem odious to you, nor feared to say so. the Interest which brought the Young French Gentleman into the Councils, has prevailed in having him appointed Lord Lieutenant for the County of Kent, & that interest was not only planted previous to the Governments taking place, but seems to have taken exuberant Root in Quebec; where his Consequence, his Interest, his Property, & his Loyalty, seem to have been blazoned in lively tropes. I shall however Yet endeavour to fall on some Scheme of getting this indepandent troop of horse established for you. Should ever my interest be courted, I can ask too; & I pledge myself to you never to sell it, but to accomplish your wishes. I am happy to find you entertain thoughts of being returned at the next Election, as it will be highly flattering to me to resign to my worthy Patron. Having struggled to put the Constitution on a good & permanent basis, I shall bow to my Constituents, thank them, & put my hand to the Plow.

The road for the New Settlement shall be asked, & if I cant get troops, I will try to get it cut by formidable Surveying party. . . .

E 27 Copy of an Account of the Sheriff's Expenses for the Election of Members for the Counties of Suffolk & Essex
[*D. W. Smith Collection, B 4, p. 106*]

August 10th 1792

	£	s	d
To cash paid for transport of Boards	0	10	0
Sheriffs officer 9 days	3	4	0
Meldrum & Parks for Boards	5	19	3
Henry Botsford making hustings	2	16	0
2 Clerks 8 days @ 37/6	30	0	0
Cash paid a man distributing Advertisements Paper &c	2	0	0
N. York Curry	44	9	3
	22	9	3
half amot. David Willm Smith Esqre	5	12	0
Returng Officer as per order	28	1	3
	7	4	9
Received of Mr. Askin	20	16	8

Received May 23 1794 the above ballance   Richd Pollard[21], Sheriff

[21]Richard Pollard was in Detroit as early as 1784, in which year he bought

E 28   ASKIN TO ALEXANDER MCKEE[22]
[*Cruikshank,* The Simcoe Papers, *II, 389*]

Detroit, August 17, 1794

I yesterday received Lt. Colonel England's orders directed to me as Senior Officer at present in the County of Essex to put the whole of the Militia of that County in a state to be ready to march at the shortest notice. In consequence of which I have wrote Capt. Fields at river à la Tranche, to examine & see what Arms & accoutrements may be wanted for to complete the Militia on this side of that river & to come immediately for them. I have ordered the same to be done at Petite Cote & I shall send to the New Settlement, tho that may not be so necessary as I suppose Lt. Colonel Caldwell[23] has taken with him from that Quarter all those who were in a situation to march.

At 11 o'clock today I will examine the arms and accoutrements of the four companies opposite the town. You will no doubt, Sir, see that is a necessity for having more officers appointed. I beg leave to mark out that there is a Joseph Beaubien of a good family & a man who is desirous of taking any Commission from you; he in my opinion would make a good Lieutenant or Ensign as you may judge fit. There is also Pierre LaBute who I understand would likewise make a good officer; these two belong to my company; Mr. Dufresne who was an officer in Lower Canada would be of great help to Major Parent who cannot read or write; there is likewise in same company a Francois Pratt who perhaps would answer well as an Ensign. Capt. Smith having a Flank Company will want two Lieuts.

---

from William Brown a tract of land three arpents by forty at Petite Côte. In the spring of 1792 he was appointed sheriff of the Western District of Upper Canada. In 1802 he was ordained a deacon, and became the first pastor of St. John's Church in Sandwich. In addition to his clerical office he continued to hold several secular appointments, including those of Probate Judge and Registrar for Essex County.

[22]Alexander McKee (1735–99) was a native of Pennsylvania who engaged in the Indian trade. In 1760 he accompanied Major Robert Rogers to Detroit. In 1772 he was appointed Deputy Agent of Indian Affairs at Fort Pitt. In 1778 he fled to Detroit with Matthew Elliott and Simon Girty. During the revolution he exerted his influence to retain the goodwill of the Indians. At Detroit he was appointed Captain in the Indian Department, then Deputy Agent, and subsequently Superintendent of Indian Affairs. For some time he made his home at Petite Côte, at the foot of the present McKee Road, Windsor, Ontario. He died at River Thames on January 13, 1799.

[23]William Caldwell (1747–1820) was born in Fermanagh County, Ireland, and migrated to America. Prior to the American Revolution he was living in western Pennsylvania. In 1775 he joined Bird's Rangers, and from 1776 to 1784 he served in Butler's Rangers. In 1783 he married Suzanne, daughter of Jacques Duperon Baby; to them were born five sons and three daughters. Caldwell and his sons took a prominent part in the War of 1812. In 1814 he was transferred to the Indian Department with the rank of Deputy Superintendent. He died at Amherstburg about 1820.

Capt. Baby's Company who lies between Major Parent's and mine has neither Lt. or Ensign, I understand there is a J. Bapt. Tourneau called Jaurette [Janette] that would make a good officer. . . .

E 29   ASKIN TO MCKEE
[*Cruikshank*, The Simcoe Papers, *II, 390*]

Detroit, August 17, 1794

Since I did myself the honor to write you this morning, I have been over the river interviewing the men, arms &c., &c. I find there is very few wanting, the people seem well disposed & ready to march when ordered but the companies are much weaker than I expected, owing to several engagés I suppose being gone away lately. Between Maisonville's & the Huron Church there is not quite 60 men & from your house to Drulliard's Mill there is no more than eleven which was meant for Capt. Smith's Company, but as Capt. Allan who joins him in the Southern Battalion has by his return to me this day 41 men, I beg you will be pleased to change the boundaries between the Northern & Southern Battalion so that Mr. Smith may get more men; for none can be spared, they now not being equal to what the Law directs. Capt. Monforton's below Capt. Allen's is strong enough, he has 29 men. In addition to those whom I mentioned this morning as thinking they might answer for officers (if you have no other in view) there is Vital Dumouchel who Capt. Baby wishes very much to have for his Lieutenant & I must again repeat that Joseph Beaubien's conduct to day gives me every reason to think that he is a very good subject & well qualified to be an officer. . . .

E 30   CAPTAIN WM. MAYNE[24] TO MAJOR GENERAL ANTHONY WAYNE[25]
[*P.A.C., C 382, p. 54; M.H.C., XXIII, 405*]

The British Port near the Island of Bois Blanc, Sept. 27, 1796

I have thought proper to send for the accomodation of the United States of America fifty barrels of Salt Pork at this period from his Majesty's provision Store according to a requisition from your First Aid du camp Captain De Butts in his letters to me of yesterday date—

From the circumstances stated in that letter, I trust his Excellency the Commander in Chief, General Prescot will approve of my conduct.

[24]William Mayne, captain in the Queen's Rangers, was sent to command the new post at the mouth of the Detroit River (subsequently known as Amherstburg) in the summer of 1796. He remained until the following summer, when he requested leave of absence to return to England.

[25]Anthony Wayne was appointed a major general in the United States Army in 1792. After defeating the Indians in 1796 his army advanced to Detroit.

E 31   WAYNE TO MAYNE
[*P.A.C., C 382, p. 57; M.H.C., XXIII, 405*]

Headquarters, Detroit
3rd October 1796

I have to acknowledge the receipt of your letter of the 27th ultimo, and am much obliged by the accomodating loan, of fifty barrels of Salt Pork from His Majesty's provision store at the post under your command, agreably to a requisition from my first aid du camp Captain De Butts, in his letter to you of the 26th of September, and I believe with you, that His Excellency the Commander in chief General Prescot will approve of your conduct upon this occasion.

Permit me to assure you Sir, that it will afford me singular pleasure, to have an opportunity in turn, of accomodating any of His Brittanick Majesty's Garrisons in Canada, with such supplies as they may occasionally want and particularly that under your charge.

F. RELIGION AND EDUCATION AFTER 1760

F 1 REPORT OF FATHER DE LAUNAY, PROCURATOR OF THE CANADIAN MISSIONS, TO THE SUPERIOR-GENERAL
[*General Jesuit Archives, Rome, gal. 110, vol. I, ff. 112–13a*]

[February 16, 1762]

... In the other missions our men continue their duties among the natives quietly and freely. Two went to the Illinois, in fear of the enemy which was occupying by force of arms the entire region of Canada—namely Fathers John Baptist de la Morinie and John Baptist Salleneuve. Father Peter Potier, who likewise betook himself to the same forest people, after a year returned to his station on the strait and was received amid the greatest manifestations of joy by his friends and with utmost humanity by the English General. ...

F 2 SALE OF LAND—POTIER TO MARANTET
[*Detroit Notarial Records, liber A, p. 114*]

Detroit, October 15, 1767

We, the undersigned, priest of the Society of Jesus, missionary of the Hurons at Detroit, residing at La Pointe de Montréal, certify that, in order to pay the debts of the said mission and to provide for the expenses of our livelihood, having been obliged to place our position before the Reverend Father Superior in Canada, we received the authority transcribed herebelow, in virtue of which authority we have sold and transferred for ever under our guarantee and that of our successors by our own deed (and not the deed of the Prince or of those who command in his name) to Sir François Gaudet Marantet, his heirs and assigns a parcel of land four arpents in width (Paris measure) by its full depth just as it was granted to us in seventeen hundred and forty-seven without any written title, the said land adjoining on the east-northeast Mr. de Longueuil's grant and on the west-southwest the land that remains to the said mission, bordering on the front the public highway and in the rear the lands not yet granted, for the said Sir Gaudet Marantet and his heirs to have and to hold the said land for ever, just as we have during the past twenty years without any interruption or disturbance; this sale is made under the above-mentioned conditions, and moreover in consideration of the sum of sixteen hundred livres which the said Gaudet Marentet will pay us in good Detroit currency upon our demand, and for which we shall give him a receipt. Done at Detroit October 15, 1767.

copy (Signed) P. Potier, Missionary of the Hurons, Jesuit

Extract from the letter of the Reverend Father Superior ... "I give full permission to sell your land since it has become useless to you, and I hope that you will be able to make a sale that will be advantageous to you...

At Quebec, July 10, 1765 ... De Glapion, J

I, the undersigned, have given to Sir Marantet one rod [perche] more than the four arpents.

copy   (Signed)   P. Potier, Jesuit Missionary. July 2, 1768

I, the undersigned, have granted to Sir Marentet Godet one arpent and one rod of land adjoining the land that remains to the mission. I have reserved on the said arpent and rod a square parcel of land that begins at the end of the mission yard and extends to the corner of the cemetery facing the church of the said mission.

copy   (Signed)   P. Potier, Jesuit Miss. July 4, 1769

F 3   POTIER TO BRIAND[1]
[Q.C.A., E.U., V–15]

Detroit, Sept. 6, 1768

I have received Your Lordship's letter confiding to my care the South Side of Detroit. This new parish consists of over sixty families of whom about one third paid their tithes last year. The Hurons whom I have served during the past twenty-four years pay no dues. The new chapel which I have built with the help of the people is in debt, and I have been obliged to sell the mission land to pay for it. I furnish the wine for the Mass, and the candles. Your Lordship will see from this that the establishment of a fabrique is useless for the present; but they have elected wardens to assist me, and as soon as I have paid off the debts on the chapel, they will begin their duties. The late Bishop Pontbriand gave me permission to use the blessings reserved to the Bishop, and I beg your Lordship to renew this faculty. I pray that Our Lord will preserve your sacred person for His glory, and for the salvation of souls. I have the honor to be, etc. ...

F 4   EXTRACT FROM THE ACCOUNT BOOK OF ASSUMPTION PARISH FOR 1775–81
[*Assumption Church Archives*]

1775

October 15—Simon Drouyard possesses a pew in the Church of the Assumption which he obtained at the auction for the sum of forty francs for one year.
November 19—Laviolette owes 6 livres for having failed to donate the blessed bread. *Paid

[1]Bishop of Quebec from 1776 to 1784.

November 21—Received from Francois Viller 23 livres, 7½ sous for a high mass. The church owes him one livre and 7½ sous.
November 25—Paid Mr. James Sterling 116 livres for a funeral pall and an antependium. The church still owes him 40 livres, perhaps a little more. *Paid
November 25—The church owes Mr. Bouron 25 livres which he gave towards the 116 livres paid to Sterling; also 2 livres that the above-mentioned paid for the mass wine.
November 25—Roy Charron still owes 6 livres for the rent of his pew.
November 25—La Palme has received a hundred nails on his wages.
November 25—Fontaine owes 6 livres to the church for having failed to donate the blessed bread.
[The items in this record are so repetitious that it is deemed sufficient to publish only the first page.]

F 5 List of Inhabitants of Petite Côte in 1778
[*Assumption Church Archives, Account Book 1775–81*]

1. Nexe [Knaggs]
2. La Boise (Robidou) (Sordillet)
3. J. B. Reaume (Charlot Reaume)
4. Theophile (olim Jos. Drouillard)
5. Chauvin (Labiroche)
6. Pare
7. Coquillard
8. J. B. Drouillard
9. Bondy
10. Robert et Jacques Peltier
11. Jaq. Belleperche et Pouget
12. Pierre Meloche
13. Simon Drouillard
14. Jos. Drouillard
15. Monforton
16. Beaugrand
17. Tourangeau
18. Pouget
19. La Jeunesse
20. Me. St. Louis (La Joie) (Langlois)
21. La Joie
22. Babi (Belair)
23. Roy et Pierre Prudhomme (chacun 2 arpents)
24. Bigras
25. Rene Cloutier
26. Boufar (6 arpents)
27. Susor
28. Etienne Jacob
29. Bernier
30. La Fonds (olim Fr. Drouillard)
31. Etienne Le Beau (Proud)
32. Fr. Lesperance
33. Gascon olim Vaudri
34. Fontaine
35. Pouget (olim Binau)
36. Jean Louis Lajeunesse (olim Ch. Reaume)
37. Tourangeau Choisi obiit)
38. La Violette
39. Renaud
40. Pajot
41. Lantailla
42. Gignac
43. Langlois (obiit)
44. Ant. Meloche
45. Montmeni
46. Saliot
47. Rau (obiit) emit
48. Bernier (olim Gignac)
49. Chapu
50. La Negresse
51. Montforton et Soumande
52. Jaq. Bezer L'Eveillé
53. Morisseau
54. J. B. Goyau (obiit)
55. Pierriche Prudhomme

Those who have lots

1. Le Vieux Le Beau (Labiroche)
2. St. Etienne
3. Bertrans (Beaugrand)
4. Alain, Le Pecheur
5. J. B. Dufour (Duroseau) (nunc alibi Meloche)
6. Pierriche Charron (nunc alibi)
7. Zach. Cloutier
8. Me. Buissonnet

F 6 GIFT OF LAND FROM THE HURONS TO FATHER POTIER
[Original deed in the Archives of Assumption University of Windsor; copy in Detroit Notarial Records, liber C, pp. 79–80]

We, the Chiefs of the Nation and Tribe of the Wyandots, commonly called Hurons, after having consulted with each other and among all the old men of our village, and wishing to give a mark of our esteem for Rev. Father Potier, Jesuit, our missionary, we can only show him our esteem by giving him two arpents of land, bordering on the Detroit River, adjoining on the east-north-east the land of Francois Gaudet, and on west-south-west the lands of our village, and in depth up to Grand Marais. Our intention is that he should possess it (he and his heirs) as if belonging to him according to the donation that we make to him without any return on our part.

In witness whereof we have given him the present at Detroit on September 22, 1780.

Teguaguiratin	Nonyacha	Totem	a turtle with a cross on its back, and also a cross on its right flipper.
Da8aton	Sachetotach		
Sindaton	Dewatonte		

In the presence of the witness
and interpreter of the Hurons—Charles Reaume

[verso] Registered at the Record-Office of Detroit in Register No. 2, pp. 79–80 by me

T. Williams[2]   Notary

F 7 DEATH AND BURIAL OF FATHER POTIER
[Assumption Church Archives, Register of Baptisms, Marriages and Burials for 1767–83, p. 82]

On the eighteenth of July, seventeen hundred and eighty-one there was buried in the sanctuary of the church of this parish on the gospel side the body of Rev. Fr. Pierre Potier, Jesuit missionary for the past 37 years. At the age of seventy-three years and three months he died on the sixteenth of this month, according to the certificate of Mr. Anthony, surgeon, from a fall on an andiron. The said burial was made by Rev. Fr. Simple, Recollet missionary, in the presence of a large number of his parishioners.

Gllme Montforton   Beaugrand   Hubert Vic: gen.

---

[2]Thomas Williams, a native of Albany, came to Detroit in 1765. He was active as storekeeper, trader, and merchant. In 1779 he was appointed justice and notary by Captain Richard Lernoult, after Philip Dejean left Detroit to join Henry Hamilton at Vincennes. Williams died at Detroit about the close of the year 1785.

F 8 AFFIDAVIT OF FRANCIS PRATT
[Detroit Notarial Records, liber C, p. 129]

Before me, the undersigned Justice, was present Mr. Francis Pratt, purchaser, as mentioned in the registered deed, Folio 77, who of his own free will has admitted and declared that it was through forgetfulness or lack of attention, that the late Father Potier had not reserved, in the said deed, the land on which are situated the church, the house, the yard and buildings and the garden enclosed with stakes. He gives up and yields all rights to the said land that might have come to him for want of any reservation of the said land being mentioned in the deed. In witness whereof he has signed this present affidavit to be used as need occurs, in the presence of the witnesses who sign with me this July, 1781.
Monforton
LaBute   Witnesses   Signed F. Pratt

F 9 INVENTORY OF THE EFFECTS OF THE LATE FATHER POTIER
[Q.C.A., PP. J., pp. 1-14]

On July 22, 1781, we—one of His Majesty's justices of the peace for the District of Quebec assisted by Sirs Monforton and Maisonville, Captains of the militia, and by Sirs Pouget and Jacques Parent, wardens of the church of Our Lady of the Assumption,—removed the seal that we had placed on the door of Father Potier's room, who died on the 16th instant, and we made an inventory of all that was found in the said room.
In the book-case were found the following papers:
A pack of letters entitled "Re our retreat to the Illinois."
A paper entitled "Agreement between Father Salleneuve and Charles Courtois October 29, 1760."
A paper entitled "Contract of Courtois and Deboyer in 1760 when I left for the Illinois."
A copy of a letter from Mr. de L'Etenduaire to Count de Vaudreuil.
[In margin] Note: Judge Williams has all these letters in his possession. H[ubert]. They have been returned H.
A small note-book—Discourse on the French clergy.
A small note-book—Anouncements of land sales and of ordinances from the commandant.
A proclamation by Governor Hamilton.
44 letters from Father Viel to Father Potier; 4 letters from Father Floquet; 3 letters from Mr. Navarre; 7 letters from Father Du Jauny; 9 letters from Father Floquet; 3 letters from Father Gibault; 3 letters from Father Glapion; 5 letters from Father Meurin; 5 letters from Father Lamolinière; 1 letter from Governor Hamilton; 1 letter from Mr. Legrand; 1 letter from Mr. Schindler; 1 letter from Major De Peyster; a small leather bag containing Father Potier's letters patent.

[There follows a list of the books. The titles of 92 volumes are given. There are also 29 pamphlets and 39 books in manuscript form.]

The Furniture and Furnishings

8 saucers, 5 cups, 1 cruet-stand, 3 earthenware cruets, 1 crystal cruet, 1 teapot without cover, 1 crystal bottle containing pepper, 2 crystal goblets, 1 earthenware jug, 3 stoneware jugs, 2 earthenware plates, 1 pewter plate and 2 pewter basins, 2 wooden dishes, 2 pairs of brushes, 1 foot-scraper, 1 mould for making hosts, 1 large iron fork, 1 large pot, 1 mirror, 2 boxes of lead, 1 pair of new shoes, 1 pair of old shoes with buckles, 2 tubs, 2 caskets, 1 box containing about 20 pounds of candles, 1 adze, 1 tomahawk, 1 small hoe, 1 woollen blanket, 4 blankets, 1 case with 4 razors, 2 large woollen blankets, 1 chamber-pot, 1 cask with old stockings, 2 empty casks, 1 casket containing 13 cotton handkerchiefs, 1 of fine linen, 9 new forks, ½ pound of thread, 1 table-cloth, 5 pairs of breeches, 3 belts, 2 cotton handkerchiefs, 1 black frock-coat, 1 jacket, 1 napkin, 5 black robes, 2 hats, 3 shirts, 1 towel, 6 shirts, 1 small cask half-filled with rum, 2 linen sheets, 1 mattress, 1 cot, 1 table-cloth, 5 handkerchiefs, 2 night-caps.

[In the margin] Gave the clothes to Laderoute, his servant. Hubert

Cash

	Pounds York Currency		
In bills in a pocket-book	34	4	8
in gold 7 Portuguese coins worth	23	8	
in silver		8	
	58		8

Notes

1 promissory note payable to order of Mr. Brulon	31	4	
1 promissory note payable to order of Mr. Andrews and Company	43	11	10
1 promissory note from Mr. Pratt payable in three months according to his agreement for the land sold to him by Father Potier	57	18	

20 silver spangles and 2 branches of porcelain.

In the Attic

1 iron stove with its stove pipe and one spit.

In the Kitchen

1 table, 2 iron-bound buckets, 1 kneading-trough, 2 frying pans, 1 pie-dish, 1 pie-plate, 1 large spoon and 1 flint and steel apparatus, 1 roasting spit, 2 andirons, 2 fire shovels, 3 iron pots, 1 duck, 2 kneading-troughs in poor condition.

In the Room off the Dining-room on the right

7 small and large pewter basins, 1 brass bowl, 2 dozen large and medium pewter plates, 15 large and small pewter molds, 2 empty casks, 2 small kegs of vinegar, 38 bags, 4 table-cloths, 1 box of old iron and 2 iron wedges, 1 buffalo robe, 4 earthenware jars, 1 linen basket, 4 small empty kegs, 6 pillow-cases and 6 stoneware saucers.

In the Room off the Dining-room on the left
1 trestle, 1 box containing 13 iron forks and one of copper, 5 table knives, 1 buffet, 2 pewter pans, 1 large and 1 small coffee-pot, 1 dozen glasses, 2 small flasks and 3 bottles, 1 coffee grinder, 12 brass candlesticks.

In the Cellar
2 large covered boilers filled with bear oil, 1 covered boiler belonging to Madam Savoyard, 1 keg full of red wine, 21 bottles filled with red wine belonging to Mr. Godet, 1 wheelbarrow wheel, 1 large cask and 6 empty kegs.

In the Dining-room
1 clock, 1 sideboard, 1 table, 10 chairs, 1 lantern, 2 andirons, 2 tripods, 7 pewter dishes, 1 chafing-dish, 1 salad-bowl.

In the Covered Passageway between the House and the Church
3 wide boilers, and in the garden 1 iron rake, 3 hoes, 1 spade and 1 wheelbarrow.

In the Bakery
In the attic 2 chests containing about 700 pounds of flour. Downstairs 6 medium-sized wide boilers, 1 wash tub and 1 chicken cage.

Done and sealed in the house of the late Reverend Father Potier on the day and year mentioned above and signed immediately.

    Guillaume Monforton, Maisonville
    Joseph Pouget   X Jos. Parent
      Williams, Judge

The church is 60 feet long by 30 feet wide and contains 34 rented pews. It is adorned with pictures; it possesses a gilt carved tabernacle; it is provided with sacred vessels and vestments necessary for divine services. There is a warden's seat and no pulpit. There is plenty of light and the windows are well glazed.

There is a house 26 feet long by 20 feet wide that was built at the expense of the inhabitants and of Father Potier in order to lodge the sexton, receive the bodies before burial and to house the children of the First Communion class.

The priest's house is large and in need of much repair. The yard 29 paces long by 10 paces wide is surrounded by cedar stakes. In it there is an almost new bakery 16 feet square, and also a chicken coop that is not quite finished.

F 10 Major De Peyster to Major Lernoult
  [*P.A.C., B 123, p. 112;* M.H.C., *X, 504*]

            Detroit 31st July 1781

The bearer of this letter, Monsieur Pougée, is deputed by the inhabitants of the Parish of L'Assomption, &c. to carry their Petition, requesting the Indulgence of a Priest in the room of Pere Potier who was killed last week by a fall which fractured his skull. The hurons also address His Excellency in a Speech and Belts, which they have requested may be presented to His Excellency by you. Immediately upon receiving the accounts of the old man's death, I sent and had an inventory taken of his Papers, among which are many volumes of Manuscripts, chiefly copies, and nothing of any consequence.

F 11   MINUTES OF A MEETING OF THE CHURCH WARDENS
[*Detroit Notarial Records, liber C, p. 128*]

On July 28, 1781, after calling a general meeting in the Church of Our Lady of the Assumption, at the close of prayer it was resolved unanimously that one or several wardens would be chosen as deputies to His Lordship in order to obtain a successor to the late Rev. Fr. Potier. For this purpose there assembled Sirs Maisonville, Marantet, Pouget, Labute, Pajot, Langlois, Bourron, Touranjeau, Susor, Bondy, Meloche and Jacques Parent, all former and new wardens, to consider the most suitable ways to request, in the name of all the people, a missionary from His Lordship, and to take the necessary steps with the Jesuit Fathers concerning the affairs of the church, the presbytery and other buildings belonging to the mission. The above-named Sirs elected Sirs Pouget and Belaire to whom they gave power of attorney and full authority to take the necessary steps mentioned above.

In witness whereof the above-named Sirs, in the name of all the people, have signed the present declaration to be used as needed.

Done in the parish house at Huron Point on the south shore of the Detroit River.

(Signed)   Maisonville   F. Marantete Godet
           J. Bondy   Monforton for Jacques Parent
           Joseph Pouget   first warden
           Touranjeau   La Bute
           Monforton for Suzor   Charles Bouron
           Pierre Meloche   Monforton for Langlois
           Monforton for Pajot

F 12   SPEECHES OF THE PRINCIPAL HURON CHIEFS IN COUNCIL WITH MAJOR DE PEYSTER, COMMANDANT OF DETROIT &C., JULY 29, 1781
[*P.A.C., B 123, pp. 107-9*]

Tiockouanhoron speaking with some branches of porcelain.

My father, I pray you to give your attention to my words, for they are the words of the chiefs, warriors, women and children who use my mouth to implore your help in the sad state in which we find ourselves. It is a matter of the greatest consequence to us.

By a belt

The death of our pious missionary Father Potier has perturbed us beyond imagination. Since that time a dark gloom has surrounded us and holds us in a pitiful position which solicits your fatherly compassion in our behalf. We ask you to join with us to obtain from His Excellency General Haldimand his help in getting for us a new missionary. Deign also to send him these words from us.

Showing a belt.

This belt is the symbol of our adoption of the Christian religion and of the chain that binds us to it. We hope to obtain today a spiritual leader as was given to us formerly.

By a belt addressed to General Haldimand

We pray your Excellency, who represents His Britannic Majesty to us, to give his attention to the request which we wish to make of him.

By another belt to the same

My father, please deign to consider the sad state of our nation since the loss of our missionary. We lament our present and future unhappy position without knowing where to turn for help. That is why we ask Your Excellency, our most solid support with His Lordship the Bishop of Quebec, to have another missionary given to your children, the Hurons of Detroit.

By another belt to His Lordship Bishop Briand of Quebec.

My father, in the name of God and of all the Huron Nation, help us in our urgent need of a missionary. The loss of Father Potier has plunged our village into a general grief which will not cease until he is replaced by another. Instructed from childhood in the principles of the Christian religion, we follow them faithfully under the direction of our spiritual leaders. But what will become of us now? The souls of our warriors will tremble henceforth at the thought of the death that awaits them at every moment; the blood of our old men and of our women runs cold at the approach of the last moment of their lingering lives; the mothers are distressed at the fate of their children; in any case, your charitable zeal, more than our words, will lead you to act in our behalf. We ask you to consider zealously our pressing need which urges you to avoid all delays, as every moment is precious in the present affair. We pray God to be favourable to us in the request that we make of you and for the preservation of Your Excellency.

By another belt to General Haldimand and the Bishop of Quebec.

My fathers, hoping to obtain from your goodness the granting of our requests for the missionary which we have asked you to give us, this belt is for him as soon as you have made your choice, to show him the road that will take him to our village and to assure him in advance of the filial and respectful affection of our nation.

By another belt addressed to the Hurons of Lorette at Quebec.

My brothers, you are of the same nation and religion as we are; that is why we ask you with confidence to join with us to obtain another missionary to replace Father Potier, who died on the 16th of July. You will know the right way to obtain such a grace. We ask you to employ all possible means to obtain this favor from our father the General and from our Bishop. We salute you all.

Names of the principal chiefs present

Tiockouanohon   Jorihoha
Toienthet   Isononcainen
Cimrathon   Tharatohat
Tihockeres

With the principal women of the Nation.

F 13   EXTRACTS FROM THE ACCOUNT BOOK OF ASSUMPTION PARISH FOR 1781

[Assumption Church Archives, Windsor, Ont.]

On November 25, 1781, the wardens and other inhabitants of the parish of the Assumption of Detroit having assembled at the sound of the bell in the usual manner for the purpose of electing a new warden in the place of Mr. Jacques Parent who is retiring from office, by a majority of the votes Mr. J. Bte. Oualette was elected as warden and he accepted the said position which he promised to fill faithfully. In witness thereof he has made his ordinary mark on the day and year mentioned above.

Mark + of J. Bte. Oualette	J. Bondy
fancoit godet	joseph pouget
charle bouron	simon drouilliar
reauomen	Hubert priest, Vicar-General

December 2, 1781—Mr. Jacques Parent who is retiring from office has turned over to Mr. Louis Suzor 309 livres and 16 sous, saying that this was all he had belonging to the church, there having been up to that time no books kept in due form. Done at L'Assomption on December 2, 1781.

Hubert priest, Vicar-General

On December 9, 1781, the old and new wardens assembled in the usual manner approved and appointed as sexton Pierre Javerai on the following mutual terms: The said Pierre Javerai shall perform faithfully all the duties assigned to him by the wardens who shall pay him from the church coffer 200 livres of 20 sous each per year, and provide him with a suitable dwelling wherever the wardens may decide on the clear understanding that the said sexton shall not demand any repayment or recompense whatsoever, nor shall he be permitted to sublet in whole or in part the dwelling that shall be provided by the church. Should the sexton not reside in the dwelling provided for him, the church reserves the right to collect the rent for the said dwelling. In addition the sexton shall be obliged to receive in his house the bodies of the deceased of the parish until their funeral, to lodge the children who are being instructed for their first Holy Communion, and to permit the people to warm themselves in the said house when they bring a load of wood to the church.

Done at L'Assomption on the day and year mentioned above.

joseph pouget Mark of Pierre + Javerai, sexton
françois meloche Pierre meloche
fancois godet La Bute

I, Pierre Javerai, certify that I have received from Mr. Suzor, chief warden, 83 livres and 6 sous as payment for my wages until the last day of January, the present to serve as receipt.

Done at L'Assomption January 20, 1782.

Witness Hubert   Mark of + Pierre Javerai

At a meeting of the wardens it was decided to give sexton Amable Bigra the sum of 20 pounds or 100 écus [crowns] as wages. Done at the parish of the Assumption January 27, 1782

Hubert priest, Vicar-General

Received from Father Hubert 50 livres for three months' wages due on the 1st instant..	50#	
Also received for one High Mass on the 17th January for Louis Goiaux	2#	10s
For one High Mass for the late Robert.............................	2#	10s
For burial and funeral service of Pierre Campeau's wife.............	6#	
For one High Mass and burial of Mr. Charles Reaume's panis [slave]..	4#	
For one High Mass for Phil. Leduc................................	2#	10s
Total paid to Mr. Gaillard, singer........................	67#	10s
February 18, 1782—Louis Gaillard		

On June 9 at a meeting of the wardens it was decided that about 4000 livres of the church money would be used to buy boards, planks, etc. for the building of a new church.

ACCOUNT OF MR. LOUIS SUZOR, WARDEN

RECEIPTS

1. The said Louis Suzor received the sum of three hundred livres and sixteen sous from his predecessor in office Mr. Jacques Parent.. 309# 16s
   Also from Mr. Pierre Meloche, former warden, for the balance due at the end of his year............................ 48#
2. The Child Jesus Collection in money................ 221# 12s
   In corn sold to Mr. Marantet....................... 93# 11s
   in 12 bushels of wheat to Mr. Pouget............... 180#
   In 2½ bushels of wheat to Roucout for a year's supply of altar breads............................ 37# 10s 532# 13s
3. Good Friday Collection...................................... 189#
   Also a note from Potevin for 204# if it is paid..................
4. Sunday Collections in the church in cash...................... 149# 9s
   N.B. In these collections there were 220 spangles that have been placed in the church coffer. 500 spangles had already been taken out of these collections and sold to Mr. Drouillard.
5. Received for rental of pews, namely from (N.B. There are 34 pews).
   Pierre Meloche Sr. for................1 pew 1 year— 7# 10s
   Labutte............................2 " 1 " — 15#

Marantet	2 " 1 " —	15#	
Joseph Drouillard	1 " 1 " —	7#	10s
André Peltier	1 " 1 " —	7#	10s
Suzor	1 " 2 " —	15#	
Bonaventure Réaume	1 " 2 " —	15#	
Mr. Réaume Sr.	1 " 3 plus—	24#	
Claude Réaume	1 " 1 year—	7#	10s
Vital Dumouchelle	1 " 1 " —	7#	10s
Jacques Charon	1 " 3 " —	22#	10s
Joseph Pilet	1 " 3 " —	22#	10s
Oualet	1 " 2 " —	15#	
N. Langlois	1 " 1 " —	7#	10s
Lesperance	1 " 1 " —	7#	10s
Janis	1 " 1 " —	7#	10s
Laurent Parent	1 " 3 " —	22#	10s
Joseph Beaubien	1 " 1 " —	7#	10s
Guillaume Goyau	1 " 1 " —	7#	10s
Tourangeaux	1 " 4 " —	30#	
Louis Deveau	1 " 1 " —	7#	10s
Antoine Meloche			309#

N.B. Poirier, Gignac, Hodienne had paid for their pews the preceding year.

6. Received from the sale of pews:

J. B. Oualet	225#		
Simon Drouillard	226#		
Charles Renaud	240#		
Antaya	232#	10s	
Gignac	240#		
Julien Parent on account of 270#	135#		1298# 10s

7. Received from Mr. Beaufait 500# for an Anniversary Service to be sung during next October for the late Paul Marsac ... 500#
8. Received from Mr. Pierre Drouillard for 870 spangles ... 404#
   N.B. 500 of these 870 spangles had been taken from the church coffer out of this year's collection.
9. Received for High Masses, burials and funerals ... 910# 10s
   Also on August 9 for the Anniversary Service of Bois-menu ... 26#
   Received from Suzor for 8 ear-rings ... 6#

Total Receipts ... 4682# 18s

N.B. Received as a present from Joseph Drouillard two silver candle-sticks worth 150#.

EXPENDITURES

1. Paid to Mrs. Janis, church laundress, for her year ending November 1, 1778 ... 49# 10s
   To same as payment for 1781 ... 6#
   To same on account for the year starting November 1, 1781, at the rate of 120# per year, by her pew rent ... 7# 10s
   June 24—To same on account 6 pounds ... 90# — 153#
2. Paid to Laderoute, former sexton, for wages up to the day of his departure ... 83# 6s
3. Paid to Bigra, sexton, from February 1, 1782, at the rate of 300# per year ...
   for wages and casual fees up to August 16 next ... 212#
   To same for having auctioned 7 pews ... 21# — 233#
4. Paid to Louis Gaillard, singer, at 200# per year, up to August 1, 1782—wages ... 150#
   To same for casual fees up to said date ... 117# — 267#
5. To Roucout for a year's supply of altar breads due January 1, 1782, 2½ bushels of wheat ... 37# 10s
6. To Father Hubert for salary to August 1, 1782 ... 215#

RELIGION AND EDUCATION AFTER 1760

7. To Mr. Rankin, merchant, for cloth for the sexton's robe....................................		52#	
To Mr. Pouget for making said robe...............		12#	64#
To Mrs. Janis for soap for the church.............			15#
To Guilbeau for 10 pounds of candle..............			37# 10s
To Fovel for getting some palms...................		12#	
To same for fence around the sexton's lot.........		60#	72#
Paid for vestments and candles bought at Montreal by Father Hubert.................................			157#
Paid for wax, candle-stick and surplice by Mr. Pouget			109# 10s
Paid for 1 pound of incense......................			3#
Paid for the expenses of the pastor's trip from church money..			232# 2s
			1684# 18s

The receipts being 4682# and 18s and the expenses being 1684# and 18s, therefore the receipts of Mr. Louis Suzor exceed the expenses by the sum of 2998#, which sum the said Mr. Louis Suzor, warden, has deposited in the church coffer along with 200 spangles.

Done at Detroit in the parish of the Assumption on August 11, 1782.

        joseph pouget   francoit gaudet
        J. Bondy   fr. meloche
                           Hubert priest, Vicar-General

ACCOUNT OF MR. JOSEPH POUGET, CHIEF WARDEN, FROM AUGUST 15, 1782 TO 1783.

RECEIPTS

1. Mr. Joseph Pouget received the sum of 2998# from Mr. Louis Suzor when the latter retired from office..............			2998#	
Received as stipends for High Masses, funerals and burials etc...........................			1336#	10s
Donations to the Church........................	85#	10		
Money in Sunday Collections.....................	205#			
Money in the Child Jesus Collection..............	171#			
Money in the Good Friday Collection.............	115#			
Collection in flour 840 pounds...................	630#			
in corn 11 bushels.....................	198#			
in oats 7 bushels......................	70#			
Various collections, spangles, porcelain..........	1258#	5	2732#	15
Pew rents......................................			246#	
Total Receipts............			7313#	5

EXPENDITURES

Paid to Father Hubert for his salary up to August 15, 1783		284#	10
To Gaillard, singer, for wages and casual fees...........	346#		
To same on new account...............................	45#	391#	
To Bigra, sexton, up to last April for wages & fees.......		311#	
To Mrs. Janis for laundry work........................		22#	10
For Mass wine...		255#	
For candles & funeral of Mr. Marsac....................		56#	
For glue and starch...................................		15#	
For a complete set of vestments and candles............		687#	8
Paid in money for the pinery..........................	4200#		
Paid in flour etc. to same.............................	698#	5098#	
Total Expenditures................		7120#	8

The total expense of the pinery was 17740# and 10s, the church paid 5098# and Father Hubert gave the sum of 12642# and 10s. Closed above account by which it appears that the Receipts were 7313# 5s and the Expenditures 7120# 8s. The Receipts exceed the Expenditures by the sum of 192# 17s, which amount the said Mr. Pouget has turned over to Mr. Oualet, chief warden.

        Maisonville   godet
        J. Bondy   Hubert priest, Vicar-General
        joseph + pouget

...

On September 9, 1787, after the mature deliberation of a large assemblage composed of the most eminent inhabitants of the parish of the Assumption of Detroit and of the principal Huron chiefs meeting together to deal with the business of their corporation, it was decided that a part of the church would be occupied by the Huron Nation. To put it more clearly from the back of the church beginning at the nave up to the second window inclusive, no one at all shall have a right in the said area except the said Indians, recognized as Christians and the legitimate possessors of the part in question for having manifested their zeal and for having contributed towards the expense and building of the said church as much as was in their power.

In consideration of the glory of God and for the benefit of peace and concord that must unite the faithful, we have issued the present document to serve in case of need and for the comfort of the interested parties.

However, notice must be taken that if the said Indians wish to distinguish their chiefs or other persons of rank in their nation, they will be obliged to have made at their own expense seats, pews and other special furnishings provided that they conform to the laws and usages of our Holy Mother the Church.

Done on the ninth of September of the above-mentioned year in the priest's house in the presence of Father Dufaux, undersigned missionary priest, and several others as appears hereinafter.

    Payet, missionary priest   F. X. Dufaux
    Claude Reaume   Charles Reaume

...

ACCOUNT OF MR. JEAN BAPTISTE TOURNEUX, CHIEF WARDEN, FROM JANUARY 1, 1792 TO JANUARY 1, 1793.

RECEIPTS

1. Mr. Jean Baptiste Tourneux received the sum of 58# 9s from Mr. Antoine Meloche who is retiring from office	98#	9s
Stipends for funerals, High Masses and burials	771#	10s
Pew rent	1150#	
Child Jesus Collection	275#	14s
Other donations to the Church	38#	
	2293#	13s

EXPENDITURES

Wages and fees of Bigras, sexton	548#	18s
Wages and fees of Beauchant	147#	15s
Wages and fees of Mr. Perthuis	126#	
Salary and fees of the pastor	220#	
To Mrs. Bigras for laundry work	40#	
For a woolen carpet	60#	
For palms	7#	10s
For farm expenses	38#	
For white Mass wine	121#	10s
For candles	120#	
For stearic candles	48#	
For altar breads, incense, starch, soap, etc.	45#	

Paid in cash to Frerot for the pulpit............................ 285#
Paid to Morand for the wood of the pulpit...................... 36#

1843# 13s

Closed the present account by which it appears that the Receipts being 2293# 13s and the Expenditures 1843# 13s, the Receipts exceed the Expenditures by 450#, which sum Mr. Tourneux has turned over to Mr. Boufard when the latter took office.

F 14 GIFT OF LAND FROM THE HURON INDIANS TO THE REVEREND F. X. HUBERT AND THE SISTERS OF THE CONGREGATION
[*Detroit Notarial Records, liber C, pp. 158–60*]

[Detroit, March 4, 1782]

Know all men by these presents that we the chiefs & principal leaders of the Huron or Wyandot nation of Indians at Detroit, for ourselves & by & with the advice & consent of the whole of our said nation, in consideration of the good will, love & afection which we and the whole of the said nation have & bear unto the Reverend Francois Xavier Hubert grand vicar of Detroit, & the sisters of the congregation, & also for divers other good causes & considerations us the said chiefs & rest of our nation hereunto moving, have given, granted, aliened, enfeoffed & confirmed & by these presents do give, grant, alien, enfeoff & confirm unto the said Reverend Francois Xavier Hubert & the said sisters of the congregation, a certain tract of land of six acres or arpents in front & forty arpents in depth, bounded in front by a certain little rivulet or creek running back of the Huron village, which rivulet or creek to be the front boundary until it discharges itself into the River Detroit, thence along said river to James Rankin's fence,[3] thence along said fence a south southwest course as far as it extends at present. On the east northeast by Francois Pratt's farm, in the rear and part of the west southwest by Indian lands & the other part of the west south west by James Rankin's lands, as also a road of sixty feet wide, on the west south west & joining Francis Pratt's farm from the said rivulet or creek to the river Detroit, with all & singular the appurtenances &c. unto the said tract of land appertaining or in any wise belonging & the Reversion & Reversions, Remainder & Remainders, Rents & services of the said Premises & also all the estate, right, title, interest, property, claim or demand whatever of us the said chiefs or of any one whatever of the said nation of, in & to the said messuage, tenement & premises & of, in & to every part thereof TO HAVE AND TO HOLD the said messuage, tenements, lands, hereditaments & premises hereby given & granted or mentioned or intended to be given & granted with their & every of their

[3]On June 20, 1775, the chiefs of the Wyandotte Nation (Hurons) "put their heads together and gave to James Rankin's children a small piece of land beginning at a little run of water just below the Huron Church." A photographic copy of this deed of gift is preserved in the George F. Macdonald Collection, Windsor, Ontario. In 1897 the original was in the hands of Mr. P. B. Hansford of Wyandotte County in the State of Kansas.

appurtenances unto the said Francois Xavier Hubert & the said sisters, their heirs & assigns for the only proper use & behoof of them the said Francois Xavier Hubert & the said sisters, their heirs & assigns forever. And the said chiefs for themselves & in behalf of the whole of their nation, their heirs, executors & administrators do covenant, promise & grant to & with the said Francois Xavier Hubert and the said sisters, their heirs & assigns by these presents, that they the said Francois Xavier Hubert & the said sisters, their heirs & assigns shall and lawfully may from henceforth & for ever after peaceably and quietly have, hold, occupy, possess & enjoy the said messuage, tenements, lands, hereditaments & premises hereby given & granted or mentioned or intended to be given & granted with their & every of their appurtenances free, clear & discharged or well & sufficiently saved, kept harmless & indemnified of, from & against all former & other Gets, grants, bargains, sales, jointures, feoffments, dowers, estates, entails, rents, rent charges, arrearages of rents, statutes, judgments, recognizances, statutes merchant & of the staple, extents & of, from & against all former & other titles, troubles, charges & incombrances whatsoever had, done or suffered or to be had, done or suffered by them the said chiefs or by anyone whatever of the said nation, their heirs, executors or administrators or any person or persons lawfully claiming or to claim by, from or under them or any or either of them. And by these presents do make this our act & deed irrevocable under any pretence whatever & have put the said Francois Xaxier Hubert & the said sisters in full possession & seizin by delivering them a piece of the said tract on the premises. In witness whereof we the said chiefs for ourselves & in behalf of our whole nation of Ouindats or Hurons have unto these presents set the marks of our different tribes at Detroit the fourth day of March in the year of our Lord one thousand seven hundred and eighty two.
(signed) Doyantate
    Dewatonte

    Seals

F 15 Re a Foundation of the Congregation of Notre-Dame at Detroit

[L'Histoire de la Congrégation de Notre-Dame de Montréal, V, 345–53]

In 1755 the inhabitants of Detroit had requested Bishop Pontbriand to establish a house of our institute in their town. With the same object in view they had also presented a request to Marquis Duquesne de Menneville . . . but nothing resulted. However, the project of this foundation had not been abandoned, and in 1782 it was revived in a more lively manner than ever before. Father Hubert, pastor of the Church of the Assumption among the Hurons near Detroit, former superior of the Quebec Seminary, later named successor to Bishop

D'Esglis, whose heart was set on this foundation, wrote to this purpose, and Bishop Briand supported his request by enclosing the following letter:

Quebec, March 26, 1782

My dear Sister,

I can add nothing to Father Hubert's enclosed letter. I could not give you any motives more pressing or more analogous to those of your institute than the ones he mentions. Masses without morals and without the knowledge of religion which reforms them, that was the great objective in the minds of the zealous and saintly founders of your useful congregation. If your institute agrees, you will have an understanding with Father Montgolfier with regard to the choice of personnel and the rest. I beseech Our Lord to inspire your community to consent to take on this great work of charity. May He also grant to those chosen for this work the courage and zeal to undertake it, the wisdom, prudence and all the other virtues necessary to conduct it well and to render their work and solicitude useful for the glory of God and for the salvation of those poor peoples.

With much consideration I remain etc.

J. Ol. Bishop of Quebec

After having read the Bishop's letter to her council, Sister St. Ignace replied to it as follows:

Your Lordship:

With the most respectful submission I have received the letter that Your Excellency so kindly wrote to me. Although we cannot fail to realize the great temporal burden, and perhaps the spiritual harm that might come to our community from the proposed new establishment of a mission at Detroit, the matter seems so advantageous to the glory of God, so consistent with the obligations of our state of life and with the sentiments of zeal animating us, that authorized by Your Excellency we could not reject it completely. But may we be permitted to state that the project cannot be carried out immediately. Although it appears that Father Hubert has taken just and reasonable steps to facilitate our first trip, and to procure for us a place of residence, these are only temporary aids, and the question of a permanent establishment must be considered. The protection and zeal of this priest could easily be taken away before the project is completed . . . and what will happen to our dear sisters isolated in a country so distant, so impassable and perhaps without any spiritual help?

Although we are not lacking in zealous sisters, we do not have any free at present who are disposed to undertake this work. The time does not seem favorable to start new foundations at such a distance when we have much difficulty in maintaining the completely erected houses in the vicinity. Finally, even if it were possible to undertake this work it would seem necessary to be careful not to enter into a contract that is impossible or that could be detrimental in many ways.

As a result of these considerations it appears necessary to take time to consider the conditions on which we could enter upon this work, and we hope that Your Excellency will grant us his approval.

I have the honor to be, etc.

Montreal, June 12, 1782

Sister St. Ignace

On June 21 Sister St. Ignace wrote to Father Hubert, pastor of the Church of the Assumption at Detroit:

Dear Father,
On May 30 I informed you that I had received the two letters that you had so kindly written to me, and also the 2400 livres that I have placed on deposit. I wrote to the Bishop concerning the conditions that the community demands for the mission at Detroit. I shall not fail to write you as soon as I receive His Excellency's reply. Notwithstanding the desire that we all have of contributing to the common good as far as our condition permits, we cannot help realizing the many difficulties entailed in such a distant mission. I believe that much thoughtful consideration must precede this foundation.

The community joins me in expressing our best wishes and in asking you to give us a remembrance in your Holy Sacrifices of the Mass.

I have the honor to be etc. . . .

Sister St. Ignace

. . .

After pondering the advantages and disadvantages of this mission, the congregation decided not to undertake it.

F 16   Hubert to Bishop Briand
[Q.C.A., Ev. Q., II, p. 36]

Detroit, September 26, 1784

Mr. Baby comforted me greatly when he told me that your health was improving. That is the only report that I have received this year.

Mr. Payet has not yet returned from his mission. I do not expect him before two weeks.

In a few days I am going to enter into a new rectory, which is large and beautiful for this part of the country. A new church is planned for next year. I would like to be able to reform the morals as easily as building a new rectory; but alas! what obstacles are encountered; passions are pretty nearly the same. We bring back one, and another leaves. The profanation of the Sundays appears to be the cause of other troubles, and unfortunately it is increasing. The time of divine mercy has not yet arrived. We must wait for it.

F 17   Fréchette[4] to Hubert
[Q.C.A., E.U., V–46]

L'Assomption de Detroit, April 24, 1786

Having received no news since your departure from Detroit, I do not know how to address you. However, no matter where you may be, please be assured of my respect and of my submission to all your wishes.

---

[4]Pierre Fréchette (1761–1816), a native of Quebec, was ordained a priest on December 18, 1784. In autumn of 1785, he succeeded Father Hubert as pastor of

I take advantage of the first reliable occasion to send you news of your parish. Last winter a sort of grippe and scarlet fever made the rounds, which caused me great anxiety. However, God in His infinite goodness gave me enough health and strength to be able to attend all those who had need of me. Many people died, especially young people. I buried a man named Picotte, whom God in His infinite mercy brought back to his duty some time before his death, and who gave me much consolation in his last days upon earth. I also buried old man Repus, and the wife of poor Pelletier, the warden. As you know she left behind a large family. I am not going to give you an account of the morals of the inhabitants, since you know them better than I do. I am quite satisfied with the parish. God has completed in several persons the work that you had happily begun, and I am pleased to tell you that there are very few, if any, who have not presented themselves to the tribunal of penance during the Easter season. God has touched even the heart of Deveau, who has been reconciled and who appears desirous of doing what is right. I have chased from my parish Madam Tourangeau, called the blue woman, who had taken refuge here last fall. I also made Madam Morisseau leave Simon's mill; she was behaving very badly. I put somewhat of a stop to the balls and dances last winter by representing to the people the above-named sickness as a punishment for their disorders and debaucheries.

Work has begun for the church. Last winter the people hauled the stone and the wood for the lime; everyone seems well disposed to work as soon as the seedings are finished. I made a collection last winter, and I took in a goodly sum. In general I am quite satisfied with the parish, and I even dare flatter myself that the people fear and love me at the same time. Nobody is trying to cause me any trouble, on the contrary everybody is trying to help me. There is only François Meloche who was foolish enough last winter to threaten to sue me for the candles used at the funeral of his sister, Madame Pelletier. After having shown him that they belonged to me, he was so ashamed of his mistake that he doesn't dare show his face at the rectory any more. There is only one thing that troubles me, and that is the fact that Mr. Payet gives me reason to believe and he has even told several people that he intended to ask for my present parish if he should come back this fall. That would disturb me greatly. You know the difficulty I experienced on leaving my country. If that should happen I beg you and even feel obliged in conscience to ask you to recall me to Lower Canada. With the experience that I have, I can see that for many reasons it would be impossible for me to go anywhere else.

Assumption parish, but in the following year exchanged parishes with Father Dufaux who had just come to take charge of Ste. Anne's Church. Fréchette continued to serve Ste. Anne's for ten years, leaving Detroit for Lower Canada shortly before the American occupation in July 1796.

F 18   Dufaux[5] to Hubert
[Q.C.A., E.U., V–47]

Detroit, August 24, 1787

. . .
I received your letter of June 18 enjoining me to rely upon Fr. Payet for all that you left at Assumption, except the books that I found without any reference to the quantity, and Fr. Potier's manuscripts which I shall hand over to Fr. Payet. The land is in the enjoyment of Mr. Pouget. I keep my animals on the neighbours' farms. The furniture is in such small quantity that I am ashamed to make a list of what is left at the rectory. There are 9 plates, 2 dishes, 3 old table-cloths, 1 decanter and 2 glasses. The rest is not worth mentioning. I borrowed from several obliging persons the most necessary pieces of furniture, since I was not in a position to obtain them myself without buying them on credit—a thing I can't make up my mind to do. Money is so rare that I have scarcely received a hundred crowns during the whole year to pay wages of my good servant Bigras. The best inhabitants who were in a position to help out in good deeds three or four years ago do not even possess a dollar, and they are all in debt. Mr. Ouellette for whom I married two children during the past six months has not been able to pay me for the marriages. He admitted to me that he did not have a single cent to meet this obligation. Out of six marriages that I performed only one was able to pay the stipend, the others are on credit. As for low masses I have not even received a money stipend for thirty since my arrival. The collections on Sundays and Holydays amounted to 11 livres and 10 sous. In the Child Jesus collection I received about 80 bushels of wheat which I employed to have some work done for the church, because I could not sell it [the wheat].

I supplied all the needs of the church in wax, candles, wine, 100 planks for the floor, laundry soap, starch, mending, etc., all usually at my own expense. I did not find a single piece of linen in fit condition to use for the Holy Sacrifice. I obtained a new supply of everything without it costing the church a red cent. I have also looked after many other small expenditures for the work on the church and for its maintenance.

I did not find a single building in which I could keep a chicken. There was hardly any fence at all. I had a building 26 feet long by 16 feet wide erected at my own expense. If I received some assistance in this undertaking from the inhabitants, I believe they were well repaid from the food and drinks of brandy that I had to give them.

In the same way I had Mouton's small house moved near the rectory.

---

[5]François-Xavier Dufaux (1752–96), a Sulpician, was the son of the Montreal contractor who built Fort Rouillé at Toronto. In 1786 he was sent to Detroit where by agreement he took up the pastorate of Assumption parish. There he remained until his death on September 11, 1796.

I had it recoated, joints tightened and a stone chimney erected. I paid ten crowns a barrel for the lime; it took five barrels. I also paid for the window panes, nails and labor. There was no other way of lodging the teachers that I had brought with me following your advice. I stayed three days at the fort, where I celebrated Mass twice. Many people were present, but none to bid me welcome or to offer me the least assistance. Where was I to lodge the teachers? In the fort at a rental of one hundred dollars besides the other necessary housekeeping expenses? They would have required a man to look after their needs; living and clothing are frightfully dear. What revenues could they have received to provide for their necessities? There are four or five mixed (boys and girls) schools in the fort. The pupils are nearly all English, because they are the only ones who have the desire and means to have their children educated. I immediately realized my unfortunate situation, that I had left a peaceful position in order to take on a lot of trouble. I went to see Father Fréchette, and I told him my troubles and difficulties. He acquainted me with his troubles, and he assured me that he had shed more than a hatful of tears over the arrangements that you had made with Mr. Mouton. With nothing on one side of the river and a lot of trouble on the other, he appeared inclined to take the parish of the fort, where he is at present, rather than stay at Assumption and try to make arrangements for the teachers. And so I stayed in his place. Immediately I spoke to Mouton, and I asked him if he wanted to stay with me and continue to serve me as he had served you. He said he did. Well, I said, stay on and you will have reason to be satisfied. That was my intention according to the recommendation that you had given me. Two or three days go by; I am served only cabbage soup and a dish of cabbage for dinner and supper. An Indian brings me a turkey and two ducks for which I was very grateful. I give them to Mouton asking him to prepare some meat soup which I needed badly. The next day I was served onion soup, one roasted duck and the two wings of the turkey. That's all the meat that I tasted during the ten days that Mr. Mouton stayed with me. It was necessary to have the small house moved speedily near the rectory, and I asked seven or eight persons to lend me a hand. With a bit of help and money it was accomplished in a short time. I asked Mouton if it would be possible to offer some refreshments to those who were helping me. Gruffly he replied that there was some onion soup. He served some, and the men all shrugged their shoulders at seeing me treated in this manner. I asked if there was some pork, eggs or butter; nothing of the kind. Ten days go by on a lenten fare that did not help me to recuperate from a difficult 54-day trip. In short he told me one day that neither he nor his wife nor his children were disposed to serve anyone. He said that Fr. Hubert used to wash the dishes with the little boys. I told him that I had never done that type of work and that I would be very awkward trying to do so, and that he had to make up his mind. He showed me a small piece of paper authorising him to dispose of all your belongings in his possession. For one week he carried things away and left me with only what I have mentioned above. I now close this subject or I could relate a thousand other truths sadder than the rest.

While I was having the small house moved, the Misses Ademard and Papineau stayed with Mr. Marentette for about three weeks. Then they moved into that little house that serves as a dormitory for them and their boarders. The large *salle des habitants* is used for a classroom. They have eight boarders and five day students. They live under a mission rule. In order to encourage them I let them keep the revenue from the boarders as well as from the day students. I pay all the expenses for the board of the teachers and their pupils. Out of eight boarders, only three pay two pounds per month, namely, a Miss Baby and two small English girls from the home of Mr. Macomb. The parents set the price. There are three others who give what they can, namely, Perthuis, Ademard and Dumouchelle. Two Beneteau girls are boarded gratis; they promised me that God would keep their account and they were accepted on those conditions. In general all the girls are doing very well and afford much satisfaction.

All winter long up to the time of the First Communion they [the teachers] catechised about twenty girls every day of the week except Thursday. During the same period of time I taught catechism to the boys four times a week right up to the day of the First Communion which was on 27th of June. There were thirty children in the class—eighteen girls and twelve boys. They all received their second communion on the feast-day of the parish, on which occasion I was pleased to observe the same dispositions as were evidenced on the day of their First Communion. The parents seemed to appreciate the unsparing efforts made to instruct their children. All the inhabitants admit the necessity and advantage of giving an education to their children.

Two weeks in advance I announced the plenary indulgence that you sent me for the feast of the Assumption. On the two Sundays preceding the feast I explained the meaning of a plenary indulgence and showed the people how important it was to take advantage of it. During those two weeks a large number came to confession. On the eve of the feast I entered the confessional at a quarter after twelve (noon), and I did not leave until ten thirty at night. On the day of the feast I heard from five o'clock until twelve thirty (noon).

On the ninth of August I solemnly blessed the new church. After the blessing Father Fréchette sang the Mass and I took up the collection. I received about 500 livres in notes for wheat, some silver-plated pieces and currency. Besides I received 240 dollars from the Indians in silver-plated goods, porcelain and other merchandise peculiar to them, based on what it costs them.

Small-pox is bringing terror to Detroit. The Indians fear it very much, and the French are not exempt. It is raging at Sandusky. It even struck a young boy near here in the Rankin home. Major Mathews was notified and he came with a doctor to verify it. He had the boy and his family transported down to the mouth of the river. It is reported that the father caught the disease from the child and in his frenzy drowned himself.

There are in the parish 620 communicants plus about ten families that returned from Sandusky this spring. About 600 made their Easter duty. The parish tithes amounted to 500 bushels of wheat, 150 bushels of corn, 10 bushels of peas and 56 bushels of oats. I still have 250 bushels of wheat which I can't dispose of on any terms. The rest was used for my own livelihood, for alms and for work on the church.

During the past year there were 33 baptisms, 6 marriages, 7 funerals of adults and one of a child.

There is hardly any more talk of balls and dances, horse races and drunkenness. The times are too bad to devote one's time to such amusements. It is difficult to make a living in the warm season. As for wine one cannot think of using even the smallest quantity. At 24 francs and 10 sous a gallon we can do without it. 45 livres for a sheep; I haven't tasted mutton at Detroit. 12 livres for a turkey etc. It is necessary to live on pork, which it is very difficult to keep. There was no hunting this year.

F19   DUFAUX TO HUBERT
[*Q.C.A., E.U., V-53*]

Detroit, November 5, 1787

I take advantage of Major Mathews' return to Quebec to reaffirm my respectful and obedient sentiment towards your Lordship. I believe this will be the last and the safest opportunity this year. Mr. Mathews appeared at Detroit only long enough to be regretted. He won all hearts by his judicious court hearings, and personally I am much indebted to him for the hearings that he gave me. I beg your Lordship to second the thanks that I have expressed to him on several occasions. I paid him a few visits, and he did me the honor of coming to visit me in my house. He examined all the work going on at the church, the buildings and outbuildings of the parish. He visited the teachers, enquired about the number of pupils, visited their classroom and the small house that they use as a dormitory. He seemed pleasantly surprised with what he saw and gave it his approval.

Since Father Payet's departure the outside walls of the church have been covered with siding and the sacristy soon will be. The inside of the sacristy, partitions, stairs, closets, etc., are finished, and the most important matter of all is that the workmen have nearly all been paid. I hope to have everything paid off before the end of the year. I take full advantage of the fact that I have with me the Misses Papineau and Ademard who freely devote their leisure time to the service of the church. It would have been very difficult for me to find at Detroit people who would have been willing and able to do what they did. With a very poor diamond and some keys they cut about 400 panes of glass for the side windows and the oval window of the church, and puttied nearly a thousand panes. Workmen wanted 30 cents for cutting panes of glass and 10 cents for puttying them. They have saved the church that expense and much more in the work that they do every day for the adornment and upkeep of the church. The present intention is to put everything in the best possible condition without placing the church in debt, and to work for education as the habitants request it. The most unfortunate circumstance is that nearly all are in debt, and instead of making repayments the majority are going farther into debt. Money is so rare that there is no longer any talk of paying in cash. Nearly all the transactions are made by barter. The King takes a small amount of flour, one fifth of what each farmer can supply, i.e., anyone who subscribed for 1000 pounds is cut down to 200 pounds, at 24 livres a hundredweight, and 4½ livres for corn paid in merchandise that is excessively high-priced, especially when it is imported. One pound of putty is priced at one crown; one pound of nails 40 cents; one pound of salt 30 cents. It is surprising the amount of nails and putty that went into the building of the church. All is paid and I am not in debt to any merchant.

After having been so poorly housed in the old church, I am quite happy to have a moderately decent place of worship. The pews of the old church have been moved to the new, and each owner retains his former title. The new pews, however, are rented by the year to the highest bidder for his lifetime under the following conditions: 1. He will have the pew made. 2. He will pay the rental yearly during the month of January, otherwise the church re-enters into its rights. 3. If the holder vacates his pew for any reason whatever, he must warn the head warden three months in advance so that the church will not suffer any loss. About half of the new pews have been awarded. Some people protested against this arrangement but I did not pay any attention to them, and now they are greatly humiliated. The sale of pews is continuing as before, and none dares say anything. At the auction the pews sell for about 25 livres.

I have no great difficulties concerning spiritual matters. I obtained from Major Mathews orders under penalty of a fine of five pounds for what troubled me most, namely, those who work on Sundays and Holydays, those who stay at the door of the church during the services, those who make the rounds on New Year's Day, those who hold amusement meetings way into the night at any time of the year.

We still owe merchants and others 5000 livres for the building of the rectory, a debt that is increased daily by the interest, and which will not soon be paid off because of bad will or lack of means on the part of the inhabitants. The merchants are threatening to have the rectory sold for debts, but I don't believe they'll go through with that plan. Detroit is not a good place for building. Your Lordship started, and besides encountering many obstacles and difficulties it cost you all your savings. I finished the building program, and I will not say how much it cost me. I leave it to the Lord to reckon what I would like to do for love of Him; according to His pleasure He changes a perishable fortune into a better one, and momentary consolations into tears, to teach us that we must attach ourselves to the Consoler rather than to consolations. Magnificent and just in His rewards, He knows best whether to reward His true servants in this life or in the next. Sit nomen Domini benedictum. . . .

F 20   DUFAUX TO HUBERT
[Q.C.A., E.U., V-59]

Detroit, August 3, 1788

I have just received the ratification of the powers that were conferred on me by the late Bishop Dorilée [D'Esglis] of Quebec, along with a circular letter and a private one outlining my duties. It is my intention to do all I can to fulfill the hopes that you have placed in me for the greater good of your people at Detroit, a people for the most part not very zealous for its education, and still less able to help in procuring that advantage that it hardly recognizes. They admit the good conduct, the zeal and the talents of the teachers. Still there are only eight to ten pupils, including boarders and day students. That number is not increasing. The times are indescribably hard among the inhabitants who have no outlet for their products. They are obliged to go into debt every day, and to give the little that they possess to satisfy the wishes of their creditors. They don't sell any stock because large quantities are arriving from the colonies and are sold at a wretched price. They are forced to keep theirs and often to see it perish from local disease—another plague that is only too common at Detroit. What is one to do or undertake in such hard times? It does not seem opportune to start any new buildings. It is better not to bother the people. In any case I have made up my mind to maintain everything patiently this year, and if conditions do not appear any brighter I shall return [to Lower Canada], and I'm asking you that permission in advance.

For the past month and a half I have had a very bad case of trembling fever. It has left me very thin and extremely weak. The Misses Adhemar and Papineau, who appreciate very much your kind remembrance, have also been sick with the fever for more than two months. They seem a little better now, but I think it will be a long time before they are completely recovered. Neither one has a strong constitution.

I am not going to detail my feelings about all these trials; I shall simply say that I ask the Lord every day to grant me his grace to turn them to good use. . . .

F 21   DUFAUX TO HUBERT
[*Q.C.A., E.U., V-79*]

District of Hesse, August 22, 1790

During the present month I received by Mr. Belle Cour your letter in reply to the one I wrote to you last January. Major Mathews and Mr. Powell also received letters, and the latter hastened to my house to read to me the contents of his letter in an effort to soothe my grief and dispel my secret anxieties of the past eight months. . . . I confess most sincerely that I love, esteem and respect most heartily my Bishop, and that I pray for his preservation. Hence it is easy to realize how grieved I was to see that, by a most awful calumny, I was the cause of trouble to Your Excellency. From that fact you can understand how eager I am to know and follow your wishes, and how I esteem the powers that you have granted me. When I left Montreal my sentiments were all for the glory of God's Holy Name. I felt obliged to make the sacrifice of my country and of loving hearts in order to carry out Your Excellency's wishes. If your hopes have not been entirely fulfilled it is not my fault, nor is it a crime. The times and circumstances were not favorable. My departure was so hurried that I did not have time to make certain family arrangements. Now my temporal and other affairs suffer from my absence. My health, always precarious, makes me decide to return to Montreal next spring, and to ask Your Excellency in advance to grant me that permission.

I do not hesitate to state that I shall leave the parish of the Assumption in a better condition than you found it on your arrival at Detroit. This is true with regards to the works of the church, its ample supply of clean and suitable vestments, and also with regards the instruction of youth. The zeal, care and exertion of Miss Papineau will long be remembered. Her virtuous christian conduct as well as that of Miss Adhemar leave no room for criticism by decent people. On the contrary they are esteemed by them. I think that I shall go back as I came, and not leave here anyone who helped me in whatever good I accomplished at Detroit. I feel obliged to do so out of gratitude.

Since I have been at Detroit I have seen only one good crop. The last three look more like famine than plenty, and the present one augurs nothing but want. The drought has been so great that there will hardly be any corn, vegetables, potatoes or small grain. Disease among the animals is not only continuing but is increasing day by day. I dare say that there is not one farmer who has not lost horses or cattle, and some have lost everything. Times are hard, everything is dear and there is no money. The farmer is in debt, he is pressed for payment, the merchant compounds his interest. It is necessary to pay the costs of the opulence, pomp and amusements contracted during the currency of the pounds. Today people would get down on their knees before a dollar. What is one to do or undertake? With reason would I fear becoming that man "qui coepit edificare, et non potuit perficere."

Diligent instruction is still being given at my expense to seven or eight pupils, boarders and day students. I am just barely able to keep it up. I receive no support from anyone; everybody is in incredibly straitened circumstances. Jealousy, calumny, drunkenness and amusements are vices common everywhere, and, as a very respectable missionary remarked, the priests are accused of everything. I am convinced of this from the letters that my confrere and I received from Your Excellency last autumn. I would be inconsolable if I did not feel certain that God who is the witness of the truth will reward the great difficulties that I have undergone.

At present I am not having any trouble or difficulty with anyone; Captain Maisonville is away. I would have been pleasantly surprised if on Captain Maisonville's return I had received a letter as satisfying as the one I received by Mr. Belle Cour, in answer to mine of last January 28. Hardly am I consoled when I am undeservingly burdened and overwhelmed by new troubles and grief. Would that Your Excellency were a witness to my conduct in order to render it its due reward!

1. Is it possible for me or Fr. Fréchette or anyone else in my place to serve the Hurons better than Your Excellency served them during four years. I have married them, heard their confessions, buried them whenever there was a request, and through an interpreter I readily baptize their children whenever they want to bring them. On all occasions I have been charitable towards them. What more were you able to do? What more can I do now that they are less numerous and scattered here and there as they were beginning to be in your time.

2. It is not true that I sold or caused to be sold a pew intended for the chiefs. I don't even know that they have one in the church.

3. It is not true that I have reduced the space alloted to them in the church. One glance can verify that fact. The space is still there ready to receive their pews, seats or other furnishings erected at their expense, as stated in the act passed by Father Payet and which I signed with him under obedience. Father Payet must have given Your Excellency a copy of this act which now makes all the parishioners complain because this reserved space spoils the order in the church with pews on one side and none on the other. Now they say, but too late, that it would have been better not to have accepted anything from the Indians.

Re the parish hall.

1. It is not true that I took possession of their hall without asking for it. It was offered to me on my arrival, when I told them of Your Excellency's plans regarding schools that you had strongly recommended to me.

2. It is not true that the inhabitants grumbled because it was used as a classroom.

3. It is not true that the inhabitants were deprived of their hall. They have always used it and still do. My large room is also used by the men only, and, as Your Excellency can understand, good order is maintained in the rectory, the men on one side and the women and girls on the other. Everyone is pleased with the order and convenience without any expense to anyone except the pastor.

. . .

Now with regard to his Honor the Judge. On his arrival at Detroit I received his visit. I was suffering from the fever at the time. He told me that on saying goodbye to the General he asked him where he would hold court at Detroit, and that Major Mathews spoke up and said that he knew me and thought that he would be able to make some temporary arrangements while awaiting a later decision. He immediately mentioned the old church and asked to see it. I had it opened for him, and he seemed worried when he saw that it required a lot of preparations. He told me that he had a few urgent cases to try, and that they might require three or four sittings. Then I offered him very politely the parish hall for these sittings, on Thursdays when there is no school. A few inhabitants urged on by Captain Maisonville expressed their displeasure and decided to present me with a request for the key to their hall. I received them politely and said to them: "My brethren, in acting as I did towards the judge I thought that as your pastor I should show the courtesy that we all must have towards persons endowed with the power of the gracious government under which we live. If I had acted differently I would have sinned against politeness, prudence and religion. We must be very tactful and show ourselves in every way zealous, respectful and faithful to the government, because every day we are the recipients of favors with regard to our religion etc. etc. You especially who enjoy the advantage of not paying any rent or sales taxes etc." I had not finished speaking when they admitted they were in the wrong, and regretted their action, and that they realized that I had acted politely, prudently and religiously. There were ten in the group. I asked them what they wanted me to do with their written petition. They said that I could tear it up and throw it in the fire. Since that day I have not heard anything except from Your Excellency's letter that Captain Maisonville has just sent me, and to which I am replying immediately by an opportunity that is leaving tomorrow morning and which may be the last of the season. It is now midnight and I will not have time to recopy my letter which I have written hurriedly. I beg Your Excellency to excuse me.

As for the blessed bread that Your Excellency orders me to have presented to Captain Maisonville first, I have already told the sexton to do so. He never requested it of me nor did he do so in your time; no doubt he was not aware of his right or had failed to exercise it. I hope that in eating it he will sanctify himself, and that once sanctified he will pay the tithes that he owes me. . . .

F 22   DUFAUX TO HUBERT
[*Q.C.A., E.U., V-90*]

February 4, 1792

. . .
I am still maintaining the girls' school, and the progress of the pupils under Miss Papineau's care is so remarkable and flattering that I feel obliged to report again to Your Excellency, and to assure you that the results seem to be approaching the objective you had in mind. There are now 12 boarders and 5 or 6 day students who attend class from morning till night. Their lodging quarters are much too small, and I am waiting until spring to build an addition. If Miss Papineau, the parents and the children continue their good work, I shall do my best to put up a suitable residence and to provide for the necessities of life. That is what I intend to do with the grace of God and the help of Divine Providence.
. . .

F 23   WM. MONFORTON TO ALEXANDER MCKEE
[M.H.C., *XX, 312*]

Petite Côte, Jan. 28, 1793

Inclosed the return of my company which you have asked for by Mr. Thomas Smith, as officer of Militia, I regard the commission which you have given him an order from you and which I will punctually discharge as I have always done those of your predecessor. And I would surely have been present with my officers at the Assembly which was convoked for you if I had had any knowledge of it, of which I am very mortified.

Accustomed at all times to receive orders regarding the service in writing, I have never made it a point to go each Sunday to the church to learn there in a publication what concerns the Captains of the Militia.

F 24   DUFAUX TO HUBERT
[*Q.C.A., E.U., V-116*]

October 9, 1795

You will find enclosed a letter that Father Burke[6] wrote to ask me to assign a place of honor in my church to Mr. François Baby as repre-

[6]Edmund Burke (1750–1820), a native of County Kildare, Ireland, was educated for the priesthood in Paris, and came to Canada in 1786. Shortly afterwards he was named professor of philosophy and mathematics at the Seminary of Quebec. An ardent royalist, in 1794 at the request of Lieutenant-Governor Simcoe he was sent to Detroit for the purpose of quieting the unrest among the Indians. With the title of Vicar-General of Upper Canada he remained in the western country until the summer of 1796, spending some months of this time at Raisin River (now Monroe, Michigan). For three months in the autumn of 1796

sentative of His Royal Highness. Mr. Baby did not wait for my assignment, but sent Joseph Reaume (a firebrand) to ask me permission to go into the church to take measurements for a pew. I replied that the church door was not locked in the day-time and consequently he could go in, but that I was surprised that Mr. Baby was taking this step before receiving the order that I had in my possession to assign him a place of honor. I intended to give him Father Burke's order without taking anything upon myself. In brief, at his own expense he had a pew made that is higher, wider and deeper by at least four or five inches than any other pew. Moreover, there is a platform inside that raises it by one step covered by an ample green carpet. Unknown to me the said pew was erected in the place occupied by the school girls who are there observed by Miss Victoire, their teacher—i.e., between the railing and the first pew in the row of the warden's pew. He took possession of it on Sunday at the Post-Communion of the Mass to which he came with his wife and her sister, both born of Protestant parents and Protestant herself. A little later and they would have missed Mass. Your Lordship can imagine whether this royal court stamping diagonally across the church and climbing into that raised and carpeted pew with a continual click-click caused distractions among the congregation during the rest of the Mass. This incident was followed by a lot of talk. The people did not fail to ask me by what order Mr. Baby was claiming that place of honor and that distinctive pew. Moreover, the wardens and the chief people of the parish consulted amongst themselves and sought advice from the wiser men in order to act for the best. There was no lack of English and French counsellors who assured them that Mr. Baby had no precedence in church in his own right nor as deputy of the honorable Alexander McKee, the Lord Lieutenant of our county. On being reproached for tolerating such an abuse, the warden met with two other wardens and the three went and told Mr. Baby to remove his pew within a week, otherwise he would put it out of the church until he could produce an order from Your Lordship giving him the right to possess such a place of honor in the church.

It is impossible to imagine to what extent Father Burke has disturbed our parishes. For the past two weeks he has been at Ste. Anne's and Assumption trying to elaborate titles for Mr. Baby and sugar-coating pills to have them swallowed more easily by my wardens. But he did not succeed. He is causing trouble everywhere. He does not scruple about absenting himself from his parish for two or three Sundays in a row, and likewise for the feasts of All Saints, All Souls, and Ascension, etc. He follows no ecclesiastical rule or regulation, hardly ever wearing his habit. There are many other things that I don't want to mention that lead to much public slander. Nearly all the people I meet speak ill of him.

---

he was in charge of Assumption Parish. In 1801 he was appointed Vicar-General of Nova Scotia, and in 1818 he became Vicar-Apostolic of Nova Scotia.

Do not imagine, Your Lordship, that it is out of jealousy or vengeance that I speak thus about him; rather it is because these matters are public, and I think it is my duty to inform you. I hope to receive answer by the first opportunity with regard to Mr. Baby's pew, and also with regard to the answers I gave to your last letter. I told Father Burke that I thought it possible to come to a fairer conclusion, namely, since we have a pew of honor set aside by an ordinance for the captains of the militia, and since this pew contains three seats, the first could be assigned to the lieutenant colonel, the second and the third to the majors because they rank above the captains. No, he replied, all the officers must have special seats. I believe this is an abuse that should not be started at Detroit, where the churches are so poor. There is already a section reserved for the Indians that takes up one quarter of the church and that does not bring in any revenue.

F 25 COPY OF A LETTER FROM HIS EXCELLENCY JOHN GRAVES SIMCOE TO THE REVEREND EDMUND BURKE, VICAR-GENERAL OF UPPER CANADA
[*Assumption Church Archives, Account Book 1781—, p. 41*]

Niagara, 7th of June, 1796

Having been informed that great difficulties have arisen respecting the occupation of a pew due to the Government in your church, at which I am greatly surprised; and the Bishop of Quebec leaving to me to determine who is the person who should have the enjoyment of it; I therefore pronounce that the said pew and the honors pertaining thereto are one of the privileges to which the Lieutenant, or, in his absence, the Deputy Lieutenant, has an undoubted right. You will accordingly be pleased to give directions that the same conduct which was observed formerly towards the French Commandant be now kept towards the person who will in future occupy the pew in question.
a true copy
Edmund Burke V.G.

I have ordered Mr. Dufaux, missionary at Assumption, as well as the wardens and their successors to carry into execution the tenor of the aforesaid letter from His Excellency the Lieutenant-Governor, and in order to forestall future disputes I have ordered that the same practice be observed in all the churches of Upper Canada.
Edmund Burke, Vicar-General of the diocese of Quebec with a special commission for Upper Canada.

Given at Assumption July 2, 1796

F 26   DUFAUX TO HUBERT
[Q.C.A., E.U., V–124]

Detroit, September 2, 1796

I take advantage of this opportunity to inform Your Excellency that the Bishop of Baltimore has provided for the care of the parish of Ste. Anne of Detroit. He has sent Father Levadou, Sulpician, who for the last three and a half years had been laboring in the Illinois country with the powers of a vicar-general. He is a short, worthy and respectable priest fifty years old. He appears to have a great attachment and loyalty for the American government and for his bishop. And I feel the same way towards mine. I go to him for confession, and he comes to me. I hope that we shall live in close fraternal relations, even though we belong to different dioceses and observe the discipline and ceremonies proper to each. He appeared surprised that in these parts we kept lent and Saturdays also. I told him truthfully that in my parish two thirds of the people had kept the whole lent this year. There is also much difference in the observance of the feasts and the solemnities. They no longer sing *Domine salvum fac regem*. It is now replaced by *Domine salvum fac populum*. He has presently gone to get acquainted with the people at River Raisin, and on his return he will allow his parishioners to choose freely to continue paying tithes as formerly. He plans to do this by passing an enactment signed by everybody, which will give him a right to collect the tithes. Otherwise under his government there would be no way of forcing payment or of obtaining a decent income. There are no fees for dispensations; he grants them gratis whenever he judges them reasonable. In his diocese they perform marriages at any hour of the day, hear confessions of individuals in their homes, clergymen, even the bishop, dress in civies. He has not yet adopted our practices except for the fact that the day after his arrival he sang a Solemn High Mass on the feast of the Assumption (August 15), and at Vespers he sang a solemn *Te Deum* in thanksgiving for the safe arrival of General Wayne and for the possession of the posts. Then he gave benediction of the Blessed Sacrament while singing and making three signs of the cross in the manner of bishops.

Father Levadou seemed grieved that Father Fréchette did not wait until he was relieved by a successor to whom he could have left his furniture at a reasonable price, and have given necessary information about the manners and character of the people. . . . As for myself he reproved me for having ceased to exercise my ministry at the post as soon as it was ceded to the Americans. He said that neither the Bishop of Quebec nor his vicar-general could prevent me from exercising the ministry in a place where he had no jurisdiction. He also said that in favor of the common welfare I could use epi(ei)keia [equity] until revocation, and that such action would have been very acceptable to the

Bishop of Baltimore. But what was I to do? Once bitten twice shy. I indicated to you in my last letter that Father Burke had strongly advised me to act in this way. I had to comply or refuse to follow the orders of Your Lordship.

I went alone to pay my compliments to Colonel Hamtramck, but he was absent. Nevertheless he came to my house with seven officers to return my visit, saying that he was sorry he was away when I called. To be sure I received him with all the politeness of a gentleman. A few weeks later General Wayne arrived and I again went to pay my respects along with Father Levadou. He expressed to me his sincere pleasure of making my acquaintance, and invited me and my confrere to have dinner with him a few days later. We accepted the honor of his invitation. After dinner, as is the custom, the general drank to the health of various people, and then placing me on his right he asked me to offer my toast. I offered it to *unanimous peace*, and all together we drank a bumper. Then I stood up and announced that I was the general's very humble servant. The colonel also very politely invited me to dine with him. Everything went off very respectably. I don't believe I ever was shown so much politeness, and all because I did not do any harm or cause any harm to be done to them. My course of conduct is to stick to duty without stressing or forgetting the duties of my station.

The general and all the officers detest Father Burke for the alarm that he caused them among the Indians when he was in the Department of Indian Affairs. It's a good thing he has gone away, and I don't believe it will ever be advantageous for him to return to these parts.

His Majesty's loyal subjects on the American side are disqualified from holding office. There is no longer any Lord Lieutenant, Chevalier de Joncaire is Colonel of the militia, Cicot is a major and Sirs Robiche Navarre, Buffet, Voyer, Lemay, Habette and a few others are justices of the peace. The judges of the Court of Common Pleas will not be appointed until the Governor's return from Mackinac. Father Levadou plans to obtain missionaries for the Indians through Congress as a surer way of attaching them to the Government. He hopes to obtain some assistance next year to attend to his parishes. There is left only enough space to assure Your Lordship that I remain your respectful and obedient servant.

F 27   THE INHABITANTS OF L'ASSOMPTION TO HUBERT
[*Q.C.A., E.U., V–130*]

Detroit, September 19, 1796

We presume that you are going to mingle your tears with ours when trembling with emotion we announce to you the death of our dear Father Dufaux, who died on the eleventh of this month at ten o'clock in the evening. The whole parish joins you in offering to the God of all goodness sincere prayers for the repose of his soul. Our children and the poor have lost a father, and we would be inconsolable if we did not feel assured that he is now our advocate before God and that his blessed soul is enjoying eternal rest.

After all, Your Excellency, we have been your parishioners, and you are still our pastor. Our whole parish beseeches you with joined hands not to leave us languish long without the spiritual help that you are in a position to give us. We want to live and die in the religion of our fathers, and we are ready to shed the last drop of our blood for the faith of Jesus Christ. You know better than we do, Your Excellency, that too long a delay can cool the ardor of youth. If we dared, we would ask you for one who has spent many years amongst us, one whose merit and virtues are so well known to us, namely, dear Father Fréchette. This would not be the least of our many obligations to you.

We have the honor to be, Your Excellency, your very humble and obedient servants.

        Labadie Maisonville
        B. Antaya Joseph Pouget
               Parent

F 28 THE REVEREND E. BURKE TO THE PARISHIONERS OF THE CHURCH OF THE ASSUMPTION

[*Assumption Church Archives, Account Book 1781 —, p. 40a*]

[L'Assomption, Jan. 7, 1797]

We Edmund Burke, priest, vicar-general of the Diocese of Quebec, to all who may be interested in these presents, Greetings.

Having informed Father Jean B. Marchand, missionary priest at L'Assomption in the County of Essex, and Mr. Charles Reneau, chief warden of the said mission, of an extract from a letter written by His Lordship Jean François Hubert, Bishop of Quebec, addressed to the honorable James Baby, Lord Lieutenant of the County of Kent and Member of the His Majesty's Executive Council in the Province of Upper Canada, bearing the date of April 1, 1796, and quoted by His Lordship the aforementioned Bishop of Quebec in the letter addressed to us on the October 13, 1796, which states: "that the Government has a right to a seat of honor, and that the seat must be occupied by the person to whom the government awards it, which takes the matter out of his jurisdiction, and that as soon as His Majesty's representative shall present himself, neither the pastor nor the wardens will have any obligation except to leave free a suitable place for the first pew of the church, whose design must conform with the surroundings and the other pews, etc." And having also informed the said Jean B. Marchand, missionary, and Charles Reneau, chief warden, of the order from His Excellency J. G. Simcoe, Lieutenant Governor of the Province of Upper

Canada, addressed to us bearing date of June 7, 1796, of which a collated copy is to be found in the Register of the said church, which awards the said place of honor due to the Government with all the honors appertaining thereto to the Lieutenant or in his absence to the Deputy Lieutenant of this county; We the above-mentioned Edmund Burke, priest, Vicar-General of the Diocese of Quebec, in accordance with the above orders sent to us by His Excellency the Lieutenant Governor of Upper Canada, and by His Lordship the Bishop of Quebec, have ordained and by these presents do ordain that the first place in front on the epistle side along the wall to be assigned to the Lieutenant or in his absence to the Deputy Lieutenant of this County of Essex in order that he may there erect a pew of conventional design, forbidding by the authority of above-mentioned Lieutenant Governor of Upper Canada and of the above-mentioned Bishop of Quebec anyone from disturbing him in the possession of the said place of honor.

Done at L'Assomption January 7, 1797.

Edmund Burke V. G. entrusted with a special mandate for Upper Canada in matters spiritual.

I, priest, pastor and missionary certify that on January 8, 1797, at the sermon of the parochial Mass, did promulgate the said ordinance.

Marchand priest

F 29 MARCHAND[7] TO HUBERT
[Q.C.A., E.U., V-132]

L'Assomption du Detroit,
January 31, 1797

In spite of the precautions we had taken to get here promptly, we arrived only on Christmas Day in the evening. In two weeks we reached Fort Erie on November 5, but we were unable to set sail before the evening of the thirtieth. After coming in sight of the Sandusky Islands the west wind became so furious that we had to turn around on the feast of St. Francis Xavier [December 3]. After running great risk of being cast on the shore below Presqu'isle in a frightful cold, and after much tossing we finally returned to Fort Erie on the second Sunday of Advent, where we anchored about ten o'clock in the morning. Without wasting any time we made preparations for the trip by land. On the day after the feast of the Immaculate Conception [December 8] we went down to Niagara. In the morning of the feast of St. Lucy [December 13] Mr. Pratt and I, each riding on horse-back, carrying a few clothes as well as provisions for ourselves and our horses, started on our way to

[7]Jean-Baptiste Marchand (1760–1825), a Sulpician, was Superior of the College of Montreal when he was named pastor of Assumption Church in 1796. He arrived at his new charge on Christmas Day of that year, and continued to serve the parish until his death in 1825.

Detroit by the Grand River of the Mohawks. After a day's march from the River of the Mohawks we came upon the River La Tranche [Thames], which we followed down for nearly eighty leagues, sixty of which were through the woods. There were a few houses along our way, and we had to sleep outside only two nights with some slight suffering from cold and rain. The last eighteen leagues are settled just like the road from Niagara to the Grand River (from 9 to 9 arpents)[?] and in the whole distance to Niagara there are only 12 Catholics at the lower end of the Thames River, 10 out of the 12 are French-Canadians.

The day after my arrival I went to the church where I met Father Burke to whom I gave the letter of my appointment that I had obtained in your name from the Coadjutor-Bishop. He immediately installed me and I sang the High Mass. He expressed much joy at my arrival, about which he had been very anxious because of the bad news that had spread about Detroit that we were in the islands. The joy that was apparent at our arrival, the fine welcome that I received from the inhabitants who expressed gratitude for your kind remembrance to them and for acceding to their request by sending them a priest so soon—all these circumstances make me hope for much consolation in this place. I didn't experience an hour's sickness during the whole trip and I am still very well.

The only difficulty I found in the parish was with regard to a pew of honor requested by the King. On the 7th instant Father Burke notified me and the chief warden of Your Lordship's orders as well as those of Governor Simcoe on this matter. He drew up an ordinance which I read at the sermon the following Sunday, complying with the order that he gave me viva voce. He was present and he spoke on this topic in an attempt to calm the minds of the people. Nevertheless immediately after Mass the pew, that Mr. Baby had had installed relying upon Father Burke's ordinance, was thrown out of the church and the place was auctioned off and awarded the following Sunday to a man named Goyeau who erected a pew last Saturday. Mr. Baby has instituted action against those who removed the pew and the case is being followed seriously. Following your orders I did not take any part in this dispute. I simply told Mr. Baby and Goyeau: "I have nothing to do with this; you both think you're authorized to erect the pew, you're running all the risks."

I found the church and sacristy in very good order and fully furnished with clean linens and vestments. But I can't find anything relating to the fees of the pastor or of the church. In the rectory I found only a clock, a stove, a mattress, a few dishes, a few pieces of kitchen furniture, three chairs and the armchair of the late Father Potier. With regard to the library, I did not find the list of books that you left me. Father Levadou was satisfied with 60 volumes and there remain 540 volumes, some good and some bad, but good enough for a parish priest. Not more than a hundred volumes are damaged or belong to broken sets.

The parish is made up of only 150 inhabitants including the 12 at River Thames, 5 along the shore of Lake Erie and 4 on La Rivière aux Canards. As for the Hurons, there remain only four or five lodges with few occupants at La Rivière aux Canards. Fort Malden is an infant establishment where there are only two or three Catholics. Outside of Niagara and Kingston which can be more easily served from Montreal, the only mission that could be attended from this place is Sault Ste. Marie where there are only ten or twelve inhabitants. However, if Your Lordship decides to send a priest to reside with me, I shall be very happy. I am quite circumspect in my dealings with Father Levadou, because he is suspected of being very much opposed to the King's interests at this place. I don't know if there is any good reason for thinking so; in any case I'm being cautious. . . . I did not think that my letter would be so long; I beg you to excuse me and to believe me when I say that I am your very respectful and obedient servant.

F 30 EXTRACT FROM THE MINUTES OF THE EXECUTIVE COUNCIL (LANDS)
[*Cruikshank and Hunter,* The Russell Papers, *III, 256*]

COUNCIL CHAMBER, York 1st July 1799

Curate & Wardens of the Church of Notre Dame L'Assomption. Praying that the possession of the Church of Notre Dame may be confirmed in manner following Vizt.

One lot of ground of about eight square acres, which has long been appropriated for the Church & Church Yard;

One lot of three arpents in front by forty in depth for the Church and Curate with the back Concessions, or as far in depth until intercepted by other Lines;

And also that part of the Church possessions which was sold to Thomas Pajott towards defraying the expense of its building.

Referred to the Acting Surveyor General.

G. LOYALISTS AND LAND BOARDS

G 1 INDIAN DEED TO JACOB SCHIEFFELIN[1]
[*P.A.C., B 103, pp. 385–8; Detroit Notarial Records, liber c, p. 283*]

[Detroit, Oct. 13, 1783]

KNOW ALL MEN BY THESE PRESENTS that we the Principal Village Chiefs and War Chiefs of the Ottawa Nation residing near Detroit, for and in consideration of our affection and esteem which we the said Chiefs have & bear unto Lieutenant Jacob Schieffelin, Secretary of the District of Detroit, as also for the better maintenance support Livelihood and Preferment of him the said Lieutenant Jacob Schieffelin, Have given, granted, aliened, conferred and confirmed unto the said Lieutenant Jacob Schieffelin his Heirs and Assigns All that tract or parcel of Land of seven miles in front and seven miles in the DEPTH bearing the same width throughout laying and situated on the south side of the Detroit and directly opposite the Island commonly called Isle au Bois blanc near the mouth of said River, bounded in the Front by the Detroit river in the rear by unlocated Lands, on the North East side by the Point of the bank near the old Huron Town, and on the South West side by unlocated Lands along Lake Erie (the front of said Tract is partly bounded by Lake Erie) together with all and singular Lands, tenements, Meadows, Pastures, feedings, Trees, Woods, underwoods, commons, common of Pasture, ways, paths, passages, waters, water courses, casements, profits, commodities, Royalties, Privileges, Franchises, Liberties, advantages emoluments, Hereditaments and appurtenances whatsoever to the said Tract of Land and Premises hereby mentioned or intended to be granted and confirmed unto the said Lieutenant Jacob Schieffelin as aforesaid or any part or Parcel thereof, belonging or in any wise appertaining or therewithall commonly held and occupied or enjoyed or accepted, reputed taken or known as part or parcel of, or belonging to the same, and the Reversion and Reversions, Remainder & Remainders, Rents, Services, Issues and Profits of all and Singular the said Premises with their appurtenances and all the Estate, right, Title, Interest, Property, Claim, challenge and Demand whatsoever of us the said Chiefs, of in and to the said Capital, Lands, tenements and Premises and of in and to every part and parcel thereof. To have and to hold the said Capital Lands, tenements, hereditaments and all and singular other the Premises hereby granted and confirmed or mentioned or intended so to be with their and every of their appur-

---

[1]Jacob Schieffelin served in the Indian Department and as secretary to Lieutenant-Governor Henry Hamilton at Detroit. He subsequently engaged in business in Montreal and in New York.

tenances unto the said Lieut Jacob Schiefflin his Heirs and Assigns to the only proper use and Behoof of him, the said Lieut Jacob Schiefflin his Heirs and Assigns forever—and the said Chiefs for themselves, their nation, their Heirs, and successors Do convenant, grant and agree to and with the said Lieutenant Jacob Schieffelin his Heirs, and Assigns, shall and Lawfully may from time to time and at all times hereafter peaceably and quietly have, hold, use, occupy, possess and enjoy the said Capital, Lands, tenements, hereditaments and Premisses hereby granted and confirmed or mentioned or intended to be hereby granted and confirmed, with their and every of their appurtenances, free, clear and fully discharged or well and sufficiently saved, kept harmless and indemnified of, from and against all former and other gifts, grants, Bargains, Sales, Jointures, Feoffments, Dowers, Estates, entails, Rents, rent charges, Statutes Judgments, Recognaisances, executions, statutes —Merchant and of the Staple extents and of from and against all former and other Titles, Troubles, Charges and incumberances whatsoever had, done or suffered by we the said Chiefs of the Ottawa Nation our Heirs, Successors or assigns or any other Person or Persons Lawfully claiming or to claim, by, from, or under him, them or any of them. In witness whereof we the several Chiefs have hereunto affixed our hands and Seals at Detroit the thirteenth day of October one Thousand seven Hundred and Eighty Three (1783).

Sealed and delivered in presence of us—
Cicot—Temoin
Gn Lois Lafontaine   Temoin
Arch Thompson
David Gray   } temoins
T. Perlier benac

SIGNATURES	TOTEM
Kiwitchiwene	Tribe of Eagle
Neanigo	The Fork
Negig	Sturgeon
Poquash	Sturgeon
Chiminatawa	Sturgeon
Okitchinoyon	Wolf
Assoguaw	Bear

G 2   CAPTAIN ALEXANDER MCKEE TO SIR JOHN JOHNSON[2]
[*P.A.C., B 115, p. 164;* M.H.C., *XX, 190–1*]

Detroit 11th Oct. 1783

I am just informed of a circumstance which is my duty to inform you of—which is that of a Deed obtained for a considerable Tract of Land

[2]Sir John Johnson (1752–1830) was born in New York, the son of the famous Superintendent of Indian Affairs, Sir William Johnson. On the death of Sir

near the mouth of the Detroit River in a Clandestine manner from a few drunken Indians who are not the real owners, by Mr. Jacob Schiefflin, Secretary for the Indian Department here. At the same time he was acquainted that proper application was making in the name of a number of officers and Loyalists who are determined to settle in this country whereas on the contrary his intentions is to make sale of it, and expects through the friendship of Governor Hamilton, and sanction of the beforementioned Indians to have it confirmed to him, but I flatter myself this timely notice will prevent its taking place until I am able to send for further particulars—As it may be the cause of trouble between the Indian Nations.

G 3   CAPTAIN BIRD[3] TO CAPTAIN MATHEWS
[P.A.C., B 105, pp. 374–5; M.H.C., XX, 191–2]

Rivers Mouth October 15, 1783

. . .

A few days ago he (Schiefflin) privately assembled a few chiefs who really have not the power to grant the Land, gives them liquor and obtains from them a territory including the little spot the Hurons were counciling about for the Loyalists and others.

This Grant he sends down to Governor Hamilton by this vessel to get it by this means confirmed.

We discovered it by accident, somebody seeing the grant which was registered yesterday by Mr. Schiefflin (with Justice Williams) after the vessel sailed.

Capt. Caldwell was informing several of us yesterday that he had actually heard Mr. Schiefflin get such a grant in the manner before mentioned. I took Mr. Schiefflin's part. he himself came in just at the time. I asked him before them all, if he had done so, and he immediately denied it, tho' (as we are since informed) he came that minute from obtaining it.

If such a thing should be proposed for Mr. Schiefflin, I flatter myself Dear Sir you will mention the above circumstances. Capt. McKee has wrote to Sir John to beg he will mention the matter to the General. If you think proper this may be shown to Governor Hamilton.

William in 1774, the son succeeded to his title and his immense estate on the Mohawk River. During the Revolution he raised two battalions of troops in the Mohawk country for the royal service. At the end of the war he abandoned his possessions in the State of New York and went to Canada, where in 1785 he was made Superintendent-General and Inspector-General of Indian Affairs. From 1786 to 1791 he was a member of the Legislative Council of the Province of Quebec.

[3]Captain Henry Bird came to Detroit from Niagara in the autumn of 1778, and planned the construction of Fort Lernoult. During the Revolution he led expeditions to the Ohio and Kentucky frontiers. In 1796 he was living in retirement in England.

Pray pardon this scrawl, I write it on a Trunk in a hurry. My respects if you please to Major Lernoult.

p.s. Mr. Schiefflin might have been a proprietor with us had he mentioned any such inclination.

G 4   GENERAL FREDERICK HALDIMAND TO SIR JOHN JOHNSON
[*P.A.C., B 115, p. 184;* M.H.C., *XX, 199*]

Head Quarters Quebec
15th Nov. 1783

I have been favored by your letter of the 10th Instant covering an extract of a letter from Mr. McKee, the substance of which is of a very extraordinary nature; I enclose for your information a copy of a letter upon the same subject and I have made inquiry of Governor Hamilton if the application therein mentioned had been made to him. He had not received anything of the kind so that there is a possibility that Mr. Schiefflin may not have procured the grant which may also be supposed from his having denied the fact to Captain Bird; but if he really has and has had the Presumption to have it registered (which can be very easily ascertained) I must desire that you will direct Mr. McKee to strike him immediately off the List as Secy. & to assemble such Council as may be very necessary upon the occasion & express to the Indians your disapprobation of Mr. Schiefflin's conduct, in such terms as you think fit. He is the more culpable, having in the course of his duty been witness to Lt. Gov. Hamilton's displeasure on a similar occasion and his positive commands against any practice of the kind. . . .

G 5   HALDIMAND TO LIEUTENANT-GOVERNOR HAY
[*P.A.C., B 123, pp. 442-5;* M.H.C., *XI, 409-10*]

Headquarters Quebec
26th April, 1784

. . . In answer to the other subjects of your letter, I have to acquaint you that the claims of individuals, without distinction, upon Indian Lands at Detroit, or any other part of the Province are INVALID, and the mode of acquiring lands by what is called Deeds of Gift, is to be entirely discountenanced, for by the King's instructions, no private Person, Society, Corporation, or Colony, is capable of acquiring any property in lands belonging to the Indians, either by purchase of, or grant of conveyance from the said Indians, excepting only where the lands lye within the limits of any colony, the soil of which has been vested in Proprietaries, or corporations only shall be capable of acquiring such property by purchase, or Grants from the Indians. It is also necessary to observe to you that by the King's instructions, no Purchase of Lands belonging to the Indians, whether in the name or for the use of the Crown, or in the name or for the use of Proprietaries of Colonies be made, but at some general meeting at which the Principal Chiefs of each Tribe claiming a proportion in such lands are present; and all tracts so purchased must be regularly Surveyed by a Sworn Surveyor in the presence and with the assistance of a Person deputed by the Indians to attend such Survey, and the said Surveyor shall make an Accurate Map of such Tract, describing the Limits, which map shall be entered upon the Record with the deed of conveyance from the Indians.

These instructions lay totally aside the claim of Mr. Scheifflin (which you will hear at Detroit) to an Indian Grant of Land even had he obtained it by less unworthy means than He did.

Some application to, or offer from the Indians at Detroit for Lands has been made in favor of the Officers and Interpreters who have served during the war with them—Should it be renewed on your arrival there you will please to communicate the circumstances to me, describing particularly the Tract of Land, the persons applying for it &c. and such part of the Transaction as may concern the Indians must, at the same time, to be reported to Sir John Johnson thro Mr. McKee, His Deputy at Detroit. — . . .

Your Last Query, "What you are to look upon as an Established precedent "for demanding & collecting all dues, Perquisites, &c, &c.," I am at a loss to understand. Quit Rents, and all dues whatever belonging to the Crown, must be regularly demanded, collected and accounted for to the Receiver General of the Province, as well in future as for six years back, for which the Lieutenant Governor, &c., several Commanding Officers, must be accountable. In regard of Perquisites, I am ignorant of any accruing to the Crown, or to Lieutenant Governors in any part of this Province.

P.S.—Inclosed is a Warrant for the last year's allowance for House Rent, and an order for the Bell promised to the Hurons.

G 6 HAY TO HALDIMAND
[*P.A.C.*, B 123, p. 466; M.H.C., XI, 435–6]

Detroit 22nd July 1784

I take the opportunity of Commodore Grants going to Quebec, to inclose to your Excellency a list of the names of those who claim Indian Lands in the vicinity of this Place, from Grants recorded in the Recorders office, and as I understand by the knowledge of the Commanding Officers here since the year 1780, by which it will appear your Excellency's orders to me to discountenance such proceedings, is something too Late to have any effect, as almost all the Land between the Lakes

Erie and Huron on both sides the Streight is claimed and a great part settled upon and improved—If it is your Excellency's pleasure this should be stopp'd nothing but your Excellency's publick and positive orders will affect it.

As Lieut. Governor Hamilton knows the most of the claimants he can inform your Excellency many of them are very unworthy any indulgence in that way. . . .

I am informed several of the reduced Provincial Officers and many of the Soldiers wish to settle on the South side of Detroit rather than anywhere else—

Several have built upon and improved Lands who have no other Pretensions than the Indians consent possession, Captains Bird and Caldwell are of the number, at a place they have called Fredericks Burg. . . .

G 7   HALDIMAND TO HAY
[*P.A.C., B 64, pp. 158–60;* M.H.C., *XX, 246*]

Quebec 14th August 1784

Captain Caldwell late of Lieut Col. Butler's Rangers, being one of the officers to whom the Huron and other neighbouring Indian Chiefs at Detroit have given a Tract of Land, situated at the mouth of the River Detroit, about seven miles square, for the purpose of settling amongst them has, in the name of the Persons concerned renewed their application for my sanction to settle thereon, and has represented to me that the Indians are equally desirous with them for the speedy and effectual settling of the same as well from a political view, as on account of the Regard they bear them, having so long served in the field together. Altho' it is not in my power to gratify the wishes of the Persons concerned in this undertaking, and of the Indians by confirming their gift immediately without conforming to His Majesty's Instructions, communicated to you in my Letter of the 26h April last, I consider the intended Settlement as a matter that may prove of infinite utility to the Strength and Interest of this Province, and wish to give it every encouragement in my power, I therefore wait with impatience for your report upon this matter. In the mean time, in order to make speedy provision for the maintenance of these His Majesty's Loyal Subjects now dismissed from His Service, I have agreed they shall carry on their Improvements with every diligence in their Power, until the Land can be laid out & granted agreeably to the King's Instructions, and the mode in practice in the lower parts of the Province. You will please therefore to communicate the same to them, and give such orders as shall be necessary for that purpose. It will be expedient that Mr. McKee should explain to the Indians the nature and intention of the precautions the

King has taken to prevent their being iniquitously deprived of their Lands, and that they formally, in council, make over to the King, by deed, the tract in question, for the purpose they wish. Their deed must be transmitted to Sir John Johnson to be properly confirmed by the governor of the Province when regular grants will be given to the persons who are to be proprietors of the Land. The Intended Settlement being at the entrance of the River and by Capt. Caldwell's Report, a place where it may hereafter be necessary to establish a Post, I would have two thousand yards from the centre of such place on all sides reserved for that purpose.

I am concerned that the great distance and Difficultys of the Transport precludes a possibility of giving the Settlers the assistance I could wish in the article of Provisions, but what can, without purchasing, must be done for them as well in that respect, as in all others, that do not interfere with the King's Service, and that are not of any material expence to government.

I have directed Sir John Johnson (who superintends the settling of the Loyalists in the Upper part of the Province) to furnish to Capt. Caldwell a proportion of Implements for clearing Land and Building, in like manner as to the Loyalists here.

G 8 HAY TO PHILIP FRY, DEPUTY SURVEYOR
[*P.A.C., Q 304, pp. 76–8;* M.H.C., *XXV, 145–6*]

March 25, 1785

As it is necessary before the gentlemen designed by the Commander in Chief to settle on the lands near the mouth of the River, given by the Indians to the King for that purpose, can make Improvements, their Lots should be measured off; You will please to begin at the lower side of Captain Caldwell's fenced field, and measure his lot of six acres in front up the River. From thence measure what land lies between his Boundary and Captain Bird's house & make a Memorandum of the same. Then begin at the lower end of Captain Caldwell's fenced field again, & measure due south, a lot of six acres in front for Mr. McKee, where he began his Improvements; then another of six acres in front for Mr. Elliott; Then another of four acres in front for Captain Joncaire; Then two lots of four acres to be reserved for Sir John Johnson & myself—his to be first.

Then as many lots of four acres in front as there is land until you come upon Lake Erie—in the same South course. No. 2 being the first after the 2 Lots reserved as above and for Mr. Thomas McKee. No. 3. for Mr. S. Girty. No. 4. for Mr. A. St. Martin. No. 5. for Mr. D. Baby. No. 6. for Captain Lamothe. No. 7. for I. Chene. No. 8. for Captain Chabert. No. 9. for Captain Reaume. The remainder, if any, will be disposed of to other officers of the Indian Department.

G 9   CERTIFICATE OF PHILIP FRY, DEPUTY SURVEYOR
[*P.A.C., Q 304, pp. 78-9*]

[Detroit, March 25, 1785]

Know all men by these Presents that I, Philip R. Fry, Sworn Deputy Surveyor for the Upper District of the Province of Quebec, have laid out the Lands granted by the Indians to the Loyalists at the mouth of the River Detroit, by Lieut. Governor Hay's directions in the following manner vizt.

I began 3 acres below a small creek opposite the Island Bois Blanc, on the East side of the said River, and measured off six acres in front for Captain William Caldwell. Then six for Alexander McKee. Six for Captain M. Elliott. The following Lots beginning next Captain Elliotts— No. 1. four acres in front for Joncaire Chabert. No. 2. Thomas McKee. —These two vacant lots not numbered. No. 3. Simon Girty. No. 4. Anthony St. Martin. No. 5. Duperon Baby. No. 6. Captain William Lamothe. No. 7. Chevalier Chabert. No. 8. Isidore Chene. No. 9. Captain Charles Reaume. On a due South course towards Lake Erie; The Division Lines of all the said Lands run due East, till they bound upon the Indian Lands, in the rear of the said grant.

G 10   EXTRACT FROM THE MINUTES OF THE COUNCIL OF UPPER CANADA, TUESDAY THE 8TH DAY OF JANUARY 1793
[*Fraser,* Third Report of Archives of Ontario, *1905, pp. 222-3*]

Read the Petition of Captain Alexander Harrow, for land adjoining Captain Bird's farm, at the mouth of Detroit River. Read several petitions for Locations in the Indian Officers' land and the reserve, near the mouth of the Straight of Detroit.

Several Extracts from the register of the Land Board of the Western District, and other papers relative to a tract of land ceded by the Indians to their Officers in 1784, were produced to the Honorable Council by Captain Caldwell, who also gave other Information himself, relative to the said tract—the papers were accordingly read.

The Honorable Council were pleased to resolve, that a Township be laid out of the Tract in question, at the mouth of the Detroit River, to be called the Township of Malden; To commence on the Streight, at the south boundary of the Indian land, thence along, and following the Course and Bank of the River and Lake, with the Stream, untill it strikes the West Boundary of Lot No. 97, in the Two Connected Townships, County of Essex—thence North up the said Boundary of the lots 97, in the 1st and 2nd Concessions, as heretofore surveyed, (and said to be 76 acres from the Lake to the rear of the 2nd Concession) from thence East, until it intersects a line produced South, from the rear of the Indian land near River Canards, thence North, along the said line, till it strikes the Easternmost Extremity of the South Boundary of the Indian land, and thence West along the said Boundary to the place of beginning on the Streight.

Colonel McKee, Captain Elliott and Captain Caldwell to be the Patentees of the Township.

The persons who have been settled under the authority of the late Governor Hay, and who have actually made improvements are to be confirmed in such improvements, to the extent of 200 Acres each.

The Marsh, it appears, has been granted to the sons of Captain Caldwell by the Honorable Council of the Province of Quebec,

The Indian Officers have it at their option, to complete their Quota of land in the said Township.

The land laying between Captain Bird's lot, and the Indian land, being reserved for Government, Captain Harrow's Petition for that tract is rejected.

In all respects the Township of Malden, to be subject to such general regulations as are, or may be hereafter framed for the Government of Townships.

Especial Care to be taken that the reserve be made of two Sevenths. A Copy.

(signed) D. W. Smith, Acting Surveyor General

G 11 REPORT OF THE LAND COMMITTEE RE THE GRANT OF A CERTAIN MARSH AT DETROIT

[*P.A.C., Q 39, pp. 84-5; M.H.C., XI, 626*]

To His Excellency the Right Honourable Lord Dorchester, Governor General of His Majesty's Provinces in North America &c.

The Committee appointed by your Excellency to examine petitions for the Waste Lands of the Crown, now lying on the Council Table.

Humbly Report...

"The Petition of Captain Caldwell late of Lieut. Colonel Butler's Rangers praying for a grant of lands to his Sons William and James, of a certain marsh at Detroit"—

"The Committee on the information of Major Matthews humbly set forth that the marsh pray'd for, is situated at the entrance to the River of Detroit, on the North side of Lake Erie, it is about two miles in front, by six in depth, and is only fit for Grazing Cattle.—It lies between a small grant made by Indians to some officers of the Indian Department, who served in the war in that Country, and a later grant from the same, of six leagues which Captain Caldwell procured at a considerable expence to himself and which he gave up to Government for the purpose of extending the settlement occupied by disbanded Rangers and meritorious Loyalists—If it is your Excellency's pleasure to grant the land pray'd for, the Committee conceive that the improvement of the marsh would be of public benefit.—When Major Matthews laid out the Settle-

ment for Rangers & Loyalists the marsh was left out, unfit for Improvement"—
Council Chamber By order of the Committee
Bishop's Palace (signed) "HUGH FINLAY
Quebec 13th Octr 1788 in the Chair"

G 12 EXTRACTS FROM THE DIARY OF DAVID ZEISBERGER[4]
[*Translated from the original German Manuscript and edited by Eugene F. Bliss, Cincinnati, 1885*]

Wednesday, May 4, 1791. . . . Here, when we landed, we met Br. Sensemann, his wife, and Michael Jung, with some Indian brethren who saw us coming, and prayed for us. The others who had been separated from us in the storm came, some the next day, others not till three days afterward. We rejoiced together and thanked the Saviour, who had again brought us together. The Sensemanns, who had sailed from Sandusky with a good wind April 21, got into the river here the same evening at ten o'clock, and came to anchor. They found a house which belongs to Capt. Elliot, where they took shelter, and the next day they unloaded the ship and stored everything in the house, for which they got help from the inhabitants, so that in one day the ship was unloaded, and also sailed for Detroit. We examined the country and encamped with the Indian brethren for the most part on McKee's plantation, where no one lived, for it had been vacated for us, where there is much cleared land for planting. Next to this is Elliot's plantation, where also we got much cleared land and a house to live in.

Friday, May 6. The brethren were busy putting up huts on McKee's land, for which they found in abundance timber and material on the islands over against us. There lived here only a few white settlers beyond Elliot's farm, near us. He came today with Mr. McKee's son and two officers from Detroit, who remained here on the 7th, pointing out to us how far we had to go and could make use of the cleared land.

Tuesday, 17. We brought all the cattle over the river by boat, and though this was a weary work, and often by windy weather not to be done, yet everything went off well.

Sunday, 29. At the sermon, which Br. Sensemann delivered, and which we had to have in the open air on account of the much needful work, especially in planting, many blacks and also whites were present. Some Baptists, among them John Missemer, the preacher, who have held meetings on the lake seven or eight miles from here, came back from

[4]David Zeisberger (1721–1808) was born in Moravia and came to America with his parents in 1736. In 1740 he arrived at Bethlehem, Pa., the chief centre of Moravian influence in America. A large part of his missionary labours was devoted to the Delaware tribe in Ohio and Michigan, and finally at Fairfield on the River Thames. For full treatment of this story see Elma E. Gray, *Wilderness Christians: The Moravian Mission to the Delaware Indians.*

there and called on us. They were very friendly and cordial, invited us to attend their meetings, and told us in what place it would be held a week hence, and where they would have the breaking of bread in two weeks. We did not accept the invitation on account of our Indians, and could not also make plain to them our reason.

Saturday, June 17. Our meeting-house was so far done that Sunday, 19, Trinity Sunday, we could have the first sermon in it, where we first read something, the first part of the church litany, at which were present whites and blacks from the neighbourhood. . . .

Tuesday, 21. . . . The meeting-house was to-day chinked, doors and benches made, and the bell put in place.

Saturday, 25. We had again the first communion since we had it in Pettiquotting. Our number was small, for many remained away, who in the intervening time have made themselves unworthy of it, and have lost it.

Tuesday, July 12. Several Indian brethren, among them Samuel and Abraham, went to Detroit, the sisters with baskets and brooms, for now here they can again sell such things.

Tuesday, 19. Elliot, who came from the fort yesterday, asked for some of our people to help in the harvest, which was granted under the condition that they should be kept sober, for Simon Girty has caused trouble in the neighbourhood among us, by making our Indians drunk, and he has paid them in rum.

Monday, November 20. . . . With some of our Indians, who came by water from Detroit, came also Mrs. Dolson, to visit her two children, who are at school here with Br. Sensemann.

Tuesday, December 13. From the eastward settlement on the lake came some white people, Germans and English, who stayed here a couple of days and attended our meetings. They complained about their pastor, who is a German from the States, with whom they made an agreement for preaching, but since they could not pay enough, being poor, he gave the matter up, though they had built him a house and done other services for him. . . .

Monday, January 9, 1792. . . . Judge Powell came back from the farthest settlement on the lake in a sledge. He called upon us, and we had a talk with him about our moving away from here in the spring. . . . He approved the plan. . . . He advised us, therefore, to lay it before Mr. McKee in writing, who would bring it before the board.

Monday, February 6. Most of our brethren went off to the bush to make preparations for sugar-boiling.

Monday, April 2. Samuel went to Detroit, and took there with him Dolson's two children.

Thursday, April 12. We assembled early for the last time here in our chapel. . . . Then the canoes were laden, and towards noon we went away, we whites making the start, and sailed with a good wind, but after we had gone half way this changed, so that we had to land upon Fighting Island and remain over night. Nine canoes followed us here and stayed by us. Br. Michael Jung, who could not bear wind and cold, went with the brethren by land, whom we did not see again till we were at Retrenche....

G 13 THE CHIEFS OF THE OTTAWA AND CHIPPEWA NATIONS OF DETROIT CEDING LAND AT RIVER CANARD AND BOIS BLANC, MAY 15, 1786
[*P.A.C., Q 58–2, pp. 451–4; M.H.C., XXIV, 27–8*]

Know all men by these Presents, that we the principal Village & War Chiefs of the Ottawa & Chipewa Nations of Detroit, for & in consideration of the good will, friendship & affection which we have for Alexander McKee, who has served with us against the Enemy during the late War, have by & with the consent of the whole of our said nations given, granted, enfeoffed, alienated & confirmed & by these Presents do give, grant & enfeoff, alien & confirm unto His Majesty George the Third, King of Great Britain, France & Ireland &c &c &c, a certain tract or parcel of Land situated on the South Side of the Detroit River, beginning at the line granted on the seventh day of June one thousand seven hundred & eighty-four, by the Ottawas & Hurons to the Indian officers, & running an easterly course along said line, until it arrives at the end of seven English miles, from thence a northerly course, bearing always in breadth seven English miles from the said Detroit River till it strikes the most northern branch of the River Canard, thence down the said branch & River Canard to the mouth thereof, & from thence down the River Detroit, to the place of beginning. Also an Island in the mouth of the said River Detroit, commonly known by the name Bois Blanc, with all & singular the appertenances unto the said Tract of Land & Island belonging, or in any wise appertaining & the Reversion & Reversions, Remainder & Remainders, Rents & services of the said Premises & all the Estate, Right, Title, Interest, Property, Claim or Demand whatever, of us the said Chiefs, or anyone whatever of our said Nations, of, in & to the said Tract or Parcel of Land, or of, in & to every part & Parcel thereof & to hold the said Lands & premises, hereby given & granted, or mentioned or intended to be given & granted unto His said Majesty, George the Third, His Heirs & Successors for the only proper use & behoof, of His said Majesty George the Third, His Heirs & Successors forever—& we the said chiefs for ourselves, & the whole of our said nations, our & their Heirs, Executors, Administrators do covenant, promise & grant to, & with His said Majesty George the Third, his heirs & successors by these presents, that His said Majesty, his heirs & successors, shall & lawfully may, from henceforth, & forever after peacably & Quietly, have, hold, occupy, possess and enjoy the said

Tract or Parcel of Land, hereby given & granted, or mentioned, or intended to be given & granted with all and every of its appurtenances, free, clear & discharged or well & sufficiently saved, kept harmless & indemnified of, from & against all former & other gifts, grants, bargains & sales, & of, from & against all former & other Titles, Troubles, charges of incumbrances whatever, had, done or suffered, or to be had, done or suffered, by any of us Chiefs, or by anyone whatever, of the said nations, our & their Heirs, Executors or Administrators; and by these Presents do make this our Act & Deed irrevocable under any pretense whatever of the said nations, & have put His said Majesty in full possession & Seizin by allowing houses to be built on the premises; In witness whereof we the said Chiefs, for ourselves & the said nations, have unto these Presents affixed the marks of our difft Tribes at Detroit, aforesaid, the fifteenth day of May in the twenty sixth year of the Reign of our Sovereign Lord George the Third, of Great Britain, France & Ireland King, Defender of the Faith &c &c in the year of our Lord one thousand seven hundred and eighty six.
signed in the presence of

    Thomas Williams signed (with totems)
    John Clark   Shaboque Chipawas
    Daniel Field   Nayquoscan   Eagle Tribe
             Squashawa Ottawa Bear Tribe
             Niquelon
             Kingewano   " Wolf Tribe
             Tickcomegosson
             Misquecapowee
                       Pontiac
                       Assinowee

G 14 MAJOR ROBERT MATTHEWS TO HALDIMAND
[*P.A.C., B 76, p. 289;* M.H.C., *XX, 288-9*]

Detroit, 3rd August, 1787

. . .

It will concern you, Sir, to hear that your good intentions have been frustrated & Your orders not attended to by the late Govr. Hay, respecting the settlement at the mouth of the river, which was given for that purpose by the Indians to Mr. McKee and other officers who served with them and for which you gave Captain Caldwell Tools &c. It is true he did not prevent the officers from settling on the Land but he put so many others who were not intended by the Indians or officers, that the Rangers were excluded & of all the men that were brought by Caldwell for that purpose, there is not a man yet settled, the ground, indeed, is too little to contain many and Caldwell foreseeing that, obtained a grant adjoining to it six Leagues upon the Lake, this he gave me upon behalf of government & I went down lately to survey & lay it out—but was driven home by bad weather & want of Provisions before I had got half thro' with it—. As soon as I dismiss this vessel I shall return & finish it. I have got together about 60 fine fellows whom I shall place on it before I go down—In the event of giving up this Post, very advantageous ones may be taken at the mouth of the River, & on an opposite Island, between which ships must pass in a channel about 400 yards. A mile above is a fine situation for a town with as much Timber as can be wanted, and an excellent stone quarry upon the spot; here also may be a battery to command the upper part of the channel where any craft so small as to pass round the Isle au bois blanc above mentioned must fall into to get up. . . .

G 15 LIST OF DISBANDED TROOPS AND LOYALISTS TO BE SETTLED ON THE NORTH SIDE OF LAKE ERIE, FROM A CREEK 4 MILES FROM THE MOUTH OF THE RIVER DETROIT, TO A SMALL CREEK ABOUT A MILE AND HALF BEYOND CEDAR RIVER
[*P.A.C., R.G. I, L 4, vol. II, pp. 188–92; Fraser,* Third Report of the Archives of Ontario, *1905, pp. 88–91*]

No.	Names	Remarks	Lot No.
1	John Sheifflin	Lieutenant Detroit Volunteers	43
2	Edwd. Haizil	"	74
3	Ante. de Quindre	Lieutenant Indian Department	45
4	Fras. de Quindre	" "	71
5	Fonte. de Quindre	" "	35
6	Dage. de Quindre	" "	11
7	Simon Girty	" "	52
8	Joseph Bonde	" "	55
9	Nichs. Guin	Lieutenant Minute Man	65
10	I. B. Chicott	" "	76
11	Thos. Reynolds	Commissary Provisions	88
12	Col. Andrews	Son of Capn, Andrews, lost in the Ontario	85
13	Walter Roe	Wr. Officer Marine department	25
14	Harry Fecer	Engaged Smith "	80
15	James Tracey	Private 4th Regt. 10 Years, 3 years man	64
16	Thomas Hall	" Kings Regiment "	40
17	William Dugan	" " "	5
18	John Pardo	" " "	47
19	Thomas Ashworth	" " "	84
20	Walter Dalton	Sergeant 47, Drafted to the Kings	42
21	Nichs. Lichemburg	Private 60 Regiment	75
22	—— McCarthy	" 84 "	72
23	Duncan Cameron	" "	94
24	Danl. McPherson	" "	86
25	—— Vancamp	" R1 Reg. New York	44
26	Vancamp Junr	" "	20
27	Alex. Fraser	Guards 10 years, and Sergt. Nova Scotia Volunteers	87
28	Samuel Hall	Private Queens Rangers	19
29	Alex. Clarke	Sergeant McAlpins Corps	2
30	Randal McGilles	" Lt. Col. Butlers Rangers	90

G 15 (cont'd.)

No.	Names	Remarks	Lot No.
31	Peter McDonell	" "	73
32	Daniel Fields	Corporal "	89
33	Edwd. Nevill	" "	51
34	Andrew Hamilton	" "	67
35	John Elliot	Private "	81
36	Eley Wilcox	" "	83
37	Pat Hill	" "	57
38	Pat Johnson	" "	22
39	John Arnold	" "	27
40	John Moss	" "	21
41	John Cameron	" "	50
42	Samuel Newkirk	" "	58
43	John Top	" "	17
44	Helmes Yoger	" "	16
45	Nathl. Lewis	" "	59
46	James Empson	" "	60
47	John Clearwater	" "	61
48	Thomas Parsons	" "	62
49	William Munger	" "	56
50	John Dalton	Private Lt. Col. Butlers Rangers	37
51	John Wright	" "	15
52	Samuel Finlay	" "	14
53	Jos. Springfield	" "	91
54	Jacob Ruhart	" "	93
55	William Yarnes	" "	13
56	Jacob Quant	" "	92
57	Joseph Fry	" "	36
58	John Young	" "	46
59	John Williamson	" "	23
60	Jacob Segar	" "	77
61	Thomas Harper	" "	28
62	Thomas Dyker	" "	96
63	Leonard Scratch	" "	12
64	John Wormwood	" "	82
65	Luke Casety	" "	31
66	John Goodnight	" "	24
67	Benjamin Knapp	" "	66
68	Micl. Harnes	" "	32
69	John Carnwall	" "	97
70	Christ. Winter	" "	79
71	Henry Ramsey	" "	33
72	James Wood	" "	3
73	Francis Robert	Serg.-Major Detroit Volunteers	4
74	Jos. Brone	" "	95
75	I. B. Souvraint	" "	10
76	I. B. Begras	Corporal "	18
77	Joseph Robert	Private Detroit Volunteers	54
78	Francis Vallade	" "	34
79	I. B. St. Eudre	" "	41
80	William Scott	" "	78
81	Jonathan Deane	" "	53
82	Nathl. Miller	" "	29
83	Jon. Countryman	" "	26
84	John Smith	Soldier at the taking of Quebec, & in the 84th	49
85	Charles Philipley	Soldier 44 10 years, & Volunteer all the war	48

G 15 (cont'd.)

No.	Names	Remarks	Lot No.
86	Christian Bunsack	Soldier 29th, 8 years, a 3 years Man	9
87	James Girty	Partizan all the war	8
88	George Girty	" "	7
89	Danl. McKillip	Serg. Butlers Rangers	63
90	Jas. Windall	Private 8 Regr. 3 Years Man	6
91	Thomas Smith	Loyalist, came into Niagara in 76 with a plan of fort Stanwix & Intelligence	30
92	Robert Surphlet	Loyalist came in with Mr. McKee	
93	Frederick Arnold	Loyalist Came in Since the War	
94	Amos Weston	Blacksmith, many years with Stedman	
95	John Waters	Loyalist, in many Years	
96	James Robertson	Private in Butlers Rangers	
97	John Little	Loyalist	
98	Adam Dorkney	Loyalist in many Years, much persecuted	
99	Thomas Gaubb	Loyalist in many Years with Stedman	
100	Gregg	Loyalist, Express in the War	
101	Daniel Garret	" " "	
102	Frederick Fisher	Loyalist, Prisoner by the Indians, much attached	
103	Thomas Alexander Clarke	2 years from England, a Millwright	
104	John Gordon	Loyalist	
105	John McLean	"	
106	Jacob Snyder	"	
No.	Names	Remarks	
107	Harbour	Loyalist	
108	Fox	Loyalist in Since the war	
109	Holmes	" "	
110	Reynolds	" "	
111	McDunach	" "	
112	Chalmers	" "	
113	Robert Dowlar	" "	
114	Henry Wright	" "	
115	James Little	"	
116	Jacob Lans	German troops taken with Lord Cornwallis	
117	Robert Dennison	Volunteer to Post Vincenne	
118	Richard Whittle	" "	
119	John Lebour	Private in Butlers Rangers	
120	Charles Dice	Loyalist	
121	James Steward	Loyalist Sent on many Scouts	
122	James Rogers	Long Prisoner with Indians, attached to us	
123	John Prinnie	Private Butlers Rangers	
124	Thomas Williams	Blacksmith Indian Department	
125	William Cook	Warrant Officer, Royal Artillery	
126	Thomas Kelly	Three years, provincial Navy	
127	West	Sergeant 52nd Regiment	
128	James Understone	Master Provincial Navy	

N. B.—Nos. 68, 69, 70, including a beautiful Plain are reserved for Towns.
Nos. 38 and 39 are given to Mr. McGregor, Major of Militia, as a mark of attention for his long services at this Post.
The Lots now given are 4 acres in front, and 38 back, and are intended for the purpose of immediate settlement. The back Lots will be hereafter laid out, and distributed to those who occupy the front, in the proportions directed by Government for their families.
Detroit, 1st October, 1787

(signed) R. Mathews, Major Commanding
A true Copy. Quebec, 18 June, 1790.   John Collins, D.S.G.

G 16 LIST OF DISBANDED TROOPS AND LOYALISTS SETTLED AT THE MOUTH OF THE RIVER DETROIT, IN THE NEW SETTLEMENT, DETROIT 15TH DECEMBER
[*P.A.C., R.G. I, L 4, vol. II, p. 208*]

SECOND CONCESSION

No.	Names	Remarks	Lot No.
			1
1	John Reynolds	Loyalist	2
2	Michael Scheffre	Soldier in the German corps	3
3	George Reynolds	Loyalist	4
4	George Myers	Soldier in the German corps	5
5	George Dickins	Native of Pennsylvania	6
6	Henry Wright	Native of old England	7
7	Frederick Harboth	Served in German Corps	8
8	Valantine Oyler	Loyalist	9
9	Morrice Willcox	"	10
10	Julious Rapely	"	11
11	Frederick Rapely	"	12
12	John Timberman	"	13
13	Joseph Speckman	"	14
14	John Messamore	"	15
15	John Shipley		16
16	George Dyce	a German	17
17	Henry Sherman	Served in German Corps	18
18	Nathan Miller	Native of Scotland	19
19	Nicholas Clengenborner	a German	20
20	George Schelsteel	a German	21
21	Jacob Dix	Loyalist	22
22	John McLean	Native of Ireland	23
23	Thomas Fares	Loyalist	24
24	Joseph Fares	"	25
25	Edward Butler	Ireland	26 27 28
		a great marsh	29
26	Wyndel Wyley	German	30
27	James Denachooe	Ireland	31
28	David Hartley	Loyalist	32
29	Peter Mellott	"	33
30	William Lockhart	Scotland	34
31	John Cray	Ireland	35
32	Thomas Kelly	" served on the Lakes	36
33	John Ritchie	Scotland	37
34	Ebenezar Loveless	Served on Burgoyne's expedition	38
35	Joseph Bents	Served in German Corps	39
36	James Baker	Butler's Rangers (a black man)	40
37	Alexander Grant	Loyalist	
			41
			42
38			43
			44
			45
39	Frederick Fisher	Loyalist	46
40	John Pastmis	Loyalist	47
41	George Pastmis	"	48
42	Charles Taylor	Canadian	49
43	William Yearns	Private in Butler's Rangers	50
44	Adam Stoutmyre	Served as Boatswain on Lake Erie	51
45	James Understone	Served as Naster on Lake Erie	52
46	Andrew Ulse	Loyalist	

[Signed] F. Close
Major Commanding

G 17 INDIAN DEED OF PRESENT SOUTHWESTERN ONTARIO TO KING GEORGE III, MAY 19, 1790
[*Detroit Notarial Records, liber C, pp. 374–7;* Indian Treaties and Surrenders *(Ottawa, 1905), I, 1–5*]

KNOW ALL MEN BY THESE PRESENTS that we the principal Village and War Chiefs of the Ottawa, Chippewa, Pottowatomy and Huron Indian Nations of Detroit for and in consideration of the sum of Twelve hundred Pounds Currency of the Province of Quebec at Five shillings per Spanish Dollar for valuable Wares and Merchandise to us delivered by the hands of Alexander McKee, Esquire, Deputy Agent of Indian Affairs, the receipt whereof we do hereby acknowledge, have by and with the consent of the whole of our said Nations, given, granted, enfeoffed, alienated and confirmed, and by these presents do give, grant, enfeoff, alien and confirm unto his Majesty George the Third, King of Great Britain, France and Ireland, Defender of the Faith &c. &c. &c. a certain Tract of Land beginning at the mouth of Catfish Creek, commonly called Rivière au Chaudière on the North side of Lake Erie, being the Western extremity of a Tract purchased by his said Majesty from the Messesagey Indians in the year One Thousand seven hundred and eighty Four and from thence running westward along the border of Lake Erie and up the Streight to the mouth of a River known by the name of Channail Ecarté and up the main branch of the said Channel Ecarté to the first fork on the South side, then a due east line until it intersects the Rivière à la Tranche, and up the said Rivière à la Tranche to the North West corner of the said cession granted to his Majesty in the year one Thousand Seven Hundred and Eighty Four, then following the western boundary of said tract being a due South direction until it strikes the mouth of Catfish Creek or otherwise Rivière au Chaudière being the first offset;

RESERVING a Tract beginning at the Indian Officers Land at a small run near the head of the Island of Bois Blanc and running upwards along the border of the Streight to the beginning of the French Settlement above the Head of the Petite Isle au D'Inde; then a due East line seven miles, and then South so many miles as will intersect another East line run from the mouth of said Run or Gully near the head of said Island of Bois Blanc:

AND another Tract beginning at the mouth of Rivière au Jarvais commonly called Knagg's Creek, running up along the border of the Streight to the Huron Church and one hundred and twenty arpents in depth with all and singular the appurtanences unto the said Tract of Land belonging or in any wise appertaining, and the reversion and reversions, remainder and remainders, rents and services of the said premises and all the Estate, right, title, interest, property, claim or demand whatsoever of us the said Chiefs or any other person or persons whatsoever of our said Nations of, in, and to the said Tract of Land, or of, in, and to every part and parcel thereof excepting the Reserve aforesaid.

TO HAVE AND TO HOLD the said Lands and premises hereby given and granted, mentioned or intended to be given and granted unto his said Majesty George the Third, His Heirs and Successors for the only proper use and behoof of His said Majesty George the Third, His Heirs and Successors for EVER.

And we the said Chiefs for ourselves and the whole of our said Nations our and their Heirs, Executors and administrators do covenant, promise and grant to and with His said Majesty George the Third, His Heirs and Successors by these presents that His said Majesty, His Heirs and Successors shall and lawfully may from henceforth and for ever after peaceably and quietly, have, hold, occupy, possess and enjoy the said Tract of Land hereby given and granted, mentioned or intended to be given and granted with all and every of the appurtenances free, clear, and discharged or well and sufficiently saved, kept harmless and indemnified of, from and against all former and other gifts, grants, bargains and sales, and of, from and against all former and other titles, troubles, charges or incumbrances whatever, had, done or suffered or to be had, done or suffered by any of us the said Chiefs, or by any one whatever of the said Nations ours and their Heirs, Executors or administrators; and by these presents do make this our act and Deed irrevocable under any pretence whatever, and have put His said Majesty in full possession and seizin by allowing houses to be built upon the premises.

IN WITNESS whereof, we the said Chiefs, for ourselves and the said Nations have unto these presents made the marks of our different Tribes and affixed our seals at Detroit, District of Hesse in the Province of Quebec, this Nineteenth day of May, in the Thirtieth Year of the Reign of our Sovereign Lord George the Third, King of Great Britain, France and Ireland, Defender of the Faith &c. and in the year of Our Lord one thousand seven hundred and ninety 1790.

Signed, sealed and delivered in the present of us in full Council: (Signed)

Patrick Murray, Major
  Commanding Detroit
Richard Porter,
  Capt. 60th Regt.
Charles Ingram,
  Capt. 60th Regt.
John Buller,
  Capt. 60th Regt.
J. Hesselbergh,
  Lieut. 60th Regt.
John Robertson,
  Lieut. 60th Regt.
David Meredith,
  Lt. R. R. Artillery
E. Cartwright,
  Lieut. 60 Regt.

Jo. Jordan,
  Lt. 60 Regt.
Samuel Gibbs,
  Ens. 60 Regt
G. Westphal.
  Adjt. 60th Regt
Jas. Henderson,
  Surgeon
A. Grant,
Alex Harrow,
  Lt. Condr. N.D.P.
P. Frichette, Ptre. Miss
Adhemar St. Martin,
Gregor McGregor,
  Major Detroit Militia
John Martin,
  Ens. Militia
William Robertson,
T. Smith
  Lieut. Militia

Thomas Reynolds,
  asst. Comss. and Storekeeper
Henry Hay, Ensign
Wm. Harffy,
Ottawa Nation (signed)
Egouch—i-ouay
Wawish kuy
Nia ne go
Ki wish e ouan
Atta wa kie
Onagan
Endashin
Maug gich a way

Chippewa Nation (signed)
Wasson
Ti e cami go se
Essebalc
Ouit a nis a

Nangie	Penash	Son din ou
Chabou quai	Shebense	Dou yen tet
Wabandisgais	Key way te nan	Ted y a ta
Mesh qui ga boui	Huron Nation (signed)	Tren you maing
Pottowatomy Nation (signed)	Sastaritsie	She hou wa te mon
Skanesque	Ta hou ne ha wie tie	Meng da hai
E. sha ha	Skahoumat	Tsough ka rats y wa
Mettego chin	Mondoro	Rou nia hy ra
	Te hatow rence	

Recorded by me this 22d day of June 1790, at L'Assomption in the District of Hesse. Register No. C, pp. 374–377

    T. Smith, C.C.P.
    District of Hesse

G 18   INDIAN SPEECH TO SIR JOHN JOHNSON AT THE HURON VILLAGE
[*P.A.C., C 249, pp. 353–4;* M.H.C., *XX, 308–9*]

                                                                                      August 16, 1790

Duyenty a Huron Chief.
Father,

    We now inform you of a matter of importance to us—When our forefathers were living they were always at war and fighting with different Nations of Indians and were drove from place to place untill at last they came to the River Kannard and other places about it, where then Sastareche fixed his seat, and said this Ground I appoint for the present Generation and the Posterity that is to come after them. I have made it known to all Nations around me that this Ground I intend to stand upon—and here we must perish before any other power dispossess us of it.

    Speech of Egouch-a-way, a principal Ottawa Chief:
Father,

    You desired us to inform you of the Bounds of the Lands reserved for the Huron Confederacy, at the sale we made in May last to the King, which Bounds begin at the first creek or run nearly opposite to the Upper end of the Island of Bois Blanc to run thence up the Straight or River of Detroit to a painted post at the Lower end of the French settlement which was fixed by us and Major Murray who then was Commanding Officer at Detroit to run from the painted post an East Course about seven miles into the woods, then a South course until it intersects a Line running an Easterly course from the beginning at the before mentioned run, in order to take in our Sugar Camps, this Father is the true Bounds agreed upon and fixed by the whole Confederacy.

G 19   MINUTES OF A MEETING OF THE LAND BOARD FOR THE DISTRICT OF HESSE, HOLDEN AT THE COUNCIL CHAMBER OF DETROIT, FRYDAY,
                                          4 MAY, 1792
[*Fraser*, Third Report of the Archives of Ontario, *1905, pp. 181–2*]

    The Board think it pertinent to remark in this place (to prevent any surprize which may originate from seeing persons in these 2 Connected townships apparently occupying 3 and 400 acres) that the Lots are irregularly laid out, the largest of them containing no more than about 152 Acres, and many of them no more than 114—which will induce the Board in a few instances to grant a second lot, or half a Lot more to a petitioner, in order to make him up about 200 Acres actually—in the rear, or second Concession of this township, from the number of swamps, no one will ever accept a location unless they can have 2 or 3 Lots making from 9 to 12 Acres in front; and in this tract even little good ground will be found—this second Concession has been once deserted already.

G 20   SCHEDULES OF LOTS IN TWO CONNECTED TOWNSHIPS
[Third Report of the Archives of Ontario, *1905, pp. 76–8*]

District of Hesse. The Lots contain about 200 acres each.
First Concession

Lots	Names of Grantees	Date of Location
1		
2	Alexander Clarke	Sept. 10, 1790
3	William Wright	May 4, 1792
4	Robert Dennison	Sept. 30, 1791
5	John Hocust	May 4, 1792
6	Joseph Windale	Sept. 10, 1790
7		
8		
9	Christian Bonsack	Sept. 10, 1790
10	Michael Shaver	May 4, 1792
11		
12	Leonard Scratch	Sept. 10, 1790
13	Martin Tofflemire	Sept. 10, 1790
14	James Steward	Sept. 10, 1790
15		
16	Adam Darkness	May 4, 1792
17	John Top	Sept 10, 1790
18		
19	Samuel Hall	May 27, 1791
20	Asa Holmes	Sept. 10, 1791
21	John Moss	Sept. 10, 1791
22		
23	Wm. Harpur	April 22, 1791
24	James Empson	Nov. 25, 1791
25		
26	Joseph Countryman	Sept. 10, 1790
27	Jacob Arner	Sept. 10, 1790
28	Joseph Vallade	July 29, 1791
29	Richard Whittle	Sept. 10, 1790
30	Thomas Smith	Oct. 22, 1790
31		
32	Edward Butler	June 3, 1791
33	Henry Ramsay	Sept. 11, 1790
34	Jean Baptiste Vallade	May 27, 1791
35		
36	James Little	Oct. 29, 1790
37	John Dalton	Sept. 11, 1790
38, 39	Gregor McGregor, Esq.	April 22, 1791

LOYALISTS AND LAND BOARDS

G 20 (cont'd.)

Lots	Name of Grantees	Date of Location
40	Thomas Hall	Sept. 11, 1790
41	Samuel Weston	April 15, 1791
42	Thomas Jones	May 13, 1791
43		
44	Louis Viseneau	Oct. 22, 1790
45	Richard Cornwall	Oct. 22, 1790
46	John Little, Jun.	May 11, 1792
47	John Pardo	Sept. 11, 1790
48	Charles Filpley	Sept. 11, 1790
49	John Smith	Sept. 24, 1790
50	John Cray	April 22, 1791
51	Edward Nevel	Sept. 9, 1791
52		
53	John Daine	Sept. 24, 1790
54		
55	Joseph Bondé	May 4, 1792
56	William Monger	Mch. 23, 1792
57		
58	Thomas Little	May 4, 1792
59		
60	John McClaine	April 22, 1791
61	John Clearwater	22 July 1791
62	John Joseph Waters	4 May, 1792
63	Daniel McKillip	3 June, 1791
64	James Tracey	Sept. 11, 1790
65	James Wilcox	4 May, 1792
66	Benjamin Knapp	Sept. 11, 90
67	Andrew Hamilton	do
68 } 69 } 70 }	Reserved for a town	
71	François Dequindre	22 July, 1791
72	Edward McCarty	24 June, 91
73	John Snider	Sept. 11, 90
74	John Stockwell	do
75		
76	John Baptiste Cicot	4 May, 1792
77	Henry Wright	4 May, 1792
78	William Scot	do
79	Amos Weston	Sept. 11, 90
80	Harry Facer	do
81	James Robertson	do
82	Elisher Wilcox, Senr.	22 April, 91
83	Elisha Wilcox, Sen. (say Jun.?)	Sept. 11, 90
84	Thomas Ashworth	do
85		
86	Rudolph Hoffman	4 May, 1792
87	George Jacob Rudhart	Sept. 11, 90
88	Thomas Reynolds	22 April, 91
89	Prince Robertson	Sept. 10, 90
90	Joseph Drouillard	24 June, 91
91	Andrew Woolche	4 May, 1792
92	Daniel Cameron	do
93	Cameron, John	22d April, 91
94	{ ½ to Daniel Cameron { ½ to John Cameron	4 May, 92 do
95	Joseph Baro	April 15, 91
96	John Gordan	22d Octb. 90
97		

G 21   MINUTES OF A MEETING OF THE LAND BOARD FOR THE DISTRICT
OF HESSE, OCTOBER 22, 1790
[Third Report of the Archives of Ontario, *1905, pp. 59–60*]

Present: Major Smith, W. D. Powell, Esquire, A. Grant, Esquire.

The board received 10 petitions for so many lots of the 12 unlocated ones easternmost in the New Settlement, at the mouth of the Strait of Detroit, and having examined the schedules for Location before the board, find no other interfering petitions for the specified lots, prayed for, the board therefore, willing to establish such settlers, having examined into their loyalty, characters and pretensions, and seeing no special cause why they should not be located, proceeded to administer the directed oaths and declaration, and they having taken, declared and subscribed the same, the board delivered to them, severally and separately, single lots of about 200 acres each, as follows—

Marten, for Henry Tofflemire, Lot No. 1, easternmost; Henry Racus, Lot No. 3, easternmost; Nicholas Weatherhold, Lot No. 4, easternmost; George Lichelstil, Lot No. 6, easternmost; Aug Fred Weizbach, Lot No. 7, easternmost; Philip Fox, Lot No. 8, easternmost; Jonas Fox, Lot No. 9, easternmost; Henry Hoffman, Lot No. 10, easternmost; George Dice, Lot No. 11. easternmost; John Lipps, Lot No. 12, easternmost.

In the case of Henry Tofflemire, the Board took into consideration the remarkable circumstances of his Father, the petitioner's sufferings as known to a part of the Board, His being a Prisoner of war to a British officer who had not authority over the Indians to rescue his children, captured at the same time, from Slavery; His wonderful exertions to support so large a family, and to pay so heavy a ransom for one of his children to the Indians, induce the Board to meet the Father's Petition and readily grant a certificate for a single Lot to his eldest son, who, being presented to the Board, although not of full age, appears fully equal to such an Improvement of the Lot granted as becomes a useful settler.

N.B. Lot No. 2 was granted by the Land Board to John Wirt on June 3, 1791.

Lot No. 5 was reserved for public uses.

G 22   MINUTES OF A MEETING OF THE LAND BOARD OF THE COUNTIES
OF ESSEX AND KENT, AT THE COMMANDANT'S QUARTERS, DETROIT,
20TH DECEMBER, 1793
[Third Report of the Archives of Ontario, *1905, p. 246*]

The Board having received information relative to the application made by Andrew Ulcoch, on Friday the 29th day of November, for leave to erect a grist mill on Mill Creek, in the New Settlement Lake Erie, and also a petition signed by most of the respectable Inhabitants, representing the distress they are in, and praying that a Mill Seat may be granted to Andrew Ulcoch who is a Miller—

The Board having taken the same into Consideration, grant him Lot No. 1, which appears to be unoccupied, with a small Tract of vacant Land supposed to be about twenty-five yards in breadth on the East Side of the Creek, for the purpose of building a Mill on, for the benefit of the Settlement.

G 23 MINUTES OF THE LAND BOARD MEETING ON FEBRUARY 8, 1793, RE THE CLAIMS OF THE INHABITANTS OF L'ASSOMPTION SETTLEMENT FOR A SECOND CONCESSION
[Third Report of the Archives of Ontario, *1905, p. 224*]

Agreeable to the Advertisement of the 18th of January, the Board proceeded to receive the Claims of the Inhabitants of the L'Assomption Settlement for a second Concession in their rear in order the better to supply them with wood for the convenience of fencing, as well as for their family purposes, and agreed to grant a second Concession to each of the Inhabitants possessing the front lots.

NAME	LOTS	NO. OF ACRES IN FRONT	NAME	LOTS	NO. OF ACRES IN FRONT
Francis Pratt	No. 64	2	Jacque Parent	No. 107	2
Jacques Marontet	" 65	3	Laurant Parent	" 108	2
Domk. Marontet	" 66	2 & 43 ft	Baptiste Beaubien	" 109	3
Jacques Parent	" 67	3	Jacques Charon	" 110	3
Laurant Parent	" 68	3	André Peltier	" 111	3
Claude Reaume	" 69	2	Josh. Basiné	" 112	1
Bapte. LeDuc	" 70	3	Pierre Letourné	" 113	4½
Bapte. Ouillet	" 71	3	Louis Peltier	" 114	3
Bapte. Mayea	" 72	3	Louis St. Louis	" 115	4
Josh. Muillar	" 73	2	Bpte. Chapoton	" 116	3½
Terese Janis	" 74	3	Antoine LaBadie	" 117	3
....	" 75		Charles La Marshe	" 118	2
Andrew Benetto	" 76	2	D. Le Piconiere	" 119	2
Madame Baby	" 77	2*	——— Demouchelle	" 120	2
J. B. Tournée	" 78	2	Pierre St. Louis	" 121	2
Madame Baby	" 79	3	Julien Le Bute	" 122	3
Madame Baby	" 80	3	Bapte. L'Anglois	" 123	3
Vital Demouchelle	" 81	½	Jacques Belparche	" 124	3
Vital Demouchelle	" 82	½	——— Desaunier	" 125	3
Louis Goyon	" 83	2	Benjn. Marsac	" 126	3
Josh. L'Esperance	" 84	2	Jacques Louisant	" 127	3
Julian Parent	" 85	2	John Askin, Esqr.	" 128	3
....	" 86	2	Madame Marsac	" 129	6
Pierre Le Bute	" 87	4	Bapte. Molosh	" 130	3
P. P. De La Salline	" 88	2	——— Basiné	" 131	3
Francois Marontet	" 89	3	Antoine Labadie	" 132	3
Charles DeLisle	" 90	2	Andre Landroche	" 133	3
Antoine Langlois	" 91	4	Bapte. Soulier	" 134	3
Joncaire Chaubert	" 92	3½	Bapte. Paré	" 135	3
Josh. Beaubien	" 93	3	Josh. Morant	" 136	3
Alex. Maisonville	" 94	5½	Alexis Peltier	" 137	3
....	" 95	4	Louis Campeau	" 138	3
....	" 96	4	Antoine Robert	" 139	3
Bonavant. Reaume	" 97	4	Simon Molosh	" 140	3

*The second concession to this lot is granted to Bapte. Bruger.

G 23 (cont'd.)

NAME	LOTS	NO. OF ACRES IN FRONT	NAME	LOTS	NO. OF ACRES IN FRONT
Antoine Labadie	" 98	3	....	" 141	3
Baptiste Pilette	" 99	2	——— Leficore	" 142	3
Josh. Berthiaume	" 100	3	P. T. Reaume	" 143	—
R. T. Reaume	" 101	3	P. T. Reaume	" 144	1½
Francois Malosh	" 102	3	Madam Molosh	" 145	1½
Baptiste La Badie	" 103	4	Bapte. Paré	" 146	3
Julien Parent	" 104	3	Michael Wool	" 147	3
Jacques Molosh	" 105	2	Penish Campeau	" 148	3
Francois Molosh	" 106	2	Capt. Maisonville	" 149	6

G 24 MINUTES OF A MEETING OF THE LAND BOARD FOR THE DISTRICT OF HESSE, HOLDEN AT THE COUNCIL CHAMBER OF DETROIT, FRYDAY, 10 MAY, 1792, RE THE PETITION OF THE INHABITANTS OF PETITE CÔTE FOR THEIR CONTINUATIONS

[Third Report of the Archives of Ontario, *1905, pp. 183–4*]

The petition of the inhabitants of the Petite Cote was read praying for their contimuations; The Board does not think the petition unreasonable, so far as relate to their 2 Concessions, as most of the lots there are about three acres in front, which in the first and second concession together will give little more than 200 Acres to each Lot, and they presume that the inhabitants will be ready to assist the Deputy Surveyor in laying out the second Concession. The Captain of Militia and chief Inhabitants are to be consulted as to the most proper places for roads from the 2d Concession which must be determined on before Grants can be made for that Concession.

The petition of others settled on River Canards, was also read, the Survey was referred to, by which it appears that the people who are settled on River Canards, come within the first Concession of the Settlements of the Strait.

The Board direct enquiry to be made whether the settlers on the Strait near River Canards, or those on that River, were established first, and whether the people who have set down on River Canards have done it, since the Board's prohibition to settle on the Waste Lands of the Crown —without their authority.

G 25 D. W. SMITH, SECRETARY OF THE LAND BOARD, TO P. MCNIFF,[5] DEPUTY SURVEYOR

[Third Report of the Archives of Ontario, *1905, p. 184*]

Detroit, 11 May, 1792

You are to proceed to the North Boundary of the Reserve at River

[5]Patrick McNiff was a deputy surveyor in Canada for about ten years. He was reputed to be an agitator. When the Americans occupied Detroit in 1796 he

Canards on the bank of the Water's Edge and there commence your survey—marking off a road space on the King's waste land from the Reserve upwards on the Strait—proceeding from thence Eastward along the said boundary forty acres, at the end of which you will mark a road between the 1st and 2nd concessions of the Petite Cote (having regard at the same time to the road space along the said boundary), you will proceed thence on your line 40 Acres more, and there mark another road between the second and third concessions, Thence back on your line 40 Acres, to the road space between the first and second Concessions, thence along said road in a due north direction laying out the 2d Concession as you go along in Lots of 3 Acres fronting on said road, whose side lines are to be at right angles with the Road—till you come to the boundary of the Reserve at River au Jarvais; marking at the end of and between every 15 lots, a road space to lead from the front of the 2d to the third Concession—all such roads being of the width directed by the General Rules and Regulations and order of the Board.

G 26 McNiff to D. W. Smith
[Third Report of the Archives of Ontario, 1905, pp. 187–8]

Detroit, 31 May, 1792

Pursuant to an order of the Land Board of the District of Hesse, dated the 11 May, instant, I did on the 26 Instant, commence to run and mark the line between the Reserve at River Canards and the Land at Petite Cote, which I effected for one Concession; I also endeavoured to continue that line the depth of the 2nd Concession, but was obstructed by the marshes, that are between the Branches of River Cannards, which marshes I could not pass either with, or without a Canoe—there not being water sufficient for a Canoe, and the mudd too soft to pass on foot. I endeavoured by different offsets to get clear of the Marsh but in vain being still headed by it—which obliged me to discontinue that line and commence to run the division line between the first and second Concession, from the Reserve at River Cannards upwards to the Reserve at the Huron Church.

In the course of my continuing this line—I found settled on the front of the second Concession, on Lots No. 5,6,7,8,9 and 10, Six Inhabitants, some with considerable improvements. From Lot No. 11 to No. 29, a continued Marsh and Swamp in most places covered with water a considerable depth, from No. 29 to the end of my line a plain and marsh with very little wood. I also find settled nearly in the rear of Colonel McKee and others, several others who claim land in front above the Huron Church, they are said to be settled on the third Concession; between their improvements and the River no wood, land being all a plain. On Lot No. 35, I find Druillards Water Mill to be five

---

did not choose to remain a British subject, and automatically became an American citizen.

Arpents west of my line; the Mill is said to be fifty five arpents back from the River.

The whole distance that I have run from Lot No. 12 upwards, the 2nd Concession can only be deemed useful for the little wood that may be on it, the land being of no value.

G 27 Minutes of the Land Board of the District of Hesse, at the Council House, at Detroit, on Friday the 20th Day of July, 1792, Re the Side Lines at Petite Côte
[Third Report of the Archives of Ontario, *1905, p.192*]

Petite Cote. The Board having received by Captain Monforton a written agreement signed by the Majority of the Inhabitants of Petite Cote dated the 15th of July 1792 and lodged with the Board, setting forth that the old French side Lines run between the S. and E., and that they wish they should be continued in the same direction, and on reference to the Deputy Surveyor's Map, having found that more of their fences now run South 73 East—than any other Course, and being desirous to put the Inhabitants to as little expense as possible, from an attention to their Ease, direct that South 73 East—should be the Standard as to the side Lines of the 1st Concession or old Grants, and that due East should also be the standard for the Continuation or second Concession and further direct that the Inhabitants employ some proper Surveyor to draw their side Lines in the direction above mentioned—in order to facilitate the Board in granting if possible the second Concession prayed for by the Inhabitants and that twelve of the Inhabitants possessing the Lots next the Reserve, with also those people settled in their Rear do attend the Board on Friday next the 27th Instant, in order finally to determine on the Claims, and if possible grant the Lots in the second Concession to those who have well founded Pretensions.

G 28 D. W. Smith to Captain Monforton
[Third Report of the Archives of Ontario, *1905, pp. 184–5*]

Detroit, May 11, 1792

The Petition of the Inhabitants of Petite Cote for their continuations has been taken up by the Land Board for the District of Hesse, who think it reasonable so far as it relates to their 2d Concession which the Deputy Surveyor is ordered to lay out—and it is presumed the Old Inhabitants will lend him such assistance as will enable him to carry the Survey into execution, as at present he cannot get that assistance from hence.

But before any certificate can be granted for Lots in either the 1st or 2d Concessions, it is highly necessary that spaces for roads, to lead from the River to the 2d Concession should be adopted; you will, therefore, in conjunction with your company, report where such roads may be most conveniently made, as well for the good of the people in general, as the settlement in particular—immediately below Turkey River seems to point itself out as a convenient and central site for a principal Road, one between that and River au Jervaise, and another between Turkey River and the Reserve, may perhaps suffice.

It appears from the Surveyor's Report that almost all the farms contain more in front than specifyed by their Contracts, or by your return, so that wherever the lot may fall for the public Good, the Individual can have little or no cause of complaint.

Should there be any settlers who have usurped lands since the formation of the board, but most particularly since their prohibition to settle on the King's waste Lands without authority, they perhaps cannot claim the same indulgences as the older Inhabitants, who have settled under some kind of authority, although without deeds "en roture".

It is presumed also, that although a transfer of property has thrown 2 or 3 lots in front into the possession of an individual, yet it is not reasonable, or consistent with the public good to suppose such individual can expect more than one Lot in the Continuation.

You will be careful that the inhabitants who render assistance to the Deputy Surveyor do not imbibe the idea that this Service will entitle them to any peculiar preference for their second Concessions, merely an account of their assistance; but in order to repay them fully for their labour, the Board have directed that the front of the second Concession be extended in a due north direction from the end of 40 Acres (taken on the north boundary of the Reserve) from the River, which on account of the Curvilineal front of the Strait, will extend the first Concession of nearly all the Old Inhabitants to about 50 Acres—which will be an acquisition much more than adequate to any trouble they be at. The Board do not wish that any of the people who may have settled without authority since their formation should be employed with the Surveyor, lest they should bring that forward as a pretense to be secured in their usurpations. Should it be quite convenient to you to come to the fort, I shall be happy to have a personal interview with you—which I make no doubt will be also a satisfactory opportunity to the Surveyor of meeting you.

I have the honor, &c., Per order of the board. . . .

G 29   E. J. O'BRIEN, SECRETARY OF THE LAND BOARD, TO MCNIFF
[Third Report of the Archives of Ontario, *1905, pp. 220-1*]

Detroit, February 5th, 1793

Sir—The Land Board of the Counties of Essex and Kent finding that the report made by you of the late Survey you were desired to make in the rear of the L'Assomption Settlement is not as satisfactory as they flattered themselves to have received from you, direct that you do immediately proceed to the said Settlement, and commencing at the Huron Church, draw a line between the land granted to the Church by the Hurons, and the Reserve made by them, running according to the Grant made in 1750 by the Marquis De Lajonquire to Monsieur Longuiele, N.N.W., or to what may be considered as such by Monsieur Dufault, the present Curate residing at the Huron Church, and Monsieur Pratt, who also lives there, at the distance of Eighty french Acres so as to leave room for a second Concession in the rear of the L'Assomption Settlement, and after there leaving such room for a public road as is directed by the Chequered Plan, then run a line at right Angles in rear of the ground allotted for the second Concession of the L'Assomption Settlement, so as to extend the length directed by the Chequered Plan for the front of a Township (a copy of which the Board have given you) in the rear of which, you will proceed to complete a Township agreeable to said Plan, and continue it as far as unforeseen or unavoidable Circumstances will allow you, but certainly four Lots deep—

G 30   REPORT FROM MCNIFF
[Third Report of the Archives of Ontario, *1905, pp. 224–5*]

Detroit, 2nd March, 1793.

Pursuant to the order of the Land Board for the Western District, of the 5th of February, 1793, directing a survey of the back Concessions in the rear of L'Assomption, I did on the 13th of February last commence between the Church Land and the Indian Reserve and run back S28d, 30E. the distance of Six Concessions, at which distance the Land proved so wet and Swampy could not continue that line to its end. I therefore proceeded to the head line of the third Concession and run it the distance of nine miles marking and numbering the Lots as I went, chiefly low wet land, few lots fit For Culture. That line ended I commenced at the head line of the 4th Concession, and run it to the end of the 14th Lot which terminated in a Swamp full of water where originates Petite River, River au Peche, River Puce and Belle River—I then commenced at the head line of the 5th Concession and continued it to the end of the 8th lot ending in a Swamp, then commenced at the head of the 6th Concession and continued that line cross Six Lots ending in the foregoing Swamp; here ends my Actual Survey. I then proceeded to examine the land on River au Peche, River au Puce, Belle River and River Ruscom, they all appear to originate in One Swamp, on each of these Rivers Several good Farms may be had nearly in the following proportion, Vis.:

On River au Peche .. 10. Navigable at certain Seasons about 4 miles.
On River au Puce .... 15. Navigable at certain Seasons about 2 miles.
On Belle River .... 20. Navigable at certain Seasons about 6 miles.
On River Ruscom .. 14. Navigable at certain Seasons about 4 miles.

Those Farms supposed to have the same breadth with farms ordered by the present established order of survey, but to front on each side of the River which will give two fronts on each River, and not to front on Lake St. Clair, a thing from the face of the Country not practicable, I have entered each of these Rivers with a Boat; and have gone up two of them, Vis.: River Ruscom and Belle River, a considerable distance, which I have already communicated to His Excellency the Governor, the entrance into each of them (River Ruscom excepted) are closed up at certain times with sand, but in a short time are open again. But instead of dividing the land on these Rivers, conformable to the present Established order of Survey of farm lots, I would recommend the allotments to be made so that each farm should be six Acres wide and no more and extend back the distance of 34 Acres which will give each of the occupants 204 Acres, and will make them sufficiently content, they cannot extend back from the front on each River at most more than 20 and 24 Acres before they descend into a Swamp. My reason for recommending in the present instance this deviation from the General Plan is, that Settlers having six Acres in front of good land and extending back from 20 to 24 Acres, will have no objection to take 10 or 14 Acres in the rear of swampy Land which may answer all the purposes of having wood for Fuel and Fencing, by this deviation from the General Rule, half as many more Settlers can be placed on the Space of land as can be done if the General Rule is attended to. . . .

G 31 ORDER OF SURVEY FOR LOTS ON STREAMS FLOWING INTO LAKE ST. CLAIR
[Third Report of the Archives of Ontario, *1905, p. 227*]

Detroit, March 29th, 1793

You are directed by the Land Board of the Counties of Essex and Kent to Proceed with as much expedition as possible to survey the lots reported by you to be on River Ruscom, Belle River, Riviere aux Pêches, Riviere aux Puces and La Petite Riviere, and lay them out in the Manner mentioned by you in your report of the 2nd Instant to be most suitable for Settlement as the land presents itself. You will make the usual reserves for Government and the Church, as directed by the Order of His Excellency the Lieutenant-Governor and Council.

Should you, when on this survey, consider that confining the front Lots to five Acres would be equally convenient to the Settlers, it is considered by the Board that such a survey would be most eligible, as it would make room for a greater Number of Settlers. You will, of course, extend the depth of each lot in proportion so as to make two Hundred Acres in each Lot.

To Mr. McNiff, Deputy Surveyor

I am, Sir,
Your obedient Servant,
E. J. O'Brien, Secretary

G 32   REPORT FROM THE DEPUTY SURVEYOR RE LOTS ON STREAMS FLOWING INTO LAKE ST. CLAIR
[Third Report of the Archives of Ontario, *1905, p. 228*]

Detroit, April 11th, 1793

Pursuant to the Orders of the Land Board of the 29th Ultimo I did proceed to survey and lay out into lots the land on the River Ruscom, Belle River, River aux Puces and River aux Pêches; on the first are fourteen lots of tolerable good land, on the second fourteen lots, on the third fourteen lots, twelve of which are exceedingly good, on the fourth fourteen lots, thirteen of which are exceeding good. Many more lots of excellent land may be had in the forks or Branches of the last two Rivers, but they cannot be conveniently settled by an uniform survey corresponding with what is already done from the number of Branches they form, and these Branches in many places near to each other; this, with their very Serpentine Courses, render it impossible to front lots on any of them, without crossing them in several places; on the West Bank of the two last Rivers very good Roads may with ease be made to their Forks, where I find Springs of excellent Waters but no Mill seat, for where the Bank is high on one side, the opposite side is very low. . . .

G 33   R. G. ENGLAND[6] TO D. W. SMITH
[*Cruikshank,* The Simcoe Papers, *I, 324–5*]

Detroit, May 1st, 1793

(Private)

In my last by the Speedwell I mentioned to you the difficulties I had in fitting out and getting Mr. McNiff to proceed on the Survey directed by you of the River Thames. . . .

. . . I hope the purpose of his expedition will be fully answered but I have very strong doubts, and if I am to judge by the sketch of the survey he made on the South Shore of Lake St. Clair and which he presented to me, I apprehend the Governor will be disappointed in the information he expects from him on his return. I will answer for it there was never such a sketch delivered by any Surveyor as a guidance for granting nearly sixty lots of land of six acres in front. If my information is correct there are as many more lots on those rivers, but for some reason I do not comprehend Mr. McNiff reports there are not more lots than he mentioned in his sketch.

The 16th Inst. is fixed for granting those lots which are much sought after, and I hope before then to hear from you about the propriety of establishing those settlements without making the usual Reserves. The

[6]Lieutenant-Colonel Richard G. England of the Twenty-fourth Regiment was the last British Commandant at Detroit, serving there in 1791 and again from 1793 to 1796. As Commanding Officer he was an *ex officio* member of the Land Board.

sketch marks seven lots in front on each side of the rivers and four rivers, so that each river produces but fourteen lots, except the front is divided into two, which in some I am informed may be done. . . .

G 34 AGREEMENT OF SALE FROM WILLIAM SMITH TO JOHN ASKIN
[*Cruikshank and Hunter,* The Russell Papers, *I, 130*]

Memorandum of an Agreement between William Smith of the River Thames & John Askin of Detroit Merch't as follows, Vist.

Said Smith sells to said Askin Three Lots of Land on the West Side of the Belle River for the Sum of Sixty Pounds N.Y. Curr. They are No. 8, 9 & 10 and contain Two Hundred Acres of Land Each, & he obliges himself to give up to said Askin the Certificates he holds for the Occupation of said Lands and so soon as he gets Grants of the same he obliges himself to transfer them over to said Askin Agreeable to Law, however should there be any fees of Office said Askin is to pay them & the above mentioned sixty Pounds are to be paid as follows: Six pounds now in Cash & Twenty four pounds more in one year from the date hereof. The remaining thirty Pounds to be paid in goods out of Said Askin's store at the rate he usually sells at any time that said Smith chooses and finds in said store what Answers his purpose & for the true performance of this Agreement according to the real Intention & Meaning thereof Each party binds himself in the Penal Sum of One Hundred Pounds N.Y. Cur. Detroit.
January the 17th 1797
Witness A. Maisonville

Endorsed—Received, January the 17th 1797—the six pounds mentioned on the other side.

G 35 DEPUTY SURVEYOR IREDELL[7] TO SURVEYOR GENERAL'S OFFICE
[*Ont. Dept. of Public Records and Archives, Crown Land Papers, shelf 5, no. 1, p. 109*]

Jan. 30, 1798

. . . In surveying and locating of the lots in Tilbury I did not advert to your Instructions in regard to the Reserve being made on the principle of the Chequered Plan—as six lots on front of that Township was granted by the Land Board where there is only five in the Chequered Plan in a Concession, and a special grant of the Council in favor of Jos. Moore (covering an improvement made by the Indians) 3rd of August 1795, and two recommendations of Mr. Maisonville in favor of Charron and Lepoint countersigned by Mr. Small 4th of August, 1795—

[7]Abraham Iredell was a deputy surveyor in the Western District. After the American occupation of Detroit he resided on the Thames River, at the present townsite of Chatham, Ontario.

Charron being an actual settler, tho since sold to Moore—I'll forbear locating more lots in that township until you direct me what lots to reserve.

G 36 CERTIFICATES FOR LOTS OF LAND BOUGHT BY ASKIN
[*B.H.C., Askin Papers MSS, carton for 1796*]

Sept. 14, 1796

List of Certificates for Lots of Land Bought by John Askin Sr. & to be laid out in the name of

Jacques Gravelle	Laurent Boismier	Vincent Maheux
J. B. Prudhomme	Simon Leduc	Pierre Solo
Nicholas Drouillard	François Martin	J. B. Bonvouloir
Joseph Blanchard	Claude Solo	Charles Chauvin
Hypolite Janisse	Toussaint Chesne	Gabriel Lapointe Jr.
André Peltier Jun	Alexis Dubois	Jacques Gabourie
J. B. Lemay		

Sent to Iredell [Surveyor]

G 37 ASKIN TO D. W. SMITH AT NEWARK
[*Quaife,* The John Askin Papers, *II, 100–1*]

Detroit April 3d 1797

... I am under many Obligations to you for your Friendly information & Advice not to purchase Lands untill Granted under the Great Seal of the Province. This I will attend to in the future, but I have like most others bought a good many last year say about 80 Lots several of which I have made improvements on as you may recollect I mentioned in former letters and I should hope Government would not deprive me of Lands which in my possession will in all probability be sooner settled than if in those to whom the Certificates were given. Had it pleased His Excellency Governor Simcoe to be as liberal to my family as he was to many other I would not have been necessitated to lay out money that I could badly spare in order to secure to them some fixed property after I was gone, however when a man is gone away it may not be fair to speak against him therefore I will drop the subject so far as it relates to him, but I rely too much on the Generosity of the Administrator & Council to suppose that they would deprive me of Lands which I have purchased fairly and from those who are British subjects and according to the Regulations were entitled to Lands; I depend on your friendship to Settle this matter and if for forms sake the Grants must be given in the Names of those who got the Certificates its all the same I know they will readily Transfer them over to me after wards I have their Sales of them & Power of Attorney to receive the Deeds. They are mostly all situated in the Rivers Ruscum, Belle Riviere, Puce and Peches & along the Lake between these Rivers, under cover herewith you have a list of their names & by a Map transmitted to you by Mr. Iredell you will see their situations.

... I learn Government wishes or Intends to have a purchase made from the Indians at the Huron Church in order to lay out a Town the situation is high and good but the Distance from the Water side owing to a Swamp is rather Great for people in Trade in particular. Whilst I was a Member of the Board I allways opposed Cardins lands being given away to any person & wanted them to be reserved for some public purpose as a Town—their Situation having Advantages over any other that I know for that purpose but as it has pleased the Government to give them to Mr. Maisonville I should be glad he had deeds for them, his selling them to us would answer two good purposes namely that of our removing & several others speedily to the other side & furnish him with the means of paying some debts that he owes. ...

G 38   ASKIN TO THE HONORABLE RICHARD CARTWRIGHT[8] AT YORKE
[*Quaife*, The John Askin Papers, *II, 144–7*]

Detroit 12 July 1798

Tho I wish to be as little troublesome to my old acquaintances as possible, yet in the present case, my interest as well as that of Mssrs Isaac Todd & James McGill is so deeply concerned, that I am obliged to call on all my friends not only to exercise their personal influence in my behalf but also to call to their aid such as are capable from their situations, of giving any, provided you and them think me right after you have heared what I have to say.

Some years ago, when the Governor's proclamation declared that Lands should be given to certain persons on the Certificate of a Magistrate, finding many of those who possessed these Certificates were disposed to sell them, and being desirous by every means in my power to render my property more valuable for the sole purpose of discharging as far as in my power lay the heavy balance I owed the best of men, I accordingly purchased several at the rate of from £10 even to £50 for each 200 acres & never entertained any doubt as to their validity, having as every British Subject should a perfect reliance on the word or proclamation of the Servants of Government. Those who obtained the Magistrates Certificate carried them immediately to Mr. Iredell the Deputy Surveyor and mentioned at the same time where they wished to take up those Lands, and as I purchased them I reported to Mr. Iredell likewise my having done so & that as soon as the country was surveyed where these people made their choice I would wish to locate

[8]Richard Cartwright was a successful merchant of Kingston, Ontario, who took an active part in the politics of Upper Canada. He served as a member of the Executive Council from its formation in 1792 until his death in 1815. He also served as Justice of the Court of Common Pleas in the Districts of Mecklenburg and Luneburg.

the Lands I purchased in said place, not from the goodness of the Lands but their situation as being nearer some others I had got. I also frequently mentioned to the Acting Surveyor General my Friend what I had done and was doing and for a certain time did not understand that there was any objections to such purchases. I afterwards learned some doubts arose; but when the Legislature in the last years Sessions passed that most equitable law respecting the Purchase of Lands, I then was perfectly satisfied that they were mine, and that if my purchases were proved to be fair and honest before the Commissioners, Deeds would be issued in my name. I therefore begged the acting surveyor General would order that part of the Country to be laid out in Lotts where those I purchased of had made choice, and where I still wished to take up these lands.

. . . I understood that it was once supposed that several Magistrates had given certificates to people undeserving for the purpose of purchasing them, I deny any such conduct in me. I have therefore transmitted by my son in order to show it to you & other friends a list of the names of the people of whom I got the Lands, what Magistrates signed their Certificates and their present place of abode. . .

I now, agreeable to my Friend Mr. Smith's letter Memorialize the President & Honorable Council to direct that the Lands I claim may be surveyed and allotted to me or to those of whom I got them and that when the Commissioners come here if my pretensions are found good that Deeds may be granted me for them.

I do not recollect having ever been more interested in any event than this as my worthy Friends Messrs James & Andrew McGill have agreed in their settlement with me to take 40 of these Lotts in lieu of £4000 & I was to give them free of charges. Should I not obtain Grants for these lands I purchased I will not be able to fulfill my engagements with them & consequently ruined. And tho you and Mr. Hamilton are not of the Executive Council yet you have influence with those that are and if you find my claims right & just I hope & firmly believe from your general character exclusive of your friendship that you will have my Memorial supported so as to obtain what I ask for, and think my just due. . . .

I have laid out about £500 in improvements, etc. on Lotts I purchased from those who had Land-Board Certificates which is more than those I purchased of would have done in a long time.

I am Dear Sir with real regard your most obedient humble servant. . . .

H. THE FIRST TOWNS—SANDWICH AND AMHERSTBURG

H 1 LISTS OF PERSONS RESIDING IN DETROIT IN 1796 WHO ELECTED TO REMAIN BRITISH SUBJECTS
[M.H.C., *VIII, 410–11*]

Augustin Amelle
Lauret Maure
James McIntosh
Robt. Innis
Rt. Pattinson
Robt. Grant
Jonathan Schifflin
John Martin
D. McRae
Wm. Forsyth
Francis Bertrand
Pre. Gabarne
Hugh Heward
Wm. Fleming
Charles Chovin
James Donaldson
Louis Moore
James Condon
Pre. Dolorme
Alex. Harson
Thomas Smith
John Askin, Sr.
Pierre Vallee
John McKirgan
James Smith
Joseph Mason
John Anderson
Agnes [Angus] McIntosh
Conrad Showler
Charles Roque
John Little
Ch. Poupard
In. Robital
Nicholas Boyer
John Fearson
Benoit Chapoton
James Cartwright
Gabriel Hewes
Robt. Forsyth
Antoine Chauvin

Jeane Bt. Pere
Jean Bt. Montroi
Thomas Green
Francis Primo
Charles Petre
Pre. Lanoux
Redmond Condon
Joseph Bernard
John Grant
George Sharp
James Vincent
Louis Barthy
Alex. Duff
Batiste Boete
John Daine
William Harfy
Samuel Edge
John Langloi
Jas. Guthrie
John Whitehead
Wm. Thorn
Jonathan Nelson
Geo. Meldrum
A. Iredell
J. Bte. Barthe
J. Bte. Barthe, Jr
Robt. Nichol
Alex. Maisonville, fils
Jean. Bt. Bernard
John Reul
Mathew Dolson
Wm. Park
Wm. Smith
Robt. McDougall
John McGregor
John Askin, Jr
Joseph Borrelle, pere
James McGregor
Robt. Goine

John Clark
James Fraser
J. Portier Benac
Wm. Hands
Francis Rassette
Simon Drouillar
Geo. Jacob Rudhart
Pierre Rell
Basile Durocher
Alexis Crait
Joseph Borrell, fils
Alexis Borrell, fils
Richard Money
Noel Delisle
Wm. Mickle
Wm. Baker
John Cain
R. McDonnell
John McDonnell
John Wheaton
Louis Coutre
Amable Latour
Wm. Mills
James Anderson
Peter Blanch
Isaac Ganize, pere
John Lagord
Bt. Telemain dit
——— St. Louis
Bte. Monmerell
Richard Donovan
Isaac Gragnier, fils
Franc Lenaire
Sam'l Eddy
Dominique Druillard
Bapt. Druillard
Bapt. Rousseau
Phillip Bellanger
Joseph Grenist

189

H 2 A MEMORIAL FROM SEVERAL MAGISTRATES OF DETROIT TO
COLONEL SARGENT[1]
[*Quaife,* The John Askin Papers, *II, 112–13*]

Detroit, 12 July, 1797

We the undersigned Majestrates, and Sherif of Wayne County in the territory of the United States of America, impressed with every degree of attachment to the Government of the United States and most Sincere wishes for the Safety of this Country and its Inhabitants, have Sincerely to regret its present Situation; and for its Safety, disagreable apprehensions from the dangers that at present MENACE its tranquility from an approaching Ennemy, as well as from internal and increasing factions. Twelve months ago, we Knew of no more than Ten of its Inhabitants that were avowed British Subjects, they remaining here for one year after the evacuation of this place by the British, during that period, they with Some other Emissaries, found means by indirect insinuations and circulating-papers to corrupt the minds of the Inhabitants and alienated their affections from the Government of the States to Such a degree, that it was with difficulty that the Sherrif could procure a Jury of real Citizens to attend the last Sessions, or Ballifs to do their duty. Some Scores (It is said Some hundreds) of the Inhabitants having signed the Said circulating papers declaring themselves British Subjects Which gives us reason to fear, that little or no dependance could be put in the Militia of the Country If called upon. This being truly the State of the Country, WE feel the greatest anxiety for its Safety. We therefore conceive it our duty to transmit you every part of our apprehensions, and the causes exciting them, hoping that you will See the propriety of vesting Sufficient power in the Commander in Chief now here, or the commanding-Officer, for the time being to take Such Steps as may check the progress of the present prevailing faction, and prevent a further corruption of the Inhabitants, we by experience finding it out of the power of the civil authority at present to do it.

Signed: James Abbott Senior
James May
Nathan Williams
Charles F. Girardin
Joseph Voyer
Patrick McNiff   } Esq
Herman Eberts
John Dodemead
Joncaire chabert
Antoine Beaubien
Robert Abbott
Daniel Sawyer

[1] Winthrop Sargent served in the Indian War 1791–4, and at this time was acting Governor of the Northwest Territory.

H 3   PETER RUSSELL[2] TO ROBERT PRESCOTT[3]
[*Cruikshank and Hunter,* The Russell Papers, *I, 149*]

West Niagara, 28th Feby. 1797

It having been resolved in Council last June, that application should be immediately made to the Commander in Chief for the purchase of the Huron Reserve on the Detroit River for the purpose of laying off a Town thereon to be the Capital of the Western District of this Province, and not knowing whether any Measures have been taken for this purpose, I am advised by the Council to request Your Excellency will be pleased (if it should be judged expedient to purchase the Huron Reserve) to give directions for purchasing the Gore near the Huron Church, described in the inclosed Minutes of Council; and I beg leave in consequence to submit their Request to your Excellency's Consideration.

H 4   PRESCOTT TO RUSSELL
[*Cruikshank and Hunter,* The Russell Papers, *I, 163*]

Quebec 11th April 1797

I hope you will excuse my declining to give my sanction to the purchase of the Huron Reserve, which has been recommended by the Council of Upper Canada. The ground being wanted merely for Civil Purposes, I really cannot (as Commander in Chief) take upon me to direct it to be purchased without having the authority of the Secretary of State for such a Measure.

H 5   RUSSELL TO PRESCOTT
[The Russell Papers, *I, 181–2*]

Upper Canada York May 30th 1797

The Request I had the honor of making to your Excellency in my letter marked No. 11, for the purchase of the Gore near the Huron Church, is I believe conformable to the mode hitherto practised by the Civil Government of this Province, when the Welfare thereof called for the purchase of any additional Lands from the Indian Proprietors. But a letter which I have lately received from Colo. McKee the Dy. SuperIntendt. Genl. having informed me that the Genl. Orders for the Government of the Indian Dept. of the 20th December 1794, direct that "When Indian Territory shall be wanted by any of the King's Provinces the Governor or Person administering the Government of the

---

[2]Peter Russell (1733–1808) was born in Cork, Ireland, and was educated at Cambridge. He served in America during the Revolution and then went back to England. In 1792 he came to Canada, having been appointed by Simcoe Receiver-General of the Province of Upper Canada. On Simcoe's withdrawal in 1796, Russell, as President of the Council, succeeded to the governorship, retaining the position until 1799. He died in Toronto, September 30, 1808.

[3]The Lieutenant-Governor of the Province of Lower Canada.

respective Province will make his requisition to the Commander in Chief and also to the SuperIntdt. Genl., or in his absence to the Dy. SuperIntdt Genl. accompanied with a Sketch of the Tract required, who will endeavour to find out the probable price to be paid therefor in Goods (the Manufacture of Great Britain) and report the same to the Commander in Chief that measure may be taken to get them out from England by the first opportunity". I beg leave to renew my requisition to your Excy. conformable thereto that a purchase may be made as soon as possible of a Gore near the Huron Church on the Detroit River (which had been reserved for the Indians, when a Cession was made by them to the Crown of a Tract described in the Deed of Cession. "A Tract beginning at the mouth of River aux Jarvais, commonly called Knaggs Creek, running up the Border of the Strait to the Huron Church and 120 arpents in depth") and to transmit herewith a Sketch thereof for your Excellency's Information; having sent a similar requisition and sketch to the Deputy Superintendent General, that he may endeavor to find out what the Wyandots may be disposed to part with this spot for, and transmit the Provisional Agreement to your Excy. without loss of time.

I am induced to take the liberty of troubling your Excellency again upon this Subject, from the absolute necessity I feel myself under of providing immediately some convenient place for the District Town, to which the former Inhabitants of Detroit may resort after the first of June, when they must make their selection of the Government which they mean to reside under. Else we may probably lose a very extensive Commerce of considerable value to Great Britain, and a numerous Body of Loyal and respectable Subjects, who might be compelled by the nature of their Trade to remain on the American side of the River, unless they can obtain one equally convenient to it on this, and the situation of this Spot has been represented by them to be best suited to their purpose of any we possess. It is moreover within the Parish of L'Assomption wherein the sittings of the Courts have been established by Statute; and from the smallness and Barrenness of the Tract required it is presumable the amount of its purchase cannot become an object of any Consequence.

H 6 PRESCOTT TO RUSSELL
[The Russell Papers, *I, 191*]

Quebec 21st June 1797

I have received your Letters marked Nos. 15, 16 and 17, under date of the 30th May.

The objection I made formerly to Purchase the Gore near the Huron Church on the Detroit River, from the Wyandot Indians, arose first from not being then possessed of sufficient and necessary powers to Sanction Civil concerns in the Province of Upper Canada, and secondly from conceiving that the vast tracts of waste Lands situated to the Southward of Amherstburg were still unconceded, and under such circumstances would afford the Lieut. Governor and Council of Upper Canada sufficient choice of Land to fix on for a Town, without having recourse to purchase from the Indians—But as Governor General I have no objection to give my Sanction to the Purchase if that spot is found actually to be the best calculated for Commercial purposes and sufficient for a District Town, to which the former Inhabitants of Detroit may resort, and Merchants may likewise remove, who seated themselves within the Fort of Amherstburg on the first evacuation of Detroit—

As soon as I am informed how the Indians incline to this measure, and the requisition is received for such Goods as may be agreed upon with them to compleat this Purchase, I will embrace an early opportunity of transmitting it home for His Majesty's approbation.
. . .

H 7 LIST OF PERSONS WHO HAVE DRAWN LOTS IN THE TOWN OF SANDWICH
[*Fraser,* Twentieth Report of the Archives of Ontario, *1931, pp. 42–3*]

14th. August, 1797

Council Chamber at Newark
Present: His Honor Peter Russell, Esquire, President, &c. &c.
Read a list of persons who have drawn lots in the town of Sandwich. With the sanction of the magistrates and consent of the parties applying for lots in the proposed town of Sandwich, the choice of lots was referred to drawing by hazard, and the following is the choice made by the persons to whose lot it fell to draw in the front street (called Russell Street).

	Russell Street East side	Bedford Street West Side	Bedford Street East Side
Lot 1.	Richard Pattinson	George Sharp, Esq.	not drawn
Lot 2.	Gregor McGregor	Antoine Dufresne	William Harffy*
Lot 3.	Hon. James Baby	Francis Baby, Esq.	Jean Baptiste Barthe
Lot 4.	James Allen	John Askin, Esq.	Dr. Robt. Richardson
Lot 5.	Col. McKee	William Park, Esq.	Alexis Maisonville
Lot 6.	Angus McIntosh	Capt. McKee	Wm. Caldwell, Esq.
Lot 7.	Joseph Borelli	Not drawn	Porlier Benac
Lot 8.	William Hands	Reserved	Reserved
Lot 9.	John McGregor	Reserved	Reserved
Lot 10.	John Martin	Thos. McCrae	Not drawn
Lot 11.	Geo. Meldrum, Esq.	Jonathan Scheifflin	Robt. McDougall
Lot 12.	Robert Innis	Walter Roe, Esq.	Capt. Harrow
Lot 13.	Alexander Duff	Baptiste Baby	Mathew Elliott
Lot 14.	Hon. Alex. Grant	Wm. Shepherd	Abraham Iredell
Lot 15.	Alex. McKenzie	Richard Pollard	James Leith
Lot 16.	John Askin, Jr.	Prideaux Selby, Esq.	Mathew Dolson

* Such part as does not interfere with William Hands farm.

(Signed) W. Roe
C. P. and Sessions, W.D.

The persons herein mentioned are recommended for the lots opposite their names.

Approved.
Confirmed.

Copy

(Signed) J.E.
(Signed) Peter Russell
(Signed) Peter Russell
(Signed) D.W.S.

H 8 MINUTES OF THE EXECUTIVE COUNCIL (LANDS) RE LOTS ADJOINING THE BABY MILL
[*Ontario Archives, Microfilm of the Minutes of the Executive Council (Lands) at York*]

Council Chambers at York 13th July 1799.

Hoble James Baby—Stating that he has a Mill opposite to the Town of Sandwich, Western District, round which there is a Reserve of one square Acre for the use of the said Mill.[4] That Petitioner finds that West half of Lot No. 2 and East half of Lot No. 4,[5] adjoining said Mill are vacant, and not applied for—and praying that they may be granted to him.

Recommended for the broken front in front of Lot. No. 3, that in front of the Southern half of No. 2, and that in front of the Northern half of No. 4, in Russell Street Sandwich.

H 9 DIRECTIONS RESPECTING RESERVES AND SURVEYS IN THE TOWN OF SANDWICH
[*Toronto Public Library, Reference Division, David W. Smith Collection, Series B, vol. IX, p. 191;* The Russell Papers, *I, 253*]

A Reserve to be laid off equal to the Quantity of land taken into the present Town of Sandwich—and whatever land may remain afterward behind the Town, to be divided into Lots of 24 acres each which are to be given as Park Lots to those settlers who build the first Houses in the Town—which they will be confirmed in upon their producing a Certificate at the Surveyor General's Office from the Town Wardens of their having actually built a good Dwelling House there and residing in it either in their own Persons or by a good sufficient Tenant. Descriptions may be sent to the Attorney General of the Land granted to Mr. Allison that Deeds may issue thereon. 19 August 1797.

To the Honorable D. W. Smith, Esq.

Peter Russell

[4]This mill was later sold to Mr. Hypolite Lasalline, and is reported to have ground as much as 100 bushels of wheat in a day during the war of 1812–13.

[5]Mr. Baby was confused in his directions. He must have forgotten that the mill was below the bend in the river. The northern and southern half of lots 2 and 4, as employed in the recommendation, is a more proper description.

H 10 Certificate of First Houses in the Town of Sandwich and Assignment of Park Lots

[*Toronto Public Library, Reference Division, David W. Smith Collection, Series A, vol. VIII, pp. 245-7;* The Russell Papers, *II, 104*]

I do hereby certify, that the Petitioners John McGregor, Richard Pattinson and Robert Innis have finished their buildings at Sandwich, in the W. District agreeable to His Honor the President's instructions.
York Feby 26, 1798

R. Pollard

York, March 5, 1798

Sir, you will be pleased to assign to Messrs. McGregor, Richard Pattinson & Robert Innis—Park Lots of 24 Acres each in the neighbourhood of Sandwich as a Douceur for having built houses in that Town, agreeable to the Promise made to the Inhabitants, who should build the first houses there.

I have the honor to be Sir &c
Peter Russell

I do hereby certify that the Petitioner Wm. Park Esqr. has built a house in the Town of Sandwich, in the W. District agreeable to His Honor the President's Instructions.
York March 5th, 1798   Richard Pollard, Sheriff W.D.

An assignment of a Park Lot of 24 acres to issue to Wm. Park Esqr. as the Builder of the 4th House in Sandwich.

Peter Russell

The Honble. D. W. Smith &c.
Endorsed:—His Honor 5 March 98.

H 11 Minutes of the Executive Council re Gaol and Court House for the Western District

[The Russell Papers, *I, 109*]

Council Chamber at Newark
12th Decr. 1796

No. 5. Memorial from the Magistrates in General Quarter Sessions, held at L'Assomption Western District, Stating that a paragraph of a letter from His Honor, Peter Russell Esqr. Administering the Government of the Province, to James Baby & Alexr. McKee Esquires, Lieutenants of the Counties of Kent & Essex, being laid down before them—as follows:

"You will also be pleased to recommend it to the Justices at their Quarter Sessions to report to me the State of the Prisons, what repairs they may want, & whether new ones are necessary, & how far the Inhabitants of the District are capable of bearing the whole or part of the expence, that provision may be made without delay for building at least one sufficient Gaol in each District which is absolutely indispensible, for the prevention of disorder in every community;" to which they represent that the late evacuation of territory has so much curtailed the number of Inhabitants of the Western District that it is entirely out of their power to erect a Gaol & Court House therein. That the present County Rates or Assessments are not sufficient to pay the necessary expences for the internal regulation thereof—They further beg leave to observe, that the debts actually incurred by the District, cannot by the present Assessment be satisfied in less than three years altho' they have reason to hope that if the Government should be disposed to afford the District a loan of seven hundred & fifty pounds currency, the remainder towards effecting the erection of a Gaol and Court House may be collected within the District, they further judge it proper to add that as the Season is now at hand, when the materials can be procured for the purpose of building they request that an answer may be conveyed to them by the River Thames.

By Order of the Magistrates
W. Roe, C. P. & Sess. W.D.

Resolved that an offer be made to the Magistrates of the Western District of the Store house lately built by Government at Chatham to be used as a Prison either in the place where it now stands or to be removed by them to any other more proper situation—but the Magistrates are desired in case they resolve on removal to inform this Board before they do it of the place they shall chuse for that purpose.

H 12   PRIDEAUX SELBY[6] TO RUSSELL
[The Russell Papers, II, 45–6]

Sandwich 22d December 1797

The great Misfortune we have lately sustained by the loss of our Jail & Court House by Fire will, I trust, be accepted as an Apology for the freedom I now presume to take in addressing your Honor on the Subject thereof, with a view of obtaining by your generous Assistance the means, and I believe the only means, of carrying on the public Business—

With a disposition very much to be commended, a certain Description of the Magistrates, in Consideration of the high assessments, and the Weight of our debt, advanced between three and four Hundred Pounds by way of Loan, in order to compleat this most necessary Building; and at the Moment of our approach to respectability, all our Hopes, all our

---

[6]Prideaux Selby was a lieutenant in the Fifth Infantry and for a time Assistant Secretary of Indian Affairs at Detroit. From 1809 until his death at Toronto in 1813 he was a member of the Executive Council for Upper Canada. At the time this letter was written he was Chairman of the Bench of Justices for the Western District of Upper Canada.

Exertions, and I may justly add, all our Power as Magistrates, ceased at once. In a special Session which I directed to be called the day subsequent to the Conflagration, there appeared some ground to warrant a Suspicion that the Building was set on fire by a Young Man, the son of one of the Prisoners, who is a free negro—But I fear we shall not be able to produce such Evidence as may induce a Jury to convict him—

Under all the Circumstances in which this Calamity has involved the District, I beg leave to assure your Honor that all our Dependance now is placed in the assistance of the Executive Government of the Province without which there is not a ray of Hope left us for the accomplishment of Subordination to the Laws, or the suppression of Vice—

I persuade myself your Honor will receive favorably this humiliating Picture of our Present distress; and that your Benevolence will guard us against the Introduction of Anarchy by affording us another Opportunity of recording your generous Protection of the Western District.

H 13 RUSSELL TO THE DUKE OF PORTLAND[7]
[*The Russell Papers, II, 125*]

Upper Canada 21st March 1798

I beg leave to lay before your Grace a letter which I have lately received from the Chairman of the Bench of Justices in the Western District of the Province, soliciting assistance from me to enable the District to rebuild its Jail and Court House which has been destroyed by fire—

In consequence of repeated Representations from the Magistrates of the District, that since the United States had obtained possession of Detroit, Multitudes of Deserters from their Army were daily dispersing themselves among the Settlements on this side of the River, & committing every Species of Crime that can blacken a Newgate Kalendar; and that for want of a Jail, (which they were too poor to build at their own Expense) they were incapable of suppressing those Enormities unless Government should think proper to give them a secure place for confining Criminals and other Offenders against the Laws; I immediately consulted the Executive Council upon the Subject of their application; and by its advice & Consent I permitted the Magistrates of the Western District to cause a Block house, that had been erected at Chatham for a store, to be removed from thence to Sandwich and converted into a Jail and Court House for the use of the Western District—We were induced to permit this Removal by the great Expense it would apparently require to secure the Block house from tumbling into the River (it having been unfortunately built upon a point of land which the stream was gradually washing from under it); and by the necessity Government

---

[7]From 1794 to 1801 the Duke of Portland was Secretary of State for the Home Department.

was under to provide a trusty Person to look after the Block House & Gun Boats at Chatham, so few people seemed inclined to build Houses and reside there—

This recent Misfortune having placed the Western District in a Situation which calls for Relief with equal force with the one it was in before this favor was granted it; I should not have hesitated about assenting to the Magistrates' present Request, was I not restrained by the Reasons I have stated in my letter to their Chairman—I have therefore taken the liberty of suspending my compliance with it, until I shall be honored with your Grace's answer to this letter; and I have in the meantime requested the Officer Commanding at Amherstburg to give up to the Sheriff one of the unemployed vessels in the Detroit River, which he may make use of as a temporary Prison—

H 14 SCHEDULE OF TIMBERS CONTRACTED FOR BY MR. AUGUSTIN ROY FOR THE PURPOSE OF BUILDING A GAOL AND COURT HOUSE AT SANDWICH

[*George F. Macdonald Collection, Wm. Hands*[8] *Papers*]

[Undated]

Oak Timbers			Running feet
240 pieces......20 feet long............12	inches by 6................		4,800
50 pieces......13 feet long.......... 8	inches by 6................		650
Pine Timbers			
30 pieces......27 feet long............ 7	inches by 4................		810
4 pieces......35 feet long............ 7	inches by 4................		140
4 pieces......30 feet long............ 7	inches by 4................		120
2 pieces......60 feet long............ 9	inches by 9................		120
2 pieces......40 feet long............ 9	inches by 9................		80
15 pieces......25 feet long............ 7	inches by 4................		375
30 pieces......15 feet long............12	inches by 4................		450
40 pieces......20 feet long............ 4½	inches by 6................		320

425 pieces containing..running feet 8,665

Total four hundred and twenty five pieces of timber, containing eight thousand six hundred and sixty five feet running measure, at eleven pence half penny, New York currency per foot is four hundred and fifteen pounds, three shillings and eleven pence half penny New York currency dollars at Eight Shillings.

his
Augustin + Roy
mark
William Hands

---

[8]William Hands was engaged in trade at Detroit as early as 1781. At the time of the American occupation of Detroit he signified his intention of remaining a British subject, and in 1799 built a house that is still occupied at the corner of Rosedale and Sandwich streets, Windsor. This property had been donated by the Huron Indians to Jean B. Reaume, from whom Hands purchased it in 1794. Hands held many local offices at Sandwich, being sheriff, treasurer, postmaster, customs officer, and register of the Surrogate Court for the Western District. He died at Sandwich, February 20, 1836.

H 15 Russell to the Anglican Bishop of Quebec[9]
[*The Russell Papers, II, 97*]

Upper Canada York
22nd February, 1798

... Yet it is at the same time my wish that no time should be lost in placing a discreet good Clergyman at Sandwich and giving him a Church there; because its Vicinage to a Military Frontier of the United States whose Soldiers are daily deserting to this Side exposes it to a most dangerous Contagion; which if not early opposed by the improved Morals of its Inhabitants may spread wide and be ultimately productive of every Evil that can be apprehended from a total disregard to all the Duties we owe to God and Man. The Necessity of such an antidote is moreover strongly impressed on my mind by a letter which I have just received from the Chairman of the Bench for the Western District, where he implores my immediate assistance towards rebuilding their Jail which has been lately burnt—as they have no proper place to confine the Multitudes of American Deserters who are daily committed by the Magistrates for every Crime that can blacken a New Year Kalendar.

H 16 The Anglican Bishop of Quebec to Russell
[*The Russell Papers, II, 178*]

Quebec 12th June, 1798

... I see, and feel very strongly, Sir, the force of your reasoning relative to the expediency of placing, as soon as possible, a discreet good Clergyman at Sandwich. The manifold evils which immediately flow in, wherever there is a total suspension of Religious and Moral instruction, acquire, undoubtedly great additional activity from the local circumstances mentioned by you; but they are of themselves and in all cases, of a nature so malignant as to produce a perversion in principle, and a profligacy in practice utterly inconsistent with the duties of good men, and of good subjects—They are evils no less of political than of moral consideration, and, feeling them to be such, I can not but deeply regret the long delays that have already taken place, and the ground that has perhaps irrevocably been lost. ...

H 17 Russell to the Duke of Portland
[*The Russell Papers, II, 200*]

Upper Canada
York 4th July, 1798

... The Western District being the only one which has reported to me its appointment of Wardens to take charge of the Monies to be

[9]Rt. Rev. Jacob Mountain, the first Anglican Bishop of Quebec.

collected & appropriated for the building a Church therein, I have as yet drawn on the Lords of the Treasury towards this Service for only two Hundred Pounds in favor of the Wardens of Sandwich, to enable them to build an Episcopal Church in that Town.

H 18   MARRIAGE REGISTER FOR THE WESTERN DISTRICT
[George F. Macdonald Collection]

Marriage Register for the Western District of the Province of Upper Canada, pursuant to an Act of the Legislature of said Province, passed in the thirty third year of King George the Third, entitled, "An Act to confirm and make valid, certain Marriages heretofore contracted in the Country now comprised within the Province of Upper Canada, and to provide for the future solemnization of Marriage within the same".

W.R.C. Pe.[10]

SAMPLE ENTRIES OF MARRIAGE CONFIRMATION (pp. 9–10)
Province of Upper Canada
Western District

I Angus Mackintosh[11] of Detroit Merchant do solemnly swear in the presence of Almighty God that I did publicly intermarry with Archange St. Martin at Detroit aforesaid on the seventeenth day of June One thousand seven hundred and eighty three, and that there is living issue of the said Marriage, Duncan Mackintosh born on the Twenty fourth day of September One thousand seven hundred & Eighty five, Alexander Mackintosh born on the Twenty third day of August One thousand seven hundred and Eighty Seven, Anne Mackintosh born on the first day of April One Thousand seven hundred and Ninety, Archange Mackintosh born on the Twenty fifth day of April One Thousand Seven hundred and Ninety three & Isabelle Mackintosh born on the seventeenth of March One thousand seven hundred and ninety five.

signed Angus Mackintosh

I Archange St. Martin do solemnly swear in the presence of Almighty God that I did publicly intermarry with Angus Mackintosh of Detroit Merchant on the seventeenth day of June . . . [rest as above].

signed Archange St. Martin

---

[10]Walter Roe was granted a lot in the New Settlement in 1787, and was listed as a warrant officer in the Marine Department. On the organization of the judicial department of the District of Hesse he undertook the practice of law. He was for some years Clerk of the Court at Detroit. On August 7, 1801, he fell into the river and was drowned.

[11]Angus McIntosh was born near Inverness, Scotland, in 1762. He came to Detroit in early manhood, and in 1783 married Mary Archange Baudry dit Desbuttes dit St. Martin. On the American occupation of Detroit McIntosh removed to the south side of the river, where he built a mansion called Moy House (at the foot of present Moy Avenue). He prospered in trade as a factor of the North West Company. His wife died at Moy House, July 13, 1827, and was buried in Assumption cemetery. In 1831 McIntosh returned to Scotland where he died January 25, 1833.

I William Harffy Esquire, one of his Majestys Justices of the Peace for the said Western District, do hereby certify, that on the thirty first day of May in the year of our Lord One thousand seven hundred and ninety six, I administered an Oath to Angus and Archange Mackintosh, of Detroit, to the effect herein before set forth, agreeable to an Act passed in the second Session of the Legislature of his Majesty's said Province of Upper Canada, entitled "an Act to confirm and make valid certain Marriages, heretofore contracted in the Country now comprised within the Province of Upper Canada, and to provide for the future solemnization of Marriage, within the same." In Testimony whereof I have hereunto set my hand, and affixed my seal, at Detroit aforesaid, in the Province aforesaid, the day and month and year above written.

(signed) Wm. Harffy J.P.[12] W.D.

Registered the 2nd of June, 1796
W. Roe C. Pe & Sess. Wn. Dt.

SAMPLE ENTRY OF MARRIAGE (pp. 14–15)
Western District
Province of Upper Canada

Whereas Thomas McKee and Theresa Askin, both of the said District, were desirous of intermarrying with each other, and there being no Parson or Minister of the Church of England, living within eighteen miles of them, or either of them, they have applied to me for that purpose. Now these are to certify that in pursuance of the powers granted by an Act of the Legislature of this Province, passed in the thirty third year of His Majesty's Reign, I Prideaux Selby, Esquire, one of His Majesty's Justices of the Peace, having caused the previous notice by the statute required to be given, have this day married the said Thomas McKee and Theresa Askin together, and they are become legally contracted to each other in Marriage.

Petite Cote, Parish of L'Assomption, this seventeenth day of April, in the year of Our Lord, One thousand seven hundred and ninety seven.

Present at this Marriage.
(signed)
A. McKee
John Askin   (signed) P. Selby J.P.
Alex Grant—A. Grant
J. Bte. Barthe—P. Grant
Wm. Harffy—A. Askin
Alex Duff.

[12]William Harffy was sent to Detroit as hospital mate in the spring of 1781. In 1786 he succeeded Dr. George Anthon as surgeon of the garrison. He was later garrison surgeon at Amherstburg, where he died shortly prior to June 2, 1802.

LIST OF MARRIAGES CONFIRMED, VALIDATED OR PERFORMED AND REGISTERED BEFORE THE YEAR 1800. THESE ARE ALL REGISTERED BY W. ROE, C.P. & SESS. W.D.

William Macomb and Sarah Dring—Married July 18, 1780; attested Feb. 17, 1796, before Angus Mackintosh J.P. W.D.; registered Feb. 19, 1796.

Walter Roe and Anne Laughton—Married March 1, 1790; attested Feb. 16, 1796, before Wm. Harffy J.P. W.D.; registered Feb. 19, 1796. (This marriage had been performed by Alexander Grant J.P. D.H.)

William Hands and Mary Abbott—Married Dec. 10, 1789; attested May 30, 1796, before Wm. Harffy J.P. W.D.; registered May 31, 1796.

Angus Mackintosh and Archange St. Martin—Married June 17, 1783; attested May 31, 1796, before Wm. Harffy J.P. W.D.; registered June 2, 1796.

Allan Bellingham and Monica Baby—Married by Wm. Park J.P.[13] W.D. March 22, 1795; registered July 1, 1796.

Peter Laughton and Catherine Harsen, both of the River St. Clair—Married Sept 14, 1788; attested before Wm. Park J.P. W.D. Sept. 26, 1796; registered Oct. 5, 1796.

Thomas McKee and Theresa Askin—Married at Petite Côte April 17, 1797, by Prideaux Selby J.P.; registered April 22, 1797.

George Reynolds and Mary Everitt of the River Thames—Married May 29, 1797, by Wm. Shaw J.P.; registered June 14, 1797.

Gregor McGregor and Susan Robert—Married August 12, 1776; attested before Thos. Smith J.P.[14] W.D. May 1, 1796; registered Sept. 8, 1798.

Pierre Labadie otherwise Badichon and Anne Purday both of the Township of Sandwich—Married by Abraham Iredell J.P. Oct. 1, 1798; registered Oct. 2, 1798.

John Askin and Archange Barthe—Married June 21, 1772; attested before Wm. Harffy J.P. Feb. 27, 1798; registered Jan. 29, 1799.

Alexander Grant and Theresa Barthe—Married Sept. 30, 1774; attested before Thomas Smith J.P. Feb. 27, 1798; registered Jan. 26, 1799.

John Sparkman and Susanna Stedman—Married Dec. 17, 1787; attested before Alex. Grant J.P. on April 26, 1796; registered Jan. 23, 1799.

John Pike and Mary More both of Raleigh Township—Married at Sandwich by P. Selby J.P. Oct. 11, 1799; registered Oct. 16, 1799.

[13]William Park was for a long time a partner in the firm of Meldrum and Park of Detroit. Subsequent to the American occupation of Detroit he crossed the river and made his home at Petite Côte. He was among the first four to build a house in the town of Sandwich, where he died October 4, 1811.

[14]Thomas Smith was a deputy surveyor and notary. In the summer of 1788 he was appointed Clerk of the newly instituted Court of Common Pleas. He was intensely loyal to Great Britain, and in 1796 he elected to remain a British subject, and removed to Petite Côte on the south bank of the Detroit River. There he died March 3, 1833.

H 19   REPORT OF THE GRAND JURY RE TOWN OF SANDWICH
[*P.A.C., R.G. 1, E 1 State C, pp. 66–8; available on microfilm at the Ont. Dept. of Public Records and Archives*]

Council Chamber at York 8th August 1800.

Present
The Hone. John Elmsley Chief Justice
   Hone. Aeneas Shaw
   Hone. John McGill

Read the following Presentment from Grand Jury of the Western District.

S. 24

The Grand Jurors of Our Lord the King for the Western District upon their oath present:

1st. That the greatest number of Lots in the Town of Sandwich granted by Government to Individuals in the Month of July 1797 are still unimproved, although the period of three years appointed to improve has since elapsed; and the Settlement of the said Town has been impeded in consequence of the long indulgence granted to the manifest injury of those Persons who have already built, and to the Country at large; and that His Majesty's bounty has been abused, by many of those who had Lots without any intention of improving them; but have actually sold them to others, who could not originally obtain grants. We also Represent as a grievance, that many have obtained Deeds for their Lots, although they remain still unimproved, contrary to the Regulation made by His Honor the President.

2nd. It has been Represented to us by many individuals, as a particular hardship, that they cannot obtain a grant of a Lot, although there are only seven or eight Houses in the whole Town, but that some of them (all British subjects) have been obliged to purchase, and others cannot obtain Lots upon any terms in a suitable situation for their Commerce.

3rd. We strongly recommend to the worshipful Bench, to forward this Representation without delay to His Excellency the Governor, and to entreat him to forfeit all the vacant or unimproved Lots in the Town of Sandwich, and to grant them to the first applicants, under a restriction and penalty that good and sufficient houses shall be built thereon in a certain limited time; by which means the County Town would soon be settled, and add not a little to the wealth of the District.

4th. We further Represent to your Worships, that all the Brush should be cut, and the Streets opened in the said Town immediately, and that all those who hold Lots, whether improved or not, shall be obliged to give a stated labor for that purpose, and we also Recommend your attention to the Roads between Amherstsburgh and Sandwich, particularly about the dangerous River Canard which is almost impassable.

Jury Room Sandwich 8th July 1800.
Signed R. Pattinson, Foreman, Alex Duff, John McGregor, Robert Innis, Thomas Forsyth, Hipolite, Janis, J. B. Tourneux, Fr. Pratte, Louis Goyeaux, Claude Reaume, Jacque Parent, Julien Parent, Antoine Bouffard, fils, Paul LaSaline, Joseph Pillet—

I certify the foregoing to be a true copy of the Presentment Filed and Read before the grand Jury in general Quarter Sessions at Sandwich, this 8th day of July 1800.

(signed) W. Roe CP&S W District.

Recommended, that a Surveyor be employed to examine and Report the improvement made on each individual Lot in Sandwich.

H 20 ALEXANDER McKEE TO RUSSELL
[The Russell Papers, *II, 285*]

Amherstburg 17th October 1798

I take the Earliest Opportunity of informing you that I was in hopes that the meeting of the several nations at this place to receive their annual supplies would have been so general as to put it into my Power to have got the Deeds for Sandwich perfected but some Chiefs of the several tribes of Hurons being absent who were deemed by them necessary to be present, that Nation declined doing anything in the business untill their return; and as the other Nations will be always ready I Judged it best to defer the matter untill all the parties concerned should be present at the same time in Order to compleat the business to the satisfaction of the whole.

H 21 SIR JOHN JOHNSON TO RUSSELL
[The Russell Papers, *III, 212–13*]

Fort George 26th May 1799

The Indians being all out in their hunting grounds, and not likely to return to the neighbourhood of Malden or Sandwich for a considerable time, and finding that Hurons had not finally agreed to the sale of the Land around Sandwich, I thought it most adviseable for the good of the service that Capt. Claus[15] who had gone with me in the Capacity of acting Depy. Superintendt. Genl. should return to this Post as the most Central and nearest the seat of Government leaving Capt. McKee to transact the business of the Department at Amherstburg & I have no doubt the Hurons will readily come into the measure of granting a part of the reserve near the Fort and to confirm the purchase of Sandwich when

---

[15]Captain William Claus, grandson of Sir William Johnson, succeeded Colonel Alexander McKee as Deputy Superintendent-General and Deputy Inspector-General of Indian Affairs.

a Power may be given to Captain McKee to finish that Business should it not be thought necessary to send Capt. Claus for that purpose.

H 22   CAPTAIN THOMAS MCKEE[16] TO CAPTAIN WILLIAM CLAUS
[*P.A.C., C 252, p. 317;* M.H.C., *XX, 657–8*]

Amherstburg 4th Sept. 1799

My letter of the 17th August informs you of the meeting with the Wyandots on the 10th and that no occasion might be let slip which might facilitate the compleating of the Sandwich purchase, I informed the Chiefs of that Nation, that as I understood the greatest part of them were preparing to go to their hunting grounds, and were desirous of receiving their share of the goods sent up for the payment of the said purchase, I had no objection to comply with their request to have the goods immediately, provided they appointed two or three Chiefs who meant to stay at home to execute the Deed in the name of their Nation as soon as the Chiefs of the Ottawas & Chippewas could be conveniently assembled. This they readily complied with, and their share of the goods was delivered accordingly: of course there is now no kind of difficulty in finishing the business as soon as you can come up, or send me an authority for that purpose. I would by no means have taken this step without orders had I not been well assured of the necessity and propriety of permanently finishing the business with the Wyandotts, who heretofore made a considerable difficulty in it. You will please also to pardon my having proposed to this Nation without your permission to give to the Crown sixty feet of road through their reserve between Amherstburg & Sandwich, without which these Townships were not connected, nor could the Commissioner of High Ways or overseers compel statute labor so that the road might be made safe and commodious.

The Wyandots immediately agreed to give it, and I submit to you the propriety of obtaining an authority to accept the same, and of inserting the description thereof in the Sandwich Deed.

H 23   SALE OF THE HURON CHURCH RESERVE
[*Treaty No. 12,* Indian Treaties and Surrenders *(1905), I, 30–2*]

[Sept. 11, 1800]

To all whom these presents may come, Greeting.

WHEREAS we, the principal Chiefs, Warriors and people of the Ottawa, Chippewa, Powtawatamie and Wyandot nations of Indians, being desirous for a certain consideration, hereafter shown, of selling and disposing of a certain parcel or Tract of Land, situate, lying and being on

---

[16]Captain Thomas McKee was the son of Colonel Alexander McKee. On April 17, 1797, he married Thérèse Askin, and in 1799 they were living at Petite Côte. He died in Lower Canada in the spring of 1815.

the South East side of the Detroit River and known by the name of the Huron Church Reserve unto His Britannic Majesty King George the Third our Great Father; Now know ye that we the said principal Chiefs, Warriors and people of the Ottawa, Chippewa, Powtawatamie and Wyandot Nations for and in consideration of Three Hundred pounds Quebec Currency, value in goods estimated according to the Montreal price, and now delivered to us, the receipt whereof we hereby acknowledge, Have given, granted, sold, disposed of and confirmed, and by these presents Do give, grant, sell, dispose of and confirm forever unto Captain Thomas McKee, Superintendent of Indian Affairs for and on behalf of His said Britannic Majesty King George the Third His Heirs and Successors, all that parcel or Tract of Land known and called as aforesaid by the name of the Huron Church Reserve, beginning at a stone Boundary between the lands of the said Captain Thomas McKee and the said Huron Church Reserve; from thence following the windings up the said River to a certain Creek, about one hundred and fifty-seven yards above a windmill belonging or lately belonging to Messieurs Baby; thence South seventy-three degrees East forty-three Chains and sixty-four Links; thence South Twenty-eight degrees East one hundred and thirty-four chains and two Links; and thence north seventy-four degrees West one hundred and sixty-one Chains and forty links till it intersects the said River Detroit, which intersection is the station or place of beginning, Containing by admeasurement One thousand and seventy-eight Acres be the same more or less, and is more particularly described by a sketch of the same hereunto annexed, and colored Red.

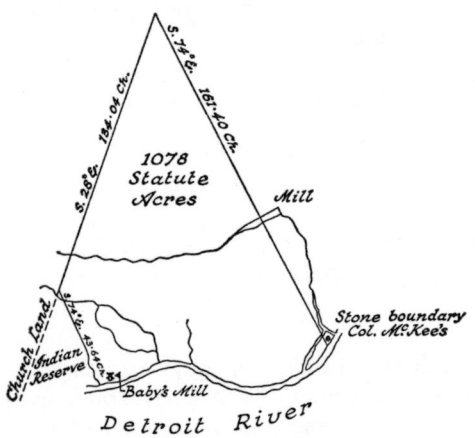

AND WHEREAS it appeared to us in Council that the ground about His said Majesty's Garrison of Amherstburg was too small and confined, and that a Road was wanted in and through the Huron Reserve to connect the Communication between the Township of Sandwich and the said

Garrison. We Did on the tenth day of August in the year one thousand seven hundred and ninety-nine, offer as a gift to the said Captain Thomas McKee, for and on behalf of His said Majesty, as follows, that is to say, an additional space of five hundred yards, extending up the stream from a painted Tree, which was the former boundary between the said Garrison and the Huron Reserve; thence East the whole Depth thereof; and from thence South until it intersects the East Line of the said former boundary; And also a space of sixty feet wide for a road of communication as aforesaid, to be laid out in such parts of the said Huron Reserve, as shall or may be thought most convenient by any persons or person acting under the authority of His Majesty's Government; And we having been informed by the said Capt. Thomas McKee that His Excellency the Commander in Chief has directed him to accept in the name of His Majesty, the said lands as a Gift from us, Now know ye, That we, the principal Chiefs of the Ottawa, Chippewa, Powtawatamie and Wyandot Nations of Indians in consideration of our good will and affection for our Great Father, His said Majesty, King George the Third, Have given, granted and confirmed, and by these presents Do give, grant and confirm, as a free and voluntary Gift to the said Captain Thomas McKee, for and on behalf of His said Majesty, His Heirs and Successors for ever, the said space of Five Hundred yards extending up the stream from a Painted Tree, which was the former Boundary, Thence East the whole depth of said Huron Reserve, and from thence south until it intersects the East line of the said former boundary as is more particularly described by a sketch thereof also hereunto annexed marked H.R.

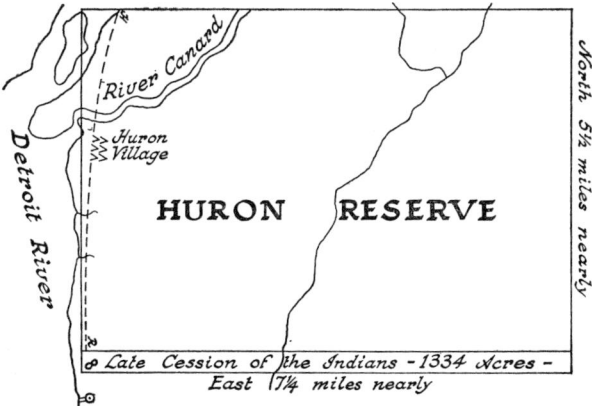

red; And also the space of Sixty feet wide in and through the said Huron Reserve for the purpose of a Road to be laid out in such parts of the same lying between the said Garrison of Amherstburg and the Township of Sandwich, as shall or may be thought most convenient by any person or persons acting under the authority of His said Majesty's Government, the whole of the two parcels or Tracts of Land last mentioned, containing Thirteen Hundred and Eighty acres or thereabouts, be the same more or less, To Have and to Hold all the said several parcels or Tracts of Land together with all the woods and waters thereon unto the said Captain Thomas McKee for and on behalf of His said Britannic Majesty King George the Third, His Heirs and successors for ever, free and clear of and from all claims, rights, privileges and emoluments which we the said Chiefs, Warriors and people of the Ottawa, Chippewa, Powtawatamie and Wyandot Nations might have before the execution of these presents, And free and clear of any pretended claims which our children or Descendants may hereafter make to the same, hereby renouncing and forever divesting ourselves, our children, Descendants and Posterity of all Title to the said several parcels or Tracts of Land and the soil, woods and waters thereof, in favour of the said Captain Thomas McKee for and on behalf of His said Britannic Majesty, His Heirs and Successors forever.

IN WITNESS WHEREOF we have for ourselves and the rest of our Nations respectively set our marks and seals this Eleventh Day of September, in the year of our Lord one thousand and Eight Hundred, having first heard this instrument interpreted openly in our several languages, and fully approved by ourselves and our respective nations.

Witnesses present at the Execution of this Instrument:
F. Baby, } Commissioners for the Province
Alex. Duff, } of Upper Canada
H. McLean, Capt.R.C.V. Commanding
Alex. McMillan, Capt. R.C.V.
L. R. C. DeLery, Capt. R.C.V.
Wm. Bachwell, Lt. R. Engineers
John Suth'd Sinclair, Lt. R. Artillery
J. I. Duchesnoy, Lieut. R.C.V.
Rob't Woolsey, Ensign R.C.Vols.
Stephen McVay, Ensign R.C.V.
Geo. Ironside, Lt. K. & Clk. 1. Dept.
Simon + Girty's Mark
T. Alexander Clarke.
Charleveaume.
John Martin.

T. McKee, S.I.A., for and on behalf of His Majesty (L.S.)
(totem) Witanis (L.S.)
(totem) Galash (L.S.)
(totem) Pshikie (L.S.)
(totem) Nakatewaquit (L.S.)
(totem) Nangy (L.S.)
(totem) Ustaiechta or Round Head (L.S.)
(totem) Ruhumatt, or One Canoe (L.S.)
(totem) Utreaupowannie or Great Batt. (L.S.)
(totem) Sahenteskon (L.S.)
(totem) Desharemoi (L.S.)
(totem) Eshkibie (L.S.)
(totem) Nashan (L.S.)
(totem) Waginai (L.S.)
(totem) Kagekumego or Otter (L.S.)
(totem) Wishawas (L.S.)
(totem) Kievehiwen (L.S.)
(totem) Kageskaiva (L.S.)
(totem) Pisortim or Turner (L.S.)
(totem) Toquish (L.S.)

[Jan. 3, 1801]

We do hereby certify that the following goods were delivered in our presence to the respective Nations of Indians, subscribers to the within Deed, being the consideration therein mentioned.

						£	s	d
Blankets	3 point, 20 pairs at 19s. 6d............................					19	10	0
	2½ " 50 " 15s. 9d.............................					39	7	6
	2 " 50 " 11s. 6d.............................					28	15	0
	1½ " 40 " 9s. 4½d					18	15	0
	1 " 25 " 7s. 10½.......................					9	16	10½
Kettles	Copper, 64 lbs. at 3s. 1½d...........................					10	0	0
	Brass, 86 " 2s. 4½d...........................					10	4	3
Pipes, gross, 10 at 2s. 7½d.................................						1	6	3
Strouds, blue, 5 pieces at 117s per piece............................						29	5	0
Tobacco, 200 lbs. at 13½....................................						11	5	0
Cloth.....	Scarlet, 12 yds at 16s. 6d............................					9	18	0
	Green, 7 " 15s.............................					5	5	0
	Blue, 7 " 15s.............................					5	5	0
Caddee, 2 pieces, containing 108 yds at 3s. 9d....................						20	5	0
Silk handkerchiefs, 3 doz. at 60s............................						9	0	0
Calico, 3 pieces at 58s. 6d..................................						8	15	16
Knives, butchers', 12 doz. at 4s. 6d...........................						2	14	0
Irish linen, 4 pieces at 3s.................................						15	0	0
Pewter Basins	12 of 1 pint		weighing 50 lbs at 1s. 9d......................			4	7	6
	8 of 1 quart							
	12 of 3 quarts							
	2 of 4 "							
Ball, 3 boxes of 112 lbs. each at 33s. 9d...........................						5	1	3
Shot, Nos. 1,2 & 3, 3 boxes of 112 lbs each at 33s. 9d...............						5	1	3
Gunpowder, 100 lbs at 1s. 10½d..............................						9	7	6
Rum, 23 galls, at 7s.....................................						8	1	0
A bullock...						13	14	2
						£300	0	½

Amounting in the whole to three hundred pounds, Quebec currency.

F. Baby ⎱ Commissioners for the
Alex. Duff ⎰ Province of Upper Canada
L. R. C. De Lery, Capt. R.C.V.
John Suthd. Sinclair, Lieut, Royal Artillery
Robert Woolsey, Ensn, R.C.V.
Geo. Ironside, Lieut. K. & Clk. I.D.
T. Alex Clark
John Martin

H. McLean, Capt. R.C.V. Commanding
Alex McMillan, Capt. R.C.V.
Wm. Backwell, Lieut Royal Engineers
B. Duchesnay, Lieut. R.C.V.
Stephen McKay, Ensn. R.C.V.
Simon + Girty's mark Charleveaume

Recorded in the Register for the County of Essex, on the third day of January, one thousand eight hundred and one, at ten o'clock in the forenoon. Libr. A. Folio 111, 112, 113, 114, 115.

P. Selby,
  Ass't Sec., Indian Agent

Richard Pollard,
  Registrar

H 24 EXTRACT FROM GOTHER MANN'S[17] REPORT TO LORD DORCHESTER
[*P.A.C., Q 47–1, pp. 116–18;* M.H.C., *XII, 32*]

December 6, 1788

. . .

Re Communication from Lake Erie to Detroit. . . . I therefore think it

---

[17]Gother Mann was a British military engineer, commanding Royal Engineers at Quebec from 1785 to 1793. He drew many of the maps and plans of fortifications that are preserved at the Public Archives of Canada.

may be safely concluded that there is no ship channel from Lake Erie up this River to the Westward of Gross Isle, and particularly when it is considered that the Waters of the Lake and River were at least three or four feet higher this year, than has ever been remembered at any former period.

The best Channel for Vessels passing this communication to or from Lake Erie, is between the Island Bois Blanc, and the East Main Shore; there is however another tolerable channel to the Westward of the Island, which I likewise examined but this unites with the former close in with the North End of the Island. I am therefore of the opinion that the best situation for a Post, will be on the Main Shore opposite to the North end of the Island Bois Blanc, as such position will command both Channels, every Vessel being obliged to come within Five Hundred yards of it. There is good and safe anchorage in the Channel between the Island and the Main Shore; that shore is also well adapted for wharfs and other conveniences for Naval or Commercial purposes; and to which a post as above described would afford good protection; and if a Battery was constructed on the South end of the Island, the whole of this Channel and Harbour would be secured. . . .

H 25 MINUTES OF THE LAND BOARD OF HESSE FOR FRIDAY, 14TH AUGUST 1789, RE GEORGE TOWN
[*Fraser,* Third Report of the Archives of Ontario, *1905, pp. 2–3*]

The Board received, and having under consideration the Letter from Mr. Secretary Motz of the 15th June, respecting the immediate settlement of George Town, have made the necessary inquiries, into the claim of Indians, or others, being obstacles to the immediate execution of the Plan, learn from Alexander McKee Esquire, Deputy Superintendant of Indians, that the land has never yet been bought from the Indians for the use of the Crown, and that he has no instructions from Sir John Johnson, the Superintendant-General on that head, but that the Indians have actually divested themselves of that land by deed bearing date 7th June, 1784—in favor of certain officers and others who served with them during the war.

The board having seen the Deed proceeded to enquire upon what authority it was received, and if the land is improved by the parties, find that upon the representation of Captain Caldwell subsequent to the Indian grant His Excellency, Sir Frederick Haldimand then commander in chief, did by letter the 14th August, 1784, to John Hay,[18] Esquire then Lieutenant Governor of Detroit enjoin all due encouragement to captains Caldwell and Elliott to settle on the land now pointed out for George Town; that in obedience to their injunction Governor Hay did actually by letter cause the lines to be run by Mr. Fry allotting six acres

---

[18]The correct name is Jehu Hay.

only in front to Captains, Bird, McKee, Caldwell and Elliott, that those gentlemen having claim by special promise from the Indians did actually occupy forty acres in front being the space fronting the whole length of the Island of Bois Blanc, in which possession they were confirmed so lately as in 1788 by Major Mathews who in person accompanied by Captain McKee one of the Board, and Mr. Hughes as surveyor extended the lines to ten arpents for each farmer and planted the Pickets for their lines which have since been run out, in conformity to those Pickets, by Mr. Thomas Smith sometime Acting Deputy Surveyor.

As Major Mathews acted under written Instructions from His Excellency the Right Honorable Lord Dorchester whereof Copy is before the Board, they conceive that it would not be agreeable to His Lordship under such circumstances to press obedience to the instructions of the 14th June in relation to the proposed establishment of George Town. . . . In this conviction the Board resolves to forbear any orders to the Deputy Surveyor on the subject of the proposed Town opposite the Island of Bois Blanc until further instructed. . . .

H 26 MEMORANDUM BY GOTHER MANN TO LIEUTENANT-GOVERNOR SIMCOE
[*Cruikshank*, The Simcoe Papers, *IV, 122–3*]

Quebec, 4th Novr. 1795

A general Statement of the Buildings which it is supposed may be necessary to be immediately provided for lodging Troops, depositing and preserving the King's provisions, and Naval and Military Stores at the undermentioned places, Vizt.

On the ground opposite the Isle aux Bois Blanc, near the entrance of the Streights from Lake Erie leading to Detroit.

Two Blockhouses to contain Fifty Men each, for the protection of the Naval and Military Stores, &c.

A Store house having dimensions about three thousand feet of flooring for Provisions Marine & General stores.

An Ordinance Store house and small Magazine having in dimensions together about fifteen hundred feet of flooring.

A Wharf contiguous to the proposed Naval yard for the King's Vessels and Boats, to take in or discharge their loading &c.

N.B. It is proposed that the several Blockhouses and Store Houses before mentioned should be constructed of good squared Log work on Stone foundations, and that the necessary materials hereafter specified should be provided at each place during the Winter, so that the Work may be begun upon at the earliest period the season will permit, and carried on with all possible dispatch.

H 27　Lieutenant-Colonel R. G. England to Simcoe
[The Simcoe Papers, *IV, 159*]

Detroit, December 16th, 1795

I received yesterday by Express a letter from Captain Green,[19] Military Secretary, enclosing a list of materials directed to be immediately provided here for building in the Spring, two Block Houses, two Stores and a wharf on the ground opposite the Island of Bois Blanc near the entrance of the Strait leading from Lake Erie to Detroit. Those buildings he mentions are for lodging Troops, depositing the King's Provisions, Naval and Military stores preparatory to evacuating this Post. Measures will be immediately taken on my part to provide the materials directed, at least such part of them as can be procured before the navigation opens.

H 28　Dorchester to Simcoe
[The Simcoe Papers, *IV, 181*]

Quebec, 25th Jany, 1796

Though the Ratification of the Treaty with the United States is not officially announced, the Evacuation of the Posts, I have reason to believe will take place at the time fixed and as a means of facilitating that measure you will desire the respective Commanding Officers to cause General Surveys to be held without delay on all the King's Stores and effects, and to make returns of all such as shall be found unfit for use, not worth removing or impracticable to remove, that orders may be given for their destruction, or otherwise, as the case may require. Such Engineer's Stores and Tools as remain at the Miamis, are to be immediately removed from thence, they being necessary to the service directed to be performed opposite the Isle of Bois Blanc. To prevent delay copies of the foregoing are forwarded to the Officers Commanding the Posts of Niagara and Detroit, that in case of not receiving your orders immediately no time may be lost in carrying the Services into execution.

H 29　England to Green
[*P.A.C., C 249, p. 77;* M.H.C., *XII, 203*]

Detroit April 25th 1796

. . .

On the 15 Inst. I reported to you, that the frame of the shed for the Temporary Deposit of Stores belonging to the Ordnance and Commissary General's Departments, was nearly finished here, and am now to

[19]Captain James Green was appointed military secretary to Lord Dorchester in 1795, and continued to serve, in this capacity, other commanders of the forces in Canada until 1807.

report that a Raft containing the Frame & Covering of this Shed, with other materials for the buildings proposed to be erected at the Entrance of the River, dropped down on the 20th Instant, to the ground where they are to be erected.

A detachment from the Garrison, accompanied with Lieutenant Cooper is also gone down to assist in Carrying into Execution as expeditiously as possible, the different services that are directed. . . .

H 30 ENGLAND TO GREEN
[P.A.C., C 249, pp. 129–30; M.H.C., XII, 209]

Detroit, May 27th, 1796

. . . All the stores that can be spared at present from this Post, except Powder, are sent to the Rivers Mouth, where they are under Cover, in the sheds ordered to be erected for that purpose, & I have directed that every exertion should be used in finishing the Block Houses, intended for the accomodation and Protection of the Troops, Materials sufficient for this service are already delivered by the several Contractors. One Captain, one Lieutenant, and Thirty men are sent down there for the protection of the Stores, and to assist in the works. More could not with propriety be spared from this very weak garrison.

Some Expense has been unavoidably incurred in the removal of the Stores, and particularly in removing the timber from the Naval Yard, All which, with the exception of some very heavy Oak Timber, now almost decayed, has been with two thousand Pickets, made into several Rafts, and towed at different times, down the River by strong Parties from the garrison—and I have the Satisfaction of Reporting that not a foot of timber that could be Converted into any use is left here. . . .

H 31 ENGLAND TO JAMES WILKINSON
[P.A.C., Wolford, Simcoe Papers, Book 8, M.G. 23, H 1, 1, 1, 3, p. 256;
M.H.C., XII, 220; Cruikshank, The Simcoe Papers, *IV, 296–7]*

Detroit, June 10th, 1796

I had the Honor of receiving by your Aide de Camp, Captain Shaumburg, your letter under date the 27th Ulto, mentioning your wish to concert with me, such Measures as may be deemed expedient for delivering up this Post to you, and requesting to know the day that it would be convenient for me to withdraw the Troops under my command from the Territory of the United States.

And in answer beg to inform you, that in consequence of orders from His Excellency Lord Dorchester, Buildings are erecting on the ground directed by His Excellency to be occupied on the opposite side of this River, for the accomodation of His Majesty's Troops and the protection of Stores, preparatory to evacuating this Post, agreeably to the Treaty of amity, commerce and navigation, concluded between Great Britain and the United States, and that those Buildings and other preparations directed by His Excellency, are now in great forwardness, but not having yet received His final orders, to evacuate the Posts under my Command, it is not possible for me to fix a Day for that purpose.

I have, however, strong reason for supposing that those orders will not be unnecessarily delayed, and when I receive them, it will afford me much Pleasure in communicating to you the time I shall be able to withdraw the Troops, and to Concert with you, such measures as may be deemed expedient for your immediately occupying the Posts under my direction.

I beg further to add that from the preparations already made, a few days will be sufficient to accomplish the Transport of the Troops and the remaining stores, to the Post, ordered to be occupied on the opposite side of this River.

To Brigadier Gen'l Wilkinson
Commanding the Troops of the United States &c.

H 32   CAPTAIN WM. MAYNE TO GREEN
[*P.A.C., C 382, pp. 47–51;* M.H.C., *XXII, 402–3*]

Detroit River Sept 8th. 1796

I have the honor to enclose to be laid before his Excellency, the Commander in Chief, abstracts of ordinance stores issued, and received at Detroit, and at this Post, between the 16th of November 1795 and the first September 1796—as also to acknowledge your letter to Captain Salmon, or Officer Commanding at this post, dated Quebec 15th August 1796, with its enclosure—

The dangerous state of the Hull of the Felicity, renders it necessary that the powder remaining for the use of this Post, as well as that for the service of The Indian Department, should be immediately removed to a more secure deposit—in consequence, on the return of His Majesty's schooner the Dunmore, (which will be then laid up at this Post) it is expedient that, that vessel should be employed, as the best temporary means of keeping the gun powder and fixed ammunition in safety until the temporary Magazine approved of to be erected, ("should the officer commanding not find a place near this Garrison of sufficient safety for the powder remaining here") is compleated—

I shall transmit the necessary Estimates of the Expences, of the work in question to Head Quarters, observing that it is finished in the most suitable and economical manner—

I have reason to fear that the merchants, who have already erected buildings on the ground within the line of defence of the Post under my Command, will not be easily reconciled to the Sentiments of the Commander in Chief on that Subject. They have not merely built temporary sheds, some of their buildings are valuable, and have cost to the amount of Many Hundred Pounds, authorised in these their proceedings by Colonel England, who hitherto commanded this district—at the same time they were to hold these lots on limited terms.

With due deference, I beg to observe I do not know of any vacant land in the vicinity of this Garrison. On the South Side, all land is claimed by Individuals, by Captain Caldwell, formerly of Colonel Butler's Rangers, by Colonel McKee, of the Indian Department, and by Captain Elliot—on the North, the vacant land has not been purchased from the Huron Indians, concerning whom, I have forwarded a letter bearing date the third Instant.

The land in the rear of this Post, beyond the proposed boundary of that which is to be reserved for Government, being 1000 yards from the River, is not Suited to the private interests of Merchants and is a perfect Swamp.

It might be feasible to purchase the Tract of Indian Land adjacent to this Garrison, for the purpose mentioned at the conclusion of your letter, but how far advantageous for Mercantile Situations that might be, I am unable to judge; the proposed land to be reserved for Government, without the line of defence, runs into that tract, near one third of a mile.

I now enclose for the Commander in Chief's inspection, a plan of a Town laid out by Colonel Caldwell on his own land, who could sell his lots to much advantage to British Subjects wishing to leave the territory of the United States, did he conceive the same would meet with the approbation of His Excellency. It may be remarked that part of this Town borders on the proposed line of defence, that circumstance might be ordered otherwise.

It is but just that such British Subjects as wish to remove with their effects within our lines should have a situation suitable to the branches of trade which many of them follow—I am convinced the Commander in Chief will see the necessity of any establishment of the kind, it being as conducive to his Majesty's interest as satisfactory to the views of his loyal Subjects.

H 33   CAPTAIN HECTOR MCLEAN[20] TO GREEN
[*P.A.C., C 250, pp. 103–10;* M.H.C., *XX, 524–5*]

Amherstburg, 3rd August
1797

I arrived here on the 22nd & took command of the Post on the 24th ultimo.

[20]Captain Hector McLean came to America with the Eighty-fourth Regiment in 1779. He was a captain in the Royal Canadian Volunteers from its organization in 1796 until its disbandment in 1802. He succeeded Captain Mayne as commander of the post at Amherstburg on July 24, 1797, and in 1802 he returned to his former home in Kingston.

I have since received your Letters of the 21st & 30th June & in compliance with the former have ordered the Board of Survey on the Gun Powder as directed; the proceedings of which I enclose for the Commander in Chief's information. The contents of the letter, conveying proposals for repairing the Ottawa &c. shall likewise be duly attended to, and shall be forwarded by me as much as possible consistent with the strength of the garrison; I have however to observe that the number of our men now at this Post is scarcely sufficient to carry on the multiplicity of work already in hand, Chiefly performed by soldiers & that should there be any additional work ordered, it will be very difficult if not impracticable to carry it into execution with our present numbers, considering that we have several old men, but ill calculated for Labourious work, I have notwithstanding the satisfaction to find the work go on cheerfully and I believe with more expedition than in the time of our predecessors. Capt. Vigneau's Company being almost all recruits & totally undisciplined I conceive it would have been more conducive to His Majesty's Service had Col. McDonell kept him at the Head Quarters of the Regt. and sent an older Company in their place, by that means they might have had a better opportunity & more leisure for instruction. I am further obliged to say that I labour under great inconvenience from the ignorance of the officers as well as the men in every point of their duty.

His Excellency may rest assured that as far as depends on me nothing shall be wanting to carry his orders completely into execution, but I repeat it our numbers are too few. Had Col. McDonell sent the Lt. Infantry or indeed any other Company we could do better particularly as I could not trust the recruits on guard until they had been some time at Drill, which made the Duty heavier on the rest. Neither the officers nor men's Quarters are yet finished. The magazine but begun a few days previous to my arrival. The Frame of the Store House not yet up and the wharf only begun. I must however do the Engineer Lieut. Cooper the justice to say that he is very assiduous & attentive. I cannot as yet pretend to pass an opinion on any thing at the Post, but I can already perceive that the expenses of the Indians are enormous particularly in the consumption of provisions & I think may in some degree be checked without the least detriment to the service but quite the reverse. I find that some time previous to my arrival here some Indians had been sent towards the Mississippi with a view to gain intelligence of the Spaniards in that Quarter, they are soon expected to return, when if they bring any intelligence it shall be communicated. My reasons for mentioning this are that I suppose His Excellency is already apprized of the apparent Hostile disposition of the Spaniards in that Quarter towards the United States, by refusing to deliver up agreeable to Treaty the Posts within their Boundary Line on the frivolous pretence of guarding against an Expedition from Canada & instead of laying out the Line of Division employing the men intended for that purpose in strengthening the Fortifications of the Natchez & Walnut hills.

H 34 McLean to Green
[*P.A.C., C 250, pp. 123–5;* M.H.C., *XII, 267*]

Amherstburg 18th August 1797

... The two small Block houses for the protection of the Stores now building and Flanking it, tho' apparently very well adapted to answer the end proposed, yet being at the distance of near half a mile from the North Block House opposite the end of Isle au Bois Blan, occupied with troops above, & ordnance stores & fixed ammunition below, it can hardly be expected, that any aid or protection they can either give or receive at such a distance will be of Consequence.

The Magazine now building however well placed according to the Original Plan, is likewise so detached from the last mentioned Block House, as to render its Situation in my opinion rather precarious in case of alarm, from any ill designing persons, in the event the powder was deposited in it. I have however the satisfaction to say that I have not the smallest Cause to suppose that there are any such in our Vicinity. In short I say that however proper the original plan of defence may be to answer the intended purpose, it is by much too extensive and by no means Calculated to afford immediate protection with the present force, in case of need; and so far from having our small force, as well as stores, separated & detached as at present, I am of opinion there ought to be some place of security for the troops and stores proportionate to our number while the whole might act in concert, covered by a small entrenchment or abbatis, which might soon be effected, and would at least set Indians at defiance.

The plan best suited in my opinion for this purpose, is near the two Block houses, & the New Store which will soon be up, for the reception of all the Stores, the Gunpowder might be lodged with safety in that part of the store under ground sufficiently secured at top, the two Blockhouses might upon an emergency Contain the greatest part of our men, if not the whole, and the laid up vessels at the wharf in front of the Store, would afford an additional security. Thus our whole force would be Compact and drawn within a small Compass to enable them to act with vigour, which might perhaps be proper in case of Alarm, tho' at present I see no appearance of anything to interrupt our tranquility, unless the Spaniards might send some emissaries to corrupt the Indians....

H 35 Requisition for Stores Proposed as Presents for Indians Resorting to the Post of Amherstburg for the Year 1797
[*P.A.C., C 250, pp. 426–8;* M.H.C., *XII, 256–9*]

						£		
Arm Bands Pairs thirty				@	11s	16	10	—
Axes Half Number Two hundred					2	20	—	—
Ball & Shot Pounds Twelve Thousand				22s per cwt		117	19	10½
Bath Coating White pieces three								
do	Grey	do	do		82	49	4	—
do	Blue	do	do					
do	Brown	do	do					

Bar Lead pounds Four hundred......................	19	3 16 11	
Basons Pewter Number, one hundred & fifty..........		14 8 1	
Blankets one point pairs Two hundred................	5 6d	55 — —	
do 1½ " do Two hundred................	6 6	65 — —	
do 2 " do Four hundred...............	8	160 — —	
do 2½ " do Five hundred...............	11	275 — —	
do 3 " do Five hundred...............	13 6	371 5 —	
Bed Lace Crimson Gro thirty-four....................	13 6	22 5 6	
do scarlet do thirty three.................	13 6	22 19 —	
do Green do thirty three.................	11 6	18 19 6	
do Blue do twenty.......................	11 6	11 10 —	
Beads, small white, pounds Two hundred.............	9	7 10 —	
Bridles number thirty..............................	3	4 10 —	
Broaches Plain do Four thousand....................	6	100 — —	
Broad Cloth Blue pieces Ten ⎫			
do Green do Five ⎬ ab't 414 Yds..........	9	186 6 —	
do Scarlet do Ten ⎭			
Bunting crimson do Five.......................	24	6 — —	
do blue do Five.......................	20	5 — —	
do white do Five.......................	18	4 10 —	
Buttons large Gilt Gro: Twelve.................	24	14 8 —	
do small " do Twelve.................	12	7 4 —	
do large plated do Twelve.................	30	18 — —	
do small " do Twelve.................	15	9 — —	
do large common do Twelve.................	21	12 12 —	
do small do do Twelve.................	10	6 — —	
Caddees Green pieces ⎫			
do Blue do ⎬			
do Purple do ⎬ about 3032 Yards..............	2 2	328 9 4	
do Brown do ⎭			
Callicoe, three colors pieces thirty five................	36	63 — —	
do two do do thirty five..............	28	49 — —	
Cambric do twelve....................	24	14 8 —	
Combs Horn Dozen Forty..........................	2	4 — —	
" Ivory do Twenty.......................	6	6 — —	
Ear bobs Pairs Four thousand.......................	6½	108 6 8	
Embossed Serge Pieces Fifty........................	53 6	133 15 —	
Feathers Ostrich Number Fifty......................	2 6	6 5	
do Fox Tail diff't colors Number one hundred...	10½	4 7 6	
Ferretting assorted pieces Twenty....................	4 9	5 18 9	
Files Smith do number Twenty two...............		4 10 —	
Files steels Gro. Two..............................	15	1 10 —	
Fish Hooks do Five............................	3	— 15 —	
Flannel white pieces Ten ab't 320 yds................	1 3	20 — —	
do Green do Ten " 360 "	1 6	20 — —	
Gorgets Number Thirty............................	23	34 10 —	
Guns common do Fifty	21	52 10 —	
do Chiefs do Three hundred & fifty.............	36	612 10 —	
do Rifled do Fifty...........................	52 6	131 5 —	
Gun flints do Ten thousand.....................	10 6	5 5 —	
Gun powder pounds four thousand...................	189	378 — —	
Gun worms Number one hundred & 44..............		— 7 —	
Hankerchiefs silk common Band piece Ten..........	60	30 — —	
do " Black " Ten...........	44	22 — —	
Hats fine not Laced Number fifty....................	3 11	9 15 —	
do course do eighty....................	3	12 0 0	
Hoes Broad Carolina do four hundred.............	1 6	30 1 0	
Iron assorted Bars Thirty ab't 12 cwt.................	23	13 16 —	
Knives Buck Handles doz. two hundred..............	3	30 — —	
do Pen do Twelve...................	5	3 — —	
Kettles Brass with Iron ears Nests Eighteen about 1760	19	139 16 —	
do Copper thick do Twelve about 1014.	2 2	109 17 —	
do Tin, w't covers do do Twelve.............	42	25 4 —	
Linen pieces one hundred...........................	45	225 — —	
Lines Cod number fifty............................	2 3	5 12 6	

Item			
do Hambro do twenty............................	2 3	2 5 —	
do Fishing do one hundred and fifty..............	3	1 17 4	
do Mackrel do twenty...........................	3	— 5 —	
Looking Glasses, oval frame, doz. ten.................	11 6	5 15 —	
do do paper " do twenty.............	4	4 — —	
Medals Large do thirty...............	26	39 — —	
Molton purple pieces Fifteen ⎫			
do green do Fifteen ⎪	48	144 — —	
do blue do Fifteen ⎬			
do brown do Fifteen ⎭			
Muslin do Twelve........................	60	36 — —	
Nails Board Casks Two............................	166	16 — —	
Needles number Three thousand......................	4 9	— 14 3	
Oiled clothes number Eighteen......................	40	36 — —	
Osnabrigs pieces Six...............................	72	21 12 —	
Pipes Gross thirty two.............................	1 6	2 8 —	
Ratteen Blue pieces Three ⎫			
New ⎪			
do Green do Three ⎬ £7.4 a piece..............		108 — —	
do Grey do Three ⎪			
do Scarlet do Three ⎪			
do Brown do Three ⎭			
Razors doz Twelve................................	5	3 — —	
Ribbon broad carcinet Crimson ps Twenty ⎫			
do do Green " Twenty ⎪			
do do Lt blue " Twenty ⎬	12	60 — —	
do do Purple " Twenty ⎪			
do do Scarlet " Twenty ⎭			
Rifle Locks, Dble Bridle. Number Fifty..............	8	20 — —	
Romals common pieces Ten ⎫	14	14 — —	
do Blue do Ten ⎭			
Sadles Number Thirty Six..........................	25	45 — —	
Sheeting Russia pieces Twenty......................	58	58 — —	
do Scotch do Fifteen........................	105	78 15 —	
Shoes men pairs one hundred........................	4 4	21 13 4	
Seine Twine pounds Sixty..........................	1 1	3 5 —	
Scissors Large pairs Six Hundred....................	5	12 10 —	
do small pairs One hundred & twenty...........	4	2 — —	
Spectacles do Twenty four....................	1 6	1 16 —	
Steel Bars Twenty four abt 1 cwt 2 q. 0 lb...........	56	4 4 —	
Striped Cotton pieces Forty........................	76	152 — —	
Spunge pounds Ten................................	10	— 8 4	
Swanskin spotted pieces Ten........................	58	29 — —	
Strouds Blue do One hundred................	70	350 — —	
Tea Bohea pounds one hundred......................	2	10 — —	
Tents Six Estimated...............................	120	36 — —	
Thread White assorted pounds Thirty.................	4	6 — —	
do all colors do Seventy..............	2 6	8 15 —	
Tobacco Carrot pounds Three thousand..............	6	75 — —	
Tomahawks Number Two hundred...................	4	40 — —	
Trunks Hair Nests Ten............................	30	15 — —	
Vermillion pounds one hundred......................	4	20 — —	
Worsted Assorted pounds one hundred & 25..........	2	12 10 —	
Wampum Black & White, one half of ea: Fifty thousand	13 6d	33 15 —	
Stlg...........................		5785 10 6½	

Amounting to Five Thousand seven hundred and Eighty five pounds ten shillings, & six pence halfpenny sterling Dollars @ 4s 6d.

Ex^d. Joseph Chew
    S.I.A.

                                          Montreal 9th Feby 1797
                       Approved   John Johnson
                                              Robt Prescott

By order of the Commander in Chief
                    JAMES GREEN M.S.

H 36 RETURN OF PROVISIONS AND RUM ISSUED TO INDIANS AT AMHERSTBURG AND CHENAIL ÉCARTÉ FROM 25 JUNE 1797 TO 24 JUNE 1798 INCLUSIVE
[*P.A.C., C 251, p. 269; M.H.C., XII, 277*]

PERIODS	NO	FLOUR		PORK		PEASE		BUTTER		RICE		CORN			RUM	
		LBS	OZ	LBS	OZ	BUSH	GALL	LBS	OZ	LBS	OZS	BUSH	GAL	PTS	GAL	PTS
From 25 June to 24 July Capt Mayne	267	4,920	8	6256	11	79	4	142	8	129	—	163	7	4	17	—
From 25 July to 24 Augt	244	6,480	—	6335	15	34	7	—	—	6	12	339	3	4	17	—
25 Augt to 24 Sept	235	7,377	—	4937	10	66	1	—	—	7	8	227	5	6	17	—
25 Sept to 24 Oct	339	12,450	—	6600	9	62	2	—	—	—	—	—	—	—	2	—
25 Oct to 24 Nov	218	8,334	—	4325	5	43	2	—	—	—	—	—	—	—	4	4
25 Nov to 24 Dec	132	5,985	—	2310	5	12	7	—	—	—	—	—	—	—	13	—
25 Dec to 24 Jany 1798	—	—	—	—	—	—	—	—	—	—	—	—	—	—	—	—
25 Jany to 23 Feby	80	6,708	—	3336	6	1	6	—	—	—	—	—	—	—	17	—
24 Feby to 24 March	—	—	—	—	—	—	—	—	—	—	—	—	—	—	—	—
25 March to 24 April	196	4,251	—	4467	12	—	4	—	—	—	—	433	3	4	7	—
25 April to 24 May	332	10,215	—	8322	9	—	4	—	—	16	8	363	3	2	80	2
25 May to 24 June	413	21,159	—	13775	14	1	—	—	—	—	—	436	5	6	34	4
		88,479	8	60678	11	302	7	142	8	48	12	1974	4	6	201	2

	RATIONS	RUM		CORN
		G	PTS	
Total expenditure for the year ending 24th June 1797	97,790	1393	0	7238
ditto 24th June 1798	76,140	201	2	1964
Difference being a demenution since last year	21,642	1191	6	7238

A. McLEAN
Capt. R C V

H 37   McLean to Green
[*P.A.C., C 250, pp. 150–1;* M.H.C., *XX, 538*]

Amherstburg, 14th Sept 1797

The Indian store being at so great a distance as Mr. Elliott's House (above a mile) makes it rather inconvenient particularly at such short notice as they give, generally at the dinner hour. This Distance likewise renders peculation the more easy & detection the less so. I think that should there be room enough when the new store is finished it would be best plan to have the Indian Stores removed, even if there should be a place built for the storekeeper, tho' in the mean time room might be made for him in any one of the Block Houses. This would save government the expense of storage now charged by Mr. Elliott on whom I cannot help making a few remarks. He lives as I am informed in the greatest affluence at an expense of above a thousand a year. He possesses an extensive farm not far from the garrison stock'd with about six or seven hundred head of cattle & I am told employs fifty or sixty persons constantly about his house & farm chiefly slaves. If the question should be asked, "How these people are fed and cloathed & how his wealth has been accumulated," I shall not undertake to give a positive answer, but the general opinion of people better acquainted with these matters is well known. . . .

H 38   McLean to Colonel Alexander McKee
[*P.A.C., C 250, pp. 337–8;* M.H.C., *XX, 565*]

Amherstburg, 28th October, 1797

. . . Perceiving a considerable number of Indians frequently remain at this Post for a length of time previous to receiving their presents & after being in possession of them are an immense expense to govt. and much to their own prejudice, by disposing of both provisions & presents for rum, there have been even between 150 & 200 Potawatamies & Chippewas here lately from the 14th to the 24th October without any requisition made for their presents, & chiefly in a state of intoxication not from any rum received in or about the garrison as I have given positive orders against it. This being I conceive an abuse of the govt. Bounty & a circumstance that calls for a remedy, it is my duty to represent it & I have no doubt of your acting upon it as may most conduce to the good of His Majesty's service. I have recommended to Mr. Elliott to give them their presents as soon as possible after their arrival at the Post & to exert his influence to encourage them to depart immediately after receiving them but to no effect. . . .

H 39   McLean to General Robert Prescott
[*P.A.C., C 250, pp. 371–2;* M.H.C., *XX, 581*]

Amherstburg, 11th November, 1797

. . .

Mr. Elliott has of late convicted himself sufficiently by giving in a false return of the Indians at Chenail Ecarté Settlement. He makes them 543 which exceeds by about 360 the number that any other can make of them.

Mr. McKee has had more prudence not to mention any number on my application for him for a return tho' better acquainted with them than the other, in which he has strongly contributed to convict Mr. Elliott tho' probably not intending it. The difference in the amount of requisition contributes still more towards it.

I have enclosed to Captain Green a Return of these Indians which I am convinced is as accurate as possible, and having written to him so fully on this and every other subject within my observation, that I shall forbear troubling you unnecessarily.

H 40   Prescott to Russell
[*P.A.C., C 250, pp. 385–7;* M.H.C., *XX, 584–5*]

Quebec, December 15, 1797

In my letter No. 28 I had the honor to inform you that the difficulty you found to decide on the misunderstanding between the officers of the Indian Department and Capt. McLean Commanding at Amherstburg, would be easily obviated by reference to my late Correspondence on Indian Affairs, and the orders & Regulations in force for the Government of the Indian Department.

I now send you an Extract from Captain McLean's letter of the 11th Nov. and copies of a correspondence between Mr. McKee, Mr. Elliott and Capt. McLean in consequence of the latter having discovered, that Mr. Elliott had imposed on him respecting the number of Indians on the Chenail Ecarté Settlement, by demanding "Provisions for Six Months for 543 Indians determined to remain there, exclusive of occasional visitors" when their number actually amounted to no more than 167 Persons—the greater number of which are since gone away to their hunting grounds.

Several attempts have been made from time to time by Mr. Elliott, to draw provisions profusely from the Stores, but they have been uniformly and with great propriety resisted by Capt. McLean, which is the cause of the misunderstanding between them. Had Mr. Elliott, and the other officers in the Indian Department, obeyed orders and conformed to the Regulations, nothing of the kind could possibly have happened.

Mr. Elliott's conduct for some time past, and in the above business more particularly, has been such as to have considerably shaken the confidence so very necessary to be reposed in Persons holding Public Employments. I am therefore to request you will inform him, that the appointment of Superintendent of Indians & Indian Affairs, which he holds during my pleasure, is forfeited, and that there is no further occasion for his services, in the before mentioned capacity.

I shall inform his Grace the Duke of Portland of the above transaction, & recommend that Major Fraser should be appointed to succeed him, whom the Duke mentioned last summer as an eligible Person for a situation in the Indian Department.

I am at the present time to request that you will please to direct Mr. McKee, the Deputy Superintendent General for Indian Affairs, to remove to Amherstburg, being a situation more central and eligible to reside at, than the Western extremity of the Province, where he lives at present, and his son Captain McKee should be charged with the duties of the North Western District, for which he was originally appointed Superintendent.

H 41   McLean to Green
[*P.A.C., C 251, pp. 22–5;* M.H.C., *XX, 590–2*]

Amherstburg 2nd Feb 1798

I had the honor of writing you by an opportunity from this place for Niagara on the 30h Dec last and acknowledging the receipt of your Letters of the 9h & 19h October and 6h November.

I have now to acquaint you for the Commander in Chief's information that Mr. Caldwell has got the contract for furnishing Government with Teams for the current year at the rate of nineteen Shillings New York Currency (about 12 Halx.) each single Team per day. Likewise the contract for Firewood at the rate of 12/6 Halifax Pr. Cord to be cut on the Garrison ground. The former being the lowest proposal for Teams and the Latter the only one made for the firewood. Mr. Caldwell would have undertaken to furnish the Government with Firewood from his own Land at 15s Halifax per Cord, but I preferred having it furnished from the Garrison ground at half a dollar less untill the Commander in Chief's pleasure is known. Indeed if the strength of the Troops admitted of their being employed to cut the firewood it might be procured at half the price, as the King's horses cou'd haul a great part of it. The same objection that existed at Detroit of the Troops being too much harrassed in fetching the garrison firewood on Batteaux having no weight here particularly while it can be furnished so near at hand on the Govt ground, in the same manner as part of the wood was provided last year at Kingston at an easy rate. So much land in the vicinity of this post having been granted to individuals & reserved for Indians & their Officers that the Garrison ground is consequently rather circumscribed & cannot furnish firewood for many years. The Policy of the Govt of this Province of granting large tracts of Land to Individuals not capable of improving,

& probably not entitled to them, has evidently been injurious to the Country in general. It is even said that the Indian Reserve of 7 miles square near this Garrison is now claimed by an Individual.

I have agreeable to His Excellency's desire signified to me in your Letter of the 19h Oct. last given notice that Lotts should be granted near this Garrison to build upon, on the ground allotted for that purpose, and have already had more applications than there are Lotts from Merchants & others, chiefly Mechanicks. I have as yet granted none, but have given them to understand that a consideration should be annexed, that unless a habitable house should be erected on the Lott before the expiration of a twelve months, it reverts to the Crown. They seemed satisfied with this condition and I have no doubt but the whole of the Lotts will be occupied within that Period.

Should the weather prove favourable the cutting and hauling of the Ship Timber will be compleated in a Fortnight. The Indians have made no difficulty in permitting the Timber to be cut on the Reserve without exacting a present, at least they have said nothing on the subject, indeed there are only four or five Families of them.

The Indian Stores have been removed on the 20th ultimo. into the Garrison to an apartment prepared for that purpose in the new store where there is sufficient room & Mr. Elliott has been told that the rent of his store was to cease.

The Superintendant & Storekeeper at this Post have come to me voluntarily to make the required apologies for their conduct last Summer & seem more submissive in consequence of the notice taken of their behavior by His Excellency. I find in the Pay Bill for the Quarter ending the 24h Decr. last a charge made of pay for Fisher and Day Indian Interpreters notwithstanding your notification to me that the Commander in Chief refused to sanction their appointment with his approbation. I declined approving of this charge & was told they had been appointed by Mr. President Russell, the Quarter was expired previous to the Commander in Chief's disapprobation being known, which was the reason for making this charge; not wishing to throw any obstacles in the way of their business, upon this signed the Pay Bill, tho it is more than probable I have done wrong, as this reason will be hardly thought sufficient.

There is a Blacksmith for the Indian Dept. paid by Govt. & allowed Fuel & Lodging equal to a Subaltern officer; he lives within a few miles of this place & I am informed has very little to do for Indians, I would therefore recommend that he should reside at this Post & when not occupied in that Line be kept constantly employed doing the necessary work of the Garrison, which will probably save the Expence of having another Blacksmith with the assistance of a Labourer from the Troops.

The District Jail & Court House having lately been burnt to the ground by accident the Magistrates in Session have applied to me for the Schooner Dunmore as a temporary security for the prisoners, to which after consulting the Storekeeper I in the mean time consented.

H 42   McLean to Green
[*P.A.C., C 251, pp. 92–5;* M.H.C., *XX, 602–3*]

Amherstburg, 13th of May, 1798

With respect to Mr. Elliot's dismissal I think it cannot fail to be attended with the very best consequences, in this part of the Country & a warning to others. The good effects of it are already visible, everything being done with great regularity, and as to the Indians I hardly think they have considered it of consequence enough to bestow a thought upon it.

A quantity of sugar has already been received here from the Indians and put into the King's store, being I believe the first donation of the kind received at this Post, none having been received during Mr. Elliott's Superintendancy and he not finding it so convenient to take it from them this year as usual. . . .

The Blacksmith engaged last Fall has since been employed & does all the work both for the Marine & Engineer Departments. His name is Francois Bertran. . . .

A room is already prepared in the new store for holding Indian Corn in Bulk of which an estimate will be transmitted.

There is I believe a sufficient quantity of Timber cut for building the intended vessel; what part of it was cut here has been hauled during the winter, and the remainder being all cedar, which was cut on the Islands by the Ottawa's crew in the winter, I expect to have here in a couple of days, Captain Grant having gone to fetch it with three vessels (the Ottawa, Maria & Miamis) in order to have it over before the hurry of the transport begins. . . .

All the Lotts on the Plan sent up are already given away, almost all to Merchants. There are a number of other applicants good subjects & chiefly meckanicks, which might probably be an useful acquisition at the Post. I shall therefore be glad to know whether another street might not be laid out back for these people, or as much land as will be sufficient to settle them in the same proportion as the first. Lieut. Cooper seems to think it might be done without inconvenience or interfering much with anything else. I wish to be instructed on this Head.

H 43   McLean to Green
[*P.A.C., C 251, pp. 187–90;* M.H.C., *XX, 620–1*]

Amherstburg, 17th of August 1798

I received on the 13th Inst. your letter of the 28th June inclosing Col. Mann's opinion relative to laying out another street for Building in the rear of those already laid out, which as well as every other part of its contents shall receive due attention. . . .

The Ship Timber is piled upon skids to prevent its receiving any injury from the wet ground.

I am happy to say that there is a visible difference in the progress of all the works carrying on here since the arrival of Lieut. Blackwell. . . .

The Indian Storekeeper's house is covered & the chimneys finished. It will soon be completed, and the foundations for the Council & Interpreters House is laid. The Indian Store will in a few days be removed to the new Indian Store. . . .

H 44 NAMES OF LOT HOLDERS IN THE TOWN OF AMHERSTBURG 1799
[*P.A.C., Tray 102-12, C-1469*]

FIRST STREET	SECOND STREET	THIRD STREET
EAST SIDE	WEST SIDE	WEST SIDE
(North to South)	(North to South)	(North to South)
Lot 1—Meldrum and Parks	Lot 1—Wm. Cornwall	Lot 1—C. O. Ermating
Lot 2—Reserved for Naval Artificers	Lot 2—A. Maisonville	Lot 2—J. Jackson
	Lot 3—F. Moonin	Lot 3—John Sparden
Lot 3—Lt. Wm. Fleming	Lot 4—Aug. Roy	Lot 4—W. Smith
	Lot 5—Jos. Reaume	Lot 5—J. P. Sparkman
Lot 4—	Lot 6—Anthe. Reaume	Lot 6—J. Whiting
Lot 5—Old Provision Storehouse	Lot 7—Wm. Mills	Lot 7—S. Bernard
	Lot 8—F. Buissonette	Lot 8—Aug. Crete
Lot 6—Mr. Reynolds	Lot 9—Paschal Reaume	Lot 9—Bourdeaux
Lot 7—Mr. Bouilli	Lot 10—Ch. Reaume	Lot 10—E. Moore
Lot 8—Mr. Dufresne	Lot 11—Frs. Billet	Lot 11—Ep. Manson
Lot 9—Mr. McIntosh	Lot 12—J. Askin, Jr.	Lot 12— ....
Lot 10—Mr. McGregor	Lot 13—F. Bertrand	Lot 13 ⎫
Lot 11—Innes and Patterson	EAST SIDE	Lot 14 ⎬ —Burying Ground
	(South to North)	Lot 15 ⎭
Lot 12—Mr. J. Allen	Lot 14—Wm. Aitken	EAST SIDE
Lot 13—Mr. Harffy	Lot 15—W. Hutchinson	(South to North)
WEST SIDE	Lot 16—School House	Lot 16—John Topp
(South to North)	Lot 17—Pierre Barron	Lot 17—De Gerard
Lot 14—Mr. Thos Forsyth	Lot 18—Frs. Labellain	Lot 18— ....
	Lot 19—Benjn. Hall	Lot 19—A. Gillis
Lot 15—Mr. Robt. Forsyth	Lot 20—Jos. Gravelines	Lot 20—Conrad Lick
	Lot 21—W. Muckle	Lot 21—Bloom
Lot 16—Mr. Alex McKenzie	Lot 22—Ch. Spinnard	Lot 22—J. Boyle
	Lot 23—Th. Conthois	Lot 23—J. Carpenter
Lot 17—Leith, Shepherd & Duff	Lot 24—Den Druyard	Lot 24—St. Martin
	Lot 25—Jos. Rowe	Lot 25—H. Botsford
Lot 18—Mr. G. Sharp	Lot 26—Sol Druyard	Lot 26— ....
Lot 19—Mr. J. Askin	Lot 27—James Duff	Lot 27— ....
Lot 20—Eben. Reynolds		Lot 28—Fearson
Lot 21—Robert Reynolds		Lot 29— ....
Reserved Lot—Occupied by Mr. Reynolds, (Depy Commissary)		Lot 30—Jos. Bisseau
		Lot 31—W. Searle
Reserved Lot—Occupied by Mr. Sparkman (Barracks Master)		

The Main Streets are 50 feet wide
The Cross Streets and Back Streets are 30 feet wide
The Lots are 60 feet in Front and 120 feet in Depth

APPENDIXES

APPENDIX I

Original Text of French and Latin Documents

A 1 Extraits de la relation de 1640–1 par Jérôme Lalement à Ste-Marie-aux-Hurons
[*Thwaites,* Jesuit Relations, *XXI, 189*]

...
Du premier bourg de la Nation Neutre que l'on rencontre en arrivant d'icy, continuant de cheminer au Midy ou Sudest, il y a environ quatre journées de chemin jusques à l'emboucheure de la Riviere si celebre de cette Nation, dans l'Ontario ou lac de S. Louys. Au deçà de cette Riviere, & non au delà, comme le marque quelque Charte, sont la plus part des bourgs de la Nation Neutre. . . .

Cette Riviere ou Fleuve, est celuy par lequel se descharge nostre grand lac des Hurons, ou Mer douce, qui se rend premierement dans le lac d'Erié ou de la Nation du Chat, & jusques là elle entre dans les terres de la Nation Neutre, & prend le nom d'Onguiaahra, jusques à ce qu'elle se soit deschargée dans l'Ontario ou lac de sainct Louys, d'où enfin sort le fleuve qui passe devant Quebek, dit de S. Laurens. De sorte que si une fois on estoit maistre de la coste de la mer plus proche de la demeure des Iroquois, on monteroit par le fleuve de sainct Laurens sans danger, jusques à la Nation Neutre, & au delà de beaucoup, avec espargne notable de peine & de temps. . . .

A 2 Extraits de la relation de 1640–1 par Jérôme Lalement à Ste-Marie-aux-Hurons
[*Thwaites,* Jesuit Relations, *XXI, 222, 230*]

...
Les Peres [Brébeuf et Chaumonot] ont parcouru en leur voyage dix-huicts bourgs ou bourgades, à toutes lesquelles ils ont donné un nom Chrestien, duquel nous nous servirons cy apres aux occasions. Ils se sont arrestez particulierement à dix, auxquels ils ont donné autant d'instruction qu'ils ont pu trouver d'audience. Ils font estat d'environ cinq cens feux, & de trois mille personnes que peuvent contenir ces dix bourgades, auxquels ils ont proposé & publié l'Evangile. . . .

Pendant toutes ces bourasques & tempestes, les Peres n'ont pas laissé de pourvoir au salut des petits enfans, vieillards, & malades qu'ils ont peû aborder, & qu'ils en ont trouvé capables. En tous ces dix-huit bourgs qu'ils ont visité, il ne s'en est trouvé qu'un, scavoir celuy de Khioetoa, surnommé de saint Michel, qui leur ayt donné l'audience que meritoit leur Ambassade. Dans ce bourg s'est refugié depuis quelques années, par la crainte de leur ennemis, une certaine Nation estrangere, qui demeuroit au delà d'Erie ou de la Nation du Chat, nommé A8enrehronon, qui semble n'estre venue en ces quartiers que pour jouyr du bonheur de cette visite, & y avoir esté conduite par la providence du bon Pasteur, pour y entendre sa voix. On les a suffisamment instuits: mais les Peres n'ont pas jugé à propos de passer encore outre à les baptizer; le sainct Esprit fera meurir cette semence qu'on a jetté dedans leurs coeurs & en son temps on ira recueillir la moisson qu'on a desja arrousé de tant de sueurs.

C'est en cette Nation que les Peres firent le premier Baptesme d'Adultes, en la personne d'une bonne vieille qui avoit desja presque perdu l'ouye. Au Baptesme de laquelle est remarquable l'affection d'une bonne femme de la mesme cabine, qui servit aux Peres de truchement, luy declarant les mysteres de nostre Foy, plus clairement & efficacement que les Peres, disent-ils, n'avoient fait auparavant à elle mesme. La pauvre femme n'eut rien à repliquer, sinon que pour estre desja vieille, elle auroit trop de peine d'arriver jusques au Ciel; en outre qu'elle n'avoit rien dont elle peût faire present aux Peres, & qu'il eut fallu attendre ses enfans qui estoient à la chasse, afin d'avoir d'eux les habits necessaires pour se parer. Il fut facile de la contenter là dessus, et elle fut enfin heureusement baptizé. Deux ou trois autres adultes ont aussi participé au bonheur de cette visite: Et quelque nombre de petits enfans, qui par advance s'en sont allez au Ciel.

A 3   EXTRAITS DU VOYAGE DE MM. DOLLIER ET GALINÉE 1669–70
[*Bibliothèque Nationale, Paris; Margry,* Découvertes, *I, 112–66; Ontario Historical Society,* Papers and Records, *IV (Toronto, 1903)*]

. . .
Enfin, nous arrivasmes à Tinaoutoua le 24 septembre, et trouvasmes que le François qui estoit arrivé le jour précédent estoit un nommé Jolliet, qui estoit parti avant nous de Montréal avec une flotte de quatre canots chargez de marchandises pour les Outaouacs, qui avoit eu ordre de M. le Gouverneur de monter jusques dans le lac Supérieur pour descouvrir où estoit une mine de cuivre dont on voit ici des morceaux qui n'ont presque pas besoin d'estre raffinez, tant le cuivre est bon et pur; (après avoir trouvé cette mine, de chercher un chemin plus facile qu'à l'ordinaire pour le pouvoir apporter au Montréal. M. Jolliet n'avait pu voir cette mine à cause que le temps le pressoit pour son retour, mais ayant trouvé aux Outaouacs des prisonniers que ces peuples avoient fait sur les Iroquois, il leur dit que l'intention d'Onontio estoit qu'ils vescussent en paix avec les Iroquois, et leur persuada d'envoyer aux Iroquois un de leurs prisonniers, en tesmoignage de la paix qu'ils vouloient avoir avec eux.

Ce fut cet Iroquois qui montra à M. Jolliet un nouveau chemin que les François n'avoient point sceu jusques alors pour revenir des Outaouacs dans le pays des Iroquois. Cependant la crainte que ce sauvage eut de retomber entre les mains des Antastoes luy fit dire à M. Jolliet qu'il falloit qu'il quittast son canot et marchast par terre plustot qu'il n'eust fallu. . . .

Cependant la maladie de M. de la Salle commençoit à luy oster l'envie de pousser plus loin, et le désir de voir Montréal commençoit à le presser. . . . et d'ailleurs le chemin que M. Jolliet avoit fait avec la nouvelle qu'il nous apprit qu'il avoit envoyé de son monde chercher une nation d'Outaouacs fort nombreuse nommée les Pouteouetamites, où il n'y avoit jamais eu de missionnaires, et que ce peuple estoit voisin des Iskoutegas, et la grande rivière que menoit aux Chaouanons nous fit envie, à M. Dollier et à moy, d'aller chercher la rivière où nous voulions entrer par le côté des Outaouacs plustost que par celuy des Iroquois, parceque le chemin nous en sembla beaucoup plus facile et que nous sçavions tous deux la langue Outaouaise.

. . . M. Jolliet nous fit offre d'une description qu'il avoit faite de sa route depuis les Outaouacs que j'acceptay, et la reduisit des lors en carte marine, qui nous a beaucoup apris pour nous conduire. . . .

...

Nous partismes donc de Tinaouataoua, le 1er octobre 1669, accompagnez de bon nombre de Sauvages qui nous aidoient à porter nos canots et nos hardes, et après avoir fait environ 9 ou 10 lieues en trois jours, nous arrivasmes sur le bord de la rivière que je nomme Rapide, à cause de la violence avec lacquelle elle marche. . . .

...

Enfin, nous arrivasmes, le 13 ou le 14, au bord du lac Erié, qui nous parut d'abord comme une grande mer, parcequ'il souffloit pour lors un grand vent du Sud. . . . Nous marchasmes trois journées le long de ce lac. . . . Au bout de trois jours, pendant lesquels nous ne fismes que 21 ou 22 lieues, nous trouvasmes un endroit qui nous parut si beau, avec une chasse si abandante, que nous creumes ne pouvoir trouver mieux où passer notre hiver. . . . Nous y cherchasmes quelque bel endroit pour faire une cabane d'hiver, et nous trouvasmes une fort jolie rivière sur l'embouchure de laquelle nous nous cabanasmes. . . .

Nous ne pouvions pas passer l'hiver sur le bord du lac, à cause des grands vents dont nous eussions esté battus. C'est pourquoy nous choisismes un fort bel endroit sur le bord d'un ruisseau, environ un quart de lieu dans le bois, où nous nous cabanasmes. . . .

...

Cependant, nous ne laissons pas de souhaiter le temps de la navigation afin de pouvoir nous rendre aux Pouteouetamites de bonne heure, et que je pusse retourner cette année au Montréal, pour renvoyer à M. Dollier les choses dont il auroit besoin dans sa mission.

Le 23 mars, jour du dimanche de la Passion, nous allasmes tous au bord du lac pour faire et planter une croix en memoire d'une si longue demeure des François, comme avoit esté la nostre. Nous y fismes nos prières, et voyant que là où nous estions estoit presque net de glaces, nous résolusmes de partir le 26 mars, le lendemain de l'Annonciation.

Mais comme la rivière par où nous avions esté au lieu de notre hyvernement estoit encore toutes gelée, [de sorte qu']il fallut faire portage de toutes nos hardes et de nos canots jusques au lac où nous nous embarquasmes, après avoir demeuré en ce lieu 5 mois et 11 jours.

...

Nous nous chargeasmes en ce lieu [Pointe aux Pins] de viande fraische et boucanée, et marchasmes jusques à une longue pointe que vous trouverez marquée dans la carte du lac Erié. Nous y arrivasmes sur un beau sable du costé du levant de cette pointe; nous avions fait ce jour là près de vingt lieues. Aussi nous estions tous fort fatiquez, ce qui fut cause que nous n'apportasmes point toutes nos hardes jusques sur la terre, mais les laissasmes sur le sable et portasmes nos canots jusques sur la terre.

La nuit vint et on s'endormit si profondément qu'un grand vent Nord-Est s'estant élevé eut le temps d'agiter le lac avec tant de force que l'eau monta de six pieds ou nous estions, et emporta les hardes du canot de M. Dollier qui estoient les plus proches de l'eau et auroit emporté toutes les autres, si un de nous ne se fust éveillé qui, estant estonné d'entendre le lac qui mugissoit si furieusement, alla voir sur le bord si les bagages estoient en seureté, et voyant que l'eau venoit déjà jusques aux hardes qui estoient placées le plus haut, s'escria que tout estoit perdu. A ce cri, on se leva et on sauva le bagage de mon canot et d'un de ceux de M. Dollier. On alluma des escorces pour chercher le long de l'eau; mais on ne put sauver qu'un baril de poudre qui flottoit, le reste fut emporté; le plomb mesme fut emporté ou enfoncé si avant dans le sable qu'on ne put jamais le trouver, mais le plus fascheux fut que la chapelle entière fut perdue, nous attendismes que le vent fust calmé et les eaux retirées pour aller chercher, le long de l'eau, si on ne trouveroit pas quelque débris du naufrage, mais on ne trouva qu'un mousqueton et un petit sac de hardes à un de nos hommes; le reste fut perdu sans ressources. Nos vivres mesmes furent tous perdus, hormis ce qu'il y avoit dans mos canot.

Cet accident nous mit hors d'estat d'estre assistez du secours des sacrements et d'en pouvoir assister les autres. Ainsi nous mismes en délibération savoir si nous devions nous arrester à quelque nation pour y faire nostre mission ou si nous retournerions au Montréal chercher une autre chapelle et d'autres marchandises nécessaires pour avoir des vivres pour retourner ensuite nous establir en quelque endroit; et cet avis nous sembla le meilleur; et comme le chemin des Outaouacs nous sembla presque aussi court du lieu ou nous estions comme par où nous estions venus, et que nous pretendions arriver à Sainte-Marie du Sault ou les Outaouacs s'ssemblent pour descendre de compagnie, avant qu'ils fussent partis, nous creumes que nous descendrions avec eux plus facilement. Ajoutez à cela que nous estions plus aises de voir un nouveau pays que de retourner sur nos pas.

Nous poursuivismes donc notre route vers le Couchant, et après avoir fait environ 100 lieues sur le lac Erié, nous arrivasmes au lieu par où le lac des Hurons, autrement dit la Mer douce des Hurons ou le Michigane se descharge dans ce lac. Cette descharge a bien une demi-lieue de largeur et tourne tout court au Nord-Est, de sorte que nous retournions presque sur nos pas. Au bout de six lieues nous trouvasmes un endroit fort remarquables et fort en vénération à tous les Sauvages de ces contrées à cause d'une idole de pierre que la nature y a formée, à qui ils disent devoir le bonheur de leur navigation sur le lac d'Erié lorsqu'ils l'ont passé sans accident, et qu'ils apaisent par des sacrifices, des présens de peaux, de vivres, etc., lorsqu'ils veulent s'y embarquer. Ce lieu estoit plein de cabanages de ceux qui estoient venus rendre leur homage à cette pierre qui n'avoit autre rapport avec la figure d'un homme que celuy que l'imagination luy vouloit bien donner. Cependant elle estoit toute peinte, et on luy avoit formé une espèce de visage avec du vermillion. Je vous laisse à penser si nous vengeasmes sur cette idole, que les Iroquois nous avoient fort recommandé d'honorer, la perte de nostre chapelle. Nous luy attribuasmes mesmes la disette où nous avions esté de vivres jusques icy. Enfin il n'y avoit personne dont elle n'eust attiré la haine. Je consacray une de mes haches pour casser ce dieu de pierre, et puis ayant accosté nos canots ensemble, nous portasmes les plus gros morceaux au milieu de la rivière et jetasmes aussi tout le reste à l'eau, afin qu'on n'en entendist jamais parler. Dieu nous récompensa aussi tost de cette bonne action; car nous tuasmes dans cette mesme journée un chevreuil et un ours.

Au bout de quatre lieues, nous entrasmes dans un petit lac qui a environ dix lieues de long et presque autant de large, appelé par Mr. Samson le Lac des Eaux Salées. Mais nous n'y avons veu aucune marque de sel. . . .

A 4   Acte de prise de possession des terres du Lac Erié
[*Bibliothèque Nationale, Paris, Fonds Renaudot, XXX*]

Nous soubsignez, certifions avoir veu afficher sur les terres du lac nommé Erie les armes du Roy de France avec cette inscription: "L'an de salut 1669, Clément IX estant assis dans la chaire de saint Pierre, Louis XIV régnant en France, Monsieur de Courcelles estant gouverneur de la Nouvelle France et Monsieur Talon y estant intendant pour le Roy, sont arrivez en ce lieu deux missionnaires de Montréal, accompagnez de sept autres François, qui les premiers de touts les peuples Européans ont hyverné en ce lac, dont ils ont pris possession au nom de leur Roy, comme d'une terre non occupée, par apposition de ses armes, qu'ils ont attachées au pied de cette croix." En foy de quoy nous avons signé le présent certificat.

                Signe: François Dollier, prestre du diocèse de Nantes, en Bretagne;
                             De Galinée, diacre du diocèse de Rennes, en Bretagne.

A 5   Visite de M. de Tonti au détroit du Lac Herié
[*Tonti, Dernières Découvertes, pp. 35–9*]

... Il (M. de La Sale) voulut, en attendant le Printems, employer le reste de l'hyver à ramasser des pelleteries, & toutes sortes de munitions pour fournir aux frais de son voiage. Ces raisons l'obligerent de s'en retourner à Frontenac sur les glaces; il commanda auparavant quinze hommes pour aller chercher les Illinois, le devancer, & lui preparer les voies, & me laisser pour commandant à Niagara avec trente hommes & un Pere Recollet. ...

... Il m'ordonna cependant d'aller à six fois vingt lieues de là reconnoitre les côtes & les terres qui sont au delà des Lacs au Nord-Est. Je m'embarquai dans un canot avec cinq hommes; après deux jours de navigation, j'arrivai au détroit de Lac Herié: C'est un canal d'environ trente lieues de long, par où ce Lac se joint avec celui des Hurons; j'allai prendre terre à un de ses bords du côté du nord: Etant là je m'informai aussitôt de nos gens; l'on m'apprit qu'ils avoient passé plus haut; le desir de les rencontrer me fit faire une revue exacte du pais; c'étoit une espece de presqu'isle en forme de cœur compris entre ces trois Lacs. Après avoir assez parcouru ces terres, je remontai dans mon canot, pour aller rendre compte de ma commission à M. de La Sale, qui durant l'espace de mon petit voiage, étoit reparti pour Fontenac, où il porta de nouvelles marchandises, & d'où quelque tems après il rapporta de nouvelles provisions & de nouveau monde à Niagara: Il y arriva le 7 Aoust de l'année 1679, accompagné de trois Peres Recollets. ...

M. de La Sale, etant de retour à Niagara disposa tout pour la continuation de son ouvrage: nous montâmes en nombre de quarante personnes dans sa nouvelle Barque vers le mi-aoust, et ayant heureusement traversé le lac Herié, nous entrâmes dans le lac des Hurons, beaucoup plus grands que les deux premiers: nous emploiames le reste du mois à le parcourir à cause du mauvais tems, et après avoir essuié la plus affreuse tempête qu'on puisse éprouver dans les mers les plus ourageuses, nous vinmes a surgir à une rade de la contrée nommée Missilimachinac.

A 6   Description par Hennepin du détroit par lequel le Lac Orléans
se décharge dans le Lac Conty
[*Hennepin,* Description de la Louisiane, *pp. 51–2*]

... Nostre navigation fut si heureuse que le dixième au matin, Feste de Saint Laurens, nous abordâmes à l'entrée du Détroit, par où le Lac d'Orleans se decharge dans le Lac de Conty, & qui est éloigné de cent lieues de la Rivière de Niagara. Ce Détroit a trente lieues de longueur, & presque partout une lieue de largeur, excepté dans son milieu, où il s'elargit & forme un Lac de figure Circulaire, & de dix lieues de Diametre que nous nomâmes le Lac Sainte Claire à cause du jour de cette Sainte que nous le traversâmes. Le Pais des deux costez de ce beau Détroit est garny de belles Campagnes découvertes, & l'on voit quantité de Cerfs, de Biches, de Chevreuils, d'Hours peu farouches & très bon à manger, de Poules d'Inde, & de toute sorte de gibier, des Cignes en quantité : nos Haut-bans étoient chargés & garnys de plusieurs bestes fauves depiecées, que nostre Sauvage & nos François tuerent : le reste du Détroit est couvert de Forests, d'Arbres fruitiers, comme Noyers, Chastaigniers, Pruniers, Pomiers, de vignes sauvages, & chargées de raisins, dont nous fismes quelque peu de vin; il y a des Bois propres à bâtir, c'est l'endroit où les bestes fauves se plaisent le plus. ...

A 7   Lettre du Marquis de Denonville à Greysolon du Lhut
(Duluth)
[*Margry,* Découvertes, *V, 23–5*]

Villemarie, 6 juin 1686

Quoyque je vous aye mandé cette automne de venir me trouver pour conférer avec nous de bien des choses qui ne se peuvent escrire, — Le R. P. Enjalran estant venu ici et s'en devant retourner à Michilimakinac, aussitost que la restitution des prisonniers aura esté faite, — vostre présence est beaucoup plus nécessaire aux Outaouas. C'est pourquoy je vous mande par celle cy de ne plus descendre, mais de vous joindre à M. de La Durantaye, qui doit estre à Michilimakinac pour exécuter les ordres que je luy envoye pour la seureté de nos alliez et amis.

Vous verrez par les lettres que j'escris à M. de La Durantaye que mon intention est que vous occupiez un poste au destroit du lac Erié avec cinquante hommes, que vous choisissiez un poste en lieu avantageux pour nous asseurer ce passage, y couvrir nos Sauvages qui vont à la chasse et leur servir d'asyle contre les entreprises de leurs ennemis et des nostres. Vous ne ferez ni ne direz rien aux Iroquois, à moins qu'ils n'entreprennent quelque chose contre vous et contre nos alliez. Vous verrez encore par la lettre que j'escris à M. de La Durantaye que mon intention est que vous alliez à ce poste le plutost que vous pourrez avec une vingtaine d'hommes seulement, que vous establirez sous le commandement de tel vostre lieutenant, que vous choisirez pour estre le plus propre pour le commandement et qui vous conviendra le plus.

Après avoir donné tous le ordres que vous aurez jugé necessaires pour la seureté de ce poste et avoir bien recommandé à vostre lieutenant de se tenir sur ses gardes, et recommandé l'obéissance aux autres, vous vous rendrez à

Michilimakinac pour y attendre le R. P. Anjelran, et apprendre ce que je luy auray communiqué de ce que je souhaite de vous. Ensuite vous vous en retournerez avec trente autres hommes, que vous recevrz de M. de La Durantaye pour les mener audit poste, où je ne doute pas qu'il ne se puisse faire quelque traite de Pelletries. Ainsi vos gens ne feront pas mal d'y porter quelque peu de marchandises.

Je ne sçaurois assez vous recommander d'entretenir avec M. de La Durantaye une bonne intelligence, sans quoy tous nos desseins deviendront à rien, et cependant le service du Roy et du public en souffriroient beaucoup.

Le poste où je vous envoye est d'autant plus de conséquence que je compte qu'il nous mettra en relation avec les Illinois, auxquels vous ferez sçavoir les choses dont le R. P. vous informera. Comptez que rien ne sçauroit estre de si important que de vous appliquer à bien executer tout ce que je vous mande et ce que je vous feray sçavoir par le R. P., à son retour de Michilimakinac.

Je vous envoye les commissions nécessaires pour le commandement de ce poste et pour vostre lieutenant.

Je ne vous dis rien de vos intérests, mais vous devez comptez que je feray avec plaisir tout ce qu'il faudra pour vos avantages, après cecy cependant.

Je répéteray encore une fois que vous ne sçauriez avoir trop d'application pour réussir en tout ce que je souhaiterois de vous pour les intérests du service du Roy. — Si vos affaires pouvoient permettre que monsieur vostre frère fust auprès de vous au printems prochain, j'en serois très aise; car, comme c'est un garçon entendu et qui vous seroit d'un grand secours, il pourroit aussi nous estre d'une grande utilité.

Je vous prie de ne rien dire de nos desseins que vous pouvez entrevoir, mais d'éluder tout cela.

A 8　La Durantaye renouvelle la prise de possession des terres des environs du détroit des Lacs Erié et Huron
[*Margry,* Découvertes, *V, 31–2*]

Olivier Morel, escuyer, sieur de La Durantaye, commandant pour le Roy au Pays des Outaouas, Miamis, Pouteouatamis, Sioux, et autres nations sous les ordres de M. le Marquis de Denonville, gouverneur général de la Nouvelle France.

Aujourd'huy, septième jour de juin mil six cent quatre-vingt-sept, en présence du R. P. Enjalran, supérieur des missions des Outaouas à Missilimakinac, de Sainte-Marie du Sault, des Miamis, des Illinois, de la baye des Puans et des Sioux, de M. de La Forest, cy devant commandant au fort de Saint-Louis aux Illinois, de M. De Lisle, nostre lieutenant, et de M. de Beauvais, lieutenant du fort Saint-Joseph au destroit des lacs Huron et Erie, Declarons à tous, à qui il appartiendra, estre venu sur le bord de la rivière Saint-Denys, située à trois lieues du lac Erie au Nord, pour, et au nom du Roy, réitérer la prise de possession des dits postes, faite par M. de La Salle pour la facilité des voyages qu'il fit et fit faire par la barque de Niagara à Missiliquinac, ès années. . . . Auquels dits postes nous aurions fait planter de nouveau un poteau avec les armes du Roy pour marquer la dite réitération de possession, et ordonné plusieurs logements estre faits pour l'etablissements des François et Sauvages Chaouanons et Miamis, de longtemps propriétaires desdits pays du destroit et lac Erie, desquels ils se seroient retirez pendant quelque temps pour leur plus grande utilité.

Le present acte passé en nostre présence, signé de nostre main et R. P. Enjalran, de la Compagnie de Jésus, de MM. de La Forest, Delisle et de Beauvais. Ainsi signé à l'original :

Enjalran, Jesuite; de la Durantaye. Le Gardeur de Beauvais, et F. de la Forest.

A 9 FRONTENAC AU MINISTRE
[*B.H.C., Cadillac Papers (French), IV, 826*]

A Quebec ce 10 octobre 1698

. . .

Le Sr de la Mothe Cadillac Capitaine des troupes de la Marine vous rendra mes lettres, et vous dira plus particulièrement tout ce qui regarde l'estat de ce pays dont il est parfaitement Instruit. Je suis persuadé que vous serez satisfait du compte qu'il vous en rendra, sy vous voulez bien souffrir qu'il vous en entretienne. Il a toujours tres bien fait son devoir lors qu'il s'est agy du service du Roy, comme je vous en ay desja Informé par plusieurs de mes Lettres, et surtout dans le Commandement des 8taouais ou il a este pendant trois ans. C'est un homme qui merite assurement l'honneur de vostre protection.

A 10 LAMOTHE CADILLAC AU MINISTRE
[*Margry, Découvertes, V, 166–72*]

Québec, 18 octobre 1700.

Il est de mon devoir de vous rendre un compte exact de tout ce que j'ay fait au sujet de l'establissement du Détroit, puisque le projet vous a esté renvoyé dans le temps que j'estois en France, et dont vous eustes la bonté de m'entretenir.

M. de Pontchartrain l'ayant renvoyé cette année à MM. de Callières et de Champigny pour le mettre incessamment en avant, au cas qu'il eust des inconveniens considérables, ils l'ont tous les deux approuvé et m'ont retenu pour faire l'establissement de ce Détroit, qui fait la distinction du lac Huron d'avec le lac Erié.

Il est fort à craindre que l'exécution de ce projet n'ait esté trop retardée par les nouvelles que nous avons, que les Anglois se sont fortifiés sur une rivière qui se dégorge dans le lac Ontario, et qu'ils ont continué leurs postes vers le lac Erié.

Si nostre colonie n'estoit pas remplie d'envieux, de désunion, de gens de cabale et d'intrigue, on n'auroit trouvé aucune opposition à se mettre en possession d'un poste si avantageux que, s'il se trouvoit séparé de tous ceux que nous avons, on seroit contraint en peu de temps de tout abandonner, puisque c'est luy seul qui fera l'entière seureté de la colonie, celle de son commerce et la ruine certaine des Colonies Angloises. C'est pourquoy il est très important qu'il ne passe point en une autre main, ce qui seroit inévitable, si on en différoit davantage la possession.

Les difficultés qu'on avoit fait naistre à contre-temps, en croyant que cet establissement pourroit nous faire perpétuer la guerre avec les Iroquois, sont maintenant levées par la paix qui a esté conclue avec eux. Cette nation n'estoit pas en estat de soustenir plus longtemps la guerre et ne s'y trouvera pas de sitost pour la recommencer. Voilà pourquoy on ne sçauroit plus à propos establir le Détroit, qui se fortifiera plus promptement que les Iroquois ne pourront se repeupler.

C'est un fait incontestable que les forces des Sauvages consistent dans l'esloignement des François et que les nostres s'augmenteront à leur esgard par la proximité, parce qu'il est certain qu'avec un peu de bled d'inde, ces gens-là ne s'embarrassent pas de faire deux cents lieues pour venir dérober quelques testes, et, lorsque nous voulons nous transporter sur leurs terres, nous sommes obligés de nous munitionner en toute manière et de faire de grands armemens, ce qui couste des despenses extraordinaires au Roy, et tousjours fort inutilement, puisque c'est vouloir prendre le lièvre avec le tambour.

Mais, au contraire, lorsque nous serons voisins de cette nation et que nous en serons à bonne portée, elle se tiendra en respect et se trouvera forcée de demeurer paisible, ne pouvant faire autrement sans vouloir se perdre sans ressource.

Ce seroit en vain qu'on formeroit cet establissement, si on ne vouloit se conformer à mon mémoire, parce que, si on n'y entretenoit simplement qu'une garnison, elle seroit sujette aux revolutions qui arrivent ordinairement dans les postes avancés; elle ne feroit aucune impression dans l'esprit des Iroquois et beaucoup moins encore dans celuy des Anglois. Pour bien réussir, il seroit bon, suivant ma pensée, de suivre les moyens suivans :

1º De s'y aller poster avec cent hommes, dont une moitié soit soldats et l'autre Canadiens, afin de faire cette expédition avec toute la diligence possible, et pour désabuser d'abord les Anglois d'y rien prétendre, ensuite leur oster entièrement l'espérance de lier aucun commerce avec nos alliés. Ces forces sont suffisantes pour la première année, parce que ce nombre m'est absolument nécessaire pour me fortifier et pour prendre de justes mesures pour la subsistance de ceux qui voudront s'y establir subséquemment.

2º L'année d'après, le fort se trouvant hors d'insulte, il est bon de permettre à vingt ou trente familles de s'y establir, d'y emmener leurs bestiaux et autres choses nécessaires, ce qu'elles feront volontiers à leurs frais et despens, ce qui pourra estre continué, comme il est permis dans tous les autres establissemens de la colonie.

3º Il n'est pas moins nécessaire que le Roy envoye deux cents hommes d'élite, qui soyent, autant qu'il se pourra, de différents métiers et mesme assez jeunes.

4º Il n'est pas expédient que j'y fasse aucun commerce, non plus que les autres officiers, soldats et habitans, avec les Sauvages, pour oster tout sujet de plainte à ceux des autres postes establis, sur quoy ils sont fort alertes, mais de joindre ce négoce dans celuy de la Compagnie générale qui est formée, où elle entretiendra un magasin pour y fournir toutes les marchandises nécessaires aux Sauvages nos alliés et Iroquois, en les leur donnant à meilleur marché que par le passé, ce qui se pourra faire facilement par la voiture des barques. Mais comme il me seroit impossible d'y subsister, sans faire aucun commerce et avec mille livres d'appointemens que j'ay seulement, qui à peine suffiront pour faire boire et manger les principaux des Sauvages à ma table, pour les mettre par ce bon traitement dans nos intérests, j'espère que vous aurez assez de bonté pour moy de faire connoistre à M. de Pontchartrain l'indispensable nécessité de les augmenter, pour ne pas tomber dans celle de ne pouvoir continuer mes services avec l'esclat qui est deu à Sa Majesté.

5º Il faut establir dans ce poste des Missionnaires de différentes communautés, comme Jésuites et autres religieux et ecclésiastiques des Missions Etrangères. Ce sont des vignerons qui doivent estre receus sans distinction pour travailler à la vigne du Seigneur, avec ordre particulièrement d'enseigner aux petits Sauvages la langue françoise, comme estant le seul moyen pour les civiliser, humaniser et insinuer dans leur cœur et dans leur esprit la loy de la Religion et du Monarque. On prend les bestes féroces en leur naissance, les oiseaux dans leurs nids pour les apprivoiser et affranchir; mais pour mieux y réussir, il faudroit que le Roy favorisast de ses libéralités et de ses aumosnes ces mesmes Missionnaires, à mesure qu'ils instruiroient chez eux les enfans des Sauvages, sur le tesmoignage que le Commandant et les officiers en rendront.

6º La troisiesme ou quatriesme année, on pourra y establir des Ursulines ou d'autres filles, à qui Sa Majesté pourra accorder les mesmes grâces.

7º Il seroit important qu'il y eust aussi un hospital pour les Sauvages malades et infirmes, n'y ayant rien de plus pressant pour gagner leur amitié que le soin qu'on prend d'eux dans leurs maladies. Les Hospitaliers de Montréal me semblent fort propres pour cela, parce qu'ils connoissent par avance l'humeur et l'inclination des Sauvages, en ayant souvent chez eux.

8º Il faudroit absolument permettre aux soldats et Canadiens mesmes de s'y marier aux filles Sauvagesses, lorsqu'elles seront instruites dans la Religion et qu'elles sçauront la langue françoise, qu'elles apprendront d'autant plus ardemment (pourveu qu'on y travaille avec soin), qu'elles préférent tousjours un François pour mary à quelque Sauvage que ce soit, sans que j'en sçache d'autre raison que la plus ordinaire, qui est que les estrangers sont préférés ou, pour mieux dire, c'est un secret de la Toute-Puissance.

9º Ces sortes de mariages affermissent l'amitié de ces nations, comme les alliances des Romains ont perpétué la paix avec les Sabins par l'entremise des filles que ces premiers avoient enlevées aux autres.

On trouvera dans l'exécution de ce projet non seulement la gloire de Sa Majesté estendue avec esclat, mais encore celle de Dieu, puisque par ce moyen son culte et sa religion seront establis au milieu des nations, et les sacrifices déplorables qu'elles font à Baal entièrement abolis.

Je ne sçaurois assez vous exprimer les mouvemens, que mes ennemis se sont donnés pour m'oster l'honneur de l'exécution de mon projet, ce qui semble ne point discontinuer. MM. de Callières et de Champigny ne s'y opposent point; au contraire, ils m'ont retenu pour cette affaire de la commencer au printemps prochain. Lorsqu'on les a veus dans cette résolution, on a fait ce qu'on a pu pour persuader que mon mémoire est impracticable, et j'ai veu vingt parties faites pour le renverser. J'ose vous asseurer qu'il n'y a rien à craindre et que tout sera favorable à cette entreprise. J'en responds sur ma vie. M. de Pontchartrain n'aura pas plustost décidé que tout le pays y applaudira, suivant la politique de tous les hommes qui sont bien aises de trouver des difficultés à tout ce qui n'est pas venu de leur sac.

Comme j'emmène mon fils avec moy au Détroit, je supplie M. le Ministre de luy vouloir bien accorder une enseigne ou un ordre pour la première vacance; on a donné celle de ma compagnie au fils de M. de Ramezay, ce dont je suis satisfait. J'espère que vous aurez la bonté de dire un mot en ma faveur à M. de Pontchartrain. . . .

B 1   CALLIÈRES AU MINISTRE
[*Margry*, Découvertes, *V, 190–2*]

4 octobre 1701

J'ay desjà eu l'honneur de vous marquer, Monseigneur, par ma première lettre du 6 d'Aoust, que j'avais envoyé le 4 de Juin les sieurs de Lamothe et de Tonty, Dugué et Chacornacle, avec plus de cent hommes, soldats ou Canadiens, pour faire l'establissement du Détroit avec un Recollet pour aumosnier des soldats et un Jésuite pour missionnaire des Sauvages. Vous verrez par les paroles de Taganissorens et des autres considérables qui les accompagnent, que j'ay jointes à cette lettre, qu'il me fit de l'opposition, en me disant d'attendre que les chefs, qui devoient venir à Montréal pour la paix, fussent arrivés : mais, comme il me parut qu'il n'avait pas mission de me parler de cet article, je ne laissay pas de poursuivre cette entreprise, dans la crainte que, si ces chefs m'avoient demandé de ne point faire cet establissement et que je leur eusse refusé, cela n'eust causé quelque obstacle à la paix, au lieu qu'en trouvant la chose faite par le départ du sieur de Lamothe, ils n'en parleroient pas. Ce qui arriva, leur ayant fait trouver les raisons de cet établissement bonnes, malgré les mesfiances que les Anglois leur en avoient données, quoy qu'ils eussent le dessein d'y aller eux-mêmes, ce que j'avois appris dès l'hyver, qui fut encore une raison pour faire presser le départ du sieur de Lamothe et de faire son detachement aussi fort qu'il est, de crainte que les Anglois ne me prévinssent. Je fis mesme promettre aux Sonnontouans, quand ils seroient de retour à leurs villages, d'y porter du bled d'inde, sur la nouvelle que j'avois eue que le sieur de Lamothe n'en trouveroit pas à Missilimakinac.

Le sieur de Chacornacle vient d'arriver présentement du fort du Détroit, qui m'a apporté des lettres du sieur de Lamothe; mais comme nous vous rendons compte dans notre lettre commune de ce que nous en avons appris, je ne vous le rappeleray point icy.

Vous verrez, Monseigneur, par ce que nous avons l'honneur de vous marquer dans la mesme lettre commune qu'en remettant le commerce de ce fort à la Compagnie, elle s'est engagée de payer les 6,000 livres que vous avez eu la bonté de faire regler pour le secours des pauvres familles de ce pays. Vous avez fait en cela une tres grande charité par le besoin qu'elles en ont, et elles vous en sont redevables.

B 2   DESCRIPTION DE LA RIVIÈRE DU DÉTROIT PAR LE SIEUR DE LAMOTHE
CADILLAC QUI Y COMMANDE
[*Margry*, Découvertes, *V, 192–4*]

8 octobre 1701

Le mestier de la guerre n'estant pas celuy d'un escrivain, je ne puis, sans ce mérite, faire le portrait d'un pays si digne d'une meilleure plume que la mienne; mais, parce que vous m'avez ordonné de vous en rendre compte, je le feray en vous disant que le Détroit n'est proprement qu'un canal ou une rivière d'une mediocre largeur et de 25 lieues de long, suivant mon estime, située nord-nord-est, et sud-sud-ouest par 41 degrés, par où s'escoulent et s'eschappent doucement et d'un cours moderé les eaux vives et cristallines du Lac Supérieur, du Michigan et du Huron, qui sont autant de mers d'eau douce dans le lac Erié, dans l'Ontario ou Frontenac et qui vont enfin se confondre dans le fleuve Saint-Laurent avec celles de l'Océan.

Ses rives sont autant de vastes prairies, dont la fraischeur de ces belles eaux tient l'herbe tousjours verdoyante. Ces mesmes prairies sont bordées par de longues et larges allées de fruitiers, qui n'ont jamais senti la main soigneuse du jardinier vigilant, et ces jeunes et anciens fruitiers, sous le poids de la quantité de leurs fruits, mollissent et courbent leurs branches vers la terre féconde qui les a produits. C'est dans cette terre si fertile que la vigne ambitieuse, qui n'a pas encore pleuré sous le couteau du laborieux vigneron, se fait un toit espais avec ses larges feuilles et ses grappes pesantes sur la teste de celui qu'elle accole et que souvent elle estouffe pour trop l'embrasser. C'est sous ces vastes allées, ou l'on voit assemblés par centaines le timide cerf et la biche craintive avec le chevreuil, bondissant pour y ramasser avec empressement les pommes et les prunes dont la terre est pavée; c'est là que la dinde soigneuse rappelle et conduit sa nombreuse couvée pour y vendanger le raisin; c'est là que viennent leurs masles, pour y remplir leur fale large et gloutonne. Les faisans dorés, la caille, la perdrix, la bécasse, la tourterelle abondante, fourmillent dans le bois et couvrent les campagnes entrecoupées et rompues par des bouquets de bois de haute futaye, qui font une charmante perspective, laquelle seule peut adoucir les tristes ennuis de la solitude. C'est là que la main de l'impitoyable faucheur n'a jamais rasé l'herbe succulente, dont s'engraissent les bœufs lainés d'une grandeur et d'une grosseur excessives.

Les bois sont de dix sortes : de noyer, de chesne blanc, du rouge, du fresne bastard, du sapin ou bois blanc et du cotonnier; mais ces mesmes arbres sont droits comme des flesches, sans nœuds et quasi sans branches que par le haut bout et d'une grandeur prodigieuse; c'est de là que l'aigle courageux regarde fixement le soleil, voyant à ses pieds de quoy satisfaire sa main fièrement armée.

Le poisson y est nourri et baigné par une eau vive et cristalline, et sa grande abondance ne le rend pas moins délicieux. Les cygnes sont en si grand nombre, qu'on prendroit pour des lys les joncs, dans lesquels ils sont entassés. L'oye babillarde, le canard, la sarcelle et l'outarde y sont si communs, que je ne veux, pour en convaincre, que me servir de l'expression d'un Sauvage, à qui je demanday, avant d'y arriver, s'il y avoit bien du gibier : « Il y en a tant, dit-il, qu'ils ne se rangent que pour laisser passer le canot. »

Peut-on croire qu'une terre sur laquelle la nature a distribué tout avec tant d'ordre sache refuser à la main du laboureur, curieux de ses fécondes entrailles, le retour qu'il s'en sera proposé ?

En un mot, le climat y est tempéré, l'air épuré pendant le jour; il y fait un vent modéré, et, pendant la nuit, le ciel, tousjours serein, respand de douces et fraisches influences, qui font gouster la bénignité d'un tranquille sommeil.

Si la situation en est agréable, elle n'en est pas moins importante, parce qu'elle ouvre et ferme la porte pour passer chez les nations les plus esloignées, et dont les vastes mers d'eau douce sont environnées.

Il n'y a que les ennemis de la vérité qui soyent les ennemis de cet establissement si nécessaire à l'augmentation de la gloire du Roy, au progrès de la Religion et à la destruction du trône de Baal.

B 3 Lettre du Père Germain à Lamothe Cadillac
[*Margry,* Découvertes, *V, 209–11*]

A Québec, ce 25 aoust 1701

Quoyque nous n'ayons pas encore eu de nouvelles positives et certaines de vostre arrivée au Détroit, nous en avons néantmoins des conjectures que vous y devez estre heureusement dès le mois de Juillet. Comme vous sçavez, Monsieur, que je prends beaucoup de part à tout ce qui vous regarde, vous voulez bien que je vous en félicite, et que je prie, comme je fais de tout mon cœur, nostre Seigneur de vouloir bénir tous vos desseins pour le bien des Missions et de la Colonie. Tandis que vous aurez ces deux choses en veue, vous ne pouvez manquer d'avoir des succès heureux dans vos entreprises, non seulement pour les affaires publiques, mais encore pour les vostres particulières. Tout le monde admire ici la générosité de ces deux dames qui ont bien le courage d'entreprendre un voyage si pénible pour aller joindre leurs maris, sans craindre les grandes difficultés, ni les fatigues ou autres incommodités qu'il faut essuyer par des chemins, si longs et si rudes pour des personnes de leur sexe. Après cela, Monsieur, peut-on faire voire une affection conjugale et un attachement plus sincères et plus solides ? Quelqu'un leur disoit agréablement, ces jours derniers, qu'elles alloient passer pour des héroïnes; mais quelques autres dames plus délicates disant à Mme de Lamothe, pour la dissuader de ce voyage, que cela seroit bon, si on alloit dans un pays agréable et où l'on pourroit tousjours avoir belle compagnie comme en France, mais d'aller à un lieu inculte et désert, où il n'y aura qu'à se beaucoup ennuyer dans une si grande solitude, qu'elles ne comprenoient pas comment on pouvoit s'y résoudre, elle leur respondit fort sagement « qu'une femme qui aime son mari, comme elle doit, n'a point de plus puissant attrait que sa compagnie, en quelque lieu que ce soit. Tout le reste luy doit estre indifférent ». Voilà quels sont ses sentimens. Je ne vous mande point d'autres nouvelles; elle-mesme vous racontera mieux de vive voix tout ce que nous pouvons avoir appris de nouveau, depuis votre départ, que je ne sçaurois le faire par escrit. Ne doutez pas, Monsieur, que je ne recommande souvent aux Ursulines vos deux chères filles, et que je ne tasche de contribuer de tout ce qui dépendra de moy à leur éducation.

Le petit Cadillac m'a promis d'embrasser une fois son frère pour moy, quand il arrivera au Détroit. S'il oublie de me rendre ce petit service, faites-lui une petite reprimande. Je n'escris à aucun de nos Pères, parce que je ne doute pas que le P. Vaillant ne soit parti pour retourner ici avant que Mme de Lamothe arrive au Détroit, et je ne sçais s'il en aura laissé quelque autre à sa place. Faites-moy la grâce de me donner quelque part dans vostre bienveillance et la justice de croire que je seray toujours, avec tout le respect possible, Monsieur, vostre très humble et très obéissant serviteur.

B 4   Extraits d'une description du Détroit par M. de Lamothe
[*B.H.C., Cadillac Papers (French), vol. I, pp. 85 sqq.*]

25, 7bre 1702

. . .

Ce pais si temperé, si bon, et si beau qu'on peut a juste titre appeller le paradis terrestre de l'Amerique Septentrionalle merite toute l'attention du Roy pour le soutenir, et le faire habiter, en sorte qu'il s'y fasse un établissement solide qui ne soit pas sujet aux revolutions ordinaires des autres postes, ou l'on ne met qu'une simple garnison.

. . .

Vous verrez ci joint le plan du fort Pontchartrain que j'ay fait faire au detroit. Je l'ay ainsi nommé par ordre de Monsieur le chr. de Calliere, et la carte du detroit. Les maisons qui y sont, sont de bonne charpente de bois de chesne blanc, qui est plein, dur et pesant comme du fer. Ce fort n'est point en risque pourvu qu'il y ait du monde suffisament pour le deffendre.

Sa situation est charmante, et tres avantageuse. C'est l'endroit le plus étroit de la rivière, et ou personne ne peut passer de jour sans être veu.

Vous savez que je suis parti du Montreal le 2e de Juin de 1701 avec 100 hommes, et trois mois de vivres, que je suis arrivé au detroit le 24e de Juillet, ayant passé par le chemin ordinaire des Utauais ou je n'ay fait que 30 portages pour en tater.

Aprez que le fort fût fait, et les logemens, je fis deffricher la terre, et je fis semer du bled françois le 7e d'Octobre, n'ayant pas eu le tems de la bien preparer. Ce bled quoique fait a la hâte est venu tres beau, et il était coupé le 21 de juillet.

J'en ay fait semer aussi ce printems comme on le seme en Canada; il y est venu assez beau, mais non pas comme celui d'automne; ainsi la terre s'étant declarée, et m'ayant fait connoitre qu'il faut imiter les labeurs de France, j'ay laissé ordre au Sr de Tonty de donner ses soins pour commencer les semences vers le 20 de 7bre, et je lui ay laissé 20 arpens de terre bien preparée. Je ne doutte point qu'il n'ait fait quelque augmentation depuis mon depart.

J'ay fait semer aussi ce printems dans le mois de May douze arpens au plus de bled d'inde qui y est venu de huict pieds de haut; il y aura été recueilli vers le 20 du mois d'Août, et j'espere qu'il y en aura beaucoup. Tous les soldats ont leurs jardins.

Je croy que ce printems prochain nous aurons 60 arpens de terre ensemencée, ainsi je m'attends d'avoir une grande quantité de grains, et je ferai batir un moulin sur les lieux pour me passer absolument du Canada pour des vivres. J'ay aussi un beau jardin ou j'ay mis de la vigne, et des fruitiers francs; il a un arpent en quarré, et on l'agrandira s'il le faut. Je n'ay fait en tout ceci que me conformer aux ordres de Mr. le gouverneur general.

Tout cela ne se jette point au moule, d'autant mieux qu'il faut tout porter au Cou n'ayant pas encore ni bœufs, ni chevaux pour tirer, ni pour labourer, et pour y parvenir il faut se donner bien de mouvemens.

J'y ay fait faire aussi une barque du port de dix tonneaux qui servira dans la rivière a divers usages.

Il y a à la droite du fort a une bonne distance un village de hurons, à qui j'ay accordé des terres au nom de Sa Majesté suivant mon ordre. Le chef de cette nation avec quattre des plus considerables en les acceptant cria avec moy par trois fois vive le Roy, et j'ay planté moimême les bornes et marqué le lieu ou je voulois qu'ils fissent leur fort et leur village. Par ce moyen j'ay mis toutes les nations sur le pied de me demander des terres, et la permission de s'y établir. La planche faite pour les autres cette nation a defriché jusqu'a present 200 arpens de terre, et fera une grande recolte.

Il y a aussi à la gauche du fort un village de Oppenago c'est a dire de loups, à qui j'ay donné pareillement des terres, même à la charge de me les abandonner, si j'en ay besoin dans la suitte, en leur en donnant d'autres plus loin. Le lieu ou ils sont pourroit servir de Commune dans la suitte. Ce sont les sauvages les plus dociles, et les plus paisibles, je suis persuadé que pour peu qu'on en prenne soin, ils seront bientôt chrêtiens. Ils s'habillent tant qu'ils peuvent à la françoise, ils sont fort caressans, ils ecorchent même tant qu'ils peuvent notre langage. Ils ont fait aussi de beaux champs de bled.

Audessus de ce village a une demi lieue plus haut il y a un village composé de quattre nations ou-tavoises à qui j'ai pareillement donné des terres. Ils y ont fait de tres beaux champs de bled d'inde; de sorte que dans l'espace d'une lieue il y a quattre forts, et environ quattre cens hommes portant les armes avec leurs familles sans la garnison.

Avant de partir du fort dix-huict Miamis sont venus de la part de leur nation pour me demander des terres, et pour prier les Sauvages qui y sont de trouver bon qu'ils s'y viennent êtablir, et se joindre à eux : ainsi cet établissement ne sauroit être en meilleur train. Ceux-ci ayant frayé le chemin, les autres ne seront plus longtems sans y venir, d'autant mieux qu'avant mon depart nous avons appris que les bleds de Missilimakinak ont été emportez cette année par la gelée comme ils l'ont été par la precedente ce qui arrive fort souvent en ce lieu la.

L'année passée ma femme, et Made Tonty partirent le dix de 7bre avec nos familles pour nous y venir joindre, leur resolution parut fort extraordinaire dans l'entreprise d'un si long et penible voyage. Il est certain que rien ne surprit si fort les iroquois que lorsqu'ils les virent. On ne sauroit croire combien ils leur firent des caresses, et principalement les iroqois qui baisoient leurs mains, et pleuroient de joye disant qu'on avoit jamais veu des femmes françoises aller volontairement dans leur pais; c'est ce qui fit dire aussi aux iroquois qu'ils connoissoient bien que la paix generale que Monsieur le Chr de Calliere venoit de faire étoit veritablement sincere, et qu'ils n'en pouvoient plus douter, puisque des femmes de cette distinction possoient chez eux avec tant de confiance.

Si ces dames donnerent des impressions favorables pour nous aux iroquois, celles que nos alliez en ont eu ne l'ont pas été moins. Ils les receurent au detroit sous les armes avec plusieurs decharges de coups de fusil. Ils ont regardé ce mouvement comme le plus considerable qu'on pouvoit faire pour leur prouver que c'etoit tout de bon qu'on vouloit s'êtablir dans ce lieu, et qu'on en vouloit faire un poste a demûre et un bon établissement. . . .

B 5   EXTRAITS D'UNE LETTRE DE LAMOTHE CADILLAC À JÉRÔME
PONTCHARTRAIN
[*Margry*, Découvertes, *V, 303 sqq.*]

Fort Pontchartrain, 31 Aoust 1703

... C'est à vous, Monseigneur, à dire si vous souhaitez que je continue de faire establir icy les Sauvages, que ce poste soit conservé, soutenu avec éclat. Si ce sont là vos sentimens, comme je le crois, peut-estre suis-je propre pour les faire exécuter; mais j'ose vous dire que les sentimens des Jésuites de ce pays sont totalement opposés aux vostres, du moins en ce point-là.

Tout cela n'a pas empesché que les Sauteurs et Mississagués ne soient venus, cette année, former encore un village dans cette rivière. Ces deux nations se sont réunies et incorporées ensemble, ayant en cela suivi mon conseil et fait ma volonté. Je l'ay ainsi jugé à propos, estimant que leur reunion leur sera avantageuse et à nous, s'il arrivoit quelque rupture avec les ennemis de l'Estat et de la Colonie.

Trente Hurons de Missilimakinak sont arrivés ici le 28 Juin, pour s'incorporer avec ceux qui y sont establis. Ainsi il n'en reste qu'environ vingt-cinq en ce lieu-là, où le P. de Carheil, qui est leur missionnaire, se tient toujours ferme. J'espère que cet automne je luy arracheray enfin cette dernière plume de l'aisle, et je suis persuadé que cet opiniastre curé mourra dans sa paroisse, sans avoir un paroissien pour l'enterrer.

Plusieurs cabanes et familles des Miamis se sont establies ici, aussi bien que des Nepissiriniens; les uns se sont incorporés aux Hurons et les autres parmi les Outaouas et les Oppenago ou Loups.

Le reste de Outaouas-Sinagos, qui sont encore à Missilimakinak, m'ont envoyé un collier en secret pour me dire qu'ils viendront joindre leurs frères du Détroit, après qu'ils auront fait leur récolte. Six grandes cabanes de Kiskakouns m'ont envoyé dire la mesme chose. Je leur ay respondu par un collier que j'allois marquer les terres, où ils pourront faire leurs champs.

... Il est bon que vous soyez instruit qu'il y a plus de cinquante ans que les Iroquois avoient chassé par la force des armes la pluspart des nations dans les extremités du Lac Supérieur, c'est-à-dire à 500 lieues dans le nord de ce poste, qui est un pays stérile et affreux, et qu'il y a environ trente-deux ans qu'on les a rapprochés dans le lieu de Missilimakinak, qui est pareillement une terre ingrate et où ils ont esté réduits à la nécessité de vivre uniquement de poisson, de la manière que je vous l'ay expliqué par une petite relation, lorsque j'estois en France, dont vous eustes la bonté de me dire que vous étiez très satisfait. Il semble donc que Dieu m'a suscité comme un autre Moyse pour aller délivrer ce peuple de sa captivité, ou comme un Caleb pour le remener dans le pays de ses pères et leur ancienne demeure, dont il ne luy restoit que de faibles idées.

Cependant le Montréal joue ici le personnage de Pharaon; il ne peut voir cette transmigration sans en frémir, et il s'arme pour la confondre. ...

... De quoi se plaint le Montréal touchant le poste du Détroit, puisque c'estoit un pays abandonné et dont la possession estoit demeurée aux Iroquois et aux Loups ? C'estoient eux qui y faisoient la chasse et dans tous ses environs, qui en apportoient les peaux, les castors et la menue pelleterie aux Anglois. C'est un fait sans réplique et il faut estre plein d'opiniastreté et d'injustice pour en disconvenir.

Donc j'ay bien pris mon temps pour commencer cet establissement. Les Iroquois s'en sont absolument retirés, ou, s'il y en reste, ils sont meslés avec nos alliés. Toute la chasse s'y fait par nos Sauvages et dont le commerce nous revient. C'est donc un avantage pour le Royaume et un bien qu'on a soustrait et arraché à l'Angleterre. Les particuliers se plaignent que la Compagnie de la Colonie en profite. Je n'en disconviens point. Je leur laisse la liberté de crier. Je voudrois seulement qu'ils eussent des yeux pour sçavoir discerner que ce n'est pas la faute de l'establissement ni de celuy qui en a donné le projet. . . .

B 7 EXTRAITS DE LA RÉPONSE DES SIEURS DE VAUDREUIL ET BÉGON
[*B.H.C., Cadillac Papers (French), vol. III, pp. 618, 621*]

Au Sud Ouest du fort en tirant vers le lac Erié sont les hurons et les Pout8atamis qui occupent une lieue de l'Etendue cy dessus :

Au Sud de l'autre costé de la Riviere sont les 8ta8ois qui conjointement avec les hurons et Pouta8atamis ont fait des deserts qui contiennent Environ deux lieues de front sur huit arpens de profondeur.

Audessus du lac Ste Claire à douze lieues du fort du Costé du Sud est un village de Mississagués et Sauteurs dont les deserts contiennent Environ trois quarts de lieue de front sur quinze arpens de profondeur.

. . .

La Nation 8ta8oise est composée de 130 hommes, celle des P8t8atamis de 150, celle des hurons de 120, et celle des Sauteurs et Mississagués de 100.

B 8 CHARLEVOIX AU DÉTROIT
[*Charlevoix,* Journal d'un voyage, *V, 376–83*]

Fort Pontchartrain, 8e juin, 1721

Le quatrième [juin] nous fûmes arrêtés une bonne partie du jour sur une Pointe, qui court trois lieues Nord & Sud, et qu'on appelle la Point Pélée. Elle est cependant assez bien boisée du côté de l'Ouest, mais celui de l'Est n'a sur un terrain sablonneux que des Cèdres rouges, assez petits, & en médiocre quantité. . . . Il y a beaucoup d'Ours dans ce Pays, & l'hyver dernier il en fut tué sur la seule Pointe Pélée plus de quatre cent.

Le cinquième . . . nous entrâmes dans le Détroit une heure avant le soleil couché, & nous passâmes la nuit audessus d'une très belle Isle, appélée l'Isle du Bois Blanc. . . .

Avant que d'arriver au Fort, qui est sur la main gauche, une lieue audessous de l'Isle de Sainte Claire, on trouve sur la même main deux Villages assez nombreux, & qui sont fort proches l'un de l'autre. Le premier est habité par des Hurons Tionnontatez, les mêmes qui après avoir longtems erré de côté & d'autre, se sont fixés d'abord au Sault Sainte Marie, & ensuite à Michillimakinac. Le second l'est par des Pouteouatamis. Sur la droite, un peu plus haut, il y en a un troisième d'Outaouais, Compagnons inséparables des Hurons, depuis que les Iroquois ont obligé les uns & les autres, à abandonner leur Pays. Il n'y a point de Chrétiens parmi eux, s'il y en a parmi les Pouteouatamis, ils sont en très petit nombre. Les Hurons le sont tous, mais ils n'ont point de Missionnaires. On dit qu'ils n'en veulent point, mais cela se réduit à quelques-uns des Principaux, qui n'ont pas beaucoup de religion, & qui empêchent qu'on n'écoute tous les autres, lesquels en demandent depuis longtems.

Il y a longtems que la situation, encore plus que la beauté du Détroit, a fait souhaiter qu'on y fît un Etablissement considérable : il étoit assez bien commencé, il y a quinze ans, mais des raisons, qu'on ne dit point, l'ont réduit à très peu de choses. . . . Le jour suivant j'allai visiter les deux Bourgades Sauvages, qui sont voisines du Fort, & je commençai par les Hurons. Je trouvai toutes les Matrones, parmi lesquelles étoit l'Ayeule de Sasteratsi, fort affligées de se voir si longtems privées de secours spirituels. Bien des choses, que j'appris en même tems, me confirmèrent dans la pensée, où j'étois déjà, que les intêrets particuliers étoient les seuls obstacles à ce que désiroient ces bonnes Chrétiennes. Il faut esperer que les derniers ordres du Conseil de Marine leveront toutes ces oppositions. M. de Tonti m'assura qu'il alloit y travailler efficacement. . . .

B 9   LA RICHARDIE AD RETZ
[*General Jesuit Archives, Rome, gal. 110, vol. II, folios 348–9*]

iunii die 21, anno 1741, in missione assumptionis beatae marie virginis apud hurones.

cum me crebro fecerit certum pater girandeau, vestrae paternitati gratum fore si initia et progressus missionis huronicae brevi compendio exponerem; filii obsequentissimi lubens fungor munere ac lum illud solum vestrae paternitati gratissimum existimans, quod ad dei gloriam pertinet. Sciat ptas va mihi primum curam puerorum instituendorum apud iroquaeos, fuisse demandatum; apud quos biennio expleto, Rd pater du parc, tunc praepositus missionis, instinctu divinitus infuso, ut comprobavit eventus, experiri cupiens utrum longe esset a regno deo, huronica gens; hanc, mihi indignissimo, delegavit provinciam: quam multis annis, sine ullo animarum lucro curans, quamvis ut puto, labore improbo: tandem aliquando gratiae divinae radius illuxit: atque corda adamantina Sancti Spiritus ignis emollivit.

ne unum quidem adveniens, reperi barbarorum, christianam fidem profitentem: quamvis ex senioribus aliqui, olim morbo laborantes, a primis missionariis sacro fonte expiati. quadraginta prope abhinc annis, gentem corde incirconsisam pulverem pedum excutientes, deseruerant. unus inter primores gentis, Hoosiens nomine, post multas temporis moras christianam fidem cognationi universae, ita fuit exemplo; et ex ipsius tota parentela, ne unus quidem spiritui Sancto restiterit. brevissimo temporis intervallo, illo e vivis sublato vix lenissima spes remanebat barbarum vulgus ad Xi dulcissimam servitutem deducenti. quippe qui, immemor altitudinis scientiae dei, profectionem prope paraveram existimans, mortuo viro principe, rei christiana, indefesso tutore, mortuam quoque spem gloria dei promovendae. dum sic incertus, ac taedio confectus vagaret animus, apparuit benignitas salvatoris, in eo quod barbari utriusque sexus et aetatis, me insperante, et re pluries frustra tentata, ad doctrinae christinae expositionem et ad publicas in compitas habitas conciones, festini properarent. gratia dei promovente ita fervebat opus divinum, ut triennio vix emenso, post mortem laudati viri principis, ne unus quidem aetnicus in tota gente remaneret.

quod ad praesens tempus spectat RRme pater, omnia, ut puto, in tuto sunt posita. barbara gens, corde non ficto, fidem vidaetur profiteri: multitudinem christianorum vix continet sacra domus, licet septuaginta cubitorum longitudinis. ter in die convenimus oraturi et audituri: quater vero diebus festis: in quibus praecipue, vix cibi capiendi, superest temporis morula. quod praestat flagrans ardor ad sacrum tribunal accedendi. quotidianus labor insumitur in visitandis aegrotis, controversiis componendis, delinquentibus corrigendis, concionibus habendis pueris instituendis; et rebus sacris administrandis. mei, misertus, prope sexagenarii, Rd pater St. Pe praepositus missionis, socium providit, qui in ista dmi vinea elaboranda totus incumbat. nunc senex, nulliusque paene valetudinis, maxime doleo Rrme pater, quod me imparem experiar in ediscendis linguis barbarorum commorantium in circuitu, nondum sacro fonte expiatorum superstitem nunc habentem, qui in hac missione rem divinam curet, lubens ad alias gentes me converterem, nisi oenitus extinctam cognoscerem memoriam, qua primis temporibus pollebam. quanvis ad illorum conversionem, omnia spero ex eo quo comburitur divinae gloriae zelo, Rdus pater St. Pe; quem zelum, antequam praeficeretur, prope extinctum lugenam; nunc vero reviviscenti gratulor. Faxit musericors Deus, ut eum, missioni amantissimae, paternitas vestra, donet praepositum, quamdiu vixerit: ut sic reflorescat religiosa disciplina in domibus Societatis: zelus observor in missionibus. quod si gratum videatur paternitati vestrae ut fusius rem missionis huronicae prosequar, ipsius obtemperabo mandatis. paternitati vestrae filius in Xo obsequentissimus,

[F. 349 verso]—Rdo admodum Patri
    in Xo
    praeposito Societatis Jesu
    generalis
        Roman

1741   Miss. Canad.

in miss assumptionis Bmae V apud hurones 21 jun. P. Armandus de la Richardie scribit jam de missione sua ne unum quidem superesse ethnicum etc. . . . lettera tutta piena di edificazione e di consolazione, communicato al Sommo Pontefice

R. 18a jan. 1742

B 11   Extraits du livre de compte de la mission des Hurons du Détroit
      [*B.H.C.*]

[1743]

Je dois à Meloche pour tous les batiments qu'il m'a fait et qu'il doit me faire 3100 livres.
Je dois à Janis pour la maçonne desdits batiments la somme de 600#............ de plus au meme 10# pour la maison du fermier et pour l'etable............de plus au meme 100# pour petites reparations et pour ce qu'il a fait pour le forgeron...........ce dernier article ne doit se payer qu'en 1744...........de plus 30# pour les cloisons. Sur quoi je lui ai paié 48# en blé............de plus paié au meme 160#............de plus 100# qu'il accepte sur ce que Cecile me

doit............de plus 227#............les 635# sont payés. ainsi je ne dois plus rien à Janis pour l'eglise et la maison............Je lui dois encore pour la maison du fermier et autres ouvrages la somme de 200# moins 21# 15s. La ditte somme est payé.

Donné a Lesperance sur ses gages 100#. Je lui dois encore 34# 10s. j'en dois à Prisq. 56. Lesperance est fini de payé.

Payé a Meloche pour mes batiments 985# qu'il a pris de Cuillerier qui me les devoit............4# sur Valet qui me les devoit............101# en chats que je lui ai donné............somme totale donnée au dit 1090#............Le meme a reçu des Caron à ma decharge la somme de 300#. total 1390#............de Binau pour ma terre 1900#............Le dit Meloche est payé de tout ce que je lui devois excepter 90# que Mini ou Bineau lui payera l'an prochain 1744, comme ledit Meloche l'a accepté............de plus au meme 10 messes qu'il m'a commandées pour Saguin............

Cette mission ne doit plus rien excepté l'envoy des provisions que Le Sieur de Couagne m'a envoyées cette année 1743.

J'ai preté a St. Martin les 161# qui me revenoient de ses travaux de forge, pour Le roy, qui doivent etre payé à Montreal.

Aujourd'hui 2 de juillet 1743 est convenu Le Sr Jean Bapt. Goyau habitant du poste du Detroit de se transporter ici avec toute sa famille dans le cours du mois Sept. de la meme année pour y prendre la ferme de la mission des Peres de la compagnie de Jesus aux conditions suivantes :

1. Les dits Peres cèdent laditte ferme audit Goyau pour le tems de 6 années; quoiqu'il ne se trouve pas bien des Rds PP. ou les Rds PP. de lui, chacun sera libre de part et d'autre en s'avertissant mutuellement un an d'avance.

2. Les dits Rds PP fourniront audit Goyau la semence de tous les grains qu'il semera sur leur terre et partageront avec lui par egale portion le provenu desdites semences, sans qu'il soit libre audit Goyau de semer pour lui ou pour les siens quoiq. ce soit sur laditte terre, sans en partager avec eux ledit provenu, a moins que ce ne fut du bled dinde qu'il voulut semer pour ses usages; et pour que les Rds Peres n'en manquent pas, il leur labourera tous les ans deux arpents de terre où ils en puissent semer pour eux seuls.

3. Il sera fait inventaire des ustensilles et harnois de chariage et labourage que lesdits Rds PP livreront audit Goyau pour qu'il rende le tout au meme etat et teneur qu'il l'aura pris.

4. Pour ce qui est des animaux il sera tenu d'en rendre à la fin de la ferme le meme nombre en meme qualité qu'il les aura reçus, ou pourra recevoir dans la suite avec la moitie du provenu desdits animaux.

5. Il fera un parque commode pour la garde et pature desdits animaux, et entretiendra avec soin la palissade de la terre qui lui sera livrée et la laissera en bon etat a la fin de la ferme.

6. Lesdits Rds PP. consentent que ledit Goyau puissent se servir de leurs animaux pour chariage et labourage tant pour français que pour sauvages. Le tout a condition qu'il leur chariera tous les hivers, tant pour leur chauffage que pour leur part des fourneaux de leur forgeron, 40 cordes de bois; et meme sera obligé ledit Goyau de preter lesdits animaux auxdits Rds PP. pour trainage ou chariage quand ils en auront besoin.

J'ai livré a Goyau en entrant dans cette ferme de L'île aux bois blancs : 6 minots et demi de pois pour semer, 5 minots d'avoine pour meme usage, avec 14 minots et demi de bléd froment pour semer, lesquels semences il rendra en quittant la ferme............de plus j'ai livré au meme une charrue garnie avec ses ruelles, toute neuve, une charette avec des roues presq. neuve; une traine neuve; 3 bœufs illinois avec une vache de meme espece, 2 juments coutants chacune 80#. Le tout coutant 400#. de plus 2 vaches du pais avec une taure d'un an.

Pour remplacer les 3 vaches qi sont mortes ou ont eté tuées entre les mains de Goyau, j'ai livré 2 genisses illinoises dont l'une m'a couté 40# et l'autre 75. Je lui ai aussi livré une taure illinoise que j'ai changé pour une vache anoliere.

Me Goyau a commencé a blanchir et à boulanger pour cette mission a la St. Michel 1743 pour la somme de 100# chaq. année.

Me Goyau a reçu une chemise 3# 10s............une pinte d'eau de vie 3#............ une p.d.d.v. 3#............3#............une paire de mitasse de molleton............une paire de mitasse de molleton............une p.d.d.v............2 minots de pois 18#............6 couvertes 54#............une paire de mitasse 3#............Me Goyau est finie de payer pour la 1ere année.

Preté à Mallet 3 pintes d'eau de vie............3 livres de poudre............5 liv. de plomb............une couverte bleue............3 grandes chemises............3 petites chemises (P. Degonor).

Reçu de Mallet 6 chevreuils............16 dindes............6 outardes............1 cigne ....8 canards............1 fesse d'ours............5 ou 6 perdrix............2 petits castors &c. (P. Degonor).

...

[1748]

J'ai fait marché avec Meloche pr la charpente de mon eglise, maison, couverture &c. pr la somme de 1000#............et pr chaque cent de planches et de madriers à 60#............et pr ce qu'il me sciera à 30# le cent.

Item avec Janis pr 2 cheminées de pierre, foyers; pr later, crepir, renduire et blanchir le tout cy-dessus que Meloche doit me faire, pr la somme de 850 liv. et trois minots de blé d'inde; et s'il renduit les dehors, je lui dois payer 300 liv de plus.

Item avec Parent pr toute la menuiserie desdits batiments, pr la somme de 1000# et 2 minots de blé d'inde : des 1000#, 400 payables ici, et les 600# payables à Montreal.

Je dois à Regis 5 minots et demi de blé d'inde que j'ai pris sur sa part. Je lui dois aussi 6 livres de peau de chevreux.

Je devrai à Morand pr 100 pieces de pin de sciage 250 liv............à Mini pr le quarré de l'eglise, et pr comble et quarré de la maison, 400 liv. en billets............à Claude et Niagara pr le chariage des planches et madriers 40 liv; de plus aux memes pr le chariage du cajeu de Mini 100 liv. moins 10 sols.

Mr Le Commandant a paye 500 liv. à Mini.

Niagara a pris la ferme de cette mission le 1er 7bre, 1748 à condition d'en partager tout le provenu avec les PP de laditte mission. Je lui ai fourni 30 minots de semence de blé francais; 4 minots de pois; une charrue neuve, rouelles et soc neufs. je lui ai livré 4 bœufs illinois, 4 vaches de meme espece; un jeune cheval et une vielle jument. De plus je lui ai avancé 150# pr se batir une maison et une etable; le tout à condition qu'il nous charira tous les hyvers 40 cordes de bois de chauffages, et qu'il labourera aussi tous les ans 3 arpens de terre pour y semer du blé d'inde au profit de la mission. En outre j'ai avancé audit Niagara la somme de 200# pour nous blanchir et nous boulanger pendant 2 ans, lesquels 2 ans expirés, il sera obligé de nous blanchir et boulanger pendant le tems de sa ferme, moyennant 100# par ans que la mission lui payera à la fin de sa ferme. Il rendra les ustensiles tels qu'il les a reçus; et les animaux il les rendra de meme, et partagera le provenu. Les souches seront aussi rendues.

[1749]

Le Sr. Chauvin le 10 avril 1749 a pris la forge de cette mission aux conditions suivantes :

1. qu'on lui livrera tous les ustensiles qui sont en nature de laditte forge;
2. qu'on lui donnera l'acier et les limes qui viendront de Montreal chaque année;
3. qu'il se batira une forge à ladite mission et une maison quand il le pourra.
4. qu'en lui fournissant le fer il sera obligé de faire et de racommoder tout ce qui sera necessaire pour les batimens et usages de la mission, et memes les armes; le tout gratuitement. Moyennant cela la mission lui cede tout le provenu de ladite forge, à condition de payer tous les ans aux missionnaires la somme de 300#.

Planches............Robert m'en a scié 126; et plus 57 planches — 7# 10s de chariage — 47# 10s de sciage............Niagara a rendu ici de chez Meloche 253 planches; de plus 90 madriers; de plus 293 planches; total 560. le chariage 39#............Regis m'a charié de chez Meloche 192 madriers de bois blanc; de plus 40 madriers de 15 pies.

Parent a pris chez nous au fort :
1. 21 madriers ou planches;
2. 15 ici;
3. 7 la meme;
4. 4 chez Meloche, et 14 chez Robert, avec 12 que Regis lui a remis.

J'ai payé a Moran 250# pr le bois de sciage que j'ai reçu de lui.
J'ai payé à Claude Campeau 82# pr ce que je lui dois, pr chariage et pr une piroguée de pierre.
Barte et Dumouchel ont fini de me payer l'acier que je leur ai vendu.
J'ai reçu de la veuve Caron 33 liv par Pagét, et 140 liv. pesant de plomb.
Meloche — Je lui ai payé 100# moins 10s sur ses ouvrages, en menues pelleteries............de plus 30# à lui payées à ma decharge par Me Caron ....de plus 100 pistoles à lui payées à ma decharge par le Sr Carignan commerçant au Detroit............de plus payé au susdit 300# par Mr Navarre ....Il est fini de payer.
Janis — Je lui ai payé 39# 10s sur ses ouvrages en menues pelleteries............ de plus 160# que Pierrot Labute et Carignan lui ont payées............de plus 60# que la Caron lui a payées pour moi............de plus 10# que je lui ai

payées............de plus 268# à lui payées a ma decharge par le Sr Gouin commerçant au Detroit............de plus 259# au susdit par Mr Navarre............ il est fini de payer.
Parent — 112# à lui payées à ma decharge par Mr. Godefroi............de plus 63# à lui payées par le P. bon............de plus 232# à lui payées à ma decharge par le Sr. Guoin commerçant au Detroit............de plus 5# pr des messes ....de plus 600# par Mr Navarre............il est fini de payer............il. a reçu 12# au dela de son payement.

J'ai payé à Lesperance le cadet la somme de 59# en deduction des 50 ecus que je lui devois pr l'année qu'il m'a servi............j'ai fini de payer au susdit les 50 ecus que je lui devois.
...

J'ai payé à Nicolas Catin la somme de 350# qu'il touchera à Montreal par le moyen de 412# qu'il y recevra en billets sur le pié de 30 pour cent, sur quoi je lui suis redevable de 43# payables ici au mois de mai 1750. Laditte somme est a l'acquit de Niagara.

[1750]
...
J'ai remis à Chauvin forgeron de cette mission la somme de 100# sur les 300# qu'il doit donner tous les ans à laditte mission pour le dedomagement de l'acier et du fer que je n'ai pu lui donner cette année 1750.
J'ai livré au Sr Roy voyageur 3 paquets pour les remettre à Montreal au Sr René de Couagne; le fret de ces 3 pacquets est de 36 liv., le portage compris : l'un est de castor pesant 92 liv : l'autre de chats couvert de 2 castors; le 3me de 48 pichous, 75 loutres, 28 chats, et 43 liv. pesant de castor............Le port de ces 3 paquets a eté payé ici par une chaudiere couverte............20 aout 1750.
...
Semences de 1750............37 minots de ....6 minots d'avoine............et 3 quarts de pois............Nota : La recolte a eté de 1050 gerbes : il faut 7 gerbes au minot, et par consequant il doit y avoir 150 minots............otez-en 40 pour la semence, restent 110, dont 55 pour notre part.
La Recolte de blé a eté de 150 minots............La recolte de blé d'inde de 40 minots, dont 7 minots et demi d'epiochons; regis en a eu le tiers............la recolte d'avoine de 16 minots............et celle de pois de 2 minots.
Oignons............800 en tresses............553 non tressés............et 347 sives ....total 1600. 240 ails, dont 180 en tresses.

B 12   EXTRAITS DU MANUSCRIT POTIER
[*Bibliothèque Municipale de Montréal, Collection Gagnon*]

[p. 195]

   Village-huron de L'ile aux bois-blancs en 1747 — 33 cabanes ou loges
      Le Petit Village (19 cabanes)
         à droite en entrant dans le village   [Personnes]
1. La La foret............grand-male............temiskam   [44]
2. Skutache............Nicolas............Le Manchot............   [34]
   angelique

3. La cabane des iroquois [7]
   à gauche en entrant...........nota : 1 marque la cabane sur la rue...........2 celle qui est derriere........... 3 celle &c.

1. Taechiaten............(maison à la françoise) [9]
1. La vielle Coin (non extat, manet etionnont8t)
1. Mathias (nova casa) [11 et des enfants]
2. La vielle S8ndak8a [9]
3. Kinench8e [7]
1. Le Bijou...........La Busquette [5]
1. La8aron...........8asanion...........8kaes...........babi, la caliere...........bedau [44 et des enfants]
2. Aa8as...........tiok8oink [51]
1. La vielle cheveux-plats [7]
2. Sastaretsi...........La vielle catherine...........La mitasse ....anien8indes...........la femme de misting8oin [40]
1. Bricon...........Sondekon...........La christofle [11]
2. L'onnonsio (ou) La vielle-noire (ou) La mal aux levres...........8a8ananta [9]
1. Le glorieux...........ozane [13]
1. Ang8irot (janus quirinus) bibax...........non extat
1. L'enien8indes...........L'œil eraillé...........enons........... Skanaret...........Sachendoa (bon ivrogne) [27 et bien des enfants]
2. Nicolas...........Le manchot (nova casa) [pas encore habités]

       Le Grand Village (15 cabanes) [Personnes]
1. Les filles d'anne [4]
2. La delonchamps [7]
1. le medecin...........son neveu...........la borgnette [5]
1. la vielle piponnette...........3 neveu de bapt. piponnette [21 et bien des enfants]
2. la veuve Ang8irot [6]
1. la babillarde...........Sent8anne [28]
1. les trois filles de toussaint (huron de lorette) [6]
1. le grand Aoes...........tonti [7]
1. la vielle reine...........Ondechonti, son fils [6]
2. N'ondaentons (nemo domi, à etionnont8t)
1. la vielle Sadendora...........grand-male [10 et des enfants]
1. la vielle Andatorenha...........la vielle marie........... les loups [32 plusieurs grands et petits pas baptizés]
1. la vielle 40 sols...........le borgne...........la puce, laurent &c [72 et des enfants]
2. Aronissa (maison françoise, brulée)...........
1. le Brutal (à etionnont8t). [12]

       etionnont8t (ou) le petit village
1. Nicolas   5. Ta8ita
2. Le Brutal   6. Sandotes
3. Nendaentons   7. La caliere
4. La vielle coin   8. Le lorretain

     Aaae ou R. blanche ou Belle Riv : 8 cab
1. Makons
2. Sadendora
3. 2 sœurs de la babillarde
4. la canerin

[p. 200]

Les trois bandes huronnes, divisées en 10
1 Oskennonto — la bande du chevreuil, en 3
   1e es8ntennonk — Sastaretsi ⎫
   2e eangontr8nnon — Mathias ⎬ hontaxen
   3e hatinnionen — aa8as ⎭
2 Andia8ich — la bande de la tortue en 4
   1e ennchensiaeronnon (aron-issa) (Saens8at)
   2e eronhisseeronnon (orontondi — le manchot)
   3e atieeronnon (babi)
   4e entihoronnon — ang8irot — S8nnonkanien
3 hannaarisk8a — la bande du loup en 3
   1e hatinnaarisk8a — Taechiaten — hondatorinke
   2e hatindesonk (les eperviers)
   3e (hotiraon (les eturgeons) le brutal
      (Hataensik (ne font qu'une bande)

3 grands chefs dans le nation huronne
   1. Sastaretsi   2. Saents8at   3. Taechiaten

B 13 EXTRAITS DE LA GAZETTE DU PÈRE POTIER
[Archives du Collège Ste-Marie, Montréal]

[p. 84]

Chron : &

(1743)
juili 18 — depart de la Rochelle
aout 5 — attaqué en mer par 3 vaiss : anglais
Oct   1 — arrivée à Quebec ou je fus 15 jours
     16 — à lorette 8 mois 8 jours

(1744)
Juin 26 — partis de Quebec pour le Detroit
sept 25 — arrivai à L'ile aux bois blancs
     28 — fis le 1er service (il etoit de 40 sols)
oct 11 — fus au fort pour la 1ere fois (vis Mr. Navarre le 12)
      * — La mission huronne fut transportée à L'ile aux bois blancs le 13 oct 1742
     28 — fus à la Riv. aux canards — Navarre y etoit depuis 5 jours : ne le vis pas
nov   3 — fus au fort avec Mr. de Longueuil par un vent & & — Navarre passa à L'ile aux bois-blancs allant à la chasse; dejeuna, repassa le lendemain avec 12 dindes

(1745)
fev   2 — commençai à faire des casseaux &
mars 23 — la foudre tomba sur la chapelle de Lorette, blessa un soldat
juil 29 — la foudre tomba proche notre maison
aout 20 — arrivée de Mr. de Muys avec la nouvelle de la prise de L'ile-royalle & — repartit le 27 du fort, et le 29 d'ici
     28 — Cuillerier passa ici conduisant 20 françois pour defendre Niagara

sept 22 — vers ce tems fus au fort avec Mr. Navarre : couchames à la riv : aux canards
oct 19 — partis pour l'hivernement, ou je fus 6 mois 18 jours — * ce meme jour le frère La tour fut blessé d'un coup de fusil par regis
dec 2 — baptisai une Louve à etionnont8t qui mourut le 11

(1746)
janv 31 — depart d'hondatorenha pour la guerre
mars 1 — La cabane d'enons brula
 15 — passai une Riv sur la glace
 20 — un chien se noya dans les glaces à la riv d'ostand8ski
 25 — la nuit du 24 au 25 le P. la Richardie eut une atteinte de paralysie
avril 4 — eus la colique — lus une lettre en huron addressée aux anciens — grand conseil
avril 16 — partis d'ontietsi & — passai par le portage d'etionnont8t ou je restai jusqu'au 30, et arrivai le 5 mai à L'ile aux bois blancs
 28 — Navarre partit de la pointe aux cedres apres m'y avoir attendu 6 jours
mai 21 — la fievre me prit matin, et dura 14 mois
 27 — enterrai la la douceur (1er enterrement)
juin 7 — Les bleds d'inde gelés
 14 — depart des 8ta8as, P8t et Sauteurs pour Montreal, dans le canot de préjan
aout 20 — Le P. dujaunai fit une retraite à L'ile aux bois-blancs
nov 6 — Navarre et Pierrot chene passerent allant à la chasse
 14 — fus à la chasse à la presqu'ile
 22 — arrivée de q : hurons de Montreal avec 4 chev.
dec 20 — Navarre et Pierrot chene passerent 7 à 8 jours à L'ile aux bois blancs

(1747)
janv 2 — arrivée de Mr Sac-epée, fils, avec la croix de S. Louis pour Mr. de Longueuil
 18 — la maison d'aron-issa brula
 23 — Mr de Longueuil et cuillerier vinrent, sur les glaces, à L'ile aux bois blancs, par un froid de sauvage
fev 15 — depart de 22 fr. pour les cha8annons
 15 — arrivée d'un onnontagués à L'ile aux bois blancs, avec la nouvelle de la defaite des cedres; partit le 16 pour le fort, et le 17 Mr. de Longueuil courut apres les 22 fr : pour les faire relacher
mars 19 — fus au fort — trouvai la riviere pleine de glaces à la pointe du Montreal
 31 — arrivée de 32 person : de Montreal pour lever les nations
avril 16 — partis pour etionnont8t, y arrivai le 20, en repartis le 24, et arrivai à l'ile aux bois-blancs le 29
mai 20 — arrivée de Nicolas à L'ile aux bois-blancs avec ses guerriers — *me rendis au fort à minuit et demi
 31 — vers ce tems-ci, antoine chapoton, Tousignan et la Borde, tués par des 8ta8as vers le Saghinan

[p. 90]

P. Marcol mihi — du 19 juin 1749 — recu le 23 oct par les chefs 8ia............

M.R.P. Pax Xi —

rien ne pouvait me faire plus de plaisir que la resolution dans laquelle vous m'avez temoigné être de faire un dernier effort pour vous perfectionner dans la langue huronne — faites donc M.R.P., voyez beaucoup les Sauvages, allez dans les cabanes, et qu'ils trouvent toujours un accès facile auprès de vous dans tous les tems. C'est le moyen de les gagner. il en coute, J'en conviens; mais le bien des ames et la gloire de dieu demande de nous ce sacrifice — rappelons-nous souvent ces sentiments de zele et de ferveur avec lesquels en quittant l'europe et nos familles, nous sommes venus dans ce païs-cy chercher une vie souffrante ou une mort prompte. confessez, parlez, instruisez, faites le catechisme. Comme le P. de la Richardie n'est plus en etat de soutenir les fatigues d'une mission, et que je compte qu'il descendra au 1er jour, je prie le Seigneur de vous remplir de son esprit, et de vous donner tout ce qui est necessaire pour conduire, gouverner, augmenter une grande mission — je suis en union de vos SS. pp avec respect.
M.R.P.-v.t.h. & o.s.

Marcol. Jes.

à Montreal ce 19 juin 1749

au P. Marcol —   du 29 Sept — [1749]   par Mr. dubuisson —

M.R.P. P.Xi —

J'ai reçu vos lettres en date du 13 de mai et du 19 de juin. je suis tres sensible aux offres de services que vous me faites dans le 1ere, et je tacherai de profiter des instructions que vous me donner dans la seconde. quoique les progrès que j'ai fait dans la langue huronne, depuis la dernière lettre que j'ai eu l'honneur de vous ecrire, ne soient pas bien considerables, je compte néanmoins être en etat, le printems prochain, de me tirer d'affaire, en cas que le P. de la Richardie descende. Ce R^d Pere continue de jouir d'une santé passable. il a retenu le f. gournay, parceque le vieux ratier, St-Come, lui a manqué de parole. Nicolas et ses adherants (à l'exception de q. familles qui se sont rangés à la mission) perseverent toujours dans leur schisme, et il est à souhaiter qu'ils continuent d'y perseverer, car, de l'aveu meme des hurons qui sont ici, ce sont des esprits si remuants et si mal-faits, que s'ils revenaient dans ce village, ils ne pourraient s'empecher de rebrouiller la terre. Aussi, le la Richardie — vue leur obstination — a pris le parti de les abandonner à leur sens reprouve — en general les hurons des païs d'enhaut sont de vilaines gueleries : fourbes, yvrognes, superstitieux, d'un orgueil Luciferien. Il faut néanmoins avouer qu'il y en a de bons parmi, mais ce sont bien : rari montes in gurgite vasto — et pour l'amour de ce petit je consens de vivre et de mourir avec eux : nous sommes rebatis en entier à l'exception d'une partie du plancher et du plafond de la chapelle, ce qui n'a pas empeché d'y dire la messe, pour la 1ere fois, le jour de la Nativité de la Ste Vierge — nous attendons Mr. de Celorum de jour en jour, cependant-nous n'en avons aucune nouvelle depuis quinze jours qu'un 8ta8ais en apporta des lettres dattées du 24 aout — il etait pour lors sur le point de quitter les Cha8annons de Sonnioto pour aller à la Riviere à la Roche, pour faire la viste aux Miamis rebelles. La saison est bien avancée, je crains que l'armée ne soit obligé d'hyverner au Detroit. Si cela est, je plains le P. bonnecamps, et votre Rce qui sans doute en a besoin.

    Je suis M.R.P. en l'union de vos SS. pp. avec soumission v.t.h & —

[pp. 90–1]
    ego D. de Longueuil — du 29 Sept. [1749] — par Mr. dubuisson —

Mr —
    c'est avec bien du regret que je vous ai vu partir d'ici. Au regret a succédé la douleur lorsque j'ai appris les avantures facheuses de votre voyage du Detroit à Montreal. j'ai eté surtout indigné contre la pointe Pelée pour le vilain tour qu'elle vous jouat. mais ma douleur s'est entierement dissipée à l'arrivée de la promotion; deja deux fois j'eus l'honneur de vous faire mon compliment à l'occasion de votre avancement, souffrez que je vous le fasse pour la 3e fois, et cela doublement tant par rapport à vous que par rapport à Mr. votre frere. fasse le ciel que vous n'en demeuriez pas là ! Nicolas est toujours le meme et au meme endroit. Le bruit court qu'il a dessein de revenir se recamper à atsand8ski, mais j'espere que nos puissances s'y opposeront. Le Sieur Tahatie arriva dernierement d'Orange avec un grand collier addressé à nicolas par le gouverneur de baston, pour le remercier d'avoir employé la hache d'onnontio contre onnontio meme, et pour l'inviter de se rendre à baston ou à Ch8agen, avec promesse que tous les magazins lui seront ouverts pour en prendre gratuitement tout ce que bon lui semblera. Mr. de Sabrevois a travaillé ... (le reste de la lettre manque).

[p. 91]
    Mr. de Celoron mihi ... le 9 Sept. 1750, apporté jean marie et cahousa a 8 h. et demi du soir ... etais couché depuis 1 heure.

M.R.P. — j'apprends de nouvelles circonstances qui me font tout apprehender pour le P. de La Richardie. Baby vient d'avouer à chauvin que les hurons fugitifs ne sont pas bien intentionnés, et que votre P. Superieur court des risques : voici en bref ce que dit Baby : il repete ce que La Miamise a deja declaré : il ne dit pas qu'on tuera, mais il avoue que c'est de valeur; interpretez s'il vous plait ce terme sauvage. quelle raison aurait Baby de faire cette nouvelle ? craint-il que les hurons de nicolas, une fois revenus à la mission ne le degradent, et ne detronent Sastaredzy ? il ne convient point d'approfondir jusques là, je ne crois pas que cette politique puisse avoir lieu : il faut plutôt croire que les hurons de Yahagué sont encore des scelerats et que l'impunité de leur crime les rend plus insolens que jamais ! — Je n'ai point voulu empecher d'autorité le voyage du P. Superieur, je lui ai donné mes conseils, et je crois qu'ils devraient prévaloir dans les occurences comme celles-ci, après des avis si souvent reiterés de la bouche meme des hurons.

    je reïtere mes instances auprès du P. de La Richardie. joignez-vous à moy pour l'engager à ne point faire une demarche qui fournit aux rebelles l'occasion de se rendre encore plus coupables. —

    Il faut que le Pere tienne un conseil avec les hurons qui l'accompagnent, ils ont grand interet d'agir avec prudence, d'autant plus qu'ils ont part aux menaces qui ont eté faites et vraisemblement ils auront leur part aussi des coups qui pourront être frappés. je vous addresse une lettre pour le P. que

je vous prie de lui envoyer par le fils du Roy qui doit partir demain. je serais faché que son zele et sa fermeté lui fut prejudiciable. Je suis avec respect M.R.P. v.t. &c
ce 9 Sept. 1750 au Detroit

Celoron

[p. 94]
   ego P. Marcol — 13 oct. 1750 par Mr. de Raymond

Mon. R.P. — Le P. de La Richardie partit d'ici le 7 de Sept. pour le pays des hurons fuyards, accompagné de trois françois qui lui servent de canoteurs. Les deux principaux chefs de ce village, avec deux autres consideres, et q. jeunes gens s'embarquerent le lendemain pour se joindre au P : à peine ces derniers furent-ils partis que le bruit se repandit qu'on devait lever la chevelure à toute la troupe des ambassadeurs. Mr. de Celoron allarmé de ce bruit depecha sur le champ des courriers avec une lettre pour le pere : ceux-ci ayant trouvé les chefs à trois lieu du detroit, la leur remirent, et s'en revinrent le soir. comme le mauvais bruit croissait d'heure en heure, Mr. de Celoron ecrivit une seconde lettre au P. Je lui ecrivis aussi pour lui donner avis de tout ce qui se debitait ici —

il y a aujourd'hui 35 jours que le Pere est parti sans que nous ayons reçu de ses nouvelles. est-il allé jusqu'au village des rebelles, n'y est-il point allé ? c'est ce que nous ignorons : ma pensée est qu'il se sera arrêté à la Riviere au Vermillion à trois journees de marche du pays des fuyards, et que de là il aura envoyé des courriers aux chefs des rebelles leur dire de venir lui parler. quoi qu'il en soit, je ne scaurais croire que le nicolaïtes osent attenter sur la vie du pere.

Le P. bon : a la fievre tremblante depuis 15 jours; le quinquinna que je lui ai donné les lui a fait passer. je souhaite qu'elle ne re-vienne pas. Je me souviens d'avoir medit de ce R.P. dans ma derniere lettre, je retracte. Mr. de Celoron travaille aussi à rassembler les Miamis, mais je doute qu'il reussira.

J'aurais bien des choses à vous dire touchant la mission, mais ce sera pour une autre occasion. Je suis avec soumission en l'union de vos SS.pp. M.R.P.

Postscriptum. Je viens de recevoir une lettre du P. de la Richardie, il me mande qu'il s'est arrêté à la riv : au vermillion, ou il attend de jour en jour les chefs des rebelles.

C 1 Extraits du journal de la campagne que le Sr. de Léry a faite au Détroit en l'année 1749
[*Archives du Séminaire de Québec; publié dans Roy,* Rapport de l'Archiviste de la Province de Québec pour 1926–7, *pp. 334–48*]

... Le 24, nous partîmes dans la nuit; à 10 heures du matin, je fis le portage de la Pointe Pelée; à une lieue de distance de lextrémité de ladite Pointe, ce portage a ¾ de lieue de long, il faut porter le canot pendant six arpents pour entrer dans un marais où il y a assez d'eau, et pour en sortir, il faut faire portage de 14 autres arpents : pour lors, vous vous trouvez à une lieue et demie de la Pointe Pelée qui est doublée et vous avez épargné 1 lieue ¾ de chemin et doublé la plus mauvaise pointe du lac. On pourrait très bien arranger ce portage de façon que les ¾ de lieue que l'on fait par eau dans le marais serait aisé, en coupant les bois qui y sont tombés. Quelques canots qui voulurent doubler la Pointe Pelée se brisèrent quoiquil ne venta point fort. La mer y brise avec force et il faut aller à ½ lieue au large parce que l'extrémité de cette Pointe est de rochers dont une partie est sous l'eau; quelquefois il s'y forme des bancs de sable; de l'endroit où nous avions couché [à la Pointe aux Pins] à venir au portage de la Pointe Pelée, il y a 14 lieues, de la Pointe Pelée à la rivière à Perthuis il y a 4 lieues, de la rivière à Perthuis à un endroit appelé le Gros Cap (et où il n'y en a point,) il y a 2 lieues, et dudit Gros-Cap à la rivière aux Cèdres où nous campâmes 2 lieues. Fait cette journée 22 lieues. Les bords du lac sont comme les jours précédents, les bois de même.

. . .

Le 25, nous partîmes du matin de la rivière aux Cèdres après avoir fait 1½ lieue nous trouvâmes la rivière Amaconce, 1½ lieue après ladite rivière, la Presqu'isle, et à une lieue plus loin que la presqu'isle, l'entrée de la rivière du Detroit. Route depuis la rivière aux Cèdres à l'entrée de la rivière du Détroit, 4 lieues — Partant de l'entrée de la rivière du Détroit, à ¾ de lieue nous trouvâmes le bout d'en bas de l'isle au Bois-Blanc, où était l'ancien village des Hurons. L'Isle aux Bois Blanc a une demi lieue de long et a la forme d'un quarré long arrondi par les angles. A une lieue du bas de l'Isle au Bois Blanc, nous trouvâmes l'embouchure de la rivière aux Canards et à une lieue plus haut, le milieu de la petite Isle aux Dindes, où nous campâmes, elle peut avoir ⅛ de lieue de long.

. . .

Le 26, à ¾ de l'Isle aux Dindes c'est à dire de la Petite Isle, car il y en a une Grande au milieu de la rivière, vis à vis la Petite, qui a une lieue de long et qui sert avec la petite de communes, pour mettre les animaux des habitans, nous trouvâmes la Rivière aux Dindes à une lieue plus haut le ruisseau de la Vieille Reine; à demi lieue dudit ruisseau, le village des Hurons avec l'église et maison des missionnaires. Nous fîmes encore ½ lieue et nous trouvâmes vis à vis le Fort où nous traversâmes et faisant le N.N.O. . . .

. . .

Le 27, je commençai à lever les plans et à prendre les connaissances nécessaires pour rendre un compte exact de la position, de la qualité des terres et des choses à faire pour les faire valoir.

. . .

Il y a des endroits au Détroit où la terre est bonne à faire de la brique, elle y valait, en 1749 50 l. le millier, elle est très bonne. Au bord de l'eau, vis-à-vis le fort, la brique est d'une excellente qualité. Il n'y a point d'épinette ni de bois de cèdre au fort du Détroit, il faut en avoir de vingt cinq lieues aux environs de la rivière à Mr. Dulude, où est la grande pinière. Sur ladite rivière il y a un moulin à scie appartenant au Sr Gervais, habitant du Détroit, qui apporte des planches et madriers au poste en cajeux; le courant est favorable pour ce transport dans lequel les bois ne courrent aucun risque.

Il n'y a point de pierre au fort du Détroit; il faut aller la chercher à 4 lieues audessous, à la rivière à la Carrière. Il faut, pour avoir de la belle pierre, entrer un quart de lieue dans le bois à la rive du sud de lad[te] rivière; elle est semblable à celle de L'Ange-Gardien de Québec. A 4 lieues ¾ audessous du fort, il y a une île qui a environ un quart de lieue de tour, où la pierre est semblable à celle de la rivière à la Carrière pour sa beauté et de la meme qualité qu'est celle de la Pointe aux Trembles de Québec, aussi la nomme-t-on Isle à la Pierre. On va chercher la pierre aux endroits ci-dessus avec de grands bateaux faits exprès, que l'on mène à la rame et à la voile. Les barques peuvent venir mouiller l'ancre à 54 toises de distance de terre vis à vis le fort.

La rivière du Détroit a de largeur depuis 60 perches du ruisseau du Moulin de Claude Campeaux en descendant la rivière, endroit où est pris le point pour la traverser, en alignant à une petite coullée ou ruisseau qui est audessus du village des Hurons ... de 115 perches de 18 pieds de long qui font ensemble 11 arpents ½. — Le chenal de la rivière du Détroit se trouve plus à la côte du O. qu'à celle de l'E. .... — On concéda des terres de trois arpents de front sur 40 arpents de profondeur, à 22 habitants, sur la rivière à prendre depuis le Ruisseau de la Vieille Reine à la Rivière aux Dindes, que vous trouverez marquée sur la carte 40 depuis la rivière 33 jusqu'à la rivière 32.

POSITIONS DES VILLAGES SAUVAGES

Le village des Hurons est à la coste du sud de la Rivière du Détroit à demi lieue audessous du Fort marqué C.

Le village des Outa8ois est à la même coste, à ½ quart de lieue au dessus du Fort, marqué sur la carte D.

Le village des Poute8atamis est à ½ lieue audessous du Fort à la coste du nord, marqué B.

AOUT

...

Le 26, je partis du fort du Détroit avec deux canots armés de chacun cinq hommes, j'avais pris la précaution de mettre dans chaque un double des papiers touchant les observations de mon voyage, en cas de quelque accident arrivé à l'un desdits canots. Je vins coucher à lentrée de la rivière du Détroit à six lieues du Fort.

Le 27, je couchai à la Pointe Pelée, à 15 lieues de l'entrée de la Rivière Détroit.

C 4 RAPPORT DE JOSEPH GASPARD CHAUSSEGROS DE LÉRY SUR SON VOYAGE AU DÉTROIT EN 1749
[*Archives de la Marine, Le ministère de la France d'outre-mer, Carton #9, 546: Amérique Septentrionale*]

Les Terres qui bordent la Rivierre du Détroit sont la plus grande partye très bonnes et rien de plus avantageux pour nous que leur Establissement, surtout dans le cas d'une guerre prochaine. La derniere nous a donnée des preuves, que les hurons, outa8ais, et Poute8atamis, qui sont les trois nations sauvages qui l'habite avec un village de Sauteurs qui sont a son entrée au Bord du Lac Huron, sont plus portez à en donner la possession aux Anglais qu'à nous la conserver, n'ayant pas de moyens qu'ils n'ayt mis en usage, pour non seulement nous en chasser, mais même massacrer tous les français du poste.

Les trois villages sont environ a demye lieue du fort français. L'on pourray en placer dans la Riviere aux Ecorces et a la grande presqu'Isle. Mais le nombre de français qui habitent cette Riverre n'est pas encore suffisant pour eloigner ces Sauvages de la vue du fort, lesquels pouroient encore nous jouer quelques trahisons.

Etant ou ils sont a la vue du fort, l'on peut voir leur moindre mouvements et y porter remede. D'ailleurs les hurons, et outa8ois qui sont les plus mauvais sont du costé opposé a notre fort et il faut pour y traverser des préparatifs dont on peut s'apercevoir.

Les Poute8atamis, du même costé du fort ne nous laissent rien a craindre puisqu'ils sont de tous les sauvages les plus fidel aux français, quoique cependant ils n'en recoivent pas plus de présent dont ils m'ont parue beaucoup se plaindre.

Il faudray donc commancer par Etablir le Bas de la Rivierre du Détroit, et cela vis a vis L'Isle aux Bois Blanc ou etoient en 1748 le village des hurons.

Pour cela il seray à propos de choisir dans le Gouvernement de Quebec, ou les habitans sont les meilleurs Terriens du Canada, des familles, dont les Chefs eussent la reputation d'etre bon travaillant, et leur faire les avantages suivant; sans quoi il me paroist difficil qu'ils soient en etat de former une nouvelle colonie au Détroit.

Il faudray premierement que le Roy transporta a ses frais, les habitans et leur petit menage au Détroit. Ensuite qu'il les nourrie deux années aux vivres du Détroit, qu'il donna a chaque habitans et a plusieurs ensemblent.

Scavoir

Une Charrue garnye a deux habitans
Un bœuf a chaque habitans
Une Vache a deux habitans
Un Cheval a deux habitans
Un Cochon a deux habitans
Une Scie de long, une de travers et Sciot par six habitans

A chaque habitans

Une vache [hache ?]	2 paires de souliers
Une pioche	un fusil
Une plaine	8 l. de poudre et 24 l. de plomb
Une ferrée	un casse testes
Une herminette	une paire de mitasse
Une tarriere d'un pouce	une couverte de 4 points
une chaudiere	La semance pour une année de la terre qu'ils auray mis en valleur la premiere année de leur arrivée.

Tous les habitans Canadiens scavent se servir des outils cy dessus mentionnée et seront en etat en ayant, de faire leurs maisons, granges, et etables, et même des forts de bois dans l'occasion.

A l'Egard des Bestiaux nécessaire l'on peut en faire venir des Isllynois a peu de frais.

La distance de l'Entrée de la Rivierre du Détroit au fort est de six lieues. L'on pourray faire un petit fort a l'Entrée de ladte. Rivierre qui y batteray et sur le Lac Errie, qui garderay le passage; car de la maniere dont les choses sont actuellement, il ne seray pas difficile aux Ennemis d'empêcher les Convois et courier de parvenir au fort français, ce qui metteray ces anciens et nouveaux Etablissements de cette Rivierre dans le cas d'estre totallement Ruinée.

Les terres de l'Est de la Rivierre sont Bordée de prairies de façon que les habitans n'ont pas de bois a abattre pour faire leurs champs, et semer leurs grains. Il faut seullement lever la terre a la charue et couper quelques fredoches. Les terres y sont bonne et poussent du bled, de l'orge, de l'avene, des poix, et générallement toutes sortes de grains. L'on y fait du bled d'automne.

Le premier aoust j'ay plantée dans le jardin du Roy de la vigne de France que j'avais portée de Montréal. Elle etois bien prises et poussay bien quand j'en suis party. Il y en avay trois pieds de blanche, et quatre de violettes.

Il y a dans ce jardin des pêches, des poires, des pommes, qui sont fort bonnes. Les habitans en ont aussi sur leurs habitations, ainsy que des légumes et autres jardinage qui y sont en abondance.

Les habitans du lieu disent qu'il est impossible que l'on mette les nouveaux habitans en village par la grande quantitée d'étourneaux qui mangent le grain. Il est vray qu'il y en a beaucoup et qu'il faut du monde a les garder. Mais il est vray aussy que les habitans qui habitent le Détroit a présent n'aiment pas l'ouvrage. Ils ont cependant en cette année une Belle Recolte.

Il seray necessaire tant pour la suretée du fort français que pour en imposer et faire craindre les nations sauvages d'avoir au Détroit de l'artillerie dont je joins icy l'etat.

Scavoir

8 pieces de canons du calibre de 4 l. }
2 " " " " de 3 l. } leurs Boulets et affust
18 pierriers

Le transport de cette artillerie est moins difficile que l'on ne pense. L'on peut du fort de Niagara faire transporter des Batteaux dans le Lac Errie et l'artillerie cy dessus.

Les costes du Portage de Niagara ne sont point un obstacle. L'on peut en eviter une partye en détournant le chemin dans les bois. Pour moy je trouve la chose faysable et ce transport nécessaire pour la suretée du Détroit.

Les Anglais qui ont pris a présent la routte de la Grande Rivierre peuvent la continuer jusqu'au Detroit, et l'attaquer sans que l'on ayt aucune connaissance au fort de Niagara, ce qui nous metteray dans le cas de ne pouvoir y porter aucun secour.

Il est donc nécessaire de garnir le Détroit, et le mettre à l'Epreuve de quelques facheux Evenements, n'y ayant point a douter que sy ce poste passay entre les mains des Anglais, les pays d'enhault ne fussent entierrement perdue pour nous.

Mais si l'on y met des troupes, des habitans et de l'artillerie, nous pouvons estre assurée que quelques tentatives que fassent nos Ennemis, ils ne pouront reussir, quoique même les sauvages vinsçent a leurs prêster la main, ce qu'ils ne feront point, quand ils verront des trouppes, de l'artillerie, et des habitans.

Ce poste etant bien garny nous sommes en etat de nous conserver les pays d'enhault, et du produit des terres que l'on fera valloir, de nourrire la garnison du Détroit, et même celle du fort de Niagara, au moyen d'une Barque sur le Lac Errie. L'on pouray la construire dans la Rivierre du Détroit, ou dans le Lac Errie. Il y a du bois de construction de quoy faire une grande quantitée de vaisseaux de toutes grandeurs.

Le Détroit etably peut fournir a toute heure des détachements pour porter remedes aux affaires qui pourroient arriver a Niagara, aux Ouyatanons, aux

Misamis, a Michelimimakina, a St. Joseph par eaux et par terre, a la Baye et généralement dans tous les postes et même a la Louisiane.

L'Enceinte d'a présent du fort du Détroit est de pieux debouts; par la suite L'on poura en faire de pierre. Elle y est très bonne ainsy que la chaux, et le sable.

Fait à Quebec le 22 Octobre 1749

C 5   CONTRAT DE JEAN BAPTISTE ET RENÉ LEBEAU POUR CONDUIRE UN CANOT AU POSTE DU DÉTROIT
[*B.H.C., Montreal Papers, vol. XII, p. 4088*]

Pardevant Les Notaires Royaux de la ville et jurisdiction Royalle de Montreal y residant soussignez — furent presents Jean Baptiste et René LeBeau pere et fils voyageurs demeurant en cette ville lesquels ont reconnus et confesse s'estre engage et par ces presentes s'engage à Sieur Jean Baptiste Godefroy Escuyer demeurant en cette ville en sa maison sise Rue St-Jean Baptiste a ce present et acceptant les dits susnommés pour à sa première requisition partir de cette ville dans un canot chargé de marchandises, aider à le mener et conduire jusqu'au poste du Detroit du Lac Erie pour estre libre au dit lieu, avoir soing, pendant toutes les routes, des canots, marchandises, pelteries, vivres, ustensiles, chercher le profit dudit Sieur, eviter son dommage, et l'en avertir s'il vient à sa connaissance, obeir en tout ce qu'il leur sera commandé de licitte et honnête, et enfin faire tout ce que peut et doit faire de bons et fideles engagés voyageurs sans pouvoir quitter le dit service sous les peines des ordonnances et de perdre leurs gages. Cet engagement ainsi fait pour et moyennant la somme de cent cinquante livres, scavoir cent livres pour le dit LeBeau le pere et cinquante pour le dit LeBeau le fils, le tout en argent ayant cours en ce pays.

Que le dit Sieur Godefroy promet et s'oblige bailler et payer aux dits engagés pour leur gages et salaires sitot l'arrivé engagés en cette ville. [Mot illisible] de tout dépense dommages et intéret. Car ainsi sont convenu chacun en droit fait et promettant et obligant et renoncant &c. Fait et passé au dit Montreal es estudes des dits notaires soussignez, l'an sept cent, quarante sept le deuxieme jour de Juillet après-midi et ont signes à l'exceptions desdits engagés susnommés, lesquels ont declaré ne scavoir ecrire ni signer, de ce enquis lecture faire suivant l'ordonnance.

Signez   Godefroy   A Dehemar
Fr. Simonnet
Notaire Royal

C 6   EXTRAITS DU REGISTRE CICOT
[*B.H.C.*]

LOUIS PLICHON — a eté envoié de Montreal et Est arrivé au Detroit le 26 juillet 1749 avec sa femme et deux Enfants pour prendre une terre qui lui a eté concedée de 3 arpents de large sur 40 de profondeur Située a la cote du Sud, joignant au Nord Est Louis Gervais et Sud ou Est les terres non concedées. la cinquieme Ration dont il est parlé cy contre a eté accordée a un des freres de sa femme qui Est venu le trouver en 1750.

APPENDIX I

CI-CONTRE

A lui delivré par grace	A luy delivré pour rendre ou paier
4 rations pour 4 personnes depuis le 26 Juillet 1749 jusqua pareil jour 1750. Et depuis le 26 Juillet 1750 — cinq rations jusquau 26 Jan. 1751. 2 chevreuls en viande 2 L. de farine 1 pioche 1 hache 1 charue complette 1 faux 1 faucille 2 tarrieres 1 truie 7 volailles 80 cloux a couvrir 4 L. de poudre 4 L. de plomb	20 minots de froment Rendu 1 minot de mais Rendu 1 vache R 1 Bœuf Rd 1755 Le 5 Juin a prit une vache au Roy a terme. Tue par les hurons Reçu dud. Pelichon 2 mts de froment qu'il a delivré a Pierre Mongardon dit Brindamour le . . . 1754 suivant le billet qu'il doit raporter. 18 mts de Bled le 10e Mars

PIERRE DINAN — a eté envoié de Montreal et est arrivé au Detroit le 26 Juillet 1749 avec sa femme trois garcons et trois filles pour prendre une terre qui lui a eté concedée de 3 arpents de large sur 40 de profondeur, située a la Cote du Sud, joignant au Nord Est Louis Plichon et au Sud-Ou-Est les terres non concedées.

A lui delivré par grace : 8 rations pour 8 personnes depuis le 26 Juillet 1749 jusqu'au 26 Janv. 1751.

[Suit la liste des ustensiles d'agricultures etc.]

JEAN BAPTISTE DROUILLARD — Envoié de Montreal, arrivé au Detroit le 26 Juillet 1749 avec sa femme 5 garcons et 3 filles pour prendre une terre de 3 arpents de large situé a la cote du Sud joignant au Nord-Est Pierre Dinan et au Sud-Ou-Est les terres non concedées.

A lui delivré par grace : Dix rations pour dix personnes depuis le 26 Juillet 1749 jusqu'au 26 Janvier 1751. etc.

JEAN BAPTISTE LEBEAU — Demeurant au Detroit depuis plusieurs années lorsqu'on fit monter sa famille qu'il avait laissée en Canada. Comme il etait Censé habitant du lieu, M. de Sabreuvois ne juge pas de lui donner la ration. Il lui a été concedée une terre de 3 arpents tenant au Nord Est au voisin de Drouillard et au Sud Ou Est aux terres non concedées.

A lui delivré par grace : trois rations pour sa femme, un garcon et une fille, depuis le 26 Juil 1749 jusqu'au 26 Janv. 1751.

PIERRE BECQUET — Etait au Pais d'ouabache lorsque Sa femme arriva au Detroit le 24 Juil. 1749 pour s'y establir sur une terre. Elle avait avec elle deux garcons et une fille. On lui conceda une terre, mais ne pouvant la defricher par elle même M. De Sabreuvois lui permit d'aller chercher son marit qui etait aux Ouyas ou il est mort. Et la concession n'a pas eu lieu.

Delivré a sa femme par grace : 4 rations pour 4 personnes depuis le 24 Juillet 1749 jusqu'au 24 d'Octobre suivant. etc.

JACQUES PILET — Etait au Detroit depuis nombre d'années lorsque sa famille qu'il avait laissée a Boucherville vint l'y trouver pour s'y etablir sur une terre. Censé qu'il etait du Detroit, M. De Sabreuvois ne voulut point luy donner de ration. Elle fut accordée a sa femme, son fils Joseph et trois filles qu'elle avait amenés avec elle. Et il a eté concedé a ce dit Joseph une terre de 3 arpents Située a la Cote du Sud, avec des ustensiles d'agricultures, son pere se contentant de faire valoir une petite piece de terre dans l'isle aux cochons dont la proprieté n'est pas a luy.
Delivré par grace a sa famille : 5 rations pour cinq personnes depuis le 26 Juillet 1749 jusqu'au 26 Janv. 1751. etc.

LOUIS EDELINE — arrivé au Detroit avec son fils pour s'etablir sur une terre qui lui a eté concedée de 3 arpents de large sur 40 de profondeur, située a la Cote du Sud.
A lui delivré par grace : Deux rations pour deux personnes depuis le 26 juillet 1749 jusqu'au 26 Janv. 1751. etc.

FRANÇOIS LEDUC dit PERSIL — Venu au Detroit le 26 Juillet 1749 dans l'escorte obtint une terre de 3 arpts a la Cote du Sud, et dix-huit mois de vivres suivant le reglement.
A lui delivré par grace : la ration depuis le 26 Juillet 1749 jusqu'au 26 Janv. 1751. etc.

LOUIS VILLERS — soldat marié au Detroit obtint une terre en 1749, ou il s'est etabli la même année, sur la Cote du Sud. Un nommé Louis Morain son beau frere eut une concession de 3 arpents attenant que Louis Villers a unie a la sienne sous le bon plaisir de Monr. de Celoron pour quoy il est parlé cy contre de deux pioches et 2 haches a cause dud. Louis Morain qui devait s'en servir, comme Villers a defricher sa terre,
a luy delivré par grace : 2 rations et ½ depuis le pr. 9bre 1749 jusqu'au pr. May 1751, pour luy, sa femme et un enfant. etc.

RENÉ LEBEAU — Monté au Detroit en 1749 garcon, pour s'etablir sur une terre qui lui a eté concedée a la Cote du Sud. Il est descendu à Montreal en 1751, ou il s'est marié et a amenée sa femme a laquelle il a eté accordé une ration.
A lui delivré par grace : une ration depuis le 26 Juil. 1749 jusqu'au 26 Janv. 1751. Une autre ration pour sa femme depuis le 10 d'aoust 1752 jusqu'au 10 fevr. 1754. etc.

BAPTISTE MALLET — cordonnier du Detroit descendit a Montreal en 1749 avec sa femme et un garcon qu'il avait et obtint l'année suivante d'y remonter avec sa famille dans les canots du Roy sur la promesse qu'il fit de s'y etablir sur une terre qui lui a eté concedée de 3 arpents de large a la Cote du Sud.
A luy delivré par grace : trois rations pour trois personnes depuis le 3 d'aoust 1750 jusqu'au 3 fev. 1752. etc.

FRANÇOIS MALLET — Le veuf, monta au Detroit en 1750, et amena une fille et un garcon, pour s'etablir sur une terre qui lui a eté concedée à la Cote du Sud de 3 arpts de large. Son fils a disparu en 1752.
a lui delivré par grace : pour trois personnes depuis le 3 d'aoust 1750 jusqu'au 3 fev. 1752 — trois rations. etc.

LOUIS BINAU — Monté au Detroit en 1750 pour s'etablir sur une terre qui lui a eté concedée a la Cote du Sud de 3 arpts de large. il etait alors suivi de sa femme et de sept enfants.
A lui delivré par grace : cinq rations et demie depuis le 3 d'aoust 1750 au 3 fev. 1752. etc.

JACQUES BIGRAS — Parut avec une nombreuse posterité le 19 d'aoust 1750 au Detroit pour s'etablir sur une terre qui luy fut concedée en premier lieu a la cote du nord. Ses remontrances luy en obtinrent une autre à la Cote du Sud de 3 arpents ou est a present etablie sa veuve. 3 grands garçons qui auraient deus etre l'appui de leur mère l'ont abandonnée, ce qui l'a engagé a se remarier a Antoine Brizare qui a entré dans tous les droits du defunt s'etant chargé de toutes les dettes.
a luy delivré par grace : huit rations a commencer du 19 d'aoust 1750, jusqu'au premier 7bre 1751. Et depuis ledit pr. 7bre 1751 jusqu'au 19 fev. 1752 quatre rations et demie. etc.

NICOLAS TAVERNIER dit ST. MARTIN — soldat envoié au Detroit pour tenir garnison eut permission de se marier avec la fille de Bigras et s'etablit sur une terre de 3 arpents qui luy fut concedée a la Côte du Sud. Il est mort dans les 8 prs mois de son mariage laissant une veuve sans enfants.
a luy accordé en consideration de son etablissement et de son mariage, une ration d'habitant depuis le 9 Janvier 1751 que celle de soldat luy fut retranchée jusqu'a sa mort en aoust 1751. etc. aussi un cercueuil.

JOSEPH METEIER — monté au Detroit avec sa femme et une petite fille en 1750 arrivé le 19 d'aoust pour s'etablir sur une terre de 3 arpts a la cote du Sud.
a lui delivré par grace : 2 rations ½ depuis le 19 d'aoust 1750 jusqu'au 19 fev. 1752. etc.

PIERRE DUFOUR — Demeurant au Detroit avec une grosse famille composée de 5 garçons, 2 filles et leur mère. Il demanda une terre qui luy fut concedée à la cote du Sud vis-avis l'isle aux Dindes.
A lui accordé par grace : cinq rations ½ depuis le pr. 7bre 1750 jusqu'au pr. mars 1752. etc.

LOUIS ANTOINE DESHÊTRES fils — venu de S. Joseph avec son père. On luy a concedé une terre sur la Cote du Sud près du village des Outaouais dont il est interprete.
A luy delivré une ration comprise dans les huit dont il est parlé de l'autre [i.e. de son père].

LOUIS REVEAU — du Bourg de Vif paroisse de St. Jean a 2 lieues de Grenoble, etait de la garnison du Detroit depuis plusieurs années lorsqu'il obtint la permission de se marier avec la fille ainée de Pierre Dinan, et une terre de 3 arpts a la Côte du Sud sur laquelle il s'est etabli. Sa femme a reçu sa ration chés son père en 1749 et 1750.
a lui accordé par grace : 1 ration a commencer du Pr. Janvier 1750 jusqu'au Pr. Juillet 1752. etc.

PIERRE DURAND dit MONTMIREL — Soldat monté au Detroit en 1750 pour tenir garnison, eut permission de se marier avec la fille de Pierre Dinan, pour s'etablir sur une terre qui lui fut accordée sur la Côte du Sud sur laquelle il a fait un petit defrichement.

A lui delivré par grace : 2 rations pour luy et sa femme depuis le pr. Janvier 1751 jusqu'au Pr. Juillet 1752. etc.

JEAN VALE dit VERSAILLES — Idem que Montmirel.

A luy delivré par grace : 2 rations pr lui et sa femme depuis le 9 Janv. 1751 jusqu'au 9 Juillet 1752. etc. aussi 5 minots de froment a Drouillard pour tailler et lever sa maison.

JEAN FRANÇOIS LEBEAU — fils de Baptiste LeBeau canadien monta au Detroit en 1749, passager dans les canots marchands, obtint une terre, mais l'on ne jugea pas a propos de luy accorder les bonnes graces du Roy que lorsqu'il auroit pris une femme. Le Nicolas Tavernier cy devant nommé, etant mort, il a Epousé sa veuve qui lui a merité une ration.

A lui delivré par grace : une ration pour lui seul a commencer du 20 7bre 1752 jusqu'au 20 mars 1754. etc.

FRANÇOIS PRUD'HOMME — du Government de Montreal monta au Detroit en 1751 avec une assé grosse famille pour s'etablir sur une terre a luy concedée a la Cote du Sud vis-avis l'isle aux D'Indes.

A luy accordé par grace : cinq rations pour sept personnes depuis le Pr. 7bre 1751 jusqu'au Pr. mars 1753. etc.

JOSEPH ST. AUBIN — Idem que F. Prud'homme.

A luy delivré par grace : 6 rations depuis le Pr. 7bre 1751 jusqu'au Pr. mars, 1752. Et 5 rations ½ depuis ledit Pr. Mars 1752 jusqu'au Pr. Mars 1753. etc. aussi 10 L. de tabac et 5 L. de poudre pr. le tirage de sa maison.

CHARLES CAMPAU — l'on peut le dire enfant du Detroit et en consideration des travaux qu'il a faite sur une terre et de son mariage avec la fille de Prud'homme il a eu les avantages marqués cy-contre.

A lui delivré par grace : une ration depuis le 14 7bre 1752 jusqu'au 14 Mars 1754. etc.

CHARLES BUTAU — Canadois de Montreal monta au Detroit en 1751, prit connaissance du Pais, obtint une terre a la Côte du Sud, et descendu en 1752 pour remonter avec sa famille. Pourquoy il a obtenu ce qui est porté cy contre.

A lui delivré par grace : quatre rations pour 5 personnes a commencer du 23 aoust 1752 jusqu'au 24 fev. 1754. etc.

Aussi 3 L. de poudre et 9 L. de plomb pour faire tirer sa maison par Deline.

SIMON BERGERON — A lui delivré en consideration de ce qu'il s'est marié avec la fille de Jean Bte. LeBeau pour une ration a lui, sa femme aiant eu ses vivres a son arrivée de Montreal.

C 8   Extrait du rapport du Père Bonnecamps
[*Thwaites,* Jesuit Relations, *LXIX, 150–99*]

... J'ai demeuré trop peu de tems au Détroit pour pouvoir vous en faire une description exacte.... C'est la Touraine et la Beauce du Canada....

De plus, on doit regarder le Détroit comme un des postes les plus importants de la Colonie. Il est à portée de donner du secours à Michilimakinac, à la Rivière St. Joseph, à la Baye, aux Miamis, aux Ouitanons et à la Belle Rivière, supposé qu'on y fasse des établissements. Ainsi on ne sauroit y jetter trop de monde; mais où le prendre ce monde ? Ce n'est pas au Canada. Les colons que vous y envoyates l'année dernière se sont contentés de manger la ration que le Roy leur donnoit; quelques uns même d'entre eux emportés par leur légéreté naturelle, ont quitté le pais et sont allés chercher fortune ailleurs. Combien de pauvres laboureurs en France seroient charmés de trouver un pais qui leur fourniroit abondamment de quoi les dédomager de leurs travaux et de leurs sueurs !

C 9   CONCESSION AU CHEVALIER DE LONGUEUIL
[*Registre des Actes Notariaux du Détroit, liber A, pp. 44–5*]

[Québec, le premier avril 1750]

Le Marquis de Lajonquière Chevalier de l'ordre Royal et Militaire de St. Louis, Chef de l'Esadre des armées navalles de Sa Majesté, Gouverneur, et Lieutenant général pour le Roy en toute la nouvelle France et pays de La Louisianne.

François Bigot conceiller du Roy en ses conseils, Intendant de Justice, police, finances et de La Marine en dits pays.

Sur la demande qui nous a été faite par Mr. Le Chevalier de Longueuil de L'Ordre Royal et Militaire de St. Louis, Lieutenant du Roy de la ville et chateau de Quebec, de lui accorder et concéder une terre de douze arpents de front sur quarante de profondeur située sur la rivière du Détroit du lac Erié, tenant d'un cotté à l'ouest sud ouest au terrain de la Mission des Hurons, et à l'est nord est aux terres non concédées, bornée par une ligne qui court nord nord ouest et sud sud est, par le devant sur ladte. Rivière du Détroit, et dans la profondeur par une ligne est nord est et ouest sud ouest joignant pareillement aux terres non concédées. Nous en vertu du pouvoir à nous conjointement donné par Sa Majesté avons donné, accordé et concédé, donnons, accordons et concédons à titre de Cens et Rentes des maintenant et pour tourjours au dit Sieur de Longueuil, pour lui, ses hoirs et ayant cause à l'avenir une concession de terre située sur le Détroit du lac Erié de la contenance de douze arpents de front sur quarante de profondeur, bornée sur les Rumbs de vent designés cy devant pour en jouir faire et disposer par ledit Sieur de Longueuil ses hoirs et ayant cause aux Charges Clauses et Conditions cy après; Savoir que ledit Sieur le Longueuil ses hoirs et ayant cause seront tenus de porter leurs grains moudre au Moulin Banal lorsqu'il y en aura un Etably, à peine de confiscation des grains et d'amende arbitraire, d'y tenir ou faire tenir feu et lieu dans un an d'icy au plus tard, de couvrir les déserts des voisins à mesure qu'ils en auront besoin, cultiver laditte terre, y souffrir les chemins qui seront jugés nécessaires pour l'utilité publique, faire les clôtures mitoyennes ainsi qu'il sera reglé et de payer par chaque an au receveur du domaine de Sa Majesté en ce pays ou au commis dudit receveur qui résidera au Détroit un sol de Cens par chaque arpent de front et vingt sols de Rente par chaque vingt arpent en superficie faisant pour les dits douze arpents de front sur quarante de profondeur douze sols de Cens et vingt quatre livres de Rente, et en outre trois minots de bled froment pour les dits douze arpents de front, le tout payable par chaque année au jour et feste de la St. Martin dont la première année échouera au onze novembre mil sept cent cinquante un, les dits Cens portant profit des lots et ventes saisine et amende avec touts autres droits Seigneuriaux et Royaux quand le cas y échouera suivant la Coutume de la ville prévôté et vicomté de Paris; Sera cependant loisible au dit Sieur de Longueuil de payer les dits vingt quatre livres de Rente et douze sols de Cens en pelterie au prix du Détroit juaqu'à ce qu'il y ait une monnaie courante d'establie, reservant au nom du Roy sur ladte. habitation tous les bois dont Sa Majesté aura besoin pour charpente et construction des bâtiments et forts qu'elle pourra établir par la suite, ainsi que la propriété des mines, minières et mineraux s'il s'en trouvoit dans l'étendue de laditte concession, et seront lesdits Sieurs de Longueuil, ses hoirs et ayant cause tenus de faire incessament alligner, borner et mesurer laditte concession dans toute sa largeur et profondeur à ses depens, et d'executer les clauses portées par le présent titre, et de prendre un brevet de confirmation de sa Majesté dans deux ans à peine de nullité des présentes.

C 10 Concession à Alexis Delisle
[*Registre des Actes Notariaux du Détroit, liber A, p. 346*]

[Detroit, le 24 novembre 1751]

CELERON, MAJOR COMMANDANT DU DETROIT ÉRIÉ ET DES POSTES DU SUD
Nous avons en vertu ou en consequence des ordres de MM. le General & Intendant concédé à Alexis Delisle une terre de deux arpents de large sur quarante de profondeur, au sud de cette rivière, située sur le bord du Detroit, joignant à l'ouest sud ouest à Hyacinthe Reaume, et d'autre coté à l'est nord est aux terres non concédées, bornée par une ligne qui court sud sud est, et nord nord ouest, pour en jouir selon les contrats ci devant accordés aux habitants de ce lieu, et particulièrement aux conditions qu'il défrichera et cultivera la de. terre, et y tiendra feu et lieu d'aujourd'hui en un an sous peine de nullité des présentes.

C 11 Concession à Pierre Réaume
[*A.P.C., G 1, La Nouvelle France et Détroit, p. 10*]

[Detroit, 24 novembre 1751]

CELORON, MAJOR COMMANDANT AU DETROIT & DES POSTES DU SUD
Nous avons en conséquence des ordres de Mm. le Général & Intendant concédé à Pierre Reaume un emplacement [en remplacement] d'une concession de deux arpents qui lui a été ci-devant accordée prèst de ce fort et dont la trop grande proximité est contraire aux ordres réitérés de M. le Général par lesquels il nous enjoint d'observer une distance de cinq arpents de banlieue pour ce fort, une autre concession au Sud de cette rivière de trois arpents de large sur le bord du Detroit et de quarante de profondeur, joignant à l'ouest-sud-ouest à celle de Jacques Gaudet et d'autre coté à l'est-nord-est aux terres non concédées, bornée par une ligne qui cours sud-sud-est nord-nord-est, pour en jouir suivant les contrats cy devant accordés aux

habitants de ce lieu, et particulièrement aux conditions qu'il défrichera et cultivera la dite terre et y tiendra feu et lieu d'aujourd'hui en un an sous peine d'en être déchu, tous ainsy qu'au moyen des présentes, il ne lui reste aucune proprieté de celle de deux arpents qui lui avait été accordée prèst de ce fort.

C 12 Concession à la veuve Vien
[Registre des Actes Notariaux du Détroit, liber A, p. 313]

[Detroit, le 24 novembre 1751]

Nous avons en consequences des ordres de Monsieur le General & Intendant concedé à la veuve Vien deux arpents de terre de large sur le bord du Detroit au sud de cette rivière, sur quarante de profondeur joignant à l'ouest sud ouest la terre du Sr. Chauvin, et à l'est nord est les terres non concedées, bornée par une ligne qui coure sud sud est, et nord nord ouest pour en jouir au terme des contrats ci devant accordés aux habitants de ce lieu, et particulièrement aux conditions qu'elle defrichera et établira la ditte terre d'huy en un an sous peine de nullité des présentes.

C 15 Louis Gervais prend possession d'une terre
[George F. Macdonald Collection, Windsor, Ontario]

Je certifie qu'il a eté concedé en mil sept cent quarante neuf par Mr. De Sabrevois Commandant au Detroit, une terre de trois arpents de front à Louis Gervaise attenant et joignant les terres des Hurons, de laquelle terre il a pris possession en laditte année et en a payé les rentes au Roy conformément aux quittances que je luy en ay données en vertu de ma commission de Receveur des rentes, ce que j'affirme veritable, et pour avoir moy même mesuré laditte terre par ordre.
Fait au Detroit le 24e may mil sept cent soixante six.

Navarre

C 18 Donation des Ottawas à Charles Réaume
[En possession de Mme Frank Fortin, 2317 Riverside Drive, Windsor, Ont.]

Nous les principaux chefs des differentes bandes du village des outaouas du Detroit, soussignés de notre marque tant en notre nom qu'en celuy de toute la nation —
Reconaissons : En presence de William tocker, un de nos interpretes, qu'en consideration de la sincere amitié et affection que nous avons pour Charles Reaume avons de notre bonne volonté, donnés, concedés, et abandonnés, donnons, cedons, et abandonons, au suddt. Charles Reaume, a luy, ses hoirs & ayant causes, une terre de trois arpents de frond sur le coté du sud, de la rivière du Detroit, et de quatre vingts arpens de profondeur : borné par devant par la riviere dudt. Detroit et en profondeur par les terres non concedés, tenant d'un coté à celle que nous avons donné à Pierre Reaume pere et de l'autre coté a celle donné à Jean Baptiste Meloche, de laquelle terre il jouiras, useras, et disposeras, en toute proprieté luy, ses hoirs et ayant causes, comme d'un bien a luy appartenant, promettant, tant en notre

nom, qu'en celuy de toute la nation entiere ne jamais l'inquieter, n'y troubler dans la paisible possession de ladte terre presentement donnée. Fait & passé au Detroit le 10e Juin, mil sept cent soixante & seize.

Isidore Chene	d'Egouchi8ay	marque [animal]
temoin	de Michimandac	marque [animal]
	Chamyanda8a	marque [poisson]
		poisson
		oisseau

C 22   LE COMMANDANT DE PEYSTER À F. COMPARÉ
[*Registre des Actes Notariaux du Détroit, liber C, p. 352*]

[Detroit, le 24 octobre 1781]

François Comparé père
En consequence d'un Certificat de Monsieur Bénac Arpenteur et autres preuves à l'égard des terres concedées à la Petite Rivière par les Outawas, il vous est ordonné de reculer votre maison, grange, clôtures et autres bâtiments jusqu'à ce qu'il y a trois arpents de terre de large entre vous et Antoine Robert père pour Pierre Meny selon les intentions des dits sauvages.

D 2   CONTRAT DE MARIAGE
[*Registre des Actes Notariaux du Détroit, liber B, p. 96*]

PAR DEVANT Phillipe Dejean Notaire au Détroit y résidant soussigné fut présent Jean Bte. Gignac aussi résidant au susdit lieu du Détroit, natif de la Paroisse du Cap Santé Diocese de Québec fils majeur de Joseph Gignac, et de Magdelaine Galernau ses père et mère stipulant pour lui et en son nom d'une part, Sieur Jean Bte. Le Beau veuf de feu Catherine Dudevoir stipulant pour Dame Catherine Le Beau leur fille, veuve de Simon Bergeron decédé en ce poste à ce présent et acceptant pour elle et en son nom d'autre part; lesquels en la présence et de l'avis & conseils des Sieurs et Dames leurs parents & amis pour ce assemblés, scavoir de la part du susdit Sr. Jean Bte. Gignac les Sieurs René Cloutier, François Drouillard, François Langlois. Et de la part de la susditte Catherine Le Beau le sudit Sieur Jean Baptiste Le Beau son père, les Sieurs Thomas Pageau, Antoine Rouchau dit Lafond, Jean Bte. Antaya, et Victoire [*sic*] Morrisseaux gendre de laditte Dame Catherine Le Beau. Ont fait les Conventions et accords de mariage qui suivent. C'est à sçavoir que le susdit Sieur Jean Baptiste Le Beau a promis et promet donner la susditte Dame Catherine Le Beau sa fille au dit Sieur Jean Baptiste Gignac, qui promet la prendre pour sa future et legitime Epouse par loy de mariage, et icelui faire célébrer & solemniser en face de notre mère Sainte Eglise C. A. & R. le plutost que faire se pourra, ou lorsqu'un des deux partis en requerera l'autre.

Seront les futurs Epoux uns et communs en tous biens meubles et immeubles & Conquêts suivant l'usage et coutume de la Vicomté de Paris Derogeant expressement à touts autres lois et coutumes contraires. Se prennent les dits Sieurs futurs Epoux avec les Biens et Droits à eux appartenants et en ce qu'iceux peuvent consister sans qu'il soit besoin d'en faire ici aucune designation.

Le dit Sieur futur Epoux a doué laditte Dame future Epouse de la somme de trois cent livres de douaire préfix une fois payé à l'avoir & prendre sitost que Douaire aura lieu sur tous les biens des futurs Epoux qui les y a hypothéqué, à fournir et faire valoir ledit douaire duquel laditte future épouse jouira et sera saisine sans être tenu d'en faire demande en justice et sera propre le susdit Douaire aux enfants qui naîtront dudit futur mariage. Et au defaut d'enfans demeurera et appartiendra à laditte Dame future Epouse.

Arrivant à la dissolution du futur mariage par le prédécés dudit futur Epoux laditte Dame future Epouse aura et prendra pour son préciput la somme de cent cinquante livres Tournois, et lui sera loisible & à ses enfans s'il y en a et au defaut d'enfants à ses plus proches heritiers d'accepter laditte communauté ou d'y renoncer. En ce cas la elle prendra tout ce qu'elle aura apporté audit mariage avec ses hardes & joyaux, sa chambre garnie, ainsi que les biens qui lui seront prevenus d'héritage.

Et pour faire insinuer le présent contrat au Greffe du susdit Détroit & partout ailleurs où besoin sera Les dittes parties ont Elu pour leur procureur, Général et Spécial le porteur d'icelui à qui ils donnent pouvoir d'en requerir acte.

Car ainsi &c. promettant &c obligeant &c. fait et passé au Détroit Etude dudit notaire l'an mil sept cent soixante dix sept, le vingt unième septembre avant midi. Et ont les susdits Sieurs futurs Epoux declaré ne savoir signer de ce enquis lecture faite ont cependant fait leur marque ordinaire présence de leur parents & amis.

Catherine + Le Beau	Jean Baptiste + Gignac	Rene + Cloutier
J. Bte + Antaya	François + Langlois	Antoine + Rouchau
Victorin + Morisseau	Largeau	Thomas + Pageau

P. Dejean, Notaire

D 4   Inventaire des biens de feu Joseph Pillet, habitant établi a la Côte du Sud
[*Registre des Actes Notariaux du Détroit, liber A, p. 317*]

le 10 juin, 1767

le 10 juin, 1767

Une terre de six arpents de front sur quarante de profondeur avec une maison, une grange neuve, une vieille, un hangard, et autres petits bâtiments estimés à	4000 livres
quatre bœufs de tire et deux taureaux	700
trois vaches et deux taures	400
trois veaux de l'année	100
un vieux cheval	50
deux juments, une pouliche, et un poulain	250
huit cochons	160
six petits cochons	10
deux douzne. et demi de poulles	30
une marmite	30
une cuve et deux cuvettes	20
un poêle de fer	230
douze cents clous à latte	12
une tourtière & son couvert	40
une bêche, trois haches, un crock, un sciot et autres ferrailles	80
cinq vieilles chaudières	15
une vieille tourtière	6

une marmite	20	
trois chaudières	15	
deux poêles à frire	6	
deux fer à repasser, un gril, deux petits trepieds, une cuillère à pot, une fourchette à viande, et une lanterne	12	
vingt trois livres d'etain	23	
cinquante livres de fer	37	10
une paire de chenêts, une pelle à feu, et une crémaillère	20	
une vieille calèche	40	
une carriolle ferrée avec son travail et chaine	25	
une charrette, une dte. sans roues	40	
une charrue	35	
un lit de plume, une paillasse, une couverte	40	
un lit de plume, une paillasse, une couverte, une contrepointe	80	
des harnois, courrois, chaines etc	50	
une chaine à tirer des pièces	15	
deux tables, une huche, un vieux coffre, six chaises, une petite armoire	40	
un miroir	6	
	6637	10
en argent monnoyer	162	
à ajouter qui est dû à la communauté	876	10
à deduire pour les dettes passives 1160		
	6516	

J. B. Faignan
Pierre Meloche
Nicolas Langlois
Charles Morand
Joseph Pouget

D 6 Contrat d'acquest entre Claude Landry et Benjamin Chappue
[*Quaife*, The John Askin Papers, *I, 60–1*]

Pardevant nous Gabriel LeGrand Notaire au detroit y Resident sousigné fut present Le sr Claude Landry dit s^t andré demeurant sur sa terre a la Coste du sorois du dit detroit ou nous nous sommes transporté pour ce qui suit Cest a savoir que Le dit Sr Claude Landry nous a declaré de sa franche Et Bonne Volonte Et sans Contrainte Confesse avoir Vendu du Consantement dangelique Leduc son Epouse qui Lauthorise a Cet Effet a Lexecution des presente avoir Vendu quitté Cedé Et deLaissé Des maintenants Et a toujours Et promis faire jouir Et garantir de tous troubles Et Empeschement quelconques provenants de ses faits, Une terre de trois arpents de front sur quarante de profondeurs fixe et située a La coste du sud sur Le Bord de La Rivièrre du dit detroit Bornée dun costé au nord Est a Ginac Et de Lautre Costé au sorois a LeVeillié Et par derrierre au terre non Consedée, circonstance Et dependance aussi Une maison dessus de seize pieds sur dix sept de piece sur pi[e]ce, sans aucune Reserve telle quelle se comporte et se tends de toute parts, a Benjamin Chappue habitants a ce present acceptant pour luy ses hoirs Et ayant Cause Et qui nous a dit bien La Connoistre pour Lavoir Venu Et Visitée Et dit Estre Contants Et satisfait, La ditte terre appartenants au dit Vendeurs qui la Reprisee de Charles Bergante a qui pierre Coquelliard La Voit Vendue, Et par faute de payment Le dit S^r S^t andré a Rentré dans sa terre Et qui soblige de Remettre tous Les papiers Concernant La ditte terre Entre les mains du dit acquereurs ses hoirs Et ayant Cause Cette Ventes ainsy faitte pour par le dit acquereurs Usser faire Et disposer a toujours aux Charges Des cens Et Rentes droits seigneuriaux

Et servitudes accountumee, La ditte terre Relevant du domaine du Roy, Et En outre moyennants La cantité de cent minots de Bled fromant et soixante minots de bled dainde qui ont Eté payé Contant, et dont Le dit S^t andré Et femme tienne Generallement Quitte Le dit acquereurs pourquoy Le dit s^r s^t andré a transporté au dit Benjamin Chappue ses hoirs Et ayant Cause a La venir tous droits de proprietté, quil peut avoir Et pretendre sur La ditte terre Voulant que Le dit acquereurs Et siens en sois mis Et Resseu En bonne Et paisible possesion Et saisine par qui Et ainsy quil apartiendre En Vertu des presentes Constituant pour Cet Effet son procureurs irrevocables Le porteurs dicelles Luy En donnant pouvoir Cai ainsy &^{c} promettant &^{c} obligeant Renonçant &^{c} fait Et passé au detroit maison du dit s^t andré par nous notaire sousigné apres midy Le neuf juillet mil sept cent soixante quatorze presence du s^r jacques Godefroy habutants Demeurant au detroit, Et jean LaRue demeurant a La Coste du sud tous deux temoins qui ont signé Et pour Le dit Claude Landry Et angelique Leduc sa femme ont declaré ne savoir signer dont fait Leurs marque ord^{re} apres lecture faitte, Et dans La minutte Est Ecrit jacques Godefroy, jean LaRue par sa marque, s^t andré, et angelique Leduc ausi par leurs marque Et Legrand notaire qui a delivré La presente Coppie Qui Est Veritable Et conforme a la minutte Le vingt deux avril mil sept cent soixante seize.

Legrand notaire

D 8 PÉTITION POUR UN MOULIN À EAU À LA RIVIÈRE AUX DINDES
[*Registre des Actes Notariaux du Détroit, liber C, p. 8*]

Nous sousignés tous habitants de la Petite Côte, Paroisse de L'Assomption du Detroit, reconnaissons que pour le bien publique il serait nécessaire d'avoir un Moulin à l'eau dans la ditte côte qui fut en état de moudre les grains dans les saisons les plus avantageuses pour l'utilité des dits habitants, et qu'il ne se trouve de place pour cette effet qu'à la Riviere aux Dindes sur la Domaine du Roy, connaissant la capacité et en etat de faire le dit Moulin que le Sieur Simon Drouillard, nous supplions Mons. le Commandant de lui accorder la permission de bâtir le dit Moulin, et en jouir pour lui et ses hoyrs. En foy de quoy nous avons signés le présent au Detroit le premier juillet mil sept cent quatre vingt.
Signé :

J. Bondy	+ Antoine Cloutier	+ Charles Renot
Joseph Pouget	+ J. Baptist Lebeau	Pierre Belaire
Charles Reaume	Pierre Meloche	+ Charles Fontane
+ Rene Cloutier	+ Pierre Parrez	J. B. Baushomme
+ Theofil Lemay	Touranjeau	+ J. B. Faignant
+ Jacques Belleperche	+ J. B. Drouillard	+ Augus. Pinparre
+____ Tuotte	+ J. B. Pitre	+ Francois Lesperance
+ Antoine Lafont	+____ Charron	+ Francois Dufour
Baptist Dufour	George Knaggs	+ Pierre Proux
		+ Louis Reveau

En consequence d'un placet signé de plusieurs habitants de la petite cote, je permet à Simon Drouillard de faire batir un moulin a l'eau sur la riviere au dinde —

Donné au Detroit ce 11eme Juillet 1780
(Signé) At S. DePeyster

D 9 LE RÉVÉREND J.-F. HUBERT AU GÉNÉRAL HALDIMAND
[*A.P.C., B 74, pp. 225–6*]

De la Pointe de Montréal du détroit
21 Xbre 1781

Votre Excellence m'ayant honoré de la permission de lui écrire, c'est pour moi un devoir de le faire. Je vais donc l'informer de mon arrivée au détroit le 8–9bre dernier. J'ai été 22 jours à Lisle Carleton occupé à rendre aux Matelots canadiens les secours spirituels qu'ils demandoient depuis longtems. Ce voyage quoique long a été pour moi des plus gracieux; il me sembloit que les lettres de votre Excellence à Messieurs les Commandants des differents Postes, leur transmettoient les sentiments de bienveillance dont votre Excellence m'a honoré.

Le P. de Charlevoix n'a point exagéré dans son histoire du Canada, en disant de ce pays, que tout en est beau, beau climat, belles rivières, belles prairies, belles Forêts, mais surtout beau & bon terrain et très fertile. Votre Excellence a donc raison d'etre surprise que ce pays ne nourisse pas ses habitans. Je crois en avoir trouvé la cause dans le prix du bled trop modique; il y a 8 ans, il ne valoit que 5# alors un habitant trouvoit plus vite et avec plus d'inclination, au bout de son fusil, ou de sa ligne de quoi faire 5# qu'avec son minot de bled, de là les terres négligées; mais presentement que le bled, se vend un Louis, il quitte volontiers le fusil et la ligne pour prendre la charue. Selon moi c'est un mal pour un bien que le bled soit cher, cela fait que tous en veulent faire, insensiblement l'homme s'adonnera à la culture des terres, y formera ses enfants & domestiques par la ceux cy se déferont peu à peu de leur inclination pour les voyages et la chasse et seront forcés de devenir laboureurs utiles, au lieu de chasseurs faineans.

Le tems ne m'ayant pas encore permis de faire d'autres remarques sur ce pays, je finis cette lettre par souhaiter de longs & heureux jours à votre Excellence, et l'assurer du très profond Respect avec lequel je suis, mon très illustre général,

E 1 LETTRE DE MR. LE MARQUIS DE VAUDREUIL À MR. DE BELESTRE, COMMANDANT AU DÉTROIT, À LA SUITE DE LA CAPITULATION DE MONTRÉAL À L'ARMÉE ANGLOISE LE 8 SEPTRE, 1760
[*Archives du Séminaire de Québec, Viger, « Ma Saberdache, » M, tome I, pp. 158–60*]

Je vous apprends, Monsieur, que j'ai été dans la nécessité de capituler à l'armée du Général Amherst. Cette ville est, vous savez sans défense, nos troupes étoient considérablement diminuées, nos moyens et ressources totalement épuisés. Nous étions entourés par trois armées qui, réunies, formoient au moins 30,000 hommes. Le Général Amherst étoit au six de ce mois à la vue des murs de cette ville. Le Général Murray à portée d'un de nos faubourgs; et l'armée du lac Champlain étoit à La Prairie et à Longueuil. Dans ces circonstances, ne pouvant rien espérer des efforts, ni même du sacrifice des troupes, j'ay pris sagement le parti de capituler avec le Général Amherst, à des conditions très avantageuses pour les colons, et particulièrement pour les habitans du Détroit. En effet, ils conservent le libre exercise de leur religion, et sont maintenus dans la possession de leur biens meubles, immeubles et leurs pelleteries; ils ont aussi le commerce libre comme les propres sujet du Roi de la Grande Bretagne. Les mêmes conditions sont accordées aux militaires, et ils peuvent commettre des procureurs pour user en leur absence de leurs droits; eux et tous les citoyens en général peuvent vendre aux Anglois ou aux François leurs biens, et en faire passer le produit en France, ou l'emporter avec lui, s'ils jugent à propos de s'y retirer à la paix. Ils conservent leurs Nègres et Panis, mais ils sont obligés de rendre ceux qu'ils ont pris aux Anglois. Le Général Anglois a déclaré que les Canadiens devenoient Sujets de Sa Majesté Britannique, et par cette raison le peuple n'a point été conservé dans la Coutume de Paris. A l'egard des troupes, il leur a été imposé la condition de ne point servir pendant la présente guerre et de mettre bas les armes : elles doivent être envoyées en France. Vous ferez donc, Monsr., rassembler les officiers et soldats qui sont dans votre poste, vous leur ferez mettre bas les armes, et vous vous rendrez avec eux à tel port de mer que l'on jugera à propos, pour de là passer en France. Les Citoyens et habitans du Détroit seront conséquemment sous le commandement de l'Officier que le Général Amherst aura destiné pour ce lieu : vous ferez passer copie de ma lettre aux Miamis et 8cactanons, supposé qu'il y eût quelques soldats, afin qu'eux et les habitans s'y conforment. Je compte avoir le plaisir de vous voir en France avec tous vos messieurs. Me de Belestre jouit d'une parfaite santé.

E 4   EXTRAITS DU JOURNAL DE LA CONSPIRATION DE PONTIAC
[*B.H.C.*]

. . . ses deux nations composoient environ quatre cents hommes, ce nombre ne Luy paraissait pas encore suffisant : il Sagissait de mettre dans leurs projets La nation huronne, qui divisé en deux Bande etoient gouverné par deux chefs différent et de différent caractère. Et cependant tous étoient conduit par le Supérieur, père Jésuite, Leur missionnaire. Les deux chefs de cette dernière nation, se nommoient, L'un také du mesme caractere que pondiak et l'autre se nommait téata, homme fort circonspect, d'une prudence consommée; ce dernier n'était pas facil à entrainé n'étant point d'un naturel à mal faire, ne voulu point écouté les deputés de pondiak, Les renvoya comme ils etoient venus; ceux cy aux premiers de cette dernière nation, de qui ils furent écoutés et reçus colliers de guères pour se joindre à pondiak et ninivois. . . .

12ieme May. — Le Jeudi 12e de May, jour de la feste de Lascencion de notre Seigneur, pondiak qui ne connaissait ni feste, ni dimanche, que tous Les jours Lui était Egaux, ne fesant profession d'aucune S. religion ordonna dès Le matin que Ses gens Se tinrent près pour quand Les hurons viendrait pour frapé tous ensemble. Et craignant que Les hurons Luy manquassent de parole, il envoya un de Ses chefs avec plusieurs jeunes gens chez eux pour Leur dirent de ne pas manqué Sitôt que Leurs missionnaires auroient fini de venirent se joindre aux poux et qu'il n'attendaient que Leurs arrivé pour frapé. Les hurons Leurs promirent et Leurs tins La parole — quoy que pondiak attendissent Les hurons pour faire commencer L'attaque du fort il avait fait néanmoins avancer Ses gens pour semparé des derrières des granges et des écuries autour du fort pour tous aporté à premier signe et pour empêché que personne ne sorte du fort.

Teata et Baby tous deux chefs de la Bonne bande des hurons, que Jusque à présent avait gardé La neutralité et qui Laurait voullu La gardé plus Longtemps, se voyant forcé par menace firent assemblé Leurs bande qui composoient autour de soixant hommes et Leur dirent. Mes frères vous voyez tous également comme nous les risques que nous Courons tous et que dans La Situation ou sont Les affaires nous n'avons plus d'autre ressource ou de nous joindre à nos frères Les Outavois et Les poux ou Bien d'abandonner nos terres et de fuir avec nos femmes et nos enfants, ce qui est bien de valeur, nous ne serons peut estre pas à peine partis pour nous en aller, que Les outavois et Les poux et ceux mesme de nostre nations, tomberons Sur nous et tuerons nos femmes et nos enfans, et encore nous contraindrons de faire Comme eux, aulieu que en Lefaisant aprésent, nous assure que nos familles seront tranquille dans nostre village, nous ne scavons pas quelle sont Les desseins du Maître de La Vie sur nous, peut Estre Esce Luy qui inspire cette guerre à nos frères, Les Outavois, si ce nest pas Luy qui L'ordonne, il sçaura Bien nous faire connaître Sa volonté et nous serons toujours Bien a mesme de nous retire sans estre tache du sang des Anglois, faisons ce que nos frères exige denous Et ne nous Epargnons point, tant incontinent après cette harangue ils prirent chaqu'un un Casse teste et chantèrent La guerre et invitèrent Leurs gens à en faire autant. En attendant l'heure de La messe, que Leurs femmes chantèrent et qu'ils furent entendre Bien devotement. La Messe finit chaqu'un fut à Sa Cabane sarmé de ce qui Leurs étaient nécessaire pour frapé et traversssèrent La rivière au nombre de douze Canots, droit chez Les poux qui firent des cris de Joye de les voir arrivé, et ses mesme cris étoient un signal pour pondiak de la venu des hurons, qui devinrent plus taquin aux feux que tous Les autres Sauvages ensemblé. . . .

14eme May. — Le père potier, Jésuite missionnaire des hurons, qui par cette qualité Et par Le pouvoir qu'il a sur eux en avoit rammené une partie, Surtout La Bande, dans Les Bornes de la tranquilité en Leurs refusant Les Sacraments, Et qui pour achevé de Les maintenir tout, avait Besoin d'aide, pria Mr. La Boise, domicilié du fort, qui pour Lors étoit chez Luy depuis quelque tems de voulloir Bien traversé La rivière et d'aller prié de sa part Les plus anciens et Les plus Sensés des habitans, ceux qu'ils Sçavaient estre aimé et Considére des Sauvages de venir se joindre à Luy pour arresté Le Cour de cette Orage, qui en menaçant L'anglois, paroissait menacé Les français, Ce qu'il fit, ces derniers qui Connoissoient et respectoient Le père Jésuite, pour un très digne religieux, Le regardoient comme un Saint Sur terre, à sa demande ne furent aucune difficulté de se transporter chez Luy et traitèrent ensemble de quelle façon il fallait se prendre pour adoucir pondiak et Les représentations qu'il falait Luy faire pour s'engager à finir cette guerre intestine. . . .

17e May. — Pondiak qui en commençant cette guerre n'avait pas eu soin de faire des provisions pour la Subsistance de ses guerriers fut obligé d'avoir recours à la Supercherie pour vivre, Luy et tout son monde, pour cela il fut avec quatre chef de sa nation en contrainte chez tous Les habitans dans Les Coste pour Leurs demander des vivres de bonne volonté ou de force ou bien qu'ils tueroient Les animaux domestique ce qu'ils avaient dejà Commencé de faire. Bien que cependant il y avoient des habitans qui en nourissoient jusqu'a vingt et cela n'empêchait pas qu'ils ne fissent de dégas. Les habitans qui craignoient que Les Sauvages ne se bandassent contre eux, accordèrent à la demande des chefs et chaqu'un nourrissaient par ensemble Les Sauvages qui étoient de leurs Costé, de sorte que pondiak et ses gens tiroient Leurs Subsistance dans La Coste du Nord, ninivois et Les poux tiroient dans la Coste du sorouest, et Les hurons dans Les Costes de L'est et du Sud. . . .

16e Juin. — Sur Les trois heures Les chefs de la bonne bande des hurons qui, depuis que père poitier pour Les arresté Leurs avoient refusé Les Sacrements, ils n'avoient plus frapés, vinrent cette journée Sur les trois heures après midy pour parlé ils entrèrent dans le fort par une fausse porte et traitèrent de paix avec Le Commandant fesant Bien des excuses touchant ce qu'ils avaient fait. Le Commandant Les écouta et Leur donna un pavillon qu'ils acceptèrent en signe d'union et S'en retournèrent Sans autre conclusion que Le pavillon.

18e Juin. — Ce mesme jour à midi, Le père dujonois, Jesuite missionnaire des Outaouis de Michelimakinak arriva avec sept Sauvages de cette nation et huit Sauteux du même endroit, commandé par un nommé Kinonchamek fils du grand chef de cette nation, par eux L'on Sçu La defaite de Mrs. Les anglais dans ce poste par Les Sauteux Le deux de ce mois.

Le Père Jésuite fut logé avec Son Confrère Le missionnaire des Hurons. . . .

23e Juin. — Les Sauvages ne vinrent point tiré Sur Le fort de la journée par ce qu'ils étaient occupé du projet qu'ils avaient fait de prendre La barque qu'ils Sçavaient estre à L'entré du Lac, ils passèrent dès le petit matin par derrière Lefort en grand nombre pour aller rejoindre ceux qui étoient deux jours auparavant partis et furent tous ensemble dans l'isle au dinde qui est un espèce de petit Détroit parce que La rivière est fort étroite à cette endroit, Les Sauvages dans cette isle firent un retranchement avec des corps d'arbres qu'ils Buchèrent et qu'ils couchèrent Sur le bord de la rivière du costé que La Barque devait passé, ils mirent aussi de la terre raporté avec des branches de sorte que S'ils eussent été vue dans Leurs retranchements, ils ne craignaient pas, Le Boulet et dans cette retraite ils attendirent La barque au passage. . . .

7e Juillet — Pendant Le tems qu'une partie de ses Mrs. étaient a donné L'epouvante au Camp de Pondiak, Les poux vinrent avec Mr. Gommelin pour demander à faire La paix avec Mr. Le Commandant, ce qui Leurs fut accordé a Condition qu'ils demeureroient neutre et qu'ils rendroient Les prisonniers, ce qu'ils promirent et ne tinrent point. Le mesme jour Les deux bandes de hurons tinrent conseil entre eux pour venir au fort faire La paix avec Mr. Le Cdt. . . .

8e Juillet — Sur les deux heures après midy Les hurons vinrent pour traiter avec Mr. Le Commandant Suivant Le Conseil qu'ils avaient tenu la veille à Leurs Villages. Mr. Le Commandant Leurs fit ouvrir La porte et ils Les admit dans Lefort et tinrent conseil sur la place d'Armes où ils demandèrent à faire La paix avec ses Mrs., il leur fut répondu * * * * que s'ils voulaient rendre tous les prisonniers et les marchandises et resté tranquille sur Leurs natte que tout Leur sotisses seraient pardonné et que Lepassé serait oublié, ils répondirent qu'ils voulaient retourner à Leurs village pour parlé à Leurs frères, de la mesme maniére et de Les faire consentir et ils se retirèrent résoud à tout ce que l'on exigeaient deux, promettant de venir La Landemain. . . .

9e Juillet. — Sur Les quatre heures Les hurons revinrent Comme ils L'avoient promis La journée précédente et ammenèrent avec eux sept prisonniers, cinq hommes dont Le Commandant de la presquisle était du nombre, une femme et un enfant qu'ils rendirent à Mr. Le Commandant et demandèrent La paix, il Leur fut repondu qu'il faloit qu'ils rendent toutes Les marchandises qu'ils avaient pris aux marchands jusqu'à une aiguillé de fil et que après La paix leur serait accordée, ils se retirèrent promettant d'apporté tout Les merchandises qu'ils avaient dans Leur villages. . . .

11e Juillet. — Sur les dix heures du matin, Les hurons vinrent S'acquiter de leurs promesse rapportant toutes Les marchandises qui avaient été prises aux marchands sur Le Lac et dans La rivière et La paix furent conclus entre eux et ces Mrs. . . .

E 19   POWELL À HUBERT
[*Archives de l'Archêveché de Québec, E.U., V–65*]

Au Détroit le 26me Decembre 1789

Mon egard pour la Justice et L'Equité ne permet pas la reponse de Mr. Dufaux à la lettre qu'il vient de recevoir de son Evêque sans l'appui de mon temoignage, tel qu'il peut valoir, depuis que j'ai l'honneur de le connoitre.

Rien ne peut être plus eloigné de tout ce qui doit donner atteinte a sa loyauté que la conduite de ce monsieur dans toutes les occasions ou il est permis à un bon sujet de marquer son attachement. Il ne s'arrête pas aux préceptes, il y ajoute l'exemple. Dans la disette qui menaça la garnison de ce poste, il sacrifioit son interêt en cédant au prix du taux tout ce qu'il avoit du bled jusqu'à presque manquer son necessaire.

A mon arrivée voyant la difficulté que j'eus à trouver une salle d'audience il m'offrit l'ancienne Eglise, et jusqu'à ce qu'on pourroit l'arranger m'accorde la salle de son Presbytère, marque de son respect pour la commission du roi et bien public qui manqua de lui susciter un procès avec ses paroissiens que sa prudence et sa fermeté lui sauva. Preuve qu'il n'y fut porté que par un empressement à faire son devoir. Je n'avois pas alors l'honneur de lui être connu. Je ne doute que le retour du courier ne l'ait blanchi dans l'Esprit de Milord Dorchester, et n'ait chassé du vôtre, monseigneur, l'odieuse soupçon qu'on a sçu y susciter, mais je me sentirois coupable de ne pas temoigner la conviction ou je suis que sa mission fera honneur à son ordre.

E 20   EXTRAIT DE LA COPIE D'UN JOURNAL DATÉ DÉTROIT 8 JANVIER 1791
[*A.P.C., Q 51–2, pp. 790–1*]

. . . Les habitants, tant du fort du Detroit que ceux des campagnes de ce coté du fort ont repondu qu'ils seroient toujours prêt, comme ils l'avoient toujours été à defendre le Gouvernement et leurs proprietés, et obéiroient au premier ordre provenant de Milord ou ses representants. Que cette assemblée, si toute fois elle étoit faite par des marchands, qui peut estre desiroit pour l'interest de leurs commerce, les engager à une guerre, dans laquelle les sauvages seuls paroissoient avoir part, et qui, peut estre même n'auroit pas la Sanction de Milord, ils n'iroient pas. La Compagnie de Maisonville et celle de l'autre bord, ont fait a peu près même reponse, ont objecté et representé qu'ils n'avoient point de Chevaux, la maladie sur les Animaux ayant été considerables se plaignent beaucoup de ce que les Sauvages dernierement ont detruit leurs animaux, et pillié dans quelques maisons, des farines et autre choses, qu'ils ont representés et qu'il n'est du pouvoir de personne de payer les dommages, lesquels precedement avoient toujours été payés, et qu'ils n'yroient pas volontairement après cela les aider, mais que lorsque le service reelle le requereroit, qu'ils ne feroient pas moins qu'ils avoient déjà faites cinquante deux ayant été au Poste avec le Gouverneur Hamilton.

F 1   DE LAUNY, PROC. MISS. CANAD. AD SUPERIOREM GENERALEM
[*General Jesuit Archives, Rome, gal. 110, vol. 1, f. 112*]

16 Febr. 1762

. . .

In caeteris missionibus nostri sua apud barbaros munia quiete et libere exercent. Dua ad Illdinenses se contulerunt metu hostium qui omnen armis Canadensem tractum occupabant, nempe PP. J. Baptista de la Morinie et J. Ba. Salleneuve. P. Petrus Potier, qui pariter sese apud eosdem sylvestres receperat, post annum ad suam stationem in freto remeavit et maxima gaudi testificatione a suis popularibus, summa humanitate ab Anglo Duce exceptus est. . . .

F 2   VENTE DE TERRE — POTIER À MARANTET
[*Registre des Actes Notariaux du Détroit, liber A, p. 114*]

Detroit le 15 Octobre, 1767

Nous soussigné praitre de la Compagnie de Jesus Missionnaire des hurons au Detroit y Resident a la pointe de Montreal, certifions qu'aiant eté obligé pour satisfaire aux dettes de la ditte mission et pour fournir aux frais de notre subsistence de faire nos representations a notre Reverend Pere Superieur de la Residence de Canada, nous en aurions reçu en reponse les pouvoirs transcrit au bas des presentes, en vertue desquels pouvoirs nous avons vendu et transporté pour toujours sous notre garantie et celles de nos successeurs de nos faits et actions (et non des faits du Prince, ou des personnes qui commandent en son non) au Sr. françois gaudet Marantet pour lui et ses hoirs ayant cause une terre de quatre arpent de large mesure de Paris sur toute la profondeur telle qu'elle nous a été concedée en mil sept cent quarante sept sans aucun titre par ecrit, Ladte. terre tenant d'un coté à L'est nord est à la concession de Mr. de Longueuil et à L'ouest sud ouest a la terre qui reste a la ditte mission, tenant par le devant au Chemin public, et dans la profondeur aux terres non concedées, pour par Ledit Sieur gaudet Marantet et Les Siens jouir de laditte terre en toute proprieté et a perpetuité, comme nous avons fait depuis vingt ans sans interruption et sans trouble, cette vente faite aux conditions susdittes, et en outre pour et moyennant la somme de Seize cens livres que le Sr. Gaudet Marantet nous payera en bonnes especes de monnoyes ayant cours au Detroit dans tel tems qu'il

nous plaira, et dont nous lui donnerons qittance en son lieu. Fait au Detroit le quinze octobre mil Sept cens soixante sept.
pour Copie   Signe   P. Potier Missionnaire des hurons, jesuite

extrait de la lettre du Reverend Pere Superieur . . . je vous donne tout permission de vendre votre terre puisqu'elle vous est devenu inutile, et je vous souhaite que vous tro [uverez a] faire une vente qui vous soit avantageuse. . . .
a Quebec Le 10 juillet 1765 . . . De Clapion J.

Je Soussigné ai donné au Sr. Marantet une perche de plus des quatre arpens.
Pour Copie   Signé   P. Potier, Missionnaire Jesuite
Le 2 Juillet 1768

Je soussigné ai concedé au Sr. Marantet Godet un arpent et une perche de terre tenant a celle qui reste a la mission : je me suis réservé sur le dt. arpent et perche un terrain quarré qui prend du bout de la cour de la Mission, et qui va jusqu'au Couin du cimetiere qui regarde l'eglise de Laditte mission.
Pour Copie   Signé   P. Potier Miss. Jes.
Le 4 Juin 1769

F 3   POTIER À BRIAND
[Archives de l'Archevêché de Québec, E.U., V–15]

Detroit, 6 Sept., 1768

J'ai reçu la lettre de votre grandeur par laquelle elle confie à mes soins les habitants de la cote du sud du Detroit; cette nouvelle paroisse consiste en soixante et quelques familles, dont le tiers, environ, m'a paié les dixmes l'an passé. Les hurons que je dessers depuis vingt quatre ans, ne paient point de dixmes. La nouvelle chappelle, que j'ai batie avec l'aide du public, est endettée; j'ai été obligé de vendre la terre de la mission pour l'acquitter. Je fournis le vin pour le sacrifice, et le luminaire. Votre grandeur jugera par là que l'establissement d'une fabrique est inutile pour le présent : on a cependant elû des marguilliers pour m'aider, dès que j'aurai acquitté les dettes de la chapelle, ils feront leurs fonctions. Feû, Mgr. Pont-briand m'avoit accordé la permission de faire les benédictions reservées aux evêques, je prie votre grandeur de me la continuer. Je supplie notre Seigneur de conserver votre personne sacrée pour sa gloire et le salut des âmes. J'ai l'honneur d'etre avec tout le respect et la soumission possible, Mgr., v.t.h. et t.o.s. . . .

F 4   EXTRAIT DU LIVRE DE COMPTE DE L'ÉGLISE DE L'ASSOMPTION 1775–81
[Archives de l'Eglise de L'Assomption]

1775
Le 15 Octobre Simon Drouyard a un banc dans L'eglise de La Somption qui La hû a la criée poure la some de quarante frant poure un année [Pas écrit par le Père Potier].
19 Nov : 75 — La violette doit 6# pour avoir manquer à donner le pain beni. *Paié
21 Nov : 75 — reçu de fr. viller 23# 7s et demi pour une grand'messe. L'eglise lui redoit 1# 7s et demi
25 Nov : 75 — paié à Mr. james Sterlin 116# pour un drap mortuaire et un

devant d'autel. L'eglise lui redoit 40#, peut-etre quelque chose de plus. * paié
25 Nov : L'eglise doit 25# à Mr. bouron qu'il a fourni sur les 116# paié à
Sterlin; item 2# que Le Susdit a paié pour le vin des messes.
25 Nov : 75 — Roy Charron redoit 6# jour le louage de son banc.
25 Nov : 75 — La palme a reçu un cent de clous sur ses gages.
25 Nov : 75 — fontaine doit 6# à L'eglise pour avoir manquer de donner le pain beni.

F 6 Donation des Hurons au Père Potier
[*Archives de l'Université de l'Assomption; Registre des Actes Notariaux du Détroit, liber C, pp. 79–80*]

Nous, les Chefs de la Nation et Tribu des 8endatte, vulgairement nommé Huron, apres nous être consulté entre les anciens de notre village, et voulant donner des marques de notre estime au R. Père Potier, Jesuite, notre Missionaire, nous ne pouvons luy temoigner quant [qu'en] luy donnant deux arpents de terre à prendre sur le bord de la Rivière du Détroit tenant du côté de l'est nord est à François Gaudet et du côté de l'ouest sud ouest à nos terres de notre village, et la profondeur jusqu'au Grand Marais. Nos intentions sont qu'il en jouisse luy et ses hoyrs comme à luy appartenant suivant la donation que nous luy en faisons sans aucun retour de notre part. En foy de quoy nous luy avons donné le présent au Detroit, le 22 Septembre 1780.

Teguaguiratin	Nonyacha	
Da8aton	Sachehotach	Totem tortue
Sindaton	Dewatonte	

Presence Temoin et Interprette des Hurons — charle reaume
[verso] Enregistré au Greffe du Détroit sur le Registre No. 2, folio 79 & 80 par moy
                                                              T. Williams Notaire

F 7 Mort et inhumation du Père Potier
[*Registre des Baptêmes, Mariages et Enterrements de l'Eglise de l'Assomption 1767–83, p. 82*]

Le dix-huit juillet mil sept cent quatre vingt un a été inhumé dans le chœur de l'église de cette paroisse du coté de l'Evangile le corps du R. P. Pierre Potier Jésuitte, Missionnaire depuis environ 37 ans; agé de soixante treize ans et trois mois décédé le seize du courant, suivant le certificat de Monsr. Anthony, chirurgien, d'une chute sur un chenêt. Ladite inhumation faite par le R. P. LeSimple Recollet Missionnaire présence d'un grand nombre de ses paroissiens.
Gllme Monforton   Beaugrand   Hubert Vic : Gen

F 8 Déclaration de François Pratt
[*Registre des Actes Notariaux du Détroit, liber C, p. 129*]

PARDEVANT nous juge soussigné fut présent le Sieur Francois Pratt acquéreur mentionné à l'acte enregistré folio 77 lequel de son bon gré et volonté a reconnu et déclaré que ce fut par oubli ou faute d'attention que feu Père

Potier n'avait pas reservé dans le dite acte le terrain ou se trouvent situé et sis l'Eglise, la maison, cour et bâtiments, et le jardin entouré de pieux debout, auquel terrain il renonce et cède tous et tels droits qui pourrait lui être donner faute d'y être mentionné aucune reserve du dit terrain, en foi de quoy il a signé cette présente declaration pour servir et valoir en présence des témoins qui ont signé avec nous ce juillet 1781.

Signé F. Pratt

Monforton témoin
La Bute

F 9 Inventaire des effets du feu Père Potier (copie)
[*Archives de l'Archevêché de Québec, PP. J., pp. 1–14*]

L'an mil sept cent quatre vingt un le 22 de juillet nous un des juges a paix de sa Majesté pour le district de Québec assisté des Srs Monforton et Maisonville Capitaines de Milice et des Srs Pouget et Jqs Parant Marguilliers de L'Eglise de notre Dame de L'Assomption avons levé le scellé que nous avions posé à la porte de la chambre du pere Potié decedé le seize du courant et nous avons fait inventaire de tout ce qui s'est trouvé dans la dte chambre.

S'est trouvé dans la Bibliotèque les papiers suivants.
Un paquet de lettres intitulé — Au sujet de notre retraite aux Illinois
Un papier intitulé — Accord fait entre le pere Salleneuve et Charles Courtois 29 8bre 1760.
Un papier intitulé — Contrat de Courtois et de Deboyer en 1760 lorsque je partis pour les Ilinois.
Une copie d'une lettre de Mr. de L'Etenduaire à Mr. le Compte de Vaudreuil.
[En marge] Na. Mr. Williams juge a toutes ces lettres entre ses mains. H. Elles ont été remises. H.
Un petit cayer — discours du clergé de France.
Un petit cayer — annoncant la vente des terres et des ordonances des commandants.
Une proclamation du gouverneur Amilton.
44 lettres du pere Viel au Pere Potié.
 4 " du père floquet
 3 " de Mr. Navarre
 7 " du pere dujauné
 9 " du pere floquet

Suite des Lettres

3 lettres du Père Gibault
 3 " du Père Glapion
 5 " du Pere Murin
 5 " du pere Lamoliniere
 1 " du gouverneur Amilton
 1 " de Mr. Legrant
 1 " de Mr. Shindler
 1 " de Mr. Le Major Depeyster
Un petit sac de cuir contenant les lettres patantes du Pere Potié.

Suivent les livres

[39 livres, manuscrits, 29 brochures et les titres de 92 tomes]

Suivent les meubles

huit secoupes, cinq tasses, un porte-huillier, trois huilliers de fayance, un de cristal, un pot a the sans couvert, une bouteille de cristal avec du poivre, deux gobelets de cristal, un pot de fayance, trois pots de grai, deux assiettes de fayance, une assiette et deux bassins d'Etein, deux plats de bois, deux paires de brosses, une decrotoire, un moule à hosties, une grande fourchette de fer, une marmite, un miroir, deux Boittes de Plomb, une paire de souliers neuf, une paire vieux avec les boucles, deux cuves, deux cassettes, une caisse contenant environ vingt livres de chandelles, une herminette, un casse-tête, une petite pioche, une couverte de laine, quatre couvertes, un Etui avec quatre rasoirs, deux grand couvertes de laine, un pot de chambre, un barril avec de vieux bas, deux barrils vides, une cassette contenant treize mouchoirs de cotton, un de toile fine, nœuf fourchettes neuves, une demi livre de fil, une nape, cinq paires de culotes, trois ceintures, deux mouchoirs de cotton, une redingotte noire, une veste, une serviette, cinq robes noires, deux chapeaux, trois chemises, un essuie-main, six chemises, un quart a motié de Rum, deux draps de toile, un matelas, une couchette, une nape, cinq mouchoirs, deux bonets de nuit.

[En marge] — Donné les hardes a Laderoute son domestique. Hubert

Suit L'Argent

Dans un porte feuille en papier	Pounts York	34	4	8
en or Sept Portugaises — egal a		23	8	
en argent blanc			8	
		58		8

Suivent les Billets

un billet a ordre de Mr. Brulon	31	4	
un " a yd de Mr. Anders et Cgnie	43	11	10
un " de Mr. Prat payable en trois mois suivant son contrat de terre a lui vendu par le Pere Poitié	57	18	

vingt epinglettes d'argent et deux
Branches de Porcelaine

S'est trouvé dans le grenier

Un poele de fer et son tuyau et une tourne broche

S'est trouvé dans la cuisine

Une table, deux seaux ferrés, un huche, deux poiles a frire, une tourtiere, une Liche frite, une cuiller a pot et un briquet, une broche a rotir, deux chenets, deux pelles a feu, trois marmittes de fer, un canar, deux mechantes huches.

S'est trouvé dans la chambre en entrant au Refectoire à Droit

Sept bassins d'etein petits et grands, une punoise de cuivre jaune, deux douz d'assiettes grandes et moyennes d'etein, quinze moules d'etein, petits et grands, deux quarts vides, deux petits barrils de vinaigre, trente et huit poches, quatre nappes, une caisse de ferrailles et deux vieux coins de fer, une robe de bœuf Ilinois, quatre pots de terre, une mane a lessiver, quatre petits barrils vides, six taies et six secoupes de grai.

S'est trouvé dans la chambre entrant au Refectoire à gauche

Un Baudet, une boette contenant treize fourchettes de fer et une de cuivre, cinq couteaux de table, un Buffet, deux pots d'etein, deux cafetieres une petite et une grande, une douz de verres, deux petits flacons et trois bouteilles, un moulin à caffé, douze chandellier de cuivre jaune.

Dans la cave

Deux grand chaudieres couvertes pleines d'huile d'ours, une chaudiere couverte appartenant a Mdme Savoyar, un quart plein de vin rouge, vingt et une bouteilles pleines de vin rouge dont le vin appartient a Mr. Godet, une roue de brouette, une tonne et six quarts vides.

S'est trouvé dans le Refectoire

une pendule, un dressoir, une table, dix chaises, un fanal, deux chenets, deux tripiers, sept plats d'etein, un rechau, un saladié.

S'est trouvé dans le chemin couvert qui conduit de la maison a l'eglise trois chaudières evasées et au jardin un rateau de fer, trois pioches, une beche et une brouette.

S'est trouvé dans la boulangerie

au grenier

deux coffres contenant environ sept cens livres de farine

en bas

six moyenes chaudières evasées, une cuve a lessive et une cage a poules. Arreté et clos dans la maison du feu R. P. Potier le jour et an que de l'autre part ainsi signés a la minute

Gllme Monforton,   Maisonville
Joseph Pouget   + Jos Parant
Williams juge

L'Eglise est de soixante pieds de long sur 30 de large contenant 34 bancs payant Rante — bien ornée de tablaux, tabernacle en sculpture doré, pourvu de vases sacrés et autres ornements et linges necessaire pour le service divin. Banc d'œuvre et point de chaire — bien eclairée et bien vitrée.

Une maison faite aux frais des habitants et ceux du Pere Potier de 26 pieds de long sur vingt de large pour loger de Bedeau, recevoir les corps et les enfants pour la première communion.

La maison du pere est grande et en besoin de beaucoup de reparations.

La cour est entourée de pieux de cedre de 29 pas de long sur dix de large dans laquelle se trouvent une Boulangerie de 16 pieds carrée presque neuve, et un poulier qui n'est pas encore achevé.

F 11   PROCÈS-VERBAL D'UNE ASSEMBLÉE DES MARGUILLIERS
[*Registre des Actes Notariaux du Détroit, liber C, p. 128*]

L'an mil sept cent quatre vingt un le 28 de juillet après la convocation d'une assemblée generale tenue dans l'église de notre dame de l'Assomption à l'issue de la prière a été délibéré d'un consentiment unanime qu'il serait élu parmi les marguillers un ou plusieurs deputés auprès de sa Grandeur pour obtenir un successeur au feu R. P. Potier. A cet effet ce sont assemblés les Sieurs Maisonville, Marantete, Pouget, Labute, Pajot, Langlois, Bouron, Touranjeau, Suzor, Bondy, Meloche et Jacques Parent tous anciens et nouveaux marguillers pour délibérer sur les voyes les plus convenables tant pour faire la demande au nom de tout le public à sa grandeur d'un missionaire que pour faire les demarches necessaires auprès des Reverends pères Jesuites pour tout ce qui concerne les affaires de l'église et du Presbitère et autres bâtiments appartenants à la mission, et ont les dit Sieurs susnommés élu les personnes des Sieurs Pouget et Belaire qu'ils ont chargés de leur

procuration et plein pouvoir pour faire les demarches necessaires et cy dessus mentionnées, en foy de quoy ont les dits Sieurs cy nommés au nom de tout le public ont signés le présent acte pour servir au besoin. Fait et passé dans la Maison presbitériale à la pointe des Hurons au sud de la rivière du Detroit.
  (Signés)

Maisonville	F. Marantete Godet
J. Bondy	(Monforton pour Jacques Parent
Joseph Pouget	Marguiller en charge)
Touranjeau	La Bute
Monforton pour Suzor	Charles Bouron
Pierre Meloche	Monforton pour Langlois
Monforton pour Pajot	

F 12 Discours des principaux chefs Hurons en conseil au Major De Peyster commandant au Détroit &c. 29 juillet 1781
[*A.P.C., B 123, pp. 107–9*]

          Tiockouanhoron parlant avec des Branches de porcelaine
  Mon pere, je vous prie de faire attention à mes paroles ce sont celles des chefs, des guerriers, des femmes et des enfants, qui se servent de ma bouche pour implorer votre secours, dans le triste état où nous nous trouvons : L'affaire est de la dernière conséquence pour nous.
                        Par un collier
  La mort de notre pieux missionnaire le père Poitier a jetté dans nos esprits un trouble inconcevable, depuis ce tems, d'épaisses ténèbres nous ont environné et nous tiennent dans un état pitoyable, qui sollicite votre compassion paternelle en notre faveur : nous vous prions de vous joindre à nous, pour obtenir de Son Excellence le Général Haldiman, son appuy pour nous avoir un nouveau missionnaire : d'aignés aussi lui faire parvenir ces paroles de notre part.
                        en montrant un collier
  Ce collier est le simbole de notre adoption à la religion chretienne et de la chaine qui nous y attache, nous esperons obtenir aujourd'huy, un conducteur spirituel comme on nous les accordait précédement.
          Par un collier addressé au Général Haldiman
  Nous supplions Votre Excellence qui nous représente sa Majesté Britannic, de prêter son attention à la demande que nous voulons lui faire.
                Par un autre collier au même
  Mon Pere, d'aignés s'il vous plait considerer le triste état de notre nation, depuis la perte de notre missionnaire : nous gémissons sur notre malheureux sort présent et à venir, sans sçavoir à qui recourir : c'est pourquoi nous sollicitons votre Excellence comme notre plus Solide appuy auprès de sa grandeur, Monseigneur L'Evêque de Quebec pour faire avoir un autre missionnaire aux Hurons de Detroit vos Enfants.
         Par un autre collier à Monseigneur Briant Evêque de Quebec
  Mon père, au nom de Dieu et de toutte la nation huronne, secourés nous dans le pressant besoin où nous sommes d'un missionnaire, la perte du pere Poitier a laissé une desolation generalle dans nos villages, qui ne cessera que lorsque vous l'aurés remplacé par un autre : instruits des l'enfance des prin-

cipes de la Religion Chrétienne, nous les suivons avec fidélitée, sous la direction de nos conducteurs spirituels : mais auhourd'huy que deviendrons-nous ? les ames de nos guerriers frémiront desormais a l'aspect de la mort qui les attend a chaque instant, le Sang de nos vieillards et de nos femmes se glace par avance a l'approche du dernier momment de leur vie languissante, les meres se désolent sur le sort de leurs Enfants, enfin votre charitable zele vous en dira plus que nous, pour vous solliciter en notre faveur : je vous prie de le consulter et le pressant besoin ou nous sommes, qui vous engage à éviter tous délais et retardement car tous les instants sont precieux dans l'affaire presente : nous prions Dieu de nous être favorable dans la demande que nous vous faisons, et pour la conservation de votre grandeur.

Par un autre collier addressé a Son Excellence le Général Haldiman, et à sa Grandeur l'Evêque de Quebec.

Mes Peres, Espérant obtenir de votre bontée l'effet de nos demandes pour le Missionnaire que nous vous prions de nous accorder, sitôt que vous aurés fixé votre choix ce collier s'addresse à lui, afin de lui indiquer la Routte qui le conduira à notre village, nous l'assurons par avance de l'affection filiale et respectueuse de notre nation.

Par un autre collier addressé aux Hurons de Lorette à Quebec.

Mes freres vous estes de la même nation et Religion que nous, c'est pourquoi nous vous prions avec confiance de vous joindre a nous pour nous obtenir un nouveau missionnaire pour remplacer le pere Poitier, qui est mort le 16e de juillet : vous devés être en état de connaitre les vrays moyens dont on doit se servir pour obtenir une telle grace. nous vous prions donc de mettre tout en usage pour nous obtenir cette faveur de notre père le Général, et de Monseigneur notre Evêque : Nous vous saluons tous.

Au Detroit le 29e juillet 1781.

Noms des principaux Chefs présents
Tiockouanorhon   Jorihoha
Toienthet   Isononcainen
Cimiathon   Tharatobat
Tiockeres
Avec les principales dames de la nation

F 13   EXTRAITS DU REGISTRE DES COMPTES, ELECTIONS &C. DE LA PAROISSE DE L'ASSOMPTION, 1781 —
[*Archives de L'Eglise de l'Assomption*]

Le vingt cinq novembre mil sept cens quatre vingt un les Marguilliers & autres habitants de la paroisse de L'Assomption du Détroit étant assemblés au son de la cloche en la maniere ordinaire pour procéder à l'Election d'un nouveau marguillier à la place du Sr. Jacques Parent sortant de charge, à la pluralité des voix a été Elu le Sr. J. bte. Oualette en qualité de marguillier, lequel a accepté la dite charge et a promis s'en acquitter avec fidelité. en foy de quoy il a fait sa marque ordinaire les jour & an que dessus.

Marque + de J. bte. Oualette   J. Bondy
fancoit godet   joseph pouget
charle bouron   simon drouilliar
reauomen   Hubert ptre. Vic. Gen.

Le 2 Decembre 1781 — Le Sieur Jacques Parent sortant de charge a remis au Sr. Louis Suzor trois cens neuf livres seize sols étant tout ce qu'il nous a dit avoir à l'Eglise, n'ayant eu jusqu'à présent aucun compte en règle. à L'Assomption le 2 Xbre 1781.

Hubert ptre Vic. Gen.

Le neuf Decembre mil sept cens quatre vingt un Les Marguilliers anciens & nouveaux assemblés en la maniere ordinaire ont approuvé et nommé pour Bedeau pierre Javerai aux conditions suivantes de part et d'autre que le dit Pre Javerai s'acquittera de son emploi avec fidelité en tout ce qui lui est marqué, de la part des Marguilliers qui la lui payeront de la caisse de la fabrique deux cens livres courant de vingt sols par an et le logement convenable pour le bedeau dans les endroits que les Marguilliers jugeront, et à condition expresse que le dit bedeau n'exigera aucun remboursement ny dedomagement quelconque, ny ne pourra sous louer en tout ou en partie le logement qui lui serait fourni par la fabrique. La dite fabrique se reservant le droit de percevoir le Loyer du dit emplacement dans le cas que le bedeau n'y demeurerait pas. De plus le bedeau sera obligé et tenu de recevoir les corps morts de la paroisse jusqu'à leur Enterrement, Loger les enfants qui se font instruire pour la 1ere. Communion, de souffrir les personnes qui auront apporté un voyage de bois se chauffer dans la dite maison.
Fait à L'Asomption les jour & an que dessus.

    joseph pouget   Marque pierre + Javerai Bedeau
    francois meloche pierre meloche
    fancoit godet   La Bute

Je pierre Javerai certifie avoir reçu de Mr. Suzor Marguillier en charge 83# 6s pour solde de mes gages jusqu'au dernier de Janvier dont Quittce.
a L'Assomption Le 20 Janv. 1782.

        Hubert témoin   marque de + pre Javerai

Il a été décidé dans l'assemblée de Messieurs les marguilliers que l'on donnerait au bedeau Amable Bigra la somme de vingt pounds ou cens Ecus pour Gage. a la paroisse de L'Assomption le 27 Janv. 1782

Hubert ptre. Vic. Gen.

Reçu de Monsieur Hubert cinquante livres pour trois mois de Gages Echues le 1er du Courant..	50#	
de plus reçu pr. 1 gde messe le 17 Janv. Ls. Goiaux.................	2#	10s
pr. 1 yd.................feu Robert..............................	2#	10s
pr. Enter & service de la fe. de Pre. Campeau......................	6#	
pr. 1 gde messe & Ent. du panis de Mr. Ch. Reaume................	4#	
pr. 1 gde messe pr. Phil. Leduc....................................	2#	10s
Total payé a Mr. Gaillard Chantre.............................	67#	10s
Le 18 Fevr. 1782—Louis Gaillard		

Le 9 Juin Messieurs les marguillers assemblés a Eté décidé que l'on emploieroit environ quatre mille livres argent de l'Eglise a acheter planches, madriers &c. pr. la batisse d'une nouvelle Eglise.

Hubert ptre. Vic. Gen.

    joseph pouget

COMPTE DU SR. LOUIS SUZOR MARGUILLIER
CHAPITRE IER
RECETTES

1. fait recette le dit Ls. Suzor de la somme de trois cens neuf livres seize sols a lui remis par le Sr. Jacques Parent son prédécesseur.. 309# 16s
de plus du Sr. Pre. meloche ancien marguillier pour ballance duë a la fin de son année.................. 48#
2. reçu de la quête de l'enfant Jesus en argent......... 221# 12s
en bled d'inde vendu a Mr. Marantet.............. 93# 11s
en 12 minots bled froment a Mr. pouget........... 180#
en 2½ yd a Roucout pr. 1 an d'hosties.............. 37# 10s 532# 13s
3. Quête du Vendredi St.................. 189#
plus un billet de 204# de Poitevin, s'il est payé, pr. mre.
4. Quête des Dimanches dans L'Eglise—en argent— 149# 9s
Na. dans ces quêtes il y avait 220 Epinglettes qu'on a remis dans la caisse de l'Eglise. On en avait deja pris 500—vendues a Mr. Drouillard de cette même quête.
5. Reçu pour rente de bancs, Scavoir de (Na. il y a 34 bancs)

Srs. Pre Meloche pere pr 1 banc 1 année............ 7# 10s
Labutte................2......1.............. 15#
Marantet...............2......1.............. 15#
Jh. Drouillard..........1......1.............. 7# 10s
André Peltier..........1......1.............. 7# 10s
Suzor.................1......2.............. 15#
Bon:Réaume..........1......2.............. 15#
M. Réaume Pere.......1......3 et plus......... 24#
Claude Réaume.......1......1.............. 7# 10s
Vital Dumouchelle....1......1.............. 7# 10s
Js. Charon...........1......3.............. 22# 10s
Jh. Pilet.............1......3.............. 22# 10s
Oualet...............1......2.............. 15#
N. Langlois..........1......1.............. 7# 10s
L'Espérance.........1......1.............. 7# 10s
Janis................1......1.............. 7# 10s
Laurt. Parent........1......1.............. 7# 10s
Jh. Beaubien.........1......3.............. 22# 10s
Guille. Goyau........1 banc 1 année............ 7# 10s
Tourangeaux.........1......1.............. 7# 10s
Ls. Deveau...........1......4.............. 30#
Ant. Meloche........1......1.............. 7# 10s 309# 0s

Na. Poirier, Gignac, Hodienne, avaient payé leurs bancs en entrant L'année précédente.
6. Reçu pr. adjudication de bancs de J-bte. Oualet..... 225#
Simon Drouillard............................. 226#
Charles Renauld............................. 240#
d'Antaia................................... 232# 10s
de Gignac.................................. 240#
de Julien Parent a Compte de 270#............. 135# 1298# 10s

7. reçu de Mr. Beufait cinq cens livres pour L'Eglise qui fera chanter un service pour défunt Mr. Paul Marsac dans le courant d'Octobre prochain cy... 500#
8. Reçu de Mr. Pre. Drouillard pr. 870 Epinglettes............. 404#
Na. dans ces 870 Epinglettes on en avait pris 500 dans le coffre de L'Eglise de la quête de cette année
9. Reçu pour gdes. messes, enterrements et services.............. 910# 10s
plus du 9 aoust pr. le service de bois menu.................. 26#
reçu de Suzor pr. 8 pends. d'oreille........................ 6#

Total de la Recette.................. 4682# 18s
Na. Reçu en present de Joseph Drouillard
deux flambeaux d'argent de 150#

APPENDIX I

CHAPITRE 2D—DÉPENSES

1.	Payé a Mde Janis blanchisseuse de L'Eglise pour solde de son année échuë le 1er 9bre 1778..........	49#	10
	a yd pr solde de 1781.........................	6#	
	a yd a compte de l'année depuis le 1er 9bre 1781, a raison de 120# par an. par la rente de son banc......	7#	10
	Juin 24—a yd a compte 6 pounds..................	90#	153# —
2.	Payé a ladéroute ancien bedeau pour solde jusqu'au jour de son départ...........................		83# 6
3.	a Bigra Bedeau depuis le 1er fev. 1782 a 300# par an ... Pr gages et Casuel jusqu'au 16 aoust prochain..	212#	
	a yd pr avoir crié 7 bancs.......................	21#	233#
4.	Payé a Ls. Gaillard chantre a 200# par an. Jusqu'au 1er aoust 1782. pr gages.................	150#	
	a yd pr. Casuel jusqu'au dit jour..................	117#	267#
5.	a Roucout pour l'année d'hosties Echuë le 1er Janv. 1782, par 2½ bled...........................		37# 10
6.	a M. Hubert pr honoraire jusqu'au 1er aoust 1782...		215#
7.	a M. Rankin marchand pr Etoffe pour la roble du bedeau......................................	52#	
	a M. Pouget pr façon de ladite roble..............	12#	64#
	Pr Savon pr L'Eglise a Mde. Janis.................		15#
	a Guilbeau pr 10 livres de chandelle..............		37# 10
	a Fovel pr aller chercher des rameaux.............	12#	
	a yd pr Cloture de L'emplacement du bedeau......	60#	72#
			1177# 6
	Payé pour ornements et cierge achetés a M'réal par M. Hubert.....		157#
	Pr Cire chandelier et surplis acheté par M. Pouget................		109 10
	Pr 1 livre d'encens...		3#
	Payé pr les frais du voyage de M. le Curé argt de la fabrique.......		232# 2
			1684# 18

La recette étant de quatre mil six cens quatre vingt deux livres dix huit sols et la dépense étant de seize cens quatre vingt quatre livres dix huit, partant la recette du Sr. Louis Suzor excede la depense de la somme de deux mil neuf cens quatre vingt dix huit livres—laquelle somme ledit Sr. Ls Suzor marguillier a remis dans le coffre de L'eglise, ainsi que deux cens vingt Epinglettes. Arrêté au Détroit paroisse de L'assomption le 11 aoust 1782—

      joseph pouget   francoit gaudet
      J. Bondy   fr. meloche
                Hubert ptre. vic. gen.

COMPTE DU SR. JOSEPH POUGET MARGUILLIER EN CHARGE DEPUIS LE 15 AOUST 1782—JUSQUE 1783

CHAPITRE PREMIER

RECETTES

1.	Fait recette le Sieur Joseph Pouget de la somme de deux mil neuf cens quatre vingt dix huit livres a lui remise par le Sr. Louis Suzor sortant de charge..		2998#	
	De plus reçu pour honoraires de grand-messes, services, enterrements &c..		1336#	10
	Plus dons faits a L'Eglise................	85#	10	
	Quête des Dimanches en argent..................	205#		
	Quête de L'enfant Jesus argt.....................	171#		
	Quête du Vendredi St. argt.....................	115#		
	Quête en farine 840 livres........................	630#		
	en bled dinde—11 minots.................	198#		
	en avoine—7 minots.................	70#		
	Quêtes diverses Epinglettes, Porcelaine...........	1258#	5	2732# 15
	Plus pr rentes des bancs........................		246#	
	Total de la recette................................		7313#	5

CHAPITRE SECOND
DÉPENSES

Payé a Mr. Hubert pr. honoraire jusqu'au 15 aoust 1783............		284#	10
a Guillard Chantre jusqu'au 1er 7bre pour gages & Casuel	346#		
a yd a Compte nouveau.............................	45#	391#	
a Bigra Bedeau jusqu'au mois d'avril dernier pr. Gages & honoraires.............................		311#	
a Me. Janis pr. solde de Blanchissage................		22#	10
Pr. Vin de messes.................................		255#	
Pr. Luminaire & Service pr. M. Marsac...............		56#	
Pr. empoix & amidon..............................		15#	
Pr. 1 ornement complet & Cierge...................		687#	8
Payé en argent pr la piniere......................	4200#	5098#	
Pr. yd en farine &c..............................	898#		
Total de la dépense....................		7120#	8

Na. La Depense totale de la piniere a été dix sept mil sept cens quarante livres dix sols, L'Eglise a fourni 5098# et Mr. Hubert a fourni la somme de douze mil six cens quarante deux livres dix sous.

Arrêté le Compte cy dessus par lequel il appert que la recette etant de 7313# 5s et la dépense de 7120# 8. La Recette excède la dépense de la somme de cent quatre vingt douze livres dix sept sols que Mondit Sr. Pouget a remis au Sr. Oualet marguillier en charge.

      Maisonville   godet
      J. Bondy
      joseph + pouget Hubert pt. Vic Gn

L'an mil sept cent quatre vingt sept, le neuf de Septembre, après la mure deliberation d'une nombreuse assemblée composée des plus notables habitants de la paroisse de L'assomption du detroit et des principaux chefs hurons réunis pour proceder aux affaires de leur fabrique: certifions qu'il a été decidé qu'une portion de l'eglise serait employée par la nation huronne.

C'est à dire pour parler plus clairement que depuis le bas de l'eglise, en prenant au milieu de la nef jusques à la seconde fenêtre inclusivement personne n'aurait droit positivement dans la dite portion de l'eglise que les dits Sauvages, reconnus pour chretiens, et legitime possesseurs de la partie en question, pour avoir manifesté leur zele, et cotisé aux frais et a l'edification de la dite église en tout ce qui etait a leur pouvoir.

En consideration de la gloire de dieu pour le bien de la paix et de la concorde qui doit unir les fideles nous avons delivré le present acte pour servir au besoin et à la satisfaction des parties interessées.

Cependant il est a remarquer que si les dits Sauvages veulent distinguer leurs chefs, et autres personnes de Marque parmi leur nation, ils seront obligés de faire faire eux mêmes et a leur propre depends: sieges, bans, et autre commoditées distinctives pourvu qu'ils se conforment aux loix et usages etablis par les constitutions de notre mere la Ste. Eglise. —

Fait et passé le neuf Septembre (de l'année susdite) dans la maison présbiteriale en presence de Messire dufaux prêtre missionaire, soussigné, et de plusieurs autres comme il parait cy après. —

    payet ptre missionaire   F. X. Dufaux
    claude réaume   Charles reaume

COMPTE DU SIEUR JEAN BAPTISTE TOURNEUX MARGUILLER EN CHARGE DEPUIS LE 1ER JANVIER 1792 JUSQU'AU 1ER JANVIER 1793.

RECETTES

1. fait recette le sieur jean baptiste tourneux de la somme de cinquante huit livres neuf sols a lui remise par le sieur antoine meloche sortant de charge. 58# 9s
de plus honoraire des services, grandes messes et enterements....... 771# 10s
rente des bans... 1150#
queste de l'enfant jesus.. 275# 14s
autres dons faits a l'eglise.................................... 38#

2293# 13s

DÉPENSES

pour gage et honoraire de bigras bedeau........................ 548# 18s
pour gage et honoraire de beauchant............................ 147# 15s
pour ditto de Mr. perthuis..................................... 126#
pour ditto du Mr. le curé...................................... 220#
pour blanchissage à la bigras.................................. 40#
pour un tapis de leine... 60#
pour rameaux... 7# 10s
pour fret de la terre.. 38#
pour vin blanc de la messe..................................... 121# 10s
pour chandelle... 120#
pour bougie.. 48#
pour hosties, encens, enpoie, savon &c......................... 45#
payé a frerot pour la chair en argent.......................... 285#
payé a morand pour le bois de la chair......................... 36#

1843# 13s

arreté le present compte par lequel appartient que la recette etant de 2293# 13s et la depense de 1843# 13s, la recette excede la depense de 450# que Mr. Tourneux a remis à Mr. Boufard entrant en charge.

Dufaux ptre.

F 15 ETABLISSEMENT DE LA CONGRÉGATION DE NOTRE-DAME À DÉTROIT
[L'Histoire de la Congrégation de Notre-Dame de Montréal, *V, 345–53*]

En 1755, les habitanta de Détroit avaient fait des instances auprès de Mgr de Pontbriand pour avoir une mission de notre Institut dans leur ville; ils avaient présenté une requête au Marquis Duquesne de Menneville dans le même but . . . mais la chose était demeurée sans résultat. Cependant le project de cette fondation n'avait point été abandonné; et, en 1782, on s'en occupa d'une manière plus active que jamais. M. Hubert, curé de l'Assomption chez les Hurons, près du Détroit, ex-supérieur du Séminaire de Québec, nommé plus tard successeur de Mgr d'Esglis, qui avait pris cet établissement fort à cœur, ayant écrit à cet effet, Mgr Briand voulut appuyer sa demande en y joignant la lettre qui suit :

Québec, 26 Mars, 1782

« Ma très honorée Sœur,

Je n'ai rien à ajouter à la lettre ci-jointe de M. Hubert; je ne pourrais vous donner de motifs plus pressants et plus analogues à votre Institut que ceux qu'il vous donne : des peuples sans mœurs et sans connaissance de la religion qui les réforme, c'est le grand objet qu'ont eu en vue les personnes zélées et saintes qui ont institué votre utile Congrégation. Si votre maison consent, vous vous entendrez avec M. Montgolfier pour le choix des personnes et pour le reste. Je prie Notre-Seigneur qu'Il inspire à votre communauté de consentir à cette bonne et grande œuvre; et qu'Il donne à celles que l'on choisira le courage et le zèle de l'entreprendre, la sagesse, la prudence et toutes les autres vertus nécessaires pour le bien conduire, pour rendre leurs travaux et leurs soins utiles à la gloire de Dieu et au salut des pauvres peuples.

« Je suis avec bien de l'estime, Votre ... etc.

+ J. Ol. Evêque de Québec. »

Sœur Saint-Ignace après avoir communiqué à son Conseil la lettre de Monseigneur, y répondit ainsi :

« Monseigneur,

J'ai reçu avec la plus respectueuse soumission la lettre que Votre Grandeur m'a fait l'honneur de m'écrire. Quoique nous ne puissons pas nous dissimuler la grande charge temporelle, et peut-être le préjudice spirituel que pourra occasionner à notre communauté le nouvel établissement qu'on nous propose d'une mission au Détroit, la chose nous paraît si avantageuse à la gloire de Dieu, si conforme aux obligations de notre état et aux sentiments de zèle dont nous sommes animées, qu'autorisées par Votre Grandeur, nous ne saurions nous y refuser absolument. Mais qu'il nous soit permis, Monseigneur, de représenter qu'il nous paraît impossible de l'exécuter sur le champ. Quoiqu'il semble que M. Hubert ait pris des précautions justes et raisonnables pour nous en faciliter le premier voyage et pour nous y procurer un asile, ce ne sont que des secours passagers, et il devrait être question d'un etablissement pour toujours. La protection et le zèle de ce Monsieur peuvent nous manquer avant que l'affaire soit entièrement finie ... et que feront nos chères Sœurs isolées dans un pays si éloigné, si impracticable, peut-être sans secours spirituels ? ...

« Quoique nous ne manquions pas de Sœurs zélées, nous n'en avons point à la main, pour le présent, disposées à entreprendre cet ouvrage. Les circonstances ne nous paraissent pas favorables pour entreprendre de nouveaux établissements dans des endroits si éloignés, dans le temps que nous avons beaucoup de peine à soutenir nos établissements voisins et tout formés. Enfin, fût-il possible de l'entreprendre, il nous paraît nécessaire de prendre quelques précautions pour ne pas former un engagement insoutenable, et qui pourrait devenir préjudiciable en bien des manières.

C'est en conséquence de ces réflexions qu'il nous paraît nécessaire de prendre du temps pour réfléchir sur les conditions auxquelles nous pourrions nous prêter, et nous espérons que Votre Grandeur voudra bien nous donner son approbation.

« J'ai l'honneur d'être avec le plus profond respect,
Monseigneur,
Votre très humble et très obéissante servante,
Sœur Saint-Ignace.

Montréal, 12 juin 1782. »

Le 21 juin, Sœur Saint-Ignace écrivait à M. Hubert, curé de L'Assomption de Détroit:

Monsieur,

J'ai eu l'honneur de vous marquer le 30 mai que j'avais reçu les deux lettres que vous m'avez fait l'honneur de m'écrire, et les deux mille quatre cents livres que je conserve en dépôt. J'ai écrit à Monseigneur pour les conditions que la Communauté demande pour la mission de Détroit; je ne manquerai pas de vous écrire aussitôt que j'aurai reçu la réponse de Sa Grandeur.

Nous ne pouvons nous dissimuler, nonobstant le désir que nous avons toutes de contribuer au bien, autant que notre petite condition le permet, à quel point une mission si éloignée sera, à bien des égards, pénible à notre Communauté. Plus d'une réflexion raissonnable doit, je crois, précéder cet établissement.

Agréez, s'il vous plaît, les très humbles respects de la Communuté. Elle se joint à moi pour vous supplier de nous accorder un précieux souvenir dans vos saints sacrifices.

J'ai l'honneur d'être,
    Monsieur,
        Votre très humble servante,

                      Sœur Saint-Ignace

...

Après avoir pesé les avantages et les désavantages de cette Mission, la Communauté dut y renoncer.

F 16   Hubert à Mgr. J.-O. Briand
[Archives de l'Archevêché de Québec, Ev. Q., II, p. 36]

Détroit, 26. 7bre 1784.

Monsr. Baby m'a entrêmement consolé en me disant que votre Santé se rétablissoit. C'est la seule nouvelle que j'en aie reçue cette année.

Mr. payet n'est point encore de retour de sa mission; Je l'attends dans 15 jours.

Je vais entrer dans quelques jours dans un nouveau presbitaire, qui est beau pour le pays et grand. L'on se propose une nouvelle Eglise pour l'année prochaine; Je désirerois pouvoir reformer les mœurs aussi facilement que de rebatir un presbitaire; mais hélas, que d'obstacles; les passions sont presque les mêmes. Nous en ramenons un, il en sort un autre. La profanation des dimanches me paroit la source des autres miseres, et malheureusement elle augmente; Le moment de la miséricorde divine n'est point encore arrivé. Il faut l'attendre.

F 17   Fréchette à Hubert
[Archives de l'Archevêché de Québec, E.U., V–46]

L'Assomption du Detroit le 24 avril 1786

N'ayant appris aucune nouvelle depuis votre départ du Detroit, je ne scais comment m'addresser à votre égard, cependant, Monsieur, en quelque place que vous soyez, je vous supplie d'être persuadé de mon respect et de ma soumission a toutes vos volontés.

Je profite de la premiere occasion qui me parait assuré pour vous donner des nouvelles de votre paroisse. Il a couru cet hiver une espece de grippe et de fievre rouge qui, m'a donné beaucoup de tourment; cependant Dieu par son infinie bonté m'a donné assez de santé et de force pour satisfaire à tous ceux qui ont eu besoin de moi; il est mort bien du monde et surtout des jeunes personnes. J'ai enterré un nomme Picotte, que Dieu par sa misericorde infini a ramené à son devoir quelque tems devant sa mort et qui m'a bien donné de la consolation sur la fin de ses jours. J'ai enterré aussi le vieux Répus, et la femme du pauvre Pelletier, Marguillier, laquelle, comme vous scavez a laissé une nombreuse famille. Je ne vous rend point compte des meurs des habitants, vous les connaissez mieux que moi. Je suis assez content de la paroisse, Dieu a fini en plusieurs l'ouvrage que vous aviez heureusement commencé, et je vous marque avec plaisir qu'il n'en reste que bien peu, si toute fois il en reste, qui ne se soient presenté au tribunal de la penitence dans le temps pascal; jusqu'a Deveau à qui Dieu a touché le cœur et qui s'est enfin reconnu et qui me parait avoir envie de bien faire. J'ai chassé de ma paroisse Madame tourangeau, dite la bleux, qui était venue s'y refugier cette automne. j'ai fait partir aussi du moulin de Simon madame Morisseau qui s'y comportait très mal. j'ai areté un peu les bals et les danse cet hiver en leur representant la maladie ci-dessus nommée, comme une punition de leurs desordres et de leurs débauches.

Pour l'eglise on commence à travailler. on a tiré cet hiver la pierre et le bois pour la chaud; tout le monde me parait bien disposé a travailler citot que les semences seront finis. j'ai faite une quête cet hiver à laquelle j'ai assez ramassé. je suis assez comptant [sic] la paroisse en general, et j'ose même me flatter que l'on me craint et que l'on m'aime en même tems. Personne ne cherche à me faire de la peine, bien au contraire tout le monde ne cherche qu'à me rendre service; il n'y a que françois Meloche qui étant cet hiver dans les folies, a voulu me tenter procès pour les chandelles de l'enterrement de sa sœur la Pelletier, mais après lui avoir fait voir que cela m'appartenait bien, il a tant eu de honte de sa bevue, qu'il n'ose plus paraitre au presbytere. Je n'ai qu'une chose qui me fait de la peine, Monsieur, qui est que Monsieur Payet me donne à connaitre et a même dit à plusieurs qu'il voulait demander la paroisse ou je suis s'il remontait cette automne. Cela me troublerait beaucoup; d'ailleurs vous scavé la peine que j'ai resentit en laissant ma patrie. Si cela arrive je vous supplie, et je me crois même obligé en conscience de vous demander de me rappeler en Canada, parceque connaissant maintenant le monde comme je le connais, je vois qu'il est impossible que j'aille ailleurs pour bien des raisons. Je suis, Monsieur, en me recommandant à vos Sts Sacrifices

F 18   DUFAUX À HUBERT
[*Archives de l'Archevêché de Québec, E.U., V–47*]

Du Detroit, 24 Aoust, 1787

. . .

J'ai reçu une lettre de votre grandeur du 18 Juin qui m'enjoint de m'en rapporter à Mr. Payet pour tout ce qu'elle a laissé à l'Assomption excepté les livres que j'ai trouvé sans aucune notte de la quantité, et les manuscrits du P. Potier, que je livrerai à Mr. Payet. La terre est en la jouissance de Mr. Pouget; je mets mes animeaux chez les voisins; les meubles sont en si petites quantité que j'ai honte de vous faire le detail de ce qui a resté au presbiter. 9 assiettes, 2 plas, 3 vielle napes, une caraphe et 2 verres. Le reste ne vaut pas la peine de le mentionner. J'ai emprunté le plus necessaire des meubles de menage de plusieurs personnes qui m'ont rendu ce service, n'étant point en état d'en avoir par moi même, a moins de prendre a credie, a quoi je ne puis me resoudre. l'argent est si rare que j'ai a peine reçu cent ecus dans toute l'année, pour payer les gages du bon homme Bigras qui est à mon service. Les meilleurs habitants qui étoit en etat de se preter a quelques bonnes œuvres il y a trois ou quatre ans, n'ont pas seulement une piastre devant eux, et ils doivent tous; tel Mr. Houelette a qui j'ai marié deux enfants depuis six mois, n'a pas eté en etat de me payer seulement leur mariage. Il m'a avoué qu'il n'avoit pas un seul sol d'argent pour y satisfaire; sur six mariages que j'ai faits en tout, il ni en a qu'un seul qui a pu payer, le reste est a credis; pour les basses messes, je n'ai pas reçu en argent la retribution de trente, depuis que je suis arrivée. Les questes des festes et dimanches se sont monté a 11# 10S en argent. Dans la queste de l'enfant Jesus j'ai ramassé aux environ de 80 minots de bled froment, que n'ayant pu vendre, j'ai employé à faire travailler à l'eglise.

J'ai fournis à l'eglise tout son entretien de cire, de chandelles, de vin, cent madriers pour le plancher de l'eglise, le blanchissage, savon, emploie, recommodage, etc., tout généralement à mes frêts. Je n'ai pas trouvé une seul piesse de linge pour les Sacrifices en etat de servir; j'ai tout renouvellé a mes frets sans qu'il en ait couté un denier à l'eglise; mille autres petite depenses, tant pour les travaux de l'eglise que pour son entretien aux quelles je me suis pretté.

Je n'ai pas trouvé un seul batiment pour y loger une poule, presque point de cloture. J'ai fais lever un batiment de vingt six pieds sur seize a mes frets, et si j'ai eu des habitants quelques coups de main pour cet ouvrage, je crois l'avoir bien payé par la nourriture et les coups d'eau-de-vie qu'il m'a fallu verser.

J'ai pareillement fait transporté la petite maison de Mouton auprès du presbiter je l'ai fait renduire proprement et tiré les joins, monté une cheminé en pierre, payé la chaux 10 ecus la barique, il en a fallu cinq barriques, les vitres, le cloux, la facon, etc., tout a eté fait à mes depens. Je ne pouvois faire autrement pour loger les missionnaires que j'avois enmemé avec moi par votre conseil. J'ai resté trois jours au fort. J'y ai celebré deux fois la messe. Beaucoup de monde pour les entendre, mais personne pour me souhaiter le bonjour ni m'offrir la moindre assistance. Ou loger les deux missionnaires ? Dans le fort a cent piastres de loyer, outre les autres depenses pour un ménage qu'il leur auroit fallu, un homme dans leur maison pour leur donner leur besoin; la vie, l'habit d'une cherté epouvantable; quels sont les revenus qu'elles auroient pu percevoir pour subvenir a leur necessaire; 4 ou 5 ecolles dans le fort melé de garçons et de filles, et presque tous englois, car il n'y a qu'eux seule qui aient le gout de faire instruire leurs enfants et qui puissent le faire. Je vis bien daborb que j'etois dans une pénible nasse, que J'avois laissé une grande tranquilité pour me charger d'un grand embaras. J'allai trouver Mr. Frechette, je lui contai mes peines et mes embaras, il me fit part des siennes, et m'assura avec verité qu'il avoit versé plus de larmes au sujet des arrangements que vous aviez pris avec le Sr. Mouton qu'il n'en pourroit tenir dans son chapeau. Rien d'un coté, et bien mal de l'autre, il me paru disposé a prendre la partie du fort ou il est maintenant assez bien arrangé, plutot que de rester à l'assomption à la charge d'arranger les deux missionaires, ou au moins de s'y pretter. Et moi je suis resté à sa place. Aussitôt je parlai à Mouton, et je lui demandai s'il vouloit continuer de demeurer avec moi et de me rendre les service qu'il vous avoit rendu. Il me dit que oui. Eh bien, je lui dis, continuez et vous aurez lieu d'être content. Et c'etoit mon intention, suivant la recommendation que vous m'en aviez fait. Deux trois jours se passe; on ne me sert que de la soupe au choux et un plas de choux, le soir comme le midy. Un sauvage m'apporte un dinde et deux sarcelles en présent, que je payai de reconnoissance. Je les donne a Mouton en le priant de me faire faire de la soupe à la viande, que j'en avois grandement besoin. Le landemain on me sert de la soupe à l'ognon, une sarcelle rautie et les deux ailerons du dinde. C'est tout ce que j'ai gouté de viande pendant dix jours que le Sr. Mouton a resté avec moy. Il falloit avec diligence faire transporter la petite maison auprès du presbiter, et pour cela je parlai à sept ou huit personnes pour me donner un coup de main. Avec un peu d'aide et d'argent j'en suis venus à bout en peu de tems; je demandai à Mouton s'il n'y auroit pas moyen de faire prendre quelque chose à ceux qui se prettoient à me rendre service; d'un air assez revêche il me dit qu'il y avoit de la soupe à l'ognon; on leur en sert; chacun levoit les épaules de me voir traité de la sorte; je demande s'il y avoit du lard, des œufs ou du beure, rien de tout cela. Dix jours se passe en rude carême Ce n'etoit pas pour me recuperer d'un penible voyage de 54 jours. Bref il me dit un jour qu'il n'etoit ny lui, ny sa femme, ny ses enfants faits pour servir personne; que Mr. Hubert laveoit lui même la vaissele avec les petits garçons; je lui dis que je n'avois jamais fait cet office, et que je serois bien gauche a m'en acquitter, et qu'ainsi qu'il falloit qu'il prit son parti. Il me montre un papier qui l'autorisoit a l'effet de disposer de tout ce qui etoit en sa jouissance à vous appartenant. Pendant huit jours il a charié et n'a laissé que ce que je vous ai marqué cy dessus; je finis sur le chapitre ou je pourrois vous rapporter mil autres veritées tout plus pénibles les unes que les autres.

Pendant que j'ai fait transporté cette petite maison, les Mlles. Ademard et Papineau se sont retiré chez Mr. Marentet pendant environ trois semaines; ensuite elles se sont loger dans cette petite maison qui leur sert ainsi qu'a leurs pensionnaire de dortoire, la salle commune des habitants leur sert d'ecole; elles ont huit pensionaires et cinq externes; elles vivent sous un reglement comme dans les missions; je leur laisse les revenus des pensions ainsi que de leur ecolieres, pour leur donner de l'encouragement, et je les nourris gratis ainsi que leurs enfants. De huit pensionaires, il n'y en a que trois qui payent deux ponds par mois, qui sont une demoiselle Baby et deux petites engloises de chez Mr. Maccome. C'est les parens qui ont eux mêmes fixé le prix. Trois autres qui donnent ce qu'elles pouront, qui sont pertuit, Ademard et Dumouchelle; deux autres qui sont a pension gratuite, qui sont les deux Bénétot; elles m'ont assuré les deux dernieres que Dieu m'en tiendroit compte, et a ces conditions ont les a reçus. Toutes en général font fort bien et donnent quelque contentement. Tout l'hiver jusqu'à la premiere communion, elles ont eu une vingtaine de filles à catechiser tous les jours de la semaine excepté le jeudy. J'ai fais le cathechisme pendant tout ce tems aux garcons quatre fois la semaine, jusqu'a la premiere communion 27 de Juin. Il y a eu trente enfants, 18 filles et 12 garcons. Ils ont tous faits leur seconde communion le jour de la feste de la paroisse, et j'ai eu sujet d'être content dans la seconde communion des dispositions qu'ils ont apportés à la premiere. Les parents ont paru sensibles et reconnoissants des peines que l'ont s'est donné sans épargnes pour instruire leurs enfants. Tous les habitants conviennent de la necessité et de l'avantage de donner de l'education à leurs enfants.

J'ai annoncé l'indulgence pleniere que vous m'avez remis pour l'Assomption 15 jours d'avance; et les deux dimanches qui ont précédé la feste, j'ai expliqué à l'office ce que c'etoit qu'une indulgence pleniere, et fait voir combien il etoit important d'en profiter; pendant les quinze jours s'est presenté quantité de personnes a confesse; et la veille de la feste je suis entré au confessional a midy un quard, et n'en suis sortit qu'a 10½ du soir; le jour de la feste depuis cinq heures jusqu'a midy et demi.

J'ai fait la benediction de la nouvelle eglise le neuf d'aoust avec solemnité; après la bénédiction Mr. Frechette a chanté la messe pendant laquelle j'ai questé; j'ai ramassé aux environ de 500# tant en bon pour du bled qu'en argentery, et argent courant du pays; plus 240 piastres des sauvages en argenterie, porcelines, et autres marchandises à eux propres, à la valluation de ce que cela leur coute.

La picotte cause un grand effroit dans le Detroit; les sauvages en ont beaucoup de peur, et les Francois n'en sont point exempt. Elle est fortement à Sandosqué; elle a paru même sur un jeune enfant auprès de chez moi, chez la Rinkine; mais le major Malthus en a été informé, est venu avec un docteur s'assurer de la verité; il a fait transporter l'enfant et sa famille au bas de la rivierre; le pere dit-on l'a attrappé de l'enfant, et s'est noyé dans la fièvre chaude.

Il y a dans la paroisse 620 communiants, plus une dixaine de famille qui sont revenus de Sandosqué ce printemps. 600 environ qui ont satisfait à leur devoir Paschal. Il y a eu dans la paroisse 500 minots de bled froment de dimes, 150 minots de ble dinde, 10 minots de pois et 56 minots d'avoine. Il me reste encore 250 minots de bled fr., dont je ne puis me defaire a quelque condition que ce soit. Le reste a été employé pour la vie, en aumone et en bonnes œuvres pour l'eglise.

Il y a eu dans toute l'année 33 baptêmes, 6 mariages et 7 morts d'adultes, un enfant.

On ne parle presque plus de bal et de danse, de course de cheveaux, ni d'ivrognerie. L'année est trop mauvaise pour se livrer à ces sortes de divertissements. La vie est dure et difficile a avoir et a conserver dans les chaleurs; pour le vin il ne faut pas penser seulement à en faire usage en quelque petite quantité que ce soit, a 24 francs 10 ecus [*sic*] le gallon en argent, ont peu bien en sevrer. 45# un mouton, je n'en ai pas encore gouté au Detroit, 12# un dinde, etc. Il faut vivre au lard, que l'on a bien de la peine a conserver. Il n'y a point eu de chasse cette année....

F 19 DUFAUX À HUBERT
[*Archives de l'Archevêché de Québec, E.U., V–53*]

Detroit, 5 Nov. 1787

Je profite de l'occasion du Major Mathus pour assurer votre grandeur de mes sentiments respectueux et obeissants. C'est je pense la derniere occasion de l'année ou j'aurai cet avantage et la plus sure. Mr. Mathus n'a paru au Detroit que pour s'y faire regretter; il y a gagné les cœurs par toutes les audiences judicieuses qu'il y a rendu, et en mon particulier je lui suis tres redevable de celles qu'il m'a accordé. Je supplie votre grandeur d'appuier ma reconnoissance dont je l'ai plusieurs fois assuré. Je lui ai fait quelques visites et il m'a fait l'honneur de me venir voir chez moi. Il a pris connoissance de tous les traveaux de l'église, des batiments et dépendances de la cure; il a rendu visite aux maitresses d'instruction, s'est informé du nombre de leurs ecollieres, visité leur classe et leur petite maison qui leur sert de dortoire; il m'a paru surpris avec satisfaction de tout ce qu'il a vu et la appuyé de son suffrage.

Depuis le depart de Mr. Payet, l'eglise a été lambrisée en dehors, la sacristie est a la veille de l'être; les dedans de la sacristie, cloisons, escaliers, armoires, etc., etc., dicelle sont finis, et le principal de tout c'est que les ouvriers sont payé en grande partie. J'espere avant la fin de l'année avoir tout liquidé. Je profite de l'avantage que j'ai d'avoir auprès de moi les Dlles. Papineau et Ademard, qui se prêtemt gratis au service de l'eglise dans les moments libres qu'elles ont. J'aurois été fort embarassé de trouver au Détroit des personnes qui eussent pu et voulu faire ce qu'elles ont faite. Tailler avec un très mauvais diamant et des clefs environ 400 vitres pour les evantailles et l'œil de bouc de l'eglise et près de 1000 vitres qu'elles ont mastiquée; on me demandoit 30s par vitre pour les tailler et 10s pour les mastiquer. Elles ont epargnée a l'eglise cette depense et bien d'autres traveaux qu'elles y ont faite et qu'elles y font journellement, tant pour les ornements que pour l'entretien de l'eglise; l'intention présente est de mettre tout dans le meilleur etat possible sans endetter l'eglise, et de se pretter a l'instruction à la demande des habitants. Mais ce qu'il y a de plus facheux c'est que presque tous doivent et le plus grand nombre s'endette bien loin de s'acquiter. L'argent est si rare que l'on ne parle plus de payer en argent. C'est en danré que se font presque tous les marchés. Le roy prend un peu de farine, et ce que chaque habitant peut fournir est redigé a la cinquième partie; c'est à dire que celuy qui a souscrit pour 1000 livres est retranché a 200 livres, a 24# le quintal. et 4# 10s le bledinde en marchandises qui sont d'un prix excessive surtout les articles qui sont deport; un ecu une livre de mastique, 40s une livre de cloux, 30s une livre de sel, c'est immense ce qu'il a entré de cloux et de mastique dans la batisse de l'eglise, le tout est payé, et je ne me suis pas endetté chez aucun marchand. Après avoir été bien mal et bien pauvrement dans l'encienne église, je me trouve heureux dans une honnête médiocreté. Les bancs de l'encienne église ont été transporté dans la nouvelle, et chaque propriétaire jouit de ses enciens titres. Mais pour les nouveaux ils sont loué a l'année au plus haut encherisseur la vie durante de ceux à qui ils sont adjugé, à la charge, 1 — de faire faire leur banc, 2 — d'en payer le loyer annuellement dans le cours de Janvier, faute de quoi l'eglise reprend ses droit, 3 — si le locateur veut laisser le banc sous quelque pretexe que ce soit, il doit avertir le marguillier en charge 3 mois d'avance, a fin que l'eglise ne perde rien. Il y a peu près la moitier des nouveaux bancs d'adjugé; quelqu'un s'est récrier contre cet arrangement; je les ai laissé dire, et ceux sont maintenant les plus humiliés; ont continue de les adjuger ainsi, et personne ne parle ou n'ause plus parler. Les bancs se montent à la crier aux environ de 25#.

Je n'ai point de peines extraordinaires dans ce qui regarde le spirituel. J'ai obtenu de Mr. le Major Mathus des ordres sous peine de cinq ponds d'amende pour ce qui m'affligeois le plus, pour ceux qui travaillent les dimanches et jours de feste, pour ceux qui restent à la porte de l'eglise pendant les offices sous quelque pretexe que ce soit, pour ceux qui courent la guignolette au jour de l'an, et en tout tems qui font des assemblés de divertissement nuitament. . . .

Il est encore du pour la batisse du presbiter chez les marchands et autres personnes aux environ cinq mille francs, dette qui s'auguemente tous les jours par les interests et qui ne sera pas payé de citot, faute de bonne volonté ou de moyen de la part des habitants. On menace de faire vendre le presbiter, mais je n'en crois pas l'execution. Il ne fait pas bon a batir au Détroit. Votre grandeur a commencé, il lui en a coûté bien des traverse, bien des peines, et tout le fruit de ses épargnes; j'ai achevé et je ne dirai pas ce qu'il men coute. Je laisse au Seigneur le soin de compter ce que je desirerois faire pour son amour; il change quand il lui plait les fortunes perissables en une meilleure, et les consolation passageres en larmes pour nous apprendre que nous devons plutot nous attacher au consolateur qu'aux consolations; magnifique et juste dans ses recompenses, il scait a propos ou dans cette vie ou dans l'autre dedomager ses veritables serviteurs. Sit nomen Domini benedictum. . . .

F 20   Dufaux à Hubert
[Archives de l'Archevêché de Québec, E.U., V–59]

Detroit, le 3 Aoust, 1788

Je viens de recevoir la ratification des pouvoirs qui m'ont été confié par feu Mgr. de Dorilée, Ev. de Quebec, et avec une lettre commune et une particuliere de votre grandeur qui m'insinue ce que je dois faire. C'est aussi mon intention de remplir autant qu'il sera a mon pouvoir les esperances qu'elle a en moi pour le plus grand bien qu'elle veut à son peuple du Detroit, peuple en général peu zélé pour son instruction, et encore moins capable d'aider à se procurer cet avantage, qu'il ne connoit guere. On reconnoit ou on semble reconnoitre la bonne conduite, le zèle et les talents des maitresses. Cependant elles n'ont que huit ou dix enfants, tant pensionnaires qu'externes. Ce nombre n'augmente point; la misere est si grande parmi les habitants que je ne sçaurois l'exprimer, n'ayant aucune débouche de leurs danrés; ils sont obligés de s'endetter tous les jours, et de donner le peu qu'ils ont à la volonté de leurs creanciers. Ils ne vendent plus d'animeaux, il en vient des quantité des colonies qui se donnent a vil prix; ils sont obligé de garder les leurs et de les voir souvant mourir de la maladie du pays, autre fleaux qui n'est que trop commun dans le Detroit. Que faire, et quoi entreprendre dans un reigne si dure. Il me paroit que ce n'est pas le tems d'entreprendre de nouvelle establissement. C'est plutot celui de laisser le monde tranquil. Quoiqu'il en soit, mon parti est pris; je vais encore soutenir et patienter cette année, ensuite si les choses n'ont pas meilleure apparence, je me deciderai a replier, et j'en demande par avance la permission à votre grandeur.

Depuis un mois et demi je tremble des fievres qui m'ont bien mal traité; je les ai encore, mais elles commencent a me laisser; et en me laissant, elles m'ont ravie le peu d'enbonpoint que j'avois et toutes mes forces; car je suis d'une faiblesse extrême. Les Dlles. Adhemard et Papineau, qui ont été très sensibles au bon souvenir de votre grandeur, les ont aussi depuis deux mois et plus. Il me paroit qu'elles vont un peu mieux, cependant je crois qu'elles seront longtems encore avant d'être retablie, car ni l'une ni l'autre ne sont point d'un bon temperament.

Je n'entre point dans le detail de ma sensibilité sur toutes ces epreuves; je dirai seulement que je prie le Seigneur tous les jours de m'accorder son secour pour en faire un bon usage. . . .

F 21   DUFAUX À HUBERT
[*Archives de l'Archevêché de Québec, E.U., V–79*]

District de Hesse 22 aoust 1790

J'ai reçu dans le courant du présent par Mr. Belle Cour la lettre de votre grandeur en réponse à celle que je lui ai écris dans le mois de janvier dernier. Le Major Murray et Mr. Powell en ont aussi reçu, et le dernier n'a rien eu de plus pressé que de venir chez moi m'en faire la lecture, et par un effet de son attention calmer ma douleur et disciper mes secretes inquietudes depuis 8 mois. . . . J'aime, j'estime et je respecte de tout mon cœur mon Evêque et je prie pour sa conservation, voila ma confession la plus sincère. De là il est aisé de se persuadé, combien j'ai eu de douleur de me voir, par la plus affreuse calomnie, l'auteur de la peine que votre grandeur a due eprouver à mon sujet. De là aussi on peut conclure combien je suis tout devoué a étudier et a suivre son esprit et sa conduite, et combien je respecte les pouvoirs que j'en ai reçu. Quand je suis parti de Montréal j'etois dans les sentiments les plus conformes à la gloire du St. nom de Dieu, j'ai cru devoir faire le sacrifice de ma patrie et de tous les cœurs qui m'étoient devoués pour repondre aux vues et aux desirs de votre grandeur; si les succés n'ont répondu qu'en partie aux esperances, ce n'est pas ma faute, ni un crime, c'est le tems et les circonstances qui ne sont pas favorables. Mon départ a eté si prompt que je n'ai pas eu le tems de regler certains arrangements de famille. J'ai laissé mes interests temporels qui aujourd'hui souffrent avec plusieurs autres de mon absence : ma santée presque toujours debile me determine encore plus a prendre le parti de descendre le printems prochain, et de supplier premierement votre grandeur de m'en donner la permission.

Je ne crains point d'affirmer que je laisserai la paroisse de l'Assomption dans un meilleur état que votre grandeur l'a trouvé a son arrivée au Detroit &c. tant pour les travaux de l'eglise et ses ornements qui sont en une honnête quantité, propres et decents, que pour l'instruction de la jeunesse &c. Le zéle, les soins et les travaux de Mlle Papineau y seront longtems reconnus; sa conduite honnête et chretienne aussi que celle de Mlle Adhemar ne peuvent donner lieu à la critique des honnetes gens, elles en sont estimé. Je pense que je descendrai comme je suis monté, je ne laisserai personne de ceux qui m'ont aidé à procuré le bien que j'ai pu faire au Detroit, je m'y crois obligé par reconnaissance.

Depuis que je suis au Detroit je n'ai vu qu'une bonne recolte, les trois dernières ressemblent plus a la famine qu'a l'abondance, et la presente n'annonce que la disette. La secheresse a eté si grande qu'il n'y aura presque point de blé dinde, de legume, de patatte et de menu grain. La maladie depuis plusieurs années sur les animaux non seulement continue mais augmente tous les jours; j'ose dire qu'il n'y a pas d'habitant qui n'ait perdu chevaux ou bête à corne, il y en a même qui ont tout perdu. La vie est dure, tout est chere, et point d'argent. L'habitant doit, il est persecuté, le marchant retrograde, il faut payer les frêts, de l'opulence, du faste et des amusements, contractés dans le reigne des ponds. Aujourd'hui on se mettrait à genoux devant une piastre. Que faire, qu'entreprendre; je craindrais avec raison de devenir cet homme « qui coepit edificare, et non potuit perficere ».

    L'instruction se fait toujours assidument a sept ou huit enfant tant pensionnaires qu'externes, le tout a mes frêts; je soutiens et c'est tout. Je ne trouve d'apuis en personne, tout le monde est a l'etroit plus qu'on ne scauroit se l'imaginer : la jalousie, la calomnie, l'ivrognerie et les divertissements sont des vices en usage presque partout : et comme un très respectable missionaire l'a remarqué les robes noires sont accusées de tout. J'en suis convaincu par les lettres que moi et mon confrère avons reçu de votre grandeur l'automne dernier : je serais inconsolable si je n'etois pas persuadé que Dieu qui est le temoin de la verité sera le garant de la peine mortelle que j'ai eprouvé.

    Je n'ai de peine ni de difficulté avec personne pour le présent. Le Capitaine Maisonville est absent. J'aurois été agréablement surpris si j'eusse reçu au retour du Capitaine Maisonville une lettre aussi satisfaisante que celle que j'ai reçu par Mr. Belle Cour en reponse de ma lettre du 28 janvier dernier : Je suis a peine gueri et consolé, et voila que je suis chargé et accablé de nouvelles peines et d'engoises, sans l'avoir merité. Ah Monseigneur que votre grandeur n'est elle présente à toute ma conduite pour lui rendre avec justice le tribut qui lui est du!

1e Est-il possible que moi ou Mr. Frechette ou tout autre à ma place puisse mieux desservir les hurons que votre grandeur les a desservi pendant quatre ans. J'en ai marié, j'en ai confessé et enterré dans leur cimetiere en très petit nombre quand ils se sont presente et par interprette je baptise leurs enfants a toute main et autant qu'ils se presente toujours de bonne volonté, et en toute occasion je me suis montré charitable a leur egard : qu'a pu faire de plus votre grandeur ? et que puis-je faire moi-même davantage auhourd'hui surtout qu'ils sont en plus petit nombre, dispersé ça et là, comme ils commencoient a l'être de votre tems.

2e Il nest pas vrai que j'ai vendu ou fait vendre un banc destiné pour les chefs, je ne leur en connois aucun dans l'eglise.

3e Il n'est pas vrai que j'ai diminué leur place dans l'eglise; la vue en decouvre le fait, elle est encore toute entiere à même de recevoir leur bans, siéges ou autres commodités a leur frets et depends comme le porte l'acte passé par Mr. Payet ou j'ai signé d'union et par obeissance. Mr. Payet a du avoir remi a votre grandeur cet acte qui maintenant fait gemir tout les paroissiens, parcèque cette place reservée defigure l'ordre de l'eglise vû qu'il y a des bans d'un coté et point de l'autre, et ils disent maintenant mais trop tard qu'il auroit mieux vallu n'avoir rien reçu des sauvages &c. &c.

Au sujet de la salle des paroissiens.

1e Il n'est pas vrai que je me suis emparé de leur chambre sans l'avoir demandé; elle m'a eté accordée a mon arrivé lorsque je temoignai les desseins de votre grandeur au sujet des ecolles que vous m'avez si fort recommendée.

2ᵉ Il n'est pas vrai que les habitants ayent murmuré de ce que l'on y a fait les ecoles.

3ᵉ Il n'est vrai que les habitants ayent été privé de leur salle. Ils s'en sont toujours servis et s'en servent encore et non seulement leur salle mais aussi la mienne est a l'usage des hommes seulement, et comme votre gdr. peut en juger le bon ordre est dans la presbiter, les hommes d'un coté et les filles et les femmes de l'autre. tout le monde est contant dans la dessence et la commodite sans qu'il en coute rien, excepté au curé.

. . .

Enfin pour ce qui est de Mr. le Juge — A son arrivée au Detroit, j'ai reçu sa visitte. J'avois le fievres tremblantes dans le tems, il me dit qu'au moment de ses adieux a son excellence il lui demanda ou il tiendroit au Detroit son siége, et que le Major Mathus prit la parole et lui dit qu'il me connaissoit et qu'il pensoit bien qu'il pourroit prendre avec moi quelque arrangement pour quelque tems en attendant nouvelle decision : il me parla dabort de la vielle eglise. il me demanda à la voir, je la lui fis ouvrir et voyant, qu'il y avoit beaucoup d'ouvrage a faire, cela paru l'inquietté. il m'a dit de nouveau qu'il avoit quelque jugement a porter qui pressoit, et qui pouvoit peut-etre tenir 3 ou 4 séance. Alors je lui offris le plus poliment qu'il me fut possible la salle commune pour trois ou quatre séance seulement, les jeudis jours de vacance pour l'ecole. Quelques habitants excités par le Capitaine Maisonville en temoignent leur mecontentement et ils prirent le resolution de me presenter une requette très polie pour avoir la clef de leur salle : je les reçu poliment et je leur dit pour reponse : mes freres, en agissant de la maniere que j'ai agis a l'egard du juge, j'ai cru en qualité de votre pasteur devoir être l'echo des politesses que nous devons rendre vous et moi aux personnes qui sont revetus des pouvoirs du gouvernement gracieux ou nous sommes : en agissant autrement j'aurois cru manquer de politesse, de prudence et de religion. Nous devons tout ménager, nous montrer en tout zelé et respectueux, fidele au gouvernement parceque tous les jours nous en eprouvons les faveurs tant a l'egard de notre religion que &c. &c. Vous surtout qui jouissez de l'avantage de ne payer ni rente ni l'ausevente [lots et ventes] &c. Je n'avois pas finis qu'ils prirent la parole et me dirent qu'ils reconnaissoient qu'ils avoient tort, qu'ils regrettoient leur demarche, qu'ils reconnaissoient que j'avois agis avec politesse, avec prudence et religion. ils etoient six de leur bande. je leur demandai ce qu'ils vouloient que je fis de leur petition par ecris, ils me dirent que je pouvois bien la dechirer et la jetter au feu. Depuis ce tems la je n'ai plus entendu parlé de rien que par votre grandeur dans la lettre que le Cptne Maison vient de m'envoyer, et à laquelle je reponds subitement par une occasion qui part demain matin et qui sera probablement la derniere. Il est actuellement minuit. je n'aurai pas le tems de copier ma lettre, c'est a la hâte que j'ecris. je supplie votre grandeur de m'excuser.

Pour le pain beni que votre grandeur m'ordonne de faire presenter au Cptne Maisonville le premier : j'ai deja enjoins au Bedeau de lui donner. il ne me l'a jamais demandé, il ne l'avoit pas du tems de votre grandeur, sans doute qu'il ignorait son droit ou qu'il ne l'avoit pas exigé; je souhaite qu'en le mangeant il se sanctifie, et que sanctifié il me paye les dimes qu'il me doit. . . .

APPENDIX I

F 22   Dufaux à Hubert
[*Archives de l'Archevêché de Québec, E.U., V–90*]

le 4 fevrier 1792

...

Je continue toujours de soutenir les ecoles de jeunes filles, et le progrès que font les enfans sous la conduite de Mlle Papineau sont si marqués et si flatteurs que je ne puis me dispenser d'en informer de nouveau votre grandeur et l'assurer que les succès semblent repondre à la fin qu'on s'est proposée. Il y a presentement 12 pensionnaires et 5 ou 6 externes qui sont a l'ecole du matin au soir : leur logement est de beaucoup trop petit, jattends le printems pour faire un enlargie; et s'il y a de la constance tant de la part de Mlle Papineau, que des parents et des enfans je me pretterai de mon mieux pour former un logement commode et pourvoir aux necessitées de la vie. Telle est ma disposition, sous la Ste grace de dieu et les secours de la divine providence. . . .

F 24   Dufaux à Hubert
[*Archives de l'Archevêché de Québec, E.U., V–116*]

9me 9bre 1795

Cy est inclu une lettre que Mr. B[urke] m'a ecrit pour assigner à Mr. François Baby sous la qualité de representant de la personne de son altesse royale une place d'honneur dans mon eglise. Mr. Baby a précédé mon assignation, il a envoyé joseph reaume (Bout de feu) pour me demander la permission d'entrer dans l'eglise pour y prendre la mesure d'un banc. Je lui ai repondu que la porte de l'eglise n'est point fermé à la clef dans le jour et par consequent qu'il pouvoit y entrer, que j'etois surpris de ce que Mr. Baby précédoit l'ordre que j'avois de lui assigner une place d'honneur. j'entendois de lui presenter l'ordre de Mr. B. sans rien prendre sur moi. Bref il a fait faire à ses frets un banc plus haut, plus large et plus profond de quatre a cinq pouces au moins que tout autre banc avec un pond dedans qui le leve d'une marche, et un grand et ample tapi de drap verd. Ledit banc a été placé a mon insçu à la place des ecolieres qui sont sous la vue de Mlle Victoir leur metraisse — c'est à dire entre la balustrade et le pr. banc sur la rangée du banc d'œuvres. Il en a pris possession le dimanche à la messe à laquelle il sest rendu de compagnie avec son épouse et la sœur de son épouse, nées de parents protestants et protestante elle-même, après la post-communion, un peu plus tard ils auroient manqué la messe; votre grandeur peut juger si cette cour royale traversant la diagonale de l'eglise en tapant du pied, et se huchant dans ce banc tapissé, ponté et surelevé, occasionnants par leur gravité un cris cras continuel, a occasionné des distractions le reste de la messe a tout le temple, et ensuite combien de parlement : on n'a pas manqué de me demander par quel ordre Mr. Baby s'arrogoit cette place et ce banc si distinctif. De plus les marguilliers et les notables de la paroisse se sont consulté et ont consulté les plus eclairé pour n'agir que pour le mieux. Ils n'ont pas manqué de bons conseillers englais et francais qui leur ont assuré que Mr. Baby n'avoit aucune presseance dans l'eglise, ni en qualité de député de l'honorable Alexandre McKee lieutenant

Lord de notre compté. Le marguiller se voyant reprocher de tollerer un tel abut, s'est joint a deux autres marguillers et tous les trois ont été signifier à Mr. Baby de retirer son ban sous huit jours, autrement qu'il le mettroit hor de l'eglise jusqu'à ce qu'il eu la bonté de produire l'extrait d'une ordonnance approuvée de votre grandeur, qui donne droit à sa dignité de posseder une telle place d'honneur dans l'eglise.

Il n'est pas possible de s'imaginer jusqu'a quel point Mr. Burke a troublé nos paroisses. Voila quinze jours qu'il est icy, tantot à Ste Anne, tantot à l'Assomption occupé à colorer des titres à Mr. Baby et à dorer des pillules pour les faire envaller plus aisement à mes marguillers. Mais il n'a rien gagner. il met le trouble partout; il ne se fait aucun scrupul de s'absenter de sa paroisse des deux et trois dimanches de suite, pareillement dans les fêtes de la toussaints, des mors, de l'assention &c. Il vit sans regles ni reglements ecclesiastique, il n'en porte pas a peine l'habit. Bien d'autres chose que je ne veux pas dire qui donnent occasion à une infinité de medisances publiques. Je ne vois presque personne qui ne parle contre lui. Ne croyez pas monseigneur que ce soit par jalousie ni vengeance contre lui que je parle ainsi de lui, mais plutot parceque ce sont des choses publiques et que je crois devoir en informer votre grandeur. J'espere une reponse par la prochaine occasion pour ce qui regarde le banc de Mr. Baby ainsi qu'aux reponses que j'ai faits à la derniere lettre de votre grandeur. J'ai dis à Mr. Burke mon opinion que je pensois qu'on pouvoit prendre un parti plus tolerable sçavoir, comme nous avons un banc d'honneur designé par une ordannance pour les Capitaines de Milices, et que ce banc contient trois places, la premiere pourroit être assigné au lieutenant colonel, la seconde et la 3me place aux majors parce qu'ils possedent par eminance la dignité de Capitaine. Mais non il faut que tous les officiers ayent des places. Je crois que c'est un abut qu'il ne faut pas innover au Detroit, surtout ou les eglises sont si pauvres. Il y a deja une reserve pour les Sauvages qui contient le quart de l'eglise et qui ne donne aucun profit.

F 25   TRADUCTION FRANÇAISE DE LA SUSDITE LETTRE
[*Registre des Comptes &C. de la Paroisse de l'Assomption 1781 — p. 42*]

Niagara 7 Juin 1796

Ayant eté informé que de grandes difficultés se sont presentées à l'égard de l'occupation d'un Banc du au gouvernement dans votre Eglise, ce qui me surprend bien; et l'Evêque de Québec ayant laissé à moi à determiner qui est la personne qui doit en avoir la jouissance; je prononce donc que le dit Banc et toutes les honneurs qui lui appartiennent est un des privileges à qui le Lieutenant ou dans son absence le Deputé Lieutenant a un droit incontestable. Il vous plaira donc de donner des ordres que la même conduite qui a eté anciennement observée envers le Commandant français soit observée à l'égard de la personne qui à l'avenir occupera le banc en question.

Je suis, monsieur, votre très obeissant &c
J. S.

Ordonné à Mr. Dufaux, Missionaire à L'Assomption & à Messieurs Les Margulliers et à leurs successeurs de faire observer la teneur de la sus dite lettre de son Excellence le Lt. Governeur et pour prevenir les disputes desormais, ordonné que la même conduite s'observe dans toutes les Eglises du Haut Canada.

Edmund Burke Vicaire General du diocèse de Quebec specialement chargé du Haut Canada

Donné à L'Assomption ce 2 juillet 1796.

F 26 DUFAUX À HUBERT
[*Archives de l'Archevêché de Québec, E.U., V–124*]

Detroit 2me 7bre, 1796

Je profite de la présente occasion pour informer votre grandeur que l'evêque de Baltimore a pourvu à la cure de Ste. Anne du Detroit, il a envoyé Mr. Levadou prêtre de St. Sulpice qui desservoit aux Ilinois depuis trois ans et demi avec la qualité de grand vicaire; c'est un digne, petit, et respectable prêtre, agé de 50 ans; il paroit très attaché, et devoué au gouvernement americain et à son evêque : et moi je le suis au mien. Je m'adresse à lui avec confiance pour la confession, et il s'adresse à moi, j'espere que nous vivrons en bonne union et en bon confreres quoique nous soyons de differents diocèse et que nous observons la discipline et les ceremonies relatives chacun à notre propre diocèse. Il m'a paru surpris de ce que dans ces pays-cy on observoit le carême et le samedy, je lui ai assuré avec verité que dans ma paroisse les deux tiers avoient fait le carême entierement cette année. Il y a aussi bien de la difference dans les fêtes et les solemnitées. On ne chante plus chez lui *Domine salvum fac regem*. Actuelement c'est *Domine salvum fac populum*. Il est actuelement aller prendre connoissance de la rivierre aux raisins, et à son retour il doit mettre à l'option de ses paroissiens de lui payer la dime comme cy devant, lui en passants un acte signé de chacun, qui lui donnera droit de l'exiger, car sans cela il n'y auroit aucun droit de la faire payer dans son gouvernement, ou de lui assigner une pension honnête. . . . Point de componendes pour les dispenses, il les accordes gratis quand il le juge raisonable. Dans son diocèse on marie à tout heure, et on confesse les particuliers chez eux dans leur maison; les ecclesiastiques, l'evêque même sont habillés en seculier. Il n'a point cependant encore deroger à notre usage si ce n'est que le lendemain de son arrivée il a chanté une grande messe solemnelle le jour de l'assomption 15me aout. et a vepre il a chanté un solemnel *Te Deum* en action de grace de l'arrivée du general Waine et de la possession des postes, en suite le salut et la benediction du St. Sacrement en chantant et faisant trois formes de croix à la maniere des evêques.

Mr. Levadou m'a paru peiné de ce que Mr. Frechette n'a pas attendu qu'il fut relevé par un successeur à qui il auroit pu laisser ses meubles à une honête estimation et les informations necessaires pour connoitre les mœurs et le caractere des personnes. . . . pour moi il m'a un peu blamé de ce que du moment que le poste a été remi j'ai cessé d'y exercer mon ministere, disant pour raison que ni l'evêque de Quebec ny son grand vicaire ne pouvoit m'empecher d'exercer dans un lieu ou il n'avoit aucun droit; qu'en faveur du publique je pouvois user d'epikie jusqu'à revocation et que l'evêque de Baltimore m'en auroit sçu bon gré. Mais que faire un chat echaudé craint l'eau froide. Je vous ai marqué, Monseigneur, dans ma derniere que Mr. Burke m'avoit fortement insinuer d'agir ainsi, il fallut m'y conformer, ou me soustraire aux ordres de votre grandeur.

J'ai été seul présenter mes civilés au Colonel Hamtramck il etoit absent, n'importe il est venu chez moi avec sept officiers me rendre ma visite peiné de ne s'être pas trouvé à la mienne, je l'ai reçu sans doute avec toute la politesse d'un galant homme. quelque semaines après est arrivé le general Wayne, j'ai été pareillement lui presenter mes respects avec Mr. Levadou, il m'a temoigné son vrai plaisir de faire connoissance avec moi, m'a invité quelque jours apres à diner chez lui avec mon confrère nous avons accepté l'honneur de son invitation. après le repas, comme c'est la coutume, le general a porté ses sentées ensuite m'ayant fait mettre à sa droite il m'a prié de donner la mienne, je l'ai aussitot adressé à la *paix unanime*, et unaniment nous avons prie une rasade, ensuite je me suis levé et je me suis annoncé le serviteur bien humble du général de la compagnie. Le Colonel pareillement m'a fait aussi très poliment son invitation à diner chez lui. Tout s'y est passé très honnêtement. Je ne crois pas m'être attiré tant de politesse et pour d'autres raisons, que parceque je ne leur ai fait ni fait faire aucun mal. Ma conduite est, de n'être ni trop ni trop peu ce que je dois être, de m'en tenir à mon devoir seulement.

Le général et tous les officiers deteste Mr. Burke pour les horreurs qu'il leur a occasionné par la voix des sauvages, pendant qu'il etoit dans le departement sauvage. Il a bien fait de partir, et je ne crois pas qu'il lui soit jamais avantageux de revenir dans ces cantons-cy.

Les sujets loyaux de sa magesté, sur la partie americaine, sont dechu de leur commission, plus de lieutenant Lor, Mr. Le Chevallier Jonquer est colonel de la milice, Cicot major, Messrs. Robiche Navard, Buffet, Voyer, Le May, Habette et quelquautres sont juges à paix; les juges des plaidoyers commun ne seront nommé qu'au retour du Gouverneur de Makinac. . . . Mr. Levadou projette de faire venir des missionaires pour les sauvages par la voix du Congré comme une voix des plus sure pour les attacher au Congré. Il espere avoir de l'ede l'an prochain pour desservire ses paroisses. Il ne me reste plus de place que pour assurer votre grandeur que je suis avec respect et obeissance. . . .

F 27   Les habitants de l'Assomption à Hubert
[*Archives de l'Archevêché de Québec, E.U., V–130*]

Detroit 19 7bre 1796

Nous sommes persuadé d'avance que vous allez meler vos larmes avec les notres lorsq'en tremblant nous vous annoncons la mort du cher Monsieur Dufaux, decedé le onze de ce mois a dix heures du soir. Nous nous joignons a vous, Mgr., et toute la paroisse pour offrir au Dieu de toute bonté les veux les plus sincere pour le repos de son ame. Nos enfans et les pauvres ont perdu un pere, et nous serions inconsolable si nous ne nous flattions qu'il est presentement notre avocat aupres de Dieu, et que son ame bien heureuse jouit d'un repos eternel.

Enfin, Mgr., nous avons été vos paroissiens, et vous etes encore notre pasteur; toutte notre paroisse vous supplie a main jointe de ne pas nous lesser languir longtemps sans les secours spirituel que vous étes à même de nous donner. Nous voulons vivre et mourir dans la religion de nos pere, et nous sommes pret a repender jusqu'a la derniere goutte de notre sang pour la foy de Jesus Christ. Vous savez mieux que nous, Mgr., qu'un trop long retardement peut refroidir l'ardeur de la jeunesse. Oh si nous ausions vous supplier, Mgr., vous demander un sujet qui a été bien des années parmi nous et dont le merite et les vertus nous sont si bien connus, le cher Mr. Frèchette, C'est une obligation de plus que nous vous aurions qui ne tiendroit pas la derniere place parmi celle que nous vous avons toujours eu.

Nous avons l'honneur d'être avec un tres profond respect, de Votre Grandeur, les tres humble et tres obeissant serviteurs.

                                              Labadie   Maisonville
                                              B. Antaya Joseph Pouget
                                              ————   Parent

F 28   Le Révérend E. Burke aux paroissiens de l'église de L'Assomption

[*Registre des Comptes &C. de la Paroisse de l'Assomption 1781 — p. 40a*]

Nous Edmund Burke prêtre Vicaire General du Diocèse de Quebec à tous ceux que ces presentes interessent Salut —

Ayant signifié à Mr. Jean B. Marchand, prêtre Missionaire à L'Assomption dans le Compté d'Essex et à Mr. Charles Reneau Marguillier en charge de la sus dite Mission un extrait d'une lettre de Monseigneur Jean François Hubert, Evêque de Quebec, addressée à l'honorable Jacques Baby, Lord Lieutenant du Compté de Kent et Membre du Conseil executif de sa Majesté dans cette Province du Haut Canada en date du 1er Avril, 1796, et cité par sa grandeur le sus dit Evêque de Quebec dans sa lettre à nous addressée en date du 13 Octobre, 1796, lequel porte : « qu'il est dû au Gouvernement une place d'honneur, & que cette place doit etre occupée par celui à qui le gouvernement l'adjuge, ce qui met la question hors de sa competence. que dès que le representant de sa Majesté se sera expliqué le Curé ni la fabrique n'auront plus rien à faire si non de laisser la place convenable au premier Banc de l'église dont la construction doit s'accommoder au local et à la forme des autres sieges &c ». et ayant aussi signifié au sus dit Mr. Jean B. Marchand, Missionaire & à Mr. Charles Reneau, Marguillier en charge, l'ordre de Son Excellence J. G. Simcoe, Lieutenant Gouverneur de cette province du Haut Canada à nous addressé en date du 7 Juin, 1796, dont une copie collationnée se trouve sur le Registre de la sus dite Eglise, lequel adjuge la sus dite place d'honneur dû au gouvernement avec tous les honneurs qui lui appartiennent au Lieutenant ou dans son absence au Deputé Lieutenant de ce Compté; Nous le sus dit Edmund Burke ptre. Vicaire General du Diocèse de Quebec, en consequences des ordres cydessus indiqués à nous addressés de la part de son Excellence le Lieutenant Gouverneur du Haut Canada, et de sa grandeur l'Eveque de Quebec, avons statué et par ces presentes statuons que la première place en haut du coté de l'épitre le long de la muraille soit livrée au Lieutenant ou dans son absence au Deputé Lieutenant de ce Compte d'Essex afin qu'il y erige un Banc dans les formes ordinaires, faisant Defense par l'autorité du susdit Lieutenant Gouverneur du Haut Canada et du susdit Evêque de Quebec à toute personne de le troubler dans la possession de la susdite place d'honneur.

Fait à l'Assomption ce 7 Janvier 1797.

         Edmund Burke V.G.
         Spécialement chargé du Haut Canada
          quant à l'administration spirituelle.

Je prêtre Curé missionaire certifie avoir publié au prône de la messe paroissiale la dite ordonnance le 8 de janvier 1797.

                    Marchand Ptre.

F 29 Marchand à Hubert
[Archives de l'Archevêché de Québec, E.U., V–132]

          Assomption du Détroit le 31 Janvier 1797

 Malgré les précautions que nous avons prises pour nous rendre promptement, nous n'avons pu arriver ici que le jour de Noël (sur le soir). Nous nous sommes rendu au fort Erier en quinze jours, le 5 Novembre et nous n'avons mis à la voile que le trente au soir : et après avoir vu les isles de Sandoskée le vent d'ouest est devenu si furieux, quil nous a falu faire vent arrier le jour de St. Francois-Xavier, et après avoir couru tout risque d'être jetté en côte au bas de la pres[que] isle dans un froit excecif et être bien balottés, nous sommes enfin revenus au fort-Erier le second dimanche des Avents où nous avons ancré sur les dix heures du matin. Sans perdre de tems nous avons fait les preparatifs du voyage par terre, nous avons dessendu à Niagara le lendemain de la Conception, et le jour de sainte Lucie dans la matinée Mr. Pratte et moi, montés sur chaqu'un un cheval avec un peu de vivres pour nous et nos cheveaux et un peu de hardes, nous avons pris la route du Détroit par la grande Rivierre des Moak. Apres une journee de marche de la riviere des Moaks nous avons tombé sur la rivierre à la Tranche que nous avons descendu près de quatre vingt lieux, soixante toujours dans le bois, nous y avons trouvé quelque maisons et nous n'avons été obligé d'y coucher que deux nuits dehors avec un peu de misere pour le froid et la pluie. Les dix-huit dernierres lieux sont habités comme le chemin de Niagara jusqu'à la grand-rivierre de 9 en 9 arpents et il n'y a dans tout le chemin jusqu'à Niagara de 12 Catholiques en bas de la rivierre à la trenche, 10 Canadiens sur les 12.

 Le lendemain de mon arrivée je me rendis a l'Eglise où je trouvé Mr. Burke à qui je remis ma lettre de Mission que j'avois prise de Mgr. le Coadjuteur en Votre nom, il m'a aussitôt mis en exercice et je chantai la grand messe; il m'a témoigné beaucoup de joie de mon arrivée, qui l'inquietoit beaucoup par les nouvelles facheuses qui s'étoient repandu dans le Détroit que nous étions dans les isles. La joie qui a paru à notre arrivée et le bon accueil que j'ai reçu des habitans qui m'ont témoigné leur reconnoissance pour votre bon souvenir à leur egard et pour la bonté que votre grandeur a eu d'acquiescer à leur demande en leur envoyant un prêtre aussi subitement, me font esperer beaucoup de consolation en cette endroit. Je n'ai pas éprouvé une heure d'indisposition dans tout le voyage et je me porte très bien.

Je n'ai trouvé de trouble dans la paroisse qu'au sujet du banc d'honneur demandé par le Roy. le 7 courant Mr. Burke après m'avoir signifié et au marguiller en charge les ordres de Votre Grandeur et ceux du Gouverneur Symcoe à ce sujet, a dressé une ordonnance que j'ai lu au prone le dimanche suivant, après un ordre de sa part qu'il me donna de vive voix, il étoit présent et il parla à ce sujet d'une de maniere à calmer les esprits, cela n'empêcha pas qu'ausitot la messe finie, le banc que Mr. Baby avoit fait remettre s'appuyant sur l'ordonance de Mr. Burke, fut jetté hors de l'église et la place criée et adjugée le dimanche suivant au nommé Goyau qui y a remis un banc samedi dernier. Mr. Baby a pris acte contre ceux qui ont ôté le banc et l'affaire se poursuit au serieux. Je ne me suis point mêlé de cette affaire conformément à Vos ordres, je me suis con[ten]té de dire à Mr. Baby et à Goyeau. *Je ne [me] mêle de rien, vous vous croyez autorisé à mettre le banc, vous en courrez tous les risques.*

J'ai trouvé l'Eglise et la sacristie en très bon ordre et munis de tout très decemment tant pour le linge que pour les ornements, mais je ne trouve rien de certain pour le casuel tant du curé que de l'Eglise. Je n'ai trouvé au prèsbiterre que l'horloge, le poële, un matelat, un peu de vessele, quelque meubles de cuisine et trois chaises avec le fauteuil du feu R. pere Potier. Quant à la bibliotheque, je n'y ai point trouvé la liste que vous m'avez laissée, Mr. Lavadoue s'est contenté de 60 volumes et elle reste composée de 540 tant bons que mauvais, mais satisfaisante pour un curé par la qualité des livres dont il n'a guere que cent volumes gatés et depareillé.

La paroisse n'est composé que de cent cinquante habitants en y comprenant les 12 de la riviere à la Tranche, 5 aux petits Ecore dans le lac Erier et 4 sur la riviere aux Canards. Pour les Hurons il n'en res[te] que 4 ou 5 longe [loges?] peu peuplées à la rivierre au Canard. Le fort Malden est un établissement au berseau, il n'y a que 2 ou 3 Catholiques. Il n'y auroit de mission à faire ici, sans parler de Niag[ar]a ni de Kinston d'où l'on peut plus aisement communiquer de Montréal, que le Sault St. Marie où il n'y a de résidents que dix à 12 habitants. Si toute fois votre Grandeur juge appropos d'envoyer ici un prêtre avec moi, j'en serai bien content d'autant plus que je ne communique avec Mr. Levadoue qu'avec circomspection parceque on le soupçonne beaucoup d'être ici bien opposé aux interests du roi : Je ne sçai si l'on est en ceci bien fondé. Toute fois je suis sur la reserve. . . . Je ne croyois pas Monseigneur que ma lettre seroit si longue, je vous prie de me le pardonner et de me croire avec tout respect et soumission, Votre très humble serviteur.

APPENDIX II

French Commandants at Detroit 1701–60*

Antoine de la Mothe Cadillac, Commandant 1701–10
Pierre Alphonse de Tonti, Acting Commandant 1704–5
Etienne Venyard, Sieur de Bourgmont, Acting Commandant 1705–6
Charles Regnault, Sieur Dubuisson, Interim Commandant 1710–12
François de la Forest, Commandant 1710–14
Jacques Charles Sabrevois, Sieur de Fleury, Commandant 1714–17
Alphonse de Tonti, Commandant 1717–27
Francois Marie Picote de Belestre, Acting Commandant 1727–8
Jean Baptiste de St. Ours, Sieur Deschaillons, Commandant 1728–9
Louis Henry Deschamps, Sieur de Boishebert, Commandant 1729–32
Ives Jacques Hugues Pean, Sieur de Livaudiere, Commandant 1733–6
Nicholas Joseph Desnoyelles, Commandant 1736–9
Pierre Jacques Payan de Noyan, Sieur de Charvis, Commandant 1739–42
Pierre Joseph Céloron, Sieur de Blainville, Commandant 1742–4
Paul Joseph Lemoine, Chevalier de Longueuil, Commandant 1742–6
Jacques Charles de Sabrevois, Chevalier de St. Louis, Commandant 1749–51
Pierre Joseph Céloron, Sieur de Blainville, Commandant 1751–4
Jacques Pierre Daneau, Sieur de Muy, Commandant 1754–8
Jean Baptiste Henry Beranger, Interim Commandant 1758
François Marie Picote, Sieur de Belestre, Commandant 1758–60

*Adapted from "Detroit Rulers" by C. M. Burton in *M.H.C.*, XXXIV, 303–40.

APPENDIX III

Double Names or Sobriquets

Father Christian Denissen, noted Detroit genealogist, cites the following causes of the custom of double names:

(a) Owners of estates gave their holdings titles as in European nobility and often it was the title that survived; e.g., Douaire de Bondy.

(b) The prevailing custom of giving nicknames caused some double names; e.g., Poissant = Poisson-LaSalline.

(c) It was sometimes necessary to distinguish from another family of the same name; e.g., Joseph Martin for Joseph Durocher, son of Martin Durocher.

(d) Some sought to glorify the section of the country they came from by adding the name of the province, city, or town. This was a very common practice among the soldiers; e.g., Valé *dit* Versailles.

(e) Sometimes nicknames originated from the peculiar circumstances of a person's birth; e.g., Nicolas Campeau *dit* Niagara (born at Niagara when his parents were on their way to Montreal).

(f) At times the name was given by the Indians; e.g., Peltier *dit* Antaya.

(g) Sometimes the Christian name by which a certain person was known in the community was adopted; e.g., Louis Villers *dit* St. Louis.

(h) The name, or the double name, of the wife sometimes prevailed; e.g., Godet *dit* Marentette. Jacques Godet married Margaret Duguay *dit* Marentette.

Partial List of "dits" Gathered from the Eighteenth-Century Records Relating to the South Shore of the Detroit River

Villers *dit* St. Louis
Seguin *dit* Laderoute
Durand *dit* Montmirel
St. Onge *dit* Chesne
Chesne *dit* Labutte
Rocher[l]eau *dit* Lesperance
De Marsac *dit* Durocher
Reveau *dit* Lajeunesse
Delisle *dit* Bienvenu
Landry *dit* St. André
Godet *dit* Marentette
Descomptes *dit* Labadie
Labadie *dit* Badichon
Douaire *dit* Bondy
Patoca *dit* Bigot
Bernard *dit* Lajoie
Berthelot *dit* Savoyard
Leduc *dit* Persil
Serat (Cera) *dit* Coquillard

Beneteau *dit* Labaleine
Valé *dit* Versailles
Godefroy *dit* St. George
Poupart *dit* Lafleur
Morin *dit* Valcour
Fauvel *dit* St. Louis
Gendron *dit* Potevin
Desbuttes *dit* St. Martin
L'Oranger *dit* Maisonville
Dineau *dit* St. Etienne
Metayer *dit* Ladouceur
Vessière *dit* LaFerté
Deslierres *dit* Bonvouloir
Billau *dit* Lesperance
Dubord *dit* Clermont
Poisson *dit* Lasalline
Sedilot *dit* Montreuil
Casse *dit* St. Aubin
Javerais *dit* Laderoute
Plichon *dit* St. Louis

Jourdain *dit* Labrosse
Bernier *dit* Vadebonccœur
Campeau *dit* Piniche
Verchères *dit* Lajeunesse
Bezer *dit* L'Eveillé
Duberger *dit* Sanschagrain
Bernard *dit* Lafontaine
Rouchau (Rousseau) *dit* Lafond
Catin *dit* Barron
Rochereau *dit* Morisseau
Johan *dit* Laviolette
Audet *dit* Lapointe
Levron *dit* Metayer
Peltier *dit* Antaya
Jean Tourneux *dit* Jeanette (Janette)
Guillet *dit* Tourangeau
Rivard *dit* La Course

APPENDIX IV

ABSTRACTS FROM THE DETROIT NOTARIAL RECORDS

Liber A—from April 10, 1766, to Jan. 20, 1776

NAME	DESCRIPTION	PRICE	REMARKS
p. 12, Sept. 17, 1765 (registered April 1768) Pontiac to Dr. Christian Anthon	4 acres wide (French measure) east of land of Pierre Chenes	Free gift	
p. 28, May 9, 1768 (registered May 15, 1768) Pierre Tamisier to François Drouillard	3 x 40 arpents w.s.w. Thomas Pajot, E.N.E. François Prudhomme	150 bushels of wheat payable in three yearly instalments	
p. 60, Nov. 10, 1757 (registered Oct. 26, 1768) J. B. Cardinal Millet to J. B. Reau	3 x 40 arpents N.E. Baptiste LeBeau, s.w. J. B. Mallet	500 livres	J. B. Cardinal had obtained this parcel of land from his father-in-law, J. B. Mallet.
p. 61, Sept. 16, 1768 (registered Oct. 26, 1768) J. B. Reau to Jean Legras	3 x 40 arpents w.s.w. Gabriel Legrand, E.N.E. Baptiste LeBeau	1,500 livres	
p. 91, May 22, 1769 (registered June 11, 1769) Charles Fontaine to Antoine Bouffard	3 x 40 arpents, E.N.E. Aubinet w.s.w. Jacques	600 livres and 100 bushels of wheat	

[312]

APPENDIX IV (*continued*)

NAME	DESCRIPTION	PRICE	REMARKS
p. 106, Sept. 17, 1765 (registered Nov. 15, 1769) Pontiac to Lt. Edw. Abbot	4 x 80 acres east of land of Lt. John Carden	Free gift	
p. 107, Sept. 14, 1768 (registered Nov. 15, 1769) Lt. Edw. Abbot to Antoine Louis Labadie	same as above	£100 New York currency	
p. 114, Oct. 15, 1767 (registered March 8, 1770) P. Potier M.J. to François Gaudet Marantet	4 arpents and 1 perche wide E.N.E. M. de Longueuil, w.s.w. rest of lands of Huron Mission	1,600 livres	Full depth as given to us without title in 1747
p. 114, June 4, 1769 (registered March 8, 1770) Same to same	1 arpent and 1 perche wide adjoining lands of the Mission		Reserving a small square piece of land near the Church
p. 126, Sept. 3, 1765 (registered June 29, 1770) Pontiac to George McDougall	8 x 80 acres (French measure) east of land in possession of De Iteater (De Hetre)	Free gift	
p. 126–7, June 29, 1770 (registered June 29, 1770) George McDougall to Thomas Smallman	4 x 80 acres east of 4 acres McDougall has sold to Bonvouloir	Pontiac's intention when he gave 8 acres to McDougall	McDougall-to-Bonvouloir deed is in the George F. Macdonald Collection

[313]

Appendix IV (*continued*)

NAME	DESCRIPTION	PRICE	REMARKS
p. 127, July 2, 1770 (registered July 4, 1770) Thomas Smallman to Alex Maisonville	as above	£100 N.Y. curr.	George Anton, attorney for Thos. Smallman of province of Pensilvania
p. 128, Aug. 4, 1768 (registered July 4, 1770) Geo. Christian Anthon to Alex. Maisonville	land given by Pontiac	£100 N.Y. curr.	
p. 128, Sept. 17, 1765 (registered July 4, 1770) Pontiac to Leopold Chesne	4 x 80 acres (French measure) east of land granted to McDougall	Free gift	
p. 129, Sept. 17, 1765 (registered July 4, 1770) Pontiac to Pierre Chesne	4 x 80 acres (French measure) east of land granted to Leopold Chesne	Free gift	
p. 129, June 9, 1766 (registered July 4, 1770) Pierre Labutte (Chesne) to J. B. Beaubien, Jr.	same as above	1,000 livres	
p. 131, July 18, 1770 (registered July 27, 1770) Alex Maisonville to J. B. Beaubien	2½ acres w.s.w. J. B. Beaubien, E.N.E. Alex Maisonville	1,125 livres (£75)	

[314]

APPENDIX IV (*continued*)

NAME	DESCRIPTION	PRICE	REMARKS
p. 137, Aug. 16, 1770 (registered Aug. 28, 1770) Claude Landry *dit* St. André to Robert Thibaut	3 x 40 arpents E.N.E. J. B. Rowe, W.S.W. Joncaire Chabert	100 bushels of wheat, 60 bushels of corn	
p. 148, Sept. 8, 1766 (registered Dec. 18, 1770) Jacques Campeau to Pierre Javerais *dit* Laderoute	3 x 40 arpents opposite Turkey Is., S.E. Suzor, N.W. Bonaventure Reaume	Exchange for land on other side of river	Jacques Campeau was given this land by his father Louis who had bought it from Prud-homme, the original grantee
pp. 150–1, March 18, 1768 (registered Sept. 20, 1770) Charles Moran to Jacques Gravelle	3 x 40 arpents W.S.W. Pierre Reaume, E.N.E. L'Isleronde	Exchange for farm listed below	Log house 20 x 20 ft.
Jacques Gravelle to Charles Moran	3 x 40 arpents between St. Etienne and LeBeau Sr.	Exchange for farm listed above	Log house, barn 40 x 30 ft.
p. 176, Sept. 29, 1770 (registered July 30, 1771) Simon Drouillard to Duperon Baby	3 x 40 arpents E.N.E. Simon Drouillard, W.S.W. Antoine Meloche	900 livres (£60)	
p. 178, July 1, 1771 (registered Oct. 12, 1771) Ant. Rivard to George Knaggs	2 acres + 18 ft. x 40 acres N.E. A. Rivard, S.W. Laboise	4000 livres (£266 13s 4*d*)	
p. 179, May 15, 1771 (registered Oct. 12, 1771) Charles Chauvin to J. Rivard	2 acres x 40 acres E.N.E. Noel Chauvin, W.S.W. Jean Pilet	2500 livres (£166 13s. 4*d*.)	

[315]

APPENDIX IV (*continued*)

NAME	DESCRIPTION	PRICE	REMARKS
p. 196, March 26, 1772 (registered March 30, 1772) Joseph Dusseau to Dominique Labrosse	3 x 40 arpents E.N.E. Pierre Reaume, w.s.w. Bouron	4,600 livres (£306 13s. 4d.)	Includes livestock and implements
p. 206, Oct. 21, 1771 (registered April 27, 1772) René Theodore Duroseau to Gordon & MaComb	One lot 1½ arpent in breadth	£134	
p. 206, Aug. 25, 1760 (registered April 29, 1772) Charles Moran to Gabriel Legrand	3 x 40 arpents east of Chabotte, west of Jacques Campeau	Exchange for 2 x 80 arpents on other side of river	House 20 x 20 ft, barn 40 x 30 ft, implements, livestock
p. 246, July 5, 1773 (registered July 31, 1773) Jean Billout *dit* Lesperance *dit* Patoca to Sterling	3 x 40 arpents E.N.E. Joseph Pouget, w.s.w. Lajeunesse	£103 (1,545 livres)	Sold by auction after having been announced at Ste. Anne's Church
p. 277, Oct. 14, 1774 (registered Oct. 1774) Joseph Godet to McGregor & McLeod	3 x 40 arpents E.N.E. Vaudry, w.s.w. Charon	180 pounds (2,700 livres)	Owned formerly by Binau
p. 305, Feb. 18, 1775 (registered April 11, 1775) Charles Moran to Noel Chauvin	3 x 40 arpents E.N.E. Joseph Drouillard, w.s.w. LeBeau	Exchange for farm on other side of river	
p. 313, Aug. 21, 1768 (registered May 3, 1775) J. St. Aubin to Vital Goyau	2 x 40 arpents opposite the fort	Final payment of money owed to Madam Vien	This land was granted to widow Vien in 1751; copy of grant annexed

APPENDIX IV (*continued*)

NAME	DESCRIPTION	PRICE	REMARKS
p. 320, May 6, 1775 (registered May 10, 1775) Jacques Charon to Joseph Godett	4 x 40 arpents E.N.E. Duperon Baby, w.s.w. Baptiste Bigras	3,000 livres (£200)	
p. 322-3. Aug. 16, 1772 (registered May 10, 1775) J. B. Dufour to Jacques Charon	1 arpent	200 bushels of wheat payable in four yearly instalments	
p. 329, May 18, 1775 (registered May 18, 1775) Widow of B. Goyau to Isaac Williams	2 x 40 arpents E.N.E. Joseph Lesperance w.s.w. Louis Goyau	2,500 livres	
p. 333, May 29, 1775 (registered May 30, 1775) Louis Binau to Pierre Charon	3 x 40 arpents E.N.E. Gregor McGregor, w.s.w. Charles Reaume	Lifetime annual payments of: 20 bushels of wheat, 20 bushels of flour, 27½ cords of firewood	Livestock and implements included
p. 346, sale in 1752 (registered July 13, 1775) Alex Delisle to Bouron	2 x 40 arpents E.N.E. Jacques Godet, w.s.w. Hyacinthe Reaume	300 livres	Céloron granted this land to Delisle on Nov. 24, 1751; copy of grant annexed
p. 381, Jan. 20, 1776 (registered Feb. 1, 1776) McGregor & McLeod to Gregor McGregor	3 x 40 arpents E.N.E. widow Vaudry, w.s.w. Binau	£180 (2,700 livres)	

[END OF LIBER A]

APPENDIX IV (*continued*)

Liber B—from Feb. 2, 1776, to May 27, 1780

NAME	DESCRIPTION	PRICE	REMARKS
p. 11, May 11, 1776 (registered July 29, 1776) Jacques Charon to Jacques Peltier	3 x 40 arpents w.s.w. Jacques Belleperche, e.n.e. Jacques Charon	5,500 livres to be paid in six years	Vendor retains the mill located on this land
p. 62, July 27, 1776 (registered April 27, 1777) Jacques Charon to Pierre Charon & Antoine Robert	3 x 40 arpents w.s.w. Jacques Peltier, e.n.e. Joseph Bondy	3,000 livres (£200) in four yearly payments	Includes a horse-operated mill located on farm of Jacques Peltier
p. 65, Dec. 6, 1776 (registered April 7, 1777) Gregor McGregor to Charles Fontaine	3 x 40 arpents e.n.e. Widow Vaudry, w.s.w. Sieur Bineau	5,418 livres	
p. 91, Aug. 1, 1777 (registered Sept. 20, 1777) J. B. Leduc to Philippe Leduc	1 x 40 arpents e.n.e. J. B. Leduc, w.s.w. Philippe Leduc	1,666 livres, 13 sous, and 4 deniers	
p. 92, Aug. 1, 1777 (registered Oct. 20, 1777) J. B. Leduc to Joseph Mailloux	1 x 40 arpents e.n.e. Joseph Mailloux, w.s.w. J. B. Leduc	1,666 livres, 13 sous and four deniers	
p. 93–4, Sept. 19, 1777 (registered Oct. 20, 1777) J. B. Tourneur to Charles & J. B. Drouillard	3 x 40 arpents w.s.w. Sieur Bondy, e.n.e. Pierre Coquillard	2,000 francs	

[318]

APPENDIX IV (*continued*)

NAME	DESCRIPTION	PRICE	REMARKS
p. 120, Nov. 22, 1777 (registered Dec. 20, 1777) Louis Bineau to J. B. Crette	3 × 40 arpents w.s.w. Charles Reaume, E.N.E. Fontaine	4,000 livres	J. B. Crette paid 194 livres for "Lots et Ventes" Dec. 20, 1777
p. 140, March 5, 1778 (registered March 10, 1778) François Drouillard to Ant. Rousseau	3 × 40 arpents E.N.E. Etienne Jacob, w.s.w. François Lebeau	4,000 livres	
p. 154, Feb. 3, 1777 (registered May 23, 1778) James Thompson to Jacques Charon	2 × 40 arpents E.N.E. Jos. Lesperance, w.s.w. Louis Goyau	4,000 livres (£266 13s. 4d. N.Y. curr.)	Charon paid 333 livres, six sous and eight deniers for "Lots et Ventes"
p. 155, April 1, 1778 (registered May 23, 1778) Alex Maisonville to Joseph Berthiaume	4 × 80 arpents E.N.E. Themus Reaume, w.s.w. Joseph Godet	3,000 livres	If dispossessed by Indians or others only money paid will be refunded; improvements made will be lost
p. 156, April 1, 1778 (registered May 23, 1778) Alex Maisonville to Joseph Godet	4 × 80 arpents E.N.E. Joseph Berthiaume, w.s.w. Bonaventure Reaume	5,000 livres (£333 6s. 8d.)	If dispossessed by Indians or others only money paid will be refunded; improvements made will be lost
p. 157–8, May 23, 1778 (registered May 25, 1778) J. B. Crette, carpenter, to Joseph Pouget, tailor	3 × 40 arpents w.s.w. Charles Reaume, E.N.E. Fontaine	3,500 livres	

Appendix IV (*continued*)

NAME	DESCRIPTION	PRICE	REMARKS
p. 160, May 23, 1778 (registered May 29, 1778) Joseph Drouillard to Theophile Lemay	4 x 40 arpents E.N.E. J. B. Reaume, w.s.w. Noel Chauvin	8,000 livres	LeMay paid 444 livres, and 10 sous for "Lots et Ventes"
p. 166, June 10, 1778 (registered June 16, 1778) Charles Bouron to André Benito, mason	2 x 40 arpents w.s.w. J. B. Ouellette, E.N.E. Charles Bouron	3,000 livres (£200)	
p. 168, June 16, 1778 (registered June 16, 1778) Jacques Baby to Joseph Drouillard	3 x 40 arpents E.N.E. Jacques Baby, w.s.w. Tourangeau	15,000 livres (£1000 N.Y. curr.)	Sale included a stone windmill; Baby promised not to plant trees on his property that might interfere with mill
p. 171, Dec. 7, 1776 (registered July 2, 1778) Charles Fontaine to Antoine Meloche	2 x 40 arpents E.N.E. Ant. Meloche, w.s.w. Monmini	2,000 livres	
p. 172, March 22, 1778 (registered March 22, 1778) René St. Aubin to Ant. Bouffard	3 x 40 arpents w.s.w. Bouffard, E.N.E. René Cloutier	1,800 francs	Sold at auction after having been proclaimed at three successive weekly "criées"
p. 176, June 5, 1777 (registered July 10, 1788) Antoine Rivard to Jos. Dusseault & J. B. Ouellet	162 ft x 40 arpents w.s.w. George Knaggs, E.N.E. lands of the Hurons	2,250 livres (£150)	Mill included

[320]

APPENDIX IV (*continued*)

NAME	DESCRIPTION	PRICE	REMARKS
p. 183–4, Aug. 10, 1778 (Aug. 10, 1778) Joseph Delière *dit* Bonvouloir to François Marantet Godet, Jr.	1 x 40 arpents & 2 x 40 arpents E.N.E. Charles Delisle, w.s.w. Hyacinthe DeHêtre	11,000 livres	Sold at auction to settle estate after having been proclaimed at church on three successive Sundays
p. 206, April 1, 1778 (registered Jan. 25, 1779) Garat Graverat to Louis Bernard *dit* Lajoye	3 40 arpents E.N.E. Sieur St. Louis, w.s.w. Duperon Baby	800 livres	
p. 207, Jan. 25, 1779 (registered Jan. 25, 1779) Louis Bernard *dit* Lajoye to Louis Cousineau	3 x 40 arpents E.N.E. Louis Viller *dit* St. Louis, w.s.w. Duperon Baby	800 livres	
p. 218, Feb. 27, 1779 (registered April 30, 1779) Charles Reaume to Jean Louis Reveau *dit* Lajeunesse	3 x 40 arpents E.N.E. J. B. Crette, w.s.w. François Choisie	4,000 livres	
p. 230, June 3, 1779 (registered June 11, 1779) Simon Drouillard to Wm. Monforton	3 x 40 arpents N.E. Simon Drouillard, s.w. Joseph Drouillard	2,000 livres	Reserving use of a one-acre lot for lifetime of St. Etienne
p. 240, June 29, 1779 (registered June 30, 1779) Charles Reaume to Joseph Pilet	3 x 80 arpents E.N.E. Peltier, w.s.w. Pierre Reaume	3,000 livres	If dispossessed by Indians or others only money paid will be refunded
p. 248, Aug. 10, 1779 (registered Aug. 10, 1779) Joseph Reaume to Charles Chauvin	4 x 100 arpents E.N.E. Paul Marsac, w.s.w. Jacob Sheiffelin	2,500 livres	If dispossessed by Indians or others only money paid will be refunded

[321]

Appendix IV (*continued*)

NAME	DESCRIPTION	PRICE	REMARKS
p. 251, Aug. 24, 1779 (registered Aug. 24, 1779) J. B. Reaume to Martin Levris	3 x 80 arpents E.N.E. Cassety, w.s.w. François Meloche	Exchange for farm on north side of river	
p. 255, Oct. 14, 1779 (registered Oct. 15, 1779) J. B. Reaume to Charles Reaume	3 x 80 arpents E.N.E. Jos. Poupar Lafleur, w.s.w. Theophile Lemay	6000 livres (£400)	
p. 256, Oct. 15, 1779 (registered Oct. 15, 1779) Louis Cousineau to J. B. Lajeunesse	3 x 40 arpents E.N.E. Louis Viller *dit* St. Louis, w.s.w. Duperon Baby	800 livres	
p. 266, March 2, 1780 (registered March 2, 1780) Benjamin Chappu to Ant. Soumande	3 x 40 arpents E.N.E. Widow Espiegle, w.s.w. St. Bernier	2,000 livres	
p. 268, March 20, 1780 (registered March 20, 1780) Jacques Peltier to Ant. Robert, Jr.	3 x 40 arpents w.s.w. Jacques Belleperche, E.N.E. J. B. Pitre	3,600 livres	
p. 272, April 27, 1780 (registered April 27, 1780) Colin Andrews, atty. for Dan Campbell to Chas. & Ant. Campau	page torn; E.N.E. James Cassety, w.s.w. Capt. MacDougall	3000 francs (£200)	If dispossessed by Indians or others only money paid will be refunded; Improvements will be a loss

[END OF LIBER B]

APPENDIX IV (*continued*)

Liber C—*from May 8, 1780, to June 14, 1795*

NAME	DESCRIPTION	PRICE	REMARKS
p. 3, May 18, 1780 (registered same day) Marguerite Casety to Julien Parent	3 x 80 arpents w.s.w. Martin Levril, E.N.E. Geo. McDougall	3,500 livres	If dispossessed by Indians or others only money paid will be refunded
p. 40, June 2, 1778 (registered Sept. 28, 1780) Ottawa Indians to Wm. Tucker, interpreter	6 x 100 acres s.w. J. N. Chapoton, N.E. unlocated lands	In consideration of good-will, love and affection	
p. 67, Oct. 2, 1780 Ottawa Indians to James Abbot & Isaac Williams	3 leagues wide behind French farms extending to Lake St. Clair	In consideration of good-will, love and affection	
p. 68, Oct. 2, 1780 Ottawas & Ojibways to Wm. MaComb	On south shore between Rivière à Pins & Stoney Point running into the woods three leagues	In consideration of good-will, love and affection	
p. 69, Oct. 2, 1780 Ottawas to Jean Chapoton	From land of Pierre Paré to Rivière aux Puces	Out of sincere friendship	
p. 70, May 1, 1769 Ottawas to J. B. Chapoton	6 x 80 arpents next to F. Marsac	In consideration of good-will, love and affection	
p. 75, Sept. 21, 1780 Wyandottes to Pierre Drouillard	From G. Knaggs to Rivière à Gervais by 150 arpents		

[323]

APPENDIX IV (*continued*)

NAME	DESCRIPTION	PRICE	REMARKS
p. 76, Nov. 1, 1780 Isaac Williams to Pierre Drouillard	9 x 150 acres s.w. James Abbot, N.E. Hyacinthe Laselle	£100	
p. 77, Nov. 6, 1780 Pierre Potier, M.J. to François Pratt	2 x 40 arpents E.N.E. François Gaudet, w.s.w. Huron lands	3,000 livres (£200 N. Y. curr.)	
p. 79, Sept. 22, 1780 Huron Indians to Pierre Potier, M.J.	2 arpents wide extending to Grand Marais; E.N.E. François Gaudet, w.s.w. Huron lands		An expression of esteem for their missionary
p. 100, May 12, 1777 (registered May 1, 1781) Ottawa Indians to Jacob Schieffelin	4 x 100 arpents w.s.w. Wm. Tucker, E.N.E. J. B. Campau		In consideration of good-will, love and affection
p. 102, May 15, 1781 Jacob Schieffelin to Antoine Dequindre	same as above	£260 13s. 4d. N.Y. curr.	
p. 106, May 7, 1781 Chippewas to Labadie family	From Stoney Point to River La Tranche and 150 acres deep; next to MaComb's land		In consideration of good-will, love and affection
p. 107, (registered June 19, 1781) Ottawas to Antoine Robert	3 x 40 arpents between the lands of Joseph Huot & Pierre Miney		In consideration of good-will, love and affection Donation made in the late 1770's

[324]

APPENDIX IV (*continued*)

NAME	DESCRIPTION	PRICE	REMARKS
p. 110, March 1, 1781 Antoine Robert to J. B. Pitre	3 x 80 arpents w.s.w. Antoine Robert, E.N.E. Joseph Bondy	3,000 livres	
p. 116, June 5, 1781 Antoine DeQuindre to François DeQuindre & Charles Barriteau	4 x 100 arpents w.s.w. Wm. Tucker E.N.E. J. B. Campau	£266 13s. 4d.	
p. 119, July 7, 1781 Dominique Labrosse to J. B. Tourneux	3 x 40 arpents between lands of Pierre Reaume & Charles Bouron	7,500 livres (£500)	
p. 120, July 12, 1781 Pierre Cera *dit* Coquillard to Wm. Brown	3 x 40 arpents E.N.E. J. B. Paré, w.s.w. J. B. Drouillard	4,000 livres	
p. 145, March 17, 1781 J. B. Tourangeau to Pierre Fouquereau	3 x 40 arpents N.E. Widow Choisi, s.w. Pierre Prud-homme	3,500 livres	
p. 158, March 4, 1782 Huron Indians to F. X. Hubert & Sisters of the Congregation	6 x 40 arpents E.N.E. François Pratt, w.s.w. James Rankin & Indian lands	In consideration of good-will, love and affection	In 1775 the Wyandotte Chiefs gave a small piece of land near the river to James Rankin and his children; a copy of the deed is in the possession of Geo. F. Macdonald
p. 166, March 23, 1782 Wm. Tucker to Fontanet DeQuindre & Lamarche	3 x 100 arpents E.N.E. François DeQuindre and Lamarche, w.s.w. J. B. Chapoton	3,000 livres (£200)	

[325]

APPENDIX IV (*continued*)

NAME	DESCRIPTION	PRICE	REMARKS
p. 186, June 13, 1776 (registered 1781) Ottawas to a squaw called Tano	3 x 80 arpents s.e. Little River		
p. 195, Oct. 11, 1782 François Comparé to Antoine Moras	3 x 40 arpents at entrance of Lake St. Clair; w.s.w. Gregor McGregor, e.n.e. François Comparé	£100	If dispossessed by Indians or others only money paid will be refunded
p. 205, May 15, 1782 J. B. Campeau, Jr., Captain of Militia to Pierre Villaire	2 x 100 arpents e.n.e. Widow Marsac, w.s.w. J. B. Campeau	1,500 livres	If dispossessed by Indians or others only money paid will be refunded
p. 206, Nov. 15, 1782 J. B. Campau, Jr., Captain of Militia to Vital Dumouchel	2 x 100 arpents e.n.e. Pierre Villaire, w.s.w. François DeQuindre & Barriteau Lamarche	1,500 livres	If dispossessed by Indians or others only money paid will be refunded
p. 218, July 10, 1782 Joseph Lusier to Alex Grant	3 x 80 arpents on south shore of Lake St. Clair; east of John Askin, west of J. B. Parrey	£66 13s. 4d.	
p. 219, July 9, 1782 Antoine Lusier to John Askin	3 x 80 arpents on south shore of Lake St. Clair; east of Morin, west of Joseph Lusier	£66 13s. 4d.	
p. 222, Sept 10, 1782 J. B. Marsac to François Sordillet	3 x 40 arpents e.n.e. François Sordillet, w.s.w. widow of Paul Marsac	1,200 livres (anciens shellins de Québec)	If dispossessed by Indians or others only money paid will be refunded

[326]

APPENDIX IV (*continued*)

NAME	DESCRIPTION	PRICE	REMARKS
p. 224, Aug. 10, 1782 Joseph Lusier & Charles Rousseau to Wm. Brown	6 x 80 arpents on shore of Lake St. Clair E.N.E. Morin, w.s.w. Thomas Cox	1,800 livres (£120)	
p. 232, July 13, 1782 Chiefs of Wyandots to Edward Hazel	25 x 100 arpents east of Pierre Drouillard	Good-will & affection	
p. 241, May 1, 1772 Chiefs of Ottawas to Joseph Lusier	3 x 80 arpents on south shore of Lake St. Clair E.N.E. Morin, w.s.w. Charles Rousseau	Good-will & affection	
p. 249, March 27, 1783 Edward Hazel to Isaac Williams	4 x 100 arpents E.N.E. Huron lands w.s.w. Hazel	£5	
p. 259, Jan. 24, 1782 Charles Bernier to René LeBeau	2 x 40 arpents between Antoine Soumande & Etienne Laviolette	1,500 livres	
p. 261, April 22, 1783 René LeBeau to Pierre Meloche, Jr.	2 x 40 arpents between Antoine Soumande & Etienne Laviolette	£200	
p. 270, April 18, 1782 Antoine Miney to Gregor McGregor	3 x 100 arpents E.N.E. François Comparé, w.s.w. Antoine Robert	2,000 livres	
p. 273, July 3, 1783 Gregor McGregor to Hippolite Campau	3 x 100 arpents E.N.E. Antoine Moras, w.s.w. Antoine Robert	£300	

[327]

APPENDIX IV (*continued*)

NAME	DESCRIPTION	PRICE	REMARKS
p. 283, Oct. 13, 1783 (registered Oct. 16, 1783) Chiefs of Ottawas to Jacob Schieffelin	A tract of land seven miles square (later Township of Malden)	Love and affection	
p. 289, Dec. 17, 1783 Abbot & Saunders to François Drouillard	4 x 40 arpents w.s.w. Pierre Letourneau, E.N.E. Louis St. Louis *dit* Villaire	4,500 livres	
p. 300, Feb. 7, 1784 (registered Feb. 12, 1784) Antoine Soumande to John Askin	3 x 40 arpents at Petite Côte E.N.E. Pierre Meloche, Jr., w.s.w. Josephte Hippolite, négresse	£183 13s. 4d.	
p. 301, Feb. 7, 1784 (registered Feb. 12, 1784) Joseph Dugand to John Askin	3 x 40 arpents at Petite Côte between lands owned by Pierre Belaire	£100	
p. 303, Feb. 10, 1784 (registered Feb. 13, 1784) John Askin to James Donaldson	3 x 40 arpents at Petite Côte E.N.E. Pierre Meloche, Jr., w.s.w. Josephte Hippolite, négresse	£250	Sold back to Askin same day, same price
p. 308, Dec. 18, 1783 (registered Feb. 16, 1784) François Drouillard to Michel Cattin *dit* Baron	1 x 100 arpents E.N.E. François Drouillard, w.s.w. Pierre Letourneau	1,500 livres	

[328]

APPENDIX IV (*continued*)

NAME	DESCRIPTION	PRICE	REMARKS
p. 323, Feb. 18, 1784 Marsac family to Nicolas Langlois	3 x 80 arpents E.N.E. Jacques Belleperche, w.s.w. widow of Paul Marsac	3,500 livres	
p. 325, Dec. 7, 1783 J. B. Parrey to John Wilson	3 x 40 arpents at Petite Côte E.N.E. Joseph Bernier *dit* Vadeboncœur w.s.w. Pierre Cera *dit* Coquillard	7,500 livres (£500)	Includes furniture, livestock, & implements
p. 327, date missing, 1783 Joseph Hunot to Graverat & Visgar	3 x 80 arpents E.N.E. Antoine Robert, Sr., w.s.w. Peltier	3,000 francs	
p. 331, March 11, 1784 Pierre Cera *dit* Coquillard to William Scott	3 x 40 arpents at Petite Côte E.N.E. John Wilson, w.s.w. J. B. Drouillard	£300	
p. 338, April 18, 1782 Ottawas to Antoine Miney	3 x 100 arpents E.N.E. François Comparé, w.s.w. Antoine Robert, Sr.	Love & affection	
p. 352, July 30, 1784 Jean Louis Reveau to Wm. Brown	3 x 40 arpents at Petite Côte E.N.E. Joseph Pouget, w.s.w. J. L. Reveau	5,000 livres	
p. 353, June 3, 1784 Wm. Brown to Richard Pollard	3 x 40 arpents at Petite Côte E.N.E. Joseph Pouget, w.s.w. J. L. Reveau	£400	[The date is evidently incorrect in one of the last two entries]

APPENDIX IV (*continued*)

NAME	DESCRIPTION	PRICE	REMARKS
p. 363, Sept. 2, 1784 Theophile Lemay to Isaac Dolson	3 x 40 arpents at Petite Côte E.N.E. Charles Reaume, w.s.w. Joseph Bernier	£500	
p. 363, Sept. 10, 1784 Joseph Bernier to Daniel Feild	3 x 40 arpents at Petite Côte E.N.E. Isaac Dolson, w.s.w. John Williams	£200	

p. 373
NOTE: This Register was sent down to Quebec by order of the Commander-in-Chief in the year 1784, where it remained until the year 1789 when it was brought up from thence by William Dummer Powell, Esqr., first Judge of His Majesty's Court of Common Pleas for this District of Hesse, and afterwards deposited in my office in the year 1790 in the month of May and is now continued. During the interval the Records of the District were in the hands of William Monforton who acted as Notary Public to which a reference must be had.

Signed—T. Smith, C.C. Pleas
District of Hesse
May 24, 1790

[Now follows the Monforton Register. The first two years (1784–6) are missing, having been stolen from Monforton's office. The Monforton Register is sometimes referred to as Liber C1 of the Detroit Notarial Records.]

June 21, 1786 Baptiste Leduc to J. B. Ouellet	3 x 40 arpents N.E. Widow Mayou, s.w. Widow Philippe Leduc	7,000 livres (old Quebec shillings)	Reserving house and one arpent to L. Trudell
July 2, 1786 Pierre Martin Levry to J. B. Descoinge *dit* Labadie	2 x 80 arpents at Ottawas N.E. Julien Parent, s.w. J. B. Descomptes Labadie	2,800 livres (Quebec shillings)	Levry had inherited land from his mother
Aug. 9, 1786 Hyacinthe DeHêtre to Paul Poisson *dit* Lassaline	2 x 40 arpents N.E. Francois Marentet, Jr., s.w. Pierre Hubert	6,000 livres (£400 N.Y. curr.)	

APPENDIX IV (*continued*)

NAME	DESCRIPTION	PRICE	REMARKS
Jan. 2, 1787 Louis Monmeny to Jacob Askin	2 x 40 arpents at Petite Côte N.E. Antoine Meloche, s.w. Estienne Laviolette	£100	For debts owed by Monmeny to Askin
Feb. 7, 1787 Joseph Gaudet to Antoine Labadie	3 x 80 arpents N.E. Baptiste Pelleteau, s.w. Joseph Bon Reaume	3,000 livres (£200 N.Y. curr.)	
Feb. 2, 1787 John Askin to Joseph Mainville(oule)	2 x 40 arpents at Petite Côte N.E. Antoine Meloche, s.w. Estienne Laviolette	£100	
Michael Shannon to Frederick Arnoult	3 x 40 arpents at Petite Côte N.E. Joseph Pouget, s.w. J. L. Reveau	£150 N.Y. curr.	
May 1, 1787 Huron Indians to Church of the Assumption	4 x 40 arpents N.E. Charles Renau, s.w. lands not granted	Donation	
July 24, 1787 Charles Bouron to Baptiste Bruyiere	2 x 40 arpents N.E. J. B. Tourneux, s.w. Andre Benetau	Love & affection	
May 13, 1787 Marguillers of Assumption Church to Charles Renau	4 x 40 arpents recently given to church by the Huron Indians	7,600 lb. flour	Sold by auction
Sept. 8, 1787 Louis Payet to Assumption Church	3 x 40 arpents—part of a concession of 6 arpents made in 1782 by the Hurons to F. X. Hubert and Sisters of the Congregation. On May 4, 1787, at Montreal the Sisters ceded land to F. X. Hubert, Coadjutor Bishop of Quebec, who gave authority to Louis Payet who now gives the land to the Church of Our Lady of the Assumption. [Louis Payet came from Quebec to Detroit in 1787 to become pastor at St. Anne's Church. The bishop used this occasion to effect the transfer of property from the Sisters to the church. The land later became the Pajot farm on the western side of Huron Line]		

APPENDIX IV (continued)

NAME	DESCRIPTION	PRICE	REMARKS
Feb. 10, 1788 Joseph Drouillard to James Abbott	3 x 40 arpents minus three lots N.E. Wm. Macomb, s.w. Alexis Carrie	£88 N.Y. curr.	
Feb. 16, 1788 John Askin to Antoine Bouffar	3 x 40 arpents at Petite Côte N.E. Louis Suzor, s.w. Widow Rousseau	400 bushels of wheat & 40 bushels of oats	
May 6, 1788 Chippewas & Ottawas to James Allan, Wm. Caldwell, & J. Caldwell			11 miles by six miles north of Lake Erie beginning at lot 1 of land already inhabited by planters for 999 years renewable, three bushels of Indian corn annually or value thereof
May 1, 1788 Chippewas & Ottawas to Thomas McKee			Point Pelee Island for 999 years renewable, three bushels of Indian corn annually or value thereof
June 20, 1788 Louis Suzor to Martin Durocher	3 x 40 arpents at Petite Côte N.E. Antoine Bouffard, s.w. Antoine Bouffard	5,000 livres	
Aug. 8, 1787 Widow Tourangeau to François Latour	½ arpent square N.E. Monforton, s.w. Pouget	400 livres	
Oct. 19, 1788 William Scott to Philip Fox	3 x 40 arpents at Petite Côte E.N.E. George Forsyth, w.s.w. J. B. Drouillard	£230 N.Y. curr.	
June 6, 1789 James Donaldson to Gervais Houdienne	3 x 40 arpents at Petite Côte N.N.E. Louis Bourassa, s.s.w. Wm. Monforton	£150	

[332]

APPENDIX IV (*continued*)

NAME	DESCRIPTION	PRICE	REMARKS
July 23, 1789 John Cornwall to John Sparkman	Lot 97 at New Settlement, Lake Erie, and appurtenances	£209 N.Y. curr.	Appurtenances include dwelling house, one stable, crop, stock and utensils. Itemized account: 5 acres of corn planted; one acre of potatoes; one acre of turnips, 4 axes; 2 hoes; 8 pewter dishes, one tea kettle. One year-old stear; 30 hogs, one bateau; one rifle gun
Aug. 29, 1789 Estate of J. B. Drouillard to James Allan	3 x 40 arpents at Petite Côte minus lot 1 x 4 acres; E.N.E. Philip Fox, w.s.w. Joseph Bondy	£52 N.Y. curr., at auction	
Feb. 16, 1790 Edward Eazel of *Fredericksburg* sold the following stock to Jacques Baby for £50; six cows; one heifer; one sow and eight pigs, one grey horse.			
June 8, 1790 Matthew Dolsen to Henry Botsford	3 x 40 arpents at Petite Côte E.N.E. Isaac Dolsen, w.s.w. Judge Wm. Powell	£260 N.Y. curr.	
Sept. 25, 1792 Louis Bourassa to Pierre Boisnie	2 x 50 arpents N.E. François Beneteau, s.w. Charles Cloutier	1760 livres (£113 6s. 8d.)	
[After 1790 the transfers of property on the Canadian side of the Detroit River were subject to the Land Board of Hesse. However a few records found their way to the Register and are now reproduced in skeleton form.]			
p. 384, April 12, 1791 Simon Drouillard to J. B. Feré	Water mill on Turkey Creek including house, buildings equipment & lands connected with the operation of the mill		1,200 lbs. flour per year during the lifetime of Mr. & Mrs. S. Drouillard. On death of one, the payment will be reduced to 600 lbs. flour per yr.

[333]

APPENDIX IV (*continued*)

NAME	DESCRIPTION	PRICE	REMARKS
p. 392, Nov. 19, 1791 (registered March 17, 1792) Charles Bouron & wife, Marguerite Reaume to Suzanne Reaume, widow of Duperon Baby	2 x 40 arpents N.E. J. B. Tourneux *dit* Janet, s.w. André Benitau *dit* Labalaine, rear—J. B. Bruyère		Ceded on condition of the following yearly payments to provide a livelihood for Mr. and Mrs. Bouron: 1,000 lbs. flour 1 bushel salt 300 lbs. pork 1 milch cow & feed for winter 20 cords wood 3 barrels apples from orchard 12 lbs. candles 6 gallons rum 12 lbs. soap 12 lbs. grain 40 lbs. sugar 12 lbs. coffee 4 lbs. tea The whole to be reduced by half upon the death of either Mr. or Mrs. Bouron. In that event the grantee shall pay for the burial, funeral services and anniversary service
p. 396, Jan. 28, 1795 J. B. Chapoton, Jr. to Pierre Casarvan *dit* Ladebauche	3½ x 40 arpents between Antoine Labadie *alias* Badichon & Louis Villaire *alias* St. Louis	£291 13s. 4d.	

[334]

APPENDIX V

Genealogies*

Bondy

THOMAS DOUAIRE DE BONDY, born in 1636 in the parish of St. Germain, in Auxerre, France, came to Canada, and married at Quebec on July 26, 1656, Marguerite de Chauvigny.

JOSEPH DOUAIRE DE BONDY (third generation), born in 1733, married at Detroit on August 7, 1758, Marie Josephine Gamelin. Joseph was a trader.

THEIR CHILDREN

JOSEPH, born at Detroit in 1759, married there on October 8, 1781, Jeanne Meloche, daughter of Pierre Meloche and Marie Catherine Guignard.

GABRIEL, born at Detroit, October 23, 1762, married (A) on November 19, 1787, Marie Archange Pageot, daughter of Thomas Pageot and Marie Louise Villers *dit* St. Louis.

LAURENT, born (A) March 21, 1771, married (A) on November 21, 1791, Madeleine Pageot, daughter of Thomas Pageot and Marie Louise Villers *dit* St. Louis. Laurent was a captain of the militia.

CHARLES, born (A) April 6, 1784, married (A) on June 6, 1809, Archange Meloche, daughter of Jacques Meloche and Marie Joseph Bernard. Both the bride and the groom resided in Amherstburg.

Drouillard

SIMON DROUILLARD *dit* ARGENTCOUR, born at Marenne, diocese of Xaintes, France, came to Canada and married at Quebec on November 25, 1698, Marguerite Feret.

JEAN (second generation), born at St. François, Isle Orléans, February 14, 1707, married at Lachine on February 5, 1731, Elizabeth Rapin. They later settled at Detroit, where Jean died before 1756.

THEIR CHILDREN

JEAN BAPTISTE, born 1732, married at Detroit on February 25, 1754, Marie Charlotte Bigras *dit* Fauvel.

SIMON AMABLE, born at Montreal, March 4, 1734, married at Soulanges on August 29, 1757, Marguerite Martin *dit* St. Jean. Simon married (second) at Detroit on May 14, 1804, Marie Meny, widow of Jean B. Billiau *dit* Lesperance.

*Adapted from Denissen's Genealogies in the Burton Historical Collection and from the Registers of Assumption Church. The titles represent the French surnames that appear most frequently in Essex County family lists of this year (1958). (A) = Assumption Parish

MARIE ELIZABETH, born in 1735, married at Detroit on January 7, 1751, Jean Vallée *dit* Versailles, a soldier born in 1731. Marie married (second) Pierre Desnoyers (widower of Marie Louise Le Duc).

CATHERINE, born in 1737, married at Detroit on July 10, 1758, Jean B. Dubreuil.

FRANÇOIS, born in 1740, married (A) on January 13, 1766, Marie Anne Villers *dit* St. Louis, daughter of Louis Villers *dit* St. Louis and Marie Joseph Morin (Morand).

JOSEPH, born 1742, married (A) on September 23, 1771, Marie Joseph Godfroy *dit* St. Georges.

PIERRE, born in 1744, married at Detroit on November 20, 1776, Marie Angelique Descomps *dit* Labadie. Pierre was an official interpreter of the Huron language.

DUPUIS

FRANÇOIS DUPUIS, born in 1634 in the parish of St. Laurent at Morre, in the diocese of Limoges, France, came to Canada, and married at Quebec on October 6, 1670, Georgette Richer.

CHARLES DUPUIS (fourth generation), born at Laprairie December 10, 1728, married at Detroit on November 8, 1762, Marguerite Catherine Casse *dit* St. Aubin, daughter of Pierre Casse and Marguerite Fourneau *dit* Brindamour. Charles was buried at Detroit on August 31, 1767.

CHARLES, their son, born in 1763, is the only Dupuis baptism at Assumption Church in the eighteenth century, and there is no record of him marrying there. Another branch of the family came in the second decade of the next century, but that is beyond the scope of the present work.

LANGLOIS

NICOLAS LANGLOIS, born in 1640 in the parish of St. Pierre in the diocese of Rouen, France, came to Canada and married at Quebec October 26, 1671, Elizabeth Crétel.

NICOLAS (fourth generation), born at Cap Santé January 5, 1729, married at Detroit on September 7, 1761, Madeleine Pilet, daughter of Jacques Pilet and Marguerite Viau.

THEIR CHILDREN

JEAN BAPTISTE, born at Detroit in 1762, married (A) on January 13, 1789, Charlotte Réaume, daughter of Bonaventure Réaume and Jeanne Deshêtres.

JOSEPH, born at la Côte des Hurons July 18, 1763, married (A) on July 22, 1793, Marie Joseph Pageot, daughter of Jean Thomas Pageot and Marie Louise Villers *dit* St. Louis.

ALEXIS, born on the south shore December 8, 1765, married (A) on January 21, 1788, Louise Bissonet. Alexis married (second) (A) on February 8, 1808, Angélique Vessière *dit* Laferté (widow of Nicolas Janis), daughter of Louis Vessière *dit* Laferté and Catherine Esprit *dit* Champagne.

NICOLAS, born on the south shore May 19, 1767, married at Detroit on September 25, 1792, Marie Angélique Meloche, daughter of Jean Baptiste Meloche and Marie Louise Robert.

ANGÉLIQUE REINE, born (A) January 6, 1771, married (A) on October 9, 1786, Hippolyte Janis, son of Nicolas Janis and Thérèse Meloche.

ANTOINE (fourth generation), born at Cap Santé January 24, 1738, married (A) on March 19, 1773, Marie Desanges Rochereau *dit* Lespérance, daughter of Joseph Rochereau and Catherine Pilet.

THEIR CHILDREN

MARIE DESANGES, born (A) in 1773, married (A) on June 10, 1793, Pierre Chêne *dit* Labutte, son of Pierre Chêne and Marie Anne Cuillerier.

ANTOINE, born (A) July 18, 1774, married (A) on February 19, 1811, Charlotte Villers *dit* St. Louis, daughter of Pierre Villers and Charlotte Mouton.

JEANETTE, born (A) May 7, 1788, married (A) on February 9, 1808, François Pratt, son of François Pratt and Elizabeth Parent.

NICOLAS, birthdate unknown, married (A) on February 25, 1811, Julia Dequindre.

ALEXIS, born (A) November 15, 1783, married (A) on February 5, 1811, Susanne Parent, daughter of Jacques Parent and Catherine Beaubien.

JULIEN, born (A) February 9, 1786, married (A) on February 17, 1824, Rosalie Parent, daughter of Julien Parent and Susanne Meloche.

VICTOIRE, born (A) May 16, 1788, married (A) on March 5, 1810, Alexis Parent, son of Jacques Parent and Catherine Beaubien.

JOSEPH, born (A) October 22, 1790, married (A) on November 26, 1823, Félicité Malbœuf *dit* Beausoleil.

ANGÉLIQUE, born (A) October 27, 1795, married (A) on January 14, 1817, Laurent Parent, son of Julien Parent and Susanne Meloche.

MARENTETTE

NICOLAS GODET *dit* MARENTETTE, born in 1583 in the parish of St. Martin of Ige, in the diocese of Seez, in Perche, France, came to Canada with his family. In latter part of his life he resided at Montreal.

JACQUES GODET, his son, born at Montreal October 13, 1673, married at Three Rivers on November 4, 1698, Marguerite Duguay *dit* Marentette. Jacques was in Detroit on business in 1707.

THEIR CHILDREN

JACQUES GODET *dit* MARENTETTE, born at Montreal August 22, 1699, married before Father de La Richardie, Jesuit missionary of the Huron Indians, at Bois Blanc Island in the Detroit River, on August 15, 1743, Louise Marguerite Geneviève Baudry *dit* Desbuttes *dit* St. Martin. The marriage is recorded in Ste. Anne's Church Register.

Dominic Godet *dit* Marentette, born at Montreal January 25, 1705, married there on November 28, 1739, Marie Anne Françoise Cuillerier *dit* Beaubien.

François Godet *dit* Marentette, born at Montreal March 6, 1720, married at Detroit on September 8, 1755, Jeanne Parent, daughter of Laurent Parent and Jeanne Cardinal. In 1765 François was a lieutenant of the militia.

THE CHILDREN OF FRANÇOIS GODET AND JEANNE PARENT

François, born at Detroit November 10, 1756, married (A) on May 13, 1782, Marguerite Bernier.

Marie Louise, born (A) April 16, 1759, married (A) on May 16, 1776, François Berthelet. Marie Louise married (second) (A) on September 23, 1782, Antoine Ignace Dufresne.

Dominic François, born (A) May 16, 1763, married (A) on October 20, 1788, Marie Louise Archange Navarre, daughter of Robert Navarre and Marie Louise Marsac *dit* Durocher.

Jacques, born (A) July 16, 1768, married (A) on January 19, 1795, Geneviève Réaume, daughter of Claude Réaume and Geneviève Janis.

Laurent, born (A) August 10, 1769, married (A) on October 10, 1797, Marie Louise Chêne *dit* Labutte, daughter of Pierre Chêne *dit* Labutte and Marie Anne Cuillerier *dit* Beaubien.

Pierre, born (A) March 17, 1776, married (A) on July 22, 1828, Marie Josette Villers *dit* St. Louis, widow of Laurent Réaume.

Françoise, born (A) August 4, 1786, married (A) on January 7, 1812, Philippe Jacques Le Duc.

André, born (A) October 25, 1784, married (A) on January 28, 1817, Catherine Borel.

Meloche

François Meloche, born in the parish of Notre-Dame, in the city of Cogne, in the diocese of La Rochelle, France, came to Canada, and married at Montreal on October 25, 1700, Marie Mouflet.

Pierre, their son, born at Montreal September 1, 1701, married at Lachine on August 16, 1729, Jeanne Caron, daughter of Vital Caron and Marie Perthuis. Pierre moved to Detroit shortly after his marriage.

THEIR CHILDREN

Pierre, born at Detroit November 2, 1730, married there on June 10, 1754, Marie Catherine Guignard *dit* St. Etienne, daughter of Pierre Guignard and Marie Joseph Lebœuf.

Thérèse, born February 25, 1732, married at Detroit on January 7, 1750, Nicolas François Janis.

François, born at Detroit May 19, 1733, married there on November 4, 1755, Marie Françoise Lauson, daughter of Nicolas Lauson and Louise Chauvin. François moved to the south shore about 1782.

Marie Catherine, born March 2, 1737, married (third) (A) on February 7, 1764, André Peltier.

MARIE JOSEPH, born June 30, 1739, married at Detroit on January 13, 1755, François Rochereau *dit* Lespérance. They later moved to the south shore.
ANTOINE JEAN, born at Detroit September 16, 1744, married there on April 27, 1767, Marie Louise Campau. Antoine married (second) (A) on November 28, 1793, Reine Angélique Guillet *dit* Tourangeau, widow of Antoine Soumande.

OUELLETTE

RENÉ OUELLET[TE], born in the parish of St. Jacques, of Hautpas, in the diocese of Paris, France, came to Canada and married at Quebec on March 8, 1666, Anne Rivet.
JEAN BAPTISTE (fourth generation), born at Kamouraska November 3, 1737, settled at the Detroit River in 1762, and married on January 7, 1765, Jeanne Susanne Putelle then residing at la Côte des Hurons.

THEIR CHILDREN

JEAN BAPTISTE, born (A) May 20, 1766, married (A) on February 19, 1787, Geneviève Ouellette. Jean Baptiste married (second) (A) on January 18, 1803, Geneviève Janis, daughter of François Janis and Geneviève Deslières *dit* Bonvouloir.
FRANÇOIS, born (A) January 19, 1769, married (A) on November 3, 1795, Cecelia Chauvin, daughter of Noël Chauvin and Jeanne Meloche.
CHARLES, born (A) April 13, 1774, married (A) on February 11, 1801, Marie Marguerite Dumouchel, daughter of Vital Dumouchel and Madeleine Goyeau.

PARENT

PIERRE PARENT, born in 1610 in the parish of Mortagne in La Perche, France, came to Canada and married there on February 9, 1654, Jeanne Bedeau.
LAURENT (fourth generation), born at Montreal February 28, 1703, moved to Detroit and married there on May 24, 1731, Marie Joseph Douzet. Laurent married (second) on July 27, 1734, Jeanne Cardinal. Laurent was a carpenter and joiner by trade.

CHILDREN OF LAURENT PARENT AND JEANNE CARDINAL

JEANNE, born at Detroit April 23, 1739, married there on September 8, 1755, François Gaudet *dit* Marentette.
LAURENT, born at Detroit September 13, 1740, married (A) on November 28, 1771, Marie Madeleine Janis, daughter of Nicolas François Janis and Thérèse Meloche.
JACQUES, born at Detroit October 24, 1742, married there on November 18, 1771, Marie Catherine Cuillerier *dit* Beaubien. They settled at la Côte des Outaouais.
ELIZABETH, born at Detroit October 17, 1747, married (A) François Pratt on December 2, 1744.

JULIEN, born at Detroit August 6, 1755, married (A) on April 20, 1784, Susanne Meloche, daughter of François Meloche and Marie Françoise Lauson.

AGATHE, born at Detroit September 8, 1759, married (A) on October 23, 1783, Jean Baptiste Le Tourneux. Jean Baptiste was known in the community by his diminutive Christian name Jeannet (Johnnie) which appellation was corrupted into "Janette," and this became the family name of his descendants. He located on a farm where now is Janette Avenue in the city of Windsor, Ontario.

RÉAUME

RENÉ RÉAUME, born in 1643 at Congé, in the diocese of Rochelle, married Marie Chevreau, and came to Canada.

PIERRE (second generation), born at Charlesbourg July 28, 1691, married at Québec in 1722 Marie Thérèse Estève *dit* Lajeunesse. They settled at Detroit that same year. Pierre died at Detroit in 1740.

THEIR CHILDREN

MARIE-THÉRÈSE, born at Detroit January 10, 1723, married at Montreal on February 17, 1738, Joseph Charbonneau.

MARGUERITE, born at Detroit July 3, 1725, married there on January 7, 1756, Charles Bouron, born at Laprairie.

PIERRE *dit* THÉMUS, born at Detroit August 28, 1727, married there on January 7, 1754, Marie Joseph Pilet, daughter of Jacques Pilet and Marguerite Viau. Pierre *dit* Thémus married (second) at Montreal on August 22, 1763, Marie Catherine Dubois.

Another branch of the Réaume family, the children of Robert Réaume (second generation) and Elizabeth Brunet of Lachine, also came to Detroit. Robert is very likely the Robert Réaume who conducted Madame Cadillac and Madame de Tonti from Montreal to Detroit in the fall of 1701.

HYACINTHE (third generation), born at Lachine March 25, 1704, married at Montreal on November 17, 1727, Agathe Lacelle. Hyacinthe, a shoemaker by trade, brought his family to Detroit in 1733.

THEIR CHILDREN

MARIE-ANNE AGATHE, born at Montreal September 16, 1730, married at Detroit on February 14, 1751, Joseph Poupard.

JOSEPH, born at Detroit, November 2, 1739, married at Boucherville on July 7, 1766, Marie Charlotte Levasseur *dit* Carmel. They came to Detroit that same year, and later settled at Petite Côte.

JEAN BAPTISTE, born at Detroit July 9, 1741, married there on December 20, 1763, Agathe Lootman *dit* Barrois. The father of the bride opposed the marriage. His consent was necessary according to French law, but Major Gladwin requested Father Bocquet to proceed with the marriage, assuring him that according to English law and custom the parent's consent was not required. The pastor followed the usage of England "à laquelle il a plu à la divine Providence de nous assujetir" (Ste. Anne's Register).

APPENDIX V 341

MARIE-ANNE, born at Detroit February 15, 1746, married there on October 21, 1765, Pierre Baron *dit* Lupien.

MARIE JULIE, born at Detroit January 22, 1748, married there in 1764 Jehu Hay, Lieutenant of British troops, later Lieutenant-Governor of Detroit.

CHARLES, born at Detroit February 4, 1743, married Angélique Beauchamp. He passed practically his entire career serving as interpreter in the Indian Department. Later he settled at the mouth of the Detroit River in Malden Township.

PIERRE (another son of Robert Réaume and Elizabeth Brunet), born at Lachine October 6, 1709, married at Detroit on January 20, 1738, Susanne Hubert *dit* Lacroix.

THEIR CHILDREN

CHARLOTTE, born at Detroit June 18, 1738, married there on November 4, 1760, Pierre Charles Daneau de Muy, son of the former commandant at Detroit.

SUSANNE, born at Detroit September 12, 1740, married there on November 23, 1760, Jacques Baby *dit* Duperon, born at Montreal January 4, 1731.

CLAUDE THOMAS, born at Detroit August 7, 1743, married (A) on January 7, 1766, Geneviève Janis, daughter of Nicolas François Janis and Thérèse Meloche. They settled at la Côte des Outaouais.

VÉRONIQUE, born at Detroit February 2, 1745, married (A) on July 26, 1764, Gabriel Christophe Legrand, widower of Marie M. Chapoton.

BONAVENTURE, born at Detroit January 28, 1746, married (A) on January 6, 1767, Jeanne Deshêtres. They settled at la Côte des Outaouais.

MARIE LOUISE, born March 8, 1750, married (A) July 16, 1770, Alexis Cuillerier *dit* Beaubien. She married (second) (A) on March 7, 1791, Jean B. Guillet *dit* Tourangeau, son of Jean B. and Marie Pilote.

RENAUD

GUILLAUME RENAUD, born in the parish of St. Jovinus in the city of Rouen, France, came to Canada and married at Quebec on November 27, 1668, Marie de La Mare. They settled at Charlesbourg.

CHARLES (fourth generation), born at Charlesbourg, November 5, 1736, married (A) July 12, 1773, Marie Madeleine Bertrand, born at Soulanges, August 31, 1759.

THEIR CHILDREN

MARIE MADELEINE, born (A) August 24, 1774, married (A) on February 3, 1794, Jean B. Robidou.

ETIENNE, born (A) January 5, 1776, married (A) on November 17, 1794, Thérèse Bénéteau, born (A) October 15, 1778, daughter of François Bénéteau and Françoise Gagnon. Thérèse was likely one of the two Bénéteau girls who attended the first classes at Assumption in 1786.

CHARLES, born (A) January 5, 1776, married (A) on January 8, 1798, Angelique Dufour, daughter of Jean B. Dufour and Catherine Durand *dit* Montmirel.

FRANÇOIS, birthdate unknown, married (A) on August 27, 1805, Marie Josephine Meloche, daughter of Pierre Meloche and Catherine Campau.

JEAN BAPTISTE, born (A) April 20, 1780, married (A) April 15, 1799, Marie Joseph Martin *dit* Beaulieu, born at Post Vincennes in 1781.

JEAN, born (A) May 22, 1783, married (A) November 22, 1808, Geneviève Meloche, daughter of Pierre Meloche and Catherine Campau.

LOUIS, born (A) February 13, 1785, married (A) October 25, 1814, Marie-Anne Réaume, widow of Etienne Meloche, daughter of Joseph Réaume and Charlotte Levasseur.

ARCHANGE, born (A) October 18, 1786, married (A) June 30, 1801, Joseph Grondin.

JOSEPH, born (A) July 29, 1788, married (A) on February 6, 1815, Louise Quevillon.

MARIE LOUISE, born (A) June 26, 1792, married (A) on January 7, 1812, Jean B. Bertrand of Amherstburg.

ANTOINE, born (A) January 17, 1794, married (A) on June 10, 1822, Archange Bourassa.

APPENDIX VI

SUMMARY OF THE MARRIAGES RECORDED IN THE PARISH OF THE ASSUMPTION 1760–81*

SAMPLE COPY IN EXTENSO

L'an de notre Seigneur mil sept cent soixante et quatre, le dix-neuf de novembre, après la publication de trois bancs, par trois dimanches consecutifs, entre Charles Bernier, fils d'André Bernier et de Françoise Larivière, ses père et mère, de la paroisse de Charles-bourg d'une part; et de Marie Louise Gaudet, fille de Jacques Gaudet et de Marie Louise Desbutes, ses père et mère, de la paroisse de Sainte Anne du Detroit, et ne s'étant trouvé aucun empechement; je sousigné, missionaire des Hurons à la pointe de Montreal, certifie avoir reçu leur mutuel consentement, et leur ai donné la benediction nuptiale en présence de Jean Bapt. Tourangeau, de Charles Courtois, Jean Bapt. du Berger qui ont signés avec moi.
        Pi Potier M.J.
  Jean Baptiste Touranjeau, P. Charles Courtois
        duberge

TRANSLATION

In the year of Our Lord one thousand seven hundred and sixty-four, on the nineteenth of November, after having published the three banns on three successive Sundays, between Charles Bernier, son of André Bernier and of Françoise Larivière, his parents from the parish of Charles-bourg of the first part; and of Marie Louise Gaudet, daughter of Jacques Gaudet and Marie Louise Desbutes, her parents from the parish of Ste. Anne of Detroit of the second part, and no impediment having been made known; I undersigned, priest of the Company of Jesus, missionary of the Hurons at La Pointe de Montreal, certify that I have received their mutual consent, and that I have given them the nuptial blessing in the presence of Jean Bapt. Tourangeau, of Charles Courtois, and Jean Bapt. du Berger who have signed with me.
        Pi Potier M.J.
  Jean Baptiste Touranjeau, P. Charles Courtois
        duberge

[After October 1767 the clause "missionary of the Hurons at La Pointe de Montreal" was changed to "exercising the office of pastor in the Church of the Assumption at La Pointe de Montreal de Detroit." Records for 1782–6 were published in Ontario Historical Society, *Papers and Records*, VII (1906).]

*From Archives of Assumption Church, Windsor, Ontario.

Appendix VI (*continued*)

DATE	CONTRACTING PARTIES	PARENTS	PARISH OF PARENTS	WITNESSES
1760 May	Franc. Morin *dit* Valcour Magdelene Bouron			+Jean Bapt. Ro +Pi. Desnoyers +Jean Bapt. Girou +Charles LaMare +Jean Bapt. La Pointe
1764 Nov. 19	Charles Bernier Marie Louise Gaudet	André Bernier François Larivière Jacques Gaudet Marie Louise Desbutes	Charlesbourg Ste. Anne of Detroit	Jean Bapt. Touranjeau P. Charles Courtois dubergé
1765 Jan. 7	Charles Dominique Janson Marie Anne Binau	Charles Janson Geneviève Filiau Louis Binau Magdeleine Levrau	Quebec Montreal	Gabriel Paillez +Andre Benetau
Jan. 7	Jean Bapt. Goilette Susanne Patene	Jean Goilette Marie Terdi N. Patene Marie M. Bouron	Camouraska Ste. Anne of Detroit	+François Janis +Joseph Maillou +Michel Vaudri +Benj. LeBel
June 24	Jean Bapt. Ro Marie Jeanne Prudhomme	Joseph Ro Joseph. Lacroix François Prudhomme Judith Cuillerier	Cap de la Madelaine La Chine	Louis Jadot +J. B. Tourenjeau +Charles LaMare Robert Thibault +Etienne La Violette
July 15	Charles Gravelle Marie Jos. Dutau	Charles Gravelle Marie Anne Guérin Jean Bapt. Dutau Marie N.	Beaupré	Jean B. Touranjeau Charles Janson +Michael Vaudri +Charles La Mare
1766 Jan. 7	Claude Réaume Geneviève Janis	Pierre Réaume Susanne Lacroix François Janis Thérèse Meloche	Ste. Anne of Detroit Ste. Anne of Detroit	Claude Gouin Louis Jadot +Pierre Desnoyers +Joseph Maillou

APPENDIX VI (*continued*)

DATE	CONTRACTING PARTIES	PARENTS	PARISH OF PARENTS	WITNESSES
1766				
Jan. 13	François de Rouillard Marie Anne Villers	Jean B. de Rouillard Elizabeth Rapin Louis Villers Marie Jos. Morin	Rivière des Prairies Ste. Anne of Detroit	+Pierre Lajoie +Amable St. Etienne +Charles La Mare +Jean B. LeBeau
Feb. 3	Etienne LaViolette Judith Prudhomme	Jacques LaViolette Marie A. Des Lauriers François Prudhomme Judith Cuillerier	La Pointe de Levi Montreal	+Pierre Javrai +Charles La Mare +Joseph Bordeau +Louis Suzor
April 8	Louis Suzor Marie Jos. LeBeau	François Suzor Charlotte Coture Francois LeBeau Josette Bigras	St. Thomas This parish	+Pierre Prou +François Choisi +Etienne Jacob +Ignace Belanger
May 26	François LeBeau Marie Jos. Binau	Jean B. LeBeau Catherin Dudevoir Louis Binau Marie M. Levrau	Montreal La Chine	Louis Jadot Jean B. Touranjeau +Francois Rochelot +Etienne Jacob
June 7	Simon Gendron Géneviève Vanier	Jacques Gendron Marie Guion Jacques Vanier Charlotte Chamar	Ste. André dioc. Poitiers St. Michel	J. H. Cabasie Cicot Bienvenu Isidore Chêne
1767				
Jan. 7	Bonaventure Réaume Jeanne Deshetres	Pierre Réaume Susanne Hubert Antolne Deshetres Charlotte Chevalier	Ste. Anne of Detroit Ste. Anne of Detroit	+Guillaume Goyau +Laurent Parent +Augustin Boulet
May 11	Thomas Pajot Marie Louise Villers	Thomas Pajot Marie M. Gervais Louis Villers Marie Jos. Morin	Charlesbourg Ste. Anne of Detroit	+Francois Langlois +Louis Montmeni +Jean Louis Reveau Pierre Meloche
July 8	Antoine Rivard Felicité Ste-Marie	Antoine Rivard Marie Jos. Trottier Joseph Ste-Marie Marie Louise Piélalu	Batiscan La Prairie	Dominque Labrosse +Louison St. Sauveur Joseph Ste-Marie

APPENDIX VI (*continued*)

DATE	CONTRACTING PARTIES	PARENTS	PARISH OF PARENTS	WITNESSES
1768				
Jan. 23	Jacques Charron Jeanne Belleperche	Jacques Charron Marie La Pointe Pierre Belleperche Marie Campeau	Boucherville Ste. Anne of Detroit	+Rene Theodore.Du Roseau +Antoine Boufar
Feb. 9	Jean Saliot Marie M. Jourdain	Jean Saliot N. Jean Jourdain Marie Jos. Réaume	Ste. Servan of St. Malo La Baye	+Charles Bouron +François Janis +Joseph Du Saux Joseph Desbuttes
Feb. 15	Charles Fontaine Elizabeth Godefroi	Charles Fontaine Marie A. Godebeau François Godefroi Susanne Pepin	Ste. Jean of L'Ile d'Orleans Ste. Anne of Detroit	Gregor MackGregor +Etienne Langeron +Zacharie Cloutier Jean B. Foucher François Robert
Feb. 15	Louis Montmeni Agathe Prudhomme	Joseph Montmeni Angelique Forque François Prudhomme Agathe Cuillerier	St. Michel Ste. Anne of Detroit	+Charles Renaud +François Langlois +Pierre Prou Jena B. Touranjeau
June 16	Guillaume Daperon ...... Clairmont	Louis Clairmont M. Louise Bouron	Ste. Anne of Detroit	François Gaudet Pierre Meloche
Aug. 31	Pierre Tamisier Marie Jos. Morin (widow of Louis Villers *dit* St. Louis)	Jean Tamisier Pierre Morin Marie Jos. Donel	Dalman in dioc. of Perigueux St. Sulpice, Montreal	Guillaume Daperon Joseph Desbuttes
Nov. 21	Michel Vaudri Marie Jos. Tourangeau	Michel Vaudri François Lebœuf Jean B. Tourangeau Marie Jos. Pilote	La Walterie dioc. Quebec Quebec	Pierre Des Vaux Pierre Meloche +Joseph Du Sault

APPENDIX VI (*continued*)

DATE	CONTRACTING PARTIES	PARENTS	PARISH OF PARENTS	WITNESSES
1769 Jan. 2	Etienne Jacob Madeleine Godet	....Godet Marie L. Desbuttes	 Ste. Anne of Detroit	Tourangeau La France +Michael Vaudri +Charles Fontaine
1769 Jan. 7	Louis C. Brugiere Marg. Makons	......Makons Ottawa Woman	Ste. Anne of Detroit	Laframboise Nicolas Lenoir +Charles Fontaine
1770 Feb. 5	François Langlois Marie M. Prudhomme	François Langlois Thérèse Bertran Francois Prudhomme Judith Cuillerier	Cap Santé dioc. Quebec Assumption of Detroit	+Charles Renaud +Francois Choisi +Pierre Prou +Jean B. Fagnan
Feb. 12	Jean B. Paré Marguerite Le Beau	Louis Paré Josette Guai Rene Le Beau Marg. La Durantaie	Saint Joachim dioc. Quebec Assumption of Detroit	+J. B. Bigra Joseph Poupar +J. B. Le Beau
Feb. 12	François Choisi Marie Jos. Revau	Jean B. Choisi Jean Louis Revau Marie Jos. St. Etienne	Saint Thomas dioc. Quebec Assumption of Detroit	+Pierre Beaufort +Charles Fontaine +Charles Renaud +J. B. Lantailla Pierre Meloche
March 19	Jean B. Cuillerier (Beaubien) Genevieve Parent	Jean B. Cuillerier (Beaubien) Marie Anne Lotman (Baroi) Laurent Parent Jeanne Cardinal	Assumption of Detroit Assumption of Detroit	P. Dejean A. Barthe Charles Desjardin Ignace Painsoneau
July 16	Alexis Cuillerier Louise Réaume	Antoine Cuillerier Marie A. Girard Pierre Réaume Susanne Hubert	Ste. Anne of Detroit This parish	Medard Gamelin Wm. Sterling James Sterling

[347]

APPENDIX VI (*continued*)

DATE	CONTRACTING PARTIES	PARENTS	PARISH OF PARENTS	WITNESSES
July 22	René Theodore (Duroseau) Jeanne Villers	Antoine Duroseau Louise Marchand Louis Villers Josette Morin	Assumption of Detroit This parish	Baubien A. Barthe Simon Drouillard
1770 Sept. 5	Jean B. Durand Marie Crépeau	...... Durand .... Crépeau ...... Pertuis	Dioc. Quebec Ste. Anne of Detroit	Charles Courtois fils Charles Chesne Joseph Baron Baubin P. Descomps Labady
1771 March 2	Joseph Mainville Charlotte LeDuc	François Mainville Marie Paradis Pierre LeDuc Charlotte (Indian woman)	Rivière Ouelle dioc. Quebec This parish	+Philipe LeDuc +Joseph Mailou Charles Bouron +François Janis
Sept. 23	Joseph de Rouillard Josette Godefroi	Jean B. de Rouillard Elizabeth Rapin Francois Godefroi Susanne Papin	Des Cèdres Ste. Anne of Detroit	+J. B. De Rouillard Simon de Rouillard Philipe Belanger Dauphin +Jean B. Paré François de Rouillard +Guill. Goyau
Nov. 25	Joseph Valade Therese Binau	Charles Valade Geneviève Pilon Louis Binau Marie M. Levrau	Ste. Anne, Isle of Montreal Assumption of Detroit	Charles Lapalme +Charles Binau +François Jouet +André Pelletier +Jean B. Paré +Francois Le Beau
Nov. 28	Laurent Parent Marie M. Janis	Laurent Parent Jeanne Cardinal François Janis Thérèse Meloche	Ste. Anne of Detroit Assumption of Detroit	Beaubien père Dominique Labrosse

Appendix VI (*continued*)

DATE	CONTRACTING PARTIES	PARENTS	PARISH OF PARENTS	WITNESSES
1772				
Oct. 31	Pierre Becquet	Pierre Becquet Geneviève Ganier	St. Michel	Charles Courtois fils Pierre Gamelin
	Catherine Potier *dit* L'Ardoise	Charles Potier *dit* L'Ardoise Catherine Lavigne	Montreal	+Riopel
1773				
March 14	Antoine Langlois	....		+Faverau
	Marie Rochelot	Joseph Rochelot	Detroit	+Pierre Javerai
1773				
May 17	Joseph Valcour	Pierre Valcour Marie Claire	Rivière du sud	Charles Bouron Rene Laprise
	Josette Makons	Baptiste Makons	This parish	+Charles Odienne +Joseph Maillou
June 14	Louis Brouillet	Louis Brouillet Elizabeth Du Lude	Varennes	Vital Dumouchelle Philipe Belanger
	Louise Desnoyers	Pierre Desnoyers Marie L. Le Duc	Ste. Anne of Detroit	+Jean B. Pelletier
June 30	Alexis L'Oranger (Maisonville)	Alexis L'Oranger Charlotte Mogrin	Batiscan	Adhemar St. Martin Cicot fils
	Marguerite Joncair (Chabert)	Daniel Joncair (Sieur de Chabert) Marguerite Robert de la Morandière	Montreal	
July 12	Charles Renaud	Charles Renaud Elizabeth Garnau	Charlesbourg	+L'Antailla Louis Villers
	Marie M. Bertran	Jean B. Bertran Marie M. Martin	Soulanges	+Grenon +P. Deslauriers
Sept. 5	Jean B. LaPointe	Joseph La Pointe Charlotte La Violette	St. Jean (Ile d'Orleans)	Charles Bouron +Louis Bernard *dit* Lajoye
	Catherine Goiau	Jean B. Goiau Lisette Deslieres	This parish	+Etienne La Violette +Pierre Javerai *dit* La Deroute

[349]

APPENDIX VI (*continued*)

DATE	CONTRACTING PARTIES	PARENTS	PARISH OF PARENTS	WITNESSES
Oct. 23	Joseph La Pointe Marie L. (panise)	Joseph La Pointe Marie L. Lavallée	Mille-Iles	+Jean B. Bertrand +Charles Leverd +Charles Lapalme
Nov. 22	Vital Dumouchelle Marie M. Goiau	Louis Dumouchelle Louise Leclerc Jean B. Goiau Marie L. Deslieres	Montreal This parish	Dominque Labrosse Vital Goiau +Joseph DuSaux +Jos. Dumouchelle +Louis Goiau etc.
1774 Jan. 10	Jean B. Lantailla Marie C. Bergeron	Augusti Lantailla Marie Charron Simon Bergeron Marie C. Le Beau	Bertier	+Charles Renaud +Claude St. Aubin
Feb. 7	Antoine Boufar Angelique Boimie	François Boufar Marie A. Fournier Pierre Boimie Josette Courtois	St. Laurent, Ile St. Laurent This parish	+Louis Susor +Etienne Jacob Simon Drouillard +Jacques Charron +Jean B. Réaume
May 2	Zacharie Cloutier Thérèse Campeau	Zacharie Cloutier Marie M. Prisson Michel Campeau Josette Dutau	Beaupré This parish	+Charles Bernier +Etienne Jacob +Rene Cloutier +Charles Fontaine
Oct. 20	Claude St. Aubin Marie Jann (Jeanne)	Jos. St. Aubin Julienne Cuillerier Robert Jann (Jeanne) Catherine Réaume	This parish L'île-Jesus	+Jos. St. Aubin. +Charles Fontaine +Faignan +Robert Jeanne Legrand
Nov. 21	Michel Catin Marie L. Goiau	François Catin Marie Robert Jan Jean B. Goiau Marie L. Deslieres	Longueuil This parish	Bonaventure Réaume Charles Morant Vital Dumouchelle +Louis Goiau

Appendix VI (continued)

DATE	CONTRACTING PARTIES	PARENTS	PARISH OF PARENTS	WITNESSES
1775 Jan. 9	Louis Viller (*dit* St. Louis)	Louis Viller (St. Louis) Marie Jos. Morin	This parish	Guillaume Goyau Vital Dumouchelle Vital Goyau Pierre Meloche
	Charlotte Auriendo (*dit* Joachim)	Jaq. Auriendo (Joachim) Charlotte Pillette	Boucherville	Louis Viller *dit* St. Louis Lapalme +Deslauriers +Boimie
Feb. 13	Michel Vaudri	Michel Vaudri Francoise Leboeuf	Pointe aux Trembles of Montreal	
	Elizabeth Drouillard	Simon Drouillard Marguerite St. Jean	This parish	
1775 Feb. 19	Joseph Godet	Jacques Godet Marie L. Desbuttes	Ste. Anne of Detroit	Jos. Pouget Jean B. Campeau Charles Morant fils
	Jeanne Pilette	Joseph Pilette Jeanne Belleperche	This parish	+Jean Pelletier +Charles Bernier +Jean B. Reaume
Feb. 20	Jacques Bezer *dit* L'Eveillé	André Bezer Marie Bergeron	St. Etienne of Tours	+Charles Fontaine +Benjamin Chapu Pierre Ceras
	Catherine Meté	Joseph Meté Catherine Dufour	This parish	
Nov. 21	Charles Janson *dit* Lapalme	Charles Janson Geneviève Filiau	Quebec	+Charles Bouron +Louis Montmeni +François Prudhomme François Sourdilete
	Marie Gendron	François Gendron Marie LePage	Chateau-gay	
1776 Jan. 8	Pierre Campeau	Michel Campeau Josette Dutau	This parish	Charles Bouron +Antoine Meloche Joseph Drouillard Simon Drouillard
	M. Magdeleine Godefroi	François Godefroi Susanne Pepin	This parish	
Jan. 15	Ignace Tuote	Ignace Tuote Marie Laprairie	Longueuil	+Pierre L'Etourneau +Antoine Boufar +Andre Pelletier +Charles Bernier
	Lisette LeBeau	François LeBeau Josette Fauvel	This parish	

[351]

Appendix VI (continued)

DATE	CONTRACTING PARTIES	PARENTS	PARISH OF PARENTS	WITNESSES
Jan. 27	François Pratte Elizabeth Parent	Laurent Parent ...... Cardinal	This parish	Philippe Dejean Dominique Labrosse Francois Berthelot Pierre Berthelot François Pratte
March 19	Jacques St. Aubin Charlotte Bélair	Joseph St. Aubin Julienne Cuillerier Pierre Bélair M. Anne Menard	Montreal Montreal	+René Cloutier +Amable Latour Pierre Menard +Charles Bouron Pierre Ceras etc.
1776 May 6	J. Bapt. LeBeau Susanne Chauvin	Rene LeBeau Marguerite LaDurantaie Noel Etienne Chauvin M. Jeanne Meloche	This parish Ste. Anne of Detroit	+J. B. Réaume Pierre Ceras Joseph Drouillard +Charles Bernier
May 16	François Berthelot *dit* Savoyard Louise Gaudet	François Berthelot Anne Boular François Gaudet M. Jeanne Parent	La Chine This parish	François Gaudet Philipe Dejean Jos. Beaubien
July 8	Joseph Bertiome Catherine Pilette	André Bertiome Marie Bouvier Joseph Pilette Jeanne Belleperche	Machisse This parish	Jos. Bondy +Ant. Meloche Maisonville +Jaq. Charron +Jos. Godet +Pierre Charron +Jos. Pilette
1777 Jan. 8	Louis Goyau Thérèse Janis	Jean Bapt. Goyau M. Louise Deslieres François Janis Thérèse Meloche	This parish This parish	Charles Bouron +Louis Trudelle
Feb. 10	Victor Morisseau Charlotte Bergeron	Pierre Morisseau Marie A. Desnoyers Simon Bergeron Catherine LeBeau	Arpentigny This parish	Peltier père +Louis Peltier +Thomas Pajot +François Langlois +Pierre Viller +Simon Bergeron

[352]

APPENDIX VI (*continued*)

DATE	CONTRACTING PARTIES	PARENTS	PARISH OF PARENTS	WITNESSES
March 10	Pierre Charon Charlotte Campeau	Jacques Charon Marie Odet Charles Campeau Charlotte Montrey	Boucherville This parish	Antoine Robert +Jaq. Peltier +Michel Roi +Joseph Pilette
Aug. 4	Antoine Robert Thérèse Drouillard	Antoine Robert Marie L. Becquemont Jean B. Drouillard Charlotte Bigra	Ste. Anne of Detroit This parish	Jos. Bondy +Michel Roi Ant. Dufresne Simon Drouillard Etienne Languedoc +Jaq. Pelletier
1777 Sept. 15	Jean B. Rasicau Appolline Deslieres	Charles Rasicau Pelagie Lapointe Jos. Deslieres Veronique Denis	Boucherville This parish	+François Sabourin +Michel Catin +Guillaume Goyau F. Comparet +Louis Jaquemain +Michel Rasicau +Jean B. Favereau +François Le Duc
Sept. 22	Jean B. Gignac Catherine LeBeau	Jos. Gignac Marie M. Galernau Jean B. LeBeau Catherine Dudevoir	Cap-Santé Montreal	François Drouillard +Antoine Rousseau +Rene Cloutier +Thomas Pajot
Sept. 24	Michel Roy Marie J. Viller	Certain Roy Marie Parent Louis Viller Josette Morin	Montreal This parish	Louis Gaillard Jos. Soumande +Pierre Javerai
1778 Oct. 19	Charles Drouillard Marie L. Quenel	Jean B. Drouillard Charlotte Bigra Jaq. Quenel Marg. LaDurantaie	This parish This parish	+Pierre Levasseur Joseph Bondy +Jean B. Drouillard J. B. Tourangeau
Nov. 9	Pierre Lavasseur Marie A. Lesueur	Pierre Levasseur Marguerite Petit Michel Lesueur	Quebec Chambly	+Louis Trudelle +Jean B. Drouillard +Pierre Javerai

[353]

APPENDIX VI (*continued*)

DATE	CONTRACTING PARTIES	PARENTS	PARISH OF PARENTS	WITNESSES
1779				
Jan. 25	Pierre Proue	Joseph Proue Marthe Ganiere	St. Thomas	+Antoine Rousseau +Michel Roy
	Marie J. A. Binau	Louis Binau Marie M. Levrau	This parish	+Etienne Jacob +Augustin Dievins Tourangeau
Jan. 30	Antoine Rousseau	Pierre Rousseau Catherine DesSelliers	Cresança en Querci	Duberge +Aug. Dievins
	Marie J. Morin	Pierre Morin Marie J. D'Auné	St-Sulpice	+Pierre Proue
Dec. 20	Paul Marsac	François Marsac Thérèse Campeau	Ste. Anne of Detroit	Charles Moran Jos. Soumande
	Marie A. Chêne	Pierre Chêne Marie A. Cuillerier	This parish	+Jaq. Parent
1780				
Jan. 10	Louis Trudelle	Louis Trudelle Catherine Trudeau	La Longue Pointe	Alexus Delisle +J. B. Tourneux
	Susanne Desnoyers	Pierre Desnoyers Marie L. Le Duc	This parish	Philip Bellainge +Louis Trudelle +Charles Delisle +Susanne Desnoyers
Jan. 17	Jean B. Gignac	Joseph Gignac Marie M. Galernau	Cap-Santé	Joseph Pouget J. B. Bondy
	Charlotte Bertrand	Jean B. Bertrand M. Magdelene Martin	Soulanges	Labrosse Jos. Soumande
Aug. 11	Joseph Vermet	Antoine Vermet Françoise Seguin	St. Rose, Ile de Jesus	+André Peltier +Pierre Meloche fils
	Josette Campeau	Charles Campeau Charlotte Montrey	This parish	+Rene PetitVierge
Sept. 21	Pierre Réaume	Pierre Réaume Marie J. Pilette		+Alexis Chene +Pierre Javerai
	Jeanne Campeau	Michel Campeau Josette Dutau	This parish	+Jaques Charron +Charles Gravelle

[354]

APPENDIX VI (*continued*)

DATE	CONTRACTING PARTIES	PARENTS	PARISH OF PARENTS	WITNESSES
Nov. 6	Jean B. Drouillard Maire C. Drouin	Jean B. Drouillard Charlotte Bigra Jos. Drouin Charlotte Campeau	This parish This parish	H. B. Roucout +Jean B. Pitre +François Robert Joseph Drouillard
Nov. 18	Charles De Quindre M. Catherine Chêne	Ant. De Quindre, ecuyer Marie A. Picoté Belestre Pierre Chêne Marie A. Cuillerier	This parish	Jean B. Le Duc François De Quindre Charles Gouin +Magdele Trottier Ant. De Quindre Judith Gouin
1781 Jan. 8	Joseph Deganne M. Magd. Prudhomme	Joseph Deganne Catherine Menard François Prudhomme Judith Cuillerier	Ste. Anne, Montreal This parish	Pierre Belair +François Prudhomme
Feb. 27	Jacques Godrau Thérèse Bertrand	Gabriel Godrau ...... Baudouin Gilles Bertrand Thérèse Drouillet	Trois Rivières	J. Bondy François Prate +Pierre Javerai

[355]

APPENDIX VII

British Commanding Officers at Detroit 1760–96*

1760	Major Robert Rogers	1779	Major Arent S. De Peyster
1760	Captain Donald Campbell	1784	Major William Ancrum
1762	Major Henry Gladwin	1786	Captain Thomas Bennett
1764	Colonel John Bradstreet	1787	Major R. Mathews
1765	Colonel John Campbell	1788	Major F. Close
1766	Major Robert Bayard	1789	Major Patrick Murray
1767	Captain George Turnbull	1790	Major John Smith
1770	Major T. Bruce	1792	Colonel R. G. England
1771	Captain James Stephenson		LIEUTENANT-GOVERNORS
1772	Major Henry Bassett	1775	Henry Hamilton
1774	Major R. B. Lernoult	1784	Jehu Hay

*Adapted from Farmer's *History of Detroit*, p. 227.

APPENDIX VIII

Marguilliers or Wardens of the Parish of the Assumption

ELECTED BEFORE 1781
Maisonville
Marantet
Labute
Pajot
Langlois
Bourron
Touranjeau
Bondy
Meloche
Jacques Parent
Louis Suzor
Joseph Pouget

ELECTED FROM 1781 TO 1795
Jean B. Oualette
Jean B. Lantailla (Antaya)
André Peltier
René Cloutier
Claude Réaume
Charles Réaume
François Drouillard
Vital Dumouchel
Antoine Meloche
Jean B. Tourneux
Antoine Bouffard
Jacques Charon
Jean B. Fauvel
Joseph Berthiaume
Charles Reneau
François Pratt

APPENDIX IX

HOLDERS OF FARM LOTS IN ESSEX COUNTY ABOUT 1794

SURVEY OF TOWNSHIPS OF GOSFIELD AND COLCHESTER BY PATRICK McNIFF IN 1793-4*

GOSFIELD

A—Twelve Lots east of Mill Creek
1. Henry Tofflemire
2. John Wiert
3. Windal Wagaley
4. Charles Munger
5. Robert McMurray†
6. Geo. Silchesteel to Windal Wagaley
7. Philip Fox
8. Philip Fox‡
9. Jonas Fox
10. Henry Hoffman
11. Peter Williams
12. Thomas Lips

B—Thirty-two Lots west of Mill Creek
1. Andrew Uloch (Alcock)
2. Jonas Wood
3. ...... Clarke
4. Robert Dennison
5. Peter Williams
6. Joseph Windall
7. James Girty
8. George Girty
9. C. Bunach
10. Michael Shaffer
11. ...... Le Course
12. Martin Tofflemire
13. Martin Myer—at mouth of Cedar River
14. James Stewart
15. John Wright
16. Adam Falkner

17. John Top
18. Prince—a negro
19. Samuel Hall
20. Oliver Tiffeny
21. ....
22. Prince Robertson—negro
23. ....
24. James Empson
25. Ant. Sincerney
26. James Fry—negro
27. Jacob Arnett
28. William Harper
29. Richard Whittle
30. Thomas Smith Esq.
31. John Nibour or Libour
32. John Carrol

COLCHESTER
33. Henry Ramsay
34. Bapt. Vallard
35. ...... de Cout
36. James Little
37. John Dalton
38. Major McGregor
39. Major McGregor
40. Thomas Hall
41. Samuel Weston
42. Thomas Jones
43. Thomas Ferris
44. Louis Weisman
45. Richard (Cornwall)
46. John Little
47. John Pardo
48. Charles Phillipley
49. John Smith
50. ...... Fraser
51. Edward Neville

52. ...... Bondy
53. John Dean
54. ....
55. Joseph Bondy§
56. William Munger§
57. Pat. Hill
58. Thomas Little
59. John Little
60. John McLean
61. John Clearwater
62. Daniel McKillop
63. Daniel McKillop
64. James Tracey
65. Thomas Ashford
66. Benjamin Knapp
67. Andrew Hamilton
68. ⎫
69. ⎬ Reserve″
70. ⎭
71. John Stockwell
72. John Snyder
73. John Stockwell
75. John Pardo
76. Henry Wright
77. Henry Wright
78. Robert Dowler
79. Amos Weston
80. Henry Facer
81. Richard Robertson
82. Elisha Wilcox
83. Elisha Wilcox Jr.
84. James Wilcox
85. Colon Andrews
86. Rudolph Huffman
87. George Rudhurt
88. Thomas Reynolds
89. Daniel Field

*Original in Crown Lands Department, Toronto. The notes are in the margin in the original.

†Note: In the rear of lots 5–12 east of Mill Creek the following names appear: Capt. McKee, Capt. Muir, Mr. Reynolds.

‡Note: Along the shore on this lot there are two entrenchments with very deep fosses, flanked by two ravines.

§Note: Along the shore on these two lots there is an old Indian entrenchment.

″Note: Near the shore there is a burying place.

358   THE WINDSOR BORDER REGION

Holders of Lots in Malden Township#

1.
2. Captain Bird
3. William Caldwell
4. Alexander McKee
5. Matthew Elliot
6. Chatham Elliot
7. David Cowan
8. David Cowan
9. Archange McIntosh
10. Charles Reaume
11. Simon Girty
12. Francis Baby
13. Francis Baby
14. Hon. James Baby
15. Thomas McKee
16. Thomas McKee
17. Prideaux Selby
18. Prideaux Selby
19. Thos. Alexander Clarke

#Iredell map of April 17, 1796, in Crown Lands Department.

Proprietors of Lots at Petite Côte 1792–4

1. Laurent Bondy (Louis Bourassa)
2. Antoine Meloche
3. Gabriel Bondy
4. Joseph Bondy
5. Joseph Lesperance (Rocheleau)
6. Charles Renaud
7. Simon Bergeron
8. Jacques (Jacob) Bezaire
9. Guillaume Monforton
10. James Donaldson
11. Louis Bourisseau (Bourassa)
12. Francois Beneteau
13. Gervais Houdienne
14. Joseph Mainville
15. Antoine Meloche
16. Joseph Bondy
17. J. B. Antailla (Antaya)
18. Thomas Pajot (Aug. Lhuissier)
19. Charles Renaud
20. Pierre Prudhomme
21. J. B. Gignac
22. Pierre Girard
23. Jean Louis Reveau
24. Joseph Pouget (Pagot)
25. Pierre Meloche
26. Benjamin Chaput
27. Michel (Joseph) Rocheleau
28. Widow Prou (Groulx)
29. Widow Rousseau
30. Antoine Bouffard
31. Martin Durocher
32. Antoine Bouffard
33. Zacharie Cloutier
34. J. B. Bigras
35. Pierre Caradan (Ladebauche)
36. Joseph Réaume
37. John Askin**
38. John Snider
39. Wm. Park
40. John Dunhand (Messemer)
41. Geo. Meldrum
42. Richard Pollard
43. Joseph Pouget (Pagot)
44. Wm. Park
45. Guillaume Monforton
46. François (Ant.) Girardin
47. Simon Drouillard
48. Gregor McGregor
49. Thomas Smith
50. Thomas Smith
51. Joseph Bondy
52. Joeph Coté (Thomas Smith)
53. Robert Dowler (Philip Fox)
54. Judge Powell
55. Matthew Dolson
56. Isaac Dolson
57. Fred Arnold
58. J. B. Paré
59. Col. Alex McKee
60. Col. Alex McKee

SECOND CONCESSION

10. J. B. Laframboise
11. Alex. Bigra

**Note: In the rear of Lots 37 to 47 an area of 405 arpents is reserved to J. B. Feré for a water-mill.

Proprietors of Lots at the Settlement of L'Assomption 1792–4

61. Wm. Hands
62. Thomas Pajot
63. Church Lands
64. Francis Pratt
65. Jacques Marentette
66. Dominic Marentette
67. Jacques Parent
68. Laurent Parent
69. Claude Réaume
70. Baptiste LeDuc
71. Baptiste Ouellette
72. J. B. Mailloux
73. Joseph Mailloux
74. (Nicolas) Thérèse Janisse
75. J. B. Ouellette
76. André Beneteau
77. Madame Baby
78. J. B. Letourneau
79. Madame Baby
80. Madame Baby
81. Vital Dumouchelle
82. Vital Dumouchelle
83. Louis Goyeau
84. Joseph Lesperance
85. Julien Parent
86. Nicolas Langlois

APPENDIX IX

Proprietors at Assumption (*continued*)

87. Pierre Labutte
88. P. C. Poisson *dit* Lasalline
89. Francois Marentette
90. Charles Delisle
91. Antoine Langlois
92. Joncaire Chaubert
93. Joseph Beaubien
94. Alexis Maisonville
95. Government Lands††
96. Government Lands††
97. Bonaventure Réaume
98. Antoine Labadie
99. Baptiste Pillette
100. Joseph Berthiaume
101. R. T. Réaume
102. François Meloche
103. Baptiste Labadie
104. Julien Parent
105. Jacques Meloche
106. François Meloche
107. Jacques Parent
108. Laurent Parent
109. Baptiste Beaubien
110. Jacques Charron
111. André Peltier
112. Joseph Bazinet
113. Pierre Letourneau
114. Louis Peltier (Soullière)
115. Louis Villaire *dit* St. Louis
116. Baptiste Chapoton
117. Antoine Labadie
118. Charles Lamarche
119. Dagneau LePiconiere
120. ...... Dumouchelle
121. Pierre St. Louis
122. Julien Labutte
123. Baptiste Langlois
124. Jacques Belleperche
125. Desaulniers (Robert Marsac)
126. Benjamin Marsac
127. Jacques Lauzon
128. John Askin
129. Madame Marsac (L. Desaulniers)
130. Baptiste Meloche
131. ...... Bazinet
132. Antoine Labadie
133. Andre Landroche
134. Baptiste Soullière
135. Baptiste Paré
136. Joseph Morand
137. Alexis Peltier
138. Louis Campeau
139. Antoine Robert
140. Simon Meloche
141. Charles Chauvin
142. ...... Leficore
143. P. T. Réaume (Simon Campeau)
144. P. T. Réaume (Julien Parent)
145. Madame Meloche
146. Baptiste Paré
147. Michael Wool
148. Bapt. Péniche Campeau
149. Alexis Maisonville (J. B. Pitre)
150. Antoine Lesperance
151. Eneas Paré
152. Charles Lesperance
153. Alexis Campeau
    J. B. Mireau—east of Petite Riviere in tract not yet surveyed

SECOND CONCESSION
77. B. Bruce
134. Louis Peltier

THIRD CONCESSION
69. J. Beauchamp
89. Charles Bernier

††Note: 1793 to Jonathan Schieffelin.

Proprietors of Lots on Streams Flowing into Lake St. Clair, 1793–4

Rivière aux Pêches (Pike Creek)

West Side
1. Crown and Clergy Reserve
2. Charles Réaume
3. Charles Réaume
4. Joshua Réaume
5. Charles Drouillard
6. Pat McNiff
7. Crown and Clergy Reserve
8. Wm. Harffy (unsurveyed)

East Side
1. Crown and Clergy Reserve
2. Joseph Pouget
3. Sinsin Bissonet
4. Joseph Drouillard
5. James Allen
7. Crown and Clergy Reserve

Rivière aux Puces

West Side
1. L. Montigny (A. Serat)
2. John McCargin
3. Crown and Clergy Reserve
4. Joseph Voyer
5.
6. Crown and Clergy Reserve
7. Regis Binnot

East Side
1. John Deane
2. James Charron
3. Crown and Clergy Reserve
4. Martin Butler
5. Ranjard Le Cavalier
6. Crown and Clergy Reserve
7. Maurice Roche

Belle Rivière

West Side
1. Crown and Clergy Reserve
2.
3. Louis Dragon
4. Joseph Vermet
5.
6.
7. Crown and Clergy Reserve

East Side
1. Crown and Clergy Reserve
2.
3. François Valcour
4. Etienne Languedoc
5. Redman Condon
6. Pierre Griffin
7. Crown and Clergy Reserve

Rivière Ruscom

West Side
1. Crown and Clergy Reserve
2. Christopher Baraba
3.
4. André Lepage
5.
6. André Berthiaume
7. Crown and Clergy Reserve

East Side
1. Crown and Clergy Reserve
2. Théophile Metté
3.
4. Madame Labadie *dit* Badichon
5. Charles Charron
6. Gabriel Peltier
7. Crown and Clergy Reserve

BIBLIOGRAPHY

MANUSCRIPTS

CANADA

Public Archives of Canada
Transcripts of French documents obtained from the Bibliothèque Nationale, the Archives des Colonies, and the Archives de la Marine:
Série C II A, Correspondance générale, Canada.
Série G-1, Recensement des Habitants du Détroit 1750.
La Nouvelle France et Détroit.
Transcripts from the British Museum:
Series A, Bouquet Papers (1759–65).
Series B, Haldimand Papers (1773–90).
Series C, Indian Affairs (1761–1800).
Series Q, Papers pertaining to the relations of the British government with the Indian tribes of North America and to the military posts and marine interests of the Great Lakes (1762–99).
Series Q, Colonial Office Records (1760–1823).
R.G. 1, E 1, State C.
R.G. 1, L 4, vol. II.
Monforton Register.
Surveys, Maps and Plans (Map Collection).
Wolford Simcoe Papers.

ONTARIO

Department of Public Records and Archives
Crown Land Papers, Surveyors' Letters.
Records of Surveys.
Record Book of the Court of Common Pleas held at l'Assomption beginning July 16, 1789.
Maps.

Toronto Public Library, Reference Division
William Dummer Powell Collection.
David W. Smith Collection.

Archives of Assumption University of Windsor
Gift of Land from the Huron Indians.

Archives of the Church of the Assumption, Windsor
Account Books.
Registers of Baptisms, Marriages and Burials.

George F. Macdonald Collection, Windsor
Documents, Maps and Surveys.

Quebec

Archives de l'Archevêché de Québec (Quebec Chancery Archives)
Série E.U., vol. V, Correspondance avec le Détroit (1760–97).
Les Pères Jésuites.

Archives du Séminaire de Québec
J. Viger, "Ma Saberdache."

Archives de la Bibliothèque Municipale de Montréal
Collection Gagnon, Manuscrit Potier.

Archives du Collège Ste-Marie, Montréal
La Gazette du Père Potier.

Great Britain

British Museum
Add. 21, 649, Major Henry Gladwin's letter to Sir Jeffery Amherst.

France

La Bibliothèque Nationale
Le voyage de MM. Dollier et Galinée 1669–70.
Fonds Renaudot, Acte de prise de possession des terres du lac Erié.

Archives de la Marine
Rapport de Joseph-Gaspard Chaussegros de Léry.

Archives du Ministère des Colonies
Carte et noms des habitants à qui l'on a concédé des terres.

Italy

General Jesuit Archives, Rome
Letter from Armand de La Richardie.
Potier item.

United States

The Detroit Main Library, the Burton Historical Collection
Account Book of the Mission of the Hurons 1733–51.
Askin Papers (MSS).
Cicotte Book.
Cadillac Papers (French and English).
Denissen's Genealogies.
Detroit Notarial Records.
Macomb, Edgar and Macomb Ledger for 1779–1780.
Montreal Papers.
Pontiac Manuscript.
Registers of Baptisms, Marriages and Funerals at Ste. Anne's Church.
Surveys and Maps.

William L. Clements Library, Ann Arbor, Michigan
Amherst Papers.
Diary of the Siege of Detroit by Jehu Hay.
Gage Papers.
James Sterling Letter Book.
Maps and Paintings.

PUBLISHED DOCUMENTS AND COLLECTIONS

BLISS, EUGENE F., ed., *The Diary of David Zeisberger* (Cincinnati, 1885).
"The Captivity of Charles Stuart," *Mississippi Valley Historical Review*, XIII, no. I (June 1926).
CRUIKSHANK, E. A., ed., *The Correspondence of Lieut. Governor John Graves Simcoe, 1789-1796* (5 vols., Toronto, 1923-31).
CRUIKSHANK, E. A., and A. F. HUNTER, eds., *The Correspondence of the Honourable Peter Russell, 1796-1799* (3 vols., Toronto, 1932-6).
FRASER, ALEXANDER, *Third Report of the Bureau of Archives for the Province of Ontario* (Toronto, 1905).
—— *Fourteenth Report of the Bureau of Archives for the Province of Ontario* (Toronto, 1917).
—— *Fifteenth Report of the Bureau of Archives for the Province of Ontario* (Toronto, 1920).
—— *Seventeenth Report of the Bureau of Archives for the Province of Ontario* (Toronto, 1928).
—— *Twentieth Report of the Bureau of Archives for the Province of Ontario* (Toronto, 1931).
"George Croghan's Journal 1759-63," *Pennsylvania Magazine of History and Biography*, LXXI, no. 4 (October 1947).
HOUGH, FRANKLIN B., ed., *Diary of the Siege of Detroit* (Albany, 1860).
"The Journal of John Montresor," *Transactions of the Royal Society of Canada*, Series III, vol. XXII (Ottawa, 1928).
MARGRY, PIERRE, *Découvertes et établissements des Français dans l'ouest et dans le sud de l'Amérique septentrionale, 1614-1754* (6 vols., Paris, 1876-86).
Michigan Historical Collections (40 vols., Lansing, 1877-1929).
O'CALLAGHAN, E. B., ed., *Documents Relating to the Colonial History of the State of New York* (10 vols., Albany, 1856-61).
ONTARIO HISTORICAL SOCIETY, *Papers and Records* (Toronto).
QUAIFE, MILO M., ed., *The John Askin Papers, 1747-1820* (2 vols., Detroit, 1928, 1931).
ROCHEMONTEIX, CAMILLE DE, *Les Jésuites et la Nouvelle France au XVIIe siècle* (3 vols., Paris, 1906).
—— *Les Jésuites et la Nouvelle France au XVIIIe siècle* (2 vols., Paris, 1906).
ROY, P. G., *Rapport de l'Archiviste de la Province de Québec, 1927-28.*
THWAITES, R. G., ed., *The Jesuit Relations and Allied Documents* (73 vols., Cleveland, 1896-1901).

SECONDARY WORKS

ANON., *L'Histoire de la Congrégation de Notre-Dame de Montréal* (9 vols., Montreal, 1941).
BURTON, CLARENCE M., *The City of Detroit* (5 vols., Detroit, 1922).
—— *Journal of Pontiac's Conspiracy, 1763*, R. CLYDE FORD, trans. (Detroit, 1912).
CHARLEVOIX, P. F. X., *Journal d'un voyage fait par ordre du Roi dans l'Amérique septentrionale* (Paris, 1744).
DELANGLEZ, JEAN, "Louis Jolliet—Early Years," *Mid-America*, XXVII (January 1945), 3–29.
FARMER, SILAS, *History of Detroit and Michigan* (3rd ed., 2 vols., Detroit, 1890).
GRAY, ELMA E., *Wilderness Christians—the Moravian Mission to the Delaware Indians* (Toronto, 1956).
HENNEPIN, LOUIS, *Description de la Louisiane nouvellement découverte* (Paris, 1683).
Indian Treaties and Surrenders (Ottawa, 1905).
LA HONTAN, M. LE BARON, *Nouveaux Voyages de M. le baron de Lahontan dans l'Amérique septentrionale* (2 vols., La Haye, 1703).
LEBEL, E. C., "History of Assumption, the First Parish in Upper Canada," *Report of the Canadian Catholic Historical Association* (Ottawa, 1954).
LECLERQ, CHRISTIAN, *First Establishment of the French in New France*, JOHN G. SHEA, trans. and ed. (2 vols., New York, 1881).
MORRISON, NEIL F., *Garden Gateway to Canada* (Toronto, 1954).
PARÉ, GEORGE, *The Catholic Church in Detroit, 1701–1888* (Detroit, 1951).
PECKHAM, HOWARD H., *Pontiac and the Indian Uprising* (Princeton, 1947).
QUAIFE, MILO M., "The Royal Navy of the Upper Lakes," *Burton Historical Collection Leaflet*, II, no. 5 (May 1924).
RAMEAU DE SAINT-PÈRE, E., *La France aux colonies* (Paris, 1859).
STONE, W. L., *Life and Times of Sir William Johnson* (2 vols., Albany, 1856).
TONTI, HENRI DE, *Dernières découvertes de l'Amérique septentrionale de M. de La Sale mises au jour par M. le Chevalier Tonti, gouverneur du Fort St-Louis aux Illinois* (Paris, 1697).
WELD, ISAAC, *Travels through the States of North America and the Provinces of Upper and Lower Canada in 1795, 1796, 1797* (London, 1799).

INDEX

Names that appear only in the lists or in the appendixes are not included in this index. Only the more usual variants of proper names are given here. For double names or sobriquets consult Appendix III on page 311.

ABBOTT, LT. EDWARD, 62, 313
Account Book of the Mission of the Hurons, xliii, lxvi, 30–5, 247–51
Ademard, Miss, c, 138–42, 296–300
Alcock (Ulcoch), Andrew, cxii, 176, 357
Algonquin Indians, xxix, xl, 4
Allan, Capt., 115
Allan, James, cxv, 193, 332, 333
American Revolution. *See* Revolutionary War
Amherst, Sir Jeffery, lxxix, 88, 89, 98, 99, 274–5
Amherstburg, cxvii, cxxi–cxxix, 193, 197, 203, 204, 205, 207, 217, 220, 221, 222, 223, 225, 226
Anderdon Township, cv
Anjalran (Angeliran), Jean (Jesuit), 10, 11, 12, 234, 235, 236
Antaya (Antailla), J. B., 69, 76, 77, 79, 80, 119, 128, 180, 270, 271, 288, 307, 311, 350, 358
Anthon, Christian, 120, 281, 312, 314
Arbitration Boards, lxxxi, 100–2, 104
Arpent, note on, xli
Askin, John, lxxxvii, lxxxviii, cviii, cxv, cxvi, 75, 108–15, 177, 185, 186, 187, 188, 189, 193, 202, 226, 326, 328, 331, 332, 358, 359
Askin Papers, The John, lxxxvii, 108–13
Assumption Church (Parish), lxiv, lxvii, lxviii, lxxii, lxxiv, lxxxiv, xc–c, 85, 109, 115, 118, 122, 124, 126–30, 132, 142, 146, 148, 150, 153, 171, 182, 191, 273, 280, 284, 286–92, 300, 306, 307, 331
Assumption University, xcvi

BABY, ———, 36, 40, 252, 256
Baby, François, lx, lxxxvii, lxxxviii, xcvii, xcviii, 110, 145, 146, 147, 152, 193, 208, 303–4, 309, 358
Baby (Bâby), Jacques Duperon, lx, lxxxiv, xc, xci, cviii, 63, 66, 90, 102, 105, 119, 134, 160, 161, 293, 315, 320, 334, 341

Baby, James, lxxxv, lxxxvii, lxxxix, cxviii, 110, 150, 193, 194, 195, 307, 358
Baby's Mill, cxviii, 194, 206
Badichon. *See* Labadie
Baptisms: at Assumption Church, lxvi, lxvii, xcvii; at Ste. Anne's Church, xliii, lxvi
Bassett, Henry, lxiv, 68, 101, 356
Bayard, Major Robert, 101, 356
Beaubien, Joseph, 72, 114, 115, 128, 177, 288, 314, 338, 347, 359
Beauharnois, Gov. Charles de, xliii, xlvi, xlvii
Becquet (Biquette), Pierre, 45, 51, 263, 349
Bégon, Intendant, 26, 244
Belaire, ———, 70, 86, 119, 124, 272, 284, 328, 352
Belestre (Bellestre), François Marie Picoté, Sieur de, lxxvi, 65, 88–93, 274, 310
Belle Isle. *See* Isle aux Cochons
Belleperche, Jacques, 54, 71, 86, 119, 177, 273, 329, 346, 359
Belle Rivière, cxiv, cxv, 182–6, 360
Bellomont, Earl of, xxxvii
Bénac, Porlier, 68, 155, 189, 193
Beneteau (Benito), André, 72, 177, 311, 320, 331, 334, 358
Beneteau (Bennetto), François, 72, 76, 77, 311, 341, 358
Berenger (Barringer, Burrager), Capt. Henry, 90, 310
Bergeron, Simon, 53, 63, 76, 77, 79, 266, 270, 350, 358
Berthiaume, Joseph, 73, 178, 319, 352, 356, 359
Bertrand, Francis, 189, 225, 226
Bezaire (Beser, Bazor), Jacques, 69, 76, 77, 119, 311, 351, 358
Bienville (Blainville), Pierre Céloron, Sieur de, lii, lvii, lix, lx, 39, 40, 41, 51, 58, 59, 76, 256, 257, 264, 268–9, 310
Bigot, François, 57, 267

365

366 INDEX

Bigras, Amable, 78, 128, 129, 130, 136, 289–91, 295
Bigras, Jacques, 52, 119, 168, 347
Bineau, Louis, 31, 52, 56, 63, 81, 119, 265, 317, 319, 344, 345, 348, 354
Bird, Capt. Henry, lxxxii, xcii, xcvi, cxxiii, cxxvi, 156, 157, 159, 160, 161, 211, 358
Blackwell, Lieut. William, 208, 226
Bocquet, Simple (Recollet), lxxiii, xci, xcii, 60, 120, 281
Bois Blanc Island. *See* Isle aux Bois Blancs
Boishebert, Louis Henri Deschampes, Sieur de, xliii, xliv, xlvi, 310
Bolton, Lt. Col. Mason, 103
Bonaventure, Père, xlix, 34, 41, 251, 257
Bondy, Joseph, lxvii, 62, 71, 75, 77, 86, 119, 124, 126, 128, 167, 175, 272, 285, 286, 289, 290, 311, 325, 335, 352–8
Bonnecamps, Joseph-Pierre (Jesuit), xvi, 40, 57, 256, 266
Botsford, Henry, lxxxviii, 108, 113, 226, 333
Bouffard, Antoine, 70, 76, 119, 204, 312, 320, 333, 346, 356, 358
Bouquet, Col. Henry, lxix
Bourisseau (Bourassa), Louis, 76, 77, 119, 333, 358
Bouron, Charles, lix, lx, 64, 72, 81, 119, 124, 126, 281, 286, 316, 320, 331, 334, 340, 356
Braddock, Gen. Edward, lxi
Bradstreet, Col. John, 100, 356
Brébeuf, Jean de (Jesuit), xxix, xxx, 3, 229
Brehme, Lt. Dietrich, 89, 90
Brewer, Capt. David, 92
Briand, Mgr Jean-Olivier, lxxxi, xciv, 118, 124, 133, 134, 280, 285, 291, 293
Brief of Suppression, xciv
British subjects, 189, 190, 191
Bruce, Major T., 64, 356
Brûlé, Etienne, xxx
Burke, Rev. Edmund, lxxxix, xcviii, xcix, 145–7, 149–52, 303, 304, 306–9
Burton Historical Collection, xxxviii, xlviii, l, lv
Buteau, Charles, 53, 78, 266
Butler's Rangers, cv, 159, 162, 215

CADILLAC. *See* Lamothe Cadillac
Cadillac Papers, xxxix

Caldwell, James, civ, cxv, 162, 332
Caldwell, William, lxxxii, cii–cvii, cxxvi, cxxviii, 106, 110, 114, 159, 160, 161, 162, 166, 193, 210, 211, 215, 223, 358
Caldwell, William, Jr., civ, cxv, 162, 332
Callières, Louis Hector, xli, 13, 17, 20, 22, 236, 238, 242
Campau, Charles, 45, 52, 55, 78, 266, 353, 354
Campau, Claude, 32, 34, 54, 249, 250
Campau, Jacques, 100, 311, 315
Campau, Nicolas *dit* Niagara, xlix, 32, 34, 35, 54, 249, 250, 311
Campbell, Capt. Donald, lxix, 89, 91, 92, 94, 356
Campbell, Capt. John, lxix, 81, 356
Carheil, Etienne de (Jesuit), xlv, 23, 244
Carignan-Salières Regiment, xxxii, 106
Carleton, Gen. Guy. *See* Dorchester, Lord
Cartwright, Hon. Richard, 187
Casse. *See* St. Aubin
Castor, note on, xlix
Cat Nation of Indians, 3, 4, 229
Cayuga Creek, xxxv
Cedar Creek. *See* Rivière aux Cèdres
Céloron, Pierre. *See* Bienville
Census of Detroit, lvi, lxvi–lxviii, lxx, lxxi, 54–6, 63–4, 69–74, 82
Chabert, Joncaire de, 106, 160, 161, 177, 190, 349, 359
Chacornacle, 17, 239
Champigny, Jean de, 13, 236
Champlain, Samuel, xxiv
Chapoton, Jean, 55, 62, 102, 323
Chappus, Benjamin, lxxi, 76, 83, 119, 272, 322, 358
Charlevoix, Pierre F. X. (Jesuit), xlvi, 26, 86, 245, 274
Charon (Charron), Jacques, 63, 72, 86, 119, 128, 177, 186, 272, 288, 317, 318, 319, 346, 353, 356, 359
Chaumonot, Pierre (Jesuit), xxx, xxxi, 3, 229
Chauvin, ———, lx, 33, 35, 40, 54, 59, 119, 250, 251, 256, 269, 315, 316, 321, 339
Chenal (Chenail) Ecarté, cv, cix, 170, 220, 222
Chêne, Isidore, 66, 160, 161, 270, 345
Chêne *dit* Labutte, Pierre, 34, 38, 54, 64, 72, 81, 114, 121, 124, 250, 254, 282, 284, 288, 311, 314, 337–8, 354, 355, 356

Chippewa Indians, xliii, xlv, lxi, 22, 26, 30, 38, 46, 96, 165, 171, 205, 221, 254, 259, 244, 245, 323–4
Chouagen (Oswego), 40, 42, 44, 256
Chouannous (Chouanons, Shawanons) Indians, xxxvii, 5, 12, 38, 39, 230, 235, 254
Cicotte Book, lv, lvi, lx, lxvi, 49, 262
Clarke, Alexander, cxi, 167, 174, 209, 357, 358
Claus, Capt. Wm., 204, 205
Clergy and Crown Reserves, cxiv, cxv, 162, 183, 184, 359
Close, Major Farnham, cvii, cviii, cxxii, 170, 356
Cloutier, René, 70, 79, 86, 118, 270, 273, 320, 353, 356
Cloutier, Zacharie, 63, 70, 76, 118, 350, 358
Colchester Township, lxxxvi, cvi
Collins, John, cvii, 169
Collot, Gen. Victor, lvii
Company of the Colony, xlii, 17, 24, 238, 245
Comparé, François, 68, 270, 326, 331
Congregation of Notre Dame of Montreal, xcvi, xcix, 131–2, 291, 325
Constitutional Act, lxxxv, cxii
Contencineau (Coutinenceau), Jean, lxxxii
Cooper, Lieut., 216, 225
Cornwall, John, cx, 333
Côte des Hurons, lxxii
Côte de Misère, lxx
Côte des Outaouais, lxxii
Cottam, cxvi
Couagne, René de, xlviii, 31, 35, 248, 251
Courcelles, Rémy de, xxxii, 8, 233
Coureurs de bois, xxxvi
Courts, lxxx–lxxxv, 101, 105, 149
Croghan, George, lx, 62, 93
Currency, xlix, lxxi
Cuyler, Lt. Abraham, lxxxviii

DALYELL (DALZELL), CAPT. JAMES, lxxix
Dartmouth, Lord (Earl of), lxxxi, 84
De Gonnor (Degonor), Nicolas (Jesuit), xlvi, 32, 249
De Hêtre (Des Hêtres), Louis Antoine, lv, lx, 52, 64, 265, 313
Dejean, Philip, lxiii, lxxx–lxxxii, 63, 79, 82, 100, 101, 102, 347
Delaware Indians, civ, 59, 99
Delisle *dit* Bienvenu, Alexis, lx, 55, 58, 268, 311

Denonville, Jacques René de Brisay, Marquis de, xxxvi, xxxvii, 10, 11, 234
De Peyster, Major Arent S., lxiv, lxxiv, 68, 69, 86, 103, 121, 122, 124, 270, 273, 282, 285, 356
D'Esglis, Mgr. Louis-Philippe, 133, 141, 291
Desnoyers, Pierre, lx, 64, 81, 349, 354
Detroit (Le Détroit), name, xxiv, xxxix; early explorers at, xxxi–xxxiv, 7–8; Hennepin's description of xxxv, 9–10; formally claimed by French, xxxvi, 11–12; founded by Cadillac, xli; Cadillac's description of, 18–19; slow development of, xlii; Indian tribes at, xliii, xliv, 24–5; new settlers come to, lii–lviii, 48–53; occupied by British, lxxvi, 88–94; besieged by Pontiac, lxxvii–lxxx, 94–7; during Revolutionary War, lxxxii; Loyalists come to, cii–cvi; evacuated by British, cxii, cxiii
Dinan (Dineau) *dit* St. Etienne, Pierre, lvi, 44, 50, 56, 80, 263, 311
Dollier de Casson, François (Sulpician), xxxii, xxxiii, 5–7, 8, 230–3
Dolsen (Dolson), Isaac, 75, 330, 358
Dolsen (Dolson), Matthew, 75, 112, 164, 193, 333, 358
Dongan, Gov. Thomas, xxxvii
Dorchester, Guy Carleton, Lord, lxxx, lxxxiii, xciv, ciii, cv, cviii, cxxii, cxxiii, 67, 105, 107, 162, 209, 211, 212, 213
Doubles names. *See* Sobriquets
Drouillard, J. B., lxvii, 45, 50, 57, 63, 71, 81, 86, 119, 263, 273, 318, 333, 335, 344, 348, 353, 355
Drouillard, Simon, lxxiv, 63, 70, 75, 86, 115, 118, 119, 126, 128, 189, 272, 280, 286, 288, 315, 321, 333, 334, 351, 358
Dubuisson, Charles Regnault, Sieur, xcii, 310
Du Creux, map of, xxxi
Dufaux, François-Xavier (Sulpician), lxxxiv, xcvi–c, 106, 130, 136–49, 278, 290, 294–306
Duff, Alex, 189, 192, 195, 204, 208
Dufour, Jean B., 78, 86, 119, 272, 341
Dufour, Pierre, 52, 56, 78, 265
Du Jauny, Pierre (Jesuit), 38, 96, 121, 254, 277, 282
Duluth (du Lhut), Greysolon, xxxvl, xxxvii, 10, 234
Dumouchel, Vital, lx, 72, 115, 128,

177, 288, 326, 339, 356, 358
Dunmore, cxx, 214, 224
Du Parc, Jean B. (Jesuit), 28, 247
Dupuis, Charles, lxvii, 336
Duqué (Dugué), 17, 239
Durand *dit* Montmirel, Pierre, 53, 56, 265, 311
Durocher, Martin, 76, 311, 326, 329, 332. *See also* Marsac
Dussault, ———, 64, 81, 330

EDELINE (DESLIGNES), LOUIS, 45, 51, 264
Edgar, Wm., 102
Education, xcvi, xcix–ci
Election of 1792, lxxxvi, lxxxvii, 108–13
Elliot(t), Matthew, 106, 109, 111, 160, 161, 162, 163, 193, 210–11, 215, 221, 222–5, 358
England, Lieut. Col. R. G., civ, cv, 114, 184, 212–13, 356
Enjalran, Jean (Jesuit). *See* Anjalran
Episcopal Church of the Western District, cxx, cxxi, 200
Essex, town of, cxvi
Essex County: Indian village sites in, xxxviii; original boundaries of, lxxxv–vi; first election in, lxxxvii, lxxxviii
Etionnontout, 36, 38, 252, 254
Executive Council of the Province of Upper Canada, lxxxv, cxxiii
Exodus Act, lxxxv

Fabrique, cxiii, xcvii
Fairfield, cv
Fallen Timbers, battle of, lxxxiii
Farms of the early settlers, lxix–lxxiv
Feré, J. B., lxxiv, lxxv, 333, 358
Fields, Capt. Daniel, 114, 166, 168, 330, 357
Fighting Island. *See* Isle aux Dindes
Flathead Indians, xlvi, 36, 252
Fleming, Samuel, 103
Fort Duquesne, lxi
Fort Frontenac, xliii, 9, 233
Fort Lernoult, lxxxii, cxxii
Fort Malden, 153, 309
Fort Miamis, lxxxiii, 92, 212
Fort Niagara, lxxxii, 42, 48, 99, 150, 212, 261, 308
Fort Pitt, lxix, lxxvi, xc
Fort Pontchartrain, xli, 20, 22, 242, 244
Fort St. Joseph, xxxvi, xxxvii, 12, 234
Fort Vincennes, lxxxii

Fox Indians, xlii
Fraser, Major, 223
Fréchette, Rev. Pierre, xcvi, 134, 138, 143, 148, 172, 293, 297, 301, 305
Fredericksburg, cxxi, cxxiii, 159, 333
French, River, xxix
Frerot, Nicolas Jean François, xcvi, 131, 291
Frontenac, Louis de Buade, Count de, xxxix, 121, 236
Fry, Philip, ciii, 160, 161, 210

GAGE, GEN. THOMAS, lxii, lxix, lxxi, 64
Gaillard, Louis, 127, 287
Galinée, René Bréhant de, xxxii–xxxiv, 4, 8, 230, 233
Gaol and Court House at Sandwich, cxx, 194, 196, 197, 198, 224
Gaudet (Godet) *dit* Marentette, François, lx, xciii, 63, 71, 117, 120, 123, 124, 126, 128, 138, 176, 279, 281, 284, 285, 287, 288, 297, 311, 313, 321, 338, 352, 356, 359
Gaudet (Godet) *dit* Marentette, Jacques, lx, lxi, 54, 59, 176, 268, 337, 343, 351, 358
George Town, cxxii, cxxiii, 210
Germain, Lord George, 102
Germain, Joseph (Jesuit), 18, 24
Gervais, Louis, lv, 44, 45, 49, 55, 61, 79, 258
Gignac, Jean B., 69, 76, 83, 119, 128, 270, 272, 288, 353, 354, 358
Girty, Simon, 160, 161, 164, 167, 208, 358
Gladwin, Major Henry, lxxi, lxxvii, lxxix, xci, 64, 98–9, 356
Gosfield Township, lxxxvi, cviii
Gouin, ———, 34, 55, 167, 251, 355
Goyau, Baptiste, lx, 31, 32, 56, 119, 248, 249, 317, 349, 350, 352
Goyau, Madame, 32, 249
Goyau, Vital, 64, 81, 309, 316, 351
Grand River, xxxiii, 6, 42, 152, 231, 308
Grant, Alexander, lxxxv, cviii, 65, 106, 158, 172, 176, 193, 201, 202, 225
Green, Capt. James, 212–25
Green Bay. *See* Puans
Griffon, xxxv
Grosse Isle, xli, xlvii, 109, 210

HALDIMAND, GOV. FREDERICK, lxiv, xcix, ciii, cxx, 67, 74, 86, 101, 102, 103, 104, 125, 157, 159, 166, 210, 274, 285
Hamilton, Lt.-Gov. Henry, lxiv, lxxiv,

lxxxi–lxxxiii, xcv, cii, 67, 84, 102, 104, 107, 131, 155–8, 279, 282, 356
Hamilton, Ontario, xxxii
Hamtramck, Col. John, 149, 306
Hands, Wm., cxix, 189, 193, 198, 202, 358
Harffy, Wm., cxv, 172, 189, 193, 201, 226, 359
Hay, Jehu, Lieut.-Gov., lxxviii, lxxxiii, cxxi, 74, 157–62, 166, 172, 340, 356
Hay, Mrs. Jehu, lxxxviii, 340
Hennepin, Louis (Recollet), xxxv, 9, 234
Hesse, District of, lxxxiv, cviii, 105, 107, 173, 174. *See also* Western District
Hog Island. *See* Isle aux Cochons
Hospitallers of Montreal, 15, 238
Houdienne, Jarvais (Gervais), 76, 77, 128, 288, 332, 358
Hubert, Mgr Jean François, lxxxiv, xcvi, xcix, 86, 106, 120–52, 281–308, 325, 331
Hughes, Mr., surveyor, ciii, 211
Hull, Gen. Wm., cv
Huron, lxxvii, lxxix
Huron Church. *See* Assumption Church
Huron Indians, xxix; Jesuit missionaries among, xxx; dispersal from Huronia, xxxi; at Detroit, xlii, xliv, 60–1; mission established, xlvi; transferred to Bois Blanc Island, xlvii, xlviii; removed to La Pointe de Montréal, xlviii; fought with French in Seven Years' War, lx; took part in siege of Detroit, lxxviii; plea for missionary, xcv; withdrawal from Detroit, xcvii; gifts of land by, xcvi, xcvii, 120, 131, 324, 325
Huron Mission. *See* Mission of the Hurons
Huron Reserve: at la Rivière aux Canards, cv, cvi, cix, cx, cxxiii, 170, 179, 207, 215, 224; near the Church, cix, cx, cxvii, 170, 179, 186, 191–3, 205–9
Huronia, xxx

ILLINOIS INDIANS, xxxv, 9, 12, 29, 233, 235
Indians: presents, lxxx, cxx, 103, 217–21; stores, cxxiv, 221, 224, 226; tribes at Detroit, xliii–xlv, 24–6; *see also under names of tribes*
Infant mortality, lxvii
Innis, Robert, cxviii, 189, 193, 195, 204, 226

Iredell, Abraham, cxviii, 185–8, 189, 193, 202
Iroquois Indians, xxix–xxxii, xl, xlvii, 3, 8, 10, 14, 22, 23, 30, 35, 299, 230, 234, 237, 243, 244, 245, 252
Isle à la Pierre, 44, 259
Isle aux Bois Blancs, xlvii, liii, lxxxv, cii, ciii, cvii, cxxi–cxxviii, 26, 30, 32, 35, 37, 43, 46, 115, 154, 165, 171, 173, 209–12, 217, 245, 249, 251, 253, 258, 260
Isle aux Cochons (Hog Island), lxiv, lxxii, 26, 51, 82, 245, 264
Isle aux Dindes (Fighting Island), lxxix, 43, 52, 53, 97, 165, 171, 258, 265, 277
Isle aux Pêches (à la Pêche), lxiv, lxxvii, 68
Isle du Large. *See* Isle aux Pêches

JANIS, NICOLAS FRANÇOIS, lx, 30, 33, 34, 54, 64, 72, 78, 128, 177, 247, 249, 250, 288, 337–8, 344, 348, 358
Javerai, Pierre, 81, 126–7, 287, 311, 315, 354
Jay Treaty, lxxxiii, cxxiii
Jesuit, missionaries and missions, xxx, xxxi, xlv, 15, 17, 23, 238, 239, 244
Jesuit Relations, xxxi–xxxii, 3, 229
Johnson, Sir John, cii, cviii, 155, 157, 160, 173, 204, 210, 219
Johnson, Sir William, lxxx, xci, 98
Jolliet, Louis and Adrien, xxxii, xxxiii, 5, 230
Jung, Michael, 163

KENT COUNTY, lxxxv–lxxxix, cxiv–vi, 109, 110, 113, 115, 183, 195
Khioetoa, xxxi, 4, 229
King's Bench Act, lxxxiv
Kingsville, cvii
Kiskakous (Indians), 23, 244
Knaggs, George, 71, 86, 273, 315
Knaggs' Creek. *See* Rivière à Gervais

LABADIE, PIERRE DESCOMPS (DES-COMPTES) *dit*, lxix, 45, 55, 150, 177, 202, 307, 311, 312, 324, 331, 334, 348
Labutte. *See* Chêne
Lachine, xxxiii, 42
La Durantaye, Olivier Morel de, xxxvi, xxxvii, 10, 11, 235
La Galissonière, Roland Michel, Marquis de, xlvii, lii, liii, 42, 44
La Hontan, Baron de, xxxvii
Lajeunesse. *See* Reveau *dit* Lajeunesse

Lajoie, Louis, 71, 119, 31, 321, 349
La Jonquière, Jacques Pierre Taffanel, Marquis de, liii, 44, 57, 75, 182, 267
Lake Conty. *See* Lake Erie
Lake Erie: territory formally claimed by French, xxxiii, 8, 229, 233; English flotilla captured on, xxxvii; Lt. Cuyler's detachment intercepted on, lxxviii; settlement on shore of, cvii–cxiv
Lake Huron, xxix–xxxii, 3, 8, 42, 229, 234
Lake Ontario, xxix, xxxii, 3, 42, 229, 234
Lake Orleans. *See* Lake Huron
Lake St. Clair: called Salt Water Lake, xxxi, xxxii; present name, xxxv, 10; settlement on streams emptying into, civ; lots on shore of, cv
Lake St. Louis. *See* Lake Ontario
Lalemant, Jérôme (Jesuit), 3, 229
La Morinie, J. B. (Jesuit), 117, 279
Lamothe, Guillaume, 106, 111, 160–1
Lamothe Cadillac, Antoine Laumet, Sieur de, xxxix–xliii, lxxvi, cxxix, 12, 13, 17–26, 236, 239–45, 310
Lamothe Cadillac, Madame de, xlii, 20, 241
Land Board of Hesse, lvii, cviii–cxi, 77, 176–83, 210
Landry *dit* St. André, 63, 83, 311, 315
Langlois, Nicolas, lx, lxvii, 64, 72, 78, 81, 82, 119, 124, 128, 272, 329, 336–7, 349, 356, 358
La Richardie, Armand de (Jesuit), xlvi–xlviii, lxxxiv, 27, 38–41, 43, 246, 254–6
La Roche d'Aillon, Joseph de (Recollet), xxx
La Salle, Robert Cavelier, Sieur de, xxxii–xxxvii, 4–5, 8–9, 12, 230, 233, 235
Lasalline, Paul, 177, 204, 311, 330, 359
L'Assomption, settlement of, lxxiv, lxxxiv, cvii, cxiii, cxvii, cxx, 134, 151, 173, 177, 181, 182, 192, 195, 292, 293
Leamington, cxvi
Le Beau, Catherine, 79, 80, 270
Le Beau, J. B., 45, 48, 50, 63, 70, 79, 80, 85, 262, 263, 312, 347, 353
Le Beau, Jean François, 53, 56, 63, 78, 266, 319, 345, 351
Le Beau, René, 44, 48, 51, 78, 262, 264, 327, 347, 353

Le Duc, Baptiste, 54, 71, 109, 177, 311, 318, 330, 358
Le Duc, François, 44, 51, 264, 311
Legrand, Gabriel, lxxx, 83, 121, 272, 282, 316, 341
Leith, George, cviii, 108–12, 193
Lemay, Théophile, 71, 86, 119, 149, 273, 306, 320, 330
Lernoult, Major Richard, 123, 157, 356
Léry, Joseph-Gaspard, Chaussegros de, lii–lvii, 42–46, 257–61
Lesley, Lieut., 92
Lesperance, ———, xl, 30, 63, 69, 81, 119, 128, 177, 248, 288, 311, 317, 358
Levadoux, Michel (Sulpician), xcviii, 149, 153, 305, 309
Lhuissier (Lucier), Augustin, 77, 358
Littlehales, Major E. B., xlv
Livingstone, Robert, xxxvii
Livre, note on, xlviii, lxxi
Long Point, lxxxiv, cix, cxi
Longueuil, Paul Joseph Lemoine, Chevalier de, lix, lx, lxiv, 29, 37, 40, 57, 64, 109, 117, 182, 253, 256, 267, 279, 310
Lorette, xxxi, xlvi, xlvii, 36, 37, 125, 253, 286
Louisiana, xlii, lii, 48, 262
Louvigny, Montigny de, cviii

McCormick, Lieut., 90
McDonnell, Col., 216
McGill, Andrew, 187
McGill, James, 187, 188
McGregor, Gregor, 75, 106, 108, 169, 172, 174, 193, 202, 226, 317, 327, 357, 358
McGregor, John, cxviii, 193, 194, 204
McGregory, Col., xxxvii
McIntosh (MacIntosh, Mackintosh), Angus, 111, 189, 193, 200, 226
McKee, Col. Alexander, lxxxii, lxxxiv, lxxxviii, xcvii, ci–cix, cxxi, 75, 92, 104, 109, 111, 114, 115, 145, 155–66, 171, 179, 191, 193, 204, 211, 215, 221, 222, 358
McKee, Capt. Thomas, cxv, cxxi, 160, 161, 193, 202, 204–8, 223, 332
Mackinac. *See* Michilimackinac
McLean, Capt. Hector, cxxiv, cxxvi, 208, 215–17, 221–4
McNiff, Patrick, cx–cxv, cxvii, 76, 111, 178, 179, 181–4, 190, 359
Macomb, William, lxxxvii, 106, 111, 138, 202, 296, 316

Maidstone Township, lxxxvii, cxv
Mailloux, (Mayeux, Mayea), J., lx, 81, 177, 318, 358
Mainville (Menville), Joseph, 76, 77, 331, 348, 358
Maisonville, Alexis, xcviii, 62, 73, 106, 107, 108, 121, 123, 124, 143, 144, 177–8, 185, 193, 226, 279, 282, 284, 285, 301, 302, 307, 311, 314, 319, 349, 356, 359
Maisonville's Mill, lxxii, lxxxv, 108, 115, 221
Malden Township, lxxxvii, cii, cv, cxi, cxvii, cxxiii, 161, 204, 328
Mallet, Baptiste, 32, 52, 55, 249, 264
Mallet, François, 52, 56, 264
Mann, Gother, cxxii, 209, 211, 225
Marchand, Jean Baptiste (Sulpician), cxviii, 150, 307, 308
Marcol, Gabriel (Jesuit), 39, 255, 257
Marentette. *See* Gaudet *dit* Marentette
Marguilliers, xciii, xciv, 124, 126, 153, 284, 286, 331
Marriages: at Assumption Church, liii, lxiii, lxvi, lxvii, lxviii, 343–55; at Ste. Anne's Church, liii, lxvi
Marsac, ———, 55, 128, 177, 288, 311, 326, 329, 354, 359
Mathews, Robert, cii, ciii, cvii, cxxii, 104, 138, 139, 144, 156, 162, 166, 169, 211, 297, 302, 356
Maumee River, lxiii, lxxix
May, James, 112, 190
Mayne, Capt. Wm., cxxiii, cxxvi, 114, 115, 214
Meldrum, Geo., 75, 106, 113, 189, 193, 226, 358
Meloche (Molosh), Antoine, lxvii, 69, 76, 77, 119, 128, 288, 320, 339, 352, 356, 358
Meloche, Pierre, lxxvii, 30, 54, 63, 69, 70, 76, 80, 82, 86, 119, 124, 127, 247, 272, 273, 288, 338, 347, 356, 358
Mersea Township, lxxxvii
Messemer, John, civ, 75, 163, 170, 358
Metayer (Meteier), Joseph, 52, 56, 265, 311
Miamis Indians, xxxvii, 11, 22, 23, 41, 48, 57, 89, 235, 243, 244, 255, 262, 267, 275
Michigan, lxxix
Michigan Historical Collections, xxxix
Michilimackinac (Mackinac), xxix, xxxiv–xl, lxxxiii, 9, 10, 12, 17, 22, 23, 27, 48, 57, 92, 96, 233, 234, 235, 239, 243, 244, 245, 262, 267, 277
Midland, Ontario, xxx
Mill Creek, cvii, cviii, cxii, 176, 357
Millehome, François, 102
Mission of the Hurons, xlv–lii, lviii, lxvi, lxxviii, xc–xciii, 23, 27–9, 37, 45, 57, 78, 246–7, 253, 267
Mississauga Indians, xliii, 23, 25, 26, 171, 244, 245
Mohawk Indians, xxxii
Monforton, Guillaume, lvii, lxiv, 70, 74, 77, 108, 115, 119, 120–4, 145, 180, 281, 282, 284, 285, 321, 358
Monforton Register, liv
Montmigny (Montmeni, Mini), A. L., 31, 33, 119, 248, 249, 327, 329, 346
Montreal, Capitulation of, lxxvi, xcv, ci, 88, 89, 274
Montresor, John, lx, lxi, lxxviii, lxxix, 99
Moore, Joseph, 185
Morand (Moran, Morin), Charles, 33, 34, 51, 63, 78, 82, 131, 177, 249, 264, 272, 291, 316, 359
Moravian missionaries, civ, cxx
Motz, Henry, cxxii, 210
Mountain, Rt. Rev. Jacob, cxx, 199
Murray, Gen. James, 88, 173, 274
Murray, Major Patrick, cvi, 172, 356

Nau, Luc François (Jesuit), xlvi
Navarre, Robert, xlix, lxxvi, lxxviii, 34, 37, 38, 55, 62, 65, 121, 251, 253, 254, 269, 282
Navy Island, lxxvii
Neutral Indians, xxx–xxxii, 3, 229
New Settlement on Lake Erie, cvii–cxiv, 113, 114, 167, 170, 173–6, 333
Neyon, Commandant, lxxix
Niagara River, xxxv, lxxvii, lxxviii, lxxxvii, cv, 9, 12, 233, 234, 235
Nicolas, Huron chief, xlvii, 29, 30, 36, 38, 39, 41, 251, 252, 254, 255
Ninivois, 94, 275

Oath of allegiance, lxxvi, xc, 92, 94, 104
O'Brien, E. J., 181, 182
Ohio River (Belle Rivière), xxxii, lii, lvi, lxi, lxxxi, 57, 267
Ojibway. *See* Chippewa Indians
Onontio, lxxvii, 5, 40, 230, 256
Oppenago (Indians), Wolves, Loups, 21, 22, 30, 243, 244
Orange (Albany), 40, 256

Oswegachi, lxxxiii
Oswego, lxxxiii, 102
Ottawa Indians: at Detroit, xliii, 24–5, 61; take part in Seven Years' War, lxi; during siege of Detroit, lxxvii–lxxix, 94–6; withdrawal from Detroit, lxiii; gifts of land by, lxiii, 62, 323–9
Ouellette, J. B., lx, lxvii, 64, 72, 81, 109, 126, 128, 129, 136, 177, 286, 288, 295, 330, 339, 344, 356, 358
Ou(i)atanon (Indians), 48, 57, 89, 261, 267, 275
Outagami. *See* Fox Indians

PAJOT (PAGEOT, PAGEAU), JEAN THOMAS, lxvi, xcvii, xcix, cxviii, 63, 69, 76, 77, 78, 119, 124, 153, 270, 285, 331, 345, 356, 358
Panis(e) (slave), lxvi, lxviii, 88, 275
Papineau, Miss, c, 138–45, 296–303
Paré, J. B., 63, 68, 71, 75, 119, 178, 189, 329, 347, 358, 359
Parent, Jacques, xcviii, 71, 109, 121, 124, 126, 176, 204, 282, 285, 286, 339, 356, 359
Parent, Julien, 72, 128, 176, 204, 288, 323, 340, 359
Parent, Laurent, lx, lxvii, 33, 34, 54, 64, 71, 109, 128, 176, 248, 250, 288, 339, 347, 348, 352, 359
Parent Creek, lxxvii, lxxix
Park, Wm., cxviii, 111, 113, 189, 193, 195, 202, 226, 358
Pattinson, Richard, cxviii, 189, 193, 195, 204
Pawnees (Indians). *See* Panis
Payet, Rev. Louis, 130, 134, 135, 136, 139, 143, 290, 293–5, 298, 301, 331
Peach Island. *See* Isle aux Pêches
Pelee Island, cxv, 332
Peltier, André, 128, 177, 288, 311, 338, 356
Peltier, Jacques, 68, 119, 311, 318, 322
Peltier, Louis, 68, 177
Petite Côte, lvii, lix, lxv, lxix, lxxii, lxxiv, cxi, cxiii, 75, 77, 85, 114, 119, 178–81, 273, 328–31
Petuns, xxxii
Pew of honor in church, lxxxix, cvii–cviii, 145–7, 150–2, 303–4, 307–9
Pike Creek. *See* Rivière aux Pêches
Pilet, Jacques, 45, 51, 55, 264, 340
Pilet, Joseph, 51, 81, 128, 204, 264, 271, 288, 321, 351, 352
Plichon, François, lxvi

Plichon, Louis, lv–lvi, lxvi, 49, 56, 262, 311
Pointe aux Pins, lxxxv, 6, 42, 108, 231
Pointe de Montréal, xliii, xlvii, lix, lxvi, lxxiv, xcii, xciii, 38, 86, 117, 254, 274, 279, 343
Pointe Pelée, xxxiii, lxxviii, cxv, 26, 40, 42, 245, 256, 257
Poisson. *See* Lasalline
Pollard, Richard, lxxxviii, cxx–cxxi, 75, 109, 110, 113, 193, 195, 209, 329, 358
Pontchartrain, Louis Phélipaux, Comte de, xli, 13, 17, 236
Pontiac, Ottawa chief, lxi, lxxvii, lxxix, xci, 62, 94–100, 274–6, 312–14
Pontiac Manuscript, lxxviii, lxxx, 94, 274
Pontiac Revolt (Conspiracy), lxxvii, lxxviii, 94–6, 274–6
Population, lxiii, lxvii, xcii, xcvii, 56, 64, 74
Port Dover, xxxiii
Porteous, John, 102
Port Huron, Michigan, xxxvi
Potawatomi (Poux) Indians, xxxiii, lxxxiii, 4, 11, 24–7, 38, 44, 46, 93, 94, 171, 205, 221, 230, 235, 245, 254, 259, 260, 276
Potier, Pierre (Jesuit): at the Huron Mission, xlvii–l, 30, 35, 37, 40, 43, 60, 78, 250, 252; relations with the British, lxxxii, xc–xci, 95, 104, 117, 276, 279; pastor of Assumption parish, xcii–xciii, 117, 118, 120, 279, 280, 312, 324, 343; death, xciv–xcv, 120–6, 136, 281–6
Pouget, Joseph, 70, 75, 82, 119, 121, 123, 124, 126, 129, 136, 150, 272, 282, 284–90, 294, 307, 319, 356, 358
Poverty of the early settlers, lxix, 136, 140, 141, 142, 295, 298–300
Powell, Judge William Dummer, lxxxiv, cviii, 75, 106, 142, 164, 176, 278, 300, 333, 358
Pratt, François, xcv, xcviii, 71, 114, 121, 122, 131, 151, 177, 182, 204, 281–3, 308, 325, 339, 352, 356, 358
Prescott, Robert, cxxvi, 115, 116, 191–2, 219, 222
Protestant Church, civ, cxx. *See also* Episcopal Church
Provision stores, lxx, 80, 211, 212, 225
Prudhomme, François, 53, 63, 69, 266, 344–7
Prudhomme, Pierre, 76, 118, 358

INDEX

Puans (Puants), La Baye des, 12, 48, 57, 235, 262, 267

QUEBEC ACT, lxxxi

RANKIN, JAMES, 71, 129, 131, 289, 325
Réaume, Charles, 66, 71, 86, 119, 120, 126–7, 160, 161, 208, 226, 269, 273, 281, 287, 321–2, 340–1, 356, 359
Réaume, Claude, 71, 109, 128, 130, 177, 288, 340–1, 344, 356, 358
Réaume, Hyacinthe, lix, lxvii, 54, 58, 268, 340–1
Réaume, Joseph, 63, 75, 146, 226, 303, 321, 340–1, 358
Réaume, Pierre, lx, 54, 59, 64, 66, 72, 128, 288, 340–1, 345, 354
Recollet, missionaries and missions, xxx, xlv, 9, 233
Renaud, Charles, lxvii, 69, 76, 86, 119, 128, 150, 273, 288, 307, 331, 341, 349, 356, 358
Retz, Franciscus, 27, 246
Reveau *dit* Lajeunesse, Louis, 53, 56, 63, 69, 76, 78, 86, 119, 265, 273, 311, 321–2, 328, 347, 358
Revolutionary War, lxxxi–lxxxiii, lxxxix, cii, cviii, cxvii, cxxix
Reynolds, Thomas, 167, 172, 175, 226, 357
Rivard, Ant. J., 63, 311, 315, 320, 345
River Raisin, 109, 113, 305
Rivière à Gervais, lv, lvii, lix, 171, 179, 181, 192
Rivière à la Carrière, 44, 258
Rivière aux Canards (River Canard), xlix, lxxiv, xcvii, civ–cv, 37, 43, 153, 161, 165, 173, 178, 179, 203, 253–4, 258, 309
Rivière aux Cêdres, cvii, 43, 167, 258
Rivière aux Dindes (Turkey Creek), liii, lvii, lxv, lxxii, lxxiv, ci, cxvii, 43–4, 76, 85, 181, 258, 273
Rivière aux Pêches, cxiv–cxv, 182–4, 186, 359
Rivière aux Puces, cxiv–cxv, 182–4, 186, 359
Rivière La Tranche, xlv, lxxxv, cv, cxiii, 43, 108, 111, 114, 153, 171, 184, 196, 258, 309
Rivière Rouge, lxxix, cxxiii, 45, 109
Rivière Ruscom, cxiv–cxv, 182–4, 186, 360
Robert, Antoine, 55, 68, 71, 177, 270, 322, 324–5, 353, 359

Robertson, William, lxxxiv–lxxxv, cviii, 105, 112, 172
Rocheleau, François, 81, 311
Rocheleau (Rochereau), Joseph, 76, 311, 337, 349, 358
Rochester Township, lxxxvii, cxv
Roe, Walter, 167, 193, 196, 202, 204
Rogers, Major Robert, lxxvi, 89, 356
Rooseboom, xxxvii
Roy, Augustin, 119, 198, 226
Ruisseau de la Vieille Reine, liii, lv, lvii, lxx, lxxii, lxxiv, 43–4, 258
Russell, Hon. Peter, cxvii–cxx, cxxvi, 191–6, 199, 204, 222, 224
Ruthven, cxvi

SABREVOIS, JACQUES CHARLES, SIEUR DE, lii–liii, lvii, 40, 42, 45, 51, 62, 65, 75, 256, 264, 269, 310
Ste. Anne's Church, xli, xliii, lxxxi, lxxxix, xcviii, 148, 305
St. Aubin, Jacques, 54, 311, 316
St. Aubin, Joseph, 53, 266, 311, 350, 352
St. Cosme, Pierre, lxxx, 39, 55, 255
St. Denys River, 12, 235
St. Etienne. *See* Dinan
St. John's Church (Parish), cxxi
St. Louis. *See* Villers *dit* St. Louis
Ste. Marie, mission in Huronia, xxx, 3, 229
St. Martin, Adhemar, cviii, 106, 160, 161, 172, 311, 349
St. Martin, Archange, 200
St. Michel, mission of, xxxi, 4, 229
St. Pé, Jean B. (Jesuit), 28, 247
Salleneuve, J. B. (Jesuit), 117, 121, 279, 282
Salmon, Capt., 214
Sandusky, xlvi, xlvii, 29, 38, 40, 60, 89, 138, 254, 256, 297
Sandwich, Ontario, lxxxv, cxvii–cxxi, cxxix, 193–9, 203–5
Sanson d'Abbeville, map of, xxxi, xxxiii, 8, 232
Sargent, Winthrop, 198
Sastaretsy(i), liii, 27, 30, 36, 173, 246, 252
Saulteurs (Sauteux). *See* Chippewa Indians
Sault St. Louis, xlvi
Sault Ste. Marie, xliii, xlv, 7, 12, 27, 153, 232, 235, 245, 309
Schieffelin (Schiefflin), Jacob, cii, ciii, 154–7, 324
Scott, William, 112, 168, 175, 329, 332

Selby, Prideaux, 112, 193, 196, 201, 209, 358
Senecas (Indians), xxxii, xlv, 17, 239
Sensemann, Brother, 163
Seven Years' War, lx, xcii
Simcoe, Lt.-Gov. John Graves, xlv, lxxxv, lxxxviii, xcviii, ciii, cxxiii, 147, 150, 152, 186, 211, 212
Sioux (Indians), xxxvi, 11, 235
Slavery, lxvii, lxviii, 88, 275
Smith, Capt., 114, 115
Smith, David W., lxxxvii, lxxxviii, cxv, 108-13, 162, 178-80, 184, 186, 188, 194, 195
Smith, Major John, cxii, 108, 168, 176, 356
Smith, Thomas, cvii, cviii, 68, 75, 106, 112, 145, 169, 172, 174, 189, 202, 211, 330, 357, 358
Smyth, Lieut., 74, 75
Snye Carty. *See* Chenal Ecarté
Sobriquets, lvi, 311
Sonnontouans. *See* Senecas
Soumande, Antoine, 69, 119, 322, 328
Sterling (Stirling), James, xci, 101, 102, 119, 280, 316, 347
Stoney Island. *See* Isle à la Pierre
Stuart, Charles, lvii, lxi, 59
Suffolk County, lxxxv, lxxxvii, 108, 113
Sulpician, missionaries and missions, xxx, xlv
Suzor, Louis, 63, 70, 81, 119, 124, 127-9, 284, 288-9, 332, 345, 356

TAKÉ (TAKAY), HURON CHIEF, 94, 275
Talbot Road, cxvi
Talon, Jean, 8, 233
Tavernier *dit* St. Martin, Nicolas, 52, 265
Téata, Huron chief, 94, 275
Thames River. *See* Rivière La Tranche
Tilbury Township, cxv
Tiwanatawa, xxxii, 5, 230
Tobacco Indians. *See* Petuns
Tofflemire, Henry, 176, 357
Tonti, Alphonse de, xli, 17, 21, 27, 239, 242, 246, 310
Tonti, Madame de, xlii, 22, 243
Tonti, Henri de, xxxv, 8, 233
Tourangeau, J. B., 63, 70, 80, 119, 124, 128, 272, 284, 288, 311, 325, 333, 339, 343, 346, 356
Tourneux, Jean B., 72, 115, 130, 177, 204, 291, 311, 318, 325, 334, 340, 356
Transfer of British military post, cxxiii, cxxiv, 159, 210, 211-17
Treaty of Paris, 1783, lxxxiii, lxxxiv, cxvii, cxxiii
Tucker, William, 66, 323, 325
Turkey Creek. *See* Rivière aux Dindes
Turnbull, Capt. Geo., 100, 356

UNITED EMPIRE LOYALISTS, cii, ciii, cv, cvii, cix, 156, 159, 161, 162, 167, 170
Upper Canada, Province of, lxviii, lxxxv, xcviii, 147, 150, 192, 200, 305, 307
Ursulines, 15, 20, 238, 241

VAILLANT DE GUESLIS, FRANÇOIS (JESUIT), xlv, 20, 242
Valé *dit* Versailes, Jean, 53, 266, 311
Vaudreuil, Philippe de Rigaud, Marquis de, 26, 244
Vaudreuil, Pierre de Rigaud, Marquis de, lxxvi, xc, 88, 89, 90, 94, 274
Vien, Widow, lx, 59, 269, 316
Vigneau, Capt., 216
Villers (Villaire) *dit* St. Louis, 45, 51, 56, 63, 73, 78, 81, 177, 264, 311, 321, 345, 348, 353, 359
Villers, Marie Louise, lxvi, 78, 334, 336, 345
Voyageurs, xliii, liv, lix

WATER-MILL, lxxiv, lxxv, 85, 179, 273, 333
Wawyachtenok, xxxix
Wayne, General Anthony, lxxxiii, xcviii, 115, 116, 149, 306
Weld, Isaac, cxxiv
Western District, lxxxiv, lxxxv, cxx, 195-200, 203. *See also* District of Hesse
Wiley, Ann, lxxxii
Wilkinson, Gen. James, 213
Williams, Thomas, 74, 75, 120, 121, 156, 166, 281, 282
Windmills, lxxii, lxxiii
Windsor, Ontario, xxix, xxxi, xli, lv, lix, lx, lxxii
Wyandots. *See* Huron Indians
Wye River, xxx

ZEISBERGER, DAVID, civ, 163

THE CHAMPLAIN SOCIETY

PRESENT OFFICERS OF THE SOCIETY 1960

Honorary President
SIR EDWARD PEACOCK, G.C.V.O., LL.D., London, England

President
W. KAYE LAMB, PH.D., LL.D., Ottawa, Dominion Archivist and National Librarian

Vice-Presidents
GEORGE W. BROWN, PH.D., LL.D., F.R.S.C., Toronto, Professor of History in the University of Toronto

H. D. BURNS, D.CN.L., Toronto, Chairman of the Board, Bank of Nova Scotia

THE HON. LESLIE M. FROST, Q.C., Toronto, Prime Minister of the Province of Ontario

D. C. HARVEY, M.A., LL.D., D.LITT., Halifax, Archivist Emeritus of the Province of Nova Scotia

MSGR. JOSEPH THOMAS ARTHUR MAHEUX, B.C.L., D.D., Quebec, Archivist of the Quebec Seminary

LORNE PIERCE, TH.D., LL.D., LITT.D., D.ÈS L., F.R.S.C., Toronto, Editor Emeritus of the Ryerson Press

WALTER N. SAGE, PH.D., Vancouver, Professor Emeritus of History in the University of British Columbia

SIGMUND SAMUEL, LL.D., Toronto

SIR CAMPBELL STUART, G.C.M.G., K.B.E., Chairman of the Hudson's Bay Record Society, London, England

Members of the Council
A. G. BAILEY, PH.D., Fredericton, Dean of Arts, University of New Brunswick

RÉVEREND PÈRE RENÉ BEAUDRY, C.S.C., B.A., St. Joseph, N.B., of St. Joseph's College

D. G. CREIGHTON, LL.D., F.R.S.C., Toronto, Professor of History in the University of Toronto

JOHN M. GRAY, Toronto, President of the Macmillan Company of Canada

KENNETH E. KIDD, M.A., Toronto, Curator, Ethnology Department in the University of Toronto

W. L. MORTON, M.A., Winnipeg, Professor of History in the University of Manitoba

GEORGE SPRAGGE, D.PAED., Toronto, Archivist of Ontario

HAROLD C. WALKER, Q.C., Toronto

CLIFFORD P. WILSON, Calgary, The Glenbow Foundation

General Editor

J. B. CONACHER, M.A., PH.D., Toronto, Associate Professor of History in the University of Toronto

Editor, Ontario Series

P. C. T. WHITE, M.A., PH.D., Toronto, Assistant Professor of History in the University of Toronto

Honorary Secretary-Treasurer

PETER S. OSLER, Toronto

Executive Secretary-Treasurer

MRS. CYNTHIA WALKER HEIDENREICH

Correspondence should be addressed in care of The Library, The University of Toronto, Toronto 5, Ontario

PUBLICATIONS OF THE CHAMPLAIN SOCIETY
ONTARIO SERIES

1. *The Valley of the Trent.* Edited by E. C. Guillet
2. *Royal Fort Frontenac.* Translations by R. A. Preston, edited with introduction and notes by Leopold Lamontagne
3. *Kingston before the War of 1812.* Edited with introduction by R. A. Preston
4. *The Windsor Border Region, Canada's Southernmost Frontier.* Edited with an introduction by E. J. Lajeunesse, C.S.B.